INTRODUCTION
TO ECONOMETRICS

INTRODUCTION TO ECONOMETRICS
PRINCIPLES AND APPLICATIONS

Third Edition

Harry H. Kelejian
DEPARTMENT OF ECONOMICS
UNIVERSITY OF MARYLAND, COLLEGE PARK

Wallace E. Oates
DEPARTMENT OF ECONOMICS
UNIVERSITY OF MARYLAND, COLLEGE PARK

1817

HARPER & ROW, PUBLISHERS, NEW YORK
Cambridge, Philadelphia, San Francisco,
London, Mexico City, São Paulo, Singapore, Sydney

Sponsoring Editor: John Greenman
Project Editor: David Nickol
Text Art: Vantage Art, Inc.
Production Manager: Jeanie Berke
Production Assistant: Beth Maglione
Printer and Binder: R. R. Donnelley & Sons Company

INTRODUCTION TO ECONOMETRICS: Principles and Applications, Third Edition

Library of Congress Cataloging in Publication Data

Kelejian, Harry H.
    Introduction to econometrics:priciples and applications/Harry
H. Kelejian, Wallace E. Oates.—3rd ed.
      p.   cm.
    Includes index.
    ISBN 0-06-043621-2
    1. Econometrics. I. Oates, Wallace E. II. Title.
HB139.K44 1989
330'.028—dc19   88–25973
                                                                      CIP

88   89   90   91   9 8 7 6 5 4 3 2 1

For Our Children:

David, Douglas, and Melinda Kelejian
Catherine, Christopher, and Nora Oates

Contents

PREFACE
to the Third Edition

In this edition, we have sought to fill what certain readers saw as gaps in the earlier editions. More specifically, this edition contains five additions:

1. An extension of Appendix B to Chapter 1, which provides a review of basic statistical concepts. This extension introduces the concept of a joint density function and develops a number of corresponding results, some of which are used later in the text.

2. An expanded discussion of the measurement of the explanatory power of the regression model. Here we consider goodness-of-fit measures as a means for choosing between different regression models. We discuss shortcomings in the R^2 measure for this purpose and then introduce an alternative measure, namely the adjusted coefficient of determination (or $\bar{R}^2$ statistic). This measure is reported by many computer programs. We discuss its properties and indicate its relationship to the R^2 statistic. We also discuss the relationship between model-selection issues and hypothesis testing. In this framework, we caution against the "casual" or informal use of $\bar{R}^2$ or other goodness-of-fit measures to select models.

3. A discussion of autocorrelation problems in the presence of a lagged dependent variable. Since the standard Durbin-Watson test is not valid in such cases, we discuss two alternative tests.

4. A discussion of the concept of stability. Issues of stability arise in regression models that contain lagged dependent variables.

5. An expanded treatment of heteroscedasticity that includes the Goldfeld-Quandt test. For certain cases, this is a very appealing and straightforward test. These cases are discussed.

We are grateful to Ingmar Prucha for reviewing early versions of some of the new material in this edition and for providing very constructive comments. Of course, the usual disclaimer is in force.

HARRY H. KELEJIAN
WALLACE E. OATES

PREFACE
to the Second Edition

Our objective in this new edition is threefold: first, to expand the number and range of applications and illustrations of the econometric techniques developed in the book; second, to extend the analysis to encompass the estimation of nonlinear models; and, third, to correct and clarify the treatment of some theoretical issues in the first edition. Consequently, we have incorporated into the second edition several new examples of correlation and regression analysis and have added a new chapter, Chapter 8, on the estimation of nonlinear systems.

Those familiar with the first edition of the book will find a variety of new illustrations that, in some instances, take the student through actual calculations of estimated parameters and that, in other cases, draw directly on the economics literature to show how regression analysis has, in fact, been used to estimate important parameters and to test some of the central hypotheses of microeconomics and macroeconomics. The new examples involve simple correlation analysis, estimation of demand curves for real goods and for money balances, the estimation of a cost function, and a case study of heteroscedasticity that results from aggregation. We hope that these additional examples will assist the student in better understanding the formulation of econometric models, the use of actual data, and the interpretation of the results.

In practice, most econometric models are *not* linear. However, most undergraduate and graduate texts deal only with linear models on the apparent assumption that nonlinear models are too difficult to present. We are convinced that this is not so and, in consequence, introduce in Chapter 8 an extensive discussion of nonlinear models on the undergraduate level. Drawing on the earlier material in the text, the new chapter explores the issues of identification, estimation, and hypothesis testing in nonlinear models and presents an application of these techniques to an economic problem.

Our basic purpose in this edition is unchanged from that in the first edition: we seek to present a wide range of econometric techniques based on only elementary mathematical and statistical skills. For a description of our method, we refer the reader to the accompanying Preface to the First Edition.

We wish to express our gratitude to Stephen Goldfeld, Ronald Oaxaca, and Richard Quandt for their constructive comments on an early draft of our new Chapter 8. We are also indebted to the Literary Executor of the late Sir Ronald A. Fisher, F.R.S., and to Oliver and Boyd, Edinburgh, for their permission to reprint Table 2 from their book *Statistical Methods for Research Workers*.

HARRY H. KELEJIAN
WALLACE E. OATES

PREFACE
to the First Edition

The more recent evolution of economics has encompassed a remarkable development of econometric techniques and their use in economic analysis. Econometrics was once reserved for a select few, but it has now become a basic ingredient in the training of virtually all students of economics.

Despite this widespread increase in the use of econometric analysis, most texts that present a reasonable scope of results continue to presuppose a substantial level of mathematical sophistication that extends beyond that possessed by many students. Our objective in this text is to develop a wide scope of material while making only modest mathematical demands on the student. More specifically, this book does not use the calculus or matrix algebra. We assume a level of mathematical sophistication roughly equivalent to the second year of high school algebra.*

Although the exposition relies on elementary mathematical techniques, the range of material in this book corresponds to that in a typical graduate course in econometrics; the subjects covered, for instance, are roughly those presented in A. S. Goldberger, *Econometric Theory* (Wiley, 1964), and J. Johnston, *Econometric Methods,* 2d ed. (McGraw-Hill, 1972).

We derive the basic results using the "instrumental-variable" approach. This technique has two important advantages over the more commonly used least-squares method. First, it does not require calculus for its presentation; second, it permits the student to see clearly the role that each assumption plays in the estimation procedure. For instance, we develop the correspondence between normal equations and basic assumptions of the regression model; in this respect, particular stress is placed on the procedure by which a given assumption is translated into the corresponding normal equation. This is extremely useful, for later on the student can directly see consequences of the violation of a certain assumption and can better understand the techniques adopted to amend the estimation procedure. We also employ the instrumental-variable approach throughout the book; this allows a unified treatment of autocorrelation, multicollinearity, heteroscedasticity, systems problems, and the like, since all are treated in essentially the same manner.

---

*Because the student may not be familiar with some important propositions on summations, some needed results on the algebra of summations are developed in an appendix to Chapter 1.

The emphasis in this text is on what might be called "rigorous intuition." That is, results are not simply given; they are derived in an intuitive manner with an attempt to leave as few loose ends as possible. Although the standard cases and results are presented, we stress, first, the procedure by which these results are obtained, and second, their applications to actual estimation problems. Following the introduction of each new technique, we illustrate its use with numerical examples and actual studies from the economics literature. In consequence, the student working through this text should develop a good feel for both how things are done and why.

A set of problems at the end of each chapter has also been developed, and the answers to all problems are worked out and presented at the end of the text. The conscientious student is advised to work through these, as they relate both to the empirical implementation of the results in the text, and to the manipulation and understanding of the relevant concepts. In addition, we present a number of problems in which a model is described in verbal terms, and the student is asked to formalize it in terms of a regression model. These problems should give the student a better understanding of some of the difficulties involved in the specification of an economic model.

This book was written to serve as a text for a one-semester course in econometrics at either the undergraduate or masters level. By masters level we mean those graduate courses in econometrics that are geared to students who do not have either the mathematical or statistical training to work through more advanced formal presentations of econometrics. The prerequisite for this text is roughly the first two-thirds of a one-semester course in elementary statistics. For instance, the material in the first five chapters of W. C. Gunther's *Concepts of Statistical Inference* should be more than adequate. Any additional materials that may be needed to work through the text (plus a concise review of basic statistical concepts) are presented in an appendix to Chapter 1.

A brief description of the development of this manuscript may provide a better sense of its potential uses. The point of departure for this book was a set of Kelejian's lecture notes for the undergraduate econometrics course at Princeton University. The notes themselves are distributed in mimeographed form to students and the response, both on the part of the students at Princeton and elsewhere, encouraged the writing of this book. The notes, as well as early drafts of the chapters of this manuscript, have been used at the graduate level at New York University in a course for nonspecialists in econometrics, and also for a course in quantitative techniques, in the Masters Program in Public Affairs as the Woodrow Wilson School at Princeton. These are the kinds of courses for which we feel this book is suitable. In addition, a number of more advanced students in econometrics have found the manuscript helpful in providing a better intuitive understanding of results that they had worked through more formally elsewhere.

The particular collaboration for this book reflects its objective. Harry Kelejian has econometrics as his main area of interest; his research and teaching efforts have been predominantly in this field. The primary interests of Wallace Oates are problems in government finance. His familiarity with econometrics is mainly that of the practitioner, whose concern is the quantitative analysis of actual economic problems. The hope has been that this blend of interests would produce a book which is both econometrically sound and readily accessible to the uninitiated student of econometrics.

For their help and valuable suggestions on various drafts of the manuscript, we want to express our gratitude to Charles Beach, Larry Hersh, William Lawrence, Robert Plotnick, Richard Quandt, V. Sundararajan, Ira Sohn, and Meir Sokoler. None of them, however, is responsible for any deficiencies in the final product. In addition, we are indebted to the Literary Executor of the late Sir Ronald A. Fisher, F.R.S., and to Oliver and Boyd, Edinburgh, for their permission to reprint Table 2 from their book *Statistical Methods for Research Workers*. Finally, we acknowledge our great debt to Mrs. Betty Kaminiski for her expert typing, often under the most trying of circumstances.

HARRY H. KELEJIAN
WALLACE E. OATES

INTRODUCTION
TO ECONOMETRICS

CHAPTER 1
Introduction

An essential activity in any science is the systematic testing of theory against fact. Economics is no exception. Moreover, one of the most striking developments in recent decades in economics has been the increased emphasis on the development and use of statistical techniques for the analysis of economic problems. Theoretical relationships among economic variables are typically expressed in mathematical form; however, to give these relationships empirical content, economists have come increasingly to employ statistical methods of analysis to test hypotheses about these relationships, to estimate actual magnitudes, and to use these estimates to make quantitative predictions of economic events. This form of analysis is what we mean by the term *econometrics*.

In 1937, in his farewell address as Director of the London School of Economics, Lord William Beveridge chastized the economics profession for "a hundred years of political economy, in which facts have been treated not as controls of theory, but as illustrations.... There can be no science of society till the facts about society are available." In the period since Beveridge's statement, however, we have taken enormous strides both in the development of quantitative methods of analysis and in the accumulation of data with which to test economic theories. One can hardly pick up an issue of an economic journal without encountering a number of articles in which the authors support their arguments with econometric analyses.

This means that, to attain the capacity to understand and evaluate current research work in economics (as well as to engage in one's own empirical work), it is essential to have a familiarity with econometrics. As an example, the exciting and important debate between the so-called monetarist and neo-Keynesians over the relative effectiveness of monetary and fiscal policy in influencing the aggregate level of output and employment is essentially a controversy over a matter of fact: the structure of the economy and its response to these two types of policy. As such, it is a matter to be settled largely by appeal to empirical evidence, and participants in this debate have relied heavily on econometric techniques of analysis. The point is that, if one wants simply to follow this debate and examine critically the evidence advanced, one must have some knowledge of econometrics (including a recognition of its limitations and misuse as well as the interpretation of results from its legitimate application to economic problems).

Econometrics, then, is the branch of economics dealing with the quan-

1

titative analysis of economic behavior. As such, it has come to serve two critical functions. First, it provides techniques for the verification or refutation of theories. An economic theory, or a *model* in the jargon of the economist, is a set of definitions and assumptions that he can use to explain certain types of events. Typically expressed in the form of a set of equations, an economic theory describes the mechanism by which certain economic variables interact. The theory of consumer choice, for example, suggests that the quantity of a particular good that consumers will buy depends on consumer preferences, their incomes, the price of the good in question, and the prices of other goods and services. The theory leads us to expect that, as the price of a good rises, the amount purchased will typically decline.* In macroeconomics, we find theories that imply that the aggregate level of investment depends on the rate of interest. More specifically, these theories indicate that higher rates of interest will discourage spending on real capital formation (investment).

To evaluate the usefulness of these theories, we must determine their reliability in predicting economic events. As in the examples just cited, economic theories are generally put in a testable form by specifying some implied causal sequence of events: if this, then that (e.g., if interest rates rise, investment expenditure falls). This will frequently be expressed in mathematical terms by noting that one variable is a function of another and specifying the general character of the relationship. For instance, we might say $I = a - bR$, where I is the level of investment spending, R is the rate of interest, and a and b are numerical constants with positive values. In such form, the theory can be put to the empirical test of the accuracy of its predictions.

We might mention here that testing economic theories in this manner is rarely a simple matter. Causal statements of the kind described above are typically based on the assumption that other relevant factors are held constant. The proposition that higher rates of interest lead to a lower level of investment is based, for example, on the assumption that aggregate demand (among other things) is held constant. If demand is rising at the same time interest rates increase, a rise in investment (to meet the growing demand) might be found to accompany the higher rates of interest; this need not imply a refutation of the theory, for clearly the negative effect of the increased interest rates could be more than offset by the positive influence of higher aggregate demand. The problem that economists face in this regard is that the great bulk of their data come from day-to-day experience, not from controlled laboratory experiments. And rarely in the real world are "other things unchanged." For this reason, econometricians have had to devise statistical techniques through which they can in effect artificially hold

---

* We must say "typically" here because it is conceivable, in certain instances, that a positive income effect will more than offset the negative substitution effect of a price rise, so that a consumer may actually increase his purchases of a good whose price has risen.

constant the other influences on the variable in question; in this way, they can determine the effect of one variable on another. This problem, as will become clear in later chapters, is one that helps give quantitative techniques in economics their own particular character.

Econometrics, then, is of basic importance for the verification or refutation of economic theories. Its second primary function is to provide quantitative estimates of the *magnitudes* of the relationships among variables. A particular theory may suggest that a rise in price leads to a fall in quantity demanded, or that a decrease in levels of taxation will stimulate aggregate spending and output. While knowledge of the general character of these relationships is extremely valuable, it is frequently not very satisfactory for purposes of actual decision making. A businessman wants to know *how many* fewer units he will sell if he raises price by 10 percent so that he can assess the impact of this choice on his profits. Similarly, an economic advisor must estimate by *how much* a given tax cut will increase total spending; if the tax cut is too small, excessive unemployment and unused productive capacity may persist, while if taxes are reduced too much, inflation will result. For these reasons, quantitative techniques in economics must be capable of generating estimates of magnitude in addition to providing an assessment of the more general propositions typically suggested by economic theory.

It is helpful in introducing the general nature of the econometric problem to consider a particular, and incidentally quite an important, example. Suppose, as suggested above, that we are economic advisors who have been assigned the task of estimating the increase in consumer expenditure that would result from a proposed cut in individual income taxes of a specified magnitude. As a point of departure for our assignment, we might adopt for our theoretical frame of reference the famous Keynesian consumption function, which says that consumption spending depends on the level of disposable income. Suppose that, for sake of simplicity at least for our initial estimation, we assume that the relationship is of a linear form:

$$C = a + bY_d, \qquad (1.1)$$

where C is consumption expenditure, Y_d is disposable income, and a and b are parameters (i.e., numerical constants). It is clear that the value of the parameter b is of crucial importance to us. The tax cut will increase disposable income, which in turn will stimulate consumer spending; and b is the familiar "marginal propensity to consume" (MPC), whose value indicates the fraction of an additional dollar of disposable income that individuals will spend on consumption. We shall obviously need an estimate of b if we are going to evaluate the impact of the tax cut on the level of spending.

Macroeconomic theory provides some rough guidelines. The theory suggests, for example, that the value of the marginal propensity to consume, b, should lie somewhere between zero and unity; an additional dollar of disposable income will presumably lead to some increase in consumption expenditure, but part of it is also likely to be saved so that the increase in consumption will be somewhat less than the full rise in disposable income. We shall, however, need a far better estimate than this, because the impact of the tax cut on consumption spending will be far greater if $b = 0.9$ (i.e., if consumers spend 90 percent of additional income on consumption and save only 10 percent) than if $b = 0.5$.

We therefore set as our initial task the determination of an estimated value for b. One plausible way to proceed would be to examine the consumption and saving behavior of individuals with differing levels of disposable income. From such information we should be able to estimate how consumption varies with the level of disposable income. Suppose that we are able to get this information on consumption expenditure and income through a budget survey of a group of households. The information is assembled, tabulated, and depicted in Figure 1.1. A figure such as 1.1, which we shall use repeatedly in later chapters, is called a *scatter diagram*. Each point represents an observed pair of values of the two variables; in Figure 1.1, for instance, P_1 indicates a family in the budget survey that had a disposable income of $16,000 and consumption expenditure of $15,500.

Let us now consider the information given in Figure 1.1 in the light of the consumption function described by equation (1.1). We note first that the mathematical specification of the consumption function is exact; equation (1.1) says that there will be a certain specific level of consumption expenditure that accompanies each level of disposable income. Human behavior, however, is far from being so precise. In fact, the results in Figure 1.1 suggest that in most instances families with the same level of income will spend somewhat different amounts on consumption. Points P_1 and P_2, for example, indicate two families both of which had a disposable income of $16,000; but family 1 spent $15,500 on consumption, while family 2 spent only $15,000 and saved $1,000.

How can we determine estimates of a and b from this mass of seemingly inconsistent information? We know from elementary mathematics that two

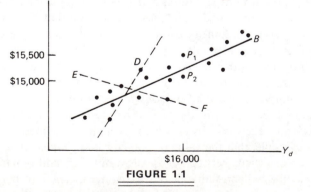

FIGURE 1.1

Information from a hypothetical budget study.

points determine a straight line; therefore, all that would seem to be necessary to determine the values of a and b in equation (1.1) are two observations. In one sense, the problem seems to be one of having too much information! Yet it seems unreasonable (and indeed it is) to disregard relevant data; we would clearly get different values for a and b depending on the particular two points we used to solve for these parameters; in Figure 1.1, for example, we could get line CD, EF, or any number of other lines depending on the particular two points we pick to determine the line.

Careful inspection of the scatter of points in Figure 1.1 does seem to suggest, however, that there is some kind of relationship between C and Y_d: as disposable income rises, the level of consumption expenditure appears *on the average* also to increase. The relationship between C and Y_d is clearly far from exact, but there does, nevertheless, appear to be some "typical" relationship between the two variables. We could simply by inspection, or by a more formal technique, fit a line such as AB to the scatter of points, a line that would represent this "typical" budgetary behavior. This would provide us with estimates of a and b, which indicate respectively the vertical intercept and the slope of the line.

This is the kind of problem with which econometrics is concerned. And, in fact, the focus of the following chapters will be the development of a systematic and sensible technique for estimating this "typical" relationship between two (and later among several) variables. In the course of this, we shall find that there are a number of questions concerning this relationship for which it is important to have answers. In the preceding hypothetical case, in which we asked the reader to consider himself in the role of an economic advisor for a proposed reduction in taxes, it would have soon become apparent that there were several further problems to be resolved, in addition to the estimation of b, before a reliable prediction of the effect of a tax cut on aggregate spending could be reached. To complete our introduction, it may prove helpful to provide a listing and brief discussion of some of these problems, since their solution is what this book is all about.

1. *Hypothesis testing.* Suppose that we have a theory that implies a causal relationship between two variables. With data for both of these variables, and perhaps for other relevant variables as well, how can we establish with some specified degree of reliability that there really exists a relationship between these variables? In terms of the scatter diagram in Figure 1.1, for example, how possible is it that the apparent "typical" relationship between C and Y_d is spurious and is simply a curious result in this particular sample?

2. *Estimates of parameters.* If there is a relationship between the two variables, how can we best make use of the available data to obtain accurate estimates of the magnitudes? Based on the information underlying the scatter diagram in Figure 1.1, what is the most effective way to generate estimates of a and b? In addition, we shall want to know by how much we can expect economic behavior to deviate from the average so that we have some idea of how useful our estimates of a and b are.

3. *Use of estimates for prediction.* Under what set of conditions or restrictions can we use these estimates to make predictions? Referring once again to Figure 1.1, what assumptions must we make in order to use the estimated value of b from our family budget survey to evaluate the effects of a tax cut on consumption expenditure? Or, on a related matter, can we forecast on the basis of this information and with some specified degree of confidence what C will be when Y_d is set at some given level?

4. *Functional form.* What is the appropriate functional form for the relationship? We assumed for simplicity a simple linear relationship between C and Y_d, but this certainly need not be the true relationship. Perhaps the MPC, that is, b, in equation (1.1) declines as income rises; the true relationship might be $C = a + bY_d^{1/2}$. How can we use theoretical results and the available data to select the particular functional relationship of the variables to estimate?

5. *Imperfections in the data.* What effect will imperfections in the available data (e.g., errors in measurement) have on our results? Do they invalidate our estimates?

6. *Feedback relationships.* Suppose we want to estimate the effect of variable X on Y, but it happens that not only does X influence Y, but Y also has an impact on X. In this case it may be difficult to discern whether the parameter estimates reflect the influence of X on Y, of Y on X, or more likely some mixture of these two effects. Feedback relationships of this kind occur with considerable frequency in economics: price determines the quantity demanded of a good, but demand also influences price; the level of aggregate spending in the economy has a powerful effect on the level of total output and income, but the level of output and income in turn influences the level of spending, and so on. This might be called the systems problem. Economic problems are often of a systems type, reflecting the interdependencies that typically characterize the functioning of an economic system. But this, we shall find, creates serious problems for the econometrician, who must try in quantitative terms to unravel these interdependencies.

These, then, are some of the problems of econometrics, and we shall proceed in the coming chapters to develop techniques to deal with them.

APPENDIX A.

Some Propositions on Summation Operations

As we indicated in the Preface, this book does not use advanced mathematical or statistical theory; we shall rely wholly on simple algebra and elementary statistics. There are, however, a few propositions concerning algebraic operations under summation signs with which some readers may be either unacquainted or perhaps a bit hazy. Since we shall use these particular propositions quite extensively, it may expedite the analysis if we present them here so that, when they appear in the text, you will be familiar with them.

Throughout this book we shall use capital sigma, $\sum$, to denote the operation of summation. For instance, let Q_1 be the quantity of a particular commodity produced in year 1; or more generally, let Q_t be the quantity produced in year t. Then the total production over years 1, 2, and 3 can be expressed as $(Q_1 + Q_2 + Q_3)$. We can economize on notation if we denote this expression by $\sum_{t=1}^{3} Q_t$, where

$$\sum_{t=1}^{3} Q_t = Q_1 + Q_2 + Q_3. \tag{1A.1}$$

More generally, the expression $\sum_{t=1}^{n} Q_t$ is defined as the sum of the first n terms of the variable Q. A simple extension of this notation enables us to express concisely intermediate sums such as

$$\sum_{t=3}^{7} Q_t = Q_3 + Q_4 + Q_5 + Q_6 + Q_7. \tag{1A.2}$$

Before continuing, you should convince yourself that the following is true:

$$\sum_{t=1}^{16} Q_t - \sum_{t=3}^{17} Q_t = Q_1 + Q_2 - Q_{17}. \tag{1A.3}$$

We shall now develop a few propositions that we shall use repeatedly in this book.

PROPOSITION I. If c is a constant (such as $c = 5$), then

$$\sum_{t=1}^{n} c X_t = c \sum_{t=1}^{n} X_t.$$

To see this, we note that by definition $\sum_{t=1}^{n} c X_t$ is the sum of the first n values of X, where each is multiplied by c. We thus have

$$\sum_{t=1}^{n} c X_t = c X_1 + c X_2 + \cdots + c X_n = c(X_1 + X_2 + \cdots + X_n)$$
$$= c \sum_{t=1}^{n} X_t. \tag{1A.4}$$

PROPOSITION II. If X and Y are two variables, then

$$\sum_{t=1}^{n} (X_t + Y_t) = \sum_{t=1}^{n} X_t + \sum_{t=1}^{n} Y_t.$$

Proposition II states that the sum of the X's and Y's is simply the sum of the X's plus the sum of the Y's. This is true because

$$\sum_{t=1}^{n} (X_t + Y_t) = (X_1 + Y_1) + (X_2 + Y_2) + \cdots + (X_n + Y_n)$$

$$= (X_1 + X_2 + \cdots + X_n) + (Y_1 + Y_2 + \cdots + Y_n) \quad (1A.5)$$

$$= \sum_{t=1}^{n} X_t + \sum_{t=1}^{n} Y_t.$$

As a generalization of both Propositions I and II, you should show that

$$\sum_{t=1}^{n} (aX_t + bY_t + cZ_t) = a \sum_{t=1}^{n} X_t + b \sum_{t=1}^{n} Y_t + c \sum_{t=1}^{n} Z_t,$$

where a, b, and c are constants and X, Y, and Z are variables.

PROPOSITION III. If $\bar{X}$ is the simple average of the first n values of the variable X, so that $\bar{X} = (\sum_{t=1}^{n} X_t)/n$, then

$$\sum_{t=1}^{n} (X_t - \bar{X}) = 0.$$

To prove this statement, we note first that

$$\sum_{t=1}^{n} (X_t - \bar{X}) = \sum_{t=1}^{n} X_t - \sum_{t=1}^{n} \bar{X}. \quad (1A.6)$$

If we multiply and divide the first term by n, we have

$$\frac{n \sum_{t=1}^{n} X_t}{n} = n\bar{X}. \quad (1A.7)$$

Next, we note that

$$\sum_{t=1}^{n} \bar{X} = \bar{X} + \bar{X} + \cdots + \bar{X} = n\bar{X}. \quad (1A.8)$$

Substituting (1A.7) and (1A.8) into (1A.6) gives us our result:

$$\sum_{t=1}^{n} (X_t - \bar{X}) = \sum_{t=1}^{n} X_t - \sum_{t=1}^{n} \bar{X} = n\bar{X} - n\bar{X} = 0.$$

From this discussion, it is more generally clear that, if K is any constant, then

$$\sum_{t=1}^{n} K = nK. \quad (1A.9)$$

PROPOSITION IV. If $\bar{X}$ and $\bar{Y}$ are the simple averages of n values of the two variables X and Y, then

$$\sum_{t=1}^{n} (X_t - \bar{X})(Y_t - \bar{Y}) = \sum_{t=1}^{n} (X_t - \bar{X})Y_t.$$

To see this, notice first that

$$\sum_{t=1}^{n} (X_t - \bar{X})(Y_t - \bar{Y}) = \sum_{t=1}^{n} [(X_t - \bar{X})Y_t - (X_t - \bar{X})\bar{Y}]$$

$$= \sum_{t=1}^{n} (X_t - \bar{X})Y_t - \sum_{t=1}^{n} (X_t - \bar{X})\bar{Y}. \tag{1A.10}$$

We shall now show that the second term in this expression is zero:

$$\sum_{t=1}^{n} (X_t - \bar{X})\bar{Y} = \bar{Y} \sum_{t=1}^{n} (X_t - \bar{X}) = \bar{Y} \cdot 0 = 0; \tag{1A.11}$$

this follows from Propositions I and III (noting that $\bar{Y}$ is a constant). This proves Proposition IV.

Extending the above one step further, we note that

$$\sum_{t=1}^{n} (X_t - \bar{X}_t)Y_t = \sum_{t=1}^{n} X_t Y_t - \sum_{t=1}^{n} \bar{X} Y_t. \tag{1A.12}$$

If we multiply and divide the last term by n, we can express (1A.12) as

$$\sum_{t=1}^{n} (X_t - \bar{X})Y_t = \sum_{t=1}^{r} X_t Y_t - n\bar{X}\bar{Y}. \tag{1A.13}$$

We leave for the reader the proof of two corollaries to Proposition IV:

$$\sum_{t=1}^{n} (X_t - \bar{X})^2 = \sum_{t=1}^{n} (X_t - \bar{X})X_t$$

and

$$\sum_{t=1}^{n} (X_t - \bar{X})^2 = \sum_{t=1}^{n} X_t^2 - n\bar{X}^2.$$

[Hint: express $\sum_{t=1}^{n} (X - \bar{X})^2$ as $\sum_{t=1}^{n} (X_t - \bar{X})(X_t - \bar{X})$.]

APPENDIX B.
A Review of Statistical Concepts

For convenience, we present here a brief review of some of the basic concepts of statistics that are used repeatedly in this book. We stress that this appendix is not intended to be a substitute for a basic course in statistics; its purpose is to provide a concise review of selected statistical concepts.

RANDOM VARIABLES

For practical purposes, a random variable can be viewed as a variable whose value is determined by the outcome of an experiment in which the outcome is subject to chance. In other words, each possible value of a random variable is associated with a particular probability of occurrence. As an example, the value of a random variable might depend on the tossing of a coin. The outcome of the toss (experiment) would be "heads" or "tails." A random variable could then be defined as a variable Y whose value is equal to one if heads appears and zero if the toss turns up tails. The statement that the possible values of Y are zero and one is often given by stating that Y is a random variable that assumes the values $y = 0, 1$. In this respect, Y and y should not be confused. Y is the random variable whose value depends on the outcome of the experiment; y simply represents the particular values (numbers) that Y might take on.

Another random variable would be W, where W is equal to the *weight* of a person selected at random from a given group of people. In this case, *the possible values* of W might be w, where perhaps $50 \text{ lb} \leq w \leq 1000 \text{ lb}$ if the group of people consists of adults. Although both Y and W are random variables, there is an important difference: W can take on any value in a range of values that is continuous, while the values of Y are not defined over a continuous interval. Variables such as W, which can have any value in a continuum, are called *continuous* random variables. Variables such as Y, which cannot assume a continuum of values, are called *discrete* random variables.

The material presented in this appendix is in terms of *discrete* random variables. The reason for this is that the analysis of continuous random variables requires the use of the calculus. For our purposes, however, we can develop the concepts we shall need later solely in terms of discrete variables.*

PROBABILITY (OR DENSITY) FUNCTION

Associated with a random variable is a probability function (sometimes called a probability density function) which gives the probabilities that the random variable will

---

* Readers who have the mathematical background may essentially translate the material below into the context of continuous random variables by replacing all the summation signs by integrals.

10

assume each of its possible values. The probability function is usually described in the form of an equation or a table. For instance, in the above example of a coin toss, the possible values of the variable Y were $y = 0, 1$ and the associated probabilities (assuming a balanced coin and a "fair" toss) are $\frac{1}{2}$ and $\frac{1}{2}$. Therefore, the probability function for Y may be written as $f(y) = \frac{1}{2}$, $y = 0, 1$. That is, if a random variable Y has a probability function $f(y)$, the statement $f(1) = \frac{1}{2}$ means "the probability that $Y = 1$ is $\frac{1}{2}$."

Another example may be helpful. Let Z be the number showing when a die is rolled. Then the range of values for Z is $z = 1, 2, 3, 4, 5, 6$, and its probability function would be $g(z) = \frac{1}{6}$, $z = 1, \ldots, 6$. Alternatively, this information could be given in the form of a table:

$$
\begin{array}{c|c|c|c|c|c|c}
z & 1 & 2 & 3 & 4 & 5 & 6 \\
\hline
g(z) & \frac{1}{6} & \frac{1}{6} & \frac{1}{6} & \frac{1}{6} & \frac{1}{6} & \frac{1}{6}
\end{array}
\tag{1B.1}
$$

Note that

$$g(1) + g(2) + \cdots + g(6) = \tfrac{1}{6} + \tfrac{1}{6} + \cdots + \tfrac{1}{6} = 1. \tag{1B.2}$$

That is, since Z must be one of the integers $1, 2, \ldots, 6$, the sum of the associated probabilities is equal to one. In short, (1B.2) states that the probability that Z will be one of the integers $1, 2, \ldots, 6$ is equal to one.

This is a general result. The sum of the probabilities corresponding to all possible values of a random variable must be equal to one. Another general result is that, since probabilities are defined to be greater than or equal to zero, the probability function must also be so defined. For instance, in the above die example, although unstated, the value of the probability function corresponding to $z = \sqrt{363}$ would be zero, since the probability that $Z = \sqrt{363}$ is zero.

INDEPENDENCE AND DEPENDENCE

Problems often arise that involve the relationship among several random variables. For instance, suppose a die is rolled twice in a random fashion. Let Z_1 and Z_2 be, respectively, the values occurring on the first and second roll. In this case, we would not expect the value of Z_2 to be influenced by the value of Z_1, and vice versa. For example, if the die is balanced, the probability of getting a 3 on the second roll, $Z_2 = 3$, would be $\frac{1}{6}$ *regardless* of the result on the first roll. This can be formalized by stating that the probability that Z_2 will take on any value is not influenced by the particular value assumed by Z_1, and vice versa. Two variables, such as Z_1 and Z_2, whose probabilities are unrelated in this manner are said to be *independent* of each other. We would thus say that Z_1 and Z_2 are independent random variables. If two variables are not independent, they are said to be *dependent*. As an example, let a single card be drawn from an ordinary deck of cards. Let $P = 1$ if a picture card is drawn, and $P = 0$ otherwise. In addition, let $K = 1$ if a king is drawn, and $K = 0$ otherwise. K and P are dependent random variables. For example, the probability that $K = 1$ would be $\frac{4}{12}$ if $P = 1$ and zero if $P = 0$. If we are not given any information concerning P, the probability that $K = 1$ would be $\frac{4}{52}$. In brief, two variables are dependent if information concerning one of them would alter the probabilities relating to the other.

The generalization of these definitions is straightforward. The random variable X_1 is independent of the random variables $X_2, \ldots, X_n$ if the probability that X_1 will take on any value is completely unaffected by the particular values assumed by $X_2, \ldots, X_n$. If there is some influence on the probabilities of X_1, then X_1 and at least one of the variables $X_2, \ldots, X_n$ are dependent.

A PRELIMINARY RESULT

Let $X_1, \ldots, X_n$ be random variables, and let Y be equal to a function of $X_1, \ldots, X_n$, say

$$Y = h(X_1, \ldots, X_n). \tag{1B.3}$$

A notation such as (1B.3) implies that Y depends upon a subset or possibly all of the variables $X_1, \ldots, X_n$. Since the X's are random variables, Y is also a random variable: its particular value would be determined by chance. In addition, if the function in (1B.3) is at all reasonable, Y will have a probability density function, just as each of the X's do. The conditions needed, and the calculations involved to determine the probability density function of Y, are beyond the level of this book. However, the results given below relating to functions of random variables do not require the calculation of this probability density function; instead they only implicitly require its existence so that the same concepts considered for the X's can also be meaningfully considered for Y. This will become clear.

EXPECTATIONS

The mathematical *expectation* (often called the *expected value*) of a random variable X, whose possible values are $x = x_1, x_2, \ldots, x_n$ and whose probability function is $f(x)$, is written as $E(X)$ and is defined as

$$E(X) = x_1 f(x_1) + x_2 f(x_2) + \cdots + x_n f(x_n). \tag{1B.4}$$

In (1B.4) we see that the expected value of X is defined as a weighted average of its possible values, where the weights are the associated probabilities. The symbol E in (1B.4) is called the *expected value operator*. As an example, the expected value of the variable Z in our die example is

$$E(Z) = 1(\tfrac{1}{6}) + 2(\tfrac{1}{6}) + \cdots + 6(\tfrac{1}{6}) = \tfrac{21}{6} = 3\tfrac{1}{2}. \tag{1B.5}$$

The expected value of a random variable is often called its *mean*, and is denoted by the letter μ with a subscript that indicates the random variable under consideration. For example, $E(Z) = \mu_Z$ and $E(X) = \mu_X$. Somewhat intuitively, the mean of a variable is a measure of its central tendency, or location; if the experiment were performed a large number of times, the mean is that value which we would expect to be the average of the variable over all the experiments.

The *variance* of a random variable X, whose possible values are $x = x_1, x_2, \ldots, x_n$ and whose probability function is $f(x)$, is usually written as σ_X^2 and is defined as

$$\sigma_X^2 = E(X - \mu_X)^2$$
$$= (x_1 - \mu_X)^2 f(x_1) + (x_2 - \mu_X)^2 f(x_2) + \cdots + (x_n - \mu_X)^2 f(x_n), \tag{1B.6}$$

where $E(X) = \mu_X$. From (1B.6) we see that the variance is defined as the expected value of the squared deviation of the variable from its mean. The variance is, in some sense, a measure of the dispersion of the random variable about its mean; it indicates, on average, how "far" from its mean the value of the random variable will be. As an example of the calculations involved, the variance of the variable Z above is

$$\sigma_Z^2 = E(Z - 3.5)^2$$

$$= (1 - 3.5)^2(\tfrac{1}{6}) + (2 - 3.5)^2(\tfrac{1}{6}) + \cdots + (6 - 3.5)^2(\tfrac{1}{6})$$

$$= \frac{17.50}{6} = 2\tfrac{11}{12}.$$

The positive square root of the variance is defined to be the *standard deviation*.

SOME PROPOSITIONS ON EXPECTATIONS

In this section we shall describe briefly some properties of expectations that we shall use frequently in the text. We note first a rather obvious statement concerning the expected value of a constant (c):

$$E(c) = c. \tag{1B.7}$$

If c is a constant with a value, say, of 5, then (1B.7) simply says that the expected value of c is 5. Since c can be nothing other than 5, it takes on the value of 5 with probability one, so that $E(5) = 5 \cdot f(5) = 5(1) = 5$.

Consider next the case where we define a new random variable, say Y, which equals a constant times another random variable. For our case of the rolling of a die, let $Y = 15Z$; for example, if the die shows a 4, then $Y = 15(4) = 60$. We find the expected value of Y by

$$E(Y) = E(15Z) = 15(1)(\tfrac{1}{6}) + 15(2)(\tfrac{1}{6}) + \cdots + 15(6)(\tfrac{1}{6})$$

$$= 15(3.5) = 52.5.$$

We thus find that the expected value of $Y = 15Z$ is simply 15 times the expected value of Z. This is a general result. Where b is a constant and X is a random variable,

$$E(bX) = bE(X) = b\mu_X. \tag{1B.8}$$

Expanding on these two propositions, let $X_1, X_2, \ldots, X_n$ be n random variables whose means are, respectively, $\mu_1, \mu_2, \ldots, \mu_n$. Let us define a variable Y as

$$Y = a_0 + a_1 X_1 + a_2 X_2 + \cdots + a_n X_n, \tag{1B.9}$$

where $a_0, a_1, \ldots, a_n$ are constants. That is, the variable Y is defined as a *linear combination* of the X's. We now note, without proof, that

$$E(Y) = E(a_0 + a_1 X_1 + a_2 X_2 + \cdots + a_n X_n)$$

$$= E(a_0) + E(a_1 X_1) + E(a_2 X_2) + \cdots + E(a_n X_n)$$

$$= a_0 + a_1 E(X_1) + a_2 E(X_2) + \cdots + a_n E(X_n)$$

$$= a_0 + a_1 \mu_1 + a_2 \mu_2 + \cdots + a_n \mu_n.$$

$$\tag{1B.10}$$

Thus, if Y is a linear combination of a set of random variables, the expected value of Y is simply equal to the sum of the expected values of the terms of which it is a function.

Suppose we now define another random variable, Q, which is equal to Z^2, where Z is the value showing when a die is rolled. The value of Q is thus equal to the square of the number appearing on the die. Taking the expected value of Q,

$$E(Q) = E(Z^2) = 1(\tfrac{1}{6}) + 4(\tfrac{1}{6}) + \cdots + 36(\tfrac{1}{6}) = 15\tfrac{1}{6}. \tag{1B.11}$$

Recalling that $E(Z) = 3.5$, we see that

$$[E(Z)]^2 = (3.5)^2 = 12.25 \neq E(Z^2) = 15\tfrac{1}{6}.$$

That is, $[E(Z)]^2 \neq E(Z^2)$. In words, the square of the expected value of Z is *not* equal to the expected value of Z^2.

This is an illustration of a more general result. That is, if $Y = g(X)$, where $g(X)$ is a *nonlinear* function of the random variable X, then, in general,

$$E(Y) = E[g(X)] \neq g[E(X)]. \tag{1B.12}$$

For instance, as we just saw, $E(X^2) \neq [E(X)]^2$; as another example, $E(e^X) \neq e^{E(X)}$.

We shall need one further result concerning expectations. Let Y now equal the product of a set of random variables:

$$Y = (X_1 X_2 \cdots X_n). \tag{1B.13}$$

In this case, unless the variables $X_1, X_2, \ldots, X_n$ are independent of each other, we have in general that

$$E(Y) = E(X_1 X_2 \cdots X_n) \neq E(X_1)E(X_2) \cdots E(X_n). \tag{1B.14}$$

We have already seen one example of this proposition, namely, that

$$E(Z^2) = E(Z \cdot Z) \neq E(Z)E(Z) = [E(Z)]^2.$$

However, if the X's are independent, then the expection of the product of the X's is equal to the product of their expectations:

$$E(Y) = E(X_1 X_2 \cdots X_n) = E(X_1)E(X_2) \cdots E(X_n), \tag{1B.15}$$

where all the X_i are independent.

RANDOM SAMPLE

Suppose we have a coin that is not perfectly balanced. For such a coin, the probability of a heads would be P, where P, in general, need not be $\tfrac{1}{2}$. The probability for a tails would be $(1 - P)$. A constant, such as P, that appears in a formula or a probability model of any sort is called a *parameter*.

Suppose we do not know the value of the parameter P, but we want somehow to obtain an estimate of it. To do this, we might toss the coin a number of times, say 100, and take $\hat{P}$ as our estimate of P, where $\hat{P}$ is the ratio of the number of heads obtained to the total tosses, namely, (number of heads)/100. To formalize this, let X_1 be a random variable whose value is equal to zero if a tails results on the first toss, or whose value is equal to one if a heads occurs. Similarly, let $X_2, \ldots, X_{100}$ be random variables whose values are zero and one corresponding, respectively, to the outcomes of tosses 2 through 100. That is, $X_i = 0$ if a tails occurs on the ith toss, and $X_i = 1$ if the ith toss is a heads.

Assuming that the probability of getting a heads on any toss is not influenced by the outcome of other tosses, the variables $X_1, X_2, \ldots, X_{100}$ would be independent. In addition, they would all have the same probability function. That is, the probability function for each X_i would be

$$
\begin{array}{c|c|c}
x_i & 0 & 1 \\
\hline
f(x_i) & 1 - P & P
\end{array}
\tag{1B.16}
$$

Random variables such as $X_1, X_2, \ldots, X_{100}$, which are *independent* and have the same *probability function*, are said to constitute a random sample. The population that is being sampled is described by the common probability function of the random variables. In the above case the sampled population (the population we are learning about) would be

$$
\begin{array}{c|c|c}
x & 0 & 1 \\
\hline
f(x) & 1 - P & P
\end{array}
\tag{1B.17}
$$

ESTIMATORS

In the example above, the manner in which we would estimate P, namely $\hat{P}$, could be described in terms of the random variables $X_1, X_2, \ldots, X_{100}$ as

$$
\hat{P} = \sum_{i=1}^{100} \frac{X_i}{100}.
\tag{1B.18}
$$

For example, if there were 80 heads out of the 100 tosses, 80 of the X_i would be one while 20 would be zero, and so $\hat{P}$ would be $\frac{80}{100} = 0.8$.

In the technical literature it would be said that, for the above example, our *estimate* of the parameter P is 0.8; on the other hand, the *formula* we used to obtain that estimate, in the above case $\hat{P}$ in (1B.18), would be called the *estimator*. That is, the estimate is a particular number that is calculated on the basis of our estimator (or formula). For example, $\hat{P}$ above tells us to add the values of the 100 random variables $X_1, X_2, \ldots, X_{100}$ and then divide by 100; this is our estimator. To obtain, however, a specific value, such as 0.80, we must actually toss the coin 100 times so that we can generate observed values for the 100 random variables. Therefore, somewhat intuitively, we may think of the *estimate* as the *ex post* or realized value of the estimator.

In general, an estimator such as $\hat{P}$ will be a function of random variables [see (1B.18)]. *The estimator must therefore itself be a random variable.* For example, $\hat{P}$ could be any of the values $0, 0.01, 0.02, \ldots, 0.99, 1.00$, depending on the outcomes of the 100 tosses of the coin. Thus, if we think of these 100 tosses as one large random experiment, it follows that $\hat{P}$ is a random variable.

UNBIASED ESTIMATORS

An estimator is said to be *unbiased* if its expectation, or mean, is equal to the parameter of which it is an estimator. That is, if $\hat{b}$ is an estimator of b, then $\hat{b}$ is unbiased if

$$
E(\hat{b}) = b.
\tag{1B.19}
$$

On the other hand, if $E(\hat{b}) \neq b$, then $\hat{b}$ is said to be a biased estimator of b.

As an example, consider again the estimator of P, namely $\hat{P}$, defined in (1B.18). Using the expression (1B.10) on expectations, we see that

$$E(\hat{P}) = E(\tfrac{1}{100}X_1 + \tfrac{1}{100}X_2 + \cdots + \tfrac{1}{100}X_{100})$$
$$= \tfrac{1}{100}[E(X_1) + E(X_2) + \cdots + E(X_{100})]. \tag{1B.20}$$

Since the probability function of each X_i is (1B.16), we see that

$$E(X_i) = 0(1 - P) + 1(P) = P. \tag{1B.21}$$

Substituting (1B.21) into (1B.20) yields

$$E(\hat{P}) = \tfrac{1}{100}(100P) = P. \tag{1B.22}$$

We thus have shown that $\hat{P}$ is an unbiased estimator of P.

As an example of a biased estimator, consider the problem of estimating the value of P^*, where $P^* = e^P$. At first this may seem like a trivial translation of the problem we just did; however, because P^* is related to P in a *nonlinear* fashion, the translation is not trivial.

The obvious estimator of $P^* = e^P$ would be $\hat{P}^* = e^{\hat{P}}$, where $\hat{P}$ is given by (1B.18). However, recall from our earlier discussion that

$$E(\hat{P}^*) = E(e^{\hat{P}}) \neq e^{E(\hat{P})} = e^P = P^*. \tag{1B.23}$$

Thus, $E(\hat{P}^*) \neq P^*$, and $\hat{P}^*$ is therefore a biased estimator of P^*. In brief, that $\hat{P}$ is an unbiased estimator of P does not imply that we can use $\hat{P}$ to obtain in a straightforward fashion, unbiased estimators of nonlinear functions of P. As we shall see in the text, this problem of nonlinear translation is a serious one in econometrics.

CONSISTENCY

Our illustrative estimator $\hat{P}$ in (1B.18) is based on a random sample of size 100. If, instead, the coin had been tossed, say, n times, we would have defined $\hat{P}$ as

$$\hat{P}_n = \sum_{i=1}^{n} \frac{X_i}{n}. \tag{1B.24}$$

Using (1B.10), it is not difficult to show that $E(\hat{P}_n) = P$ (i.e., $\hat{P}_n$ is unbiased). Further, using a formula we shall develop in the appendix to Chapter 2, we can show that the variance of $\hat{P}_n$ is

$$\sigma_{\hat{P}_n}^2 = \frac{1}{n^2}(\sigma_1^2 + \sigma_2^2 + \cdots + \sigma_n^2), \tag{1B.25}$$

where σ_i^2 is the variance of X_i. From the probability function for X_i, defined in (1B.16), we can calculate:

$$\sigma_i^2 = E[X_i - E(X_i)]^2 = E(X_i - P)^2$$
$$= [(0 - P)^2(1 - P) + (1 - P)^2 P] = P(1 - P). \tag{1B.26}$$

Substituting (1B.26) into (1B.25) yields

$$\sigma_{\hat{P}_n}^2 = \frac{1}{n}[P(1 - P)]. \tag{1B.27}$$

From (1B.27) we can see that, as our sample approaches an infinite size (as $n \rightarrow \infty$), the variance of $\hat{P}_n$ goes to zero.* Intuitively, this result together with the result that the mean of $\hat{P}_n$ is P suggests that as $n \rightarrow \infty$, the only likely value of $\hat{P}_n$ is P. More formally, it can be shown that, if the sample were of infinite size, the probability that $\hat{P}_n$ and P will differ by any amount would be zero. Symbolically, the statement is that

$$\lim_{n \to \infty} \text{Prob}(|\hat{P}_n - P| > \varepsilon) = 0, \qquad (1B.28)$$

where ε is any preassigned number, however small.

When an estimator satisfies a condition such as (1B.28), it is said to be a *consistent estimator* of the corresponding parameter. Thus, $\hat{P}_n$ is a consistent estimator of P. To generalize, $\hat{b}$ is a consistent estimator of b if

$$\lim_{n \to \infty} \text{Prob}(|\hat{b} - b| > \varepsilon) = 0. \qquad (1B.29)$$

In light of (1B.29), this condition of consistency is often written as $P \lim \hat{b} = b$. This again says that if the sample size were infinite, the probability that $\hat{b}$ will be anything other than b would be zero. Finally, if an estimator, $\hat{c}$, is not consistent, then

$$\lim_{n \to \infty} \text{Prob}(|\hat{c} - c| > \varepsilon) \neq 0. \qquad (1B.30)$$

Such an estimator is said to be *inconsistent*.

JOINT DENSITY FUNCTION: ILLUSTRATIONS

There are many cases in which the values of more than one random variable are determined by the outcome of a random experiment. As an example, consider the experiment in which a person is selected at random and this person's height, weight, and age are recorded. Let H, W, and A be, respectively, the height, weight, and age so recorded. In this case the values of three random variables, namely H, W, and A, are determined by the experiment. As another example, consider the experiment in which two coins are randomly tossed. Let $X_1 = 1$ if the first coin is a heads, and $X_1 = 0$ otherwise; similarly, let $X_2 = 1$ if the second coin is a heads, and $X_2 = 0$ otherwise. In this case, the experiment determines the values of two random variables. Clearly, our earlier discussion of independence and dependence contains still another example. It should also be clear that in general an experiment could determine the values of n random variables, where n is a positive integer.

Consider, first, the case in which two random variables are determined, say X and Y. For purposes of illustration, suppose the possible values of X are $x = 1, 2$, and the possible values of Y are $y = 1, 2$, and 3. The implication of this is that there are six possible pairs of values corresponding to X and Y, one of which will occur as the outcome of the experiment. The six possible pairs of values are (1, 1), (1, 2), (1, 3), (2, 1), (2, 2), and (2, 3) where (1, 1) corresponds to the case in which $X = 1$ and $Y = 1$, (1, 2) corresponds to $X = 1$ and $Y = 2$, and so on. To continue the illustration, suppose the probabilities for these six possible pairs of values are, respectively, 0.1, 0.2, 0.15, 0.25, 0.1, and 0.2; this indicates, for example, that $\text{Prob}(X = 1$ and $Y = 2) = 0.2$, and so on.

We define a joint density function (sometimes simply referred to as a joint density) for a set of random variables to be a function which gives the probability that the set

---

* An alternative statement of this might be that if our sample were of infinite size, the variance of P_n would be zero.

of random variables assumes each of its possible values. For the case above, this means that if $f(x, y)$ is the joint density for X and Y, where $x = 1, 2$, and $y = 1, 2, 3$, then $f(1, 3) = \text{Prob}(X = 1 \text{ and } Y = 3) = 0.15$, and so on.

The joint density $f(x, y)$ for our illustrative case can be described in table form, namely

(x, y)	$(1, 1)$	$(1, 2)$	$(1, 3)$	$(2, 1)$	$(2, 2)$	$(2, 3)$
$f(x, y)$	0.1	0.2	0.15	0.25	0.1	0.2

(1B.31)

Note that the sum of all the probabilities is unity. The reason for this is that X and Y must assume one of the six pairs of values given in the table. For purposes of reference with respect to the literature, we note that a joint density function such as that given in (1B.31) is often (equivalently) described as

x/y	1	2	3
1	0.1	0.2	0.15
2	0.25	0.1	0.2

(1B.32)

Consistent with our discussion relating to (1B.1), we define the value of the joint density $f(x, y)$ corresponding to an impossible pair of values for X and Y to be zero. As an illustration, $f(-15, 27) = f(1, 1.5) = f(52.3, 2) = 0$. The reason for this is that the probability of an impossible outcome should be zero. Somewhat more generally, we define the value of a joint density corresponding to an impossible set of values of the random variables involved to be zero.

The joint density of X and Y determines all probabilistic inferences concerning X and Y. As an illustration, from either (1B.31) or (1B.32) we see that the probability that $(X = 1 \text{ and } Y = 1)$ *or* $(X = 2 \text{ and } Y = 3)$ is $0.1 + 0.2 = 0.3$. Similarly, the probability that $(X = 2 \text{ and } Y \le 2)$ is $0.25 + 0.1 = 0.35$.

Continuing, suppose one is interested only in X and, in particular, in the probability that $X = 1$. From the table we see that $X = 1$ corresponds to the cases $(1, 1)$, $(1, 2)$, and $(1, 3)$; there are no other possibilities. Therefore, $\text{Prob}(X = 1) = \text{Prob}(X = 1 \text{ and } Y = 1) + \text{Prob}(X = 1 \text{ and } Y = 2) + \text{Prob}(X = 1 \text{ and } Y = 3) = 0.1 + 0.2 + 0.15 = 0.45$. Similarly, we see that $\text{Prob}(X = 2) = 0.25 + 0.1 + 0.2 = 0.55$. For future reference, note that $\text{Prob}(X = 1)$ is obtained from the joint density $f(x, y)$ by summing $f(1, y)$ over all possible values of y, namely $y = 1, 2, 3$.

Earlier we defined the probability density of a random variable as the function which gives the probabilities that the random variable assumes each of its possible values. In the example above, we determined that $\text{Prob}(X = 1) = 0.45$, and $\text{Prob}(X = 2) = 0.55$; there are no other possible values of X. Let $g(x)$ be the probability density of X, where $x = 1, 2$. It follows that $g(1) = 0.45$ and $g(2) = 0.55$, or in table form

x	1	2
$g(x)$	0.45	0.55

(1B.33)

Let $h(y)$, where $y = 1, 2, 3$, be the probability density of Y. Then, completely analogous to the above, we see that $h(y)$ is given by

y	1	2	3
$h(y)$	0.35	0.3	0.35

(1B.34)

In brief, the probability density of X, or of Y, can be determined from the joint density of X and Y. This is described more formally below.

JOINT DENSITY FUNCTION: A GENERALIZATION

Let X and Y be discrete random variables, and let their possible values be, respectively, $x_1, \ldots, x_n$ and $y_1, \ldots, y_m$. Let their joint density be

x, y	x_1, y_1	$\cdots$	x_n, y_1	x_1, y_2	$\cdots$	x_n, y_m
$f(x, y)$	$f(x_1, y_1)$	$\cdots$	$f(x_n, y_1)$	$f(x_1, y_2)$	$\cdots$	$f(x_n, y_m)$

$$(1B.35)$$

Let the probability density of X be $f_1(x)$, $x = x_1, \ldots, x_n$ and the density of Y be $f_2(y)$, $y = y_1, \ldots, y_m$. In light of our discussion above, the reader should have no difficulty seeing that

$$f_1(x_1) = f(x_1, y_1) + \cdots + f(x_1, y_m)$$
$$f_1(x_2) = f(x_2, y_1) + \cdots + f(x_2, y_m)$$
$$\vdots$$
$$f_1(x_n) = f(x_n, y_1) + \cdots + f(x_n, y_m).$$

$$(1B.36)$$

In summation notation, (1B.36) can be expressed as

$$f_1(x) = \sum_{i=1}^{m} f(x, y_i), \qquad x = x_1, \ldots, x_n.$$

$$(1B.37)$$

A corresponding relationship exists between $f_2(y)$ and $f(x, y)$. Specifically,

$$f_2(y) = \sum_{i=1}^{n} f(x_i, y), \qquad y = y_1, \ldots, y_m.$$

$$(1B.38)$$

JOINT DENSITY FUNCTIONS: EXPECTATIONS

Earlier we defined the expected value of X to be

$$E(X) = x_1 f_1(x_1) + \cdots + x_n f_1(x_n).$$

$$(1B.39)$$

In light of (1B.36), $E(X)$ can also be determined in terms of the joint density of X and Y. Specifically,

$$E(X) = x_1[f(x_1, y_1) + \cdots + f(x_1, y_m)]$$
$$+ x_2[f(x_2, y_1) + \cdots + f(x_2, y_m)]$$
$$\vdots$$
$$+ x_n[f(x_n, y_1) + \cdots + f(x_n, y_m)].$$

$$(1B.40)$$

Clearly, $E(Y)$ can also be determined in terms of $f_2(y)$ or $f(x, y)$.

JOINT DENSITY FUNCTIONS: EXPECTATIONS OF FUNCTIONS OF RANDOM VARIABLES

Let $h(X, Y)$ be a bounded function of X and Y; by bounded we mean that $|h(x, y)|$ is finite for all values of $x = x_1, \ldots, x_n$ and $y = y_1, \ldots, y_m$. The possible values of $h(X, Y)$ are $h(x_1, y_1), h(x_1, y_2), \ldots, h(x_1, y_m), h(x_2, y_1), \ldots, h(x_n, y_m)$.

We define the expected value of $h(X, Y)$ as

$$E[h(X, Y)] = h(x_1, y_1)f(x_1, y_1) + \cdots + h(x_1, y_m)f(x_1, y_m)$$
$$+ h(x_2, y_1)f(x_2, y_1) + \cdots + h(x_2, y_m)f(x_2, y_m) \qquad (1B.41)$$
$$\vdots$$
$$+ h(x_n, y_1)f(x_n, y_1) + \cdots + h(x_n, y_m)f(x_n, y_m).$$

The interpretation of $E[h(X, Y)]$ is clear and consistent with the univariate case given in (1B.3); specifically, the expected value of $h(X, Y)$ is defined as a weighted sum of its possible values, where the weights are the corresponding probabilities.

For purposes of illustration, consider the special case in which $h(X, Y) = X$. Then, from (1B.41)

$$E[h(X, Y)] = x_1[f(x_1, y_1) + \cdots + f(x_1, y_m)]$$
$$+ x_2[f(x_2, y_1) + \cdots + f(x_2, y_m)] \qquad (1B.42)$$
$$\vdots$$
$$+ x_n[f(x_n, y_1) + \cdots + f(x_n, y_m)].$$

Using (1B.36) this reduces to

$$E[h(X, Y)] = x_1 f_1(x_1) + x_2 f_1(x_2) + \cdots + x_n f_1(x_n) \qquad (1B.43)$$

which is identical to (1B.39). Thus (1B.39) can be viewed as a special case of (1B.41).

AN ILLUSTRATION: THE COVARIANCE OF X AND Y

Let X and Y again be the discrete random variables whose joint density is $f(x, y)$, $x = x_1, \ldots, x_n$ and $y = y_1, \ldots, y_m$. Let the mean of X be $E(X) = u_x$ and the mean of Y be $E(Y) = u_y$. The covariance of X and Y is defined as $\sigma_{X,Y}$ where

$$\sigma_{X,Y} = E[(X - u_x)(Y - u_y)]. \qquad (1B.44)$$

A discussion and an interpretation of the covariance of two random variables is given in Chapter 2.

The covariance $\sigma_{X,Y}$ can be calculated using (1B.41) by taking $h(X, Y) = (X - u_x)(Y - u_y)$. As an illustration, suppose the joint density of X and Y is given by (1B.31). Then, using (1B.40), we obtain

$$E(X) = 1[0.1 + 0.2 + 0.15] + 2[0.25 + 0.1 + 0.2] = 1.55, \qquad (1B.45)$$

and similarly

$$E(Y) = 1[0.1 + 0.25] + 2[0.2 + 0.1] + 3[0.15 + 0.2] = 2.00. \qquad (1B.46)$$

Therefore, using (1B.41), we obtain

$$\sigma_{X,Y} = E[(X - 1.55)(Y - 2.00)]$$
$$= (1 - 1.55)(1 - 2)(0.1) + (1 - 1.55)(2 - 2)(0.2) + (1 - 1.55)(3 - 2)(0.15)$$
$$+ (2 - 1.55)(1 - 2)(0.25) + (2 - 1.55)(2 - 2)(0.1) + (2 - 1.55)(3 - 2)(0.2)$$
$$= -0.050.$$

$$(1B.47)$$

JOINT DENSITY FUNCTIONS: A MORE GENERAL DISCUSSION

In this section, we generalize the basic concepts given above to the case in which three random variables are involved. Further generalization will be evident.

Consider the three discrete random variables X, Y, and W, whose possible values are, respectively, $x = x_1, \ldots, x_n$; $y = y_1, \ldots, y_m$; $w = w_1, \ldots, w_s$. In this case there are n possible values of X, m possible values of Y, and s possible values of W.

Let $p(x, y, w)$ be the joint density of X, Y, and W so that, for example, $p(x_1, y_3, w_4) = \text{Prob}(X = x_1 \text{ and } Y = y_3 \text{ and } W = w_4)$. Then a direct extension of the above discussion implies the following:

> Observation 1:   The sum of all of the values of $P(x, y, w)$ (there are *nms* of them) is equal to unity.
>
> Observation 2:   Probability statements concerning only two of the variables can be determined from the joint density of the three variables. As an illustration, a direct extension of the result in (1B.36) gives us

$$\text{Prob}(X = x_i \text{ and } Y = y_j) = p(x_i, y_j, w_1) + p(x_i, y_j, w_2) + \cdots + p(x_i, y_j, w_s). \quad (1\text{B}.48)$$

Two other illustrations which are somewhat less abstract are

$$\text{Prob}(X = 2 \text{ and } Y = 10) = p(2, 10, w_1) + p(2, 10, w_2) + \cdots + p(2, 10, w_s), \quad (1\text{B}.49)$$

and

$$\text{Prob}(X = 3 \text{ and } W = 7) = p(3, y_1, 7) + p(3, y_2, 7) + \cdots + p(3, y_m, 7). \quad (1\text{B}.50)$$

Note that in all cases the joint density is being summed over all possible values of the variable to which reference is *not made* in the probability statement.

> Observation 3:   Let the joint density of X and Y be $f(x, y)$, where $x = x_1, \ldots, x_n$ and $y = y_1, \ldots, y_m$. Then the result in (1B.48) gives $f(x_i, y_j)$—that is, the value of the joint density corresponding to x_i, y_j.

Since the calculations in (1B.48) can be carried out for each and every pair of values $(x_1, y_1), (x_1, y_2), \ldots, (x_1, y_m), (x_2, y_1), \ldots, (x_n, y_m)$, the entire joint density of X and Y can be determined from the joint density of X, Y, and W. More specifically,

$$f(x, y) = p(x, y, w_1) + p(x, y, w_2) + \cdots + p(x, y, w_s)$$
$$= \sum_{i=1}^{s} p(x, y, w_i) \qquad (1\text{B}.51)$$

where x could be any of the values $x_1, \ldots, x_n$ and y could be any of the values $y_1, \ldots, y_m$. Similarly, the joint density of X and W, say $g(x, w)$, and of Y and W, say $h(y, w)$ can be determined from the joint density of X, Y, and W. More specifically,

$$g(x, w) = p(x, y_1, w) + p(x, y_2, w) + \cdots + p(x, y_m, w)$$
$$= \sum_{i=1}^{m} p(x, y_i, w) \qquad (1\text{B}.52)$$

and

$$h(y, w) = p(x_1, y, w) + p(x_2, y, w) + \cdots + p(x_n, y, w)$$
$$= \sum_{i=1}^{n} p(x_i, y, w). \qquad (1\text{B}.53)$$

Note that in all cases, the joint density is being summed over the possible values of the variable which does *not* correspond to the density on the left-hand side of the relationship.

Our discussion thus far suggests that knowledge of the joint density of X, Y, and W implies knowledge of the joint densities of any pair of these variables. Since the density of X can be determined from the joint density of X and Y, and so on, it follows that the joint density of X, Y, and W also determines the density of X, the density of Y, and the density of W.

AN IMPORTANT RESULT CONCERNING INDEPENDENCE

Consider again the three discrete random variables X, Y, and W with joint density $p(x, y, w)$ where $x = x_1, \ldots, x_n$; $y = y_1, \ldots, y_m$; and $w = w_1, \ldots, w_s$. Again, let the density of X be $f_1(x)$ and the density of Y be $f_2(y)$; let the density of W be $f_3(w)$. Then, if X, Y, and W are *jointly independent*

$$p(x, y, w) = f_1(x)f_2(y)f_3(w). \tag{1B.54}$$

That is, if the random variables X, Y, and W are *jointly independent*, their joint density will be equal to the product of their (individual) densities. More generally, the joint density of any number of random variables will be equal to the product of the individual densities if the variables are *jointly independent*.

Recall that $f_1(x_i) = \text{Prob}(X = x_i)$, and so on. Then, one implication of (1B.54) is that, if X, Y, and W are jointly independent,

$$\text{Prob}(X = x_i \text{ and } Y = y_j \text{ and } W = w_r)$$
$$= \text{Prob}(X = x_i) * \text{Prob}(Y = y_j) * \text{Prob}(W = w_r), \tag{1B.55}$$

that is, the joint probability that $X = x_i$ *and* $Y = y_j$ *and* $W = w_r$ reduces to the product of the corresponding *individual* probabilities; there are no interactions! As an illustration, each component determining the joint probability in (1B.55) relates only to the corresponding random variable. This would generally not be the case if the variables were dependent (not independent), as we saw in our earlier discussion concerning independence and dependence.

Let $f(x, y)$ be the joint density of X and Y. Then, since $f(x, y) = p(x, y, w_1) + p(x, y, w_2) + \cdots + p(x, y, w_s)$, (1B.54) implies

$$f(x, y) = f_1(x)f_2(y)[f_3(w_1) + f_3(w_2) + \cdots + f_3(w_s)] = f_1(x)f_2(y), \tag{1B.56}$$

since the term in brackets is the sum of the density of W over all of the possible values of W, and hence is equal to one. Again, let $h(y, w)$ and $g(x, w)$ be, respectively, the joint densities of Y and W, and X and W. Then, a development similar to that leading to (1B.56) will demonstrate that

$$h(y, w) = f_2(y)f_3(w) \tag{1B.57}$$

and

$$g(x, w) = f_1(x)f_3(w). \tag{1B.58}$$

The results in (1B.56)–(1B.58) correspond to the following general result. Consider q random variables, $X_1, \ldots, X_q$, which are jointly independent so that their joint density function factors in a manner corresponding to (1B.54). Then, all subsets of these random variables are also jointly independent and so their joint densities also factor correspondingly. As an illustration, if $X_1, X_2, \ldots, X_{10}$ are jointly independent, then so are the following three variables: X_1, X_3, X_7. As another illustration if X_1, ..., X_{10} are jointly independent random variables, then so are X_1 and X_8 and hence

$$\text{Prob}(X_1 = 3 \text{ and } X_8 = 7) = \text{Prob}(X_1 = 3) * \text{Prob}(X_8 = 7). \qquad (1B.59)$$

Clearly, joint independence simplifies probability calculations.

AN APPLICATION OF THE INDEPENDENCE CONDITIONS

Suppose we have a coin whose probability of a heads is P, and therefore the probability of a tails is $1 - P$. Suppose this coin is tossed n times in a random fashion. Let $X_i = 1$ if the ith toss results in a heads, and $X_i = 0$ otherwise, $i = 1, \ldots, n$. Since the coin is tossed in a random fashion, there are n jointly independent random variables, namely $X_i, \ldots, X_n$. Note that $\text{Prob}(X_i = 1) = P$, and $\text{Prob}(X_i = 0) = 1 - P$.

Consider the probability that the first s tosses are heads and the last $n - s$ tosses are tails. Since $X_1, \ldots, X_n$, are jointly independent, this probability is [see (1B.55)]

$$\text{Prob}(X_1 = 1 \text{ and } X_2 = 1 \text{ and} \cdots \text{and } X_s = 1 \text{ and } X_{s+1} = 0 \text{ and} \cdots \text{and } X_n = 0)$$

$$= \text{Prob}(X_1 = 1) \, \text{Prob}(X_2 = 1) \cdots \text{Prob}(X_s = 1) \, \text{Prob}(X_{s+1} = 0) \cdots \text{Prob}(X_n = 0)$$

$$= P^s (1 - P)^{n-s}.$$

$$(1B.60)$$

Consider now the probability that the first $n - s$ tosses are tails, and the last s tosses are heads. The probability for this case is the same as that in (1B.60) since

$$\text{Prob}(X_1 = 0 \text{ and} \cdots \text{and } X_{n-s} = 0 \text{ and } X_{n-s+1} = 1 \text{ and} \cdots \text{and } X_n = 1)$$

$$= \text{Prob}(X_1 = 0) \cdots \text{Prob}(X_{n-s} = 0) \, \text{Prob}(X_{n-s+1} = 1) \cdots \text{Prob}(X_n = 1)$$

$$= (1 - P)^{n-s} P^s = P^s (1 - P)^{n-s}.$$

$$(1B.61)$$

To generalize, consider any particular sequence of heads and tails in this illustration in which there are s heads and therefore $(n - s)$ tails. Let $p_{s,n}$ be the probability of obtaining this particular sequence. Then, it should be clear that

$$P_{s,n} = P^s (1 - P)^{n-s}. \qquad (1B.62)$$

This result in (1B.62) will be needed at a later point.

QUESTIONS

1. Demonstrate that $\sum_{t=1}^{n} (X_t - \bar{X}) = 0$ holds in terms of the following: $X_1 = 0$, $X_2 = 5$, $X_3 = 6$, $X_4 = 1$.

2. Show that

$$\sum_{t=1}^{n} (aX_t + bY_t + cZ_t) = a \sum_{t=1}^{n} X_t + b \sum_{t=1}^{n} Y_t + c \sum_{t=1}^{n} Z_t.$$

3. Show that $\sum_{t=1}^{n} (X_t - \bar{X})(Y_t - \bar{Y})$ may be expressed as $\sum_{t=1}^{n} X_t(Y_t - \bar{Y})$.

CHAPTER 2
The Two-Variable Regression Model

One of the central problems of econometrics is the development of effective techniques for the estimation of the quantitative relationships among economic variables. In terms of our example in Chapter 1, what we need is some way to get reliable estimates of the parameters a and b in the consumption function so that, among other things, we can predict how consumption will vary with the level of disposable income. In this chapter we shall set forth the basic principles for the estimation of a relationship between two variables. We want to emphasize that this is the most important chapter in the book. It is here and in the first section of Chapter 3 that we introduce the basic conceptual structure for estimation and for the testing of hypotheses. The material in succeeding chapters (including, for example, the estimation of relationships involving several variables) consists primarily of straightforward and obvious extensions of our analysis in the two-variable case.

2.1 MEASURING THE STATISTICAL RELATIONSHIP BETWEEN TWO VARIABLES: COVARIANCE AND CORRELATION

Suppose first that we are simply interested in *describing* the statistical relationship between two variables. We have no hypotheses involving any sorts of causal relations between them; all we seek to determine at this point is whether the two variables exhibit any kind of systematic pattern of association.

As an example, suppose that we were to record the weight (L) in pounds and height (H) in inches of 30 people selected at random. As in Chapter 1, we use a scatter diagram in Figure 2.1 to depict the observations, and as before we note that there is not an exact relationship between the two variables. Two people with the same height will not in general have precisely the same weight; we can see in Figure 2.1, for example, that while the individuals represented by points P_1 and P_2 are both 70 in. tall, the first weighs 160 lb while the second weighs 180 lb. Nevertheless, there does appear to be some type of relationship between L and H. Taller people *usually* appear to weigh more than shorter persons. It thus appears that, on the average, L and H are *positively related*: larger values of H are typically associated with larger values of L.

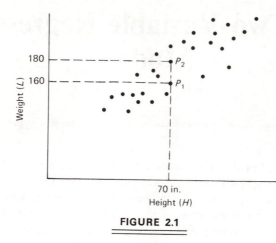

FIGURE 2.1

In contrast, the scatter diagram in Figure 2.2 suggests that the two variables considered there, the percentage change in wage rates ($\dot{w}$) and the rate of unemployment (R), are *negatively related*; the height of the points seems to decline as we move from left to right, which indicates that more rapid increases in wages are typically associated with lower rates of unemployment. Such a finding may come as no great surprise. When the economy is booming and there are few unemployed workers available, we might expect employers to bid up wages relatively rapidly in their attempts to expand output to meet the high level of demand for their products. Conversely, when aggregate demand is low and, consequently, unemployment is at a higher level, there will tend to be much less upward pressure on wages. Incidentally, a curve fitted to this scatter of points is known as a *Phillips Curve*, after A. W. Phillips, who first noted this relationship between $\dot{w}$ and R in Great Britain.*

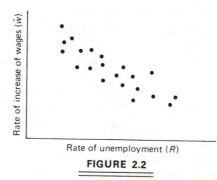

FIGURE 2.2

* See A. W. Phillips, "The Relation Between Unemployment and the Rate of Change of Money Wage Rates in the United Kingdom, 1861–1957," *Economica* 25 (Nov. 1958), pp. 283–299.

THE COVARIANCE

One question we thus want to ask about two variables is whether they are positively or negatively related: are larger-than-typical values of one usually associated with larger-than-typical values of the other (a positive relationship)? Or are larger values of the first variable normally accompanied by smaller values of the second (a negative relationship)? A parameter that captures this plus-or-minus relationship is the *covariance*. For two variables, X and Y, whose means are $E(X) = \mu_X$ and $E(Y) = \mu_Y$, the covariance $(\sigma_{X,Y})$ is formally defined as

$$\sigma_{X,Y} = E[(X - \mu_X)(Y - \mu_Y)]. \tag{2.1}$$

That is, the covariance is the expected value of the product $(X - \mu_X)$ $\times (Y - \mu_Y)$. If this covariance were positive, $\sigma_{X,Y} > 0$, this would indicate that larger-than-mean values of X, $(X - \mu_X) > 0$, are *usually* associated with larger-than-mean values of Y, $(Y - \mu_Y) > 0$, and conversely. Intuitively, the point here is simply that, if $\sigma_{X,Y}$ is to be positive, the two terms $(X - \mu_X)$ and $(Y - \mu_Y)$ must typically both be positive or both be negative. We would therefore say that if X is larger than its mean value, μ_X, then Y will typically be larger than its mean value, μ_Y. Thus, X and Y would be positively related. In contrast, if $\sigma_{X,Y} < 0$, larger-than-mean values of X will usually be accompanied by smaller-than-mean values of Y, which would indicate a negative relationship between the two variables.

The intermediate case, of course, would be the one in which $\sigma_{X,Y} = 0$. In this case, larger-than-mean values of X would be just as likely to be accompanied by smaller-than-mean values of Y as by larger-than-mean values. There are two instances in which this can happen. The first is the case in which the two variables are *independent*. For instance, if X and Y are independent,

$$\begin{aligned}\sigma_{X,Y} &= E[(X - \mu_X)(Y - \mu_Y)] \\ &= E(X - \mu_X)E(Y - \mu_Y) = 0,\end{aligned} \tag{2.2}$$

since

$$E(X - \mu_X) = E(X) - E(\mu_X) = \mu_X - \mu_X = 0.^*$$

The second is the case in which the two variables are related to each other in a particular *nonlinear* way. We shall see an example of this below. However, at this point we should note that because of this nonlinear case, a zero covariance between two variables does not imply that they are independent; instead, a zero covariance implies only that the two variables are not *linearly* related.

---

* The reader should recall (as noted in Appendix B to Chapter 1) that if the two variables are independent, the expected value of their product is equal to the product of their expected values. Note also that the mean of X, namely μ_X, is a constant, and therefore $E(\mu_X) = \mu_X$.

THE COVARIANCE ESTIMATOR

In practice we shall not generally know what the value of $\sigma_{X,Y}$ is. Typically, we shall have at our disposal only a random sample of observed values of X and Y. As before we might, for instance, have the height and weight of a certain number of people, say n, selected at random. In such a case we would say that we have a sample of size n on L and H. Suppose now that we have a sample of size n on X and Y. What we need is some way to estimate the value of $\sigma_{X,Y}$ from this sample of observations. Since $\sigma_{X,Y}$ is defined as the expected value of the product of the deviations of the variables from their means, $E[(X - \mu_X)(Y - \mu_Y)]$, the obvious way to estimate $\sigma_{X,Y}$ would be to calculate the sample average of the product of deviations of the variables X and Y from their sample averages. More formally, let the n *observed* values of our sample on X and Y be $X_1, \ldots, X_n$ and $Y_1, \ldots, Y_n$.* Then the estimator of the covariance between X and Y is

$$\hat{\sigma}_{X,Y} = \frac{\sum\limits_{t=1}^{n} (X_t - \overline{X})(Y_t - \overline{Y})}{n - 1}, \qquad (2.3)$$

where

$$\overline{X} = \frac{\sum\limits_{t=1}^{n} X_t}{n} \quad \text{and} \quad \overline{Y} = \frac{\sum\limits_{t=1}^{n} Y_t}{n}.$$

We explain below why the expression in (2.3) is divided by $(n - 1)$ rather than by n. At this point, however, we note that since $(X_t - \overline{X})(Y_t - \overline{Y})$ is the tth observed product of deviations of the variables from their sample averages, $\hat{\sigma}_{X,Y}$ is simply the average of such products.**

It will be useful to stop briefly at this point and explain our notation. In this book we shall use the symbol ^ above a variable or parameter to denote "estimator of"; thus, $\hat{\sigma}_{X,Y}$ is an estimator of $\sigma_{X,Y}$. The right-hand side (RHS) of (2.3) indicates that $\hat{\sigma}_{X,Y}$ is based on the summation of the product $(X_t - \overline{X})(Y_t - \overline{Y})$ over the entire sample, $t = 1, \ldots, n$. To simplify our notation, from here on we shall not bother to write $\sum_{t=1}^{n}$, but shall simply use $\sum$ with the understanding that, unless indicated otherwise, the summation procedure will extend over all n observations in the sample.

THE UNBIASEDNESS OF $\hat{\sigma}_{X,Y}$

We have that $\hat{\sigma}_{X,Y}$ is an estimator of the covariance between X and Y. Moreover, it can be shown that $E[\hat{\sigma}_{X,Y}] = \sigma_{X,Y}$; that is, $\hat{\sigma}_{X,Y}$ is an *unbiased*

---

* For example, X_5 would be the fifth observed value of X. In terms of our earlier illustration, where H was the height of a person and L was his weight, H_5 would be the height of the fifth observed person and L_5 would be this same person's weight.

** If the fifth observed person in our sample were 3 in. taller and weighed 15 lb more than the average of the heights and weights for the whole sample, then $(H_5 - \overline{H}) \times (L_5 - \overline{L}) = 45$. Our estimator $\hat{\sigma}_{L,H}$ for the covariance of L and H would simply be the average of these products over the entire sample.

estimator of $\sigma_{X,Y}$. The idea here is that, since $\hat{\sigma}_{X,Y}$ is generated from a random sample of X and Y, it is itself a random variable whose value will vary from sample to sample. For example, if the weight and height, L and H, of 30 people selected at random depend on the particular people chosen, then the value of the estimator of the covariance between L and H will also depend on who is selected. It follows that the value of such an estimator will vary from sample to sample. More formally, the estimator has a probability function called its *sampling distribution*. The result stated above, namely, $E(\hat{\sigma}_{X,Y}) = \sigma_{X,Y}$, implies that the mean of the sampling distribution of $\hat{\sigma}_{X,Y}$ is the value of the parameter $\sigma_{X,Y}$.

Although a formal proof is beyond the scope of this book, an example may help to clarify at a more intuitive level what it means to say that $\hat{\sigma}_{X,Y}$ is an unbiased estimator of $\sigma_{X,Y}$.* Extending the above illustration, suppose that we were to take M samples of 30 people each and measure the weight, L, and height, H, of the persons in each sample. We could then compute a value for $\hat{\sigma}_{L,H}$ for each sample, from which we would get M separate estimates of the covariance between L and H. Note that the values for the various $\hat{\sigma}_{L,H}$ will generally differ. Specifically, we would expect some of our estimates to be larger than $\sigma_{L,H}$ and some to be smaller. Now recall that the expected value of $\hat{\sigma}_{L,H}$ is $\sigma_{L,H}$. This implies that if we were to take the *average* of these M estimates, we would expect the value of that average to be the value of the parameter $\sigma_{L,H}$. Somewhat more formally, let $(\bar{\hat{\sigma}}_{L,H})$ be this average:

$$\bar{\hat{\sigma}}_{L,H} = \sum_{i=1}^{M} \frac{\hat{\sigma}_{L,H_i}}{M}, \tag{2.4}$$

where $\hat{\sigma}_{L,H_i}$ is the estimator of $\sigma_{L,H}$ that is based on the ith sample. Then $E(\bar{\hat{\sigma}}_{L,H}) = \sigma_{L,H}$. Furthermore it can be shown, under general conditions, that if M were of infinite size, the probability that $\bar{\hat{\sigma}}_{L,H}$ and $\sigma_{L,H}$ will differ by any amount, however small, would be zero.

The interpretation of this result is straightforward. In practice, we typically have only one sample. On the basis of this sample, we calculate an estimate of the covariance by the general formula given in (2.3). If this sample has been randomly chosen, it could be any one of an infinite number of samples (e.g., any of the M samples above). However, because of our averaging result above, we have no reason to believe that our estimate will exceed, or be less than, the value of the corresponding covariance parameter. In contrast, if $E(\hat{\sigma}_{X,Y}) = \sigma_{X,Y} + 5$, we would expect our computed value to exceed $\sigma_{X,Y}$. If this were the case, we would probably adjust for this bias by taking $(\hat{\sigma}_{X,Y} - 5)$ as an estimator of $\sigma_{X,Y}$.

You may still be puzzled by the fact that the denominator in equation (2.3) is $(n - 1)$ rather than the full sample size, n. Normally, in computing an average we divide the sum of the values by the number of terms included

---

* The examples that follow are not "intuitive definitions" of the concept of unbiasedness; instead, they are intuitive presentations of some results that are, under general conditions, implied by unbiasedness.

in the summation. In this case, however, although there are n terms represented in the summation in the numerator, these n terms can be *reduced* to $(n - 1)$ terms that have the same sum. There are in a sense only $(n - 1)$ "bits" of information. The reason for this is that $\overline{X}$ and $\overline{Y}$, the sample means, appear in the numerator along with the observed values of X and Y. Intuitively, to form the first $(n - 1)$ terms in (2.3), we must know X_1, $X_2, \ldots, X_{n-1}, Y_1, Y_2, \ldots, Y_{n-1}$, and $\overline{X}$ and $\overline{Y}$, where

$$\overline{X} = \frac{\sum (X_1 + \cdots + X_n)}{n} \quad \text{and} \quad \overline{Y} = \frac{\sum (Y_1 + \cdots + Y_n)}{n}.$$

With this information, we can determine exactly what X_n and Y_n must be. Under these circumstances the last term in (2.3), namely, $(X_n - \overline{X}) \times (Y_n - \overline{Y})$, contains no new information; we in effect already know, or can compute, the value of the last term in the summation from the information contained in the first $(n - 1)$ terms. This condition is often described by the statement that the numerator in (2.3) has only $(n - 1)$ *degrees of freedom*, meaning that there are only $(n - 1)$ independent bits of information. Since the numerator has only $(n - 1)$ degrees of freedom, it can be shown that

$$E[\sum (X_t - \overline{X})(Y_t - \overline{Y})] = (n - 1)\sigma_{X,Y}. \tag{2.5}$$

As a result, division by $(n - 1)$ makes $\hat{\sigma}_{X,Y}$ an unbiased estimator of $\sigma_{X,Y}$.

THE CONSISTENCY OF $\hat{\sigma}_{X,Y}$

It is also useful here, and will prove valuable for the later analysis, to explore the large-sample properties of $\hat{\sigma}_{X,Y}$. By this we mean the behavior of $\hat{\sigma}_{X,Y}$ when the size of the sample on which it is based increases without limit.

Consider, for instance, the sample mean, $\overline{X}$, of a random sample of values of X. We learn in elementary statistics that the mean of $\overline{X}$ is μ_X and that the variance of $\overline{X}$ is σ_X^2/n, where μ_X and σ_X^2 refer to the mean and variance of the random variable X, and n is the size of the sample. As the sample size n becomes continually larger, we can see that the variance of $\overline{X}$, that is, σ_X^2/n, becomes ever smaller and goes to zero as n increases beyond limit. The point here is that, as our sample becomes larger, the probability that the sample mean, $\overline{X}$, will be within a specified interval about the population mean, μ_X, becomes continually higher. In the limit when the sample becomes of infinite size, the variance of $\overline{X}$ is zero, so that the probability that $\overline{X}$ is anything other than μ_X is zero. For this reason, $\overline{X}$ is a *consistent* estimator of μ_X. More generally (as discussed in Appendix B to Chapter 1), *the property of consistency means that, for the limiting case of a sample of infinite size, the probability that the estimator will have a value which differs by any amount from that of the corresponding parameter is zero.* If an estimator (such as $\overline{X}$) is consistent, then that estimator is said to "converge in probability" to its corresponding parameter (μ_X).

It is easy to see, at least intuitively, that in the case of equation (2.3),

$\hat{\sigma}_{X,Y}$ is a consistent estimator of $\sigma_{X,Y}$. As our sample size becomes infinite, $\overline{X}$ and $\overline{Y}$ converge in probability to μ_X and μ_Y, respectively. Therefore, $\hat{\sigma}_{X,Y}$ becomes the sample average of $(X - \mu_X)(Y - \mu_Y)$ based on an infinite sample. Since $E(X - \mu_X)(Y - \mu_Y) = \sigma_{X,Y}$, it seems clear that, under general conditions, if our sample were of infinite size, then

$$\hat{\sigma}_{X,Y} = \sigma_{X,Y},$$

with probability equal to one.*

AN INTERPRETATION OF $\hat{\sigma}_{X,Y}$

Let us now interpret $\hat{\sigma}_{X,Y}$ with respect to the scatter of points in Figure 2.3. We have indicated by the dotted lines the sample averages of the observed values of X and Y and have used these lines to divide Figure 2.3 into four regions. Note the following characteristics of observations in each of these regions:

In Region I: $(X - \overline{X}) > 0$ and $(Y - \overline{Y}) > 0$,
              therefore $(X - \overline{X})(Y - \overline{Y}) > 0$.
In Region II: $(X - \overline{X}) > 0$ and $(Y - \overline{Y}) < 0$,
              therefore $(X - \overline{X})(Y - \overline{Y}) < 0$.
In Region III: $(X - \overline{X}) < 0$ and $(Y - \overline{Y}) < 0$,
              therefore $(X - \overline{X})(Y - \overline{Y}) > 0$.
In Region IV: $(X - \overline{X}) < 0$ and $(Y - \overline{Y}) > 0$,
              therefore $(X - \overline{X})(Y - \overline{Y}) < 0$.

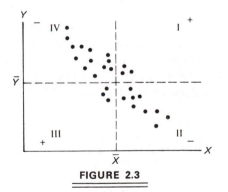

FIGURE 2.3

* As a note to more advanced readers, there are other forms of convergence in addition to the consistency property that we discussed in Appendix B to Chapter 1. One such form is called "convergence with probability one." We are not referring to this form of convergence by our statement above. Instead, we are trying to simplify notation and make the material intuitive, and so we describe

$$\lim_{n \to \infty} \text{prob} \left(|\hat{\sigma}_{X,Y} - \sigma_{X,Y}| > \varepsilon \right) = 0$$

verbally as "if the sample were of infinite size, $\hat{\sigma}_{X,Y}$ would be equal to $\sigma_{X,Y}$ with probability equal to one."

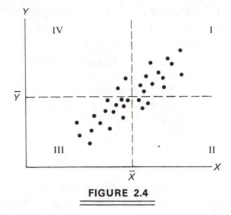

FIGURE 2.4

The observations indicated in Figure 2.3 suggest a negative relationship between the two variables. This takes the form of a concentration of points in Regions II and IV, with relatively few observations falling in Regions I and III. Since $(X - \overline{X})(Y - \overline{Y})$ is negative in II and IV and is positive in I and III, we would expect $\hat{\sigma}_{X,Y}$ in this case to be negative; or, in other words, the average of the product of deviations, $(X - \overline{X})(Y - \overline{Y})$, should be negative. If, on the other hand, the scatter of points exhibited a concentration in Regions I and III, as in Figure 2.4, we would expect $\hat{\sigma}_{X,Y}$, by a similar argument, to be positive.

Consider now the case where X and Y are *independent*, so that there exists no association between them: a high value of Y is just as likely to be accompanied by a high value of X as by a low value of X. In such a case, the scatter diagram between X and Y would not be expected to exhibit an upward or downward trend. Figure 2.5 depicts such a scatter diagram. In the figure, we see that there is a relatively even division of points among the four regions of the diagram. As a result, the positive values of $(X - \overline{X})(Y - \overline{Y})$ produced by points in Regions I and III would tend to be offset by the negative

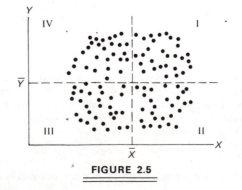

FIGURE 2.5

values generated by those points in II and IV. Thus, the calculated value of $\hat{\sigma}_{X,Y}$ would tend to be close to zero.

THE CORRELATION COEFFICIENT

In addition to knowing whether two variables are positively or negatively related, we generally want some indication of how *strongly* they are related. Figures 2.6 and 2.7, for example, present two cases of positive relationships between X and Y; however, the positive association is, in some sense, much stronger in the former case than in the latter. More specifically, we can see that once the value of X is known, the variation in Y in Figure 2.6 is small relative to that depicted in Figure 2.7*. It is highly desirable to have a measure of this characteristic of the relationship between X and Y. Unfortunately, our measure of covariance is unsuitable for indicating the *degree* of strength

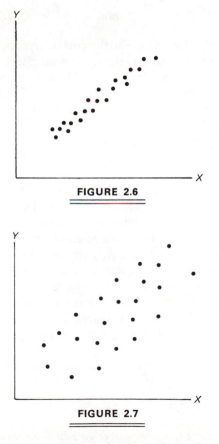

FIGURE 2.6

FIGURE 2.7

* For the more advanced reader, it can be shown that under certain conditions the conditional variance of Y, given X, varies inversely with the square of the correlation coefficient.

of the association, because its value depends on the particular units in which the variables are measured. For example, the covariance between height and weight will be much larger if we define height and weight in inches and ounces, respectively, than if we use feet and pounds.*

To get a meaningful index of the strength of the association between two variables, we need a parameter whose value is independent of the particular units of measurement. We can construct such a parameter by dividing the covariance of X and Y by the standard deviations of these two variables. More precisely, the strength of the relationship between X and Y is indicated by the correlation coefficient, $\rho_{X,Y}$,

$$\rho_{X,Y} = \frac{\sigma_{X,Y}}{\sigma_X \sigma_Y}, \tag{2.6}$$

where σ_X and σ_Y are the standard deviations of X and Y:

$$\sigma_X = +\sqrt{E(X - \mu_X)^2} \quad \text{and} \quad \sigma_Y = +\sqrt{E(Y - \mu_Y)^2}.$$

We turn now to the properties of the correlation coefficient.** Note first that it always has the same sign as the covariance. Since the denominator of equation (2.6) is always positive, it follows that the sign of $\rho_{X,Y}$ will be the same as that of the numerator, which is the covariance between the two variables. If X and Y are positively related, it follows that $\rho_{X,Y} > 0$; if they are negatively related, $\rho_{X,Y} < 0$. In the case where X and Y are independent, $\rho_{X,Y} = 0$, since $\sigma_{X,Y} = 0$. We see that the correlation coefficient possesses all the characteristics of the covariance in terms of indicating the type of relationship that exists between the variables.

However, unlike the covariance, the correlation coefficient has limits on its possible range of values. Specifically, the value of $\rho_{X,Y}$ must lie at or between plus and minus one. Moreover, the closer $\rho_{X,Y}$ is to one in either direction the stronger is the linear association (either negative or positive) between the variables; the nearer is $\rho_{X,Y}$ to zero, the weaker is the relation, with $\rho_{X,Y} = 0$ representing the absence of any linear association between the variables. In terms of Figures 2.6 and 2.7, for example, one would expect the correlation coefficient for the case of Figure 2.6 to be larger than that for Figure 2.7. In both cases, it would, of course, be positive.

We now demonstrate that if X and Y are *perfectly* and linearly related,

---

* Suppose, for instance, that our unit of measurement, instead of X, is $Z = aX$, where a is a constant. We would then have

$$E(Z - \mu_Z)(Y - \mu_Y) = E(aX - a\mu_X)(Y - \mu_Y) = aE(X - \mu_X)(Y - \mu_Y) = a\sigma_{X,Y}.$$

Thus $\sigma_{Z,Y} \neq \sigma_{X,Y}$.

** If, as in the preceding footnote, we alter our unit of measurement by using $Z = aX$ in place of X, we find that our parameter, $\rho_{X,Y}$, (unlike $\sigma_{X,Y}$) is unaffected. That is, $\rho_{Z,Y} = \rho_{X,Y}$. We leave the proof of this statement as an exercise for the reader.

then $\rho_{X,Y}$ will have a value of either plus or minus one. To see this,* consider the exact relationship

$$Y = a + bX. \tag{2.7}$$

In this instance all the points in the scatter diagram would lie precisely on a straight line with slope b and intercept a. The correlation coefficient between X and Y is

$$\rho_{X,Y} = \frac{\sigma_{X,Y}}{\sigma_X \sigma_Y}.$$

We shall show that $\rho_{X,Y} = +1$ if $b > 0$ by expressing both $\sigma_{X,Y}$ and σ_Y in terms of σ_X. We first derive μ_Y:

$$E(Y) = E(a + bX) = a + bE(X) = a + b\mu_X = \mu_Y. \tag{2.8}$$

The covariance, therefore, is

$$\begin{aligned}
\sigma_{X,Y} &= E[(Y - \mu_Y)(X - \mu_X)] \\
&= E[(a + bX - a - b\mu_X)(X - \mu_X)] \\
&= E[b(X - \mu_X)^2] = b\sigma_X^2.
\end{aligned} \tag{2.9}$$

By definition, the variance of Y is

$$\sigma_Y^2 = E[(Y - \mu_Y)^2]. \tag{2.10}$$

We can express this variance as

$$\begin{aligned}
\sigma_Y^2 &= E[(Y - \mu_Y)^2] = E[(a + bX - a - b\mu_X)^2] \\
&= E[b^2(X - \mu_X)^2] = b^2\sigma_X^2.
\end{aligned} \tag{2.11}$$

The standard deviation of Y is the positive square root: $\sigma_Y = b\sigma_X$. We can now determine the correlation coefficient:

$$\rho_{X,Y} = \frac{\sigma_{X,Y}}{\sigma_Y \sigma_X} = \frac{b\sigma_X^2}{(b\sigma_X)\sigma_X} = 1. \tag{2.12}$$

We leave it to the reader to show that if $b < 0$, then $\rho_{X,Y} = -1$. (Hint: if $b < 0$, $\sigma_Y = -b\sigma_X > 0$.)

In summary, the correlation coefficient indicates both the sign and the strength of the linear relationship between two variables. Positive and negative values of $\rho_{X,Y}$ indicate positive and negative relationships, respectively, and the closer is $\rho_{X,Y}$ to either plus or minus one, the stronger is the linear relationship, or, as it is usually put, the more highly correlated are the two variables.

---

* The following example demonstrates that $\rho_{X,Y}$ equals plus or minus one if X and Y are perfectly linearly related. Unfortunately, the proof that $\rho_{X,Y}$ cannot exceed one in absolute value, under any circumstances, is beyond the scope of this book (although it should seem intuitively reasonable).

We have also seen that if two variables are independent, the covariance, and, therefore the correlation coefficient, will be zero. Let us now demonstrate that the reverse is not true. That is, two variables may be related in a nonlinear way, yet the correlation coefficient may be zero. We reemphasize that the correlation coefficient is a measure of the *linear* relation between two variables.

TABLE 2.1

X	$P(X)$
-1	$\frac{1}{3}$
0	$\frac{1}{3}$
1	$\frac{1}{3}$

For instance, let X be a random variable and let $Y = X^2$. Then it is clear that X and Y are perfectly related in that knowledge of the value of X would enable one to predict perfectly the value of Y. Suppose, now, that the probability function of X is described by Table 2.1. That is, X takes on the values -1, 0, and 1 with equal probability. Let us now determine the covariance between X and Y:

$$\sigma_{X,Y} = E[(X - \mu_X)(Y - \mu_Y)].$$

From Table 2.1, we can see that $\mu_X = 0$, so that the expression for $\sigma_{X,Y}$ simplifies to

$$\sigma_{X,Y} = E[X(Y - \mu_Y)] = E(XY) - E(X\mu_Y). \tag{2.13}$$

Because by assumption $Y = X^2$, we have

$$\sigma_{X,Y} = E(X^3) - \mu_Y E(X) = E(X^3) \tag{2.14}$$

since $E(X) = 0$. To find $E(X^3)$, we note that X^3 will take on precisely the same values with the same probabilities of occurrence as X in Table 2.1. We thus have that

$$E(X^3) = -1(\tfrac{1}{3}) + 0(\tfrac{1}{3}) + 1(\tfrac{1}{3}) = 0. \tag{2.15}$$

$\sigma_{X,Y}$ is therefore zero. It follows from this that $\rho_{X,Y}$ is also zero.

To see intuitively what is taking place, consider the more general case where $Y = X^2$ but where X can take on a whole range of values subject to the condition that it possess a probability function that is symmetrical around zero. By the latter part of this statement, we mean simply that the probability that the value of X is between any two positive numbers, say 5 and 10, is exactly the same as the probability that it lies between the corresponding negative numbers, -5 and -10. With $Y = X^2$, we have the equation of a parabola that is tangent to the X axis at the origin, as depicted in Figure 2.8.

It may now be clear from Figure 2.8 why variables such as Y and X will, in general, have a zero correlation. All observations on X and Y must lie on the parabola, because $Y = X^2$. Because the probability function of X is symmetric about zero, for every event such as A there will be a corresponding event such as B that can occur with equal probability. As a result, the

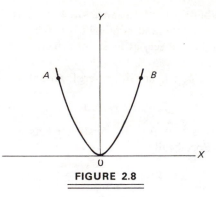

FIGURE 2.8

positive correlation between X and Y when X is restricted to positive values is offset by the negative correlation when X is restricted to negative values; therefore, the overall correlation between X and Y would be zero.

In these instances, we have cases of an exact relationship between X and Y that generates a correlation coefficient of zero. Earlier we showed that $\rho_{X,Y} = 0$ when X and Y are independent; we emphasize here that $\rho_{X,Y} = 0$ is a necessary, but not a sufficient, condition for two variables to be independent. In other words, if $\rho_{X,Y} = 0$, X and Y may, but need not, be independent; however, if X and Y are independent, then $\rho_{X,Y} = 0$. What all this implies for econometric analysis (as we shall discuss later) is that if we find a low correlation between two variables, we must still entertain the possibility that there exists some nonlinear relation between them.

THE ESTIMATOR OF THE CORRELATION COEFFICIENT

As in the case of the covariance, we shall not generally know the value of the correlation coefficient, $\rho_{X,Y}$, and an estimation problem again arises. An obvious estimator of $\rho_{X,Y}$ is*

$$\hat{\rho}_{X,Y} = \frac{\hat{\sigma}_{X,Y}}{\hat{\sigma}_X \hat{\sigma}_Y}, \tag{2.16}$$

where $\hat{\sigma}_X$ and $\hat{\sigma}_Y$ are the usual estimators of the standard deviations of X and Y:

$$\hat{\sigma}_X = +\sqrt{\frac{\sum (X_t - \bar{X})^2}{n - 1}} \quad \text{and} \quad \hat{\sigma}_Y = +\sqrt{\frac{\sum (Y_t - \bar{Y})^2}{n - 1}}. \tag{2.17}$$

Consider the large-sample properties of $\hat{\rho}_{X,Y}$. We note our earlier result that as n approaches infinity, $\bar{X}$ and $\bar{Y}$ converge in probability to μ_X and μ_Y, respectively. As a result, $\sum (X_t - \bar{X})^2/(n - 1)$ becomes the average squared deviation of X from its mean based on an infinite sample, so that it

---

* In some books the symbol r is used for $\hat{\rho}$. We prefer to use the $\hat{\rho}$ notation to emphasize that this is an estimator of ρ.

converges in probability to the variance of X, σ_X^2. It follows that $\hat{\sigma}_X$ converges in probability to σ_X (and similarly for $\hat{\sigma}_Y$). Since, at the same time, $\hat{\sigma}_{X,Y}$ converges to $\sigma_{X,Y}$, we see, at least intuitively, that $\hat{\rho}_{X,Y}$ is a consistent estimator of $\rho_{X,Y}$.

In contrast to $\hat{\sigma}_{X,Y}$, $\hat{\rho}_{X,Y}$ is not, in general, an unbiased estimator. That is,

$$E(\hat{\rho}_{X,Y}) \neq \rho_{X,Y}. \tag{2.18}$$

The reason for this is that $\hat{\rho}_{X,Y}$ is constructed as a *nonlinear* function of $\hat{\sigma}_{X,Y}$, $\hat{\sigma}_X^2$, and $\hat{\sigma}_Y^2$. Specifically,

$$\hat{\rho}_{X,Y} = \frac{\hat{\sigma}_{X,Y}}{\sqrt{\hat{\sigma}_X^2}\,\sqrt{\hat{\sigma}_Y^2}}. \tag{2.19}$$

Now it can be shown that $E(\hat{\sigma}_X^2) = \sigma_X^2$ and $E(\hat{\sigma}_Y^2) = \sigma_Y^2$. However, following our discussion of nonlinear functions in Appendix B to Chapter 1, we find here that*

$$E(\hat{\rho}_{X,Y}) = E\left(\frac{\hat{\sigma}_{X,Y}}{\sqrt{\hat{\sigma}_X^2}\,\sqrt{\hat{\sigma}_Y^2}}\right)$$

$$\neq \frac{E(\hat{\sigma}_{X,Y})}{\sqrt{E(\hat{\sigma}_X^2)}\,\sqrt{E(\hat{\sigma}_Y^2)}} = \frac{\sigma_{X,Y}}{\sigma_X \sigma_Y} = \rho_{X,Y}. \tag{2.20}$$

In summary, $\hat{\rho}_{X,Y}$ is a biased, but consistent, estimator of $\rho_{X,Y}$. This means that the bias can be considered to be unimportant if the sample size is large, because the consistency property assures us that the probability will be high that $\hat{\rho}_{X,Y}$ is close to $\rho_{X,Y}$. As we shall see later, this problem of biased, but consistent, estimators arises quite frequently in the estimation of econometric models.

A NOTE ON DEGREES OF FREEDOM

It should be pointed out that, as in the case of $\hat{\sigma}_{X,Y}$, the variance estimators $\hat{\sigma}_X^2$ and $\hat{\sigma}_Y^2$ defined by (2.17) have denominators that reflect their "degrees of freedom." That is, as before, although there are n terms in the summations corresponding to $\hat{\sigma}_X^2$ and $\hat{\sigma}_Y^2$, there are only $(n - 1)$ independent bits of information. This can be seen somewhat intuitively by noting, for the case of X, that

$$\sum_{t=1}^{n}(X_t - \overline{X}) = 0,$$

and so

$$(X_n - \overline{X}) = -(X_1 - \overline{X}) - \cdots - (X_{n-1} - \overline{X}).$$

In other words, the last term in the summation is completely dependent on the first $(n - 1)$ terms and so does not contain any new information.

---

*The following argument is not a formal proof, but simply suggests that $\hat{\rho}_{X,Y}$ is biased.

Division by the number of degrees of freedom (not by the number of observations) is, incidentally, the standard procedure for obtaining an unbiased estimator of the variance of a variable. Fortunately, for purposes of generalization, the degrees of freedom of a variance estimator (of the type considered in this book) can be obtained by a simple rule. Specifically, the degrees of freedom of such an estimator will, in general, be equal to $(n - k)$, where n is the sample size and k is the number of parameters that must be estimated in order to evaluate the numerator of the estimator. For example, the variance estimator, $\hat{\sigma}_X^2$, has $\bar{X}$ in its numerator because μ_X is not known. In this case, $k = 1$. Note that if μ_X were known, the variance of X would be estimated by the formula

$$\sum_{t=1}^{n} \frac{(X_t - \mu_X)^2}{n}.$$

A WORD OF CAUTION

Before proceeding to the linear regression model, a word of caution is in order concerning the interpretation of the correlation coefficient. Note that we have simply been measuring the extent of statistical association between two variables. We have said nothing about any causal relations between them; it is, in fact, perfectly possible for two variables to exhibit a high correlation and yet bear *no* causal relation to one another. For example, we would no doubt find a positive correlation over time between the average annual salary (in dollars) of teachers in the United States and the total output of steel. This probably does not reflect any kind of direct effect of one variable on the other, but is simply the result of the fact that, for largely different reasons, both of these variables have increased in magnitude over time. A positive or negative correlation (even if it is a very high correlation) does *not* prove that there exists a causal link between the variables.

AN ILLUSTRATION

Although the presence of a strong correlation between two variables does not prove the existence of any causal relation, such correlations can nevertheless provide valuable empirical support for a hypothesized relationship. As an example, we turn to an urban phenomenon that many observers contend is the underlying source of the ills of our central cities: the movement (or "flight") of middle and upper income families from the cities to the suburbs.* The contention is that this suburbanization of our metropolitan areas has left the center cities to cope with a residual population of relatively poor households,

---

* For an extensive econometric study of this issue, see David Bradford and Harry Kelejian, "An Econometric Model of the Flight to the Suburbs," *Journal of Political Economy*, 81 (May–June 1973), pp. 566–589.

which has proved expensive in fiscal terms and generated a cumulative process of decay in city life.

But does the evidence support this contention? To cast some light on this, we might ask what we would expect the observable and measurable consequences of this process to be and then examine the relevant data to determine if they are, in fact, consistent with these expectations. In this case, for example, we could compare different cities in the United States to see if those in which the process of suburbanization has gone farthest do, in some way, find themselves at a relatively large disadvantage as compared to their suburbs. Table 2.2 presents some data concerning this, which come from a sample of 15 large U.S. cities. Specifically, let P_i^c be the population of the ith city, and let P_i^s be the population of the suburban area surrounding the ith city. Then, for each of the 15 cities, Table 2.2 indicates the percentage of the population of the entire urban area that resides in the city itself, namely,

TABLE 2.2

City	City Share of Urban Population (percent)[a]	City-Suburb Income Ratio ($\times 100$)[b]
Baltimore	57	65
Boston	24	69
Chicago	50	73
Cleveland	38	65
Dallas	63	102
Detroit	38	82
Indianapolis	91	107
Los Angeles	34	92
Memphis	94	104
New York	49	66
Philadelphia	49	75
Phoenix	67	103
San Diego	58	98
St. Louis	33	70
Seattle	45	81

[a] Column (2) is central city population in 1970 as a percentage of the population of the entire urbanized area.

[b] Column (3) indicates for 1969 the ratio of average household income in the center city to average household income in the area outside the center city but within the metropolitan area (using the census definition of a Standard Metropolitan Statistical Area).

SOURCE: R. D. Norton, "City Life-Cycles and Municipal Expenditure Contrasts," in *Proceedings of the Seventieth Annual Conference on Taxation*, National Tax Association-Tax Institute of America (Columbus, Ohio, 1978), p. 328.

$100[P_i^c/(P_i^c + P_i^s)]$. Let Y_i^c and Y_i^s be, respectively, the average household income in the ith city and in the suburbs of the ith city. Then, for each of the 15 cities, Table 2.2 also presents data on the city-suburb income ratio, $100(Y_i^c/Y_i^s)$. If the "exodus" hypothesis is true, we would expect those cities with a relatively small fraction of their urban population (a relatively small value of $100[P_i^c/(P_i^c + P_i^s)]$) to contain a city population that is predominantly poor; for such cities we expect the income ratio $100(Y_i^c/Y_i^s)$ to be relatively low. In brief, we would expect a positive association between the variables $100[P_i^c/(P_i^c + P_i^s)]$ and $100(Y_i^c/Y_i^s)$.

The obvious procedure is to examine the data to see if they indicate such a positive association. Figure 2.9 presents a scatter diagram which is quite suggestive: larger values of the population ratio variable do appear, on average, to be associated with larger values of the relative income variable, although the pattern of association is far from "perfect."

As an illustration of the calculations involved, we now estimate the correlation between the population and income ratio variables. To simplify notation, let $X_i = 100[P_i^c/(P_i^c + P_i^s)]$, and $Y_i = 100(Y_i^c/Y_i^s)$. Then, from (2.16), the sample correlation between these variables is

$$\hat{\rho}_{X,Y} = \frac{\hat{\sigma}_{X,Y}}{\hat{\sigma}_X \hat{\sigma}_Y} = \frac{\sum (X_i - \bar{X})(Y_i - \bar{Y})/n - 1}{\sqrt{\sum (X_i - \bar{X})^2/n - 1} \sqrt{\sum (Y_i - \bar{Y})^2/n - 1}}$$

$$= \frac{\sum (X_i - \bar{X})(Y_i - \bar{Y})}{\sqrt{\sum (X_i - \bar{X})^2} \sqrt{\sum (Y_i - \bar{Y})^2}}. \tag{2.21}$$

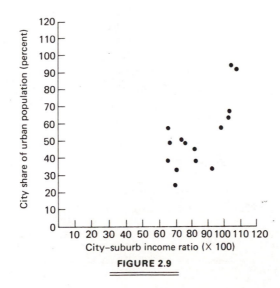

FIGURE 2.9

We can simplify the calculations if we make use of some of the identities from Appendix A to Chapter 1 [specifically (1A.10) and (1A.13)] to put 2.21 in a somewhat altered form:

$$\hat{\rho}_{X,Y} = \frac{\sum X_i Y_i - n\bar{X}\bar{Y}}{\sqrt{\sum X_i^2 - n\bar{X}^2}\sqrt{\sum Y_i^2 - n\bar{Y}^2}}. \tag{2.22}$$

The actual calculations appear in Table 2.3. It turns out that the sample correlation between these two variables is 0.71. This result is certainly consistent with the "exodus" hypothesis.

TABLE 2.3

CALCULATION OF THE
SAMPLE CORRELATION COEFFICIENT

	X_t	Y_t	$X_t Y_t$	X_t^2	Y_t^2
	57	65	3,705	3,249	4,225
	24	69	1,656	576	4,761
	50	73	3,650	2,500	5,329
	38	65	2,470	1,444	4,225
	63	102	6,426	3,969	10,404
	38	82	3,116	1,444	6,724
	91	107	9,737	8,281	11,449
	34	92	3,128	1,156	8,464
	94	104	9,776	8,836	10,816
	49	66	3,234	2,401	4,356
	49	75	3,675	2,401	5,625
	67	103	6,901	4,489	10,609
	58	98	5,684	3,364	9,604
	33	70	2,310	1,089	4,900
	45	81	3,645	2,025	6,561
Total	790	1,252	69,113	47,224	108,052

$\bar{X} = 52.7 \qquad \bar{Y} = 83.5$

$$\hat{\rho}_{X,Y} \frac{\sum X_i Y_i - n\bar{X}\bar{Y}}{\sqrt{\sum X_i^2 - n\bar{X}^2}\sqrt{\sum Y_i^2 - n\bar{Y}^2}}$$

$$= \frac{69,113 - (15)(52.7)(83.5)}{\sqrt{47,224 - (15)(52.7)^2}\sqrt{108,052 - (15)(83.5)^2}}$$

$$= 0.71.$$

2.2 THE DESCRIPTION OF BEHAVIORAL RELATIONSHIPS

In the preceding section we introduced two measures of the statistical association between two variables. With these as background, we proceed now to the issue of primary interest to us: the specification and estimation of a hypothesized economic relationship. For this purpose, let us return to the problem of the estimation of a consumption function, which we examined briefly in Chapter 1.

Economic theory suggests that consumption expenditure C is a function of disposable income Y_d; the higher is a family's level of disposable income, the higher should be its level of spending on consumption. Suppose, moreover, that we propose a linear functional form for this relationship so that

$$C_t = a + bY_{dt}, \tag{2.23}$$

where C_t is the tth value of consumption expenditure and Y_{dt} is the corresponding value of disposable income. For instance, t might refer to time periods in which case (2.23) would relate the level of consumption expenditure in time period t to the level of disposable income in period t. Alternatively, t might refer to individuals at a point in time. In this instance, (2.23) would relate the consumption expenditure of the tth individual to his disposable income.

Note first that we are specifying here a proposed causal relationship. Theory says that the level of consumption spending *depends* on the level of disposable income; as a family's disposable income increases, we expect that it will spend some portion of this increase on consumption. Second, we see that equation (2.23) specifies an *exact* relationship between C_t and Y_{dt}. If, for example, $a = 100$ and $b = 0.9$, equation (2.23) says that should $Y_{dt} = \$15,000$, then C_t would be exactly equal to $\$13,600$. As we have stressed, however, when we look at the data, we do not see an exact relationship; we do not typically find a group of points lying precisely along a straight line, but instead we see a scatter of points. The relationship between consumption and disposable income that we want to estimate is not an exact one, but is rather a typical relationship. What we have in mind is a statement of the kind that if a family's disposable income is $\$15,000$, then *on the average* the family's expenditure on consumption will be $\$13,600$. In any particular case, for a number of reasons that we shall discuss shortly, we would expect C_t to vary, in either a positive or negative direction, from its typical value.

This suggests that our simple consumption function should be written as

$$C_t = a + bY_{dt} + u_t, \tag{2.24}$$

where u_t may take on positive or negative values, but with a mean value of zero so that the mean value of C_t corresponding to a *given value* of Y_{dt} is $(a + bY_{dt})$. Suppose, for example, that our mean relationship between C_t and Y_{dt} is represented by the line AB in Figure 2.10. If $Y_{dt} = Y_{dt}^0$, the mean of C_t would be C_t^0; in general, however, whenever $Y_{dt} = Y_{dt}^0$, the

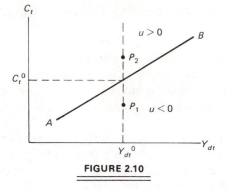

FIGURE 2.10

value of C_t would deviate somewhat from C_t^0. In some instances, $C_t < C_t^0$, as with point P_1, which would imply that $u_t < 0$; in other cases, $C_t > C_t^0$ with $u_t > 0$, as with P_2 in Figure 2.10.

The term u_t, which is of central importance in econometrics, is called the *disturbance term* (or, alternatively, the "error term"). It is the way we indicate that economic relationships are not exact, but rather represent mean behavioral patterns. This raises the issue of why we do not in economics find precise relationships that hold without exception.* Why is u_t typically different from zero? There are a number of reasons why this is true**:

1. *Variables left out.* Consider again the case of consumer expenditures. Consumption no doubt depends on a number of other variables in addition to disposable income. For instance, if C_t refers to consumption expenditures at time t, we might postulate that

$$C_t = a + b_1 Y_{dt} + b_2 L_t + b_3 \dot{P}_t + b_4 R_t + \cdots, \tag{2.25}$$

where L_t equals the stock of liquid assets at time t, $\dot{P}_t$ equals the percentage change of prices during period t, R_t equals the rate of interest during t, and so on.

On the other hand, we may feel that Y_{dt} is, at least under normal circumstances, by far the most important determinant of C_t and that the effects of the other variables will both be small and will tend to cancel out over time.

---

* There are, incidentally, some exact relationships in economics, but they are not behavioral relationships suggested by economic theory. They are what are known as "accounting identities" and are true by definition. For example, a familiar accounting identity in economics is the fundamental balance-sheet statement that

$$\text{assets} = \text{liabilities} + \text{net worth}.$$

This relationship *always* holds exactly because of the way net worth is defined:

$$\text{net worth} = \text{assets} - \text{liabilities}.$$

Net worth is defined as a residual quantity that ensures that the balance sheet balances.

** The following discussion draws on J. Johnston, *Econometric Methods*, 2nd ed. (New York: McGraw-Hill, 1972), pp. 10–11.

In this case, the disturbance term represents the sum of all these omitted terms†:

$$u_t = (b_2 L_t + b_3 \dot{P}_t + b_4 R_t + \cdots). \tag{2.26}$$

In brief, disturbance terms may arise because all the relevant factors cannot be accounted for.

2. *Unpredictable behavior of people.* The behavioral patterns of people, particularly of individuals, are rarely completely predictable. On the other hand, behavior is not generally of a purely random character either. In this respect we could look upon our consumption model (2.24) as incorporating two components: a deterministic component that relates expenditures to income $(a + bY_{dt})$ and an unpredictable (or "free will") component, u_t. In this framework the disturbance term reflects, or accounts for, "sudden urges," "changes of mind," or other changes of attitude that induce consumers to spend more, or less, than they typically do. This typical amount would be given by the deterministic component: $(a + bY_{dt})$.

In a related framework, the disturbance term can also be thought to reflect the effects of unpredictable events on economic behavior. For instance, if a friend from out-of-town were to visit unexpectedly, his host might exceed his normal budget by taking his friend out to dinner.

3. *Varying behavior among individuals.* Similarly, we all know that, because of differing attitudes, certain families have a higher propensity to save than others. If we were to use (2.24) to explain the expenditures of various families at a point in time, we could take $(a + bY_{dt})$ to represent the typical expenditure of a family whose disposable income is Y_{dt}, and let the disturbance term u_t represent deviations from this mean. That is, u_t would reflect varying attitudes toward saving; families with a relatively high propensity to save would correspond to negative values of u_t, and families with a low propensity to save would be associated with positive values of u_t.

4. *Errors of measurement.* Even if $C_t = a + bY_{dt}$ were exact, we might not be able to measure, say, C_t, with perfect precision. As a result of such errors of measurement, we may actually observe $\tilde{C}_t$, which is related to C_t by

$$\tilde{C}_t = C_t + u_t.$$

Here u_t represents the error in measurement. In this formulation, while we get an underestimate or overestimate of C_t depending on whether u_t is positive or negative, we assume that our errors tend to cancel out in the sense that if we were to take repeated measures of C_t, the average of these measures would be expected to be C_t. If we substitute $\tilde{C}_t = C_t + u_t$ into $C_t = a + bY_{dt}$, we get

$$\tilde{C}_t = a + bY_{dt} + u_t.$$

---

† We consider later the case in which these omitted terms do not tend to "cancel out."

In other words, even if the relationship between consumption expenditures and disposable income were *exact*, the relationship between *measured* expenditures and income could incorporate a disturbance term.*

We shall therefore characterize functional relationships that describe economic behavior as mean relationships and shall indicate this by the inclusion of a disturbance term, u_t, in the model. Two additional examples of such economic relationships are

$$I_t = e + fR_t + u_t \tag{2.27}$$

and

$$Q_t = g + hL_t + u_t, \tag{2.28}$$

where I = investment, R = rate of interest, Q = level of output, and L = labor input in man-hours. In each of these equations, it is clear, for example, that there are additional important variables that affect the dependent variable: investment will clearly depend on other factors, such as the demand for output, as well as the level of interest rates; in the second case, the level of output will typically vary with the quantities of other inputs that are used in combination with labor. For this reason alone, we would expect some imprecision in the relationships between these variables.

2.3 THE TWO-VARIABLE REGRESSION MODEL

Suppose that we have specified a behavioral relationship of the type just discussed. In more general terms, we have a linear relationship of the form

$$Y_t = a + bX_t + u_t, \qquad t = 1, \ldots, n, \tag{2.29}$$

where

Y_t = the tth observation on the dependent variable,
X_t = the tth observation on the independent variable,
u_t = the corresponding tth value of the disturbance term, and a and b are parameters whose values are unknown.

Equation (2.29) is a linear relationship among Y_t, X_t, and u_t that has two unknown parameters: a and b. We assume that this relationship holds for all of the specified values of t, namely, $t = 1, 2, \ldots, n$. Note that these values of t correspond to our n observations on Y_t and X_t. The value of the disturbance term, u_t, in our relationship can be expected to vary among the

---

* Note that, for purposes of illustration, we are assuming that there are no errors in the measurement of the independent variable.

different observations to reflect deviations from "typical" patterns of behavior. Unlike Y_t and X_t, we do not assume that the values of the disturbance term are observable. In passing, we also note that in equation (2.29) the dependent variable, Y_t, and the independent variable, X_t, are sometimes also referred to, respectively, as the *regressand* and the *regressor*.

Our first problem is that of estimating the values of the parameters a and b so that we can make quantitative statements about the relationship between Y_t and X_t. To do this we must first make some formal assumptions concerning the manner in which the independent variable, X_t, and the disturbance term, u_t, are generated. Indeed, the necessity of such assumptions, especially those concerning u_t, should be evident. For instance, since Y_t depends on *both* X_t and u_t, it follows that the nature of any relationship between Y_t and X_t must depend on the specifications of the disturbance term, u_t.

THE BASIC ASSUMPTIONS

1. We assume, first, that all the values of X, the independent variable, are not the same; at least one value of X must differ from the others. As we shall see, if this condition is not satisfied, we shall be unable to estimate a and b. Somewhat intuitively, if X never varies, we shall not be able to observe how Y varies with X.

This raises the issue of what does determine the particular values of X. The classical assumption is that the experimenter himself selects the values of X and then observes the corresponding or resulting values of Y. For instance, let equation (2.29) represent the relationship between the output of corn in bushels per acre of land, Y, and the input of fertilizer per acre, X, measured in pounds. To explore this relationship, the experimenter might set $X = 1$ on the first acre of land, $X = 2$ on the second acre (e.g., $X_1 = 1$, $X_2 = 2$), and so on.

It should be evident that economists are typically not in so fortunate a situation. Suppose, for example, that we wish to investigate the relationship between the rate of inflation and the rate of unemployment. In this case, we could define Y in (2.29) as the percentage change in prices from one year to the next and X as the percentage of the labor force that is unemployed during that period. It is clear that we cannot proceed to investigate the relationship between Y and X by setting the rate of unemployment at a different percentage each year and then observing the resulting rate of inflation. The rate of unemployment is determined by the functioning of the whole economy, and is, for this reason, beyond our experimental control so that we are unable to select and vary systematically the values of the independent variable. We must in this case observe *both* X and Y. We shall therefore proceed in our discussion with the assumption that, whatever mechanism generates the values of X, it does produce at least two different values of X.

2. We shall next make a set of three assumptions concerning the properties of the disturbance term itself:

2a. $E(u_t) = \mu_u = 0$,
2b. $E(u_t - \mu_u)^2 = E(u_t^2) = \sigma_u^2$,
2c. u_t is independent of u_s for $s \neq t$, and so
$$E[(u_t - \mu_u)(u_s - \mu_u)] = \text{cov}(u_t, u_s) = 0.$$

Assumption 2a states that, for every observation, the expected value of the disturbance term is zero. As a simple illustration, we might assume that for each observation the value of u_t is determined as follows. A person unknown to us flips a coin; if a head appears, he sets $u_t = 1$, but if a tail occurs, then he sets $u_t = -1$. In this case,

$$E(u_t) = \tfrac{1}{2}(1) + \tfrac{1}{2}(-1) = 0.$$

The rationale for assuming that the disturbance term has a mean value of zero is quite straightforward. We assume that our theory embodied in equation (2.29) accurately describes the mean behavior of Y corresponding to the various values of X. That is, we assume that, whatever the value of X, the mean value of Y will be $Y^m = (a + bX)$. If, however, $E(u_t) \neq 0$, this will not be the case. Suppose, for example, that u_t in equation (2.29) was consistently positive. This would imply that the mean value of Y corresponding to each value of X would exceed $(a + bX)$, which would obviously be inconsistent with our assumption that the mean value of Y is $(a + bX)$.

Alternatively, equation (2.29) can be looked upon as being derived from another equation in which the disturbance term did not have a mean of zero. For instance, suppose $E(u_t) = d \neq 0$, where d is a constant. Then we could define

$$v_t = u_t - d, \tag{2.30}$$

and note that $E(v_t) = E(u_t) - d = d - d = 0$. Using (2.30) we could then substitute $u_t = v_t + d$ into (2.29) to get

$$\begin{aligned} Y_t &= (a + d) + bX_t + v_t \\ &= a^* + bX_t + v_t, \end{aligned} \tag{2.31}$$

where $a^* = a + d$, and, as noted, $E(v_t) = 0$. We could therefore take (2.31) as our regression model.

Assumption (2b) says that the variance of the disturbance term is a constant equal to σ_u^2 and does not, therefore, vary systematically with t. If, for example, we were working with a series of observations of consumption expenditures and disposable income over time, this assumption means that the variance of the disturbance term does not become either larger or smaller as time passes.* Or, in terms of our simple example above, a violation of this assumption would take place if, upon the toss of the coin, the person unknown to us were to set $u_t = +t$ or $u_t = -t$ when, respectively, a heads or a tails appeared. In this case the expected value of u_t would still be zero,

$$E(u_t) = \tfrac{1}{2}(t) + \tfrac{1}{2}(-t) = 0,$$

but the variance of u_t clearly becomes larger with each successive observation.

The rationale for this assumption, as well as techniques for dealing with the estimation problems that arise when it is violated, are developed formally later in the book (see Chapter 6). At this point we might note that if the variance of u_t were not the same for all our observations, then all the observations would not, in some sense, be equally reliable. For instance, suppose we knew that the variance of u_t was zero for two particular observations, say the first and the second, and was some positive number for the remaining observations. Then, since the mean of u_t is zero, these two observations would, with a probability equal to one, satisfy the equation $Y = a + bX$. We would write

$$Y_1 = a + bX_1,$$
$$Y_2 = a + bX_2,$$

(2.32)

and then solve the two equations in (2.32) for a and b. In other words, we could throw away all the other observations and estimate a and b simply using these first two points. In brief, observations corresponding to small variances are, in some sense, more valuable than those corresponding to large variances. At this stage we wish all of our observations to be of equal importance, and so we make assumption 2b.

Assumption 2c states that the value of the tth disturbance term is independent of the value of any other disturbance term, say the sth. The reason for this assumption is that, for the present, we want to specify a model in which there is only one systematic or predictable force (namely, X_t) acting on the dependent variable, Y_t. If the disturbance terms were related to each other, this would obviously not be the case. For instance, suppose that u_t were negatively correlated with its immediately preceding value, u_{t-1}. Then the value of Y_t would depend, systematically and predictably, on the value of X_t *and* the value of u_{t-1}, since u_{t-1} would, at least in part, determine u_t. Although we consider such models in Chapter 6, we begin our discussion of regression analysis on a simpler level by assuming that the value of the disturbance term for one observation does not depend on its value for other observations.

---

* If, instead, we were considering a budgetary survey that indicated the consumption expenditures of families with different levels of disposable income, this assumption would imply that the variance of the disturbance term, σ_u^2, does not vary systematically with the level of disposable income. More on this in Chapter 6.

With this set of assumptions, we have characterized the disturbance term in equation (2.29) as an unobservable random variable that has a mean value of zero, a constant variance, σ_u^2, and with the property that its value in any given instance is independent of, and therefore uncorrelated with, its value on other occasions.

3. Our final assumption is that u_t is independent of all n values of the regressor X. It follows that $\text{cov}(u_t, X_t) = 0$. Since $E(u_t) = 0$ by assumption 2a, we have that

$$\text{cov}(u_t, X_t) = E[(u_t - 0)(X_t - \mu_X)] = E(u_t X_t) - E(u_t \mu_X)$$
$$= E(u_t X_t) - \mu_X E(u_t) = E(u_t X_t) = 0.$$

The assumptions thus imply that $E(u_t X_t) = 0$.

The rationale for the assumption that X_t and u_t are independent,* and therefore that $\text{cov}(u_t, X_t) = 0$, is similar to that for the assumption $E(u_t) = 0$. If either of these assumptions does not hold, then the mean value of Y_t, Y_t^m, corresponding to a particular value of X_t will in general no longer be $(a + bX_t)$. Consider, for example, the case in which X_t and u_t are positively correlated. This positive correlation implies that larger-than-mean values of u_t [positive since $E(u_t) = 0$] will tend to be associated with larger-than-mean values of X_t; similarly, smaller-than-mean values of u_t (negative) will tend to be associated with smaller-than-mean values of X_t. This implies that the mean of u_t corresponding to only *large values* of X_t will be *positive*; conversely, the mean of u_t corresponding to only small values of X_t will be *negative*. From this we see that the mean of Y_t, Y_t^m, will exceed $(a + bX_t)$ when X_t is large, and will be less than $(a + bX_t)$ when X_t is small.

We illustrate this problem in Figure 2.11. Let the line AB depict the relationship $Y_t^* = a + bX_t$. Similarly, let the line CD denote the mean value of Y_t, Y_t^m, corresponding to the various values of X_t. Then a positive correlation

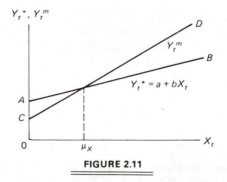

FIGURE 2.11

between the disturbance term and the regressor implies that the relationship between $Y_t{}^m$ and Y_t^* would be somewhat like that described in Figure 2.11.*

This completes our discussion of the assumptions. The specification of the relationship between X and Y in the form

$$Y_t = a + bX_t + u_t,$$

together with the assumptions we have just discussed, constitutes our basic linear regression model. Our next job is to see how we can use our assumptions to obtain estimates of a and b. In the course of the discussion, we shall come to see more clearly what the precise function of each assumption is and just how our results depend on them.

2.4 THE ESTIMATION OF THE REGRESSION EQUATION: THE INSTRUMENTAL-VARIABLE TECHNIQUE

The approach we use is known in the literature as instrumental-variable estimation, a technique that involves imposing our assumptions from the basic regression model directly on the observed sample values of X and Y.** As we shall see shortly, this enables us to generate estimators of a and b. The appeal of this approach is that it allows us to see clearly the particular importance or role of each of the assumptions we made in the regression model.

Consider, again, our basic regression equation:

$$Y_t = a + bX_t + u_t, \qquad t = 1, \ldots, n. \tag{2.29}$$

Because of our assumption that $E(u_t) = 0$, the mean value of Y_t corresponding to a given value of X_t is

$$Y_t^m = a + bX_t. \tag{2.33}$$

Equation (2.33) may be interpreted as the mean relationship between Y_t and X_t. It follows from (2.29) and (2.33) that

$$Y_t = Y_t{}^m + u_t. \tag{2.34}$$

Equation (2.34) simply states that Y_t can be expressed as the sum of its mean component and the term that causes it to deviate from its mean. Rearranging terms in (2.34), we can express the disturbance term as

$$u_t = Y_t - Y_t^m. \tag{2.35}$$

---

* We are hedging a bit here because, in theory, CD would not have to be a straight line.

** The particular form of the instrumental-variable technique that we shall employ was developed by Arthur S. Goldberger, *Topics in Regression Analysis* (New York: Macmillan, 1968).

Suppose, now, that we had estimators of a and b, say $\hat{a}$ and $\hat{b}$. In light of (2.33), our estimator of the mean value of Y_t would be

$$\hat{Y}_t = \hat{a} + \hat{b}X_t, \tag{2.36}$$

where we have simplified notation by omitting reference to the superscript in the estimator of Y_t^m. In a similar manner, our estimator of the disturbance term, which is suggested by (2.35), would be

$$\hat{u}_t = Y_t - \hat{Y}_t. \tag{2.37}$$

That is, we could obtain an estimator of the disturbance term from equation (2.35) by replacing the unknown parameters, namely a and b,, by their estimators. Again, rearranging terms in (2.37) yields an equation that corresponds to (2.34):

$$\begin{aligned} Y_t &= \hat{Y}_t + \hat{u}_t \\ &= \hat{a} + \hat{b}X_t + \hat{u}_t. \end{aligned} \tag{2.38}$$

Note that (2.38) expresses the value of Y_t in terms of our *estimators* for a, b, and u_t (namely, $\hat{a}$, $\hat{b}$, and $\hat{u}_t$), and the value of X_t.

Let us now turn to the problem of obtaining $\hat{a}$ and $\hat{b}$. One of the assumptions of our regression model is that u_t has a mean of zero: $E(u_t) = 0$. This would lead us to expect, somewhat intuitively, that if we could average n values of u_t, say $\bar{u} = \sum u_t/n$, that average would have a "small" value. More formally, we could say that $E(u_t) = 0$ implies that $E(\bar{u}) = 0$. All this suggests that if $\hat{u}_t$ is defined in (2.37), it would seem desirable for

$$\left(\sum_{t=1}^{n} \frac{\hat{u}_t}{n} \right) = 0, \tag{2.39}$$

or, multiplying across by n:

$$\sum_{t=1}^{n} \hat{u}_t = 0. \tag{2.40}$$

That is, we might like our estimator, $\hat{u}_t$, to have a property, (2.39) or (2.40), that corresponds to, and is suggested by, one of the basic assumptions concerning our disturbance term, namely, $E(u_t) = 0$.

Before continuing, it may be helpful to interpret the significance of (2.40) geometrically. From (2.38) we see that if $\sum \hat{u}_t \neq 0$, $\sum Y_t \neq \hat{Y}_t$. For purposes of illustration, suppose that $\sum \hat{u}_t = 500$. It would then follow that $\sum Y_t > \sum \hat{Y}_t$. Now consider Figure 2.12, in which the n observations on Y_t and X_t are represented by the scatter of points, and the estimated equation between Y_t and X_t, namely,

$$\hat{Y}_t = \hat{a} + \hat{b}X_t,$$

is represented by the line AB. Note that the points are generally *above* the line. The reason for this is that the height of the line corresponding to a given value of the regressor, say X_j, is $\hat{Y}_j$. However, this will generally be less than the corresponding value of the dependent variable, Y_j, since $\sum Y_t > \sum \hat{Y}_t$. It should be evident that if $\sum \hat{u}_t$ were negative, a similar argument would suggest that the scatter of points would generally lie below the estimated relationship between Y_t and X_t. Thus, the condition in (2.40) that $\sum \hat{u}_t = 0$ implies that, on balance, the points lie neither above nor below the estimated line.

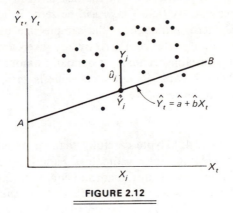

FIGURE 2.12

It may now be clear just what the role of (2.40) will be in obtaining the estimators $\hat{a}$ and $\hat{b}$. If we sum (2.38) over our n observations, we get

$$\sum Y_t = \sum \hat{Y}_t + \sum \hat{u}_t$$
$$= n\hat{a} + \hat{b} \sum X_t,$$

(2.41)

since $\sum \hat{u}_t = 0$ by (2.40). Dividing (2.41) by n, we get

$$\bar{Y} = \hat{a} + \hat{b}\bar{X},$$

(2.42)

where $\bar{Y}$ and $\bar{X}$ are the sample averages of Y and X. Since $\bar{Y}$ and $\bar{X}$ would be known from our sample, we thus have an equation in two unknowns, namely, $\hat{a}$ and $\hat{b}$. In the technical jargon of econometrics, (2.42) [or (2.41)] is known as a "normal equation."

Before proceeding to interpret this equation and to develop a second equation, it may prove helpful if we work through a somewhat more intuitive derivation of the normal equation. Let us return to our basic regression model:

$$Y_t = a + bX_t + u_t.$$

If we sum the left and right sides of this expression over all n observed values of X and Y and then divide both sides by n, we have

$$\frac{\sum Y_t}{n} = \frac{\sum a}{n} + \frac{\sum bX_t}{n} + \frac{\sum u_t}{n},$$

(2.43)

which simplifies to

$$\overline{Y} = a + b\overline{X} + \frac{\sum u_t}{n}. \tag{2.44}$$

We know from assumption 2a in our regression model that

$$E(u_t) = 0.$$

This means that the *expected value* of the last term in (2.44) will be zero. Note that this does not say that $\sum u_t/n$ *will* be zero; in general it probably will not be exactly zero, although as the sample size becomes larger, the probability that it will deviate from zero by any given amount decreases.

Our instrumental-variable technique essentially amounts to ignoring the term $\sum u_t/n$ in (2.44), because its expected value is zero. If we ignore this term (i.e., assume it to be zero), we have

$$\overline{Y} = \hat{a} + \hat{b}\overline{X}, \tag{2.45}$$

which is identical to (2.42). Note carefully that, in moving from (2.44) to (2.45), a and b are replaced by the estimators $\hat{a}$ and $\hat{b}$. The reason for this is that the relationship expressed in the normal equation (2.45) coincides with (2.44) *only* for the case where $\sum u_t/n = 0$. Only if this condition holds will $\hat{a} = a$ and $\hat{b} = b$. In general, however, since $\sum u_t/n$ will not be precisely equal to zero, $\hat{a}$ and $\hat{b}$ will not be exactly equal to a and b; they will only constitute estimators of a and b.

The next thing to see about this normal equation is what it tells us about our estimated relationship between X and Y. It says that the line we fit to our scatter of points must pass through the point that has as coordinates the mean sample values of the two variables. In terms of Figure 2.13, the normal equation indicates that point P will lie on our line.

We can now see clearly the role of our assumption that $E(u_t) = 0$. This assumption allows us to locate one point [namely, $P(\overline{X}, \overline{Y})$] on the line we shall fit to our scatter of points. Since two points determine a straight line, it is clear that if we can find one additional point, we can then determine

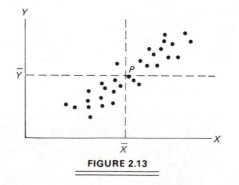

FIGURE 2.13

the equation for the line, and we shall have an estimated relationship between X and Y. To do this, we must make use of another assumption.

In the regression model, we specified as assumption 3 that the disturbance term, u_t, is independent of X_t, so that $\text{cov}(u_t, X_t) = 0$; and we showed that this implies that

$$E(u_t X_t) = 0.$$

This would lead us to expect on an intuitive level that if we had a sample of observations on u_t and X_t, their estimated covariance,

$$\hat{\sigma}_{X,u} = \frac{\sum (u_t X_t)}{n},$$

should be approximately equal to zero, since $E(u_t X_t) = 0$ implies that $E(\hat{\sigma}_{X,u}) = 0$. This suggests that a second condition we could impose on $\hat{u}_t$ is

$$\frac{\sum (\hat{u}_t X_t)}{n} = 0, \tag{2.46}$$

or, multiplying across by n:

$$\sum (\hat{u}_t X_t) = 0. \tag{2.47}$$

Return again to equation (2.38):

$$Y_t = \hat{a} + \hat{b} X_t + \hat{u}_t. \tag{2.38}$$

Multiplying both sides of (2.38) by X_t gives us

$$X_t Y_t = \hat{a} X_t + \hat{b} X_t^2 + \hat{u}_t X_t. \tag{2.48}$$

If we sum both sides of (2.48) over all n observed values of X and Y and divide by n, we obtain

$$\frac{\sum (X_t Y_t)}{n} = \frac{\sum (\hat{a} X_t)}{n} + \frac{\sum (\hat{b} X_t^2)}{n} + \frac{\sum (\hat{u}_t X_t)}{n}$$

$$= \hat{a} \overline{X} + \hat{b} \frac{\sum X_t^2}{n} + \frac{\sum (\hat{u}_t X_t)}{n}. \tag{2.49}$$

We now impose the condition that $\sum (\hat{u}_t X_t) = 0$ on the sample values, which implies that the last term in (2.49) is equal to zero; this gives us

$$\frac{\sum (X_t Y_t)}{n} = \hat{a} \overline{X} + \hat{b} \frac{\sum X_t^2}{n}. \tag{2.50}$$

We now have a second relationship between the observed values of X and Y and the still-to-be-determined values of $\hat{a}$ and $\hat{b}$. This is our *second normal equation*.

In view of the central importance of our two normal equations, it may again be helpful to use a more intuitive approach to this relationship. Beginning once again with our basic regression relationship,

$$Y_t = a + bX_t + u_t,$$

we multiply both sides by X_t to get

$$X_tY_t = aX_t + bX_t^2 + u_tX_t.$$

Next, summing all the observations and dividing by n, we have

$$\frac{\sum(Y_tX_t)}{n} = \frac{\sum(aX_t)}{n} + \frac{\sum(bX_t^2)}{n} + \frac{\sum(u_tX_t)}{n} \tag{2.51}$$

$$= a\bar{X} + \frac{b\sum X_t^2}{n} + \frac{\sum(u_tX_t)}{n}.$$

As before, we know by our assumption that the expected value of the last term in (2.51) is zero. We therefore ignore it by assuming its value to be zero. Our second normal equation follows:

$$\frac{\sum(Y_tX_t)}{n} = \hat{a}\bar{X} + \hat{b}\frac{\sum X_t^2}{n}. \tag{2.50}$$

Note again that, in going from (2.51), which contains the parameters a and b, to our normal equation (2.50), we replace a and b by $\hat{a}$ and $\hat{b}$ since $\sum(u_tX_t)/n$ will not in general be exactly equal to zero. Only where $\sum(u_tX_t)/n = 0$ will it be true that $\hat{a} = a$ and $\hat{b} = b$.

We now have two equations, (2.42) and (2.50), and two unknowns, $\hat{a}$ and $\hat{b}$. We are in a position to solve for the estimators $\hat{a}$ and $\hat{b}$. To do this, it is convenient first to multiply (2.42) by $\bar{X}$:

$$\bar{X}\bar{Y} = \hat{a}\bar{X} + \hat{b}\bar{X}^2. \tag{2.52}$$

Then we subtract this expression from (2.50) to get

$$\frac{\sum(X_tY_t)}{n} - \bar{X}\bar{Y} = \hat{b}\left(\frac{\sum X_t^2}{n} - \bar{X}^2\right). \tag{2.53}$$

We have thereby eliminated $\hat{a}$ and are left with a single equation in one unknown, $\hat{b}$. Solving (2.53) for $\hat{b}$, we get

$$\hat{b} = \frac{[\sum(X_tY_t)/n] - \bar{X}\bar{Y}}{(\sum X_t^2/n) - \bar{X}^2)} = \frac{\sum(X_tY_t) - n\bar{X}\bar{Y}}{\sum X_t^2 - n\bar{X}^2}$$

$$= \frac{\sum(X_t - \bar{X})(Y_t - \bar{Y})}{\sum(X_t - \bar{X})^2}. \tag{2.54}$$

Once we have solved for $\hat{b}$, we can simply use (2.42) to find $\hat{a}$:

$$\hat{a} = \bar{Y} - \hat{b}\bar{X}. \tag{2.55}$$

Since this is the most important single section in this book and is essential to what is to come later, it will be useful at this point to summarize what we have done and to work through a simple numerical example. We began with a hypothesized linear relationship between two variables; this relationship was not exact but instead allowed, for each value of the independent variable, some variation of the dependent variable about a mean value. We described the nature of this relationship in considerable detail in terms of a set of assumptions concerning the character of these variations in the value of the dependent variable. This constitutes what is known as the two-variable, or bivariate, linear regression model.

Our problem was to develop some means of estimating the values of the parameters of this relationship. To do this we adopted the instrumental-variable technique, by which we imposed directly on the estimator of the disturbance terms conditions that were suggested by the assumptions of the regression model itself. In particular, to obtain $\hat{a}$ and $\hat{b}$, we imposed the conditions that $\sum \hat{u}_t/n = 0$ and $\sum (\hat{u}_t X_t)/n = 0$. Each of these conditions yielded one normal equation. Or, alternatively, each allowed us to locate one point on the line we are fitting to the scatter of observed points, and with two such points we were able to solve for the estimated relationship.

AN EXAMPLE

We shall now use this technique to estimate an economic relationship. In Table 2.4 there appear the annual levels of consumption and disposable income in the United States for the years 1960–1969. You may recall earlier that in our investigation of the relationship between consumption and disposable income we focused most of our attention on the levels of consumption

TABLE 2.4

CONSUMPTION AND DISPOSABLE INCOME IN THE
UNITED STATES (billions of current dollars)

Year	Consumption (C)	Disposable Income (Y_d)
1960	325	350
1961	335	364
1962	355	385
1963	375	405
1964	401	438
1965	433	473
1966	466	512
1967	492	547
1968	537	590
1969	576	630

SOURCE: *Economic Report of the President* (Washington, D.C.: U.S. Government Printing Office, Feb. 1970), pp. 189, 195.

expenditure of individual households with differing levels of income. Using what is known as *cross-sectional analysis*, we considered the case where we had a sample of family budgetary information *at a given point in time*, and, for this point in time, we set forth to examine how consumption spending varied among families with different incomes. We might, for example, have studied income and consumption data for households for the year 1970. In cross-sectional analysis, we thus in effect hold time constant.

An alternative approach is to employ *time-series analysis*, with which we examine the behavior of an economic unit or, alternatively, the aggregate behavior of all units *over time*. For instance, we might investigate how total consumption expenditure in the economy has responded to aggregate disposable income over the years. This is what we shall do here using aggregate data for the United States. In particular, we shall use the ten observations on aggregate consumption and disposable income in the United States in Table 2.4 to estimate the influence of the level of disposable income on consumption expenditure. We first assume that

$$C_t = a + bY_{dt} + u_t,$$

and then proceed to estimate values for a and b, where b can be interpreted as the marginal propensity to consume.

We must, therefore, calculate

$$\hat{b} = \frac{\sum (C_t - \bar{C})(Y_{dt} - \bar{Y}_d)}{\sum (Y_{dt} - \bar{Y}_d)^2}$$

and

$$\hat{a} = \bar{C} - \hat{b}\bar{Y}_d.$$

The necessary computations appear in Table 2.5. The estimated equation, therefore, is

$$C = 13 + 0.89 Y_d. \tag{2.56}$$

The estimated regression line *AB*, along with the scatter of ten points, appears in Figure 2.14.* The line does seem to provide a good approximation to the pattern of association between C and Y_d, a matter about which we shall have more to say later. It is also interesting that the estimated relationship does conform to our theoretical expectations: our estimate of the marginal propensity to consume, 0.89, is positive and has a value between zero and unity, and the estimated intercept term, 13, is likewise positive.

You may have noticed in Table 2.5 that the determination of $\hat{a}$ and $\hat{b}$ required a substantial amount of computation. By making use of the properties of summation, it is possible to some extent to reduce this. In particular, note that**

$$\sum (Y_t - \bar{Y})(X_t - \bar{X}) = \sum (Y_t - \bar{Y})X_t - \sum (Y_t - \bar{Y})\bar{X}$$
$$= \sum (Y_t - \bar{Y})X_t.$$

---

*At this point, ignore the line *CD* in Figure 2.14.
**See Proposition IV in Appendix A to Chapter 1.

TABLE 2.5

(1) C_t	(2) Y_{dt}	(3) $(C_t - \bar{C})$	(4) $(Y_{dt} - \bar{Y}_d)$	(5) = (3) × (4) $[(C_t - \bar{C})(Y_{dt} - \bar{Y}_d)]$	(6) $(Y_{dt} - \bar{Y}_d)^2$
325	350	−105	−119	12,495	14,161
335	364	−95	−105	9,975	11,025
355	385	−75	−84	6,300	7,056
375	405	−55	−64	3,520	4,096
401	438	−29	−31	899	961
433	473	3	4	12	16
466	512	36	43	1,548	1,849
492	547	62	78	4,836	6,084
537	590	107	121	12,947	14,641
576	630	146	161	23,506	25,921

$$\sum C_t = 4,295 \qquad \bar{C} = 430$$
$$\sum Y_{dt} = 4,694 \qquad \bar{X}_d = 469$$

$$\sum (C_t - \bar{C})(Y_{dt} - \bar{Y}_d) = 76,038$$
$$\sum (Y_{dt} - \bar{Y}_d)^2 = 85,810$$

$$b = \frac{76,038}{85,810} = 0.89$$
$$\hat{a} = \bar{C} - b\bar{Y}_d = 430 - 0.89(469) = 13$$

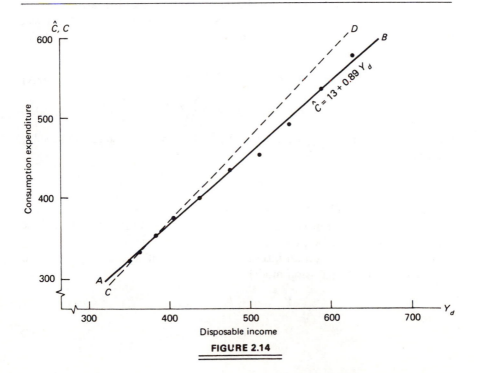

FIGURE 2.14

Similarly,

$$\sum (X_t - \bar{X})^2 = \sum (X_t - \bar{X})(X_t - \bar{X}) = \sum (X_t - \bar{X})X_t.$$

Using these relationships we can simplify, for purposes of computation, the form of $\hat{b}$:

$$\begin{aligned}\hat{b} &= \frac{\sum (Y_t - \bar{Y})(X_t - \bar{X})}{\sum (X_t - \bar{X})^2} = \frac{\sum (Y_t - \bar{Y})X_t}{\sum (X_t - \bar{X})X_t} \\ &= \frac{\sum (Y_t X_t) - \bar{Y} \sum X_t}{\sum X_t^2 - \bar{X} \sum X_t} = \frac{\sum (Y_t X_t) - n\bar{Y}\bar{X}}{\sum X_t^2 - n\bar{X}^2}.\end{aligned} \tag{2.57}$$

Even in this form, however, the determination of $\hat{a}$ and $\hat{b}$ involves a lot of work, particularly if a large number of observations are involved. Fortunately, these are calculations that can easily be done on a computer, and there are a large number of programs available that will instruct the computer to perform these tasks and produce the values for $\hat{a}$ and $\hat{b}$.

A NOTE ON ONE OF THE ASSUMPTIONS

Before proceeding to develop the properties of $\hat{a}$ and $\hat{b}$, we pause to demonstrate the importance of one of our basic assumptions: that X_t takes on at least two distinct values. To prove the point, suppose that this assumption is violated in that X_t is always equal to a particular value, such as X_0. Then, the normal equations used in determining $\hat{a}$ and $\hat{b}$, equations (2.42) and (2.50), would become

$$\bar{Y} = \hat{a} + \hat{b}X_0 \tag{2.42A}$$

and

$$X_0\bar{Y} = \hat{a}X_0 + \hat{b}X_0^2, \tag{2.50A}$$

since $\sum X_t/n = X_0$ and $\sum (X_t Y_t)/n = X_0\bar{Y}$. If we now divide (2.50A) by X_0, we have

$$\bar{Y} = \hat{a} + \hat{b}X_0,$$

which is *identical* to (2.42A). All of this means that we have only one equation, (2.42A), but two unknowns, $\hat{a}$ and $\hat{b}$. We find that we cannot solve for unique values of $\hat{a}$ and $\hat{b}$, and are thus unable to estimate a and b.

The reason for this, on an intuitive level, is that if X_t is always equal to X_0, then our basic regression model,

$$Y_t = a + bX_t + u_t,$$

becomes

$$Y_t = a + bX_0 + u_t. \tag{2.58}$$

Now, since X_0 is a constant, bX_0 can be combined with the constant term, a, so that our model becomes

$$Y_t = A + u_t, \tag{2.59}$$

where $A = (a + bX_0)$. Our regression model reduces to one that has only a constant term and a disturbance term.

If we wished to estimate A, we would again turn to our instrumental-variable technique. Specifically, we would first note from (2.59) that

$$Y_t = \hat{A} + \hat{u}_t. \tag{2.60}$$

Then our assumption that $E(u_t) = 0$ would again suggest that we set $\sum \hat{u}_t/n = 0$. Hence our normal equation would be

$$\frac{\sum Y_t}{n} = \hat{A}. \tag{2.61}$$

In other words, our estimator of A would be $\hat{A} = \bar{Y}$.*

In terms of Figure 2.15, we can see that if X_t is always equal to X_0, our scatter diagram will collapse into a series of points located vertically above X_0. Clearly, such a set of points will only enable us to estimate the mean value of Y, A, corresponding to that particular value of X, X_0.

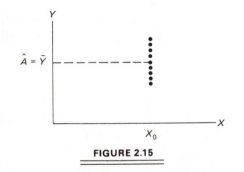

FIGURE 2.15

We thus find that if the value of X_t never varies, our instrumental-variable estimation technique will not allow us to estimate the effect of the variable X on Y, namely b, apart from that of the constant term. In such a case, we can only obtain an estimate of the combined effect $A = (a + bX_0)$. Again, intuitively, if X_t always has the same value, its effect on Y_t becomes "mixed with," or inseparable from, the constant term. We shall, incidentally, draw on this discussion in Chapter 4 when we consider a generalization of this problem in the multiple-regression case.

---

* Note that, since we have only one parameter, A, to estimate, we need only one normal equation.

2.5 THE PROPERTIES OF $\hat{a}$ AND $\hat{b}$

We now have a technique for obtaining the estimators $\hat{a}$ and $\hat{b}$. There remains, however, the question of whether or not this technique is a good one. There certainly are other ways to generate estimators of these parameters. For example, we could take *any* two points from the scatter in Figure 2.14 and solely with that information derive a line to use as an estimated relationship between consumption and disposable income. This would obviously be much easier than the procedure we went through to reach equations (2.54) and (2.55). Intuitively, you would probably feel that our technique is much the better of the two, because it makes systematic use of a great deal more information; the line AB, which we fitted to the scatter in Figure 2.14, does seem to correspond reasonably well to the behavior suggested by the observations. In contrast, if we used only two points, we could get a line such as CD in Figure 2.14, which looks like a much poorer estimate of the typical relationship between C and Y_d.

We shall now show that $\hat{a}$ and $\hat{b}$ are "good" estimators in the sense that they possess certain desirable statistical properties. In particular, we shall show that:

1. The expected values of $\hat{a}$ and $\hat{b}$ are, respectively, a and b; and
2. The variance of $\hat{a}$ and $\hat{b}$ is "relatively" small.

As a result, we shall at least know that our estimators are aimed at the right spot and, relative to other estimators, tend to have a small margin of error.

UNBIASEDNESS*

We shall show first that the expected values of $\hat{a}$ and $\hat{b}$ are in fact a and b, or, in other words, that our estimators are *unbiased*. In the proof, we make use of five properties of the operation of summation**:

$$\sum (X_t - \bar{X}) = 0, \tag{2.62}$$

$$\sum (X_t + Y_t) = \sum X_t + \sum Y_t, \tag{2.63}$$

$$\sum (X_t - \bar{X})(Y_t - \bar{Y}) = \sum (X_t - \bar{X})Y_t, \tag{2.64}$$

$$\sum (X_t - \bar{X})(Y_t - \bar{Y}) = \sum (Y_t - \bar{Y})X_t, \tag{2.65}$$

$$\sum (X_t - \bar{X})^2 = \sum (X_t - \bar{X})(X_t - \bar{X}) = \sum (X_t - \bar{X})X_t. \tag{2.66}$$

We have from the formula for $\hat{b}$ in equation (2.54) that

$$\hat{b} = \frac{\sum (X_t - \bar{X})(Y_t - \bar{Y})}{\sum (X_t - \bar{X})^2}.$$

---

* The treatment of unbiasedness follows that of J. Johnston, *Econometric Methods*, 2nd ed. (New York: McGraw-Hill, 1972), pp. 18–20.
** All of these propositions are formally proven in Appendix A to Chapter 1.

Using (2.64), we can simplify this to

$$\hat{b} = \frac{\sum (X_t - \bar{X})Y_t}{\sum (X_t - \bar{X})^2}.$$ (2.67)

If we now substitute, from our model, $Y_t = a + bX_t + u_t$ into the numerator of (2.67), we obtain

$$\hat{b} = \frac{\sum (X_t - \bar{X})(a + bX_t + u_t)}{\sum (X_t - \bar{X})^2}.$$ (2.68)

Expanding the numerator of (2.68) and using the proposition described in (2.63), we obtain

$$\hat{b} = \frac{a \sum (X_t - \bar{X}) + b \sum (X_t - \bar{X})X_t + \sum (X_t - \bar{X})u_t}{\sum (X_t - \bar{X})^2}.$$ (2.69)

Let us write (2.69) as

$$\hat{b} = \frac{a \sum (X_t - \bar{X})}{\sum (X_t - \bar{X})^2} + \frac{b \sum (X_t - \bar{X})X_t}{\sum (X_t - \bar{X})^2} + \frac{\sum (X_t - \bar{X})u_t}{\sum (X_t - \bar{X})^2}.$$ (2.70)

From (2.62), we see that the first term in this expression is equal to zero. Using (2.66) to change the form of the denominator in the second term to $\sum (X_t - \bar{X})X_t$, we find that the second term is simply equal to b. We thus have

$$\hat{b} = b + \frac{\sum (X_t - \bar{X})u_t}{\sum (X_t - \bar{X})^2}.$$ (2.71)

To simplify the notation of the following analysis, let

$$A = \sum (X_t - \bar{X})^2$$ (2.72)

and

$$w_t = (X_t - \bar{X}).$$ (2.73)

Using these definitions, the expression for $\hat{b}$ in (2.71) becomes

$$\hat{b} = b + \frac{\sum w_t u_t}{A} = b + \frac{w_1 u_1}{A} + \frac{w_2 u_2}{A} + \cdots + \frac{w_n u_n}{A}$$

$$= b + \left(\frac{w_1}{A}\right) u_1 + \left(\frac{w_2}{A}\right) u_2 + \cdots + \left(\frac{w_n}{A}\right) u_n.$$ (2.74)

We are now in a position to demonstrate that $\hat{b}$ is unbiased. Specifically, from (2.74) we have

$$E(\hat{b}) = b + E\left[\left(\frac{w_1}{A}\right) u_1\right] + E\left[\left(\frac{w_2}{A}\right) u_2\right] + \cdots + E\left[\left(\frac{w_n}{A}\right) u_n\right].$$ (2.75)

Since the terms $(w_1/A), \ldots, (w_n/A)$ depend only on the n values of the regressor X_t, and since the values of the regressor and the values of the disturbance term are assumed to be independent, we have

$$E(\hat{b}) = b + E\left(\frac{w_1}{A}\right) E(u_1) + E\left(\frac{w_2}{A}\right) E(u_2) + \cdots + E\left(\frac{w_n}{A}\right) E(u_n).$$
$$(2.76)$$

We know from the regression model that $E(u_t) = 0$. Therefore, the expected values of all but the first term are zero, and we have

$$E(\hat{b}) = b. \qquad (2.77)$$

$\hat{b}$ is thus an unbiased estimator of b.

Turning next to $\hat{a}$, we have, from (2.55),

$$\hat{a} = \overline{Y} - \hat{b}\overline{X}. \qquad (2.55)$$

Since $Y_t = a + bX_t + u_t$, it follows that

$$\overline{Y} = a + b\overline{X} + \bar{u}. \qquad (2.78)$$

Substituting (2.78) into (2.55) yields

$$\hat{a} = a + b\overline{X} + \bar{u} - \hat{b}\overline{X}. \qquad (2.79)$$

Substituting now from (2.74) for $\hat{b}$, we have

$$\hat{a} = a + b\overline{X} + \bar{u} - b\overline{X} - \left(\frac{w_1 \overline{X}}{A}\right) u_1 - \left(\frac{w_2 \overline{X}}{A}\right) u_2 - \cdots - \left(\frac{w_n \overline{X}}{A}\right) u_n.$$
$$(2.80)$$

Noting that $b\overline{X}$ and $-b\overline{X}$ cancel and taking the expected value of $\hat{a}$, we obtain

$$E(\hat{a}) = a + E(\bar{u}) - E\left(\frac{w_1 \overline{X}}{A}\right) E(u_1) - E\left(\frac{w_2 \overline{X}}{A}\right) E(u_2) - \cdots$$
$$- E\left(\frac{w_n \overline{X}}{A}\right) E(u_n) = a, \quad (2.81)$$

since $E(\bar{u}) = 0$ and $E(u_t) = 0$. Thus, $\hat{a}$ is also an unbiased estimator.

THE VARIANCES OF $\hat{a}$ AND $\hat{b}$: SOME BASICS

There remains the issue of the variances of $\hat{a}$ and $\hat{b}$. We know at this point that our method has produced estimators whose mean values are the values of the corresponding parameters. The question now arises as to the extent to which $\hat{a}$ and $\hat{b}$ can be expected to deviate from their mean values, a and b. We would hope that, compared to other techniques, our procedure yields estimators that have relatively small variances. Before deriving expressions for the variances of $\hat{a}$ and $\hat{b}$, it may prove helpful to discuss briefly just why these estimators have variances in the first place.

To begin, consider two hypothetical samples of five observations each on X and Y:

	Sample 1	Sample 2
Observation 1	(Y_{11}, X_1)	(Y_{12}, X_1)
Observation 2	(Y_{21}, X_2)	(Y_{22}, X_2)
Observation 3	(Y_{31}, X_3)	(Y_{32}, X_3)
Observation 4	(Y_{41}, X_4)	(Y_{42}, X_4)
Observation 5	(Y_{51}, X_5)	(Y_{52}, X_5).

In the subscripts for Y, the first number refers to the particular observation and the second identifies the sample. In this example, we assume that the same set of values of X occurs in the two samples. Such an assumption concerning the values of X does not, of course, imply that the values of Y will also be the same in the two samples. The reason for this is that the values of Y reflect two influences: (1) the effect of the value of X operating through the mean relationship $Y^m = a + bX$; and (2) the presence of the disturbance term, u, which is a random variable with a mean value of zero and whose value by assumption is independent of X.

Consider the first observation in each of the two samples. In the absence of the disturbance term, Y_{11} would equal Y_{12}, since Y in each case would reflect only the influence of X_1; in this instance, Y_{11} and Y_{12} would have the value $Y = a + bX_1$. If this were true for all the observations, then obviously the observed sets of values of X and Y would be identical in the two samples, and the values we would calculate for $\hat{a}$ and $\hat{b}$ would in each case equal the actual values of a and b.

The presence of the disturbance term, however, implies that the observed value of Y will deviate somewhat from that which reflects solely the effect of X. In particular,

$$Y_{11} = a + bX_1 + u_{11} \quad \text{and} \quad Y_{12} = a + bX_1 + u_{12},$$

where in general $u_{11} \neq u_{12}$. This implies that in general $Y_{11} \neq Y_{12}$. This is true also for the other observed values of Y, so that generally $Y_{t1} \neq Y_{t2}$. Since $\hat{a}$ and $\hat{b}$ are calculated directly from the observed values of X and Y, it is clear that in general $\hat{a}_1$ and $\hat{b}_1$ will not equal $\hat{a}_2$ and $\hat{b}_2$, respectively, where the subscripts refer to the samples from which the values of $\hat{a}$ and $\hat{b}$ are calculated. The disturbance term will therefore cause both the observed values of the Y and hence the calculated values of $\hat{a}$ and $\hat{b}$ to vary from sample to sample.

Now let us generalize the above. Suppose that we had P samples of a given number of observations on X and Y, where the set of values of the regressor X is the same in all the samples. Let $\hat{a}_i$ and $\hat{b}_i$ be the values of $\hat{a}$ and $\hat{b}$ calculated from the ith sample. We recall that, because the values of Y would differ from sample to sample, the values of $\hat{a}_i$ and $\hat{b}_i$ would also vary. Then, under general conditions, if P were infinite (i.e., if there were an infinite number of samples), the summations (A) and (B) in (2.82) would, with a probability of one, be equal to the variance of $\hat{a}$, $\sigma_{\hat{a}}^2$ and the variance of $\hat{b}$, $\sigma_{\hat{b}}^2$, respectively.

$$\frac{\sum\limits_{i=1}^{P} (\hat{a}_i - a)^2}{P}, \tag{A}$$

$$\tag{2.82}$$

$$\frac{\sum\limits_{i=1}^{P} (\hat{b}_i - b)^2}{P}. \tag{B}$$

In the next section we shall derive formulas for the values of the variances of $\hat{a}$ and $\hat{b}$. At this point, we should note that formally the variances developed above are said to be *conditional variances*. That is, we developed the above argument under the assumption that the set of values of X is the same across the various samples. The variation of $\hat{a}$ and $\hat{b}$ across the samples is entirely due to the variation of the values of the disturbance terms in the different samples. As one might expect, the values of the expressions in (2.82) depend, in part, on just what the common values of X are. In practice, the magnitude of a conditional variance gives the researcher an indication of just how much uncertainty is attached to his estimator, which is based on the particular set of observed values of X at hand. Finally, in passing we note that, because $E(\hat{a}) = a$ and $E(\hat{b}) = b$, we would have, under general conditions if P were infinite,

$$\sum_{i=1}^{P} \frac{\hat{a}_i}{P} = a \quad \text{and} \quad \sum_{i=1}^{P} \frac{\hat{b}_i}{P} = b, \tag{2.83}$$

with probability equal to one.

THE VARIANCE OF THE ESTIMATORS*

We shall now derive expressions first for the variance of $\hat{b}$ and then for the variance of $\hat{a}$. Beginning with our basic expression for $\hat{b}$,

$$\hat{b} = \frac{\sum (X_t - \bar{X})(Y_t - \bar{Y})}{\sum (X_t - \bar{X})^2},$$

we showed in our proof of unbiasedness that

$$\hat{b} = b + \frac{w_1 u_1}{A} + \frac{w_2 u_2}{A} + \cdots + \frac{w_n u_n}{A}, \tag{2.74}$$

where

$$w_t = (X_t - \bar{X}) \quad \text{and} \quad A = \sum (X_t - \bar{X})^2.$$

---

* We shall sometimes simplify our terminology by referring to the "variances" of $\hat{a}$ and $\hat{b}$, but the reader should remember that these are *conditional* variances. For a similar derivation of the results in this section, see J. Johnston, *Econometric Methods*, 2nd ed. (New York: McGraw-Hill, 1972), pp. 18–20.

To use (2.74) to derive an expression for var($\hat{b}$), we need to make use of a fundamental relationship for the variance of the sum of a linear combination of random variables. Specifically (and this proposition is derived in the Appendix to Chapter 2), if we have a random variable M, defined as

$$M = a_0 + a_1 Z_1 + a_2 Z_2 + \cdots + a_n Z_n, \tag{2.84}$$

where the a's are constants and the Z's are random variables, then assuming that the Z's are uncorrelated, we have

$$\text{var}(M) = a_1^2 \sigma_1^2 + a_2^2 \sigma_2^2 + \cdots + a_n^2 \sigma_n^2, \tag{2.85}$$

where $\sigma_j^2 = \text{var}(Z_j)$.

The importance of the conditional variance concept should now be apparent. In particular, if we are interested in the variance of $\hat{b}$ corresponding to a given set of values of X across samples, the n values of X can be considered to be simply n constants. It follows from (2.74) that the n values of w_t and the value of A can also be considered as constants. Under these conditions, $\hat{b}$ in (2.74) becomes simply a linear combination of the disturbance terms. Since, by assumption, these disturbance terms are independent and therefore uncorrelated with each other, and since they have the same variance, σ_u^2, we have, by applying (2.85),

$$\text{var}(\hat{b}) = \sigma_{\hat{b}}^2 = \frac{w_1^2 \sigma_u^2}{A^2} + \frac{w_2^2 \sigma_u^2}{A^2} + \cdots + \frac{w_n^2 \sigma_u^2}{A^2}$$

$$= \frac{\sigma_u^2}{A^2} \sum w_t^2 = \sigma_u^2 \frac{\sum (X_t - X)^2}{[\sum (X_t - X)^2]^2}. \tag{2.86}$$

Our result is

$$\text{var}(\hat{b}) = \sigma_{\hat{b}}^2 = \frac{\sigma_u^2}{\sum (X_t - \overline{X})^2}. \tag{2.87}$$

The expression in (2.87) is the variance of $\hat{b}$ corresponding to any particular set of values of X. Not surprisingly, we find that the variance of our estimator for b varies directly with the variance of the disturbance term; for any set of values for the X_t, the greater the variance of the disturbance term, the greater will be the variance of $\hat{b}$. Somewhat intuitively, the more uncertainty in our basic regression model, the less confidence we can have in our estimator.

In a similar manner, we can derive the variance of $\hat{a}$. Our earlier formula for $\hat{a}$ is

$$\hat{a} = \overline{Y} - \hat{b}\overline{X}. \tag{2.55}$$

Noting that $\overline{Y} = a + b\overline{X} + \overline{u}$, we can substitute (2.74) for $\hat{b}$ into (2.55) to obtain

$$\hat{a} = a + b\overline{X} + \overline{u} - b\overline{X} - \left(\frac{\overline{X} w_1}{A}\right) u_1 - \cdots - \left(\frac{\overline{X} w_n}{A}\right) u_n$$

$$= a + \overline{u} - \left(\frac{\overline{X} w_1}{A}\right) u_1 - \cdots - \left(\frac{\overline{X} w_n}{A}\right) u_n. \tag{2.88}$$

Expressing $\bar{u}$ as

$$\bar{u} = \frac{u_1}{n} + \cdots + \frac{u_n}{n}, \tag{2.89}$$

we obtain, by substituting into (2.88) and combining terms,

$$\hat{a} = a + \gamma_1 u_1 + \cdots + \gamma_n u_n, \tag{2.90}$$

where $\gamma_t = [(1/n) - \bar{X}w_t/A]$. We see that under our assumptions concerning the values of X, $\hat{a}$ also reduces to a linear combination of the disturbance terms. Therefore, applying (2.85), we find that the variance of $\hat{a}$ becomes

$$\text{var}(\hat{a}) = \sigma_{\hat{a}}^2 = \gamma_1^2 \sigma_u^2 + \cdots + \gamma_n^2 \sigma_u^2$$
$$= \sigma_u^2 \sum_{t=1}^{n} \gamma_t^2. \tag{2.91}$$

Now note that

$$\sum \gamma_t^2 = \sum \left[\frac{1}{n^2} + \left(\frac{\bar{X}^2}{A^2} \right) w_t^2 - \left(2\frac{\bar{X}}{nA} \right) w_t \right]$$
$$= \frac{1}{n} + \left(\frac{\bar{X}^2}{A^2} \right) \sum w_t^2 - \left(\frac{2\bar{X}}{nA} \right) \sum w_t. \tag{2.92}$$

It follows, since

$$\sum w_t^2 = \sum (X_t - \bar{X})^2 = A \tag{2.93}$$

and

$$\sum w_t = \sum (X_t - \bar{X}) = 0, \tag{2.94}$$

that the variance of $\hat{a}$ as given in (2.91) can be expressed as

$$\sigma_{\hat{a}}^2 = \sigma_u^2 \left(\frac{1}{n} + \frac{\bar{X}^2}{A} \right)$$
$$= \sigma_u^2 \left(\frac{A + n\bar{X}^2}{nA} \right). \tag{2.95}$$

Finally, recalling from Appendix A to Chapter 1 that

$$\sum (X_t - \bar{X})^2 = \sum X_t^2 - n\bar{X}^2,$$

we have, by direct substitution into (2.95),

$$\sigma_{\hat{a}}^2 = \frac{\sigma_u^2 \sum X_t^2}{n \sum (X_t - \bar{X})^2}. \tag{2.96}$$

As in the case of $\sigma_{\hat{b}}^2$, we find that, for any given set of X_t, the value of $\sigma_{\hat{a}}^2$ varies directly with the variance of the disturbance term, σ_u^2.

It may prove helpful at this juncture actually to compute the variances for $\hat{a}$ and $\hat{b}$ for a hypothetical sample of values for X_t and for σ_u^2. Suppose that we know on the basis of other information that the variance of the

TABLE 2.6

Y	X
8	3
12	6
14	10
15	12
15	14
18	15

disturbance term, σ_u^2, equals ten. Assume next that we have the set of observed values for X and Y shown in Table 2.6. In this case we have

$$\sum X_t^2 = 710, \qquad \sum (X_t - \bar{X})^2 = 110, \qquad n = 6.$$

Using expressions (2.87) and (2.96) we find that, for this set of values of the X_t, we have

$$\text{var}(\hat{b}) = \frac{10}{110} = 0.09, \qquad \text{var}(\hat{a}) = \frac{10(710)}{6(110)} = 10.8.$$

A MINIMUM-VARIANCE PROPERTY

We now have expressions for the variances of $\hat{a}$ and $\hat{b}$, which will prove useful later for establishing confidence intervals when we come to the problem of testing hypotheses. But first we would like to know whether these variances are large or small relative to those associated with other techniques for estimating a and b. It can be shown in this regard that there are *no linear, unbiased estimators* of a and b that have smaller variances than the $\hat{a}$ and $\hat{b}$ we have generated in this chapter. By linear estimators, we mean estimators that can be expressed as linear combinations of the values of the dependent variable Y. For instance, from (2.67), we recall that

$$\hat{b} = \frac{\sum (X_t - \bar{X})Y_t}{\sum (X_t - \bar{X})^2} = \frac{\sum w_t Y_t}{A}$$

$$= \left(\frac{w_1}{A}\right) Y_1 + \cdots + \left(\frac{w_n}{A}\right) Y_n.$$

(2.97)

And from (2.55), we have

$$\hat{a} = \bar{Y} - \bar{X}\hat{b} = \frac{\sum Y_t}{n} - \bar{X}\frac{\sum w_t Y_t}{A}$$

$$= \sum \gamma_t Y_t = \gamma_1 Y_1 + \cdots + \gamma_n Y_n.$$

(2.98)

The proof of this minimum-variance proposition, although not conceptually difficult, is somewhat long, and for that reason we have chosen to put it in the Appendix at the end of this chapter. We encourage the reader to work through the proof, but, if you prefer to take this statement on faith (at least for the time being), it will not cause any difficulties in understanding the material to come.

Not only do we have a technique for estimating a and b, but we now have reason to believe that it is a good technique. First, it generates unbiased estimators of the parameters, and, second, they are the minimum-variance estimators among the whole class of linear, unbiased estimators of a and b.

VARIANCE ESTIMATORS

There is one further piece of unfinished business regarding the variances of $\hat{a}$ and $\hat{b}$. Although we have expressions for them in equations (2.87) and (2.96), these expressions include σ_u^2, the variance of the disturbance term in the regression model. The problem is that, like a and b, σ_u^2 will generally be unknown. This means that, in order to obtain values for the variances of $\hat{a}$ and $\hat{b}$, we would first have to estimate σ_u^2. We shall now consider the problem of deriving an estimator of σ_u^2.

Recall first that

$$\sigma_u^2 = E(u_t - 0)^2 = E(u_t^2).$$

That is, the variance of the disturbance term is simply the mean value of its square. Now, from our basic regression model we know that

$$u_t = Y_t - a - bX_t = Y_t - Y_t^m. \tag{2.35}$$

Suppose we knew the values of a and b. In this case if we had a sample of size n of observations on X and Y, we could derive from (2.35) the n values for u_t. It would then be reasonable to estimate σ_u^2 by simply taking the average value for u_t^2 in the sample:

$$\frac{\sum u_t^2}{n} = \frac{\sum (Y_t - a - bX_t)^2}{n}. \tag{2.99}$$

In practice this cannot be done, because we shall not, in general, know the values of a and b. We do, however, have estimators of a and b. The obvious procedure is to obtain an estimator of σ_u^2, say $\hat{\sigma}_u^2$, from (2.99) by replacing a and b by $\hat{a}$ and $\hat{b}$. We then have

$$\hat{\sigma}_u^2 = \frac{\sum (Y_t - \hat{a} - \hat{b}X_t)^2}{n-2} = \frac{\sum (Y_t - \hat{Y}_t)^2}{n-2} = \frac{\sum \hat{u}_t^2}{n-2}. \tag{2.100}$$

Note that the denominator of (2.100) is $(n-2)$, not n, which (as discussed earlier) indicates that we have only $(n-2)$ degrees of freedom in the numerator. Two degrees of freedom are lost because two parameters are replaced by estimators. It is incidentally the case (although we shall not work through it here) that

$$E(\hat{\sigma}_u^2) = \sigma_u^2. \tag{2.101}$$

$\hat{\sigma}_u^2$ is an unbiased estimator of σ_u^2.

We now have an estimator for the variance of the disturbance term. Estimators for the variances of $\hat{a}$ and $\hat{b}$ may be obtained by simply replacing σ_u^2 by $\hat{\sigma}_u^2$ in the corresponding formulas (2.87) and (2.96). In particular, we take as our estimators of the variances:

$$\hat{\sigma}_a^2 = \frac{\hat{\sigma}_u^2 \sum X^2}{n \sum (X_t - \bar{X})^2},$$

(2.102)

$$\hat{\sigma}_b^2 = \frac{\hat{\sigma}_u^2}{\sum (X_t - \bar{X})^2}.$$

Finally, it follows from (2.101) that, since $\hat{\sigma}_u^2$ is unbiased, $\hat{\sigma}_a^2$ and $\hat{\sigma}_b^2$ are also unbiased estimators.

AN EXAMPLE

Earlier, in Table 2.5, we used data on U.S. consumption and disposable income to compute values for $\hat{a}$ and $\hat{b}$ for an estimated consumption function. You may recall that our estimated equation was

$$C = 13 + 0.89 Y_d.$$

(2.56)

We are now in a position to calculate the estimates of the corresponding variances. First, referring to Table 2.7, we calculate the value of $\hat{\sigma}_u^2$:

$$\hat{\sigma}_u^2 = \frac{92}{10 - 2} = 11.5.$$

From Table 2.5 we also have

$$\sum (Y_{dt} - \bar{Y}_d)^2 = 85,810,$$

and we find that

$$\sum (Y_{dt}^2) = 2,289,172.$$

We thus have

$$\hat{\sigma}_a^2 = \frac{11.5(2,289,172)}{10(85,810)} = 31,$$

$$\hat{\sigma}_b^2 = \frac{11.5}{85,810} = 0.0001.$$

THE LEAST-SQUARES PROPERTY OF $\hat{a}$ AND $\hat{b}$

There is one final property of our estimators $\hat{a}$ and $\hat{b}$ that we want to point out. Another approach to the problem of estimating the relationship between X and Y would be to fit a line to the scatter of points that, in some sense, is as close to the points as possible. Suppose, for example, that we were to select $\hat{a}$

TABLE 2.7

Year	C	$\hat{C}$	$\hat{u} = C - \hat{C}^a$	$\hat{u}^2 = (C - \hat{C})^2$
1960	325	325	0	0
1961	335	337	−2	4
1962	355	356	−1	1
1963	375	373	2	4
1964	401	403	−2	4
1965	433	434	−1	1
1966	466	469	−3	9
1967	492	500	−8	64
1968	537	538	−1	1
1969	576	574	2	4

$$\sum (C_t - \hat{C})^2 = 92$$

a Due to rounding, the sum of $\hat{u}_t$ is not zero.

and $\hat{b}$ so as to make the line AB in Figure 2.16 conform as best it can to the scatter of points. In this respect, consider some point, such as P_1, in the scatter. Because of the disturbance term, u_t, it will not in general lie precisely on the line, but will typically be either somewhat above or below AB. The vertical distance by which the point deviates from the line, in this case the length of the line segment $P_1 k$, represents the difference between the observed value of Y, Y_t, corresponding to X_t, and the calculated value of Y, $\hat{Y}_t$, where $\hat{Y}_t$ is obtained from the estimated relationship represented by AB:

$$P_1 k = (Y_t - \hat{Y}_t) = (Y_t - \hat{a} - \hat{b}X_t). \tag{2.103}$$

Suppose that we wanted the line AB to minimize in some sense the distance of these deviations of observed points from the line. One difficulty with simply minimizing the sum of these deviations is that, for points above the line, $(Y_t - \hat{Y}_t) > 0$, while for points below AB, $(Y_t - \hat{Y}_t) < 0$. This means that we could have a wide scatter of points about the line and yet have a very small (even zero) algebraic sum of measured deviations. In fact, we could strictly minimize this sum by placing the line AB as *high as possible*, since this would give $\sum (Y_t - \hat{Y}_t)$ a highly negative value. One way around this difficulty is to

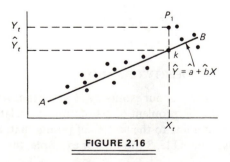

FIGURE 2.16

square these deviations (which makes them all positive), and then to minimize the sum of these squares. This is the *least-squares method* of generating estimators of a and b: find that line in the scatter diagram for which the sum

$$S = \sum (Y_t - \hat{Y}_t)^2 = \sum (Y_t - \hat{a} - \hat{b}X_t)^2$$

is minimized.

Making use of the calculus, it is a straightforward problem to determine values for $\hat{a}$ and $\hat{b}$ that will minimize $\sum (Y_t - \hat{Y}_t)^2$. If you are familiar with the basic differential calculus, we suggest that you work through this derivation, which is included in the Appendix to this chapter. What we do want you to know is that, when we compute the least-squares estimators of a and b, we get exactly the same results we reached by the instrumental-variable method. That is, the least-squares estimators are also

$$\hat{b} = \frac{\sum (X_t - \overline{X})(Y_t - \overline{Y})}{\sum (X_t - \overline{X})^2},$$

$$\hat{a} = \overline{Y} - \hat{b}\overline{X}.$$

This is important because frequently in the literature of economics one comes across equations that the author indicates he has estimated by "least-squares," and one should realize that these equations are identical to those that would be obtained by using the estimation procedure we have developed in this chapter. It just so happens that our estimation procedure also results in minimizing the sum of the squared deviations of observed values from calculated values of Y.

2.6 MEASUREMENT OF THE EXPLANATORY POWER OF THE REGRESSION MODEL

We now have a technique for estimating what we have called the mean relationship between two variables; we can obtain estimators for the parameters a and b in the regression model. However, we do not yet have a measure of how "tight" this relationship is. In Figures 2.17 and 2.18, for

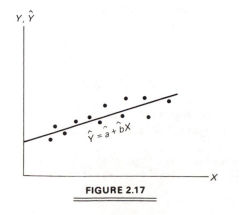

FIGURE 2.17

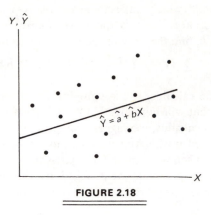

FIGURE 2.18

example, the estimated relationship between Y and X is the same. It is clear, however, that these two relationships differ in one important respect: the scatter of points is much closer to the line in the first case than in the second. In other words, we get a "tighter fit" of the observed points about the regression line.

In addition to estimators of a and b, it is important that we develop a measure of this further aspect of the relationship between X and Y.* In one sense, we want to know just how good our model is. We are presumably trying to account for the observed values of Y_t with this model. If we had no model, we could not explain the movements in Y; the best we could do in this case would be to take $\overline{Y}$ as the predicted value of Y_t regardless of the value of X_t. The question is whether or not our model allows us to do better than this, and, if so, by how much. For this reason, we shall now develop a measure of the explanatory power of our regression model; that is, we shall develop a measure of just how much of the variation in Y can be "explained" by the estimated linear relationship between X and Y.

THE COEFFICIENT OF DETERMINATION

Consider the scatter of points in Figure 2.19, to which we have fitted by our estimation technique the line $\hat{Y} = \hat{a} + \hat{b}X$. We have also indicated on the diagram the sample means, $\overline{X}$ and $\overline{Y}$, of X and Y. Recall from (2.45) that one of the properties of the estimated equation is that

$$\overline{Y} = \hat{a} + \hat{b}\overline{X}, \tag{2.45}$$

which tells us that the regression line passes through the point $(\overline{X}, \overline{Y})$, which is point C in Figure 2.19. Look next at the observation represented

---

* Actually, we already have one measure of this: the variance of the disturbance term. For instance, Figure 2.17 suggests a smaller variance of the disturbance term than does Figure 2.18.

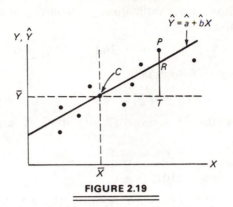

FIGURE 2.19

by P. The deviation of the value of Y at P from its sample mean value of $\overline{Y}$ is the distance PT. Some of this deviation of Y from $\overline{Y}$ is, however, "explained" by our estimated regression equation. In particular, the estimated equation accounts for RT and leaves PR of the deviation "unexplained." We can express these various distances as

$$PT = (Y_t - \overline{Y}) = \text{total deviation of } Y_t \text{ from the sample mean,}$$

$$RT = (\hat{Y}_t - \overline{Y}) = \text{explained deviation of } Y_t \text{ from } \overline{Y},$$

$$\overline{PR} = (Y_t - \hat{Y}_t) = \text{unexplained deviation of } Y_t \text{ from } \overline{Y}.$$

With this as background, we shall now develop a measure of the explanatory power of the regression equation. We recall first, from equation (2.38), that

$$Y_t = \hat{Y}_t + \hat{u}_t. \tag{2.38}$$

If we sum both sides of (2.38), we have

$$\sum Y_t = \sum \hat{Y}_t + \sum \hat{u}_t. \tag{2.104}$$

Since, however, we imposed the condition that $\sum \hat{u}_t = 0$, we have that

$$\sum Y_t = \sum \hat{Y}_t, \tag{2.105}$$

which, incidentally, if we divide through by n, implies that

$$\overline{Y} = \overline{\hat{Y}}. \tag{2.106}$$

These results will be useful later. Let us now return to (2.38), where we have $Y_t = \hat{Y}_t + \hat{u}_t$, and square both sides:

$$Y_t^2 = \hat{Y}_t^2 + \hat{u}_t^2 + 2\hat{u}_t\hat{Y}_t. \tag{2.107}$$

Summing over the whole sample yields

$$\sum Y_t^2 = \sum \hat{Y}_t^2 + \sum \hat{u}_t^2 + 2\sum (\hat{u}_t\hat{Y}_t). \tag{2.108}$$

We note next that

$$\sum (\hat{u}_t\hat{Y}_t) = 0.$$

This follows because, in our estimation procedure, you will recall that we imposed the conditions

$$\sum (\hat{u}_t X_t) = 0 \qquad \text{and} \qquad \sum \hat{u}_t = 0.$$

Since $\hat{Y}_t = \hat{a} + \hat{b} X_t$, it follows that

$$\sum (\hat{u}_t \hat{Y}_t) = \hat{a} \sum \hat{u}_t + \hat{b} \sum (\hat{u}_t X_t) = 0.$$

This means that the last term in (2.108) above is zero, so that (2.108) simplifies to

$$\sum Y_t^2 = \sum \hat{Y}_t^2 + \sum \hat{u}_t^2. \tag{2.109}$$

Next subtract $n\bar{Y}^2$ from (2.109) to get

$$\sum Y_t^2 - n\bar{Y}^2 = (\sum \hat{Y}_t^2 - n\bar{Y}^2) + \sum \hat{u}_t^2. \tag{2.110}$$

Recalling our earlier result that $\bar{Y} = \hat{\bar{Y}}$, we can now express (2.110) in the form

$$\sum (Y_t - \bar{Y})^2 = \sum (\hat{Y}_t - \bar{Y})^2 + \sum \hat{u}_t^2. \tag{2.111}$$

Equation (2.111) will prove extremely useful for our purposes, and it is important that we consider carefully the meaning of each of the terms in this expression. Note first that on the left side of (2.111) we have the sum of the squared deviations of Y_t about its sample mean; this is a measure of the variation in the dependent variable that we seek to explain with our regression equation. That is, somewhat intuitively, we would like our model to explain why the dependent variable, Y, is not always constant. In particular, we would like the movements of the variable Y to be related to, and be explained by, the movements of the variable X. In any event, let us call the first term on the left-hand side of (2.111) the *total sum of squares*, TSS.

Now consider the right-hand side of (2.111). Since $\hat{u}_t = (Y_t - \hat{Y}_t)$, $\hat{u}_t$ indicates what we have failed to explain. That is, $\hat{u}_t$ is the deviation of the observed value of Y_t from the value calculated from our regression equation, namely, $\hat{Y}_t = (\hat{a} + \hat{b} X_t)$. This last term in (2.111), $\sum \hat{u}_t^2$, is the sum of the squares of the *errors* or the unexplained portion of the variation in Y_t. We shall designate this sum as the *error sum of squares* (ESS). The difference between TSS and ESS is, from (2.111), the term $\sum (\hat{Y}_t - \bar{Y})^2$, and this obviously must represent in some sense that part of the total sum of squares that our regression model does explain. This we call the *regression sum of squares* (RSS) (i.e., the sum of squares explained by our regression model). Corresponding to (2.111) we thus have

$$\text{TSS} = \text{RSS} + \text{ESS}. \tag{2.112}$$

It may be helpful to view this relationship in terms of Figure 2.19. With reference to the observed value of Y_t represented by point P, we recall that PT represents the deviation of Y_t from its sample mean, $\bar{Y}$; PR is the deviation of Y_t from the regression line, or, in other words, that part of the variation of Y_t from $\bar{Y}$ that the regression line cannot account for; and the remaining component of PT, namely RT, is the portion of the variation of Y_t that the regression line does explain. What we have shown in (2.111) is that, if we consider the distances corresponding to PT, PR, and RT for each point in the sample, the sum of the squared distances corresponding to PT is equal to the sum of the squared distances corresponding to PR plus the corresponding sum for RT.

In summary, we have that

$$\text{TSS} = \sum (Y_t - \bar{Y})^2 = \text{total sum of squares,}$$

$$\text{RSS} = \sum (\hat{Y}_t - \bar{Y})^2 = \text{regression (or explained) sum of squares,}$$

$$\text{ESS} = \sum \hat{u}_t^2 = \text{error (unexplained) sum of squares,}$$

where $\text{TSS} = \text{RSS} + \text{ESS}$. Since $\text{RSS} \geq 0$ and $\text{ESS} \geq 0$, it follows that $\text{TSS} \geq \text{RSS}$ and $\text{TSS} \geq \text{ESS}$.

To measure the explanatory power of the regression equation, we want a measure that indicates the proportion of the variation in the Y_t that the regression equation can explain. One such measure is

$$R^2 = \frac{\text{RSS}}{\text{TSS}} = 1 - \frac{\text{ESS}}{\text{TSS}}, \qquad (2.113)$$

where R^2 is called the *coefficient of determination*. If the regression equation can explain all the variation in the Y_t (i.e., if $\hat{Y}_t = Y_t$ for all t), then $\hat{u}_t = 0$, and so $\text{ESS} = 0$. In this instance, $\text{RSS} = \text{TSS}$, and hence $R^2 = 1$. Since $Y_t = \hat{Y}_t = \hat{a} + \hat{b}X_t$, Y_t would be a perfect linear combination of X_t. Therefore, all the points in the scatter diagram between Y_t and X_t would lie on a straight line (i.e., all the disturbance terms would be zero). Such a case is described in Figure 2.20.

At the other extreme, if the regression equation explains nothing, ESS assumes its maximum value, namely, $\text{ESS} = \text{TSS}$. We see that $\text{RSS} = 0$ and so $R^2 = 0$. In this case, since $\text{RSS} = 0$, we must have $\hat{Y}_t = \bar{Y}$ for all t. This implies that $\hat{b} = 0$. To see this, substitute $\hat{a} = \bar{Y} - \hat{b}\bar{X}$ into $\hat{Y}_t = \hat{a} + \hat{b}X_t$ to get

$$\hat{Y}_t = \bar{Y} + \hat{b}(X_t - \bar{X}). \qquad (2.114)$$

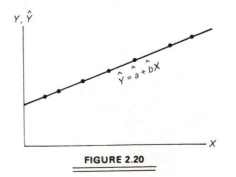

FIGURE 2.20

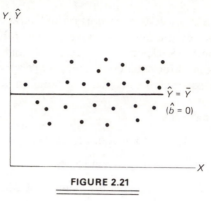

FIGURE 2.21

It follows, since all the values of X_t are not the same, $X_t \neq \bar{X}$, that $\hat{Y}_t = \bar{Y}$ implies $\hat{b} = 0$. In this case, our model is totally inadequate in that the calculated, or explained, values of Y_t, namely $\hat{Y}_t$, do not depend at all on the values of the variable, X_t. Figure 2.21 depicts one such situation.

In the more typical cases, such as those described in Figures 2.17 and 2.18, the regression equation will account for some, but not all, of the variation in Y; R^2 will lie between zero and unity. The more of the variation in Y that the equation explains (i.e., the tighter the fit of the points about the regression line), the closer R^2 will be to unity, and the weaker is the relationship between X and Y, the nearer will R^2 be to zero. R^2 thus indicates the fraction of the variation in the dependent variable that the estimated equation can account for; as a result, if $R^2 = 0.63$, for example, we say that the estimated relationship can "explain" 63 percent of the variation in the dependent variable.

$$R^2 = \hat{\rho}^2_{Y,\hat{Y}}$$

In the first section of this chapter we developed a measure of the "strength" of the linear association between two variables, which we called the correlation coefficient. This parameter was defined as the ratio of the covariance of two variables to the product of their standard deviations. We could, presumably, also use the correlation coefficient to measure the strength of the relationship in our regression equation. For instance, the correlation coefficient between Y_t and $\hat{Y}_t$, say $\rho_{Y,\hat{Y}}$, would be a measure of how closely Y_t and $\hat{Y}_t$ are related and hence would be a measure of how well our model is able to "explain" the values of Y_t.

Unfortunately, $\rho_{Y,\hat{Y}}$ will generally be unknown. It would, in practice, have to be estimated. Consistent with equation (2.16) in the first section of this chapter, the estimator for $\rho_{Y,\hat{Y}}$ would be

$$\hat{\rho}_{Y,\hat{Y}} = \frac{\sum (Y_t - \bar{Y})(\hat{Y}_t - \bar{Y})}{\sqrt{\sum (Y_t - \bar{Y})^2 \sum (\hat{Y}_t - \bar{Y})^2}} \qquad (2.115)$$

since $\bar{\hat{Y}} = \bar{Y}$. We shall now show that $\hat{\rho}_{Y,\hat{Y}}^2 = R^2$. That is, our R^2 statistic is simply the square of the estimator of the correlation coefficient between Y_t and $\hat{Y}_t$; we cannot, therefore, consider R^2 and $\hat{\rho}_{Y,\hat{Y}}$ as alternative measures of the strength of the relationship between Y and $\hat{Y}$.

Consider first the numerator in (2.115). Recalling from Appendix A to Chapter 1 that, for any two variables, say Z_{1t} and Z_{2t}, with sample averages of $\bar{Z}_1$ and $\bar{Z}_2$,

$$\sum (Z_{1t} - \bar{Z}_1)(Z_{2t} - \bar{Z}_2) = \sum (Z_{1t} - \bar{Z}_1)Z_{2t},$$

we can simplify the numerator of (2.115) to

$$\sum (\hat{Y}_t - \bar{Y})Y_t.$$

Since we know that $Y_t = \hat{Y}_t + \hat{u}_t$, we have

$$\sum (\hat{Y}_t - \bar{Y})Y_t = \sum (\hat{Y}_t - \bar{Y})(\hat{Y}_t + \hat{u}_t) = \sum (\hat{Y}_t - \bar{Y})\hat{Y}_t,$$

since

$$\sum (\hat{Y}_t \hat{u}_t) = 0 \quad \text{and} \quad \sum (\hat{u}_t \bar{Y}) = \bar{Y} \sum \hat{u}_t = 0.$$

Finally, we can put the numerator in the form

$$\sum (\hat{Y}_t - \bar{Y})\hat{Y}_t = \sum (\hat{Y}_t - \bar{Y})(\hat{Y}_t - \bar{Y}) = \sum (\hat{Y}_t - \bar{Y})^2 = \text{RSS}.$$

Note next that, for the denominator of $\hat{\rho}_{Y,\hat{Y}}$, we have

$$\sqrt{\sum (Y - \bar{Y})^2 \sum (\hat{Y}_t - \bar{Y})^2} = \sqrt{(\text{TSS})(\text{RSS})}.$$

Therefore,

$$\hat{\rho}_{Y,\hat{Y}} = \frac{\text{RSS}}{\sqrt{(\text{RSS})(\text{TSS})}} = \frac{\sqrt{\text{RSS}}}{\sqrt{\text{TSS}}}. \tag{2.116}$$

From (2.116) we can see that

$$R^2 = \hat{\rho}_{Y,\hat{Y}}^2.$$

AN EXAMPLE

For purposes of illustration, it may be useful to return to the consumption function we estimated earlier in the chapter and find the value of R^2. To simplify the computations, we note that

$$R^2 = \frac{\sum (\hat{Y}_t - \bar{Y})^2}{\sum (Y_t - \bar{Y})^2} = \frac{\sum (\hat{Y}_t - \bar{Y})\hat{Y}_t}{\sum (Y_t - \bar{Y})Y_t} = \frac{\sum \hat{Y}_t^2 - n\bar{Y}^2}{\sum Y_t^2 - n\bar{Y}^2}, \tag{2.117}$$

since as, we showed earlier, $\bar{Y} = \bar{\hat{Y}}$.

One additional step in the calculation of R^2 is that we must use the estimated regression equation to compute the calculated values of Y (i.e., the $\hat{Y}_t$). The calculations are presented in Table 2.8.

TABLE 2.8^a

$$\hat{C} = 13 + 0.89Y_d$$

C	Y_d	C^2	$\hat{C}$	$\hat{C}^2$
325	350	105,625	325	105,625
335	364	112,225	337	113,569
355	385	126,025	356	126,736
375	405	140,625	373	139,129
401	438	160,801	403	162,409
433	473	187,489	434	188,356
466	512	217,156	469	219,961
492	547	242,064	500	250,000
537	590	288,369	538	289,444
576	630	331,776	574	329,476

$$\sum C^2 = 1,912,155$$
$$\sum \hat{C}^2 = 1,924,705$$
$$\bar{C}^2 = 184,900$$
$$n\bar{C}^2 = 1,849,000$$

$$R^2 = \frac{\sum \hat{C_t}^2 - n\bar{C}^2}{\sum C_t^2 - n\bar{C}^2} = 0.99$$

^{a} Because the values of the coefficients in the regression equation are rounded off to only two significant digits, the value of R^2 generated by the above numbers is, as a result of rounding errors, slightly in excess of unity. If the coefficients are computed to a sufficient number of places, the value of R^2 is found to be 0.99.

The value of R^2 for our estimated consumption function is 0.99, which is indicative of an extremely strong association between C and Y_d. It means that the estimated regression equation accounts for 99 percent of the variation of C, and only 1 percent remains "unexplained." This confirms the tentative conclusion that we drew earlier by simply looking at the scatter diagram and regression line in Figure 2.14.

2.7 AN ILLUSTRATION: THE ESTIMATION OF A COST FUNCTION

We conclude our introduction to the bivariate regression model with an actual study from the economic literature. A central concern of the microeconomic theory of the firm is the firm's cost function. In particular, most texts present a lengthy examination of the relationship between cost and the firm's level of output. In general terms, we have that

$$C = f(Q),$$

where C is total cost and Q is the firm's output. To learn more about the form of this relationship, some economists have used regression analysis to estimate cost functions from actual data on costs and output.

One early and pioneering effort of this type was a study by Joel Dean of the cost function of a plant for the manufacture of silk stockings.* Dean assembled monthly data for the hosiery plant on its costs and its output of stockings; Figure 2.22 depicts these data in terms of a scatter diagram. Note that the points seem to cluster quite closely about the straight line in the diagram, which suggests that a linear function should provide a good description of the plant's cost function. Using the basic two-variable regression model, Dean postulated that

$$C_i = a + bQ_i + u_i, \tag{2.118}$$

where C is total monthly cost measured in thousands of dollars, Q is monthly output measured in thousands of dozens of pairs of stockings,** and u is a disturbance term. Equation (2.118) has, incidentally, some important implications for the nature of the plant's costs. Since it is a total cost function, we see that the (expected) marginal monthly cost associated with an additional unit of monthly output is simply b units of monthly costs. According to our units of measurement, this means that, if monthly output increases by one thousand dozens, monthly costs will increase by "b" thousand dollars. This, in turn, implies that an increase in monthly output of one dozen will lead to an increase in monthly costs of b dollars. The parameter "a" indicates that monthly costs will be "a" thousands of dollars if monthly output is zero; it is the firm's fixed monthly costs. Note that, if a is positive, the plant's average monthly cost will decline with output, since these fixed costs would be spread over a larger number of units of output.

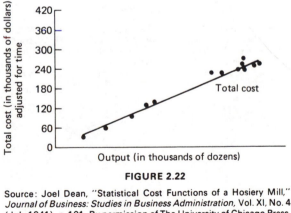

FIGURE 2.22

Source: Joel Dean, "Statistical Cost Functions of a Hosiery Mill," *Journal of Business: Studies in Business Administration*, Vol. XI, No. 4 (July 1941), p. 101. By permission of The University of Chicago Press. © 1941 by The University of Chicago.

---

* Joel Dean, "Statistical Cost Functions of a Hosiery Mill," *Journal of Business: Studies in Business Administration*, Vol. XI, No. 4 (July 1941), pp. 1–116.

** As an illustration of these measurements, a value of $C = 27$ corresponds to $27,000; a value of $Q = 17$ corresponds to 17,000 dozens or $(17,000 \times 12) = 204,000$ pairs of stockings.

Dean estimated the regression equation (2.118) by the least-squares technique which is equivalent to the instrumental-variable technique we have developed in this chapter and determined that

$$C = 2.936 + 2.00Q$$
$$R^2 = 0.95. \tag{2.119}$$

As the scatter diagram suggested, the fit is a close one: the coefficient of determination is 0.95, indicating that the estimated equation (2.119) explains 95 percent of the observed variation in total cost. In addition, the estimates of the coefficients provide some specific cost information: they indicate that the plant's fixing costs are $2936 per month and that the marginal cost of a dozen pair of stockings is $2. These cost functions are depicted in Figure 2.23. Such information is not only of interest to an economist studying cost relationships, but can also be quite valuable to the firm's management!

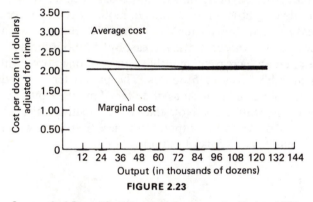

FIGURE 2.23

Source: Joel Dean, "Statistical Cost Functions of a Hosiery Mill,"
Journal of Business: Studies in Business Administration, Vol. XI, No. 4
(July 1941), p.101. By permission of The University of Chicago Press.
© 1941 by The University of Chicago.

APPENDIX.

Proofs of Three Propositions

In the text, we simply stated three propositions: one concerning the expression for the variance of a sum of uncorrelated random variables; one for the minimum-variance property of our instrumental-variable estimators; and one for a least-squares property of our estimators. Here we shall provide the proofs of these propositions.

THE VARIANCE OF THE SUM OF RANDOM VARIABLES

Let $X_1, X_2, \ldots, X_n$ be random variables, and let $a_1, a_2, \ldots, a_n$ be constants, where the means and variances of these variables are, respectively, $\mu_1, \mu_2, \ldots, \mu_n$, and $\sigma_1^2, \sigma_2^2, \ldots, \sigma_n^2$. Next define

$$Y = a_0 + a_1 X_1 + \cdots + a_n X_n. \tag{2A.1}$$

Note that, since Y is simply a linear combination of a set of random variables, Y is itself a random variable. We shall show the following:

PROPOSITION I. If the $X_1, X_2, \ldots, X_n$ are uncorrelated random variables, then, denoting the variance of Y by σ_Y^2,

$$\sigma_Y^2 = a_1^2 \sigma_1^2 + a_2^2 \sigma_2^2 + \cdots + a_n^2 \sigma_n^2. \tag{2A.2}$$

This says that if the X's are linearly unrelated to one another, then the variance of Y is equal to the sum of the variances of the X's, each multiplied by the square of its respective coefficient.

To prove Proposition I, notice first that the mean of Y, $E(Y) = \mu_Y$, is simply the mean of the right side of equation (2A.1):

$$\begin{aligned} \mu_Y &= E(a_0) + E(a_1 X_1) + \cdots + E(a_n X_n) \\ &= a_0 + a_1 \mu_1 + a_2 \mu_2 + \cdots + a_n \mu_n. \end{aligned} \tag{2A.3}$$

Next, by definition, the variance of Y is $E(Y - \mu_Y)^2$. Using (2A.1) and (2A.3), we have

$$\sigma_Y^2 = E(Y - \mu_Y)^2 = E[a_1(X_1 - \mu_1) + a_2(X_2 - \mu_2) + \cdots + a_n(X_n - \mu_n)]^2. \tag{2A.4}$$

If we expand the expression in (2A.4), we get two types of terms—squared terms and a set of cross-product terms:

$$\begin{aligned} \sigma_Y^2 = E[a_1^2(X_1 - \mu_1)^2 + a_2^2(X_2 - \mu_2)^2 + \cdots + a_n^2(X_n - \mu_n)^2 \\ + \cdots + 2a_3 a_4 (X_3 - \mu_3)(X_4 - \mu_4) + \cdots]. \end{aligned} \tag{2A.5}$$

The last term in (2A.5) is just a typical cross-product term; there may be a large number of such terms depending on how large n is. The key point is that, since the X's are by assumption uncorrelated, the expected value of each of these cross-product terms will be zero. For our illustrative cross-product term in (2A.5), we have

$$E[2a_3a_4(X_3 - \mu_3)(X_4 - \mu_4)] = 2a_3a_4E(X_3 - \mu_3)(X_4 - \mu_4)$$
$$= 2a_3a_4 \, \text{cov}(X_3, X_4) = 0, \tag{2A.6}$$

where $\text{cov}(X_3, X_4)$ is the covariance between X_3 and X_4. With the expected value of all the cross-product terms equal to zero, equation (2A.5) becomes

$$\sigma_Y^2 = E[a_1^2(X_1 - \mu_1)^2 + a_2^2(X_2 - \mu_2)^2 + \cdots + a_n^2(X_n - \mu_n)^2]$$
$$= a_1^2E(X_1 - \mu_1)^2 + a_2^2E(X_2 - \mu_2)^2 + \cdots + a_n^2E(X_n - \mu_n)^2 \tag{2A.7}$$
$$= a_1^2\sigma_1^2 + a_2^2\sigma_2^2 + \cdots + a_n^2\sigma_n^2.$$

MINIMUM-VARIANCE ESTIMATORS OF a AND b*

In the text, we showed that our instrumental-variable estimation technique produces unbiased estimators, $\hat{a}$ and $\hat{b}$, of the coefficients in the regression model. We shall now show that *our instrumental-variable estimators, $\hat{a}$ and $\hat{b}$, have the smallest conditional variance of the whole class of unbiased linear estimators of a and b.* In the literature, this is known as the *Gauss-Markov theorem.*

We note first from the text that

$$\hat{b} = \frac{\sum (X_t - \bar{X})Y_t}{\sum (X_t - \bar{X})^2} = \frac{\sum w_t Y_t}{A} \tag{2A.8}$$
$$= \sum Q_t Y_t,$$

where $Q_t = w_t/A$, with $w_t = (X_t - \bar{X})$ and $A = \sum (X_t - \bar{X})^2$. Similarly, from the text we recall that

$$\hat{a} = \bar{Y} - \hat{b}\bar{X}$$
$$= \sum \gamma_t Y_t, \tag{2A.9}$$

where $\gamma_t = (1/n) - \bar{X}(w_t/A)$. Note, as in the text, that both the γ_t and Q_t depend solely on the values of X_t. Therefore, if the values of X_t are given, we can treat the values of γ_t and Q_t as constants.

We need next to establish two properties of the weights, Q_t. Notice first that

$$\sum Q_t = \sum \left(\frac{X_t - \bar{X}}{A}\right) = \frac{1}{A} \sum (X_t - \bar{X}) = 0. \tag{2A.10}$$

Second, we have that

$$\sum (Q_t X_t) = \frac{1}{A} \sum (X_t - \bar{X})X_t = \frac{1}{A} \sum (X_t - \bar{X})^2 = \left(\frac{1}{A}\right) A = 1, \tag{2A.11}$$

since, as you will recall,

$$\sum (X_t - \bar{X})X_t = \sum (X_t - \bar{X})(X_t - \bar{X}) = \sum (X_t - \bar{X})^2 = A.$$

---

* This section draws upon J. Johnston, *Econometric Methods,* 2nd ed. (New York: McGraw-Hill, 1972), pp. 18–23.

In the text, we showed that

$$\sigma_b^2 = \frac{\sigma_u^2}{\sum (X_t - \bar{X})^2}. \tag{2A.12}$$

We can express (2A.12) as

$$\sigma_b^2 = \sigma_u^2 \sum Q_t^2, \tag{2A.13}$$

since

$$\sum Q_t^2 = \frac{\sum w_t^2}{A^2} = \frac{\sum (X_t - \bar{X})^2}{A^2} = \frac{A}{A^2} = \frac{1}{A} = \frac{1}{\sum (X_t - \bar{X})^2}.$$

Now let $\hat{b}^*$ be *any other linear estimator* of b. Then

$$
\begin{aligned}
\hat{b}^* &= \sum (Q_t + v_t)Y_t \\
&= \hat{b} + \sum v_t Y_t,
\end{aligned}
\tag{2A.14}
$$

where v_t (like Q_t) is some function of the X_t, but not the Y_t. Equation (2A.14) simply says that $\hat{b}^*$ is equal to $\hat{b}$ plus something else: namely, their difference. It follows, recalling that $\sum Q_t = 0$ and $\sum (Q_t X_t) = 1$, that

$$
\begin{aligned}
\hat{b}^* &= \sum (Q_t + v_t)Y_t = \sum (Q_t + v_t)(a + bX_t + u_t) \\
&= a \sum (Q_t + v_t) + b \sum (Q_t + v_t)X_t + \sum (Q_t + v_t)u_t \\
&= a \sum v_t + b + b \sum (v_t X_t) + \sum (Q_t + v_t)u_t.
\end{aligned}
\tag{2A.15}
$$

Taking the expected value of $\hat{b}^*$, and recalling that the values of Q_t and v_t depend only on the values of X_t and are therefore constant, we have

$$E(\hat{b}^*) = a \sum v_t + b + b \sum (v_t X_t), \tag{2A.16}$$

since $E(u_t) = 0$.

If $\hat{b}^*$ is to be an unbiased estimator of b, we must have that

$$E(\hat{b}^*) = b.$$

This implies from equation (2A.16) that, for $\hat{b}^*$ to be unbiased, we must have

$$\sum v_t = 0 \quad \text{and} \quad \sum (v_t X_t) = 0. \tag{2A.17}$$

With this information, we can now rewrite the last expression in equation (2A.15) as

$$
\begin{aligned}
\hat{b}^* &= b + \sum (Q_t + v_t)u_t \\
&= b + (Q_1 + v_1)u_1 + (Q_2 + v_2)u_2 + \cdots + (Q_n + v_n)u_n.
\end{aligned}
\tag{2A.18}
$$

We can now use Proposition I from the first section of this Appendix to obtain an expression for the variance of $\hat{b}^*$. Since $\hat{b}^*$ is a linear combination of the u_t's, and since these u_t's are uncorrelated because they are independent, the variance of $\hat{b}^*$ is

$$
\begin{aligned}
\sigma_{b^*}^2 &= (Q_1 + v_1)^2 \sigma_u^2 + \cdots + (Q_n + v_n)^2 \sigma_u^2 \\
&= \sigma_u^2 \sum (Q_t + v_t)^2 \\
&= \sigma_u^2 [\sum Q_t^2 + \sum v_t^2 + 2 \sum (Q_t v_t)] \\
&= \sigma_u^2 [\sum Q_t^2 + \sum v_t^2],
\end{aligned}
\tag{2A.19}
$$

since

$$2 \sum (Q_t v_t) = \frac{2 \sum (X_t - \bar{X})v_t}{A} = \frac{2}{A} [\sum (X_t v_t) - \bar{X} \sum v_t] = 0. \tag{2A.20}$$

From (2A.13) and (2A.19), we can see immediately that

$$\sigma_{b^*}^2 = \sigma_u^2 \sum Q_t^2 + \sigma_u^2 \sum v_t^2$$
$$= \sigma_b^2 + \sigma_u^2 \sum v_t^2.$$
(2A.21)

Since the last term in (2A.21) is obviously positive if some $v_t \neq 0$, we have that

$$\sigma_{b^*}^2 \geq \sigma_b^2.$$
(2A.22)

Notice that $\sigma_{b^*}^2$ will equal σ_b^2 only if $\sum v_t^2 = 0$, which will hold only if all $v_t = 0$; this of course implies that $b^* \equiv b$. We have thus shown that *any* other unbiased linear estimator of b will have a conditional variance greater than that of our instrumental-variable estimator. Using the same general approach, this same proposition can be shown to hold for our instrumental-variable estimator of a; we leave this as an exercise for the interested reader.

THE LEAST-SQUARES PROPERTY OF $\hat{a}$ AND $\hat{b}$

As stated in the text, the least-squares estimators are derived by minimizing, with respect to $\hat{a}$ and $\hat{b}$, the sum

$$S = \sum (Y_t - \hat{Y}_t)^2 = \sum (Y_t - \hat{a} - \hat{b}X_t)^2.$$
(2A.23)

Partially differentiating (2A.23) with respect to $\hat{a}$ and $\hat{b}$ and setting the result equal to zero, we get

$$\frac{\partial S}{\partial \hat{a}} = 2 \sum (Y_t - \hat{a} - \hat{b}X_t)(-1) = 0,$$

$$\frac{\partial S}{\partial \hat{b}} = 2 \sum (Y_t - \hat{a} - \hat{b}X_t)(-X_t) = 0.$$
(2A.24)

Multiplying equations (2A.24) by $(-\frac{1}{2})$ and simplifying, we obtain

$$\sum Y_t = n\hat{a} + \hat{b} \sum X_t \quad \text{or} \quad \bar{Y} = \hat{a} + \hat{b}\bar{X},$$
(2A.25)

and

$$\sum (Y_t X_t) = \hat{a} \sum X_t + \hat{b} \sum X_t^2.$$
(2A.26)

Since (2A.25) is identical with our first normal equation, (2.45) in the text, and (2A.26), after division by n, is identical with our second normal equation, (2.50) in the text, it follows that the least-squares estimators and our instrumental-variable estimators are *identical*.

QUESTIONS

1. Show that the intercept estimator $\hat{a}$ can be expressed as

$$\hat{a} = \sum \left(\frac{1}{n} - \bar{X} W_t \right) Y_t,$$

where

$$W_t = \frac{(X_t - \bar{X})}{\sum (X_t - \bar{X})^2}.$$

2. Consider the following regression model: $Y_t = a + bX_t + u_t$, where the observations on X_t and Y_t are

X_t	Y_t
4	8
2	6
3	5
1	7
2	4

   Estimate a, b, and σ_u^2.
3. A consumer analyst demonstrates that the consumption function $C_t = a + bY_t$ is useless, because the points (C_t, Y_t) in the scatter diagram do not lie on a straight line. He also notes that sometimes Y_t goes up but C_t goes down. He concludes that C_t is not a function of Y_t. Evaluate his argument.
4. Let $Y = 5 - 3X$. Show that the correlation coefficient $\rho_{X,Y} = \sigma_{X,Y}/\sigma_X \sigma_Y$, is equal to -1.0.
5. Let the variables X_1, X_2, and X_3 have variances $\sigma_1^2 = 1.0$, $\sigma_2^2 = 3.0$, and $\sigma_3^2 = 5.0$. Let these variables be independent. Let $Y = 13 - 2X_1 + 3X_2 - 10X_3$. Find the variance of Y.
6. It is said that middle- and upper-income families are leaving the cities because taxes in the cities are higher than taxes in the surrounding suburban area. Suppose we have data relating to a number of cities at a point in time. Formulate this hypothesis in terms of a regression model. (There is more than one way to do this!)
7. Consider the following model:

$$Y_t = a_1 + b_1 X_t + u_t, \tag{1}$$

   where the disturbance term, u_t, depends on the regressor in the following fashion:

$$u_t = a_2 + b_2 X_t + \varepsilon_t, \tag{2}$$

   where ε_t is a disturbance term that is independent of X_t and also satisfies all of our standard assumptions. Suppose that $b_2 > 0$. Demonstrate that b_1 in (1) understates the effect of X_t on Y_t.

8. Suppose that in Question 7, equation (2) were replaced by

$$u_t = a_2 + b_2 X_t^2 + \varepsilon_t.$$

Would any of our assumptions of the bivariate regression model relating Y_t to X_t be violated?

9. Set up a regression model that might describe the relationship between the age of a child and his height. Discuss whether or not such a model might have a shortcoming.

10. Consider the model

$$Y_t = a + bX_t + u_t,$$

in which we have errors of measurement in that we do not observe X_t directly. Instead, suppose that we observe

$$X_t^m = X_t + \varepsilon_t,$$

where ε_t is a disturbance term that is independent of X_t, has a mean of zero, and satisfies all of our other standard assumptions. In addition, assume that ε_t and u_t are independent. This implies the independence of X_t^m and u_t.

a. Set up the regression model relating Y_t to X_t^m.

b. Are any of our basic assumptions violated in this model?

CHAPTER 3
Applications of the Regression Model

In the preceding chapter we set forth the basic two-variable regression model and developed a technique for estimating its parameters. Using a sample of observed values for the two related variables, we can now generate estimators for a and b in the regression equation and for the variances of these estimators. We can also measure the strength of the relationship between the two variables by calculating the proportion of the variation in the dependent variable that the estimated regression equation can explain. In this chapter we shall show how economists put these techniques to work both in terms of testing hypotheses about economic behavior and in making predictions or forecasts.

3.1 HYPOTHESIS TESTING AND CONFIDENCE INTERVALS: AN INTRODUCTION

In Chapter 2 we set forth the hypothesis that consumption expenditure depends on the level of disposable income and then proceeded to estimate a linear form of this relationship. Using aggregate time-series data for the United States, we found that our estimated value for the marginal propensity to consume was positive and had a value between zero and unity; our estimate of a was also positive. These results, we suggested, would seem consistent with the standard Keynesian theory of the consumption function.

But how reliable are these results? For instance, how sure can we be that the parameter a is in fact positive? As an example, if our estimate of a were 0.001, would we be *convinced* that a is positive rather than, say, zero?

Alternatively, suppose that, on the basis of prior information, we had reason to believe that $b = 0.75$. Is our estimate of b, namely 0.89, inconsistent with the prior hypothesis that $b = 0.75$? The point is that the discrepancy between our estimate of 0.89 and our hypothesized value of $b = 0.75$ might arise from the *size of the sample* we used to obtain that estimate. As an analogy, if the average height of men in the United States is 5'10", we would not expect the average height of a group of, say, three men selected at random to be *exactly* 5'10".

These are problems of hypothesis testing. Essentially, in these problems we are interested in whether or not our parameter estimates are consistent with our prior hypotheses. A closely related problem is that of confidence intervals. For instance, we have a particular estimate of b, namely 0.89.

This is called a *point estimate*. However, if we were forced to interpret this estimate, we would probably say that the marginal propensity to consume is "around" 0.89. That is, we would probably not expect the value of *b* to be *exactly* 0.89.

We would therefore like to construct an interval about our point estimate that we felt, with a certain assurance, contained the value of *b*. The theory of confidence intervals, which we shall develop below, does just that. It enables us to expand upon our point estimate in order to produce an *interval estimate*. Such an interval is a *range of values* that, because of the way the interval is constructed, leads us to expect, with a certain level of assurance, that the value of the parameter of interest is contained in the interval. As an example, a statement of a confidence interval might be as follows: with probability 0.95, the interval $(\hat{b} \pm 0.07)$ contains the value of the parameter *b*. Finally, we shall show that, *ceteris paribus*, the only way we can have more assurance, or confidence, that our interval includes *b* is by making it wider. If we are 95 percent sure that *b* lies within 0.07 of $\hat{b}$, but we want an interval that includes *b* with probability 0.99, that new interval will have to be wider than $(\hat{b} - 0.07, \hat{b} + 0.07)$; for example, our 99 percent confidence interval might be $(\hat{b} - 0.10, \hat{b} + 0.10)$.

The problems of hypothesis testing and of confidence intervals are inter-related in the following sense. Suppose, as mentioned above, that we want to test the hypothesis $b = 0.75$. We would presumably estimate *b* and then see how close our estimate is to 0.75. If the difference between our estimate and 0.75 is very "small," we would feel that the results supported the hypothesis. If, on the other hand, our estimate differed from 0.75 by a "large" amount, we would conclude that the hypothesis is not confirmed by our observed results; we would then have good reason to believe that $b \neq 0.75$. To conduct a meaningful analysis of this kind, we must be able to distinguish between "small" and "large" differences between the hypothesized and estimated values of the parameter. As a preview, we determine what is large as compared to small by constructing a confidence interval for the parameter in question and then noting whether or not the hypothesized value of the parameter lies within the interval. As an example, if the probability were 0.95 that the interval $(\hat{b} \pm 0.07)$ contains *b*, we would reject the hypothesis with 95 percent confidence that $b = 0.75$ if, on the basis of our data, $\hat{b}$ was estimated to be 0.89. Since the width of our interval is related to the confidence we have that it contains the value of the parameter, it follows that the degree of assurance we have in the results of our testing procedure directly depends on the level of probability associated with our confidence interval.

A FURTHER ASSUMPTION

To test hypotheses and construct confidence intervals for the values of the parameters in the regression model, we must first expand upon the properties of the disturbance term, u_t, in our model. In Chapter 2 we made four assumptions about the properties of the disturbance terms themselves: they are random variables with expected values of zero; they have the same variance; they have zero covariances; and they are independent of the regressor. At this point, it is useful to introduce one further condition: we shall also assume that the disturbance terms are normally distributed; that is, their density, or probability function, is the normal curve. Since the normal distribution has only two parameters, the mean and variance, a variable that is normally distributed is completely specified by its mean and variance. We can summarize some of our assumptions concerning the disturbance term u_t by the notation $N(0, \sigma_u^2)$; in words, $N(0, \sigma_u^2)$ denotes a normally distributed variable whose mean is zero and whose variance is σ_u^2.*

With this added assumption of the normality of the disturbance terms, we can depict the basic properties of the regression model as in Figure 3.1. For any given value of X, say X_t, the mean value of Y will be $(a + bX_t)$. However, because of the disturbance term, Y is not completely determined by its mean value. If we had repeated observations on Y that all corresponded to this particular value of X, X_t, we would not expect all of the observed values of Y to be its mean value, $(a + bX_t)$. Moreover, since the deviations of Y from its mean would be caused solely by the disturbance term, it follows that these deviations would be normally distributed if the disturbance term is so distributed. For example, if we had a scatter diagram to represent the repeated observations on Y corresponding to X_t, we would expect it to resemble the scatter of points in Figure 3.1, where the "data" (observations) are more dense near the mean value of Y, $(a + bX_t)$, than farther away. The reason for this is that the height of the normal density curve tapers off as we move away from its mean (where the mean in this case is zero).**

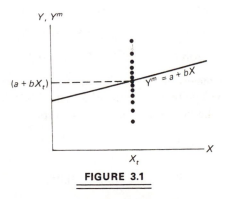

FIGURE 3.1

* $N(u_x, \sigma_x^2)$ is standard notation to indicate that a variable X is normally distributed with a mean of u_x and a variance of σ_x^2. This N is not to be confused with small n, which refers to the size of the sample.

** For convenience of exposition, we henceforth assume, throughout this book, that the disturbance term is normally distributed. Technically, however, many of the results presented below do not require this assumption.

Let us turn now to our estimators, $\hat{a}$ and $\hat{b}$, of the parameters in the regression model. Recall that, in the course of developing the variances of these estimators in Chapter 2, we showed that, for given values of the regressor, $\hat{a}$ and $\hat{b}$ are both linear combinations of the disturbance terms $u_1, u_2, \ldots, u_n$.* There is a theorem in statistics that states that linear combinations of normal variables are themselves normally distributed. For any given set of values of X_t, it follows that $\hat{a}$ and $\hat{b}$ must be normally distributed. In Chapter 2 we found that the mean values of $\hat{a}$ and $\hat{b}$ are a and b, respectively, and we developed in (2.87) and (2.96) expressions for their variances. Using these results plus our additional assumption of the normality of the u_t, we conclude that

$$\hat{a} \quad \text{is} \quad N\left(a, \frac{\sigma_u^2 \sum X_t^2}{n \sum (X_t - \bar{X})^2}\right), \tag{3.1}$$

$$\hat{b} \quad \text{is} \quad N\left(b, \frac{\sigma_u^2}{\sum (X_t - \bar{X})^2}\right). \tag{3.2}$$

This is a particularly useful result because, if our estimators $\hat{a}$ and $\hat{b}$ are normally distributed, it means that we can use standard statistical techniques to test hypotheses concerning a and b. As you will recall from basic statistics, if we have a normally distributed variable, say v, with mean μ_v and variance σ_v^2 [that is, if v is $N(\mu_v, \sigma_v^2)$], then

$$Z = \frac{v - \mu_v}{\sigma_v} \tag{3.3}$$

is the standard normal variable. In other words, Z is $N(0, 1)$. From a table for the standard normal distribution, we can make certain kinds of probability statements about the value of Z. In such a table we find, for instance, that**

$$\text{Prob} (-1.65 \leq Z \leq 1.65) = 0.90,$$

$$\text{Prob} (-1.96 \leq Z \leq 1.96) = 0.95, \tag{3.4}$$

$$\text{Prob} (-2.58 \leq Z \leq 2.58) = 0.99.$$

As an example, this means that if a value of Z were selected at random, the probability would be 0.90 that the value of Z would be between (-1.65) and $(+1.65)$. Note that the first statement in (3.4) implies that

$$\text{Prob} (Z \leq -1.65) = 0.05 \tag{3.5}$$

and

$$\text{Prob} (Z \geq 1.65) = 0.05. \tag{3.6}$$

Again, recall that the reason for this is that the normal curve is symmetric, so that if 0.90 of the area under the curve lies between ± 1.65, the 0.05 must lie to the left of -1.65, and 0.05 must lie to the right of $+1.65$.

---

* See equations (2.74) and (2.90).
** See Statistical Table 1 at the back of the book.

Assume now that σ_u^2 is known. Denoting the variance of $\hat{a}$ and $\hat{b}$ as given in (3.1) and (3.2) as $\sigma_{\hat{a}}^2$ and $\sigma_{\hat{b}}^2$, we have

$$\left(\frac{\hat{a} - a}{\sigma_{\hat{a}}}\right) \text{ is } N(0, 1) \text{ and } \left(\frac{\hat{b} - b}{\sigma_{\hat{b}}}\right) \text{ is } N(0, 1), \tag{3.7}$$

where $\sigma_{\hat{a}}$ and $\sigma_{\hat{b}}$ are the *standard deviations* of $\hat{a}$ and $\hat{b}$, respectively. In light of (3.7), we can make the same statements about $(\hat{a} - a)/\sigma_{\hat{a}}$ and $(\hat{b} - b)/\sigma_{\hat{b}}$ that we can about the standard normal variable Z of (3.3). For instance,

$$\text{Prob}\left(-1.96 \leq \frac{\hat{b} - b}{\sigma_{\hat{b}}} \leq 1.96\right) = 0.95. \tag{3.8}$$

A TEST OF $b = b_0$ AGAINST $b \neq b_0$; σ_u KNOWN

We now are in a position to construct confidence intervals and to use them in testing our hypotheses. For $\hat{b}$, for instance, we can rearrange the terms in (3.8) to obtain

$$\text{Prob }(\hat{b} - 1.96\sigma_{\hat{b}} \leq b \leq \hat{b} + 1.96\sigma_{\hat{b}}) = 0.95. \tag{3.9}$$

Equation (3.9) says that, with a probability of 0.95, the interval

$$(\hat{b} - 1.96\sigma_{\hat{b}}, \hat{b} + 1.96\sigma_{\hat{b}}) \tag{3.10}$$

includes the value of b, so that (3.10) is our 95 percent confidence interval for b. The suggested testing procedure is as follows. On the basis of our sample, calculate $\hat{b}$ and $\sigma_{\hat{b}}$. Then compute $(\hat{b} - 1.96\sigma_{\hat{b}})$ and $(\hat{b} + 1.96\sigma_{\hat{b}})$. Finally, see whether or not our hypothesized value of b lies within the interval given by (3.10). If it does not, we reject our hypothesis with 95 percent confidence. If it does, we say that the data are consistent with our hypothesis and so we accept it.

Our testing procedure is not foolproof. For instance, (3.9) implies that there is a 5 percent chance that $(\hat{b} \pm 1.96\sigma_{\hat{b}})$ does not contain b. Thus, we could reject our hypothesis concerning the value of b (such as $b = 0.75$) even though our hypothesis is correct. Somewhat more formally, we could reject our prior or, what statisticians call the *null*, hypothesis, when this hypothesis is in fact true. This form of mistake is called a *Type 1 error*; the probability of making such an error is usually denoted by α and is called the *level of significance*. In our example, $\alpha = 0.05$. Incidentally, α is also referred to as the "size" of the Type 1 error.

Suppose again that our null hypothesis (H_0) is $b = 0.75$. If we reject H_0: $b = 0.75$, and if there is no further information given to us, we are evidently left with the statement $b \neq 0.75$. In the statistical literature, this statement is referred to as the alternative hypothesis (to H_0) and is usually denoted as H_1. In other words, a full statement of our hypothesis under consideration would be H_0: $b = 0.75$, H_1: $b \neq 0.75$. That is, our testing procedure will lead to either H_0 or H_1.

A Type 1 error is not the only type of error that we could make. For instance, we could *accept* H_0 even if it is false (that is, when H_1 is true). As an example, suppose our confidence interval turns out to be (0.86 to 0.92). Suppose further that H_0: $b = 0.87$, but that the true value of b is 0.88. Then, since 0.87 is contained within our interval, we could accept H_0: $b = 0.87$. However, in this case H_1: $b \neq 0.87$ would be true. Such a possibility will always exist, since our confidence interval includes more than one value. This form of error (that of accepting the null hypothesis when it is false) is called a Type 2 error. The probability of making a Type 2 error (which is also referred to as the "size" of the Type 2 error) is usually denoted by β.

We can see that there is a lower probability of making a Type 2 error when the true value of the parameter differs a great deal from its hypothesized value. For instance, if H_0: $b = 0.75$ but, in fact, $b = 0.98$, the value of our estimator of b, $\hat{b}$, will typically be "near" 0.98, so that our confidence interval $(\hat{b} \pm 1.96\sigma_{\hat{b}})$ would usually contain a range of values centered (roughly) around 0.98. If such were the case, we would usually end up by rejecting our hypothesis that $b = 0.75$. On the other hand, if the value of b were 0.751, the confidence interval would typically include our hypothesized value of 0.75; we would thus have a high chance of committing a Type 2 error. This suggests that we are more likely to make an error of Type 2 when the hypothesized value of the parameter is *near* its true value. In brief, fine distinctions between hypotheses are difficult to make.

HYPOTHESIS TESTING: AN INTERPRETATION

In summary, our testing procedure essentially amounts to accepting or rejecting our null hypothesis on the basis of the discrepancy between our hypothesized value of the parameter and our estimate of it. To see this in more detail, consider a 95 percent confidence interval for b such as interval 2 in Figure 3.2. If the discrepancy between $\hat{b}$ and our hypothesized value of b, say b_0 (such as $b_0 = 0.75$), is so great as to exceed $1.96\sigma_{\hat{b}}$, then b_0 will lie in either interval 1 or interval 3. In such a case we would, with 95 percent confidence, reject our hypothesis that $b = b_0$. Thus we see that the determinant of what we mean by a "large" discrepancy as compared to a "small" one is simply a multiple of the standard deviation of the estimator, namely $1.96\sigma_{\hat{b}}$. This makes sense. For example, if $\sigma_{\hat{b}}$ were large, the precision of our estimator would be poor, and we would be willing to "tolerate" a larger discrepancy between our estimate and our hypothesized value of the parameter before rejecting the null hypothesis.

Interval 1	Interval 2	Interval 3
$(\hat{b} - 1.96\sigma_{\hat{b}})$	$\hat{b}$ $(\hat{b} + 1.96\sigma_{\hat{b}})$	

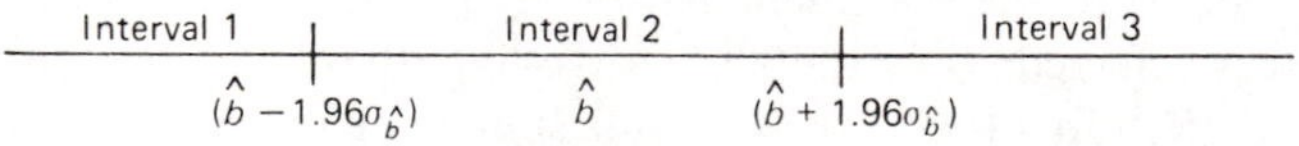

FIGURE 3.2

ACCEPTANCE AND REJECTION REGIONS

In the example above we saw that our null hypothesis would be accepted if

$$|\hat{b} - b_0| < 1.96\sigma_{\hat{b}}. \tag{3.11}$$

Manipulating the terms in (3.11), we see that the acceptance of our null hypothesis is associated with the range of values of $\hat{b}$:

$$b_0 - 1.96\sigma_{\hat{b}} < \hat{b} < b_0 + 1.96\sigma_{\hat{b}}. \tag{3.12}$$

The range of values of $\hat{b}$ defined in (3.12) is said to be the *acceptance region*. In general, an acceptance region is that range of values of our estimator that would lead to the acceptance of the null hypothesis. Conversely, that range of values of our estimator that would lead to a rejection of our null hypothesis is called the *rejection region*, or sometimes, the *critical region*. In the example above, the critical region would be

$$\begin{aligned} \hat{b} &> b_0 + 1.96\sigma_{\hat{b}}, \\ \hat{b} &< b_0 - 1.96\sigma_{\hat{b}}. \end{aligned} \tag{3.13}$$

It should be clear that an equivalent procedure for testing hypotheses would be first to establish the acceptance and rejection regions, and then, on the basis of the sample, determine which region contains our parameter estimate.

CONFIDENCE INTERVALS: AN INTERPRETATION

Before moving on, we want to discuss a bit further the interpretation of equation (3.9). Given the values of the regressor, the random variable in the probability statement is $\hat{b}$. Note that b and $\sigma_{\hat{b}}$ are constants; they are not random variables. Equation (3.9) says that the probability is 0.95 that the interval $(\hat{b} - 1.96\sigma_{\hat{b}}, \hat{b} + 1.96\sigma_{\hat{b}})$ will contain b. In other words, assume that we could take a large number of samples, say 1,000, of size 50 each. Assume, moreover, that for each of these samples the values of the X_t's are the same. Suppose that we calculate $\hat{b}$ for each sample. Since the disturbance terms would be expected to differ from sample to sample, the values of the Y_t's would differ among the samples even though the set of values of the X_t's remain unchanged. Since $\hat{b}$ depends on the Y_t's, it would vary across samples. If we then were to calculate the interval $(\hat{b} \pm 1.96\sigma_{\hat{b}})$ for each sample, we would essentially have 1000 different intervals. The essence of (3.9) is that with this procedure we would expect $0.95(1000) = 950$ of these intervals to contain the constant b.

SOME COMMENTS ON TYPE 1 AND TYPE 2 ERRORS

Our tests above were based on a 95 percent confidence interval and so had a *level of significance* of 5 percent. The choice of a level of significance is, however, at the discretion of the experimenter, and we can easily, where desired, construct tests with other levels of significance. If we wanted to be highly certain that we would not reject the hypotheses $b = 0.75$ when, in fact, it is true, we could construct a test that had a smaller probability of Type 1 error: $\alpha < 0.05$. The α usually chosen in such a case is $\alpha = 0.01$, although the researcher is free to select any value of α. For purposes of our example, suppose we wish to construct a test with $\alpha = 0.01$. Then, we would select a 0.99 level of probability in equation (3.8) and end up with the interval

$$(\hat{b} \pm 2.58\sigma_{\hat{b}}). \tag{3.14}$$

Again, we would accept or reject our hypothesis depending on whether or not the interval included our hypothesized value of b.

The confidence interval (3.14) associated with a Type 1 error of size $\alpha = 0.01$ is larger than the interval (3.10), which has a Type 1 error of size $\alpha = 0.05$. It is clear that if our confidence interval is wider, and is still centered at the same point estimator $\hat{b}$, then the probability is *higher* that we will make a Type 2 error. That is, even if H_0 is false, it is more likely to be accepted if the confidence interval is wide than if the interval is small. This indicates that as we *reduce* the likelihood of a Type 1 error, we *increase* the probability of making a Type 2 error. This *trade-off* is well known in the statistical literature: in general, with a given sample the probability of both Type 1 and Type 2 errors cannot be reduced at the same time. In short, one can only be reduced at the expense of the other. In the light of this discussion, we see that in order to construct a confidence interval for testing purposes, we must first select the probability of committing either a Type 1 or Type 2 error. Economists almost invariably test hypotheses that specify a particular value of a parameter, such as $b = 0.75$, by selecting $\alpha = 0.05$ or $\alpha = 0.01$. Typically, little or no explicit attention is given to the associated Type 2 error.

This is not the best solution. The size of the Type 1 error, which then determines the size of the Type 2 error, should be selected with care. The point is that either error may lead us to take an action (or make a decision) that has undesired consequences. We may therefore think of a loss that is associated with each type of error. Ideally, we should then weight, in some manner, the importance of these losses in determining the size of our Type 1 error. For example, suppose the government were making a study concerning the causes of riots. Assume that the null hypothesis is that a particular governmental policy has no effect in reducing the tensions that lead to riots. Suppose the alternative hypothesis is that it does. In this example, a Type 1 error would lead us to expect that the governmental policy is effective when, in fact, it is not. One consequence of this error is that funds may be wasted on an ineffective policy. The Type 2 error, on the other hand, would lead us to conclude that the policy does not work when, in fact, it does reduce the likelihood of riots. The consequence of this error is that funds will not be spent on an effective policy. Clearly, the evaluation of just how important each of these errors is would then depend on some further assumptions. For example, suppose that a number of such "antiriot" policies are to be considered, but only one can be carried out because of limited funds. Then it is clear that the Type 1 error would be extremely important, because it would lead to the waste of the limited funds and an atmosphere conducive to riots. The Type 2 error, on the other hand, would simply require the researchers to consider another policy.* Thus, in this example, α might be set at a very low value, perhaps less than 0.01.

On the other hand, suppose that funds are relatively plentiful but, to take the extreme, only one of the policies to be considered is effective. Assume further that, because funds are readily available, the government stands ready to undertake all policies that seem promising. In this case, the wasting of the funds on an ineffectual policy due to a Type 1 error may not be too serious. The only loss would be the wastage of the funds themselves. A Type 2 error, however, would lead us to believe that the effective policy is ineffective. As a consequence, the government would reject the efficacious policy and social disturbances might occur. In this case it should be clear that the Type 2 error is far more important than the Type 1 error. Therefore, under these conditions, the proper "setting" for the size of the Type 1 error would be much higher than $\alpha = 0.05$; for example, one might set $\alpha = 0.30$, or still higher, in order to reduce the size of the more costly Type 2 error. In passing, we would like to point out that a formal solution to the problem of the proper setting for α is very complicated, and the solution is well beyond the scope of this book.** We do hope, however, that you have a better understanding of at least some of the issues involved.

THE HYPOTHESIS $b \neq 0$

In practice, economists usually do not have hypotheses that specify particular values of the parameters. Often, economic theory simply suggests that two variables are related positively or negatively. Hence, the hypotheses of concern to economists are often those that specify *only* the sign of a particular parameter. Indeed, in some cases our theory only points out which variables are related; whether the relationship is negative or positive remains an empirical question.

Suppose, for example, that we are interested in how the consumption of potatoes varies with the level of family income. Our hypothesis is that

$$Q_t = a + bY_t + u_t, \tag{3.15}$$

where Q_t is the quantity of potatoes consumed by the tth family, Y_t is the

---

* We are assuming here that other policies that are effective exist and will be considered in a "reasonable" time period.

** For some background literature, see Chapter 12 of Alexander H. Mood and Franklin A. Graybill, *An Introduction to the Theory of Statistics* (New York: McGraw-Hill, 1963); and Chapters 1 and 2 in Arnold Zellner, *An Introduction to Bayesian Inferences in Econometrics* (New York: Wiley, 1971).

family's level of income, and u_t is our familiar disturbance term. In this case, it is not even clear whether we should expect b to be positive or negative. For most commodities, we believe that the quantity consumed rises with income; there is, however, a class of commodities that economists call "inferior" goods, whose consumption varies inversely with income. The idea here is that as a family's income increases, it can afford a more varied and expensive menu of foods, and we would probably not be too surprised to find higher-income families substituting to some extent other food items for potatoes. On the other hand, it is possible that wealthier families do in fact consume more potatoes than poorer families. In this case we see that, although we may believe that some relationship exists between Q and Y, we cannot even be sure of the sign of the relationship. This suggests that the hypothesis we want to test is simply $b \neq 0$, with no prior restrictions on the sign of b.

How would we test the hypothesis $b \neq 0$? Clearly we cannot simply construct, for example, a 95 percent confidence interval and see whether or not that interval includes any values of $b \neq 0$. If we did, we would *always* accept our hypothesis, because our interval would *always* include some values of $b \neq 0$. The probability of making a Type 2 error would be equal to one.

We obviously cannot have any confidence in the hypotheses we accept if our testing procedure ensures that they cannot be rejected. In order to correct for this, economists test hypotheses of the sort $b \neq 0$ by setting the size of the Type 2 error equal to a small number, usually 0.05 or 0.01. This is easily done by simply relabeling hypotheses. For example, the alternative to the null hypothesis $b \neq 0$ is $b = 0$. Therefore, the Type 2 error is to accept the hypothesis $b \neq 0$ when, in fact, $b = 0$. Suppose, however, we consider $b = 0$ as our null hypothesis, $b \neq 0$ as the alternative, and adopt a level of significance of, say $\alpha = 0.05$. Our testing procedure would then imply that the probability of rejecting $b = 0$ when, in fact, $b = 0$ is $\alpha = 0.05$. Since rejecting $b = 0$ is equivalent to accepting $b \neq 0$, we have our result. That is, as required we would have set up a test in which the probability of accepting the hypothesis $b \neq 0$ when, in fact, $b = 0$ is 0.05. In equation (3.15), for example, if there were no relationship between the quantity of potatoes consumed, Q_t, and the family's level of income, Y_t, the probability would be 0.05 that our testing procedure would lead us to believe that there is a relationship ($b \neq 0$) between these variables.

To summarize, to test the hypothesis that the value of a particular parameter, say b, is not zero, we construct the hypotheses

$$H_0: b = 0, \qquad H_1: b \neq 0, \tag{3.16}$$

and select α according to our desired level of significance. As we mentioned, economists usually set α equal to 0.05 or 0.01. If we reject $H_0: b = 0$, we say that our estimate is *significantly different from zero*; if we accept $H_0: b = 0$, we say that our estimate is *not* significantly different from zero. Note that in this latter case, we in effect say that we are unable to find a systematic relationship between the variables that meets our prescribed level of significance.

THE HYPOTHESES $b < 0$, $b > 0$

In the example above, we tested the hypotheses $H_0 \colon b = b_0$ and $H_1 \colon b \neq b_0$, where b_0 may be zero. Such a test is called a *two-tailed* test. That is, the alternative hypothesis, H_1, is that b is *either* greater than or less than b_0. Under our testing procedure, sufficiently large positive *or* negative deviations of $\hat{b}$ from the value of b specified by H_0 will lead to a rejection of the null hypothesis. Alternatively, economists are often concerned with a *one-tailed* test. Since economic theory frequently suggests the *sign* of the relationship between the variables, the hypotheses derived from theory are often of the form $b > 0$ or $b < 0$. Assume that we again wish to have a 95 percent level of confidence in the hypotheses we accept. We would then, for testing purposes, establish the hypotheses $H_0 \colon b = 0$ and either $H_1 \colon b > 0$ or $H_1 \colon b < 0$, such that the probability of committing a Type 1 error is 0.05.

The implementation of such one-tailed tests is straightforward. For example, consider the hypotheses

$$H_0 \colon b = 0, \qquad H_1 \colon b > 0. \tag{3.17}$$

These hypotheses state that b is either equal to or greater than zero. Thus, we need not concern ourselves with negative values of b. Assuming that we desire a 95 percent level of confidence in our accepted hypotheses, our testing procedure is to construct a lower bound for the value of b such that the probability is 0.95 that this lower bound is less than the value of b. This lower bound effectively provides us with a 95 percent open-ended confidence interval. As earlier, the value of this lower bound will depend on the value of our estimator, $\hat{b}$. Our testing procedure would be to determine the value of $\hat{b}$ (and therefore our lower bound) from our sample information and then determine whether or not the lower bound is greater than zero (i.e., if zero lies outside our confidence interval). If our lower bound is positive, we would reject the hypothesis $b = 0$. If not, we would accept the hypothesis and reject the alternative $b > 0$.

We derive our lower bound from the statement

$$\text{Prob}\left(\frac{\hat{b} - b}{\sigma_{\hat{b}}} < 1.65\right) = 0.95, \tag{3.18}$$

where we find 1.65 in a table of values for the standard normal curve (see Statistical Table 1). Equation (3.18) can be rewritten as

$$\text{Prob}\left(\hat{b} - 1.65\sigma_{\hat{b}} < b\right) = 0.95. \tag{3.19}$$

Recalling that $\hat{b}$, and not $\sigma_{\hat{b}}$ or b, is the variable, we see from equation (3.19) that the probability is 0.95 that the lower bound $(\hat{b} - 1.65\sigma_{\hat{b}})$ will be less than the value of the parameter b. Accordingly, we would reject the null hypothesis $b = 0$ if, on the basis of our sample information, $(\hat{b} - 1.65\sigma_{\hat{b}})$ were larger than zero. Alternatively, if $(\hat{b} - 1.65\sigma_{\hat{b}}) \leq 0$, we would accept the hypothesis $b = 0$. In this latter case, we would say that our estimate is not significantly different from zero.

In statistics, an interval such as $(\hat{b} - 1.65\sigma_{\hat{b}}) < b$ is known as a *one-tail* confidence interval. You should be able to show that, if we were testing $H_0: b = 0$ against $H_1: b < 0$ at a 5 percent level of significance, we would end up with the one-tail, 95 percent confidence interval*:

$$b < \hat{b} + 1.65\sigma_{\hat{b}}. \tag{3.20}$$

For this case, $(\hat{b} + 1.65\sigma_{\hat{b}})$ would represent our *upper* bound for the value of b. We would test the hypothesis $H_0: b = 0$ against $H_1: b < 0$ by evaluating $\hat{b}$ from our sample and then determining whether or not $(\hat{b} + 1.65\sigma_{\hat{b}})$ is less than zero. If it is, we would reject H_0; if it exceeds zero, we would accept H_0. Finally, we stress that although we have conducted the discussion in terms of the parameter b, all the testing procedures we have developed apply also to the parameter a. You can use exactly the same techniques to construct one- or two-tail confidence intervals for a to test hypotheses concerning the value of the constant term in the regression equation.

HYPOTHESIS TESTING, σ_u UNKNOWN

Throughout the preceding analysis, we have assumed that σ_u^2 and therefore $\sigma_{\hat{b}}$ and $\sigma_{\hat{a}}$, are known. This, however, is not usually the case, and it is now time to drop this assumption. As we showed in Chapter 2, when σ_u^2 is unknown, we must use an estimator for it, $\hat{\sigma}_u^2$, in order to obtain an *estimator* of the variances of $\hat{a}$ and $\hat{b}$. Our variance estimators are

$$\hat{\sigma}_{\hat{a}}^2 = \frac{\hat{\sigma}_u^2 \sum X_t^2}{n \sum (X_t - \bar{X})^2} \quad \text{and} \quad \hat{\sigma}_{\hat{b}}^2 = \frac{\hat{\sigma}_u^2}{\sum (X_t - \bar{X})^2}, \tag{3.21}$$

where

$$\hat{\sigma}_u^2 = \frac{\sum (Y_t - \hat{a} - \hat{b}X_t)^2}{(n - 2)} = \frac{\sum (Y_t - \hat{Y}_t)^2}{(n - 2)}.$$

With this modification, we can no longer use the normal curve to test hypotheses (or establish confidence intervals) concerning a and b. Instead, if we form the counterparts of (3.7), we have

$$\frac{\hat{a} - a}{\hat{\sigma}_{\hat{a}}} \quad \text{and} \quad \frac{\hat{b} - b}{\hat{\sigma}_{\hat{b}}}, \tag{3.22}$$

---

* Hint: In this case we would want an *upper bound*. We could get it by starting with an expression very similar to (3.18) with the inequality sign reversed; specifically, we would start with

$$\text{Prob}\left(\frac{\hat{b} - b}{\sigma_{\hat{b}}} > -1.65\right) = 0.95.$$

where both expressions in (3.22) are random variables that can be shown to have the t distribution with $(n - 2)$ degrees of freedom.* We follow exactly the same procedures as above, except that we use the t distribution with $(n - 2)$ degrees of freedom (see Statistical Table 2) instead of the normal distribution to determine the boundaries of our confidence intervals.

SOME EXAMPLES

To illustrate our testing procedure based on the t distribution, let us return to the consumption function that we estimated in Chapter 2. Using data for consumption and disposable income for the years 1960–1969 in the United States, we found that

$$\hat{a} = 13 \qquad \hat{\sigma}_{\hat{a}}^2 = 31 \qquad (\text{or } \hat{\sigma}_{\hat{a}} = 5.6),$$

$$\hat{b} = 0.89 \qquad \hat{\sigma}_{\hat{b}}^2 = 0.0001 \quad (\text{or } \hat{\sigma}_{\hat{b}} \doteq 0.01).$$

Let us suppose that we want to test the hypothesis that $a > 0$, and we wish to have 95 percent confidence in the hypothesis we accept.** To do this, we establish as our null hypothesis $H_0: a = 0$, and as the alternative $H_1: a > 0$, and set the level of significance equal to 0.05. Using Statistical Table 2 for the t distribution with 8 (that is, $10 - 2$) degrees of freedom, we find that the lower bound of our one-tail confidence interval for a is†

$$a > (\hat{a} - t_{n-2;0.95}\hat{\sigma}_{\hat{a}}) = [13 - 1.86(5.6)] = 2.6.$$

Since the lower bound for the interval lies above zero at the 5 percent level of significance, we accept $H_1: a > 0$. That is, we conclude that the value of a is greater than zero. Note that had we selected a 1 percent significance level, we would have had a lower bound:

$$a > (\hat{a} - t_{n-2;0.99}\hat{\sigma}_{\hat{a}}) = [13 - 2.90(5.6)] = -3.2.$$

This would have given us a confidence interval of $(a > -3.2)$, which includes zero. We would, therefore, have accepted $H_0: a = 0$ and would have concluded that a is zero. This suggests that some thought should be given to the size of the Type 1 error, because the results of our tests clearly depend on it.‡

---

* The t distribution resembles fairly closely the normal distribution and, as n becomes large, it approaches the normal distribution in the limit.

** Note: hypotheses must be established *before* the data are analyzed and the estimates determined. If not, we would clearly be guilty of circular reasoning.

† The notation used here is a common one. In general, $t_{n-2;\gamma}$ is a number such that the probability is γ that a t variable with $n - 2$ degrees of freedom is less than this number.

‡ Again, we stress that the size of the Type 1 error must be chosen *before* the data are analyzed. If not, we could accept any hypothesis of interest by simply choosing an "appropriate" size for the Type 1 error.

Finally, let us simply construct a two-tail, 99 percent confidence interval for b. From Statistical Table 2 for the t distribution, we find that the interval is

$$(\hat{b} \pm t_{n-2;0.995}\hat{\sigma}_{\hat{b}}) = 0.89 \pm 3.36(0.01) = (0.89 \pm 0.03).$$

The interval includes the range of values for the MPC from 0.86 to 0.92. From this it is clear that had we tested the null hypothesis, $H_0: b = 0.75$, against $H_1: b \neq .075$ at a 1 percent level of significance, we would have rejected H_0.

It may also be useful to point out the form in which an economist would typically report his regression results in a paper or journal article. If, for example, in an economics journal or book you were to come across the consumption function we have estimated and discussed in Chapters 2 and 3, you might find

$$\begin{array}{cccc} \hat{C} = 13 & + 0.89Y_d & n = 10 & \\ (5.6) & (0.01) & R^2 = 0.99 & \end{array} \qquad (3.23)$$

where the numbers in parentheses beneath the parameter estimates are the estimates of the corresponding standard errors (i.e., $\hat{\sigma}_{\hat{a}}$ and $\hat{\sigma}_{\hat{b}}$). With this information, the reader can easily construct confidence intervals for the various coefficients, test hypotheses, and so on.

THE t RATIO: A RULE OF THUMB

Although the precise size of the confidence interval, and therefore the results of a test, depend on the size of the sample, n, and the number of parameters to be estimated, economists do have some rough rules of thumb that they often use when looking at an estimated regression equation. For instance, if the value of the parameter estimate is more than twice the size of the corresponding estimated standard error, we can usually infer that, under a two-tail test, the parameter estimate is significantly different from zero at a 5 percent level of significance; that is, if we had considered the null hypothesis that the parameter is zero against the two-tailed alternative, these results would have lead to a rejection of the null hypothesis. If the parameter estimate is more than three times the size of the estimated standard error, it will generally be significantly different from zero at a 1 percent level of significance.

These rules of thumb are easily rationalized. For instance, if we were to test the null hypothesis $b = 0$ against the alternative $b \neq 0$, we would base our test on the interval

$$(\hat{b} \pm t_{n-2;0.975}\hat{\sigma}_{\hat{b}}) \qquad (3.24)$$

if we desired a 5 percent significance level. If this interval does not include zero, we would reject the null hypothesis. Now $\hat{b}$ could be either positive or negative, but $t_{n-2;0.975}$ and $\hat{\sigma}_{\hat{b}}$ are always positive. Hence, our confidence interval will *not* contain zero if

$$(\hat{b} - t_{n-2;0.975}\hat{\sigma}_b) > 0 \qquad \text{when } \hat{b} > 0, \qquad (3.25)$$

or

$$(\hat{b} + t_{n-2;0.975}\hat{\sigma}_b) < 0 \qquad \text{when } \hat{b} < 0.$$

These conditions can be rewritten as

$$\frac{\hat{b}}{\hat{\sigma}_b} > t_{n-2;0.975} \qquad \text{when } \hat{b} > 0, \qquad (3.26)$$

or

$$\frac{\hat{b}}{\hat{\sigma}_b} < -t_{n-2;0.975} \qquad \text{when } \hat{b} < 0.$$

Finally, we can write these conditions more compactly as

$$\left|\frac{\hat{b}}{\hat{\sigma}_b}\right| > t_{n-2;0.975}. \qquad (3.27)$$

If, therefore, the absolute value of $(\hat{b}/\hat{\sigma}_b)$ exceeds the value given by the t distribution, $t_{n-2;0.975}$, we would end up rejecting the null hypothesis that $b = 0$. In other words, we can test the hypothesis $b = 0$ against the alternative, $b \neq 0$, at a 5 percent level of significance by simply observing whether or not the absolute value of the ratio $\hat{b}/\hat{\sigma}_b$ exceeds $t_{n-2;0.975}$. We now note that economists usually work with samples that are at least of size $n = 15$. If $n = 15$, $t_{15-2;0.975} = t_{13;0.975} = 2.16$; if, on the other hand, $n = \infty$, $t_{\infty;0.975} = 1.96$. Finally, a glance at the t table shows that the value of $t_{j;0.975}$, for $13 < j < \infty$, is between 2.16 and 1.96. Hence, the rule of thumb is that, if the ratio $\hat{b}/\hat{\sigma}_b$ exceeds 2 in absolute value, we reject the null hypothesis that $b = 0$ against the two-tailed alternative at a 5 percent level of significance. For example, if the ratio $\hat{b}/\hat{\sigma}_b$ were 3, we would not even have to refer to the values of the t table; we would immediately reject the null hypothesis $b = 0$. In the literature, this ratio, $\hat{b}/\hat{\sigma}_b$, of the parameter estimator to the estimator of its standard error, is called the t *ratio*. If we desire a 1 percent level of significance, we find that $t_{15-2;0.995} = t_{13;0.995} = 3.01$, and $t_{\infty;0.995} = 2.58$. In this case we require, as a rough approximation, that the absolute value of the t ratio exceed 3 before we say that the parameter estimate is significantly different from zero.

In a manner very similar to the above, we develop the "t ratio" method of testing one-tailed hypotheses. For instance, if we were testing the hypothesis $b = 0$ against $b > 0$, we would reject the hypothesis $b = 0$, at a 5 percent level of significance, if

$$(\hat{b} - t_{n-2;0.95}\hat{\sigma}_b) > 0. \qquad (3.28)$$

Similarly, if the alternative to $b = 0$ were $b < 0$, we would reject the hypothesis $b = 0$ if

$$(\hat{b} + t_{n-2;0.95}\hat{\sigma}_b) < 0. \qquad (3.29)$$

Now (3.28) and (3.29) can be rewritten as

$$\frac{b}{\hat{\sigma}_b} > t_{n-2;0.95} \tag{3.30}$$

and

$$\frac{b}{\hat{\sigma}_b} < -t_{n-2;0.95}. \tag{3.31}$$

Again, all we need do is form the t ratio and compare it to $t_{n-2;0.95}$ as in (3.30), which corresponds to the one-tailed alternative $b > 0$, or compare it to $-t_{n-2;0.95}$ as in (3.31), which corresponds to the one-tailed alternative $b < 0$. In this case, the range of values would be $t_{13;0.95} = 1.771$, $t_{\infty;0.95} = 1.645$. Of course, a necessary condition for the null hypothesis to be rejected in either case is

$$\left| \frac{b}{\hat{\sigma}_b} \right| > t_{n-2;0.95}. \tag{3.32}$$

In some cases, to save the reader the trouble of dividing the value of the coefficient by the estimated standard error to determine the value of the t ratio, the author may perform this division and report the quotient (that is, the sample value of the t ratio itself) in parentheses below the coefficient. You should be careful to check in the accompanying notes to determine whether the number appearing in parentheses is the estimated standard error or the t ratio. In any event, it should be clear that these rules of thumb concerning the t ratios greatly facilitate the testing of hypotheses; we are often able to test hypotheses without even referring to a table of values on the t distribution because t ratios often exceed 3 or are less than 1 in absolute value.

3.2 THE PROBLEM OF FUNCTIONAL FORM

You have no doubt noticed that, throughout the discussion in Chapters 1 and 2, we assumed that the form of the relationship we wanted to estimate is linear; specifically, we assumed that

$$Y_t = a + bX_t + u_t.$$

This is clearly a most restrictive condition. Frequently, either economic theory itself or, alternatively, the scatter of observed points suggests that the relationship between two variables is a nonlinear one. But how can we deal with a nonlinear relationship in terms of a linear model?

THE PHILLIPS CURVE AND THE RECIPROCAL TRANSFORMATION

It may be helpful to introduce this problem in terms of an actual economic relationship: the Phillips Curve, which is typically regarded as a nonlinear relationship between the percentage change in wages ($\dot{W}$) and the rate of unemployment (R). Consider a simple model of the market for labor in which we have a demand for labor and a supply of labor, both of which depend on the wage rate. The model is illustrated in Figure 3.3, where the intersection of the demand and supply curves determines the equilibrium wage rate W_2. If, however, the wage rate were at W_3, the demand for labor would exceed the supply by the amount ($A_2 A_1$); in this case, we would say that there exists a positive *excess demand* for labor, which would tend to put upward pressure on the level of wage rates. Conversely, if $W = W_1$, we would have a negative excess demand (or excess supply) of ($A_4 A_3$), with an associated downward pressure on the level of wages.

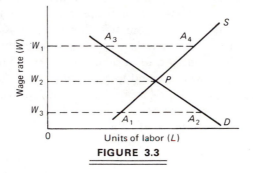

FIGURE 3.3

Let us next postulate a simple dynamic adjustment mechanism in order to capture these relationships. Specifically, we assume that the mean value of the *rate of change* in the wage rate ($\dot{W}$) from one period to the next is directly proportional to the rate of excess demand. This would seem reasonable: the larger the difference between the demand for workers by employers and the supply of labor, the greater we would expect to be the upward pressure on the level of wages. We therefore postulate that

$$\dot{W}_t = \frac{(W_t - W_{t-1})}{W_{t-1}} = \alpha D_t^* + u_t, \tag{3.33}$$

where $D_t^* = (D_t - S_t)/S_t$ is the rate of excess demand at time t, and u_t is the disturbance term.

To estimate this relationship we need observations on $\dot{W}_t$ and D_t^*. Although observations on $\dot{W}_t$ are available, we typically do not have observations (or data) on D_t^*. If we wish to have an operational model that explains wage adjustments, we must find a variable that is related to D_t^* so that we can use it as a proxy measure. It would seem plausible to assume that the rate of excess demand, D_t^*, bears a systematic relationship to the rate of unemployment, R_t, in the economy: if unemployment is very low, as is typically the case in a "tight" labor market, we would expect substantial positive excess demand; and conversely. We therefore have reason to believe that R_t and D_t^* are *negatively* related. Let us postulate the relationship

$$D_t^* = f(R_t). \tag{3.34}$$

What form should (3.34) take? The simplest assumption would be that the relation is linear, so that

$$D_t^* = e + gR_t, \tag{3.35}$$

where e and g are parameters with $g < 0$. A little thought suggests, however, that (3.35) may not be the most sensible form for this relationship. Consider Figure 3.4, in which we measure the rate of excess of demand on the vertical axis and the rate of unemployment on the horizontal axis. At point O, we have zero excess demand; D^* is positive above O and negative below. Note that zero excess demand corresponds to P in Figure 3.3, where the supply and demand for labor are equal, and there are consequently no pressures for change on the level of wages. There will, however, exist some *frictional* unemployment; that is, in a dynamic economy, some people will be in the process of moving from one job to another, but if excess demand is zero, the number of vacancies will be equal to the number of people seeking jobs. Therefore, the point E in Figure 3.4 represents the frictional rate of unemployment (that is, the rate of unemployment corresponding to zero excess demand), and corresponds to point P in Figure 3.3.

Consider next a series of periods of increasing excess demand (of continually higher values of D^*). The increased number of vacancies should reduce the time necessary for those who are unemployed to find jobs. We would therefore expect these *higher* values of D^* to be accompanied by *lower* values of R. However, as the number of vacancies continues to rise with the increases in D^*, we would not expect R to continue to fall by correspondingly equal amounts. One reason for this is that the rate of unemployment *cannot* take on negative values. Consequently, the relationship between D^* and R cannot be a linear one such as AB in Figure 3.4. All of this suggests that as D^* gets larger, the corresponding decreases in R must become smaller. Thus the relationship between these variables must be a nonlinear one, such as CD in Figure 3.4, where CD curves upward to the left of point E. To the right of this point, CD also has a negative slope, indicating that higher rates of R

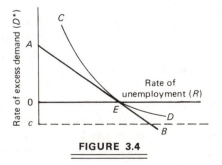

FIGURE 3.4

are associated with conditions of excess supply. For illustrative purposes, we also assume that CD curves upward to the right of the point E.

One functional form that will approximate a curve such as CD is

$$D_t^* = c + d\left(\frac{1}{R_t}\right), \qquad \text{where } c < 0, d > 0. \tag{3.36}$$

We assume here that D^* varies inversely with R. If d is positive, this will give us a curve that has a negative slope, but yet is nonlinear in that it curves upwards, indicating that the fall in R per unit increase in D^* becomes smaller as the rate of excess demand, D^*, increases. We assume that c is negative, so that D^* will be negative for the larger values of R.

We now have our proxy measure of D^*, since we have observed values for R_t. If we substitute (3.36) into our wage equation (3.33), we get a standard Phillips Curve,

$$\dot{W}_t = \alpha D_t^* + u_t = \alpha\left[c + d\left(\frac{1}{R_t}\right)\right] + u_t$$
$$= a + b\left(\frac{1}{R_t}\right) + u_t, \tag{3.37}$$

where $a = \alpha c$ and $b = \alpha d$. Equation (3.37) says that the rate of change of wages varies directly with the reciprocal of the rate of unemployment. Suppose that we have a sample of observed values for $\dot{W}_t$ and R_t. How can we estimate the parameters, a and b, for this *nonlinear* relationship? Note, we shall not attempt to estimate c and d, but rather the parameters a and b of our observable relationship (3.37).

Although (3.37) is a nonlinear relationship between $\dot{W}_t$ and R_t, it can be interpreted as a linear relationship between $\dot{W}_t$ and the *reciprocal* of R_t, namely, $1/R_t$. We can therefore apply to (3.37) the estimation technique we have developed for our linear model if we make a slight change of notation. More explicitly, suppose we define a new variable:

$$Z_t = \frac{1}{R_t}. \tag{3.38}$$

For each nonzero value of R_t, there will exist a corresponding value of Z_t, as, for example, in Table 3.1. If we simply substitute Z_t for $1/R_t$ in (3.37), we obtain

$$\dot{W}_t = a + bZ_t + u_t. \tag{3.39}$$

TABLE 3.1

HYPOTHETICAL OBSERVATION MATRIX

$\dot{W}_t$	R_t	Z_t
0.02	0.06	16.7
0.04	0.04	25.0
0.05	0.03	33.3
⋮	⋮	⋮

In other words, by making a simple transformation, we have changed the nonlinear relationship in (3.37) into a linear form in (3.39). We can then use our linear regression model and the values of $\dot{W}_t$ and Z_t to estimate the values of the parameters a and b. For example, using the formulas we derived in Chapter 2, we would have

$$\hat{b} = \frac{\sum (Z_t - \bar{Z})\dot{W}_t}{\sum (Z_t - \bar{Z})^2},$$

$$\hat{a} = \bar{W} - \hat{b}\bar{Z}. \tag{3.40}$$

Combining the results above, the estimator of the mean value of $\dot{W}_t$ corresponding to a given value of R_t would be

$$\hat{\dot{W}}_t = \hat{a} + \hat{b}\left(\frac{1}{R_t}\right). \tag{3.41}$$

We could then use equation (3.41) for prediction purposes. For example, if the rate of unemployment were 5 percent, we would predict the rate of change in wages by

$$\hat{\dot{W}} = \hat{a} + \hat{b}\left(\frac{1}{0.05}\right) = \hat{a} + 20\hat{b}. \tag{3.42}$$

The *reciprocal* transformation is just one of a number of transformations that can be used to change a nonlinear relationship between two variables into a linear one. This is of great importance, for it means that the simple linear model we have developed is not nearly so restrictive as it first appears. By a judicious use of various transformations, it is possible to put a wide variety of nonlinear relationships into a linear form. This allows us to estimate the parameters of such models using the methods we have already developed. We shall consider next, two other transformations that are widely used in econometrics.

THE LOGARITHMIC (OR LOG) TRANSFORMATION

Suppose that we want to estimate the parameters of the production model

$$Q_t = aL_t{}^b e^{u_t}, \tag{3.43}$$

where

Q_t = the level of output in period t,
L_t = the input of labor in period t,
e = a constant term that is approximately 2.718,
u_t = the disturbance term in period t, and a, b are the parameters we want to estimate.

In this model we are essentially assuming that labor is the only factor of production, an assumption we shall relax in later sections of this book.

Assuming for the moment that (3.43) is an accurate description of the

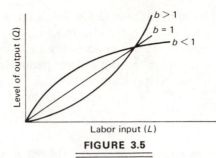

FIGURE 3.5

production function, we might be particularly interested in, or have hypotheses about, the parameter b. This is because the parameter b indicates whether there typically exist decreasing, constant, or increasing returns to scale. These cases correspond, respectively, to $b < 1$, $b = 1$, and $b > 1$, as illustrated in Figure 3.5.

Our immediate econometric problem concerning (3.43) is that it is a non-linear relationship; what we again need is a technique to transform it into a linear form so that we can apply our established estimation techniques.

The transformation we seek is the log transformation. For instance, if we take the log of each side of (3.43), we have

$$\ln Q_t = \ln a + b \ln L_t + u_t, \tag{3.44}$$

where ln is the "natural logarithm" of the variable (that is, the logarithm to the base $e \doteq 2.718$). We can see that (3.44) is linear in terms of the logs of the variables, so we make the following log transformation. Let

$$Q_t^* = \ln Q_t, \quad a^* = \ln a, \quad \text{and} \quad L_t^* = \ln L_t. \tag{3.45}$$

Making these substitutions in (3.44), we have

$$Q_t^* = a^* + b L_t^* + u_t. \tag{3.46}$$

It should now be clear that, if we make the standard assumptions concerning the disturbance term, u_t, the parameters a^* and b in (3.46) can be estimated by our instrumental-variable technique. Specifically, simply taking the natural logarithms of the observed values for Q_t and L_t, we would compute

$$\hat{b} = \frac{\sum (L_t^* - \bar{L}^*) Q_t^*}{\sum (L_t^* - \bar{L}^*)^2} \equiv \frac{\sum (\ln L_t - \overline{\ln L}) \ln Q_t}{\sum (\ln L_t - \overline{\ln L})^2}, \tag{3.47}$$

$$\hat{a}^* = \bar{Q}^* - \hat{b} \bar{L}^* \equiv \overline{\ln Q} - \hat{b} \overline{\ln L},$$

where $\bar{L}^* = \sum L_t^*/n$, and $\bar{Q}^* = \sum Q_t^*/n$.

Since we know that our estimators are unbiased, we would have

$$E(\hat{b}) = b \quad \text{and} \quad E(\hat{a}^*) = a^*. \tag{3.48}$$

Expression (3.47) provides us with an unbiased estimator of the value of the exponent of the labor-input variable in (3.43). From this we could see if our results do in fact suggest diminishing returns to labor.

Note also that our estimation procedure yields an unbiased estimator of a^*; we, however, are interested in the value of the parameter, a, since a is the parameter that appears in the production function. Since $a^* = \ln a$, we have, taking antilogs, $a = e^{a^*}$. The suggested estimator of a would be

$$\hat{a} = e^{\hat{a}^*}. \tag{3.49}$$

But $\hat{a}$ is not an unbiased estimator of a even though $E(\hat{a}^*) = a^*$. That is, $E(\hat{a}) \neq e^{E(\hat{a}^*)} = e^{a^*} = a$. You may recall that, in Appendix B to Chapter 1, we pointed out that in general the expected value of a nonlinear function, such as $E(e^{\hat{a}^*})$, is not equal to the function of the expected value, $[e^{E(\hat{a}^*)}]$; this is an example of that proposition. Fortunately, it can be shown that $\hat{a}$ is a consistent estimator of a.

To summarize, if we have a function of the general form

$$Y_t = aX_t^b e^{u_t}, \tag{3.50}$$

we can use the log transformation to put it into the linear form

$$Y_t^* = a^* + bX_t^* + u_t, \tag{3.51}$$

where * means the natural log of the corresponding variable. We can estimate (3.51) using our linear estimation technique, from which we shall get an unbiased estimator of b, and taking antilogs, a biased, but at least a consistent, estimator of a.

The log form is, incidentally, a very popular functional form for economic models, because the slope coefficient may be interpreted as the elasticity of the dependent variable with respect to the independent variable. For example, in (3.51), or (3.50), the elasticity of the mean of Y_t with respect to X_t turns out to be b.* Therefore, a model such as (3.51) implies that the elasticity is constant.

---

* For example, from (3.50) we see that, for a given value of X_t, the mean value of Y_t is $Y_t^m = aX_t^b E(e^{u_t})$. Our assumption that u_t and X_t are independent implies that $E(e^{u_t})$ is equal to some constant, say C, that will not in general be unity (e.g., $E(e^{u_t}) \neq e^{E(u_t)} = e^0 = 1$). We may express the mean value of Y_t^m corresponding to X_t as $Y_t^m = a_1 X_t^b$, where $a_1 = aC$. Next, differentiating Y_t^m with respect to X_t yields

$$\frac{dY_t^m}{dX_t} = a_1 b X_t^{b-1} = \frac{bY_t^m}{X_t}.$$

Solving for b, we obtain

$$b = \frac{dY_t^m/Y_t^m}{dX_t/X_t},$$

which is the elasticity of Y_t^m with respect to X_t.

THE SEMILOG TRANSFORMATION

A semilog transformation is often useful for formulating models involving rates of growth. Suppose, for example, that we want to estimate the average annual rate of increase in the size of the labor force in the United States over a certain period. We might suspect that over this period the labor force grew at some constant annual rate with minor variations that were the result of various random events. If so, we might postulate a relationship such as

$$L_t = a(1 + g)^t e^{u_t}, \qquad t = 1, 2, \ldots, n, \qquad (3.52)$$

where

L_t = the size of the labor force in year t,
a = a parameter,
g = a parameter that is the compound rate of growth of L_t,
u_t = the disturbance term.

Note that in (3.52) the independent variable, t, itself appears as an exponent; in (3.50), in contrast, the independent variable X_t is raised to a constant power b. However, both (3.52) and (3.50) are multiplicative, and so, as you might expect, we shall take logs in order to transform the relationship into a linear form.

Before we do, however, we should point out one property of growth paths over time. In Table 3.2 we present data for the size of the civilian labor force

TABLE 3.2

U.S. CIVILIAN LABOR FORCE
(millions of persons)

Year	L_t
1956	66.6
1957	66.9
1958	67.6
1959	68.4
1960	69.6
1961	70.5
1962	70.6
1963	71.8
1964	73.1
1965	74.5
1966	75.8
1967	77.3
1968	78.7
1969	80.7
1970	82.7

SOURCE: *Economic Report of the President* (Washington, D.C.: U.S. Government Printing Office, Feb. 1971), p. 222.

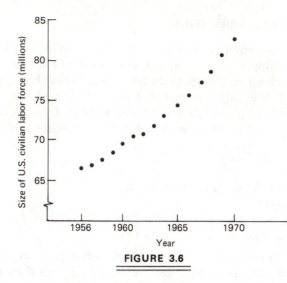

FIGURE 3.6

in the United States over the years 1956–1970. If we plot these data as in Figure 3.6, we find that the curve becomes steeper over time, which suggests that the labor force has grown more rapidly in recent years. This, however, is largely an illusion, because a given *percentage* rate of growth will generate ever-increasing *absolute* increments to the labor force from year to year because in succeeding years the size of the labor force, that is, the base from which we calculate the growth, will usually be higher than in preceding years (i.e., 3 percent of X is larger than 3 percent of Y, if $X > Y$).

If we now take the logs of both sides of (3.52), we have

$$\ln L = \ln a + t \ln(1 + g) + u_t. \tag{3.53}$$

If we let

$$L_t^* = \ln L_t,$$

$$a^* = \ln a, \tag{3.54}$$

$$b^* = \ln(1 + g),$$

we obtain

$$L_t^* = a^* + b^* t + u_t. \tag{3.55}$$

This tells us that a compound rate of growth implies a linear relationship, not between L_t and t, but rather between $\ln L_t$ and t. If instead of plotting the values of L_t over time, we had plotted the values of the log of L_t, we would have observed points about a linear path as in Figure 3.7.

To estimate the parameters of (3.55), a^* and b^*, we must have observations on $\ln L_t$ and t for each of the years in the period we are considering. To illustrate, let us return to our observed values of the size of the U.S. labor force over the period 1956–1970. The observations on L_t for each of these

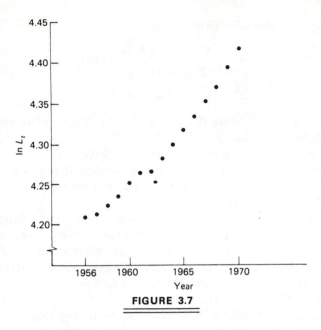

FIGURE 3.7

years immediately provide us with observations on $\ln L_t$. Observations on t are easily obtained by simply numbering the years consecutively; that is, 1956 is the first year, $t = 1$, and 1970, is the fifteenth year, $t = 15$. This is illustrated in Table 3.3.

TABLE 3.3

U.S. CIVILIAN LABOR FORCE (in millions)

Year	L_t	$\ln L_t$	t
1956	66.6	4.199	1
1957	66.9	4.203	2
1958	67.6	4.214	3
1959	68.4	4.225	4
1960	69.6	4.243	5
1961	70.5	4.256	6
1962	70.6	4.257	7
1963	71.8	4.274	8
1964	73.1	4.292	9
1965	74.5	4.311	10
1966	75.8	4.328	11
1967	77.3	4.348	12
1968	78.7	4.366	13
1969	80.7	4.391	14
1970	82.7	4.415	15

From the information in Table 3.3, we can easily calculate

$$\hat{b}^* = \frac{\sum (t - \bar{t})L_t^*}{\sum (t - \bar{t})^2} = 0.0153,$$

$$\hat{a}^* = \overline{L_t^*} - \hat{b}^*\bar{t} = 4.17.$$

Since $\ln(1 + g) = b^*$, we see that $g = (e^{b^*} - 1)$. We therefore estimate the rate of growth, g, by $\hat{g} = e^{b^*} - 1 \doteq 2.718^{(0.0153)} - 1 = 0.016$. Our estimated annual rate of growth of the labor force is 1.6 percent. For the reasons presented in the preceding section, we note that $\hat{g}$ is a consistent, but not unbiased, estimator of g. Similarly, our estimator of a, $\hat{a} = e^{\hat{a}^*}$, would be biased but consistent.

An alternative technique (which is sometimes seen in the literature) for estimating growth rates can be illustrated as follows. Take the initial value of L_t, 66.6 million in 1956, and the last observed value, 82.7 million in 1970, and then with the aid of a log table calculate the average annual rate of growth; that is, determine the growth rate per annum at which 66.6 would become 82.7 after 15 years.

This alternative procedure is not recommended. For instance, this procedure amounts to taking the first and last points in Figure 3.7 (the plot of $\ln L_t$ against t) and finding the slope of the line that connects these two points. In other words, it fits a line to only two points in the scatter. This procedure would be identical to our procedure if the sample were of size $n = 2$. For all samples of size $n > 2$, this alternative procedure would obviously be inferior to ours because of all of the information it ignores.

ON THE USE OF TRANSFORMATIONS: GENERALIZATIONS

We have seen that in many instances our *a priori* hypothesis itself may suggest a specific nonlinear form for the relationship between the variables of interest. Often we can find a transformation through which we can put such a relationship into a linear form and then simply apply our linear estimation procedure. By now, the transformations that do the trick should be obvious. For instance, if the model is

$$Y_t = a + bf(X_t) + u_t, \tag{3.56}$$

where $f(X_t)$ is some function* of X_t, we would define $Z_t = f(X_t)$, and therefore have a linear model relating Y_t to Z_t. A generalization of (3.56) is

$$g(Y_t) = a + bf(X_t) + u_t, \tag{3.57}$$

where f and g are two, possibly nonlinear, functions of Y_t and X_t. In this case we would have a linear relationship between Z_{1t} and Z_{2t}, where $Z_{1t} = g(Y_t)$

---

* We are assuming that $f(X_t)$ does not contain any unknown parameters. That is, if we had observations on X_t, we could determine the observations on $f(X_t)$.

and $Z_{2t} = f(X_t)$. Finally, a multiplicative model of the sort

$$g(Y_t) = af(X_t)^\alpha e^{u_t} \tag{3.58}$$

would be linear in Z_{1t}^* and Z_{2t}^*, where $Z_{1t}^* = \ln g(Y_t)$ and $Z_{2t}^* = \ln f(X_t)$. As an example, the reader should convince himself that the model

$$\frac{1}{Y_t} = aX_t^{2\alpha}e^{u_t} \tag{3.59}$$

is linear in $\ln(1/Y_t)$ and $\ln X_t^2$.*

In many cases, economic theory may provide little guidance to the precise form of a relationship. Theory, for example, may suggest that the quantity demanded of a commodity will vary negatively with the price, but it does not tell us whether the demand curve is likely to be of a linear, logarithmic, or a more complicated form. In such cases, the functional form of the model is sometimes determined by a simple inspection of the scatter diagram. That is, a functional form is chosen to conform to the pattern outlined by the scatter of points. This scatter diagram approach, however, may be helpful only if there are two variables involved.** Since most economic models involve many variables, we shall postpone a more thorough discussion of this problem until Chapter 5.

3.3 SCALING AND UNITS OF MEASUREMENT

In the actual calculation of a regression equation, it is important, both to simplify the computations and in some instances to facilitate interpretation of the results, to use sensible units of measurement. Consider, for example, Table 3.4 of observed values for aggregate consumption and disposable

TABLE 3.4

Year	Disposable Income (in dollars)	Consumption Expenditures (in dollars)
1960	350,000,000,000	325,000,000,000
1961	364,000,000,000	335,000,000,000
⋮	⋮	⋮
1969	630,000,000,000	576,000,000,000

* Note that $X^{2\alpha}$ can be written $(X^2)^\alpha$.

** Another, and more subtle, problem is also involved. If the form of the model is determined by *first* inspecting the data, an element of circularity exists. Theoretically, we should *first* specify our model and *then* test it in light of the data. If the form of the model is determined by an inspection of the data, a proper procedure would be to use that form and then test the model with a *new set of data*. Since economists often cannot obtain more than one sample, this element of circularity is, unfortunately, often overlooked.

TABLE 3.4A

Year	Disposable Income (in billions of dollars)	Consumer Expenditures (in billions of dollars)
1960	350	325
1961	364	335
⋮	⋮	⋮
1969	630	576

income. Suppose that we want to use these observed values of C_t and Y_{dt} to estimate a linear consumption function:

$$C_t = a + bY_{dt} + u_t.$$

Is it necessary to carry the nine zeros at the end of each observed value of C_t and Y_{dt}? The answer is no. We can save ourselves a good deal of work by simply dropping these zeros by measuring the value of each of the variables in appropriate units—in this case, in billions of dollars instead of dollars. As an analogy, astronomers measure distance in light years, not in inches.

If we measure our variables in billions of dollars, our data in Table 3.4 become the data in Table 3.4A. Using the data of Table 3.4A, we can easily estimate the parameters a and b of our consumption function. Suppose now that another researcher measured disposable income and consumer expenditures in *hundreds of billions* of dollars. His table of observed values would be as shown in Table 3.4B. Using these data, this second researcher could also estimate the parameters a and b of the consumption function. The question now, obviously, concerns the relationship between the parameter estimates based on Table 3.4A and those based on Table 3.4B.

The relationship between parameter estimates based on different units of measurements is exactly the same as the relationship between the corresponding values of the parameters. For instance, suppose we measure disposable income and consumer expenditures in billions of dollars and postulate the model:

$$c_t = a + by_{dt} + u_t. \tag{3.60}$$

The parameter a, in this model, would be the amount of consumer expenditures (in billions of dollars) that would be forthcoming if disposable income

TABLE 3.4B

Year	Disposable Income (in hundreds of billions of dollars)	Consumer Expenditures (in hundreds of billions of dollars)
1960	3.50	3.25
1961	3.64	3.35
⋮	⋮	⋮
1969	6.30	5.76

were zero; b is the marginal propensity to consume. Suppose we now divide each term in (3.60) by 100. We would get

$$C_t = A + bY_{dt} + U_t, \tag{3.61}$$

where $C_t = (\frac{1}{100})c_t$, $A = (\frac{1}{100})a$, $Y_{dt} = (\frac{1}{100})y_{dt}$, and $U_t = (\frac{1}{100})u_t$.

Equation (3.61) is a consumption function relating consumer expenditures and disposable income when these variables are defined in *hundreds* of billions of dollars. This equation was derived from (3.60) and so must be consistent with it. For instance, if $Y_{dt} = 0$, $C_t = (A + U_t)$, or multiplying by 100, $c_t = (a + u_t)$. The researcher using the data of Table 3.4A is really considering (3.60) as his model, while the data in Table 3.4B correspond to (3.61). The statement we made above says that, comparing (3.60) to (3.61), these researchers will end up with exactly the same estimate of the marginal propensity to consume, while the researcher using Table 3.4A will obtain an intercept estimate that is 100 times larger than that derived from the data in Table 3.4B. We have seen, however, that these estimates would not be inconsistent, because the variables are defined differently.

The proof of these relationships is straightforward. First, note that $\overline{Y}_d = (\frac{1}{100})\bar{y}_d$, and $\overline{C} = (\frac{1}{100})\bar{c}$. Then

$$\hat{b}_1 = \frac{\sum (Y_{dt} - \overline{Y}_d)C_t}{\sum (Y_{dt} - \overline{Y}_d)^2} = \frac{\sum (y_{dt} - \bar{y}_d)c_t}{\sum (y_{dt} - \bar{y}_d)^2} = \hat{b}_2, \tag{3.62}$$

where $\hat{b}_1$ would be the estimator of b defined by Table 3.4B and (3.61) and $\hat{b}_2$ would correspond to Table 3.4A and (3.60). For our intercept terms, we have

$$\hat{A} = \overline{C} - \hat{b}\overline{Y}_d = \frac{1}{100}(\bar{c} - \hat{b}\bar{y}_d) = \frac{1}{100}\hat{a}. \tag{3.63}$$

Let us generalize our results. Consider the model

$$y_t = a + bx_t + u_t. \tag{3.64}$$

Now let

$$Y_t = s_1 y_t, \qquad X_t = s_2 x_t, \tag{3.65}$$

where s_1 and s_2 are constants or scale factors. Substituting (3.65) into (3.64), we have the relationship between Y_t and X_t:

$$Y_t = as_1 + \left(\frac{bs_1}{s_2}\right) X_t + s_1 u_t \tag{3.66}$$

$$= A + BX_t + U_t,$$

where $A = s_1 a$, $b = bs_1/s_2$, and $U_t = s_1 u_t$. Thus, if one researcher estimated (3.64), while another first *scaled* (e.g., to eliminate unnecessary zeros) y_t and x_t as in (3.65) and then estimated (3.66), the relationship between their corresponding parameter estimates would be given by

$$\hat{A} = s_1 \hat{a}, \qquad \hat{B} = \hat{b}\left(\frac{s_1}{s_2}\right). \tag{3.67}$$

In light of (3.67), it follows that the relationships between the variances of the estimators are

$$\sigma_{\hat{A}}{}^2 = s_1{}^2 \sigma_{\hat{a}}{}^2, \qquad \sigma_{\hat{B}}{}^2 = \left(\frac{s_1}{s_2}\right)^2 \sigma_{\hat{b}}{}^2. \tag{3.68}$$

Although we shall not prove it here, it can be shown that the relationships between the estimators of the variances are exactly the same as their counterparts in (3.68):

$$\hat{\sigma}_{\hat{A}}{}^2 = s_1{}^2 \hat{\sigma}_{\hat{a}}{}^2, \qquad \hat{\sigma}_{\hat{B}}{}^2 = \left(\frac{s_1}{s_2}\right)^2 \hat{\sigma}_{\hat{b}}{}^2. \tag{3.69}$$

We see that, given the scale factors, the results of one of these studies could easily be derived directly from the results of the other.

Before presenting an example of this scaling theory, we should, perhaps, point out what may be obvious. If we have hypotheses concerning the parameters a or b in (3.64), these hypotheses may be tested either in terms of (3.64) or (3.66). For instance, the hypothesis $b = b^0$ is obviously equivalent to the hypothesis $B = b^0(s_1/s_2)$. Similar statements apply to hypotheses concerning the parameter a. Although we shall not prove it here, it can be shown that a particular hypothesis concerning a or b that is tested in terms of $\hat{a}$ or $\hat{b}$ as derived from (3.64) will be accepted or rejected *only* if the corresponding hypothesis concerning A or B that is tested in terms of (3.66) is accepted or rejected.* In other words, the t ratios for $\hat{a}$ and $\hat{b}$ are identical to those for $\hat{A}$ and $\hat{B}$.

AN EXAMPLE

Let us now consider a simple application of these principles of scaling. Suppose we are again interested in the consumption function

$$c_t = a + b y_{dt} + u_t. \tag{3.70}$$

Suppose further that we gather data on c_t and y_{dt}, estimate our parameters a and b, and finally test the hypothesis $b = b_0$. Assume now that we are informed that the data we used are inaccurate. Specifically, because of the manner in which it was collected, our figures for disposable income are consistently 10 percent too high; assume, however, that our data concerning consumer expenditures are accurate. The question is whether or not we must duplicate our entire study using corrected data.

---

*The reader can convince himself of this by noting that, in light of (3.69),

$$\frac{\hat{B} - B}{\hat{\sigma}_{\hat{B}}} \equiv \frac{\hat{b} - b}{\hat{\sigma}_{\hat{b}}} \quad \text{and} \quad \frac{\hat{A} - A}{\hat{\sigma}_{\hat{A}}} \equiv \frac{\hat{a} - a}{\hat{\sigma}_{\hat{a}}}.$$

Thus, confidence intervals for A and B based on (3.66) are simply a scaling up or down of the corresponding intervals as derived from (3.64).

Let $y_{dt}*$ be our measure of disposable income. Our measurement error implies that

$$y_{dt}* = (1.1)y_{dt},\tag{3.71}$$

where y_{dt} is the true value of disposable income. Substituting (3.71) into our consumption function (3.70), we obtain

$$c_t = a + \left(\frac{b}{1.1}\right)y_{dt}* + u_t$$

$$\tag{3.72}$$

$$= a + By_{dt}* + u_t,$$

where $B = (b/1.1)$.

Equation (3.72) is the model that relates to the use of our inaccurate data. Using our results from (3.67), we can see from (3.72) that our estimate of the intercept, a, as well as the results of any hypothesis tests concerning a, are still valid. Our estimate of the marginal propensity to consume, however, may be too low because an unbiased estimator of the MPC would be $\hat{b} = \hat{B}(1.1)$. We should multiply our estimate by (1.1). Furthermore, we must retest our hypothesis concerning the value of b. This is fairly easy to do once we note that the hypothesis, say $b = b_0$, implies the hypothesis $B = b_0/1.1$. Very little of our original work must be redone.

A final note concerns the importance in reporting results of rounding off estimates to a sensible number of significant digits. Not only does this simplify the equation, but it avoids a "spurious" accuracy. You may recall that, when we estimated the consumption function in Chapter 2, we used data in units of billions of dollars with no fractional dimension. Using these figures, we estimated the regression equation:

$$\hat{C} = 13 + 0.89Y_d.$$

The computer will typically carry the values of the estimated coefficients out to many places, so that we could have reported our results in the form:

$$\hat{C} = 13.186537 + 0.889632Y_d.$$

This, however, would obviously be rather silly. Since our basic data are correct only to the nearest billion dollars, it does not make sense to try to predict the level of consumption down to the nearest thousand dollars. This gives an illusion of precision that simply is not possible on the basis of the raw data. In presenting results, you should take some care to ensure that the number of significant digits reported is consistent with the level of accuracy the basic information will permit.

3.4 THE USE OF LAGGED VARIABLES

To this point, we have considered relationships of the form

$$C_t = a + bY_{dt} + u_t$$

and

$$\dot{W}_t = a + b\left(\frac{1}{R_t}\right) + u_t,$$

where, in time-series analysis, the subscript t refers to *time*. All of these relationships have at least one important property in common: the value of the dependent variable is related to that of the independent variable at the same point in time (or over the same period of time). For instance, our models have assumed that consumption expenditure *in 1950* depends on disposable income *in 1950*.

Often, however, economists deal with models in which all the variables do not relate to the same point in time. For example, suppose that we attempt to explain the consumption expenditure of a group of individuals who "get paid" or receive income at the end of each month. We might expect these individuals to spend a certain proportion of this income during the following month. We would therefore have a sequence over time in which expenditure in one month depended on income received in the previous month. If we let t refer to periods of one month, we would have

$$C_t = a + bY_{d(t-1)} + u_t, \tag{3.73}$$

which would indicate, for example, that

$$C_{\text{June}} = a + bY_{d(\text{May})} + u_{\text{June}}.$$

Consumption in period t would thus depend on income received during period $(t - 1)$. This is often expressed by saying that consumption "lags behind" income by one period, or that C depends on Y_d "with a one-period lag."

Another set of assumptions that leads to a model like (3.73) is as follows. Suppose that

$$C_t^p = a + bY_{dt}^e, \tag{3.74}$$

where

C_t^p = *planned* consumption expenditure for the forthcoming period t, and
Y_{dt}^e = *expected* income for the forthcoming period t.

Assume, for simplicity, that

$$Y_{dt}^e = Y_{d(t-1)}. \tag{3.75}$$

This says that people expect their income in the forthcoming period t to be the same as that in the current period, $(t - 1)$. Assume also that

$$C_t = C_t^p + u_t, \tag{3.76}$$

where C_t is actual consumption spending in period t and u_t is our disturbance term. That is, actual expenditures differ from planned expenditures by a random variable that has a mean of zero so that, on the average, actual expenditures equal planned expenditures. In this case, u_t represents the effect on actual expenditures of unforseen events such as unexpected doctor bills. In any event, if we substitute for C_t^p and Y_{dt}^e in (3.74), we obtain

$$C_t = a + bY_{d(t-1)} + u_t, \tag{3.77}$$

which is identical to (3.73).

Similar types of lagged relationships for explaining investment behavior and changes in wages may also be useful. The investment decision, for example, is not made immediately. Even if it were, the translation of that decision into investment expenditure takes time. For this reason, we might postulate that

$$I_{t-1}^d = a + br_{t-1}. \tag{3.78}$$

The investment decision, I^d, in period $(t - 1)$ depends on the rate of interest, r, in that same period. However, assume that

$$I_t = I_{t-1}^d + u_t. \tag{3.79}$$

Investment expenditure depends on the investment decision with a one-period lag. Substituting in (3.79) for I_{t-1}^d, we get a relationship like the previous one for consumption, namely that

$$I_t = a + br_{t-1} + u_t. \tag{3.80}$$

We leave it as an exercise to show that, if we incorporate a one-period lag in the Phillips Curve so that the percentage change in wages in t depends on the level of excess demand for labor in the preceding period (D_{t-1}^*), we would obtain

$$\dot{W}_t = a + b\left(\frac{1}{R_{t-1}}\right) + u_t. \tag{3.81}$$

Does such a lag seem reasonable?

The question now arises as to whether or not our model can handle the problem of estimating a relationship involving lagged variables. The answer is yes. To see this, consider the model

$$Y_t = a + bX_{t-1} + u_t, \qquad t = 1, 2, \ldots, n, \tag{3.82}$$

where we make the usual assumptions concerning the disturbance term u_t. This equation says that Y depends on X with a one-period lag. Assume that we have n observations on Y_t and X_t, which we array as in Table 3.5.

TABLE 3.5

Y	X
Y_1	X_1
Y_2	X_2
$\vdots$	$\vdots$
Y_n	X_n

TABLE 3.6

Y	X
Y_1	X_0
Y_2	X_1
Y_3	X_2
$\vdots$	$\vdots$
Y_n	X_{n-1}

Note that Y_t is not related to X_t; it depends on X_{t-1}. For this reason, we should pair values of Y with values of X from the preceding period, as in Table 3.6.

If we wanted to show our observed values of Y and X in a scatter diagram, each point in the diagram would represent a value for Y and the value of X in the preceding period. It is these points to which we would fit our regression line. Note that, in moving from Table 3.5 to Table 3.6, we lose one observation; we are unable to use Y_1 since we do not have an observed value for X_0, and we likewise cannot make use of X_n since we do not know Y_{n+1}. We see that a model with a one-period lag reduces the size of our sample by one to $(n-1)$. That is, in Table 3.6 there are only $(n-1)$ paired observations that can be used in the estimation of our model.

To estimate our lagged relationship, we simply define a variable $Z_t = X_{t-1}$. Thus, the value for Z in any time period is simply equal to the value of X in the preceding period. Our basic model, (3.82), can thus be rewritten as

$$Y_t = a + bZ_t + u_t, \qquad t = 2, \ldots, n. \tag{3.83}$$

Our estimators of a and b are

$$\hat{b} = \frac{\displaystyle\sum_{t=2}^{n} (Z_t - \bar{Z})Y_t}{\displaystyle\sum_{t=2}^{n} (Z_t - \bar{Z})^2}, \tag{3.84}$$

$$\hat{a} = \bar{Y} - \hat{b}\bar{Z},$$

where

$$\bar{Y} = \frac{\displaystyle\sum_{t=2}^{n} Y_t}{n-1}, \qquad \bar{Z} = \frac{\displaystyle\sum_{t=2}^{n} Z_t}{n-1}.$$

Note that, in this calculation, we simply drop Y_1 and X_n.

AN EXAMPLE

To illustrate this procedure, let us return to the consumption function we estimated in Chapter 2 as

$$C_t = a + bY_{dt} + u_t,$$

TABLE 3.7.

Year	Consumption (in billions of dollars)	Year	Disposable Income (in billions of dollars)
1961	335	1960	350
1962	355	1961	364
1963	375	1962	385
1964	401	1963	405
1965	433	1964	438
1966	466	1965	473
1967	492	1966	512
1968	537	1967	547
1969	576	1968	590

and let us now estimate this function with a one-period lag, so that

$$C_t = a + bY_{d(t-1)} + u_t. \tag{3.85}$$

We are postulating in (3.85) that consumption in any given year depends on the level of disposable income in the previous year.

Returning to Table 2.2 and pairing observed values of consumption with those of disposable income in the preceding year, we derive Table 3.7. Note that we now have only nine, instead of ten, observations. Applying our estimation procedure, we obtain the lagged consumption function:

$$\hat{C} = -20 + 0.98Y_{d(t-1)}, \qquad n = 9, \tag{3.86}$$
$$(0.2) \quad (44.3) \qquad R^2 = 0.99,$$

where the numbers in parentheses are the corresponding absolute values of the t ratios. We see that, like our estimated consumption function in Chapter 2, equation (3.86) has a high degree of explanatory power. However, in our lagged consumption function, the constant term is not significantly different from zero (with a t ratio of only 0.2) at a 95 percent confidence level; moreover, the estimated value of the MPC is considerably higher: 0.98 as compared to 0.89. As a result, policy prescriptions based on the lagged consumption function may differ from those based on the unlagged function. It should be clear that we need a technique that will enable us to discriminate between these two models. We shall develop such a technique in Chapter 5; in addition, we shall treat more general models of lagged relationships.

3.5 PREDICTION

In this section we turn to the second of the two primary applications of regression analysis. Earlier in this chapter we showed how our regression results can be used to test hypotheses about economic behavior. Equally important is the use of our estimated regression equation to make predictions or forecasts of the impact of certain events on economic variables. You may recall that in the introduction in Chapter 1 we examined the problem of the economic advisor who had to evaluate the impact of tax cuts of alternative sizes on the level of consumption expenditure. If, for example, our advisor knew by how much each of the alternative tax cuts would increase disposable income, it would seem that he should then be able to use his estimated relationship between C and Y_d to predict the effects of the various possible tax reductions on the level of consumption spending. Our estimated regression equations should, in this way, be of real assistance in the evaluation of the likely effects of economic policies. Regression analysis can both help us to understand in quantitative terms how the economy functions and in turn to predict the impact of the various options available to the policy maker.

At this point, we want to investigate more systematically the problem of prediction. Suppose that we have a relationship of the familiar form

$$Y_t = a + bX_t + u_t. \tag{3.87}$$

Assume initially that we know that in some future period, say f, the value of X will be X_f. For instance, if X were the level of disposable income, we might assume that X_f is the value of X that would result from a tax cut of a specific size. Our problem is that of predicting the value of Y, say Y_f, that will correspond to this specified value, X_f. Note that Y_f is the future value of Y corresponding to a *given* value of X, namely X_f.

The first thing to notice about the prediction problem is that Y_f is itself a random variable. For example, according to our model (3.87), we have

$$Y_f = a + bX_f + u_f, \tag{3.88}$$

where u_f is the value of the disturbance term in this future period. Now, by our standard specifications, u_f is unpredictable; it is a random variable that is not related to previous values of the disturbance term, or to the values of the independent variable, X. Even if we knew a and b and so could calculate $(a + bX_f)$, we would still be unable to forecast Y perfectly because of the unpredictable influence of u_f.

There will, in addition, be a second source of uncertainty or imprecision in our forecast. In general, we shall not know a and b, and so shall have to use estimates of them in order to estimate the first component of Y_f in (3.88), namely, its mean corresponding to X_f:

$$Y_f^m = a + bX_f. \tag{3.89}$$

In summary, there will in general be two distinct sources of error in our forecast: the unpredictable effect of the disturbance term, u_f, and the use of estimated values for the parameters, a and b.

We have seen in (3.88) that, given X_f, the corresponding future value of Y, Y_f is a random variable. As such, it would be desirable not only to have a point estimate or forecast of Y_f, but also to establish a confidence interval for Y_f. That is, we would want to have some measure of the likely accuracy of our forecast.

We shall next set forth a technique for using our regression results both to make forecasts and to establish such confidence intervals. We shall proceed in two steps. As noted above, since we shall not in general know a and b, we shall not know Y_t^m. We shall turn first to the problem of deriving an estimator for Y_f^m and one for the variance of the estimator. With this background, the second step will be the prediction of Y_f itself and the determination of the associated confidence intervals.

THE ESTIMATION OF Y_f^m

From (3.89) we have the expression for the mean of Y_f corresponding to X_f:

$$Y_f^m = a + bX_f. \tag{3.89}$$

Assume now that we have available the estimators $\hat{a}$ and $\hat{b}$, which are based on a sample of Y and X of size n for the periods $t = 1, 2, \ldots, n$, where, since f is a future period, $n < f$. Under our standard assumptions $\hat{a}$ and $\hat{b}$ are unbiased. From this it follows that we can use the expression $\hat{Y}_f = (\hat{a} + \hat{b}X_f)$ as an unbiased estimator of Y_f^m, since, given X_f, we have

$$E(\hat{Y}_f) = E(\hat{a} + \hat{b}X_f) = E(\hat{a}) + [E(\hat{b})]X_f \tag{3.90}$$

$$= a + bX_f = Y_f^m.$$

Returning, for example, to our estimated consumption function in Chapter 2, suppose that a proposed tax cut is associated with a level of disposable income of $500 billion. We would then estimate the mean level of consumption expenditure associated with this reduction in taxes as

$$\hat{C}_f^m = 13 + 0.89(500) = 13 + 445 = 458. \tag{3.91}$$

We note that $\hat{Y}_f$ is a point estimator of the mean of Y_f, Y_f^m, corresponding to X_f. If we wanted to obtain a confidence interval for, or test hypotheses about, Y_f^m, we would need the probability distribution (or function) of $\hat{Y}_f$. This distribution is easily derived from a basic theorem in statistics, which states that linear combinations of normal variables are themselves normally distributed. Recall that our assumption of the normality of the disturbance terms implied that $\hat{a}$ and $\hat{b}$ are normally distributed. Given X_f, $\hat{Y}_f$ is simply a linear combination of $\hat{a}$ and $\hat{b}$, and so it also must be a normally distributed random variable. The mean of $\hat{Y}_f$ is Y_f^m; further, it can be shown that the variance of $\hat{Y}_f$ is*

$$\sigma_{\hat{Y}_f}^2 = \sigma_u^2 \left[\frac{1}{n} + \frac{(X_f - \bar{X})^2}{\sum\limits_{t=1}^{n} (X_t - \bar{X})^2} \right], \tag{3.92}$$

* For a formal development of the formulas in this section, see J. Johnston, *Econometric Methods*, 2nd ed. (New York: McGraw-Hill, 1972), pp. 38–43.

where $\bar{X} = \sum_{t=1}^{n} X_t/n$, and where $X_1, \ldots, X_n$ are the observations on X on which our estimators $\hat{a}$ and $\hat{b}$ are based. We have that $\hat{Y}_f$ is $N(a + bX_f, \sigma_{\hat{Y}_f}^2)$.

Before continuing, note that the variance of $\hat{Y}_f$ increases with the square of $(X_f - \bar{X})$. This says that the farther our specified value, X_f, is from the sample mean of observations on X (which are used to construct our estimators $\hat{a}$ and $\hat{b}$), the larger is the variance of our estimator, $\hat{Y}_f$. This would seem quite reasonable. Somewhat intuitively, what it means is that the farther our forecasted value of the independent variable is from those values within the range of our observed experience, the less confidence we can have in the accuracy of our predictions. We might feel fairly confident in estimating the mean level of consumption expenditure associated with a level of disposable income that is very close to that which has prevailed in recent years. In contrast, we would probably feel a good deal less certain of an estimate of the mean level of consumption expenditure associated with a level of disposable income roughly twice the size of recent income levels.

Finally, we should note that since σ_u^2 will, in general, not be known, the variance of $\hat{Y}_f$ will not be known and so must be estimated. The suggested estimator is obviously

$$\hat{\sigma}_{\hat{Y}_f}^2 = \hat{\sigma}_u^2 \left[\frac{1}{n} + \frac{(X_f - \bar{X})^2}{\sum\limits_{t=1}^{n} (X_t - \bar{X})^2} \right], \tag{3.93}$$

which is, from our previous discussion, unbiased:

$$E(\hat{\sigma}_{\hat{Y}_f}^2) = \sigma_{\hat{Y}_f}^2. \tag{3.94}$$

The material developed above suggests that, if σ_u^2 were known, we would obtain confidence intervals, and test hypotheses concerning Y_f^m by noting that

$$\frac{(\hat{Y}_f - Y_f^m)}{\sigma_{\hat{Y}_f}} \tag{3.95}$$

is $N(0, 1)$.

If σ_u^2 is not known, we note that

$$\frac{\hat{Y}_f - Y_f^m}{\hat{\sigma}_{\hat{Y}_f}} \tag{3.96}$$

is a t variable with $n - 2$ degrees of freedom.

For example, if σ_u^2 were not known, a 95 percent confidence interval for Y_f^m would be

$$(\hat{Y}_f \pm t_{n-2;0.975}\hat{\sigma}_{\hat{Y}_f}). \tag{3.97}$$

Returning to our earlier illustration, we had $\hat{C}_f = 458$ corresponding to $Y_d = 500$. To determine a 95 percent confidence interval for C_f^m, we have

$$458 \pm 2.31 \left[3.4 \sqrt{\frac{1}{10} + \frac{(500 - 469)^2}{85,810}} \right] = 458 \pm 2.$$

THE FORECASTING OF Y_f

We turn now to what is normally the issue of central interest: the forecast of Y_f itself and the determination of the associated confidence intervals. We note first that, given X_f, our estimator (or forecast) of the future level of Y, Y_f, is *identical* to our estimator of $Y_f{}^m$, namely, $\hat{Y}_f = (\hat{a} + \hat{b}X_f)$. This follows because the unpredictable disturbance component of Y_f [see (3.88)] has a mean of zero. In other words, we would predict the *level* of Y_f simply by predicting its *mean*.

In this case the error of our forecast would be

$$e_f = Y_f - \hat{Y}_f. \tag{3.98}$$

The name, incidentally, for e_f in (3.98) is the *forecast error*. It follows from our assumptions that the forecast error has a mean of zero:

$$\begin{aligned} E(e_f) &= E(Y_f) - E(\hat{Y}_f) \\ &= a + bX_f - a - bX_f = 0. \end{aligned} \tag{3.99}$$

Assume that u_f, like $u_1, \ldots, u_n$, is normally distributed with mean zero and variance $\sigma_u{}^2$. It is then true that, given X_f, Y_f is also normally distributed with mean $(a + bX_f)$ and variance $\sigma_u{}^2$. Since our forecast error, e_f in (3.98), is a linear combination of normal variables (recall that $\hat{Y}_f$ is normal), it must also be a normal variable.

We have already determined that the mean of e_f is zero. We can determine the variance of e_f by simply noting that, given X_f, Y_f and $\hat{Y}_f$ are independent. For instance, from (3.88) we see that the only disturbance term on which Y_f depends is u_f. However, $\hat{Y}_f$ depends on the disturbance terms, $u_1, \ldots, u_n$, because $\hat{a}$ and $\hat{b}$ are constructed only in terms of the joint observations $X_1, Y_1; X_2, Y_2; \ldots; X_n, Y_n$. If each disturbance term is assumed to be independent of all of the others, it follows that, given X_f, Y_f and $\hat{Y}_f$ will be independent. From (3.98), we see that e_f is a linear sum of two independent random variables, and its variance is (see the Appendix to Chapter 2)

$$\begin{aligned} \sigma_e{}^2 &= \sigma_{Y_f}{}^2 + \sigma_{\hat{Y}_f}{}^2 \\ &= \sigma_u{}^2 + \sigma_u{}^2 \left[\frac{1}{n} + \frac{(X_f - \bar{X})^2}{\sum (X_i - \bar{X})^2} \right] \\ &= \sigma_u{}^2 \left[1 + \frac{1}{n} + \frac{(X_f - \bar{X})^2}{\sum (X_i - \bar{X})^2} \right]. \end{aligned} \tag{3.100}$$

In brief, e_f is $N(0, \sigma_e{}^2)$.

Similar to the earlier analysis, we find that an unbiased estimator of $\sigma_e{}^2$ would be

$$\hat{\sigma}_e{}^2 = \hat{\sigma}_u{}^2 \left[1 + \frac{1}{n} + \frac{(X_f - \bar{X})^2}{\sum (X_i - \bar{X})^2} \right]. \tag{3.101}$$

We construct confidence intervals (which are sometimes called *forecast intervals*) for Y_f by noting that

$$\frac{e_f}{\sigma_e} = \frac{Y_f - \hat{Y}_f}{\sigma_e} \qquad (3.102)$$

is $N(0, 1)$ or, if σ_u^2 is not known, that

$$\frac{e_f}{\hat{\sigma}_e} = \frac{Y_f - \hat{Y}_f}{\hat{\sigma}_e} \qquad (3.103)$$

is a t variable with $n - 2$ degrees of freedom. For example, if σ_u^2 is not known, a 95 percent confidence interval for Y_f would be

$$(\hat{Y}_f \pm t_{n-2;0.975}\hat{\sigma}_e). \qquad (3.104)$$

Note from (3.100) that $\sigma_e^2 > \sigma_{\hat{Y}_f}^2$, and, from (3.101) and (3.93) that $\hat{\sigma}_e^2 > \hat{\sigma}_{\hat{Y}_f}^2$. These results imply that a confidence interval for Y_f will always be wider than an interval with the same level of confidence for Y_f^m [compare (3.104) to (3.97)]. This is as it should be. There are two difficulties in predicting Y_f; one is that the parameters a and b are unknown, and the other is that the disturbance term u_f is unpredictable. On the other hand, there is only one difficulty in predicting Y_f^m, namely, that a and b are unknown.

As a final illustration, we return again to our estimated consumption equation and calculate a 95 percent confidence interval for the *level* of consumption given (as before) that $Y_d = 500$. Our interval is

$$(\hat{a} + \hat{b}Y_d) \pm t_{n-2;0.975}\hat{\sigma}_e$$

$$= 458 \pm 2.31 \left[3.4 \sqrt{1 + \frac{1}{10} + \frac{(500 - 469)^2}{85,810}} \right] = 458 \pm 8.$$

As just noted, we see that the confidence interval for our forecast of $C_f(458 \pm 8)$ is wider than that for $C_f^m(458 \pm 2)$.

3.6 AN EXAMPLE: THE ESTIMATION OF A DEMAND CURVE

We conclude our treatment of the two-variable regression model with an illustrative exercise involving the estimation of a demand curve. Table 3.8 presents some actual data on annual sales and prices of chicken in the United States. In particular, the table indicates for each year during 1948 to 1963 the consumption per capita of chicken in the United States, and its annual price deflated by the consumer price index.

We shall use these data to estimate a demand curve for chicken. Suppose we postulate the following relationship

$$Q_t = aP_t^b e^{u_t}, \qquad (3.105)$$

where Q_t is the per capita consumption of chicken at time t (during the tth year) measured in pounds, P_t is the corresponding price of chicken measured in cents per pound, and u_t is a disturbance term. As an illustration of the measurements involved, a value of $Q_t = 28.9$ implies that during the tth year the per capita consumption of chicken was 28.9 pounds; a value of $P_t = 41.4$ implies that the corresponding average price during that year was 41.4 cents per pound. Table 3.8 indicates that these figures correspond to the year 1959.

Assume that the disturbance term u_t satisfies all the assumptions of our standard model. Then, as we indicated earlier with reference to equation (3.43), the parameter b in a model, such as (3.105), can be interpreted as an elasticity. In this case, b describes the expected percentage change in the annual per capita consumption of chicken with respect to a 1 percent change in its price.

As seen earlier in this chapter, we can use the logarithmic transformation to put (3.105) into the linear form

$$\ln(Q_t) = A + b \ln(P_t) + u_t, \tag{3.106}$$

where $A = \ln(a)$, and the logarithms are taken with respect to the base e. This suggests, as already discussed, that we simply take the natural logs of both variables and then regress the log of the dependent variable, $\ln(Q_t)$, on the log

TABLE 3.8

PER CAPITA CONSUMPTION AND DEFLATED PRICE OF CHICKEN FOR 1948–1963[a]

Year	Consumption of Chicken Per Capita (pounds)	Deflated Price Per Pound (cents)
1948	18.3	75.4
1949	19.6	71.8
1950	20.6	68.0
1951	21.7	66.0
1952	22.1	65.0
1953	21.9	62.8
1954	22.8	56.4
1955	21.3	58.7
1956	24.4	50.4
1957	25.5	47.6
1958	28.2	45.8
1959	28.9	41.4
1960	28.2	41.4
1961	30.3	37.0
1962	30.2	38.6
1963	30.6	37.6

[a] Price is deflated by the consumer price index (1957–1959 = 100).
SOURCE: Frederick V. Waugh, *Demand and Price Analysis—Some Examples from Agriculture* (Washington, D.C.: U.S. Department of Agriculture, Technical Bulletin 1316, Nov. 1964), Table 5-1, p. 39.

of the independent variable, $\ln(P_t)$, in order to obtain estimates of A and b, say, $\hat{A}$ and $\hat{b}$. Our (biased) estimate of a would then be obtained as $e^{\hat{A}}$. Applying this procedure to (3.106) with the data from Table 3.8 yields

$$\ln(Q_t) = 5.87 - 0.68 \ln(P_t), \qquad (3.107)$$
$$(0.13) \quad (0.03)$$

$$R^2 = 0.97,$$

where the numbers in parentheses beneath the estimated coefficients are the respective estimated standard errors. Our point estimate of the price elasticity of demand for chicken is thus -0.68; our estimate of a to three-place accuracy is $e^{5.87} = 354$.

We now illustrate some of the techniques that were presented in this chapter in terms of the results in (3.107). For example, suppose we were interested in testing the hypothesis, at the 5 percent significance level, that the demand for chicken is not related to its price, against the alternative that it is. Our null hypothesis would then be $H_0 : b = 0$, and our alternative would be $H_1 : b \neq 0$. Taking the absolute value of the estimate of b in (3.107) and dividing it by the corresponding estimated standard error $(0.68/0.03)$ results in a very high t ratio in excess of 20; using our rule of thumb, we can therefore immediately conclude that the hypothesis $H_0 : b = 0$ would be rejected by the results in (3.107).

As a second illustration, suppose that we were interested in testing the hypothesis, at the 1 percent level of significance, that demand is price elastic against the alternative that it is not. Recall from microeconomic principles that demand is said to be price elastic if its price elasticity is less than -1 (greater than 1 in absolute value). In terms of our demand model (3.105), this corresponds to any value of $b < -1$. Thus, our null and alternative hypotheses in this case would be $H_0 : b < -1$, and $H_1 : b > -1$.

Unlike the illustrations given in previous portions of this chapter, our null hypothesis does not specify a particular value of b. Nevertheless, this hypothesis can be tested by our confidence interval procedure. To see this, first note that H_1 is a one-tail alternative which suggests that b is larger than any of its possible values as dictated by H_0. This situation is diagramed in Figure 3.8. Consistent with our discussion earlier in this chapter, we shall construct a one-tail confidence interval that has a lower bound, say LB. This confidence interval will be of the form $b \geq$ LB. If LB ≥ -1, we reject H_0; if LB < -1, we accept H_0. Note, this testing procedure *need not* automatically lead to the

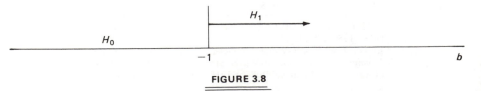

FIGURE 3.8

acceptance of H_0, which we saw was a difficulty that would arise if our null hypothesis was of the form $H_0 : b \neq 0$.

The mechanics of the analysis are straightforward. Using Statistical Table 2 for the t distribution with $16 - 2 = 14$ degrees of freedom, we find that our one-tail 99 percent confidence interval is

$$b > (\hat{b} - t_{14; 0.99}\hat{\sigma}_{\hat{b}}) = -0.68 - (2.624)(0.03) = -0.76.$$

Since $-0.76 > -1$, we reject H_0 and accept the alternative hypothesis that the demand for chicken is not price elastic.

Again consider the results in (3.107) and note that the estimated equation "fits" the observed data extremely well: the equation accounts for 97 percent of the observed variation in annual chicken consumption per capita. However, you may (and should) feel a bit uncomfortable with this for at least two reasons. First, our equation explains annual variations in chicken consumption solely in terms of price changes. But we know that, over the period 1948 to 1963, consumer incomes rose; if chicken is a normal good, we would expect rising income to account for some of the increase in chicken purchases. However, equation (3.105) omits any reference to income. By omitting an important variable (in this case, income), we may be attributing to price not only its effect on chicken consumption, but also that of income. Our estimates may, for this reason, overstate the effect that the price variable has on consumer purchases of chicken. Second, we have not, in our estimation procedure, taken account of the supply side of the market. Observed price and quantity do not result solely from the influence of demand, but rather from the interaction of supply and demand. Somehow, this should be recognized explicitly in our regression model. These are matters that we shall investigate in the remaining chapters.

QUESTIONS

1. It is claimed that performances on I.Q. tests have improved over recent years and that the mean is now over 100. Assume that I.Q. scores are normally distributed over the population. If in a sample of 100 tests the average score is 110 and the *estimated* variance is 4, test the hypothesis at the 5 percent level that the mean *population* I.Q. is greater than 100.

2. Explain why the mean is better estimated by an average based on a random sample of size 30 than one based on a sample of size 20. Are both estimators unbiased?

3. Suppose that the standard workweek in industry is 40 hours. Our hypothesis is that whenever hours deviate from 40, they will tend to move back toward 40. One way to formulate this is $\Delta H_t = \beta + \alpha(40 - H_{t-1}) + u_t$, where $\Delta H_t = H_t - H_{t-1}$, and so $H_t = (\beta + 40\alpha) + (1 - \alpha)H_{t-1} + u_t$. Suppose we estimate the following regression from quarterly U.S. data:

$$\hat{H}_t = \underset{(0.7)}{5} + \underset{(0.15)}{0.875 H_{t-1}}, \qquad R^2 = 0.98,$$

   where the estimated standard deviations are shown in parentheses below the coefficients. Should we accept or reject our hypothesis, at the 5 percent level, that the change in hours is dependent on the deviation from 40? Why?

4. Mr. A puts forth a theory suggesting that the mean height of men is 70 in. Mr. B argues that Mr. A's theory overemphasizes certain factors and hence overstates the mean. Suppose the following is the result of a random sample of size 4: 64, 74, 72, 62. Assume that the underlying probability density function is normal with $\sigma^2 = 4$. Test Mr. A's theory at the 5 percent level of significance.

5. What is the significance or importance, of our assumption that the disturbance term is normally distributed?

6. Assume that the mean height of people in the East is known to be 67 in. Suppose a coat manufacturer in the East wants to open an outlet in the West, and that he has reason to believe that people in the West are, on the average, taller. If so, he must produce coats that are somewhat longer. Suppose that this requires an extensive and expensive retooling of his machinery. Suppose also that this hypothesis concerning relative height is tested in terms of a random sample of people selected in the West. Discuss the consequences of a Type 1 and Type 2 error.

7. Explain why the linear regression model may not really be so restrictive even though many economic relationships are nonlinear. In particular, adopt an appropriate transformation and then derive the observation matrix for the model

$$Y_t = a + b\left(\frac{1}{1 - X_t}\right) + u_t,$$

when $n = 3$ and our observations on Y and X are $Y_1 = 1$, $Y_2 = 10$, $Y_3 = 12$; $X_1 = 0$, $X_2 = 0.1$, $X_3 = 0.5$.

8. Suppose that Mr. A estimates a consumption function and obtains the results

$$\hat{C} = \underset{(3.1)}{15} + \underset{(18.7)}{0.81Y_d}, \qquad \begin{array}{l} n = 19, \\ R^2 = 0.99, \end{array}$$

where the numbers in parentheses are t ratios.

a. Use the t ratio to test the hypothesis that Y_d is a statistically significant variable.

b. Determine the estimated standard deviations of the parameter estimators.

c. Construct a 95 percent confidence interval for the coefficient of Y_d. Does this interval include zero?

9. Consider the situation where an increase in the welfare benefit rate (measured as payments per family per month) leads to an increase in the demand for welfare by causing people to substitute leisure for labor. Suppose also that the increase in the demand for welfare tends in turn, through political pressure, to increase the benefit rate *in the following period*. Express these relationships by using a two-equation model.

10. Consider a situation where the number of firms that locate in a given state depends on the *relative* tax rate of that state. Assume also that, although there may be tax advantages to the residents of the state, the more firms that locate there, the higher will be the pollution rate. Express the firm location and the pollution relationships in terms of regression models.

11. Consider the standard regression model

$$Y_t = a + bX_t + u_t.$$

Suppose that we cannot measure X_t. Instead, suppose that we observe $Z_t = 5 - 3X_t$. What are the parameters in the model relating Y_t to Z_t?

CHAPTER 4
Multiple-Regression Analysis

In the preceding chapters we have explored the statistical relationship between two variables. In the case of consumption expenditure, for example, we postulated the model

$$C_t = a + bY_{dt} + u_t, \tag{4.1}$$

and developed techniques with which to estimate the values of a and b and to test hypotheses about this relationship. Typically, however, economic relationships are a good deal more complex than this; the value of a particular variable such as consumption will often depend not on a single variable but on the values of a whole set of independent variables.

For instance, suppose we assume that the level of consumption spending in period t depends not only on current disposable income but also on the value of liquid assets (A_t)* and on disposable income in the preceding period $Y_{d(t-1)}$. If consumer holdings of liquid assets are unusually high (as they were, for example, at the close of World War II), we would expect consumption expenditure to be somewhat higher than that normally associated with the prevailing level of income; conversely, if stocks of liquid assets are abnormally small, consumers may hold down their spending somewhat in order to replenish their holdings of these assets. Past income may also play a role in determining current levels of consumer spending. For instance, some expenditures undertaken in the current period may be induced by past standards of living as reflected by last period's income. For example, other things equal, the higher the income was in the previous period, the higher current consumption is likely to be. All of this means that we now have a more complicated consumption function, such as

$$C_t = a + b_1 Y_{dt} + b_2 A_t + b_3 Y_{d(t-1)} + u_t. \tag{4.2}$$

Our problem now becomes that of estimating how consumption depends on each of these independent variables; in other words, we must develop a technique with which to estimate the values of a, b_1, b_2, and b_3. Again, we would also like to be able to establish the variance of our estimators so that we shall have some measure of their precision. As a straightforward

---

* By liquid assets we shall mean private holdings of money, time deposits, savings and loan shares, and U.S. government bonds.

generalization of our preceding material, we shall now assume that we have at our disposal a set of observed values for the variables of our model; for example, corresponding to (4.2) we would have access to information such as that in Table 4.1.

At first glance, our problem appears somewhat different in character and a good deal more complicated than in the two-variable case. In particular, in the two-variable regression case we had observed values for the dependent variable and a single independent variable, and our problem was simply to estimate how the first varied with the second. Now we have observations on a whole set of independent variables, and we face what looks to be a much more difficult task of sorting out the effects of all the different independent variables. That is, to determine the effect of each independent variable we must somehow separate its effect from the influence that all the other independent variables have on the dependent variable.

In spite of this apparent complication, we stress at the outset that multiple-regression analysis (that is, the case where we have more than one independent variable) is a straightforward generalization of bivariate analysis. Initially, we shall present a multiple-regression model in which we make precisely the same assumptions concerning the properties of the disturbance term that we made in the two-variable model. Next, we shall again adopt our instrumental-variable technique by which we impose these assumptions as conditions on the estimator of the disturbance term. This will produce a set of normal equations, the solution of which will give us unbiased estimators of each of the coefficients of our model. Thus, our procedure will be almost exactly the same as in the preceding chapters; if you understand the two-variable case, you should have little difficulty with multiple-regression analysis.

TABLE 4.1

OBSERVED VALUES (billions of U.S. dollars)

Time	Consumption (C_t)	Disposable Income (Y_{dt})	Financial Assets (A_t)	Disposable Income in Preceding Year $Y_{d(t-1)}$
1960	325.2	350.0	399.2	337.3
1961	335.2	364.4	424.6	350.0
1962	355.1	385.3	459.0	364.4
1963	375.0	404.6	495.4	385.3
1964	401.2	438.1	530.5	404.6
1965	432.8	473.2	573.1	438.1
1966	466.3	511.9	601.5	473.2
1967	492.1	546.3	650.4	511.9
1968	535.8	591.2	709.6	546.3
1969	577.5	631.6	731.6	591.2

SOURCE: *Economic Report of the President* (Washington, D.C.: U.S. Government Printing Office, Feb. 1971), pp. 197, 204, 262.

4.1 THE MULTIPLE-REGRESSION MODEL

In general terms, we consider the multiple-regression model,

$$Y_t = b_0 + b_1 X_{1t} + b_2 X_{2t} + \cdots + b_k X_{kt} + u_t, \qquad t = 1, \ldots, n, \quad (4.3)$$

where

Y_t = the tth observation on the dependent variable;

X_{it} = the tth observation on the ith independent variable (or "regressor"), $i = 1, 2, \ldots, k$ if we have k independent variables;

u_t = the tth value of the disturbance term; and

b_i = the coefficient of the ith independent variable.

It will be convenient from this point on to use b_0, rather than a, to denote the constant term in the regression equation so that all the parameters in (4.3) will be b's. We shall now list the assumptions we make in the multiple-regression model; most of them will require little comment since they are the same assumptions we adopted in the two-variable case.

1. The expected or mean value of the disturbance term is zero:

$$E(u_t) = 0.$$

2. The variance of the disturbance term is a constant and therefore is independent of t:

$$E(u_t - 0)^2 = E(u_t)^2 = \sigma_u^2.$$

3. The values of the disturbance term are independent of one another so that the covariance between the disturbance terms corresponding to any two observations, u_s and u_t, is zero:

$$\mathrm{cov}(u_t, u_s) = E(u_t u_s) = 0.$$

4. The disturbance term is independent of all of the values of the regressors. More specifically, we assume that u_t is independent of $X_{1s}, \ldots, X_{ks}$, for all t and s. It follows that the covariance between the disturbance term, u_t, and each of the independent variables (regressors) of our regression equation (4.3) is zero. Again, this says that whether the experimenter sets the values of the independent variables, or whether the "economy" sets them, the particular values that are set in no way influence the value of the disturbance term. More formally, the condition of zero covariance between u_t and each X_{it} can be expressed as

$$\mathrm{cov}(u_t, X_{it}) = E[u_t(X_{it} - \mu_{Xi})] = E(u_t X_{it}) - \mu_{Xi} E(u_t) = E(u_t X_{it}) = 0,$$

where $E(X_{it}) = \mu_{Xi}$.

5. We do not have perfect multicollinearity among the regressors. That is, none of the independent variables is a *linear combination* of the others; for example, we rule out relationships such as

a. $X_{1t} = 3 - 2X_{2t} + 17X_{3t}$;
b. $X_{4t} = (X_{1t} + X_{2t} + X_{3t})/3$; or
c. $X_{2t} = 3X_{8t}$.

Nonlinear relationships, however, are not ruled out; for instance, if $X_{1t} = X_{2t}^2$, or if $X_{3t} = X_{5t}X_{6t}$, our assumption would not be violated.

The first four of these assumptions will be familiar from the two-variable model, and their justification here is exactly the same as earlier. If you are uncertain as to why we make any of assumptions 1–4, refresh your memory by referring back to the discussion of the two-variable model in Chapter 2.

The one new assumption we introduce here, assumption 5, is actually an extension of the assumption we made in Chapter 2 that the independent variable, X_t, in the two-variable case must have at least two distinct values. In Chapter 2 we saw that, in the two-variable case, if the regressor X_t never varied, so that $X_t \equiv X_0$, we would only be able to estimate a parameter, which we called A, whose value depended on both the original constant term, a, and on what is in effect a constant term created by the unchanging value of X_t, bX_0; that is, $A = a + bX_0$. In short, if the value of the regressor never varied, its effect on Y would be inseparable from the influence of the original constant term.

In our present multiple-regression case we want to ensure, not only that b_i, the effect of X_{it} on Y, is separable from the constant term, b_0, but also that it is separable from the influence of all the other X's. The force of assumption 5 is that it guarantees such separability. We shall show this formally in Section 4.2. At this point, however, consider the following intuitive illustration in which assumption 5 is violated.

Suppose that X_{1t} does vary, but is always equal to X_{2t}. Then, other things equal, if X_{1t} increases by one unit, Y_t will change by $(b_1 + b_2)$ units because, if X_{1t} is always equal to X_{2t}, X_{2t} will also increase by one unit! This suggests that only the *combined effect* of X_{1t} and X_{2t}, namely $(b_1 + b_2)$, can be estimated if $X_{1t} = X_{2t}$. There simply is no way that we can separate the effect of X_1 from X_2 on Y. This follows because if $X_{1t} = X_{2t}$, our basic model (4.3) could be rewritten as

$$Y_t = b_0 + BX_{1t} + b_3X_{3t} + \cdots + b_kX_{kt} + u_t, \qquad (4.4)$$

where $B = (b_1 + b_2)$. That is, if two regressors are always equal to each other, one of these regressors can be eliminated from our model without any loss of information. We can then consider the resulting (or "reduced") model, which contains only $(k - 1)$ independent variables; this model will contain a parameter, B above, which is the "combined" effect of the two original regressors in question. Note that (4.4) does not suggest that $b_0, b_3, \ldots, b_k$ are also unestimable. Again we shall return to this problem with more formality in Section 4.2.

We see that the multiple-regression model is essentially very similar to the two-variable model; it describes a linear functional relationship by which the values of a set of independent variables determine the value of a dependent variable. We must now develop a method to estimate the values of the parameters in this relationship.

4.2 ESTIMATION BY INSTRUMENTAL VARIABLES

Recall that the instrumental-variable technique involves imposing on the estimator of the disturbance term a set of conditions suggested by the assumptions of the regression model. In the two-variable case we imposed two conditions:

Condition   Corresponding Assumption

1. $\sum \dfrac{\hat{u}_t}{n} = 0$, or $\sum \hat{u}_t = 0$ $E(u_t) = 0$

2. $\sum \dfrac{(X_t \hat{u}_t)}{n} = 0$, or $\sum (X_t \hat{u}_t) = 0$ $E(X_t u_t) = 0$

Using these two conditions, we generated two normal equations which we then solved for the values of $\hat{a}$ and $\hat{b}$. We will take the same approach here. However, before doing so, we must extend some of our basic definitions to the multiple-regression framework. For example, our estimation procedure depends critically on the estimator of the disturbance term, $\hat{u}_t$. We must, therefore, define $\hat{u}_t$ in the context of the multiple-regression model.

If our regression model is (4.3), the mean value of Y_t associated with $X_{1t}, \ldots, X_{kt}$ is

$$Y_t^m = b_0 + b_1 X_{1t} + \cdots + b_k X_{kt}. \tag{4.5}$$

As in the two-variable case, Y_t can be written as the sum of its mean plus the disturbance term:

$$Y_t = Y_t^m + u_t. \tag{4.6}$$

If we knew $b_0, b_1, \ldots, b_k$, we could derive the value of u_t as

$$u_t = Y_t - Y_t^m. \tag{4.7}$$

Note that equations (4.6) and (4.7) are identical to their counterparts in the bivariate-regression case.

Suppose that we have estimators of $b_0, b_1, \ldots, b_k$, say $\hat{b}_0, \hat{b}_1, \ldots, \hat{b}_k$. In light of (4.5), our estimator of the mean value of Y_t would be

$$\hat{Y}_t = \hat{b}_0 + \hat{b}_1 X_{1t} + \cdots + \hat{b}_k X_{kt}, \tag{4.8}$$

where, again, the superscript m has been dropped in order to simplify the notation. The estimator of the disturbance term, which is suggested by (4.7), would then be

$$\hat{u}_t = Y_t - \hat{Y}_t$$

$$= Y_t - b_0 - b_1 X_{1t} - \cdots - b_k X_{kt}. \tag{4.9}$$

We can rewrite (4.9) as

$$Y_t = \hat{Y}_t + \hat{u}_t, \tag{4.10}$$

or, more fully, as

$$Y_t = b_0 + b_1 X_{1t} + \cdots + b_k X_{kt} + \hat{u}_t. \tag{4.11}$$

In brief, our definitions of both $\hat{Y}_t$ and $\hat{u}_t$ are also strictly analogous to those of the two-variable regression model of Chapter 2. We now have enough definitions; let us turn to estimation.

THE NORMAL EQUATIONS

As noted, we shall follow the same procedure to generate the normal equations for the multiple-regression case as we did for the two-variable case. Only now, assuming that we have k independent variables, we shall have $(k + 1)$ conditions to impose on the disturbance estimator. More specifically, we have:

	Condition	Corresponding Assumption
1.	$\sum \dfrac{\hat{u}_t}{n} = 0$, or $\sum \hat{u}_t = 0$	$E(u_t) = 0$
2.	$\sum \dfrac{(X_{1t}\hat{u}_t)}{n} = 0$, or $\sum (X_{1t}\hat{u}_t) = 0$	$E(X_{1t}u_t) = 0$
3.	$\sum \dfrac{(X_{2t}\hat{u}_t)}{n} = 0$, or $\sum (X_{2t}\hat{u}_t) = 0$	$E(X_{2t}u_t) = 0$
$\vdots$	$\vdots$	$\vdots$
$k + 1.$	$\sum \dfrac{(X_{kt}\hat{u}_t)}{n} = 0$, or $\sum (X_{kt}\hat{u}_t) = 0$	$E(X_{kt}u_t) = 0$

Note that we have $(k + 1)$ conditions and $(k + 1)$ parameters $b_0, b_1, \ldots, b_k$, appearing in our regression model.

Let us now examine just how these conditions generate a set of $(k + 1)$ normal equations. If we first sum equation (4.11) over all n sets of the observed values, we have

$$\sum Y_t = nb_0 + b_1 \sum X_{1t} + b_2 \sum X_{2t} + \cdots + b_k \sum X_{kt} + \sum \hat{u}_t. \tag{4.12}$$

If we impose our condition that $\sum \hat{u}_t = 0$, we obtain our first normal equation:

N1. $\qquad \sum Y_t = nb_0 + b_1 \sum X_{1t} + b_2 \sum X_{2t} + \cdots + b_k \sum X_{kt}.$

We obtain k more equations by multiplying (4.11) by each of the k independent variables and summing over the n sets of observed values. Specifically,

$$\sum (X_{1t}Y_t) = \hat{b}_0 \sum X_{1t} + \hat{b}_1 \sum X_{1t}^2 + \cdots + \hat{b}_k \sum (X_{1t}X_{kt}) + \sum (X_{1t}\hat{u}_t),$$

$$\sum (X_{2t}Y_t) = \hat{b}_0 \sum X_{2t} + \hat{b}_1 \sum (X_{2t}X_{1t}) + \cdots + \hat{b}_k \sum (X_{2t}X_{kt}) + \sum (X_{2t}\hat{u}_t),$$

$$\vdots$$

$$\sum (X_{kt}Y_t) = \hat{b}_0 \sum X_{kt} + \hat{b}_1 \sum (X_{kt}X_{1t}) + \cdots + \hat{b}_k \sum X_{kt}^2 + \sum (X_{kt}\hat{u}_t).$$

If we impose the conditions that $\sum (X_{it}\hat{u}_t) = 0$, $i = 1, 2, \ldots, k$, the last term in each of these equations drops out, and we obtain the remaining k normal equations:

N2. $\quad \sum (X_{1t}Y_t) = \hat{b}_0 \sum X_{1t} + \hat{b}_1 \sum X_{1t}^2 + \cdots + \hat{b}_k \sum (X_{1t}X_{kt}),$

N3. $\quad \sum (X_{2t}Y_t) = \hat{b}_0 \sum X_{2t} + \hat{b}_1 \sum (X_{2t}X_{1t}) + \cdots + \hat{b}_k \sum (X_{2t}X_{kt}),$

$$\vdots$$

N(k + 1). $\sum (X_{kt}Y_t) = \hat{b}_0 \sum X_{kt} + \hat{b}_1 \sum (X_{kt}X_{1t}) + \cdots + \hat{b}_k \sum X_{kt}^2.$

Note that the summations in the normal equations above depend only on the values of the dependent variable and the regressors. Once we have a sample of observations, we can calculate the values of these summations. Consequently, the normal equations above can be looked upon as a set of $(k + 1)$ equations in $(k + 1)$ unknowns: $\hat{b}_0, \hat{b}_1, \ldots, \hat{b}_k$. We shall, in general, be able to determine the values of these estimators by simply solving the above set of normal equations.

To illustrate, consider a multiple-regression equation in which we have two independent variables:

$$Y_t = b_0 + b_1 X_{1t} + b_2 X_{2t} + u_t.$$

The above-described procedures would generate the following set of three normal equations:

$$\sum Y_t = n\hat{b}_0 + \hat{b}_1 \sum X_{1t} + \hat{b}_2 \sum X_{2t},$$

$$\sum (X_{1t}Y_t) = \hat{b}_0 \sum X_{1t} + \hat{b}_1 \sum X_{1t}^2 + \hat{b}_2 \sum (X_{1t}X_{2t}),$$

$$\sum (X_{2t}Y_t) = \hat{b}_0 \sum X_{2t} + \hat{b}_1 \sum (X_{2t}X_{1t}) + \hat{b}_2 \sum X_{2t}^2.$$

Suppose that our computations with the observed values for Y_t, X_{1t}, and X_{2t} gave us

$$n = 10 \qquad \sum X_{1t} = 2 \qquad \sum X_{2t} = 2$$

$$\sum X_{1t}^2 = 6 \qquad \sum (X_{1t}X_{2t}) = 1 \qquad \sum X_{2t}^2 = 4$$

$$\sum Y_t = 5 \qquad \sum (X_{1t}Y_t) = 6 \qquad \sum (X_{2t}Y_t) = 7$$

Inserting these computed values into the normal equations yields

$$5 = 10\hat{b}_0 + 2\hat{b}_1 + 2\hat{b}_2,$$
$$6 = 2\hat{b}_0 + 6\hat{b}_1 + \hat{b}_2,$$
$$7 = 2\hat{b}_0 + \hat{b}_1 + 4\hat{b}_2.$$

Solving this set of equations gives us

$$\hat{b}_0 = 0.045, \qquad \hat{b}_1 = 0.727, \qquad \hat{b}_2 = 1.545.$$

Our estimated regression equation, therefore, is

$$\hat{Y} = 0.045 + 0.727X_1 + 1.545X_2.$$

This gives us an estimate of the mean value of Y associated with any particular set of values for X_1 and X_2.

As you might guess, the actual solution of the set of normal equations to determine the estimated values of the coefficients can involve an astronomical number of calculations for even a relatively small number of variables. For practical purposes, the use of multiple-regression analysis typically requires access to a computer. Nevertheless, it is important that you understand in principle how the estimated values of the coefficients are determined; this will help you not only to interpret the results properly but, with material to be presented later, also to spot difficulties.

THE PROBLEM OF PERFECT MULTICOLLINEARITY

We stated above in assumption 5 that our estimation procedure breaks down if one (or more) of the regressors is a perfect linear combination of the others. We are now in a position to see why. Suppose, for example, that X_k in (4.3) is equal to

$$X_{kt} = c_0 + c_1 X_{1t} + c_2 X_{2t} + \cdots + c_{k-1} X_{(k-1)t}, \qquad (4.13)$$

where $c_0, c_1, \ldots, c_{k-1}$ are constants; incidentally, some of these constants may be zero. Recall from the preceding discussion that we generate our $(k + 1)$th normal equation by multiplying through (4.11) by X_{kt}, summing, and then setting $\sum (X_{kt}\hat{u}_t) = 0$. If X_{kt} equals the expression in (4.13), we can derive our $(k + 1)$th normal equation by simply multiplying the first normal equation by c_0, the second by c_1, and so forth, and then summing them. For instance, in light of (4.13), we could express the left-hand side of the $(k + 1)$th normal equation as

$$\sum (Y_t X_{kt}) = c_0 \sum Y_t + c_1 \sum (Y_t X_{1t}) + \cdots + c_{k-1} \sum (Y_t X_{(k-1)t}).$$

The reader is encouraged to convince himself of this proposition by working through an example of a multiple-regression model with three independent variables.

But this means that the $(k + 1)$th normal equation is not an independent equation; it is a linear combination of the first (k) equations. We want to derive estimators for the $(k + 1)$ parameters (namely, $\hat{b}_0, \hat{b}_1, \ldots, \hat{b}_k$), but we have only k independent equations. Consequently, we cannot in general solve uniquely for our estimators of the parameters. More intuitively, our problem is that since one of our independent variables is in effect always a weighted sum of the values of the other independent variables, we are unable to separate its influence on the dependent variable from that of the others.

It is the case, however, that we can estimate the combined effects of such variables. For instance, if we substitute (4.13) into (4.3), we obtain

$$Y_t = (b_0 + b_k c_0) + (b_1 + b_k c_1)X_{1t} + \cdots$$

$$+ (b_{k-1} + b_k c_{k-1})X_{(k-1)t} + u_t \qquad (4.14)$$

$$= d_0 + d_1 X_{1t} + \cdots + d_{k-1}X_{(k-1)t} + u_t,$$

where, in general, $d_i = (b_i + b_k c_i)$. In equation (4.14), we have only k parameters, namely, $d_0, d_1, \ldots, d_{k-1}$. If there are no other relationships of the sort (4.13), we have k regressors that satisfy our fifth assumption. In brief, we can now derive, and solve uniquely, k independent normal equations involving the estimators $\hat{d}_0, \hat{d}_1, \ldots, \hat{d}_{k-1}$.

Since $d_i = (b_i + b_k c_i)$, we cannot treat our estimator of d_i as an estimator of b_i; we are in general unable to estimate the effect of X_i on Y. There is one exception to this: the case where $c_i = 0$. For example, if $c_5 = 0$, then $d_5 = b_5$ so that we can treat our estimator of d_5 as an estimator of the value of b_5. In terms of (4.13), we can see that a particular c_i is zero if the value of X_k does not depend on the value of X_i.

In general, we cannot estimate the coefficient of a "degenerate" regressor, such as X_{kt}, which is a linear combination of the other regressors. But we can estimate the coefficients of some of the other independent variables in the regression equation. For example, if

$$X_{2t} = 3 - 17X_{1t} + 8X_{5t},$$

then except for $c_0 = 3$, $c_1 = -17$, and $c_5 = 8$, all of the c_i's $= 0$. Consequently, all of the original b_i's, except b_0, b_1, b_2, and b_5, can be estimated. In conclusion, we urge the reader *not* to memorize this result, but rather to learn the technique we have derived: if one (or more) of the regressors is linearly related to some of the others, simply use the linear relationships to substitute out the "degenerate" regressors and then estimate the parameters of the reduced regression model. Finally, determine which parameters of the original regression model may be estimated by comparing the parameters of the original regression model to those of the reduced regression equation.

4.3 PROPERTIES OF THE ESTIMATORS AND HYPOTHESIS TESTING

AN INTERPRETATION OF THE ESTIMATORS*

As we have stressed throughout this chapter, to estimate the effect of a particular independent variable, such as X_k on Y, we must separate out, or account for, the effects of the other independent variables. Only then can we isolate the impact of X_k on Y. Although it is not immediately clear from our earlier set of normal equations, this is exactly what our estimation procedure does. In the Appendix to this chapter, which we strongly encourage the reader to work through at some point, we use an alternative approach to derive the expressions for the estimators, $\hat{b}_i$. With this technique, you can see clearly just how our estimation procedure accomplishes this sorting out of the effects of the different independent variables. In addition, with the explicit expressions for the estimators given in the Appendix, it is easy to show that, like the two-variable case, these estimators are unbiased.

At this point, however, we shall simply provide a brief and highly intuitive discussion of what we show in the Appendix. Suppose that we undertake to estimate in equation (4.3) the effect, other things equal, that a unit change in X_k has on Y, or, in other words, to estimate the value of b_k.

We know that b_k will be unestimable if X_k is a linear combination of the other X's. Let us assume that X_k is not such a linear combination. This, however, does not imply that X_k is totally unrelated to the other regressors. For instance, in a consumption function, X_k might be liquid assets and X_1 might be disposable income. If so, we would certainly expect X_k to be positively related to X_1; however, like the height and weight of a person, these two variables should not be perfectly related.**

Generalizing a bit, in our regression model (4.3), X_k might be related, though not perfectly, to some or all of the regressors. If so, this suggests that we could, at least partially, explain the value of X_k in terms of the values of the other regressors. Suppose we tried to do this with a linear regression equation relating X_k to the other regressors:

$$X_{kt} = c_0 + c_1 X_{1t} + \cdots + c_{k-1} X_{(k-1)t} + v_{kt}, \qquad (4.15)$$

where v_{kt} is some disturbance term. Suppose also that we estimate the parameters, $c_0, \ldots, c_{k-1}$ of (4.15) by our instrumental-variable technique† and obtain as our estimators $\hat{c}_0, \hat{c}_1, \ldots, \hat{c}_{k-1}$. Using these estimators, our

---

* This is a difficult section. Aside from an understanding of formula (4.19), the other material in this section can be omitted on a first reading without loss of continuity.

** In a sense, the liquid assets of a person are not completely determined by his income. For example, two people may have the same income, but different liquid assets.

† Our normal equations would be generated by setting

$$\sum \hat{v}_{kt} = 0, \sum (\hat{v}_{kt} X_{1t}) = 0, \ldots, \sum (\hat{v}_{kt} X_{k-1}) = 0.$$

explained (or calculated) value of X_k corresponding to $X_1, \ldots, X_{k-1}$ would be

$$\hat{X}_{kt} = \hat{c}_0 + \hat{c}_1 X_{1t} + \cdots + \hat{c}_{k-1} X_{(k-1)t}. \qquad (4.16)$$

Since we have assumed that X_{kt} is not a *perfect* linear combination of the other regressors, we know that in general $X_{kt} \neq \hat{X}_{kt}$. We can therefore express X_{kt} as

$$X_{kt} = \hat{X}_{kt} + \hat{v}_{kt}, \qquad (4.17)$$

where $\hat{v}_{kt}$ is that part of X_{kt} which the other independent variables cannot account for: $\hat{v}_{kt} = X_{kt} - \hat{X}_{kt}$. The term $\hat{v}_k$ is often called the *residual* in the regression relating X_k to $X_1, \ldots, X_{k-1}$.

As one might guess, $\hat{v}_{kt}$ is crucial to the estimation of b_k, because it represents that part of X_{kt} which, in a sense, is independent of the other regressors. For instance, from (4.17) and (4.16), we see that if $\hat{v}_{kt} = 0$, we would have perfect multicollinearity, and b_k would be unestimable. It turns out, as is shown in the Appendix, that we can express our estimator of b_k as

$$\hat{b}_k = \frac{\sum (\hat{v}_{kt} Y_t)}{\sum \hat{v}_{kt}{}^2} = \frac{\sum (X_{kt} - \hat{X}_{kt}) Y_t}{\sum (X_{kt} - \hat{X}_{kt})^2}. \qquad (4.18)$$

That is, the solution of our normal equations for $\hat{b}_k$ can be expressed as (4.18). Note that the values of the residual $\hat{v}_k$ depend only on the values of X_1 through X_k and thus are observable. A similar relationship holds for our other estimators. Specifically, we show in the Appendix that

$$\hat{b}_i = \frac{\sum (\hat{v}_{it} Y_t)}{\sum \hat{v}_{it}{}^2} = \frac{\sum (X_{it} - \hat{X}_{it}) Y_t}{\sum (X_{it} - \hat{X}_{it})^2}, \qquad i = 1, \ldots, k, \qquad (4.19)$$

where $\hat{v}_{it}$ is the residual in the regression of X_i on all of the other regressors.* In brief, our estimator, $\hat{b}_i$, depends only on that part of X_i, namely, $\hat{v}_i$, which is *not linearly associated with the other regressors*. Alternatively, our estimator $\hat{b}_i$ can be obtained by using only that part of X_i which is not perfectly multicollinear with the other regressors.

Now let $\hat{Y}_{ti}$ be that part of Y_t which is perfectly multicollinear with all

---

* Note the similarity between the formula for $\hat{b}$ in the two-variable case and that for $\hat{b}_i$ in (4.19). In the two-variable model in Chapter 2, we showed that

$$\hat{b} = \frac{\sum (X_t - \bar{X}) Y_t}{\sum (X_t - \bar{X})^2}.$$

As an exercise, the reader should demonstrate that this formula for $\hat{b}$ from the bivariate model is simply a special case of (4.19). That is, in the bivariate case $\hat{X}_t = \bar{X}$. (Hint: in the bivariate case, the equation corresponding to (4.15) would be $X_t = c + v_t$.)

of the regressors *except* X_{it}.* Then $(Y_t - \hat{Y}_{ti})$ would be that part of Y_t which is not multicollinear with these regressors. We note next that, since $\hat{v}_{it}$ in (4.19) is such that

$$\sum \hat{v}_{it} = 0, \quad \sum (\hat{v}_i X_{jt}) = 0, \quad j \neq i, \tag{4.20}$$

we must have

$$\sum (\hat{v}_{it} \hat{Y}_{ti}) = 0. \tag{4.21}$$

It follows from (4.21) that, since $Y_t = \hat{Y}_{ti} + (Y_t - \hat{Y}_{ti})$, we can express our estimator. $\hat{b}_i$, in (4.19) as

$$\hat{b}_i = \frac{\sum \hat{v}_{it}(Y_t - \hat{Y}_{ti})}{\sum \hat{v}_{it}^2} = \frac{\sum (X_{it} - \hat{X}_{it})(Y_t - \hat{Y}_{ti})}{\sum (X_{it} - \hat{X}_{it})^2}. \tag{4.22}$$

It should now be clear just how our procedure "separates" the effects that the various regressors have on the dependent variable, Y_t. The estimator $\hat{b}_i$ in (4.22) depends only on the values of X_{it} and Y_t *after* the linear influence of all of the other regressors has been subtracted out of *both* variables! Somewhat intuitively, our procedure reduces a multivariate case to a bivariate case by subtracting out the influence of the "other variables."

THE VARIANCES OF THE ESTIMATORS

You should work through the derivation of (4.19) in the Appendix to this chapter. In particular, the more formal treatment there allows us, first, to show that $\hat{b}_i$ is an unbiased estimator of b_i (that is, that $E(\hat{b}_i) = b_i$). Second, we develop expressions for the conditional variances of the $\hat{b}_i$. More specifically, we show that

$$\text{var}(\hat{b}_i) = \sigma_{\hat{b}_i}^2 = \frac{\sigma_u^2}{\sum \hat{v}_{it}^2}, \quad \text{for } i = 1, 2, \ldots, k, \tag{4.23}$$

where σ_u^2 is the variance of the disturbance term in the original multiple-regression equation (4.3).**

---

* This could be obtained by regressing Y_t on all of the regressors with the exception of X_{it}, and then calculating its predicted value. For example, we would consider the regression model

$$Y_t = \gamma_0 + \gamma_1 X_{1t} + \cdots + \gamma_{i-1} X_{(i-1)t} + \gamma_{i+1} X_{(i+1)t} + \cdots + \gamma_k X_{kt} + w_t,$$

where w_t is some disturbance term. Then, using our instrumental-variable technique, we would obtain $\hat{\gamma}_0, \hat{\gamma}_1, \ldots, \hat{\gamma}_{(i-1)}, \hat{\gamma}_{(i+1)}, \ldots, \hat{\gamma}_k$ and then

$$\hat{Y}_{ti} = \hat{\gamma}_0 + \hat{\gamma}_1 X_{1t} + \cdots + \hat{\gamma}_{i-1} X_{(i-1)t} + \hat{\gamma}_{i+1} X_{(i+1)t} + \cdots + \hat{\gamma}_k X_{kt}.$$

** Once again, note the similarity between the expressions for the variance of b in the two-variable case and $\hat{b}_i$ in the multiple-regression equation. The difference again is that the term $\sum (X_t - \bar{X})^2$ in the denominator of the expression for the variance of b in the two-variable model is replaced by $\sum \hat{v}_{it}^2 = \sum (X_{it} - \hat{X}_{it})^2$.

CONFIDENCE INTERVALS AND THE TESTING OF HYPOTHESES:
SOME PRELIMINARIES

If we continue to assume, as we did in the two-variable case, that the disturbance terms are normally distributed, it will then be true that, given the values of the regressors, each of the estimators, $\hat{b}_i$, is normally distributed. This follows because each $\hat{b}_i$ is a linear combination of the disturbance terms, and, as we discussed in Chapter 3, linear combinations of normal variables are themselves normally distributed. Our results may be drawn together, symbolically, as*

$$\hat{b}_i \quad \text{is} \quad N(b_i, \sigma_{b_i}^2), \qquad i = 0, 1, \ldots, k, \tag{4.24}$$

where

$$\sigma_{b_i}^2 = \frac{\sigma_u^2}{\sum \hat{v}_{it}^2}.$$

Our remaining difficulty is that we cannot determine the variances of the estimators because in general σ_u^2 will be unknown. We need to construct an estimator of σ_u^2 from our sample of observations. Since σ_u^2 is actually the mean of u_t^2,

$$\sigma_u^2 = E[u_t^2],$$

it would make sense, if we knew the values of the b_i, to take as our estimator of σ_u^2 the sample average:

$$\frac{\sum u_t^2}{n} = \frac{\sum (Y_t - b_0 - b_1 X_{1t} - \cdots - b_k X_{kt})^2}{n}. \tag{4.25}$$

Unfortunately, we do not know the values of the coefficients, but we do have estimators for them. We can replace each of the b_i in (4.25) by its estimator and obtain as an estimator for the variance of the disturbance term:

$$\hat{\sigma}_u^2 = \frac{\sum_{t=1}^{n}(Y_t - \hat{b}_0 - \hat{b}_1 X_{1t} - \cdots - \hat{b}_k X_{kt})^2}{n - (k + 1)}. \tag{4.26}$$

Note that the denominator in (4.26) is $[n - (k + 1)]$; this reflects the loss of $(k + 1)$ degrees of freedom in the numerator that results from the estimation of $(k + 1)$ parameters. As in the two-variable case, it is again true that

$$E(\hat{\sigma}_u^2) = \sigma_u^2.$$

---

*The regressor corresponding to b_0 is $X_{0t} \equiv 1$, $t = 1, 2, \ldots, n$. Therefore $\hat{v}_{0t}$ would be the residual in the regression of X_{0t} on all of the other regressors $X_{1t}, \ldots, X_{kt}$:

$$X_{0t} = e_1 X_{1t} + e_2 X_{2t} + \cdots + e_k X_{kt} + v_{0t}.$$

Note that this regression equation does not include a constant term because the constant term is the dependent variable. In contrast, the regression equations defining the other v_{it}'s, such as (4.15), do contain constant terms, because one of the variable regressors is the dependent variable. In brief, X_{0t} should be looked upon as just another regressor.

Our estimator in (4.26) is unbiased. Using (4.26), we can estimate the variance of each $\hat{b}_i$ by

$$\hat{\sigma}_{\hat{b}_i}^2 = \frac{\hat{\sigma}_u^2}{\sum \hat{v}_i^2} . \qquad (4.27)$$

CONFIDENCE INTERVALS AND THE TESTING OF HYPOTHESES

We are now in a position to construct confidence intervals for the individual coefficients. Using our results from Chapter 3, we note that since $\hat{b}_i$ is normal [$\hat{b}_i$ is $N(b_i, \sigma_{\hat{b}_i}^2)$], we have that

$$\frac{\hat{b}_i - b_i}{\sigma_{\hat{b}_i}}$$

is $N(0, 1)$. Then, exactly as in the two-variable case, confidence intervals may be established and hypotheses may be tested in terms of the normal curve if σ_u^2, and hence $\sigma_{\hat{b}_i}^2$, is known. For instance, the reader should prove to himself that a 95 percent confidence interval for b_i, based on the normal curve, is

$$\hat{b}_i \pm 1.96\sigma_{\hat{b}_i}.$$

As in the two-variable case, σ_u^2 is typically not known and so must be estimated. Consequently, we generally establish confidence intervals or generate t ratios to test hypotheses in terms of the t distribution. To do this, we note that

$$\frac{\hat{b}_i - b_i}{\hat{\sigma}_{\hat{b}_i}} \qquad (4.28)$$

is a t variable with $(n - k - 1)$ degrees of freedom. Note that the degrees of freedom of the t variable in (4.28) is always equal to the denominator of the variance estimator in (4.26). As a point of comparison, recall that in the two-variable case $k = 1$ and so, with two parameters to estimate, we had a t distribution with $(n - 2)$ degrees of freedom.

Using (4.28) we can adopt precisely the same procedure we developed in Chapter 3 to test hypotheses concerning any of the individual coefficients. For example, suppose we have the following model:

$$Y_t = b_0 + b_1 X_{1t} + \cdots + b_9 X_{9t} + u_t, \qquad t = 1, \ldots, 25, \qquad (4.29)$$

and wish to test, with a Type 1 error of size 0.05, the hypotheses

$$H_0 \colon b_3 = 0,$$
$$H_1 \colon b_3 \neq 0,$$

where we have a sample of 25 observations.

In this problem we have $n = 25$ and $k = 9$, so

$$\frac{\hat{b}_3 - b_3}{\hat{\sigma}_{\hat{b}_3}}$$

would be a t variable with $(25 - 9 - 1 = 15)$ degrees of freedom. We find in Statistical Table 2 for the t distribution that a 95 percent confidence interval for b_3 would be

$$(\hat{b}_3 \pm 2.131\hat{\sigma}_{\hat{b}_3}). \tag{4.30}$$

Continuing as we did in Chapter 3, we would now use our sample to evaluate $\hat{b}_3$ and $\hat{\sigma}_{\hat{b}_3}$, substitute these values into (4.30), and then see whether or not the resulting interval covers our hypothesized value of zero. If it does, we would accept H_0; if it does not, we would reject it. Alternatively, we could simply evaluate the t ratio and, following our rule of thumb, compare its absolute value to 2. In this case, of course, the exact cut-off value would be 2.131. In any event, it should be clear that, once we are given a result such as (4.28), problems concerning hypothesis testing and confidence intervals are solved in exactly the same manner in the multiple-regression case as they were in the bivariate-regression case.

4.4 THE COEFFICIENT OF MULTIPLE DETERMINATION

In the preceding sections we constructed techniques for estimating and for testing hypotheses concerning the individual coefficients in the multiple-regression model. There remains the further issue of the explanatory power of the regression equation as a whole. What portion of the variation in the dependent variable can be explained by all the independent variables taken together?

R^2 FOR THE MULTIVARIATE CASE

We developed such a measure, R^2, for the two-variable case in Chapter 2. Recall that R^2 possessed a value between zero and unity that indicated the fraction of the variation in Y that could be accounted for by the est··.ated regression equation. Following a similar procedure here, we shall show that the same formula for R^2 with the same interpretation is also applicable to multiple-regression analysis.

Consider our basic multiple-regression model

$$Y_t = b_0 + b_1 X_{1t} + \cdots + b_k X_{kt} + u_t. \tag{4.31}$$

We noted earlier that if (4.31) is estimated by our instrumental-variable technique, Y_t can be expressed as

$$Y_t = \hat{Y}_t + \hat{u}_t, \tag{4.32}$$

where

$$\hat{Y}_t = \hat{b}_0 + \hat{b}_1 X_{1t} + \cdots + \hat{b}_k X_{kt}, \tag{4.33}$$

and $\hat{u}_t$ is such that

$$\sum \hat{u}_t = 0, \qquad \sum (\hat{u}_t X_{it}) = 0, \qquad i = 1, \ldots, k. \tag{4.34}$$

Now sum (4.32) over our sample to obtain

$$\sum Y_t = \sum \hat{Y}_t + \sum \hat{u}_t. \tag{4.35}$$

Since $\sum \hat{u}_t = 0$, we have, as in the bivariate-regression case,

$$\sum Y_t = \sum \hat{Y}_t. \tag{4.36}$$

Dividing through (4.36) by n indicates that the sample average of Y_t is equal to the sample average of $\hat{Y}_t$:

$$\bar{Y} = \bar{\hat{Y}}. \tag{4.37}$$

Return to (4.32) and square both sides of the equation:

$$Y_t^2 = \hat{Y}_t^2 + \hat{u}_t^2 + 2\hat{Y}_t\hat{u}_t. \tag{4.38}$$

Summing over the sample, we obtain

$$\sum Y_t^2 = \sum \hat{Y}_t^2 + \sum \hat{u}_t^2 + 2 \sum (\hat{Y}_t\hat{u}_t). \tag{4.39}$$

The last term in (4.39) is equal to zero; to see this note that

$$\sum (\hat{u}_t\hat{Y}_t) = \sum \hat{u}_t(\hat{b}_0 + \hat{b}_1 X_{1t} + \cdots + \hat{b}_k X_{kt})$$

$$= \hat{b}_0 \sum \hat{u}_t + \hat{b}_1 \sum (\hat{u}_t X_{1t}) + \cdots + \hat{b}_k \sum (\hat{u}_t X_{kt}) = 0,$$

in light of (4.34). Equation (4.39) thus simplifies to

$$\sum Y_t^2 = \sum \hat{Y}_t^2 + \sum \hat{u}_t^2. \tag{4.40}$$

We next subtract $n\bar{Y}^2$ from each side of (4.40):

$$\sum Y_t^2 - n\bar{Y}^2 = (\sum \hat{Y}_t^2 - n\bar{Y}^2) + \sum \hat{u}_t^2. \tag{4.41}$$

Recalling from (4.37) that $\bar{Y} = \bar{\hat{Y}}$, we can express (4.41) as*

$$\sum (Y_t - \bar{Y})^2 = \sum (\hat{Y}_t - \bar{Y})^2 + \sum \hat{u}_t^2, \tag{4.42}$$

which is identical to the corresponding equation for the two-variable case derived in Chapter 2.

Remember that we described this relationship as

$$\text{TSS} = \text{RSS} + \text{ESS}, \tag{4.43}$$

where $\text{TSS} = \sum (Y_t - \bar{Y})^2$, $\text{RSS} = \sum (\hat{Y}_t - \bar{Y})^2$, and $\text{ESS} = \sum \hat{u}_t^2$. The total sum of squares (TSS) is the variation of the dependent variable about its sample average, which we seek to explain with our regression equation. That is, our regression model is supposed to tell us why Y_t is not constant. That part the equation cannot explain is the error sum of squares (ESS); the

---

* We use here a proposition from Appendix A to Chapter 1, which says that for any variable Z_t,

$$\sum (Z_t - \bar{Z})^2 = \sum Z_t^2 - n\bar{Z}^2.$$

difference then between the TSS and ESS must be the part the regression equation can account for, namely RSS, the regression sum of squares.

As in the two-variable case, we use as our measure of the explanatory power of the regression equation the fraction of the variation in the observed values of Y that the estimated regression equation can account for. We thus have

$$R^2 = 1 - \frac{ESS}{TSS} = \frac{RSS}{TSS} = \frac{\Sigma (\hat{Y}_t - \bar{Y})^2}{\Sigma (Y_t - \bar{Y})^2}, \qquad (4.44)$$

where R^2 is called the *coefficient of multiple determination*.

In review, if we have a perfect fit so that the calculated value of Y in every case equals its observed value, $Y_t = \hat{Y}_t$, each $\hat{u}_t$ would be zero and so ESS = 0; therefore RSS = TSS, and R^2 achieves its maximum value of unity. At the other extreme, where the estimated equation explains none of the variation of the dependent variable, ESS is as large as possible, which is to say ESS = TSS, so that RSS = 0 and hence $R^2 = 0$. The closer to unity is R^2, the greater the explanatory power of the estimated regression equation. Finally, although we do not present the proof (since it is identical to that for the two-variable case), we point out that R may again be shown to be nothing more than the estimator of the correlation coefficient between Y_t and $\hat{Y}_t$.

A COMMENT ON R^2

Since $R^2 = 1 - ESS/TSS$, it obviously depends upon both ESS and TSS. Of these two determinants of R^2, only ESS relates to the explanatory power of the model. TSS is simply a measure of the sample variation in the variable we seek to explain; it is in no way dependent upon the characteristics of the model used to explain Y_t. Thus, R^2 relates to the explanatory power of the model because ESS does.

Consider now the case in which there are two researchers who wish to explain the n values of Y_t, $t = 1, \ldots, n$. Suppose researcher 1 considers the model (4.31), and researcher 2 considers the model

$$Y_t = b_0 + b_1 X_{1t} + \cdots + b_k X_{kt} + b_{k+1} X_{k+1,t} + \cdots + b_{k+r} X_{k+r,t} + u_t. \quad (4.45)$$

That is, researcher 2 includes in his model all of the regressors considered by researcher 1 and then some—namely $X_{k+1,t}, \ldots, X_{k+r,t}$. Let ESS_1 and ESS_2 be, respectively, the error sum of squares obtained by researchers 1 and 2. Then as we will demonstrate below

$$ESS_2 \leq ESS_1, \qquad (4.46)$$

whether or not the additional regressors considered by researcher 2 are relevant! Let R_1^2 and R_2^2 be the coefficients of determination obtained by researchers 1 and 2, respectively. Since $R_1^2 = 1 - ESS_1/TSS$ and $R_2^2 = 1 - ESS_2/TSS$, it follows from (4.46) that

$$R_1^2 \leq R_2^2. \qquad (4.47)$$

Again (4.47) holds whether or not the additional regressors are relevant. The inequalities in (4.46) and in (4.47) will *always* hold; we note, however, that it will typically be the case in practice, that unless $ESS_1 = 0$ and $R_1^2 = 1$,

$$ESS_2 < ESS_1 \quad \text{and} \quad R_2^2 > R_1^2. \tag{4.48}$$

The results described above indicate that the R^2 statistic will typically increase, and never decrease, if additional variables are added to the model whether or not those additional variables are relevant. The reason for this is as follows. In the appendix to Chapter 2, we showed that in the bivariate regression model, our instrumental-variable estimators are identical to the least-squares estimators. This equivalence also holds in the multiple-regression case. That is, our instrumental-variable estimators of the coefficients of a linear multiple-regression model are identical to the estimators which would be obtained by the least-squares approach.

Let $\hat{b}_0, \ldots, \hat{b}_k$ be the estimates of the regression coefficients obtained by researcher 1. Then these estimates are such that the error sum of squares

$$ESS_1 = \sum_{t=1}^{N} (Y_t - \hat{b}_0 - \hat{b}_1 X_{1t} - \cdots - \hat{b}_k X_{kt})^2 \tag{4.49}$$

is as small as possible. This follows from the equivalence of our instrumental-variable and the least-squares procedures. Now let $\tilde{b}_0, \ldots, \tilde{b}_k, \tilde{b}_{k+1}, \ldots, \tilde{b}_{k+r}$ be the estimates obtained by researcher 2. Then again by the equivalence to the least-squares procedure, these estimates are such that ESS_2 is as small as possible when

$$ESS_2 = \sum_{t=1}^{N} (Y_t - \tilde{b}_0 - \cdots - \tilde{b}_k X_{kt} - \tilde{b}_{k+1} X_{k+1,t} - \cdots - \tilde{b}_{k+r} X_{k+r,t})^2. \tag{4.50}$$

The reason that ESS_2 will never exceed ESS_1 is that one possible set of values $\tilde{b}_0, \ldots, \tilde{b}_{k+r}$ is

$$\begin{aligned} \tilde{b}_i &= \hat{b}_i, \quad i = 0, \ldots, k \\ \tilde{b}_{k+j} &= 0, \quad j = 1, \ldots, r. \end{aligned} \tag{4.51}$$

In this case ESS_2 would be equal to ESS_1. It follows that the explanatory power of model two as measured by R^2 could never be less than that of model one. Typically, however, other values for $\tilde{b}_1, \ldots, \tilde{b}_{k+r}$ will be obtained and so $ESS_2 < ESS_1$ and, correspondingly, $R_2^2 > R_1^2$.

AN ADJUSTED COEFFICIENT OF DETERMINATION: $\bar{R}^2$

Researchers often wish to compare their models in terms of various measures of the "goodness" of the model. Our discussion suggests that if the R^2 statistic is taken to be one such measure, caution is in order. If the R^2 statistic will never decrease, and indeed will typically increase, when additional variables are added to the model (whether or not they are relevant), a researcher can produce a superior model by this measure simply by adding additional regressors!

The difficulty with the R^2 statistic is that there is, in a sense, no penalty for increasing the number of independent variables used to explain the dependent variable. For this reason, an adjusted form of the R^2 statistic is sometimes used. This form, so to speak, incorporates such a penalty.

The adjusted coefficient of determination is often called the "R-bar squared" statistic and is denoted as $\bar{R}^2$. In general, suppose we consider a linear regression model that has an intercept term and that has p regression coefficients in total; for example, for (4.31), we have $p = k + 1$, and for (4.45) we have $p = k + r + 1$. Then, the adjusted coefficient of determination is

$$\bar{R}^2 = 1 - \frac{\text{ESS}/(n - p)}{\text{TSS}/(n - 1)} \tag{4.52}$$

where n is the sample size, and ESS and TSS are again the error and total sums of squares for the model under consideration.*

$\bar{R}^2$ could increase, stay the same, or decrease if additional regressors are added to the model. The reason for this is that such additional regressors will typically decrease ESS, but they will also decrease $n - p$. Therefore, the direction of change of $\text{ESS}/(n - p)$ is not predictable, and so neither is the direction of change of $\bar{R}^2$.

Researchers often feel that if an "important" variable, or set of variables, is added to the model, the reduction in ESS will more than outweigh the reduction in $(n - p)$ and so $\bar{R}^2$ will increase. For certain intuitive notions of "importance," this will undoubtedly be the case. However, we stress that this is not a formal result, and counterexamples can be produced. For instance, in (4.45) suppose $r = 1$ and that $X_{k+1,t}$ is "important" because its coefficient $b_{k+1} \neq 0$. In this case the dependent variable, Y_t, actually depends upon $X_{k+1,t}$ (along with the other regressors). Despite this "importance," it could still turn out that $\bar{R}_2^2 < \bar{R}_1^2$, where $\bar{R}_2^2$ is the adjusted coefficient of determination corresponding to (4.45), and $\bar{R}_1^2$ corresponds to (4.31).

Since many researchers feel that $\bar{R}^2$ will increase if "important" variables are added to a model, but will decrease if "unimportant" variables are added, the $\bar{R}^2$ statistic is often used to compare models. For example, suppose the models under consideration are (4.45) and (4.31). Then, some researchers will take the "true" or "preferred" model to be the one with the higher $\bar{R}^2$.

We stress that while this procedure has intuitive appeal, it does not have a formal basis; we do not, therefore, recommend its use. The reason for this is that such comparisons are a form of test of the truth or validity of one model versus the other. The properties of this test, such as its Type 1 and Type 2 errors, are not known. Therefore, in effect, researchers who evaluate models

---

* In light of (4.52) and (4.44), it can be shown that $\bar{R}^2 \leq R^2$. If $R^2 = 1$, then $\bar{R}^2 = R^2$. But if $R^2 < 1$ and if $p \geq 2$, then $\bar{R}^2 < R^2$. For the interested reader, we provide a formal proof of these results in Appendix B to this chapter.

in terms of the $\bar{R}^2$ statistic in this straightforward manner are using a test whose properties are unknown.

The appropriate test procedure for evaluating (4.45) relative to (4.31) is as follows. First, consider the case in which $r = 1$. In this case the null hypothesis of interest is $H_0 : b_{k+1} = 0$. Clearly, if $b_{k+1} = 0$, then (4.31) is correctly specified; if $b_{k+1} \neq 0$ then (4.31) is not correctly specified but (4.45) is. Suppose for ease of presentation, that the alternative is $H_1 : b_{k+1} \neq 0$. Finally, suppose we wish to have a Type 1 error of 0.05. Then, given our typical modeling assumptions as described in Section 4.1, H_0 would be rejected in favor of H_1 if $|\hat{b}_{k+1}/\hat{\sigma}_{\hat{b}_{k+1}}| > t_{n-k-2;0.975}$ where $\hat{b}_{k+1}$ is our instrumental-variable estimator of b_{k+1}, and $\hat{\sigma}_{\hat{b}_{k+1}}$ is the corresponding estimator of the standard deviation of $\hat{b}_{k+1}$. This test procedure has already been discussed in Section 4.3.

Now consider the case in which $r > 1$. In this case the null hypothesis of interest is

$$H_0 : b_{k+1} = b_{k+2} = \cdots = b_{k+r} = 0. \tag{4.53}$$

Clearly, if H_0 in (4.53) is true, the model in (4.31) is correctly specified. A procedure for formally testing hypotheses of the form in (4.53) against a "two-tail" alternative is described in Appendix B to Chapter 5. Again, unlike the $\bar{R}^2$ test, the procedure described in Appendix B to Chapter 5 is such that the size of the Type 1 error can easily be set equal to a desired level—such as 0.05. The upshot of all this is that one model should not be preferred to another simply because it has a higher $\bar{R}^2$ statistic.

The reader may be puzzled as to why we have included a discussion of the adjusted coefficient of determination, $\bar{R}^2$, while recommending strongly against its use. The rationale for this discussion is twofold. First, many computerized regression programs print out values for both R^2 and $\bar{R}^2$. If we were to ignore $\bar{R}^2$, you might wonder what this strange statistic is. And, second, as we have indicated, some researchers compare the "goodness-of-fit" of their models by comparing the values of $\bar{R}^2$. We want to urge caution in accepting such a test, for as we have indicated, it does not have a sound formal basis.

As a final point, we note that there is a formal procedure for testing hypotheses of the sort described in (4.53) which is based on comparisons of $\bar{R}^2$ statistics; actually, there is also one based on comparison of R^2 statistics. However, both of these formal procedures turn out to be identical to the widely used procedures described in Appendix B to Chapter 5. Since the computational burdens of these tests are not less than the tests described in Appendix B, and since they do not offer additional insights, we will not describe them in this book.

4.5 MULTIPLE-REGRESSION ANALYSIS: TWO ILLUSTRATIONS

Having developed the principles of multiple-regression analysis, we shall now examine two actual multiple-regression studies to observe the technique in use and to interpret the results of these studies.

A MULTIVARIATE CONSUMPTION FUNCTION

In the beginning of this chapter we suggested that the level of consumption expenditure may depend on a number of variables in addition to the level of current income. Economists have in fact constructed a number of theories of consumption and have carried out extensive econometric tests of these theories. Albert Ando and Franco Modigliani, for example, have postulated a "life-cycle" theory of consumption in which they contend that the current level of consumption of an individual depends on the expected value of his future, lifetime stream of income.* As a simple operational test of this hypothesis, they suggest that

$$C_t = b_0 + b_1 Y_{dt} + b_2 A_{t-1} + u_t, \tag{4.54}$$

where current disposable labor income, Y_{dt}, serves as a proxy variable for expected income from labor services, and A_{t-1}, the net worth of consumers at the end of period $(t - 1)$, is a measure of expected nonlabor property income. That is, consumers enter the period t with A_{t-1}, which provides them with rental or interest income. Ando and Modigliani then set out to estimate the values of the coefficients in (4.54) with multiple-regression analysis. Using annual data on consumption expenditure, disposable labor income, and net worth, all measured in billions of current dollars for the years 1929–1959 (with the exclusion of the war years 1941–1945), they assemble 25 joint observations on these variables. With these time-series data they then employ the multiple-regression technique to estimate equation (4.54) and find that

$$\hat{C}_t = 5.33 \quad + 0.767 Y_{dt} + 0.047 A_{t-1} \qquad N = 25,$$
$$\quad (1.46) \quad (0.047) \quad (0.010) \qquad R^2 = 0.999. \tag{4.55}$$

(Note: the numbers in parentheses below the estimated coefficients are the respective standard errors.)

The first things we notice about the Ando-Modigliani results are that the estimated coefficients, as expected, are positive and that the estimated MPC from disposable labor income is between zero and unity. The estimated equation thus appears to be consistent with the postulated properties of consumption behavior.

Let us next note from (4.55) that, in all three cases, the parameter estimates exceed three times the estimates of the respective standard errors. From our rules of thumb concerning t ratios, this implies that, if any of the null hypotheses $b_0 = 0$, $b_1 = 0$, or $b_2 = 0$ had been considered against either a one- or two-tailed alternative, it would have been rejected at the usual 5 percent or 1 percent level of significance on the basis of the results in (4.55).

As a further illustration, suppose that we were to test the hypothesis that

---

* "The 'Life Cycle' Hypothesis of Saving: Aggregate Implications, and Tests," *American Economic Review*, 53 (March 1963), pp. 55–84.

b_1, the MPC from disposable labor income, equals one-half against a two-tailed alternative:

$$H_0 : b_1 = 0.5,$$

$$H_1 : b_1 \neq 0.5.$$

For 22 degrees of freedom and a 5 percent level of significance, we find in Statistical Table 2 that the critical value of t is 2.07; from (4.55) the calculated t ratio is

$$\frac{0.767 - 0.5}{0.047} = \frac{0.267}{0.047} = 5.7 > 2.07.$$

We would reject the null hypothesis at the 5 percent level on the basis of the results in (4.55).* When you have had a bit more practice with regression analysis, you will find that you can perform many of these tests almost by inspection. In the above case, for example, it is clear at a glance that $\hat{b}_1 = 0.767$ is easily more than two standard errors (2×0.047) away from the hypothesized value of $b_1 = 0.5$. Consequently, the hypothesis $b_1 = 0.5$ can be rejected without any involved calculations.

Finally, we note that the equation formulated by Ando and Modigliani has great explanatory power. With $R^2 = 0.999$, the two independent variables are able to account for over 99 percent of the variation in the observed values of consumption. If we accept the operational form of their theory, these empirical results appear to be consistent with their view of consumption behavior.

In interpreting these results, it is important to recognize that it is quite possible that the findings are consistent with other theories as well. While we can say that the empirical results are consistent with the theory, we cannot say, therefore, that all other theories of consumption are incorrect. This is why empirical work on a particular problem in economics is typically a continuing process in which evidence favorable to, or inconsistent with, a hypothesis accumulates; the empirical support for a hypothesis depends on the extent of the findings that are consistent with that hypothesis and, equally important, that are not consistent with competing hypotheses.

A STUDY OF CITY TAXATION

To conclude this chapter we shall examine another multiple-regression study, this time making use of cross-sectional data. In these days of critical urban problems, the mayors of most major cities are anxiously searching for sources of additional revenues with which to meet their rising budgets. The problem has become one largely of trying to levy new taxes or to raise the rates of existing taxes without doing significant damage to the city's econ-

---

* It should be clear that H_0 would also have been rejected at the 1 percent level of significance.

omy. In particular, it has been alleged by many observers that the high levels of tax rates in the cities have hastened the exodus of the middle class to the suburbs and have discouraged shoppers from purchasing goods and services in the cities. One of the major sources of revenues in many U.S. cities is a tax on retail sales; such taxes, it is argued, have led to a loss of retail sales in the city and have thereby contributed to the decline of the city's economy.

Is this true, and, if so, is it of significant quantitative importance? This is a difficult question to answer, but let us give some thought as to how we might use econometric analysis to get at the problem. If, in fact, higher sales-tax rates in central cities than in their respective suburbs do induce losses in sales in the city, we would expect to find, *other things equal*, that the larger the *differential* between the sales-tax rate of a given city and its suburban communities, the lower will be the level of retail sales per capita in the city. If we could obtain a sample of cities for which we could determine retail sales per capita and the size of this sales-tax differential, we could presumably regress the sales variable on the tax-differential variable and then examine the sign and magnitude of the coefficient estimate and carry out the appropriate tests.

While such an approach seems plausible enough, there is one problem inherent in this method that should make us feel uneasy. Our hypothesis is that, other things equal, a higher sales-tax differential should be associated with a lower level of sales, but within our sample of cities other things obviously are not equal. The level of retail sales in a particular city clearly depends on a number of other important variables besides taxes, variables such as the level of income and the relative size of the suburban population. For example, the wealthier are the city's residents, the higher should be the level of sales per capita; in addition, the larger is the suburban population, the more potential city shoppers there are and the higher should be the city's retail sales. Ideally, what we should like to do is to control for the effects of these other determinants of city sales so that we can then isolate or "separate out" the effects of the sales-tax differential.

This suggests that we should employ multiple-regression analysis. In particular, we could regress the sales variable on a set of independent variables that would include not only our tax variable, but also the other important determinants of city sales. Just such a study has been carried out by John Mikesell.* Mikesell postulates that

$$Y_t = b_0 + b_1 X_{1t} + b_2 X_{2t} + b_3 X_{3t} + b_4 X_{4t} + u_t, \qquad (4.56)$$

where

Y_t = retail sales per capita in the tth city,
X_{1t} = sales-tax differential for the tth city,
X_{2t} = per capita income in the tth city,

* "Central Cities and Sales Tax Rate Differentials: The Border City Problem," *National Tax Journal* 23 (June 1970), pp. 206–213.

X_{3t} = ratio of the city population to the population of the whole metropolitan area for city t, and

X_{4t} = area in square miles of the tth city.

The sales-tax differential variable is defined as

$$X_{1t} = \frac{1 + t_c}{1 + t_s},$$

where t_c is the sales-tax rate in the city and t_s is the average sales-tax rate in the surrounding suburban municipalities. An increase in the tth city's sales-tax rate with t_s unchanged will increase X_{1t} and would, according to equation (4.56), thereby induce a fall in city sales per capita, since we are assuming $b_1 < 0$.

Mikesell was able to assemble data for all these variables for a sample of 173 central cities and their respective suburbs in the United States. He then used these data to estimate (4.56) by the multiple-regression technique and found that

$$\hat{Y} = 4.5 - 7.44X_1 + 0.43X_2 - 0.11X_3 - 0.08X_4 \qquad N = 173,$$
$$(2.94) \quad (0.10) \quad (0.04) \quad (0.02) \qquad R^2 = 0.26, \tag{4.57}$$

where the numbers in parentheses are the corresponding estimated standard errors. We note immediately that the coefficient of the tax variable, X_1, has the anticipated negative sign and is well over twice the size of the corresponding standard error, which implies a t ratio in excess of 2. This suggests that there does in fact exist a negative association between city retail sales and the sales-tax differential in the sense that, at a 5 percent level of significance, we can reject the null hypothesis $b_1 = 0$ in favor of the alternative $b_1 < 0$. Note, moreover, that the estimate of b_1 suggests that the magnitude of the effect is typically quite sizable; an increase of one percentage point in the differential between city and suburban sales taxes is associated, *on average*, with approximately a 7 percent reduction in retail sales in the central city.*

We should also recognize that these results are a good deal more persuasive than would be a simple regression of city sales on the tax variable. With these

---

* Equation (4.56) is a slight simplification of Mikesell's results. In fact, he postulates a multiplicative relationship of the form

$$Y_t = b_0 X_{1t}{}^{b_1} X_{2t}{}^{b_2} X_{3t}{}^{b_3} X_{4t}{}^{b_4} e^{u_t},$$

so that, taking logs, we have

$$\ln Y_t = \ln b_0 + b_1 \ln X_{1t} + b_2 \ln X_{2t} + b_3 \ln X_{3t} + b_4 \ln X_{4t} + u_t.$$

We shall examine multiplicative relationships of this kind in the next chapter, but we note here that they are a straightforward generalization of our treatment in the preceding chapter of the log transformation.

multiple-regression results, Mikesell has explicitly accounted for the effects of per capita income, the city-suburban population ratio, and city area on sales. In other words, we can say that the effect of the tax variable on city retail sales has been measured with the effects of these other variables accounted for. Mikesell's results are thus consistent with the proposition that sales-tax differentials have induced significant reductions in retail sales in the central cities.

APPENDIX A.
Properties of the Estimators

The purposes of this appendix are to develop more rigorously the estimators, and their variances, for the regression coefficients, and then to prove that these estimators are unbiased. Moreover, as we showed intuitively in the text, the approach we shall use provides some additional insights into how multiple-regression analysis sorts out the effects of the different independent variables.

In the text we suggested that at least some of the independent variables of a regression model may be related, although not perfectly, to some or all of the others.

As in the text, we shall attempt to explain the last independent variable in terms of the others by way of the regression model:

$$X_{kt} = c_0 + c_1 X_{1t} + \cdots + c_{k-1} X_{(k-1)t} + v_{kt}. \tag{4A.1}$$

Suppose we estimate the parameters of (4A.1) by our instrumental-variable technique. To do so we would set $\sum \hat{v}_{kt} = 0$, $\sum (\hat{v}_{kt} X_{1t}) = 0, \ldots, \sum (\hat{v}_{kt} X_{(k-1)t}) = 0$ to get a set of normal equations:

$$\sum X_{kt} = n\hat{c}_0 + \hat{c}_1 \sum X_{1t} + \cdots + \hat{c}_{k-1} \sum X_{(k-1)t}$$

$$\sum (X_{kt} X_{1t}) = \hat{c}_0 \sum X_{1t} + \hat{c}_1 \sum X_{1t}^2 + \cdots + \hat{c}_{k-1} \sum (X_{1t} X_{(k-1)t}) \tag{4A.2}$$

$$\vdots$$

$$\sum (X_{kt} X_{(k-1)t}) = \hat{c}_0 \sum X_{(k-1)t} + \hat{c}_1 \sum (X_{1t} X_{(k-1)t}) + \cdots + \hat{c}_{(k-1)} \sum X_{(k-1)t}^2.$$

Note that in (4A.2) there are k unknowns: $\hat{c}_0, \hat{c}_1, \ldots, \hat{c}_{k-1}$, and k equations so that, given our assumptions, we can in general solve for the unknowns. This would enable us to construct

$$\hat{X}_{kt} = \hat{c}_0 + \hat{c}_1 X_{1t} + \cdots + \hat{c}_{k-1} X_{(k-1)t}. \tag{4A.3}$$

The estimator of v_{kt} would be

$$\hat{v}_{kt} = X_{kt} - \hat{X}_{kt}. \tag{4A.4}$$

Rearranging the terms in (4A.4), we have

$$X_{kt} = \hat{X}_{kt} + \hat{v}_{kt}. \tag{4A.5}$$

Note carefully what we have done to this point. We have separated the value of X_k into two components. The first part, $\hat{X}_{kt}$, is that part of X_k which is directly related to the other regressors; it is, in a sense, that part of the variation in X_k that can be accounted for by the other X's. In contrast, $\hat{v}_{kt}$ is that part of X_k that cannot be accounted for or "explained" by the other independent variables. Note again, that if $\hat{v}_{kt} = 0$ for all t, we would have perfect multicollinearity [see (4A.5) and (4A.3)] and b_k would be unestimable. For this reason, we might expect $\hat{v}_{kt}$ to play a crucial role in the estimation of b_k.

With this in mind, let us recall from the text of this chapter that we had $(k + 1)$ normal equations determining the $\hat{b}_i$, one of which was

$$\sum (Y_t X_{kt}) = \hat{b}_0 \sum X_{kt} + \hat{b}_1 \sum (X_{1t} X_{kt}) + \cdots + \hat{b}_k \sum X_{kt}^2. \tag{4A.6}$$

We know from (4A.5) that X_{kt} can be expressed as the sum of $\hat{X}_{kt}$ and $\hat{v}_{kt}$; we also know that $\sum \hat{v}_{kt} = 0$, $\sum (\hat{v}_{kt} X_{it}) = 0$, for $i = 1, 2, \ldots, (k - 1)$, and, therefore, since $\hat{X}_{kt}$ is a linear combination of $X_{1t}, X_{2t}, \ldots, X_{(k-1)t}$, [see (4A.3)] that $\sum (\hat{v}_{kt} \hat{X}_{kt}) = 0$. If we replace X_{kt} everywhere in (4A.6) by $(\hat{X}_{kt} + \hat{v}_{kt})$ and eliminate all terms that equal zero, we obtain

$$\sum (Y_t \hat{X}_{kt}) + \sum (Y_t \hat{v}_{kt})$$
$$= \hat{b}_0 \sum \hat{X}_{kt} + \hat{b}_1 \sum (X_{1t} \hat{X}_{kt}) + \cdots + \hat{b}_k \sum \hat{X}_{kt}^2 + \hat{b}_k \sum \hat{v}_{kt}^2. \tag{4A.7}$$

The sum of the first $(k + 1)$ terms on the right-hand side of (4A.7) is simply equal to $\sum (Y_t \hat{X}_{kt})$:

$$\sum (Y_t \hat{X}_{kt}) = \hat{b}_0 \sum \hat{X}_{kt} + \hat{b}_1 \sum (X_{1t} \hat{X}_{kt}) + \cdots + \hat{b}_k \sum \hat{X}_{kt}^2. \tag{4A.8}$$

To see this simply substitute

$$Y_t = \hat{b}_0 + \hat{b}_1 X_{1t} + \cdots + \hat{b}_k X_{kt} + \hat{u}_t$$

into the summation on the left-hand side of (4A.8) and note that

$$\sum (\hat{u}_t \hat{X}_{kt}) = \hat{c}_0 \sum \hat{u}_t + \hat{c}_1 \sum (\hat{u}_t X_{1t}) + \cdots + \hat{c}_{(k-1)} \sum (\hat{u}_t X_{(k-1)t}) = 0.$$

The reason for all this is that if we substitute (4A.8) into (4A.7), we obtain

$$\sum (Y_t \hat{v}_{kt}) = \hat{b}_k \sum \hat{v}_{kt}^2, \tag{4A.9}$$

and solving for $\hat{b}_k$:

$$\hat{b}_k = \frac{\sum (Y_t \hat{v}_{kt})}{\sum \hat{v}_{kt}^2}. \tag{4A.10}$$

In brief, $\hat{b}_k$ depends only on the Y_t's and the $\hat{v}_{kt}$'s, where the $\hat{v}_{kt}$ represent the "independent" variation in X_{kt}.

The generalization of (4A.10) is straightforward. In general,

$$\hat{b}_i = \frac{\sum (Y_t \hat{v}_{it})}{\sum \hat{v}_{it}^2}, \tag{4A.11}$$

where $\hat{v}_{it}$ is the residual in the regression of X_{it} on all the other X's. That is, the estimator of each b_i can be expressed in terms of the values of Y_t and the values of a term, $\hat{v}_{it}$, that represents the "independent" variation of the corresponding regressor, X_{it}.

UNBIASED ESTIMATORS

In the preceding section we showed that

$$\hat{b}_i = \frac{\sum (Y_t \hat{v}_{it})}{\sum \hat{v}_{it}^2}. \tag{4A.11}$$

In order to show that $\hat{b}_i$ is unbiased, we rewrite the basic model of the text (4.3) as

$$Y_t = b_0 + b_1 X_{1t} + \cdots + b_i (\hat{X}_{it} + \hat{v}_{it}) + \cdots + b_k X_{kt} + u_t, \tag{4A.12}$$

where $(\hat{X}_{it} + \hat{v}_{it})$ is substituted for X_{it}. Next, multiply (4A.12) by $\hat{v}_{it}$, sum over the n observations, and then substitute for $\sum (Y_t \hat{v}_{it})$ in (4A.11) to obtain

$$\hat{b}_i = b_i + \frac{\sum (\hat{v}_{it} u_t)}{\sum \hat{v}_{it}^2}. \tag{4A.13}$$

In obtaining (4A.13), we used the normal equation conditions $\sum \hat{v}_{it} = 0$, $\sum (\hat{v}_{it} X_{jt}) = 0$, if $j \neq i$, and, therefore, $\sum (\hat{v}_{it} \hat{X}_{it}) = 0$. Note that $\hat{v}_{it}$ does not depend on the values of u_t; $\hat{v}_{it}$ depends only on the given values of the X's. Since we are assuming that u_t is independent of the X's, for any given set of X's, the $\hat{v}_{it}$ would also be given and we would have

$$E(\hat{b}_i) = E(b_i) + E\left[\frac{\sum (\hat{v}_{it} u_t)}{\sum \hat{v}_{it}^2}\right]$$

$$= b_i + \left(\frac{\hat{v}_{i1}}{\sum \hat{v}_{it}^2}\right) E(u_1) + \cdots + \left(\frac{\hat{v}_{in}}{\sum \hat{v}_{it}^2}\right) E(u_n) \tag{4A.14}$$

$$= b_i.$$

Our estimator of b_i is unbiased.

VARIANCES OF THE ESTIMATORS

It is also a simple matter now to derive the conditional variance of $\hat{b}_i$ from (4A.13). Specifically, let us expand (4A.13) to get

$$\hat{b}_i = b_i + \left(\frac{\hat{v}_{i1}}{\sum \hat{v}_{it}^2}\right) u_1 + \left(\frac{\hat{v}_{i2}}{\sum \hat{v}_{it}^2}\right) u_2 + \cdots + \left(\frac{\hat{v}_{in}}{\sum \hat{v}_{it}^2}\right) u_n. \tag{4A.15}$$

Letting $M_{it} = \hat{v}_{it}/\sum \hat{v}_{it}^2$, we have

$$\hat{b}_i = b_i + M_{i1} u_1 + \cdots + M_{in} u_n. \tag{4A.16}$$

That is, $\hat{b}_i$ is a linear combination of the disturbance terms. Using the formula in Chapter 2 for the variance of a linear sum of uncorrelated random variables, we have

$$\text{var}(\hat{b}_i) = M_{i1}^2 \sigma_u^2 + M_{i2}^2 \sigma_u^2 + \cdots + M_{in}^2 \sigma_u^2. \tag{4A.17}$$

Let $A = \sum \hat{v}_{it}^2$. Then $M_{it}^2 = \hat{v}_{it}^2/A^2$. With this, (4A.17) can be rewritten as

$$\text{var}(\hat{b}_i) = \frac{\sigma_u^2}{A^2} (\hat{v}_{i1}^2 + \hat{v}_{i2}^2 + \cdots + \hat{v}_{in}^2)$$

$$= \frac{\sigma_u^2 (\sum \hat{v}_{it}^2)}{A^2} \tag{4A.18}$$

$$= \frac{\sigma_u^2}{A^2} A = \frac{\sigma_u^2}{A}.$$

In brief,

$$\text{var}(\hat{b}_i) = \frac{\sigma_u^2}{\sum \hat{v}_{it}^2}, \qquad \text{for } i = 1, \ldots, k. \tag{4A.19}$$

APPENDIX B.
The Relationship Between R^2 and $\bar{R}^2$

In the text, we indicated that $R^2 \geq \bar{R}^2$. Here we provide a proof of this proposition. Consider the linear regression model

$$Y_t = b_0 + b_1 X_{1t} + \cdots + b_k X_{kt} + u_t, \tag{4B.1}$$

which has an intercept term and k regressors so that the number of coefficients is $p = k + 1$. If we consider models for which $k \geq 1$, then $p \geq 2$. For such a model, let R^2 and $\bar{R}^2$ be, respectively, the coefficient of determination, and the adjusted coefficient of determination. Then, we will show below that

$$\bar{R}^2 < R^2 \tag{4B.2}$$

unless $R^2 = 1$, in which case $\bar{R}^2 = R^2 = 1$. Since, in practice, R^2 will typically be less than unity, the result in (4B.2) indicates that $\bar{R}^2$ will typically be less than R^2.

To obtain (4B.2), note from (4.52) that $\bar{R}^2$ can be expressed as

$$\bar{R}^2 = \left(1 - \frac{\text{ESS}}{\text{TSS}}\right) + \frac{\text{ESS}}{\text{TSS}} - \frac{\text{ESS}/(n-p)}{\text{TSS}/(n-1)}. \tag{4B.3}$$

Since $R^2 = 1 - \text{ESS}/\text{TSS}$, it follows that $\text{ESS}/\text{TSS} = 1 - R^2$. Also note that

$$\frac{\text{ESS}/(n-p)}{\text{TSS}/(n-1)} = \frac{\text{ESS}}{\text{TSS}}\left(\frac{n-1}{n-p}\right). \tag{4B.4}$$

It then follows from (4B.3) that $\bar{R}^2$ can be expressed as

$$
\begin{aligned}
\bar{R}^2 &= R^2 + \frac{\text{ESS}}{\text{TSS}} - \left(\frac{\text{ESS}}{\text{TSS}}\right)\left(\frac{n-1}{n-p}\right) \\
&= R^2 + \left(\frac{\text{ESS}}{\text{TSS}}\right)\left(1 - \frac{n-1}{n-p}\right) \\
&= R^2 + (1 - R^2)\left(1 - \frac{n-1}{n-p}\right) \\
&= R^2 + (1 - R^2)\left(\frac{n-p}{n-p} - \frac{n-1}{n-p}\right) \\
&= R^2 + (1 - R^2)\left(\frac{1-p}{n-p}\right) \\
&= R^2 - (1 - R^2)\left(\frac{p-1}{n-p}\right).
\end{aligned}
\tag{4B.5}
$$

Clearly, if $R^2 = 1$, $\bar{R}^2 = R^2$. If $R^2 < 1$ and $p \geq 2$ then $(1 - R^2)(p-1)/(n-p) > 0$. It then follows from the last line of (4.58) that $\bar{R}^2 < R^2$.

1. Consider the following regression model: $Y_t = a_0 + a_1 X_{1t} + a_2 X_{2t} + u_t$.

   a. List the standard assumptions underlying this model.
   b. Write out the normal equations and indicate the particular assumption corresponding to each equation.
   c. Suppose that in our sample, $n = 100$, and $\sum X_1 = \sum X_2 = \sum X_1 X_2 = 0$, and $\sum Y = 10$, $\sum (YX_1) = 30$, $\sum (YX_2) = 20$, $\sum X_1^2 = 35$, and $\sum X_2^2 = 3$. Estimate a_0, a_1, and a_2.

2. Consider the model $Y_t = a_0 + a_1 X_{1t} + a_2 X_{2t} + a_3(X_{1t} - X_{2t}) + a_4 X_{1t} X_{2t} + \varepsilon_t$. Under our standard assumptions, which parameters cannot be estimated? Why?

3. Consider the following regression model: $Y_t = b_0 + b_1 X_{1t} + b_2 X_{2t} + u_t$, where the observations on X_1, X_{2t}, and Y_t are

X_{1t}	X_{2t}	Y_t
1	2	7
2	1	8
1	3	5
3	1	6
1	2	4

Write out the normal equations.

4. It is said that middle- and upper-income families are leaving the cities because of relatively high taxes, high crime rates, high housing costs, and also because they desire "more space." Set up a regression model that could be used to test such a hypothesis. Explain the relative merits of cross-sectional and time-series data for testing these hypotheses.

5. Assume that $D_{1t} = a_0 + a_1 P_{1t} + a_2 P_{2t} + \cdots + a_k P_{kt} + b\bar{P}_t + cY_t + u_{1t}$, where D_{1t} is the demand for commodity 1, P_{1t} is the price of commodity 1, $P_{2t}, \ldots, P_{kt}$ are the prices of $(k - 1)$ other goods, $\bar{P}_t = \sum_{i=1}^{k} (P_{it})/k$ is the general price level, and Y_t is income. In brief, we believe that the demand for commodity 1 depends on its price, the price of other goods, the general price level, and income.

   a. Are any problems likely to arise in the estimation of the model?
   b. Can any of the parameters of the above model be estimated? Which ones? Demonstrate.

6. Consider the following model: $Y_t = b_0 + b_1 X_t + b_2 X_t^2 + \varepsilon_t$.

   a. Does the above equation have perfect multicollinearity?
   b. Suppose we have the following observations:

Y	-1	-1	2	4
X	0	1	2	5

   Write out the normal equations.

CHAPTER 5
Further Techniques in Multiple-Regression Analysis

In the preceding chapter we generalized the basic estimation technique for the two-variable regression model to the case of a multiplicity of independent variables. In this chapter we shall examine some additional techniques that can be employed in multiple-regression analysis. More specifically, we shall first extend our previous analysis of lagged variables to the multiple-regression case; in this connection we shall develop three methods for estimating various forms of lagged relationships. Second, we shall introduce the concept of "dummy" variables; such variables enable us to account for some of the qualitative influences that enter our economic relationships. For instance, the use of dummy variables may enable us to account for the effects of such things as racial or religious factors on certain types of behavior. This technique will allow us to incorporate into our analysis variables that we cannot normally measure in conventional quantitative terms. Lastly, we shall return to the issue of functional form and see how we can use multiple-regression analysis to estimate many different types of relationships.

5.1 THE ESTIMATION OF LAGGED RELATIONSHIPS

We showed in Chapter 3 that the two-variable model can be used to estimate equations in which the dependent variable depends on the value of the independent variable in an earlier period. For example, recall that we considered the case where consumption expenditure in a particular period depends on the level of disposable income in the preceding period; formally, we had

$$C_t = a + bY_{d(t-1)} + u_t. \tag{5.1}$$

There is no necessary reason, however, why current consumption should depend solely on disposable income in the immediately preceding period; levels of income in yet earlier periods, as well as in the current period, may also have some influence on consumption spending. If this is true, we could have a relationship of the form

$$C_t = a + b_0 Y_{dt} + b_1 Y_{d(t-1)} + \cdots + b_k Y_{d(t-k)} + u_t. \tag{5.2}$$

This type of relationship is called a *distributed lag*. This means that the value of the dependent variable at any given time depends on a weighted sum of past values of the independent variable. Somewhat intuitively, we may think of the dependent variable, in this case, C_t, as adjusting "sluggishly" to the current value of the independent variable, Y_{dt}, because of the "inertia" built up from the past (lagged) values of the independent variable.

An example of a formal model in which such a relationship between C_t and Y_{dt} might result is one in which consumption expenditures in time t are assumed to depend on the income expected in period $t + 1$, but where expected income, in turn, is determined as a weighted sum of levels of income in preceding periods. For instance, suppose that

$$C_t = a + b Y^e_{d(t+1)} + u_t, \tag{5.3}$$

where $Y^e_{d(t+1)}$ is the income expected in period $(t + 1)$. Suppose further that expected income is simply a weighted sum of current and past incomes:

$$Y^e_{d(t+1)} = \alpha_0 Y_{dt} + \alpha_1 Y_{d(t-1)} + \cdots + \alpha_k Y_{d(t-k)}. \tag{5.4}$$

Substituting (5.4) into (5.3) yields

$$C_t = a + b_0 Y_{dt} + b_1 Y_{d(t-1)} + \cdots + b_k Y_{d(t-k)} + u_t, \tag{5.5}$$

where $b_0 = b\alpha_0$, $b_1 = b\alpha_1$, and so on. Thus, C_t would respond sluggishly to Y_{dt}, because Y_{dt} is only one factor in the determination of $Y^e_{d(t+1)}$.

At any rate, we could in principle simply estimate equation (5.2) directly with our multiple-regression technique. Suppose that we postulate that current consumption expenditure depends on current income *and* on income in the preceding nine years; we would therefore have the equation

$$C_t = a + b_0 Y_{dt} + b_1 Y_{d(t-1)} + \cdots + b_9 Y_{d(t-9)} + u_t. \tag{5.6}$$

To estimate (5.6), we could have data in the form indicated in Table 5.1. Using the data for consumption and disposable income corresponding to the entries in Table 5.1, where each row is a joint observation, we could use the multiple-regression technique to obtain $\hat{a}, \hat{b}_0, \hat{b}_1, \ldots, \hat{b}_9$. That is, assuming we have the data described in Table 5.1, we could simply relabel, or define, $Y_{d(t-1)}$ as X_{1t}, $Y_{d(t-2)}$ as $X_{2t}, \ldots,$ and $Y_{d(t-9)}$ as X_{9t}, and then estimate the consumption function (5.6) as if it were an ordinary multiple-regression equation of the form

$$C_t = a + b_0 Y_{dt} + b_1 X_{1t} + b_2 X_{2t} + \cdots + b_9 X_{9t} + u_t. \tag{5.7}$$

Our observations on $X_{1t}, \ldots, X_{9t}$ are contained in Table 5.1.*

TABLE 5.1

C_t	Y_{dt}	$Y_{d(t-1)}$	$Y_{d(t-2)}$	$\cdots$	$Y_{d(t-9)}$
C_{1950}	$Y_{d(1950)}$	$Y_{d(1949)}$	$Y_{d(1948)}$	$\cdots$	$Y_{d(1941)}$
C_{1951}	$Y_{d(1951)}$	$Y_{d(1950)}$	$Y_{d(1949)}$	$\cdots$	$Y_{d(1942)}$
$\vdots$	$\vdots$	$\vdots$	$\vdots$	$\vdots$	$\vdots$
C_{1970}	$Y_{d(1970)}$	$Y_{d(1969)}$	$Y_{d(1968)}$	$\cdots$	$Y_{d(1961)}$

* The reader should convince himself, for example, that $X_{2(1951)} = Y_{d(1949)}$.

While this may well be an appropriate form of the relationship to estimate in some instances, it does present some problems. Recall from Chapter 3 that when we introduced a one-period lag into our two-variable relationship, we lost one observation. In the present case matters are worse because, for each additional lagged value of disposable income we include in equation (5.2), we lose yet another observation. For instance, suppose that we only had observed values for consumption and for disposable income for the ten years 1960 through 1969 and that we set out to estimate equation (5.6), in which consumption depends on current income and on income in the preceding nine years. In this case, we would lose nine of our ten observations! That is, the only year for which we would have observations for *all* of the variables appearing in (5.6) would be 1969:

$$C_{1969} = a + b_0 Y_{d(1969)} + b_1 Y_{d(1968)} + \cdots + b_9 Y_{d(1960)}. \qquad (5.8)$$

The relationship for consumption prior to 1969 would require data on disposable income prior to 1960, which would not be available. As a result, we would not have enough complete observations with which to estimate our regression equation.*

Another problem associated with the estimation of a model such as (5.6) is that if k is "large" (which would usually be taken to mean $k \geq 5$), there will be a large number of parameters to estimate. In addition, these parameters will correspond to variables that are strongly related to each other. As one might expect (and as we show formally in the next chapter), this makes it difficult to separate the effects of the various independent variables on the dependent variable. In other words, under these conditions, the variances of our estimators of the regression parameters will be large.

These are two basic problems associated with distributed-lag analysis. First, observations are lost due to the lags, and second, there are often too many parameters to estimate reliably. To deal with these problems, economists have developed models for distributed-lag analysis that either reduce the number of observations lost due to lagging and/or reduce the number of parameters to be estimated. We now present two such models.

---

* The reader should be able to demonstrate that, if we only have one joint observation, we would only have *one* independent normal equation because all of the normal equations would be proportional to the first. For instance, in relation to equations (5.7) and (5.8), the proportionality factor in the second normal equation would be $Y_{d(1969)}$, in the third it would be $Y_{d(1968)}$, etc. [Hint: the only observation on (5.7) or (5.6) would be for $t = 1$, where time period 1 denotes the year 1969.] The normal equations would be obtained from the conditions:

$$\sum_{t=1}^{1} \hat{u}_t = \hat{u}_1 = 0, \sum_{t=1}^{1} (\hat{u}_t Y_{dt}) = \hat{u}_1 Y_{d1} = 0, \sum_{t=1}^{1} (\hat{u}_t X_{1t}) = \hat{u}_1 X_{11} = 0, \cdots \sum_{t=1}^{1} (\hat{u}_t X_{9t}) = \hat{u}_1 X_{91} = 0.$$

Thus, the second normal equation would be Y_{d1} times the first, the third would be X_{11} times the first, and so on. This result is a special case of a more general result which states that if a regression model has k parameters, we must have at least k joint observations in order to estimate the parameters.

THE KOYCK LAG

The first model is the Koyck lag.* This model makes an assumption concerning the parameters of the distributed-lag relationship that permits a translation of the lagged relationship into a much simpler form. It results both in fewer lags *and* in fewer parameters to be estimated. Unfortunately, this "simpler" form also turns out to have serious complications that are often overlooked. Because the Koyck lag model has been widely used, we present it and point out its shortcomings. In addition, its presentation will serve as an important vehicle for our later discussions.

Suppose we postulate that, although consumption depends on disposable income in earlier years, the impact of income in the more distant past is less than that of income in more recent years. More specifically, let us hypothesize that current consumption is a weighted sum of present and past levels of disposable income (plus a disturbance term), where the weights diminish successively for more distant periods. The Koyck lag formulation assumes that these weights decline geometrically. For example, let λ be a constant that is between zero and one. Then, with reference to (5.2), the Koyck formulation would be

$$b_i = \lambda^i b_0, \qquad i = 1, 2, \ldots, k. \tag{5.9}$$

Substituting (5.9) into (5.2), we would have

$$C_t = a + b_0 Y_{dt} + (b_0\lambda)Y_{d(t-1)} + (b_0\lambda^2)Y_{d(t-2)} + \cdots + (b_0\lambda^k)Y_{d(t-k)} + u_t. \tag{5.10}$$

Equation (5.10) says that consumption depends on both present and past levels of income, but since λ raised to higher powers becomes continually smaller, the coefficients for earlier years become progressively smaller as we reach farther back into the past.

We shall now see the implications of the Koyck lag formulation. If we lag (5.10) by one period and then multiply through by λ, we get

$$\lambda C_{t-1} = \lambda a + (\lambda b_0)Y_{d(t-1)}$$
$$+ (\lambda^2 b_0)Y_{d(t-2)} + \cdots + (\lambda^{k+1}b_0)Y_{d(t-k-1)} + \lambda u_{t-1}. \tag{5.11}$$

If we now subtract (5.11) from (5.10), we obtain

$$C_t - \lambda C_{t-1} = (a - \lambda a) + b_0 Y_{di} - \lambda^{k+1}b_0 Y_{d(t-k-1)} + (u_t - \lambda u_{t-1}). \tag{5.12}$$

Rearranging the terms in (5.12), we have

$$C_t = (a - \lambda a) + b_0 Y_{dt} + \lambda C_{t-1} - (\lambda^{k+1}b_0)Y_{d(t-k-1)} + (u_t - \lambda u_{t-1}). \tag{5.13}$$

* L. M. Koyck, *Distributed Lags and Investment Analysis* (Amsterdam: North Holland, 1954).

If we now assume that k is big (there are a large number of lagged years involved), the next-to-last term in (5.13), $(\lambda^{k+1}b_0)Y_{d(t-k-1)}$, will be small. Thus, as an approximation, we shall set this term equal to zero.* Also, for notational simplicity let $a^* = (a - \lambda a)$. Then (5.13) simplifies to

$$C_t = a^* + b_0 Y_{dt} + \lambda C_{t-1} + (u_t - \lambda u_{t-1}). \qquad (5.14)$$

Now let

$$v_t = (u_t - \lambda u_{t-1}). \qquad (5.15)$$

Since v_t depends only on disturbance terms, it is reasonable to consider v_t itself as a disturbance term. Let us *for the moment* make the assumption (which, unfortunately, has often been made in the literature) that v_t satisfies all the assumptions in the regression model concerning properties of the disturbance term. In this case, (5.14) could be expressed as

$$C_t = a^* + b_0 Y_{dt} + \lambda C_{t-1} + v_t, \qquad (5.16)$$

where a^* is a constant and where

$$E(v_t) = 0,$$
$$E(v_t^2) = \sigma_v^2,$$
$$E(v_t v_{t-i}) = 0,$$
$$E(v_t Y_{dt}) = E(v_t C_{t-1}) = 0.$$

Note what a tremendous simplification (5.16) represents over (5.2). The effects of *all* the lagged values of disposable income on current consumption are captured in a single term: the value of consumption itself lagged by one period. One would need only to estimate the value of λ instead of the coefficients for each of the lagged values of income. In other words, if the Koyck lag model and the assumptions concerning v_t are accepted, the parameters of a model such as (5.2) could be estimated in terms of a model such as (5.16) whose estimation would require the loss of *only one observation*!

To be more specific concerning the estimation procedure, (5.16) would be considered as a multiple-regression model involving the parameters a^*, b_0, and λ. A direct application of our instrumental-variable technique would yield the estimators of these parameters, $\hat{a}^*$, $\hat{b}_0$, and $\hat{\lambda}$. With them, one could obtain estimators of all of the parameters of (5.2). For instance, assuming that there are an infinite number of lags (k is infinite),

$$\hat{b}_i = (\hat{\lambda}^i)\hat{b}_0, \qquad i = 1, 2, \ldots, \qquad (5.17)$$

and since $a^* = (a - \lambda a)$, it follows that $a = [a^*/(1 - \lambda)]$, so that the estimator of a would be

$$\hat{a} = \frac{\hat{a}^*}{1 - \hat{\lambda}}. \qquad (5.18)$$

---

* If, of course, we assume that $k \to \infty$ while $Y_{d(t-k-1)}$ remains finite, this term will be zero. This is the usual assumption made in the literature.

To express the results more generally, the Koyck lag assumptions (including the assumption that k is infinite) enable one to put a model of the form

$$Y_t = a + b_0 X_t + b_1 X_{t-1} + \cdots + u_t \tag{5.19}$$

into the simplified form

$$Y_t = a^* + b_0 X_t + \lambda Y_{t-1} + v_t, \tag{5.20}$$

in which one need estimate only three parameters, a^*, b_0, and λ. The relationship between the parameters of (5.19) and (5.20) is

$$a = \frac{a^*}{1 - \lambda}, \qquad b_i = \lambda^i b_0, \qquad i = 1, 2, \ldots . \tag{5.21}$$

By explicitly converting the model into one involving only a single lagged value of a variable, the Koyck lag formulation results in the loss of only one joint observation. The appeal of the Koyck model should now be obvious.

As noted above, however, there are some troublesome problems with the Koyck model. Recall, first, that in deriving the equation to estimate, it was simply assumed that the disturbance term

$$v_t = (u_t - \lambda u_{t-1})$$

satisfied all the conditions we normally impose on disturbance terms. Unfortunately, this will *not* generally be true. If, in the original equation (5.19), u_t satisfies the assumptions of the regression model, v_t in (5.20) generally will not. More specifically, the values of v_t will have a nonzero correlation with one another and also with one of the independent variables—the lagged value of the dependent variable, Y. For example, if $v_t = (u_t - \lambda u_{t-1})$ and $v_{t-1} = (u_{t-1} - \lambda u_{t-2})$, then v_t and v_{t-1} will not be independent of one another since they have a term in common, namely, u_{t-1}. Thus, we would not expect $E(v_t v_{t-1}) = 0$. Indeed, under our usual assumptions concerning u_t, we have

$$E(v_t v_{t-1}) = E[(u_t - \lambda u_{t-1})(u_{t-1} - \lambda u_{t-2})]$$
$$= E(u_t u_{t-1} - u_t \lambda u_{t-2} - \lambda u_{t-1}^2 + \lambda^2 u_{t-1} u_{t-2}) \tag{5.22}$$
$$= -\lambda \sigma_u^2 \neq 0.$$

We have found that the covariance between successive values of the disturbance terms in equation (5.20) will not be zero. We leave it as an exercise for the reader to show that, similarly*:

$$E(v_t Y_{t-1}) \neq 0. \tag{5.23}$$

---

* Hint: Since from (5.20) Y_t directly depends on v_t, Y_{t-1} will depend directly on v_{t-1}. $Y_{t-1} = a^* + b_0 X_{t-1} + \lambda Y_{t-2} + v_{t-1}$. Therefore, Y_{t-1} will obviously be related to v_t, since v_t and v_{t-1} are not independent. To demonstrate (5.23) formally, simply multiply Y_{t-1} by v_t and take expectations. In doing this note that $E(Y_{t-2} v_t) = 0$.

In summary, if we begin with an equation of the form of (5.19) that satisfies all the assumptions of the regression model, the Koyck transformation of this equation will in general lead to violations of some of these assumptions.* Furthermore, the consequences of these violations are serious. For instance, as we shall show in a later chapter, (5.23) implies that the estimators of b, b_i, and λ will not only be biased, but will not even be consistent!**

In addition to the estimation problems outlined above, the Koyck formulation is quite restrictive in that it assumes that the impact of past periods declines successively in a specific way. This will surely not always be the case. For example, because of a habit effect, it might well be true that the level of income in the immediately preceding period has a larger impact on consumption than income in the current period; such a relationship would clearly be inconsistent with the Koyck lag formulation. It would thus be extremely useful to have a distributed lag model that is more flexible than the Koyck lag and that also does not lead to violations of the assumptions of the regression model.

THE ALMON LAG†

Although the violations introduced by the Koyck lag procedure can be dealt with in the framework of a somewhat more general model to be developed later, the solution is not simple. This difficulty can be circumvented through the use of the Almon lag technique. We stress that this latter method does not, like the Koyck formulation, reduce the number of observations that are lost due to the presence of lagged variables; however, the Almon method does reduce the number of parameters to be estimated. Moreover, it possesses two distinct advantages over the Koyck procedure. First, it does not violate any of the assumptions of the regression model. And second, as we shall see, it is far more flexible than the Koyck method in terms of the forms of admissible lag structures.

Returning to a general formulation of a lagged relationship, let us assume that the model we wish to estimate is again of the form

$$Y_t = a + b_0 X_t + b_1 X_{t-1} + \cdots + b_k X_{t-k} + u_t, \qquad (5.24)$$

where the disturbance term u_t satisfies the usual assumptions. As before,

---

* We shall develop techniques to deal with violations of the assumptions of the regression model in Chapters 6 and 7.

** This is because the third normal equation of the regression model (5.20) is based on the condition that $\sum (\hat{v}_t Y_{t-1}) = 0$, which is no longer consistent with (5.23). More on this later.

† Shirley Almon, "The Distributed Lag Between Capital Appropriations and Expenditures," *Econometrica*, 33 (Jan. 1965), pp. 178–196. The discussion in this section draws on the explication of the Almon technique by Ray Fair and Dwight Jaffee, "A Note on the Estimation of Polynomial Distributed Lags," *Econometric Research Memorandum No. 120*, Princeton University, Feb. 1971.

we might expect the coefficients of the X's corresponding to more distant periods to be less than those corresponding to the more recent periods. On the other hand, certain considerations suggest that in a model such as (5.24), this need not be true; in some cases, the b's may actually increase at first (that is, $b_1 > b_0$) and then begin to taper off. For instance, because of, say, lags in recognition, time delays in gathering information, or the time element involved in making decisions, a variable such as investment expenditures may actually be more responsive to what demand conditions were a few periods back than to what they are today. In brief, under different assumptions, one would expect different patterns of values of the b's in a model such as (5.24).

The Almon technique, unlike the Koyck, does not assume such a rigid relationship among the b's. Instead, it assumes that whatever the pattern of the b's may be, that pattern can be described by a polynomial. For example, if the b's are expected to increase at first and then decrease, their pattern may be somewhat like that in Figure 5.1.

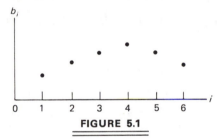

FIGURE 5.1

Suppose we assume that we can draw a smooth curve through the points in Figure 5.1, as we have done in Figure 5.2. We now wish to describe the curve in Figure 5.2 algebraically. In mathematics, there is a theorem that states that, under general conditions, a curve may be approximated by a polynomial. The rule for determining the degree of the polynomial* is that the degree should be at least one more than the number of turning points in the curve. Applying this rule to Figure 5.2, we could approximate the curve by a second-degree polynomial. Specifically, using the Almon technique, we would assume

$$b_i = \alpha_0 + \alpha_1 i + \alpha_2 i^2, \tag{5.25}$$

---

* Recall from algebra that the "degree of a polynomial" refers to the highest power to which the variable is raised. Thus,

$$Y = b_0 + b_1 X + b_1 X^2$$

is a second-degree polynomial, while

$$Y = b_0 + b_1 X + b_2 X^2 + b_3 X^3$$

is a polynomial of the third degree.

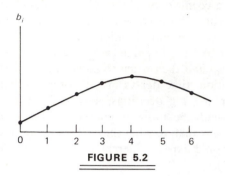

FIGURE 5.2

where α_0, α_1, and α_2 are constants to be determined. Note that, if equation (5.25) approximates the curve in Figure 5.2, we must have

$$b_0 = \alpha_0 \quad (\text{set } i = 0),$$

$$b_1 = \alpha_0 + \alpha_1 + \alpha_2 \quad (\text{set } i = 1),$$

$$b_2 = \alpha_0 + 2\alpha_1 + 4\alpha_2 \quad (\text{set } i = 2), \quad\quad (5.26)$$

$$\vdots$$

$$b_k = \alpha_0 + k\alpha_1 + k^2\alpha_2 \quad (\text{set } i = k).$$

The expression for each b_i in (5.26) is derived directly from (5.25) by simply setting i equal to the value of the subscript of the particular coefficient.

Equation (5.25) may at first seem a bit strange in that the value of the lagged weight, b_i, is related to the length of the lag itself, i. Actually, we already encountered a similar relationship in the Koyck technique. There we assumed

$$b_i = \lambda^i b_0. \quad\quad (5.27)$$

In equation (5.27), b_i is again related to i. The only difference between (5.27) and (5.25) is the form of the equation.

Before we implement the Almon technique, let us demonstrate briefly just how flexible it is. Suppose we felt that the b's followed a pattern such as the one in Figure 5.3. We would then simply assume that

$$b_i = \alpha_0 + \alpha_1 i + \alpha_2 i^2 + \alpha_3 i^3, \quad\quad (5.28)$$

which implies that

$$b_0 = \alpha_0,$$

$$b_1 = \alpha_0 + \alpha_1 + \alpha_2 + \alpha_3,$$

$$b_2 = \alpha_0 + 2\alpha_1 + 4\alpha_2 + 8\alpha_3, \quad\quad (5.29)$$

$$\vdots$$

$$b_k = \alpha_0 + k\alpha_1 + k^2\alpha_2 + k^3\alpha_3.$$

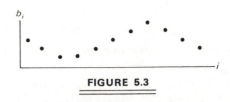

FIGURE 5.3

More generally, to use the Almon method, all we have to do is count the number of turning points in our assumed pattern for the b's and then express the b's as a polynomial in i, where the degree of the polynomial is one plus the number of turning points in the curve. In Figure 5.4, we depict a number of possible lag patterns along with the degree of the corresponding polynomial.

We shall now show how to use the Almon technique to estimate a lagged relationship. Let us return to the general formulation expressed earlier:

$$Y_t = a + b_0 X_t + b_1 X_{t-1} + \cdots + b_k X_{t-k} + u_t. \qquad (5.24)$$

Suppose that our economic theory suggests that a second-degree polynomial is appropriate to describe the form of the lag. We would take

$$b_i = \alpha_0 + \alpha_1 i + \alpha_2 i^2. \qquad (5.30)$$

If we replace the b's in (5.24) by their expressions in (5.30), we have

$$Y_t = a + \alpha_0 X_t + (\alpha_0 + \alpha_1 + \alpha_2) X_{t-1}$$
$$+ (\alpha_0 + 2\alpha_1 + 4\alpha_2) X_{t-2} + \cdots + (\alpha_0 + k\alpha_1 + k^2\alpha_2) X_{t-k} + u_t. \qquad (5.31)$$

Rearranging terms in (5.31) gives us

$$Y_t = a + \alpha_0 \left(\sum_{i=0}^{k} X_{t-i} \right) + \alpha_1 \left(\sum_{i=1}^{k} i X_{t-i} \right) + \alpha_2 \left(\sum_{i=1}^{k} i^2 X_{t-i} \right) + u_t. \qquad (5.32)$$

Let us now simplify our notation by defining

$$Z_{1t} = \sum_{i=0}^{k} X_{t-i}, \qquad Z_{2t} = \sum_{i=1}^{k} i X_{t-i}, \qquad \text{and} \qquad Z_{3t} = \sum_{i=1}^{k} i^2 X_{t-i}. \qquad (5.33)$$

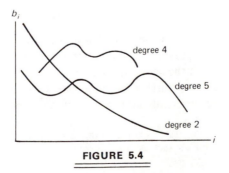

FIGURE 5.4

Then, we can rewrite (5.32) as

$$Y_t = a + \alpha_0 Z_{1t} + \alpha_1 Z_{2t} + \alpha_2 Z_{3t} + u_t. \tag{5.34}$$

Equation (5.35) is an ordinary multiple-regression model relating Y_t to Z_{1t}, Z_{2t}, and Z_{3t}. We can easily generate estimators of a, α_0, α_1, and α_2 by our standard estimation technique. Let $\hat{a}$, $\hat{\alpha}_0$, $\hat{\alpha}_1$, and $\hat{\alpha}_2$ be these estimators. Then, from (5.30), we can see that our estimators of the b's are

$$\hat{b}_0 = \hat{\alpha}_0,$$

$$\hat{b}_1 = \hat{\alpha}_0 + \hat{\alpha}_1 + \hat{\alpha}_2,$$

$$\hat{b}_2 = \hat{\alpha}_0 + 2\hat{\alpha}_1 + 4\hat{\alpha}_2, \tag{5.35}$$

$$\vdots$$

$$\hat{b}_k = \hat{\alpha}_0 + k\hat{\alpha}_1 + k^2\hat{\alpha}_2.$$

Note that by this technique we are able to obtain estimators for the k parameters, $b_0, \ldots, b_k$, by simply obtaining estimators for the three parameters α_0, α_1, and α_2. Now, it can be shown that, in any case in which there are more b's than α's, the estimators of the b's obtained from the Almon technique are better (in the sense of having smaller variances) than the *direct* estimators of the b's that would be obtained by applying the multiple-regression technique directly to (5.24).* Unfortunately, we cannot give a simple expression for the variance of the estimators, $\hat{b}_0, \ldots, \hat{b}_k$, obtained with the Almon technique. However, in practice the computer will provide us with estimates of these variances so that we can conduct the usual statistical tests concerning the values of each of the regression coefficients.

Generalizations of and variations on the Almon technique are straightforward. For instance, suppose that equation (5.24) were expanded to include another variable:

$$Y_t = a + b_0 X_t + b_1 X_{t-1} + \cdots + b_k X_{t-k} + cW_t + u_t, \tag{5.36}$$

where W_t is another independent variable. If we again assume that the b's abide by a relationship such as (5.30), we can go through exactly the same steps and reduce (5.36) to an equation identical to (5.34) with the single exception of the presence of the term cW_t:

$$Y_t = a + \alpha_0 Z_{1t} + \alpha_1 Z_{2t} + \alpha_2 Z_{3t} + cW_t + u_t. \tag{5.37}$$

That is, our inclusion of additional variables in no way affects our analysis. In fact, we can even apply the Almon method to each of several lagged independent variables in the same equation!

We want to make two further observations concerning the use of the Almon lag procedure. First, the user may want to impose some "endpoint"

---

* As one might expect, this result is based on the assumption that the assumed relationship between the b's and the α's, such as (5.30), is true.

restrictions on the values of the b's. We might, for example, wish to specify that either (or both) b_0 or b_k equals zero. Because of delays in receiving information, for instance, we might believe that the value of the independent variable in the current period has no effect on current behavior (i.e., on the value of the dependent variable in this period); that is, in equation (5.24), $b_0 = 0$. The dependent variable, Y, would in this case depend only on the lagged values of X in (5.24). On the other hand, perhaps because of the way decisions are made, we might believe that values of X lagged k or more periods have no effect on Y so that, in equation (5.24), $b_k = 0$.

One way of incorporating into our model information such as, say, $b_k = 0$, is simply to drop X_{t-k} from our basic equation (5.24) and proceed as before. This, however, is not the way it is generally done. In practice, the information that either $b_0 = 0$ or $b_k = 0$, or both, is translated using the basic assumptions such as (5.30) into a condition on the α's and then the resulting equation is estimated. Although the proof is beyond the scope of this book, this somewhat indirect approach is taken because, under certain assumptions, the variances of the resulting unbiased estimators are smaller than if the direct approach (of simply dropping X_t and X_{t-k}) is taken. For the interested reader, Appendix A to this chapter treats this issue in more detail; it shows how the Almon technique *can* incorporate these conditions, but suggests reasons in practice for adopting the direct approach. This is of some importance, incidentally, because most computer programs for the Almon lag require the user to specify his endpoint restrictions (if any).

Second, you have no doubt noted that we have presented the material in this section as if the researcher knows both the length of the lag in his regression model (that is, the value of k) and the general pattern of the b's so that the order of the polynomial can be determined. In practice, neither k nor the pattern of the b's may be known. In such a situation, we recommend the following procedure. First, choose a degree for the polynomial, say d, that is high enough to accommodate any "reasonable" pattern of the b's. In most cases a third or fourth degree polynomial should be sufficient. Then suppose the maximum "reasonable" lag you believe to be consistent with the relationship under consideration is k^*. As an example, if quarterly data are being used, k^* might be 12 or 16, which corresponds to 3- and 4-year lags. If monthly data are used, perhaps one would take $k^* = 36$. In any event, once you have selected d and k^*, estimate the relationship under consideration for $k = d, d + 1, \ldots, k^*$, where d is the degree of the polynomial. We consider only lags of $k \geq d$ because we are assuming that the length of the lag is at least as long as d (there are at least as many b's as there are α's).* *All* of the regression equations corresponding to the various values of k should be estimated with the same data. Note that this requires that we discard the first k^* observations and use only the remaining $(n - k^*)$

---

* Recall that the purpose of the Almon lag procedure is to reduce the number of parameters to be estimated. This would not occur if $k < d$.

observations to estimate the regression equations. This will permit us to compare the R^2-statistics for the various equations since they will all be based on the same sample. Thus, we should take as our value of k that which maximizes the R^2-statistic. Under certain assumptions, it can be shown that this procedure will lead to consistent estimators of both k and the regression parameters.

AN EXAMPLE

Simply to illustrate the procedure for estimating an Almon lag structure, we return to our now-familiar consumption function. In Table 5.2 we reproduce the ten observations on consumption expenditure and disposable income for 1960–1969 that we used to estimate our illustrative consumption equation back in Chapter 2 (See Table 2.2). We shall use these data once again for estimation purposes. However, in this case, we assume that consumption expenditure depends on disposable income with a distributed lag. More specifically, let us postulate that consumption depends on disposable income in the current year *and* in the four preceding years; in addition, we shall assume that the lag takes the form of a second-degree polynomial. Our specification of the consumption equation thus is

$$C_t = a + b_0 Y_{dt} + b_1 Y_{d(t-1)} + b_2 Y_{d(t-2)} + b_3 Y_{d(t-3)} + b_4 Y_{d(t-4)} + u_t,$$

$$(5.38)$$

where

$$b_i = \alpha_0 + \alpha_1 i + \alpha_2 i^2.$$

TABLE 5.2

CONSUMPTION AND DISPOSABLE INCOME
IN THE UNITED STATES
(billions of current dollars)

Year	Consumption (C)	Disposable Income (Y_d)
1960	325	350
1961	335	364
1962	355	385
1963	375	405
1964	401	438
1965	433	473
1966	466	512
1967	492	547
1968	537	590
1969	576	630

SOURCE: *Economic Report of the President* (Washington, D.C.: U.S. Government Printing Office, Feb. 1970), pp. 189, 195.

In order to put our consumption equation in the Almon form, we must calculate

$$Z_{1t} = \sum_{i=0}^{4} Y_{d(t-i)}, \qquad Z_{2t} = \sum_{i=1}^{4} i Y_{d(t-i)}, \qquad \text{and} \qquad Z_{3t} = \sum_{i=1}^{4} i^2 Y_{d(t-i)}.$$

The values for the Z's along with those for the dependent variable appear in Table 5.3. Note that, as a result of introducing a four-period lag, we have "lost" four of our observations so that Table 5.3 contains data for only six years. To illustrate the calculations, we obtain the value for $Z_{3(1969)}$ by computing:

$$Z_{3(1969)} = Y_{d(1968)} + 4Y_{d(1967)} + 9Y_{d(1966)} + 16Y_{d(1965)}$$

$$= \quad 590 \quad + \quad 2{,}188 \quad + \quad 4{,}608 \quad + \quad 7{,}568 \quad = 14{,}954.$$

Using the newly generated data in Table 5.3, we can use our standard procedure to estimate the equation

$$C_t = a + \alpha_0 Z_{1t} + \alpha_1 Z_{2t} + \alpha_2 Z_{3t} + u_t. \tag{5.39}$$

The estimated equation is

$$\hat{C}_t = -43.5 + 1.02 Z_{1t} - 1.44 Z_{2t} + 0.35 Z_{3t}. \tag{5.40}$$

With our estimated values for the α_i, we can compute estimates for the b_i:

$$\hat{b}_0 = \hat{\alpha}_0 = 1.02,$$

$$\hat{b}_1 = \hat{\alpha}_0 + \hat{\alpha}_1 + \hat{\alpha}_2 = 1.02 - 1.44 + 0.35 = -0.07,$$

$$\hat{b}_2 = \hat{\alpha}_0 + 2\hat{\alpha}_1 + 4\hat{\alpha}_2 = 1.02 + 2(-1.44) + 4(0.35) = -0.46,$$

$$\hat{b}_3 = \hat{\alpha}_0 + 3\hat{\alpha}_1 + 9\hat{\alpha}_2 = 1.02 + 3(-1.44) + 9(0.35) = -0.15,$$

$$\hat{b}_4 = \alpha_0 + 4\hat{\alpha}_1 + 16\hat{\alpha}_2 = 1.02 + 4(-1.44) + 16(0.35) = 0.86.$$

TABLE 5.3

Year	C_t	Z_{1t}	Z_{2t}	Z_{3t}
1964	401	1,942	3,667	10,821
1965	433	2,065	3,859	11,347
1966	466	2,213	4,104	12,030
1967	492	2,375	4,392	12,826
1968	537	2,560	4,742	13,860
1969	576	2,752	5,112	14,954

Our estimated consumption equation with a four-period Almon lag is thus*

$$\hat{C}_t = -43.5 + 1.02Y_{dt} - 0.07Y_{d(t-1)} - 0.46Y_{d(t-2)} \tag{5.41}$$
$$\phantom{\hat{C}_t = } (3.3) \quad (5.3) \quad\quad (0.9) \quad\quad\quad (2.8)$$

$$- 0.15Y_{d(t-3)} + 0.86Y_{d(t-4)} \quad R^2 = 0.99.$$
$$(1.9) \quad\quad\quad (4.3)$$

In addition to the estimated values of the coefficients, we have included the absolute values of the t ratios and the coefficient of determination. This additional information is provided by most computer programs with the Almon lag option.

5.2 THE USE OF DUMMY VARIABLES

To this point we have dealt exclusively with variables that we can measure in quantitative terms, such as the level of disposable income or the rate of change in wage rates. Frequently, however, we may believe that certain variables of great importance are of a qualitative character. We might, for example, believe that the level of aggregate consumption expenditure depends not only on disposable income, but also on whether or not the country is in a period of war or peace. During wartime, moral suasion and frequently actual controls restrict the availability of consumer goods so that, for any given level of disposable income, we might expect a lower level of consumption than in years of peace. But how could we possibly introduce a variable for peacetime or wartime into the regression equation?**

One approach to this problem would simply be to estimate two separate consumption functions; we would use data from periods of war to estimate a "wartime consumption function" and data from years of peace to get a "peacetime consumption function." We would thus obtain two different consumption equations. There is, however, a more efficient procedure involving the estimation of only one equation if we are willing to make certain assumptions.

Suppose that we hypothesize that wartime controls do not alter the marginal propensity to consume out of disposable income, but instead simply reduce the average propensity to consume. That is, in terms of Figure 5.5, we postulate that the consumption function during war years has the same slope as during peacetime, but has a lower intercept (or smaller constant

---

* In this case, the estimated equation does not conform very well to our expectations. The signs of the coefficients of the lagged values of the income variable suggest that more thought should be given to the formulation of the consumption function.

** For a more advanced treatment of the following discussion, see Arthur S. Goldberger, *Econometric Theory* (New York: Wiley, 1964), pp. 218–227.

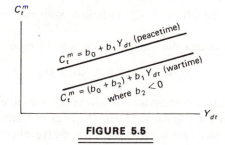

FIGURE 5.5

term). With this assumption, we can express both the wartime and peacetime consumption functions in terms of a single regression equation:

$$C_t = b_0 + b_1 Y_{dt} + b_2 D_t + u_t, \qquad t = 1, \ldots, n, \qquad (5.42)$$

where

$$D_t = 0 \quad \text{for peacetime years,}$$

and

$$D_t = 1 \quad \text{for war years.}$$

Equation (5.42) says that during peacetime, when $D_t = 0$, we have

$$C_t = b_0 + b_1 Y_{dt} + u_t, \qquad (5.43)$$

while in periods of war, when $D_t = 1$,

$$C_t = (b_0 + b_2) + b_1 Y_{dt} + u_t, \qquad (5.44)$$

where presumably $b_2 < 0$.

Suppose the time period under consideration is such that the years $t = 5$ through $t = 9$ were years of war, and the remaining years were times of peace. Then, corresponding to equation (5.42), we would have a set of data such as that in Table 5.4. Using these data, we could estimate the values of

TABLE 5.4

t	Consumption Expenditure	Disposable Income	D
1	C_1	Y_{d1}	0
$\vdots$	$\vdots$	$\vdots$	$\vdots$
4	C_4	Y_{d4}	0
5	C_5	Y_{d5}	1
6	C_6	Y_{d6}	1
7	C_7	Y_{d7}	1
8	C_8	Y_{d8}	1
9	C_9	Y_{d9}	1
10	C_{10}	Y_{d10}	0
$\vdots$	$\vdots$	$\vdots$	$\vdots$
n	C_n	Y_{dn}	0

the coefficients in equation (5.42) with our standard multiple-regression technique.

Suppose that we in fact did this and obtained the equation

$$\hat{C}_t = 40 + 0.9Y_{dt} - 30D_t, \tag{5.45}$$

where, say, the t ratio corresponding to the D_t variable was of sufficient size to suggest that the parameter b_2 in (5.42) is not zero. We would then conclude that the war had a significantly negative effect on consumption expenditures. The estimated consumption function would be

$$\hat{C}_t = 40 + 0.9Y_{dt}, \qquad \text{for years of peace,} \tag{5.46}$$

and

$$\hat{C}_t = 10 + 0.9Y_{dt}, \qquad \text{for war years.} \tag{5.47}$$

If consumption expenditures are measured in billions of dollars, a comparison of (5.46) and (5.47) would then suggest that, *for corresponding levels of income*, consumption expenditures were 30 billion dollars less during years of war. Figure 5.6 depicts these functions. In the figure, we see that the wartime consumption function, DE, is simply a line with the same slope as the peacetime function, AB, but with a vertical intercept of 30 less than AB.

Alternatively, we might have hypothesized that wartime conditions reduced the marginal propensity to consume, but not the constant term in the consumption equation.* In this second case, our regression equation including both periods would be

$$C_t = b_0 + b_1 Y_{dt} + b_2(Y_{dt}D_t) + u_t, \tag{5.48}$$

where, again,

$$D_t = 0 \qquad \text{in peacetime,}$$

$$D_t = 1 \qquad \text{in wartime.}$$

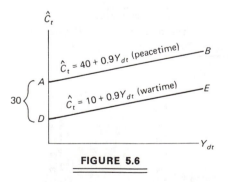

FIGURE 5.6

---

* In practice, one would presumably decide whether the intercept, or alternatively, the MPC, shifted by studying the forms of wartime controls adopted, etc.

This equation says that in years of peace we have

$$C_t = b_0 + b_1 Y_{dt} + u_t, \qquad (5.49)$$

since $D_t = 0$, while during periods of war,

$$C_t = b_0 + (b_1 + b_2) Y_{dt} + u_t, \qquad (5.50)$$

where we would expect $b_2 < 0$. As before, we could use data such as those in Table 5.4 to estimate equation (5.48). The resulting estimated relationship would be similar to the curves depicted in Figure 5.7; in the figure, the war-time consumption function has a lesser slope than, but the same vertical intercept as, the estimated peacetime function.

A variable such as D in the above equations is called a "dummy" variable; it takes on a value of unity if some condition holds and a value of zero if it does not. The use of dummy variables is an extremely powerful extension of regression analysis. As can be seen, it allows us to expand the scope of our analysis to encompass variables (often of crucial importance) that we cannot measure in quantitative units. With dummy variables, we can take account of the effects of important qualitative factors that influence the values of our dependent variable.

Consider again the first example above, in which we assumed that the intercept changed, but the MPC remained the same during the war years. If, instead of the dummy-variable approach, we had formulated two consumption functions, one for the war years and one for years of peace, we would have estimated *four*, rather than three, parameters. Under our assumption that the MPC was the same in wartime and peacetime, we would have ended up with two estimates of *one parameter*. Our problem would then be to use these two estimates to obtain some single "best" estimate of the MPC. In such a case we would probably attempt to develop some technique for "averaging" the two estimates.

It can be shown that, if the two estimates were combined in an "optimal" (to be defined) way, the result would be *identical* to that produced by the dummy-variable procedure. More formally, let $\hat{b}_{1p}$ be the estimator of the MPC that is based on the peacetime equation and data, and let $\hat{b}_{1w}$ be the corresponding estimator derived from the wartime equation and data. Under our standard assumptions, these estimators would be unbiased. If these

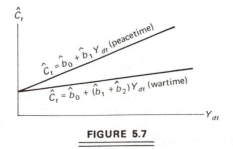

FIGURE 5.7

estimators were combined in such a way that the result is an unbiased Estimator of the MPC with the smallest possible variance, then that resulting estimator would be *identical* to the estimator produced by the dummy-variable technique. Somewhat intuitively, the dummy-variable technique uses all of the available sample information, as well as our prior knowledge concerning parameter shifts, in the most efficient manner.

We can, incidentally, use as many dummy variables as we like as independent variables in a regression equation, providing that we have a sufficient number of observations to allow us to estimate the equation. For example, suppose that we wanted to explain the consumption behavior of different households. In addition to the level of disposable income, we may believe that the household's level of consumption spending depends on a number of its characteristics: the presence or absence of children, whether or not the household unit owns its own house, its race, the age of the head of the household, and so on. If we were to obtain all this information for a sample of households, we could, for example, estimate the equation

$$C_t = b_0 + b_1 Y_{dt} + b_2 F_t + b_3 H_t + b_4 R_t + b_5 A_t + u_t, \qquad (5.51)$$

where

C_t = consumption expenditure of the tth household;

Y_{dt} = disposable income of the tth household;

$F_t = \begin{cases} 1 \text{ if the household has children,} \\ 0 \text{ if no children;} \end{cases}$

$H_t = \begin{cases} 1 \text{ if the household owns its own home,} \\ 0 \text{ if not;} \end{cases}$

$R_t = \begin{cases} 1 \text{ if the household is white,} \\ 0 \text{ if nonwhite;} \end{cases}$

$A_t = \begin{cases} 1 \text{ if the head of the household is over 50 years of age,} \\ 0 \text{ if 50 or less;} \end{cases}$

u_t = the disturbance term.

AN ILLUSTRATION

The range of application of dummy variables is virtually unlimited. Another example involving a very different sort of problem comes from a recent study by one of the authors.* The issue under study was whether or not the formal character of a country's political constitution has a systematic impact on the extent of decentralization in the nation's public finances. Or, in short, is the constitution itself important in determining the relative share of fiscal activity of the central government in the public sector as a whole?

* W. E. Oates, *Fiscal Federalism* (New York: Harcourt Brace Jovanovich, 1972), chap. 5.

Having already ascertained the importance of certain other variables (such as population size and the level of per capita income), the procedure was to introduce a dummy variable with a value of one if the country had a "federal" constitution (i.e., one guaranteeing some political autonomy to decentralized levels of government) or a value of zero in the absence of a federal constitution (i.e., where the scope of authority of decentralized levels of government is determined by the central government itself). Using cross-sectional data for a sample of 53 countries, the estimated equation was

$$\hat{G} = \underset{(12.1)}{96} - \underset{(1.3)}{1.21 \ln P} - \underset{(2.3)}{0.004Y} - \underset{(5.5)}{0.6Z} - \underset{(4.7)}{15.9F} \qquad \begin{matrix} N = 53, \\ R^2 = 0.65 \end{matrix} \qquad (5.52)$$

(the number in parentheses below the estimated coefficient is the absolute value of the t ratio), where

G = central-government share of total public revenues (as a percentage);

$\ln P$ = natural logarithm of population size (in thousands);

Y = per capita income in U.S. dollars (1965);

Z = social security contributions as a percentage of total public current revenue;

$F = \begin{cases} 1 \text{ for countries with federal constitutions,} \\ 0 \text{ for countries with nonfederal constitutions.} \end{cases}$

The results in equation (5.52) are clearly consistent with the hypothesis that the existence of a federal constitution contributes to an increased degree of decentralization in the public finances. The coefficient of the dummy variable, F, has a negative sign and possesses a t ratio in excess of 4, so that we can easily reject the null hypothesis of no association between G and F at the usual 5 percent level of significance. The magnitude of the coefficient suggests that, after allowing for the effects of population size, income, and so on, the central government in federal countries collects, on average, about 16 percentage points less of total public revenues than do the central governments in countries without federal constitutions. The constraints imposed formally by political constitutions would thus appear to be of considerable importance in determining the degree of decentralization in public fiscal activity.

SOME FURTHER RESULTS

Dummy variables have also proved very useful in separating out both seasonal and regional differences in behavior. The levels of automobile sales, as a result of the introduction of new models in the fall, or the output of various crops, which depends on weather conditions, obviously vary systematically with the seasons of the year. If we were working with quarterly or monthly data for these variables, we could introduce dummy variables corresponding to the various seasons to take account of these effects. Likewise, where we expect regional differences in behavior, we can allow for this by introducing dummy variables for the various regions.

To see how this is done (and to point out one pitfall to avoid), consider the following example. Suppose that we are trying to understand the relationship between the output of a particular good and the input of labor in its production, where we believe that certain systematic seasonal forces are at work. We might, therefore, postulate that

$$Q_t = b_0 + b_1 L_t + b_2 S_t + b_3 H_t + b_4 F_t + b_5 W_t + u_t, \qquad (5.53)$$

where

$Q_t =$ units of output in the tth quarter;

$L_t =$ units of labor input;

$S_t = \begin{cases} 1 \text{ for the quarter April–June,} \\ 0 \text{ for other quarters;} \end{cases}$

$H_t = \begin{cases} 1 \text{ for the quarter July–September,} \\ 0 \text{ for other quarters;} \end{cases}$

$F_t = \begin{cases} 1 \text{ for the quarter October–December,} \\ 0 \text{ for other quarters;} \end{cases}$

$W_t = \begin{cases} 1 \text{ for the quarter January–March,} \\ 0 \text{ for other quarters.} \end{cases}$

Note that we have inserted a dummy variable for each of the four quarters of the calendar year. In terms of Figure 5.8, our model says that the mean level of output, Q_t^m, is equal to $(b_0 + b_1 L_t)$, where b_1 is the common slope of the four lines, plus a further amount (possibly negative) that depends on the season.

Suppose that we try to estimate equation (5.53). In its present form, we would find that it is impossible to estimate, because there exists perfect multicollinearity among the regressors. That is, our assumption that the independent variables are not perfectly and linearly related is violated. Specifically, we have

$$S_t + H_t + A_t + W_t \equiv 1. \qquad (5.54)$$

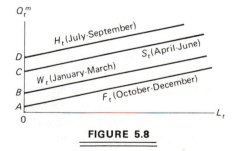

FIGURE 5.8

We know that, in any given quarter, one of these variables will have a value of unity and the others will be zero; their sum must always be one. Recall from the preceding chapter that, when there is perfect multicollinearity, we are unable to estimate uniquely the coefficients because we do not have a sufficient number of normal equations.

This problem is, however, easily resolved by simply dropping one of the dummy variables from the equation and changing some of our interpretations. For instance, suppose we delete W_t from equation (5.53) to obtain

$$Q_t = b_0 + b_1 L_t + b_2 S_t + b_3 H_t + b_4 F_t + u_t. \tag{5.55}$$

We have now eliminated the linear dependence among the regressors and so will be able to estimate the five parameters in equation (5.55). During the winter months, January–March, S_t, H_t, and F_t will be zero and so the "constant" term in our equation will be b_0. That is, in Figure 5.8, b_0 would correspond to the vertical intercept, OB. Similarly, referring again to equation (5.55), we see that the coefficients of each dummy variable indicates how the effect of the corresponding season *differs* from that of the winter season; for instance, during the spring quarter (April–June), when S_t has a value of unity, we have

$$Q_t = (b_0 + b_2) + b_1 L_t + u_t. \tag{5.56}$$

In Figure 5.8, the vertical intercept of the curve corresponding to the quarter April–June, namely OC, is equal to $(b_0 + b_2)$; b_2 thus indicates the direction and magnitude by which the effect of the spring quarter *differs* from that of the winter quarter. For instance, from Figure 5.8 we would expect b_2 to be positive. Similarly, from Figure 5.8, we would expect $b_3 > 0$ and $b_4 < 0$.

We are now in a position to review. If we have *four* seasons and if we believe that the level of our equation varies according to each season, we take one of the seasons as our standard and consider the effect of the other seasons *relative* to it. In the above example, we chose the winter season as our standard; if we had dropped S_t and included H_t, F_t, and W_t in our equation, we would have had the spring season as our standard. In this case, b_0 would represent the height of the equation during the spring season. In a sense, all of this can be summarized by stating that, if we have four seasons and we believe that the vertical intercept of our equation varies according to each season, we should formulate an equation that contains four parameters that describe these intercepts of the equation. Since the constant term is one such parameter, we only need *three* dummy variables. Note that we were unable to estimate the parameters of our original equation (5.53) because that equation contained *five* "intercept" parameters, b_0, b_2, b_3, b_4, b_5, but there were only *four* intercepts associated with the four seasons. One of the dummy variables was redundant. Our generalization is that if, because of regional variation (or what-have-you), one expects k different levels of the equation, one would only have to use $(k - 1)$ dummy variables. To review this discussion for yourself, you might return to the consumption equation we used at the beginning of this section and consider what would happen if we had put in equation (5.42) a dummy variable for war years,

$$W = \begin{cases} 1 \text{ during war years,} \\ 0 \text{ during peace,} \end{cases}$$

and a second dummy variable for years of peace,

$$P = \begin{cases} 1 \text{ during peacetime,} \\ 0 \text{ during wartime.} \end{cases}$$

Specifically, you should be able to show that, if both W and P are included, the resulting equation cannot be estimated. Second, you should convince yourself that one equation covering both the war and peace periods can be formulated with *either* W or P.

5.3 MORE ON FUNCTIONAL FORM

In Chapter 3 we examined a variety of transformations that allow us to put nonlinear relationships into a linear form so that we can then use our standard linear regression model. The use of these transformations is easily generalized to the multiple-regression case. We shall not dwell on this at any length; rather we shall simply take one particular example, the logarithmic transformation, and expand our analysis of the two-variable model to the multiple-regression case. We shall then develop some additional useful transformations that become possible when we are not restricted to our earlier two-variable formulation.

THE GENERALIZED LOGARITHMIC TRANSFORMATION

Recall that in Chapter 3 we examined a simple production relationship of the form

$$Q_t = aL_t^b e^{u_t}, \tag{5.57}$$

in which L_t, the quantity of labor used in period t, was the only variable factor in the production of Q_t. By taking logs in (5.57), we were able to express this production function as

$$\ln Q_t = \ln a + b \ln L_t + u_t. \tag{5.58}$$

We then transformed (5.58) into a linear form,

$$Q_t^* = a^* + bL_t^* + u_t, \tag{5.59}$$

by letting

$$Q_t^* = \ln Q_t,$$
$$a^* = \ln a,$$
$$L_t^* = \ln L_t.$$

In this form we used our regular estimation procedure to obtain the unbiased estimators, $\hat{a}^*$ and $\hat{b}$, of the parameters in (5.59), and we then took $e^{\hat{a}^*}$ as a biased, but at least consistent, estimator of a.

An obvious limitation of (5.57), however, is its inclusion of only a single variable factor of production. Goods and services are typically produced with the use of a variety of inputs, which suggests that a more realistic production function should allow for variable quantities of several factors. Let us consider a generalized form of (5.57) that accomplishes just this:

$$Q_t = b_0 F_{1t}{}^{b_1} F_{2t}{}^{b_2} \cdots F_{kt}{}^{b_k} e^{ut}, \tag{5.60}$$

where each of the F_t's represents the quantity of a particular factor of production used during period t. For example, F_{1t} might indicate the quantity of labor used in period t, F_{2t} the amount of capital, F_{3t} the amount of land, and so on. A production relationship of this particular form is known as a Cobb-Douglas production function.* What we need to know are the values of the b's in this relationship so that we can see how output varies with differing quantities of the various inputs. For instance, we might be interested in knowing whether or not the production of a particular commodity exhibits increasing returns to scale. By this, we mean that, other things equal,** if we were to double the inputs of all factors of production, would output more than double? If so, we say that we have increasing returns to scale; if output precisely doubles, then there are constant returns to scale; and if output less than doubles, there exist decreasing returns to scale.

This is easily determined with a Cobb-Douglas production function by simply taking the sum $\sum_{k=1}^{i} b_i$. To see this, we shall take a simple example and leave the generalization as an exercise. Suppose that we have a commodity, Q, which is produced with the use of only labor and capital such that

$$Q_t = b_0 L_t{}^{b_1} K_t{}^{b_2} e^{ut}, \tag{5.61}$$

where L_t and K_t represent the amounts of labor and capital, respectively, used in the production of Q during period t. Suppose next that we double the inputs of labor and capital; let $Q_t{}'$ be the resulting level of output. We would then have

$$Q_t{}' = b_0(2L_t)^{b_1}(2K_t)^{b_2} e^{ut} = b_0(2^{b_1})(L_t{}^{b_1})(2^{b_2})(K_t{}^{b_2})e^{ut}$$

$$= 2^{(b_1+b_2)} b_0 L_t{}^{b_1} K_t{}^{b_2} e^{ut} = 2^{(b_1+b_2)} Q_t. \tag{5.62}$$

From the last equation in (5.62), we can see that if $(b_1 + b_2) > 1$, output

---

* The Cobb-Douglas production function possesses a number of interesting and convenient properties, which have made it of considerable use in economic analysis. For a discussion of these properties, see James M. Henderson and Richard E. Quandt, *Microeconomic Theory*, 2nd ed. (New York: McGraw-Hill, 1971), pp. 79–85.

** This "other things equal" condition relates to the disturbance term. That is, in the discussion we are assuming that the disturbance term does not change when inputs are changed.

will more than double and we shall have increasing returns to scale; if $(b_1 + b_2) = 1$, output exactly doubles and there are constant returns to scale; and finally, if $(b_1 + b_2) < 1$, output less than doubles, which indicates decreasing returns to scale. More generally, in (5.60), you should be able to show that the cases of increasing, constant, or decreasing returns to scale correspond, respectively, to the cases where $\sum_{i=1}^{k} b_i$ exceeds unity, equals unity, or is less than unity.*

Empirically, our problem is to estimate the value of the b's in order to determine the character of the production relationship for a particular commodity. To get (5.60) into an estimable form, we use the logarithmic transformation; taking the log of (5.60), we obtain

$$\ln Q_t = \ln b_0 + b_1 \ln F_{1t} + b_2 \ln F_{2t} + \cdots + b_k \ln F_{kt} + u_t. \quad (5.63)$$

Next we define

$$Q_t^* = \ln Q_t,$$

$$b_0^* = \ln b_0,$$

$$F_{it}^* = \ln F_{it}.$$

Substituting into (5.63), we now have

$$Q_t^* = b_0^* + b_1 F_{1t}^* + b_2 F_{2t}^* + \cdots + b_k F_{kt}^* + u_t. \quad (5.64)$$

Using our standard technique on the variables defined in (5.64), we can obtain the unbiased estimators, $\hat{b}_0^*, \hat{b}_1, \ldots, \hat{b}_k$, of the parameters in (5.64). In this way, we obtain unbiased estimators of the elasticities of output with respect to each of the factors of production. As in the two-variable case, a biased but consistent estimator of b_0 would be $\hat{b}_0 = e^{\hat{b}_0^*}$. Finally, using the results described in Appendix B to this chapter, we could test the hypothesis as to whether or not there are constant returns to scale.

POLYNOMIAL FORMS OF INDEPENDENT VARIABLES

Economists often want to consider the possibility that the relationship between economic variables is nonlinear without really being sure just what form the relationship may take. For instance, consider the effect that age may have on an individual's consumption expenditures. It is possible that as an individual ages and his range of experience increases, his knowledge of different activities may induce an expansion in his level of expenditures for consumer goods and services. However, beyond a certain age, the individual may begin to "slow down" and actually reduce his level of consumption

---

* Another useful property of the Cobb-Douglas production function (5.60) is that each b_i may be interpreted as the elasticity of output with respect to factor i. That is, if F_i is increased by 1 percent, and all other inputs are held constant, output Q will increase by b_i percent. The reader should note, however, that each factor is indispensable in the production process in the sense that if any $F_i = 0$, output, Q, will also be zero.

expenditures. Such a relationship between consumption spending and age (when the other relevant variables, such as income, are held constant) is depicted by the solid curve *A* in Figure 5.9.

On the other hand, it may be the case that, as an individual ages, his demand for security, and therefore savings, increases and, consequently, his consumption expenditures may decline steadily. Such a relationship appears as the broken curve *B* in the same figure. Still again, in this example, the consumer's expenditures may decline only very slowly at first but then, as age advances, begin to decline at an increasing rate. This last relationship is illustrated by the dotted curve *C* in Figure 5.9.

For another example of variables for which any of a variety of nonlinear relationships is plausible, consider the effect that changes in the cost of living have on wage adjustments as measured by money-wage changes. It is, of course, possible that cost of living changes are fully reflected in changes in wages. That is, other things equal, if over the past year the cost of living went up by *X* percent, wages would be adjusted upward by *X* percent.* On the other hand, it is conceivable that "small" changes in the cost of living are not recognized and consequently do not lead to corresponding wage increases. In this case we might assume that only "large" changes in the cost of living are reflected in wage adjustments. These possibilities are outlined respectively by curves OA_1 and OA_2A_3 in Figure 5.10.

In line with these examples, we want to turn our attention to the problems of estimating and testing the relationship among variables when the form of the relationship is not certain. We shall generalize our results in terms of further examples in a later section of this chapter.

We begin (using the case of two variables for simplicity) by assuming that the dependent variable *Y* is related to the independent variable *X* in an uncertain way. This assumption may be expressed as

$$Y_t = f(X_t) + u_t, \qquad (5.65)$$

where u_t is our disturbance term. Equation (5.65) simply states that the *t*th

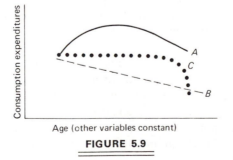

FIGURE 5.9

---

* We might want to add to this some further increase in wages to reflect rises in productivity.

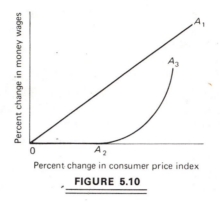

FIGURE 5.10

value of Y, Y_t, depends on the tth value of X, X_t, and on the disturbance term, u_t. Because we do not know the specific form of $f(X_t)$ in equation (5.65), to make some progress in estimating the relationship between Y_t and X_t we must obviously either find out what $f(X_t)$ is or, alternatively, employ some approximation to it. We take the latter approach by recalling a theorem we stated and used in connection with the Almon lag technique. Specifically, the theorem states that, under general conditions, a function (or curve) may be approximated to any degree of accuracy by a polynomial. If so, we may apply this theorem to our unknown function in (5.65) to obtain

$$f(X_t) \doteq a_0 + a_1 X_t + a_2 X_t^2 + \cdots + a_k X_t^k. \tag{5.66}$$

In general, the more accuracy desired, the higher the degree (k) of the polynomial must be. In a sense this follows from our discussion concerning polynomials in the Almon lag technique. In that section we indicated that the number of turning points on the graph of a polynomial was *at most* one less than the degree of the polynomial. From this we might conclude that higher-degree polynomials are more flexible in form than ones of lower degree. This indicates that, if we want a closer approximation, we need a higher-degree polynomial so that it can possess sufficient flexibility to follow closely the form of the unknown function. Typically, the more complex the form of the function being approximated, the higher must be the degree of the polynomial.

This is illustrated in terms of our unknown function $f(X_t)$ in Figure 5.11. Here we assume that our unknown function $f(X_t)$ has the form indicated by the solid curve AB. Now this curve may be approximated, although poorly, by the straight line that results if we employ a polynomial of degree one ($k = 1$). The approximation improves if we use instead a polynomial of degree two ($k = 2$). The approximation can be made still better by taking $k = 3$, and so on.

Assume that we have a number of hypotheses concerning the general form of the relationship between Y_t and X_t. Assume, further, that the most

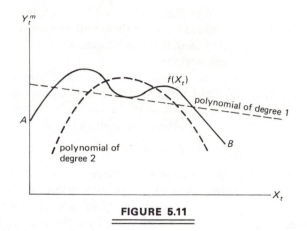

FIGURE 5.11

complicated of these hypotheses suggests that a value of $k = k_m$ would be "adequate" for the approximation in (5.66).* By "adequate" we mean that the "approximately-equal-to" sign, $\doteq$, in (5.66) may be replaced with little loss of accuracy by an equals sign. We note also that, if a polynomial of degree k_m is an adequate approximation to our most complicated hypothesized form, it is also an adequate approximation to all of the simpler forms being considered.

Under this assumption concerning k_m, we may substitute $k = k_m$ in (5.66), and this in turn into (5.65) to get

$$Y_t = a_0 + a_1 X_t + a_2 X_t^2 + \cdots + a_{k_m} X^{k_m} + u_t. \tag{5.67}$$

Equation (5.67) may be converted to our standard model by the substitutions

$$Z_{it} = X_t^i, \qquad i = 1, \ldots, k_m. \tag{5.68}$$

That is, if we substitute (5.68) into (5.67), we shall get

$$Y_t = a_0 + a_1 Z_{1t} + a_2 Z_{2t} + \cdots + a_{k_m} Z_{k_m t} + u_t, \tag{5.69}$$

which is of the standard form.

Let $\hat{a}_0, \hat{a}_1, \ldots, \hat{a}_{k_m}$ be the estimators of the parameters of (5.69). Then the estimated relationship between Y_t and X_t is

$$\hat{Y}_t = \hat{a}_0 + \hat{a}_1 X_t + \cdots + \hat{a}_{k_m} X_t^{k_m}, \tag{5.70}$$

because our estimator of $f(X_t)$ would be given by

$$\widehat{f(X_t)} = \hat{a}_0 + \hat{a}_1 X_1 + \cdots + \hat{a}_{k_m} X_t^{k_m}. \tag{5.71}$$

Consider now the problem of testing whether or not the variable Y_t depends on the variable X_t. At first glance, it might appear that this hypothesis can be tested by simply testing the hypotheses, one after another, that

* For most economic applications, a value of $k_m = 3$ would be reasonable.

$a_1 = 0, a_2 = 0, \ldots, a_{k_m} = 0$ in (5.69). We would presumably conclude that Y_t and X_t are significantly related if *any* of these null hypotheses are rejected. Conversely, if we accept all of these null hypotheses, the conclusion would be that Y_t and X_t are not significantly related.

Unfortunately, we cannot test these hypotheses concerning a relationship between Y_t and X_t in this fashion because of what we might call a "fallacy of composition." That is, the hypothesis in this case relates to more than one parameter. In particular, the hypothesis we wish to test is

$$H_0 : a_1 = a_2 = \cdots = a_{k_m} = 0. \tag{5.72}$$

In Appendix B to this chapter we develop a procedure for testing hypotheses such as (5.72). At this point, however, we point out that, if the hypotheses $a_1 = 0, a_2 = 0, \ldots, a_{k_m} = 0$ are tested, one after another, at a certain level of significance, say 5 percent, and *accepted*, the hypothesis in (5.72) may still be *rejected* at the 5 percent level of significance. In other words, a hypothesis that relates to more than one parameter, say k_m as in (5.72), cannot in general be properly tested at a given level of significance by breaking it up into k_m hypotheses each of which relates to a single parameter and then testing these hypotheses sequentially at that level of significance.

The extension of the above estimation technique to the case in which the regression model includes additional regressors is straightforward. For instance, suppose our model were

$$Y_t = b_0 + b_1 X_{1t} + b_2 X_{2t} + f(X_{3t}) + u_t, \tag{5.73}$$

where u_t is again our disturbance term, and where we again assume that the particular form of $f(X_{3t})$ is uncertain. Then, following our procedure above, if our hypotheses concerning $f(X_{3t})$ suggest that $k = k_m$ would yield an adequate polynomial approximation, we would assume that

$$f(X_{3t}) = a_0 + a_1 X_{3t} + \cdots + a_{k_m} X_{3t}{}^{k_m}. \tag{5.74}$$

Substituting (5.74) into (5.73), we have

$$Y_t = A + b_1 X_{1t} + b_2 X_{2t} + a_1 X_{3t} + \cdots + a_{k_m} X_{3t}{}^{k_m} + u_t, \tag{5.75}$$

where $A = a_0 + b_0$. Again, letting

$$Z_{it} = X_{3t}{}^i, \qquad i = 1, 2, \ldots, k_m, \tag{5.76}$$

we can write equation (5.75) as

$$Y_t = A + b_1 X_{1t} + b_2 X_{2t} + a_1 Z_{1t} + \cdots + a_{k_m} Z_{k_m t} + u_t, \tag{5.77}$$

which is in the standard form. It follows that, subject to the polynomial approximation, we can obtain the unbiased estimators $\hat{A}, \hat{b}_1, \hat{b}_2, \hat{a}_1, \ldots,$ $\hat{a}_{k_m}$ of the parameters in (5.77).

Note that in this case we would not be able to obtain separate estimators of a_0 and b_0, because only their sum, A, appears in (5.77). Unlike the simple case above, we would only be able to estimate $f(X_{3t})$ up to an additive constant. In other words, we would only be able to estimate the variable part of $f(X_{3t})$, say $f_v(X_{3t})$:

$$\widehat{f_v(X_{3t})} = \hat{a}_1 X_{3t} + \cdots + \hat{a}_{k_m} X_{3t}^{k_m}. \tag{5.78}$$

Normally, however, the important part of $f(X_{3t})$ is its variable component, because this component describes the manner in which Y_t varies with X_{3t}.

At this stage, it should be clear that we can extend the above technique to the case in which there are, in general, any number of regressors. It should also be clear that we can extend this procedure to encompass a model where more than one of these regressors enter the model in an unspecified manner.*

COMBINATIONS OF FUNCTIONAL FORMS

To draw together our discussion of functional form, we emphasize that it is perfectly legitimate to use several different transformations in the same regression equation. In fact, you may have noticed that, in some of our earlier examples, one or more variables would appear in a logarithmic, or perhaps a reciprocal, form, while others were subject to no type of transformation at all. As a further example, consider the following more complex version of a Phillips Curve relationship:

$$\dot{W}_t = b_0 + b_1 \left(\frac{1}{R_t}\right) + b_2 \pi_{(t-1)} + b_3 \dot{P}_t + b_4 \dot{P}_t^2 + b_5 \ln G_t + u_t, \tag{5.79}$$

where

$$
\begin{aligned}
\dot{W} &= \text{percentage change in wages during period } t, \\
R_t &= \text{rate of unemployment in period } t, \\
\pi_{(t-1)} &= \text{rate of business profit in period } (t-1), \\
\dot{P}_t &= \text{percentage change of prices in period } t, \\
\ln G_t &= \text{natural logarithm of the rate of growth of the labor force in} \\
&\quad\ \text{period } t, \\
u_t &= \text{the disturbance term.}
\end{aligned}
$$

Note that in the same equation we would employ the reciprocal transformation, the log transformation, a lagged relationship, and a polynomial form for one of the independent variables. At this point we are considering (5.79) in order to demonstrate transformation techniques. However, in practice there would be "reasons" (economic hypotheses) behind each of these transformations. For instance, we saw in Chapter 3 that a linear relationship between $\dot{W}$ and R is not very plausible (because R is constrained from assuming negative values), and that a reciprocal transformation makes sense. With respect to the profits' variable (π_{t-1}), we might expect unions involved

---

* For instance, consider a model of the form

$$Y_t = a_0 + f_1(X_{1t}) + f_2(X_{2t}) + a_1 X_{3t} + u_t.$$

in wage negotiations to use the rate of profits (which normally would be available for the *preceding* accounting period) as one element in the bargaining process. If profits last period were unusually high, the union might feel justified in demanding a correspondingly larger increase in wages. Similarly, we might consider the polynomial form for the price variable, because the relationship between wage adjustments and price adjustments may not be linear if "small" price changes go largely unnoticed while large price changes signal demands for wage increases (see Figure 5.10). Finally, because the growth of the labor force is associated with an increase in the supply of labor, it may have an effect on the bargaining position of workers. In this respect, we saw in Chapter 3 that the relevant variable for the growth in the labor force is typically the percentage (rather than the absolute) increase, so that the size of the change is measured relative to the level of the existing supply of labor. For illustrative purposes, in (5.79) we would adopt the logarithmic transformation for the variable G_t. The point of all this is simply that the selection of functional form is not basically a process of trial and error; we should make use of whatever theoretical and institutional information we have in determining the most appropriate forms for our functional relationships.

Returning to the wage equation, we can put (5.79) into a linear form by simply employing the following set of transformations*:

$$Z_{1t} = \left(\frac{1}{R_t}\right),$$

$$Z_{2t} = \pi_{(t-1)},$$

$$Z_{3t} = \dot{P}_t,$$

$$Z_{4t} = \dot{P}_t^2,$$

$$Z_{5t} = \ln G_t.$$

Substituting these transformations into (5.79) gives us a linear form for our equation:

$$\dot{W}_t = b_0 + b_1 Z_{1t} + b_2 Z_{2t} + b_3 Z_{3t} + b_4 Z_{4t} + b_5 Z_{5t} + u_t. \quad (5.80)$$

We can easily calculate the value of the Z's from our observed values for R, π, $\dot{P}$, and G, and then, using these values for the Z's and our standard estimation procedure, calculate $\hat{b}_0$, $\hat{b}_1$, $\hat{b}_2$, $\hat{b}_3$, $\hat{b}_4$, and $\hat{b}_5$.

All this should suggest the wide range of flexibility inherent in multiple-regression estimation. Econometricians, particularly in the earlier days of regression analysis, were often criticized for their primary reliance on linear forms for relationships. However, you should now be able to see that, with an imaginative and sensible use of transformations, the multiple-regression model is capable of handling a vast variety of quite complex functional forms.

---

* Actually, the transformation $Z_{3t} = \dot{P}_t$ is unnecessary and is made only for consistency of notation.

5.4 AN ILLUSTRATION: THE DEMAND FOR MONEY

A central issue in monetary economics is the theory and measurement of the demand for money.* In fact, a great deal hinges on this issue, for the potential effectiveness of both fiscal and monetary policy in influencing aggregate economic activity depends on the form of the money demand function and the values of its parameters. Economic theory suggests that the demand for *real* money balances (nominal money balances adjusted for the general price level so as to hold constant their purchasing power) should depend on at least three sorts of variables: income, rates of interest on bonds (or rates of return on other financial assets), and, perhaps, net worth. In brief, as peoples' incomes rise, they will demand more money balances for transactions purposes; as interest rates rise, they will wish to reduce their money holdings since the effective opportunity cost of holding cash balances (which, at least until recently, earn no interest) will have increased; and as peoples' net worth rises, they will tend to increase cash balances as one form in which to hold their increased wealth. We can summarize all this by postulating that

$$M_d = f(Y, r, W), \qquad (5.81)$$

where

M_d = demand for money balances,
Y = real income,
r = rate of interest, and
W = wealth (or net worth),

where we would expect the partial effect of the interest rate to be negative and the partial effect of the income and wealth variables to be positive.

A number of economists have done extensive econometric work aimed at estimating equations corresponding to (5.81). These efforts have drawn on a variety of functional forms involving several of the transformations we examined in this chapter; they also often include lagged values of certain variables. As an example, we present the results of one such study by Martin Bronfenbrenner and Thomas Mayer.** Their point of departure is a multiplicative money demand function of the form:

$$M_{dt} = b_0 Y_t^{b_1} r_t^{b_2} W_t^{b_3} M_{d(t-1)}^{b_4} e^{u_t}, \qquad (5.82)$$

where u_t is a disturbance term and all of the other variables have been defined in reference to (5.81). Taking the logarithm of both sides of (5.82), Bronfenbrenner and Mayer obtain the standard linear form

$$\ln M_{dt} = \ln b_0 + b_1 \ln Y_t + b_2 \ln r_t + b_3 \ln W_t + b_4 \ln M_{d(t-1)} + u_t. \qquad (5.83)$$

---

*For a detailed treatment, see David E. Laidler, *The Demand for Money: Theories and Evidence*, 2nd ed. (New York: Dun-Donnelley, 1977).

**Martin Bronfenbrenner and Thomas Mayer, "Liquidity Functions in the American Economy," *Econometrica*, 28 (1960), pp. 810–834.

For purposes of interpretation, assume that u_t satisfies all of our standard assumptions, and rewrite (5.83) as

$$(\ln M_{dt} - b_4 \ln M_{d(t-1)}) = B + b_1 \ln Y_t + b_2 \ln r_t + b_3 \ln W_t + u_t, \quad (5.84)$$

where $B = \ln b_0$. In this form we see that a model such as (5.83) can be interpreted as explaining the *difference* between the current value of the dependent variable, $\ln M_{dt}$, and its lagged value which is multiplied by the factor b_4. For instance, suppose we felt that the log of the demand for money simply fluctuated randomly about a trend line that increased at, say, 3 percent. In this case, our expectations concerning the values of the coefficients in (5.83), or (5.84), would be $b_4 = 1.03$, and $B = b_1 = b_2 = b_3 = 0$; we would believe that the demand for money is not responsive to the income, interest rate, and wealth variables.

Using annual data for the United States for the period 1919–1956, Bronfenbrenner and Mayer estimated equation (5.83) by the least-squares technique and obtained

$$\widehat{\ln M} = 0.11 + 0.34 \ln Y - 0.09 \ln r - 0.12 \ln W + 0.72 \ln M_{t-1} \quad (5.85)$$
$$\quad\quad (.003) \quad (.09) \quad\quad (.01) \quad\quad (.08) \quad\quad (.06)$$

$$R^2 = 0.99,$$

where the figures in parentheses beneath the parameter estimates are estimated standard deviations. In order to illustrate results, the calculated t values corresponding, respectively, to the income, interest rate, wealth, and lagged money variables are, approximately, 3.8, 9, 1.5, and 12. When we use our rule of thumb, these results suggest that, if we consider the null hypothesis $H_0 : b_3 = 0$ against the alternative $H_1 : b_3 \neq 0$ at a 5 percent level of significance, we would accept H_0. In contrast, were we to consider *any* of the other null hypotheses $H_0 : b_i = 0$ against $H_1 : b_i \neq 0$, where $i = 1, 2, 4$, again at the 5 percent level, we would reject H_0.

The null hypothesis $H_0 : b_2 = 0$ is of particular interest to monetary economists. The rejection of this hypothesis would give them reason to believe that at higher interest rates people hold a smaller fraction of their wealth in the form of money balances so as to take advantage of the higher return available from bonds and other interest-bearing financial assets. An important implication of this result is that fiscal policy has some impact on aggregate demand; if the demand for money is not responsive to the interest rate, fiscal policy will merely induce offsetting changes in private expenditure with no net effect on total spending in the economy.*

---

* On this point, see Laidler, *op. cit.*, chap. 2. In brief, if money demand is totally unaffected by changes in the rate of interest, the LM curve will be vertical. In consequence, a tax cut or increase in government expenditure will simply drive up interest rates and "crowd out" an equivalent amount of private expenditure. In this case, the level of money GNP depends solely on the size of the money supply.

APPENDIX A.

Endpoint Restrictions
in the Almon Lag Technique

This appendix examines the use of endpoint restrictions with the Almon technique for estimating lag structures. As we mentioned in the text, an economist may often feel he knows, not only the pattern of the b's, but also the exact value of either, or both, b_0 and b_k. This value, incidentally, is typically zero. If we know the values of these parameters, we should try to incorporate this information into our estimation procedure.

For instance, suppose we felt that the pattern of the b's is similar to that depicted by the curve A in Figure 5A.1. The b's in this case first decline, then increase, and, finally decline until the last b is zero. In this pattern we could impose one endpoint restriction, namely, $b_k = 0$. On the other hand, suppose we felt that the pattern of the b's is like that described by curve B in Figure 5A.1. In this case, there could be two endpoint restrictions, namely, $b_0 = b_k = 0$.

In general, the experimenter may impose either, or both, of these endpoint restrictions. The procedure is a straightforward generalization of our existing technique; consider again equation (5.24) and suppose that $k = 10$ (our equation has ten lags in it):

$$Y_t = a + b_0 X_t + b_1 X_{t-1} + \cdots + b_{10} X_{t-10} + u_t. \tag{5A.1}$$

First, ignoring the endpoint restrictions, suppose the assumed pattern of the b's suggests a third-degree polynomial:

$$b_i = \alpha_0 + \alpha_1 i + \alpha_2 i^2 + \alpha_3 i^3, \qquad i = 0, \ldots, 10. \tag{5A.2}$$

Then, substituting the expression for each b as given in (5A.2) into (5A.1), we have

$$Y_t = a + \alpha_0 Z_{1t} + \alpha_1 Z_{2t} + \alpha_2 Z_{3t} + \alpha_3 Z_{4t} + u_t, \tag{5A.3}$$

where

$$Z_{1t} = \sum_{i=0}^{10} X_{t-i}, \qquad Z_{2t} = \sum_{i=1}^{10} i X_{t-i},$$

$$Z_{3t} = \sum_{i=1}^{10} i^2 X_{t-i}, \qquad Z_{4t} = \sum_{i=1}^{10} i^3 X_{t-i}.$$

Let us now impose our endpoint condition. Specifically, suppose we believe that $b_{10} = 0$. Then, from (5A.2), we have

$$b_{10} = \alpha_0 + 10\alpha_1 + 100\alpha_2 + 1000\alpha_3 = 0. \tag{5A.4}$$

It is clear from (5A.4) that, if we impose the condition $b_{10} = 0$, we must have

$$\alpha_0 = -10\alpha_1 - 100\alpha_2 - 1000\alpha_3. \tag{5A.5}$$

That is, the condition $b_{10} = 0$ implies a restriction on the relationship among the

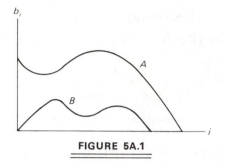

FIGURE 5A.1

α's. This, essentially, is our solution. We simply go back to (5A.3) and substitute (5A.5) for α_0. This gives us

$$Y_t = a + \alpha_1 Q_{1t} + \alpha_2 Q_{2t} + \alpha_3 Q_{3t} + u_t, \qquad (5A.6)$$

where

$$Q_{1t} = Z_{2t} - 10 Z_{1t},$$

$$Q_{2t} = Z_{3t} - 100 Z_{1t},$$

and

$$Q_{3t} = Z_{4t} - 1000 Z_{1t}.$$

Equation (5A.6) is in standard form, and so α_1, α_2, and α_3 may be estimated by our standard multiple-regression technique. Suppose that $\hat{\alpha}_1$, $\hat{\alpha}_2$, and $\hat{\alpha}_3$ are our estimators. Then, from (5A.5), our estimator for α_0 would be

$$\hat{\alpha}_0 = -10\hat{\alpha}_1 - 100\hat{\alpha}_2 - 1000\hat{\alpha}_3. \qquad (5A.7)$$

Finally, the estimators of the b's would follow from (5A.2):

$$\hat{b}_0 = \hat{\alpha}_0$$

$$\hat{b}_1 = \hat{\alpha}_0 + \hat{\alpha}_1 + \hat{\alpha}_2 + \hat{\alpha}_3$$

$$\vdots \qquad\qquad (5A.8)$$

$$\hat{b}_9 = \hat{\alpha}_0 + 9\hat{\alpha}_1 + 81\hat{\alpha}_2 + 729\hat{\alpha}_3$$

$$\hat{b}_{10} = 0.$$

In brief, imposing the endpoint condition $b_{10} = 0$ enabled us to substitute for α_0 and thereby eliminate it from our standard Almon regression model (5A.3). We leave it as an exercise for the reader to show that, if we wish to impose both $b_0 = 0$ and $b_{10} = 0$, we would end up substituting expressions in α_2 and α_3 for both α_0 and α_1 in our regression model (5A.3). Thus, both α_0 and α_1 would disappear from the equation we actually estimate.

In the text we stated that this indirect method of imposing endpoint restrictions yields unbiased estimators that have smaller variances than those produced by the direct method (of simply dropping X_t and X_{t-k} from the analysis). This is true *only under a particular assumption*. The assumption is that the endpoint parameters lie on the same polynomial curve as the other nonzero parameters. For example, if the endpoint restrictions are $b_0 = b_{10} = 0$, we must assume that the value of the polynomial is zero when $i = 0$ and $i = 10$. This is what we did with respect to $b_{10} = 0$ in our example above (5A.4).

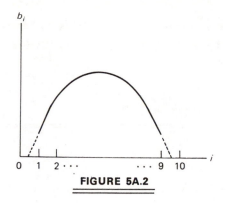

FIGURE 5A.2

In practice, however, this assumption may *not* be satisfied. For example, suppose that $k = 10$ and that $b_0 = b_{10} = 0$. Suppose, further, that the nonzero parameters $b_1, \ldots, b_9$ lie on a second-degree polynomial such as that outlined in Figure 5A.2. The assumption that the value of the polynomial is zero for $i = 0$ and $i = 10$ implies that, if we project the polynomial, it will cross the i axis at $i = 0$ and $i = 10$. Figure 5A.2 shows that this need not be the case. In the figure, the polynomial crosses the axis (as indicated by our projected dashed lines) somewhere between $i = 0$ and $i = 1$, and $i = 9$ and $i = 10$. Thus, if we go through the above manipulations, such as (5A.4), we will end up imposing restrictions that are simply invalid. The consequence is that the resulting estimators will be *biased*. In brief, one should not impose ·endpoint restrictions unless careful analysis suggests they are valid. For this reason, the direct method of dealing with information concerning the values of endpoint parameters (e.g., simply delete X_t from (5A.1) if its coefficient, b_0, is believed to be zero) seems more promising.

APPENDIX B.

Tests of Hypotheses Involving More Than One Regression Parameter

Consider the regression model

$$Y_t = a_0 + a_1 X_{1t} + \cdots + a_k X_{kt} + u_t, \qquad t = 1, \ldots, n, \qquad (5B.1)$$

where we assume that the regressors, $X_1, \ldots, X_k$, and the disturbance terms satisfy all of our standard assumptions. This includes the assumption that the disturbance terms are normally distributed.

It often happens in models such as (5B.1) that economists wish to test hypotheses that relate to *more than one parameter*. These hypotheses usually come in two forms. The first relates to linear restrictions on the coefficients of (5B.1). Some examples of such hypotheses are

$$a_1 = a_2,$$

$$a_3 = 2a_5, \qquad (5B.2)$$

$$a_0 + a_1 + a_2 + \cdots + a_k = 1.$$

The second form of such hypotheses relates to the significance of a set of the regressors. For instance, suppose we wish to test the hypothesis that Y_t does not depend on X_1, X_2, or X_3 in (5B.1). Then we would be interested in testing the hypothesis

$$a_1 = a_2 = a_3 = 0. \qquad (5B.3)$$

In both these cases, the hypotheses described in (5B.2) and (5B.3) are taken as the null hypotheses, and the alternative hypotheses are taken to be simply the complement of the null (i.e., not H_0). For example, the alternative to the null hypothesis described in (5B.3) would be the hypothesis that at least one of the parameters a_1, a_2, a_3 is not zero. Similarly, the alternatives to the hypotheses described in (5B.2) would be

$$a_1 \neq a_2,$$

$$a_3 \neq 2a_5, \qquad (5B.4)$$

$$a_0 + a_1 + \cdots + a_k \neq 1.$$

Fortunately, there is a very straightforward technique for testing such hypotheses. In particular, the testing procedure may be outlined as follows.

Step 1. Impose the null hypothesis under consideration on the regression model. For instance, if the hypothesis is $a_1 = a_2$, we would rewrite the regression model (5B.1) as

$$Y_t = a_0 + a_1(X_{1t} + X_{2t}) + a_3 X_{3t} + \cdots + a_k X_{kt} + u_t. \qquad (5B.5)$$

As another example, if the null hypothesis were $a_1 = a_2 = a_3 = 0$, we would have

$$Y_t = a_0 + a_4 X_{4t} + \cdots + a_k X_{kt} + u_t. \qquad (5B.6)$$

Finally, as a third illustration, if the null hypothesis were $a_1 + 2a_2 + 5a_3 = 10$, we would have $a_1 = 10 - 2a_2 - 5a_3$, and so

$$Y_t = a_0 + 10X_{1t} + a_2(X_{2t} - 2X_{1t}) + a_3(X_{3t} - 5X_{1t})$$

$$+ a_4X_{4t} + \cdots + a_kX_{kt} + u_t, \quad (5B.7)$$

which we could rewrite as

$$(Y_t - 10X_{1t}) = a_0 + a_2(X_{2t} - 2X_{1t}) + a_3(X_{3t} - 5X_{1t})$$

$$+ a_4X_{4t} + \cdots + a_kX_{kt} + u_t. \quad (5B.8)$$

Step 2. Estimate the resulting restricted form of the model and determine the error sum of squares, ESS_R.*

Step 3. Estimate the *original* (unrestricted) form of the regression model, (5B.1), and determine the error sum of squares, ESS_U.

Step 4. Determine the difference in the number of parameters between the restricted and unrestricted regression models. Let d be this difference. For instance, corresponding to the hypothesis $a_1 = a_2$ in (5B.2), $d = 1$. For a second example, the hypothesis in (5B.3) implies that $d = 3$.

Step 5. Calculate the ratio

$$\frac{(\text{ESS}_R - \text{ESS}_U)/d}{\text{ESS}_U/(n - k - 1)}, \quad (5B.9)$$

where n is the number of observations and $(k + 1)$ is the number of parameters in the *original* (unrestricted) model. The null hypotheses we have been discussing are accepted or rejected on the basis of the magnitude of the ratio in (5B.9). For example, suppose the null hypothesis under consideration is *false*. Then the restricted regression model would be based on a false hypothesis and hence would be improperly specified. The original regression model, on the other hand, would be properly specified. This suggests that ESS_R and ESS_U should differ by a large amount. In particular, we would expect $\text{ESS}_R > \text{ESS}_U$.

On the other hand, suppose the hypothesis under consideration is *true*. Then the restricted regression model would be properly specified. However, the original, or unrestricted, regression model would *also be properly specified!* Although this may seem strange, it is not difficult to see just why this is true. In the full specification of our model, the only assumption we made concerning the regression parameters is that they are *constants*. Clearly this assumption will be satisfied whether or not the hypotheses in (5B.2) or (5B.3) are true. The condition that, say, $a_1 = a_2$, does not violate any assumptions relating to a model such as (5B.1). Similarly, because zero is a constant, if it were the case that $a_2 = a_3 = 0$, this again would not lead to a violation of any of our assumptions in (5B.1).

In a later chapter we shall suggest that if the hypothesis under consideration is true, there are benefits, which relate to the properties of estimators, in considering the restricted form of the regression model. However, at this point we need only note that, if both the restricted and unrestricted forms of the regression model are properly specified, we would expect ESS_U and ESS_R to differ by only a "small" amount. All of this may be summarized by noting that "large" values of the ratio

* Recall from Chapters 2 and 4 that $\text{ESS} = \sum (Y_t - \hat{Y}_t)^2$.

in (5B.9) suggest that the null hypothesis under consideration is false, and "small" values of this ratio suggest that it is true.

To formalize, it can be shown* that, if the null hypothesis being considered is true, the ratio in (5B.9) is an F variable with d and $(n - k - 1)$ degrees of freedom, $F_{d, n-k-1}$.

Step 6. Since small values of this ratio are associated with the *acceptance* of the null hypothesis, we would accept H_0 at the, say, 5 percent level of significance if

$$\frac{(\text{ESS}_R - \text{ESS}_U)/d}{\text{ESS}_U/(n - k - 1)} < F_{d,n-k-1}^{0.95}, \tag{5B.10}$$

where $F_{d,n-k-1}^{0.95}$ is such that

$$\text{Prob}(F_{d,n-k-1} < F_{d,n-k-1}^{0.95}) = 0.95. \tag{5B.11}$$

We can obtain $F_{d,n-k-1}^{0.95}$ from any standard table on the F distribution. For purposes of reference, we have included as Statistical Table 3 at the end of this book such a table for the F distribution.

As an example, suppose we are considering the hypothesis $a_1 = a_2 = a_3 = 0$. Assume further that $n = 49$ and $k = 8$. We find in Statistical Table 3 that $F_{3,40}^{0.95} = 2.84$. Suppose we determine that $\text{ESS}_R = 35$ and $\text{ESS}_U = 20$. Our ratio would then be

$$\frac{(35 - 20)/3}{20/40} = \frac{15/3}{1/2} = 10 > 2.84.$$

As a result, we would reject, at the 5 percent level of significance, the hypothesis that $a_1 = a_2 = a_3 = 0$.

---

* See Arthur S. Goldberger, *Econometric Theory* (New York: Wiley, 1964), pp. 173–177.

QUESTIONS

1. Consider the production function $Q_t = (1/A)L_t^a K_t^b e^{u_t}$, where Q_t, L_t, and K_t are output, labor, and capital in time t, and u_t is the corresponding disturbance term. Assume that $E(u_t) = 0$, $E(u_t^2) = \sigma^2$ and that u_t is independent of L_t and K_t. Suggest a method for estimating A, a, and b.

2. Suppose that the amount of private investment in a given year depends on the rate of interest and the political party of the president. That is, it may be the case that investment will be higher if the president is a Republican rather than a Democrat. Formulate a time-series regression model assuming that there are only two parties.

3. Consider the model $C_t = a_0 + a_1 F_t Y_t + a_2 Y_t^{1/2} + a_3(1/A_t) + u_t$, where C_t is consumption expenditures of the tth household, Y_t is its income, F_t is its family size, and A_t is its liquid assets. Convert this model into a linear model.

4. Suppose that you want to estimate the simple linear consumption function $C_i = a + bY_i + u_i$ across n individuals. How would you take account of a possible shift in the function between urban and rural consumers if the intercept is assumed to be affected by the residential location of the individual?

5. Assume that the investment expenditures of a firm depend on the rate of interest, the rate of profits, and the change in sales as an indication of expectations.
   a. Set up the corresponding regression model.
   b. Suppose that during the sample period the profits for this firm have been, in each and every time period, 15 percent. Discuss any resulting problems of estimation.

6. Assume that the rate of investment in a given period t, I_t, depends on the interest rate in that period, r_t, sales in that period, and seven lagged values of the rate of sales, S_t. Assume that the weights corresponding to the lagged values of S are such that they first increase, reach a peak, and then decrease.
   a. Set up an unrestricted form of this model.
   b. Set up the Almon form of this model.
   c. Write out the normal equations for the Almon form.

7. Consider the multiple-regression model

$$Y_t = a + b_0 X_t + \cdots + b_6 X_{t-6} + \varepsilon_t.$$

   Suppose that we employ the Almon technique with a polynomial of degree 4 to estimate the parameters of this model. Suppose that our results are $\hat{a}_0 = 1$, $\hat{a}_1 = 3$, $\hat{a}_2 = 5$, $\hat{a}_3 = 4$, and $\hat{a}_4 = -10$.
   a. What would be our estimate for b_2?
   b. Suppose that we assume $b_0 + b_1 + \cdots + b_6 = 1$. Express this information in terms of a restriction on the α's in the Almon polynomial approximation.

8. It is sometimes said that the empirical results of a regression model should not be used to predict events that lie considerably outside the scope of experience. Discuss. (Hint: consider some of the assumptions underlying the polynomial approximations.)

9. Convert the following Koyck model into a simpler form:

$$Y_t = a_0 + a_1 X_t + b_0 Z_t + b_1 Z_{t-1} + \cdots + u_t,$$

where

$$b_i = b_0 \lambda^i, \qquad i = 1, 2, \ldots.$$

10. Consider the following Almon lag model:

$$Y_t = b + b_0 X_t + b_1 X_{t-1} + \cdots + b_{10} X_{t-10} + u_t,$$

where we assume the quadratic approximation

$$b_i = \alpha_0 + \alpha_1 i + \alpha_2 i^2, \qquad i = 0, 1, \ldots, 10.$$

Suppose that $b_5 = 3$. Derive the corresponding restrictions on the α's and hence the restricted form of the regression model.

11. Suppose that consumer expenditures, C_t, depend on income, Y_t, and on the rate of interest, r_t, if r_t exceeds 0.05. If r_t does not exceed 0.05, C_t depends only on Y_t. Formulate this relationship as a regression model.

12. Convert the following model into a multiple linear regression model, and then write out the normal equations:

$$\log Y_t = a_0 + a_1 e^{X_{1t}} + a_2 \left(\frac{1}{1 + X_{1t} X_{2t}}\right) + u_t.$$

CHAPTER 6
Problems in
Regression Analysis

In the preceding chapters we have developed techniques for estimating the relationship among a set of variables and have learned how we can use this information to test hypotheses and to predict the effect of a change in one variable on another. These techniques are dependent on a number of assumptions that, you will recall, were enumerated and discussed in our presentation of the regression model. In practice, however, economists sometimes find that it is virtually certain (or, in other cases, at least very likely) that one or more of these assumptions is violated by the character of the functional relationship or, alternatively, that serious difficulties arise from the particular set of observed values for the variables. Much of the recent work in econometrics has been directed to developing modified estimation techniques to deal with these problems.

This will be the subject of these last two chapters of the book. Here we shall examine the types of circumstances that either generate violations of the assumptions of the regression model or at least create difficulties in its use or effectiveness, and shall then discuss the ways in which we can "patch up" our estimation procedures to take account of these problems.

6.1 MULTICOLLINEARITY

We have already, in several places, discussed the problem of multicollinearity. Formally, you will remember, this problem arises when at least one of the independent variables is a linear combination of the others, with the result that we have too few independent normal equations and, hence, cannot derive estimators for all our coefficients. As a brief review, suppose that, in

$$Y_t = b_0 + b_1 X_{1t} + b_2 X_{2t} + u_t, \tag{6.1}$$

equation (6.1), the values of X_1 and X_2 are always precisely identical, so that we have

$$X_{1t} = X_{2t} \qquad \text{for } t = 1, 2, \ldots, n.$$

This means that every movement from period to period in X_1 is exactly matched by the same movement in X_2. If this is true, we simply cannot separate the influence of X_1 on Y from that of X_2. Recall, however, that we can still estimate the combined effect of X_1 and X_2 on Y; that is, substituting

X_{1t} for X_{2t} in (6.1), we can estimate the value of $b_3 = (b_1 + b_2)$ in (6.2),*

$$Y_t = b_0 + (b_1 + b_2)X_{1t} + u_t = b_0 + b_3 X_{1t} + u_t. \tag{6.2}$$

If the multicollinearity of X_{1t} and X_{2t} continues to hold in periods beyond our sample, the estimated form of equation (6.2) would be useful for the prediction of future values of the dependent variable, Y_t.

The case we have just described is called one of "perfect" multicollinearity: one (or more) independent variable is an *exact* linear combination of the others. This case usually arises from the way in which the regression equation is formulated, such as the instance we discussed in the preceding chapter where dummy variables were included for all four (instead of just three) of the seasons. As another example, suppose that we postulated a consumption function of the form

$$C_t = b_0 + b_1 Y_{dt} + b_2 Y_{d(t-1)} + b_3(\Delta Y_{dt}) + u_t, \tag{6.3}$$

where Y_{dt} reflects the influence of current income on consumption, $Y_{d(t-1)}$ indicates the effects of past income levels or habit, and $\Delta Y_{dt} = (Y_{dt} - Y_{d(t-1)})$ reflects an "expectation effect" stemming from recent changes in levels of income. Since $\Delta Y_{dt} = (Y_{dt} - Y_{d(t-1)})$ is a linear combination of Y_{dt} and $Y_{d(t-1)}$, we would be unable to estimate all the coefficients in (6.3). We leave it as an exercise to put (6.3) into a form that could be estimated and possibly used to predict values for C_t.

These then are cases of *perfect* multicollinearity. However, this problem comes in all degrees, and it is typically less-than-perfect multicollinearity that causes most of the headaches for researchers. Somewhat intuitively, the problem arises when the independent variables are highly, although not perfectly, correlated. For example, assume that we are attempting to estimate the demand function in (6.4),

$$Q_t = b_0 + b_1 P_t + b_2 Y_t + u_t, \tag{6.4}$$

for a particular group of commodities, say imports, where we postulate that the quantity demanded (Q) depends on the level of prices of domestically produced goods (P) and on the income level (Y) of consumers. The higher is the level of domestic prices, the more of the now-cheaper, foreign-made goods people will want to buy, so that we would expect b_1 to be positive. Likewise, the higher are consumers' incomes, the more of nearly all goods and services (including imports) we would expect them to buy, so that b_2 will presumably also be positive. When we look over our data, we note (as is usually true) that over periods of rapid domestic inflation, imports increase and, likewise, during times of rising incomes, imports also grow. The difficulty is that periods of rapidly rising incomes have generally been times of high inflation, and conversely. Or, in other words, there exists a high (although not a perfect) positive correlation between P and Y. The effect of

---

* Formally, we can estimate (6.2) because we have reduced the number of parameters to be estimated by one, so that it is now equal to our number of independent normal equations.

this high correlation is to make it difficult to separate the influences of P and Y on Q. If imports are rising rapidly at the same time that *both* income and domestic prices are increasing, it may be hard to determine the relative effects of the inflation and the higher incomes in inducing the increase in imports.

"IMPERFECT" MULTICOLLINEARITY: SOME CONSEQUENCES

How does the researcher know when he has a serious problem of multicollinearity on his hands? As we indicated, multicollinearity comes in degrees and may or may not in particular cases prove troublesome. There is, however, a set of regression results that, perhaps, can only be interpreted in terms of a high degree of "imperfect" multicollinearity: a large coefficient of determination (R^2) accompanied by *statistically insignificant* estimates of the coefficients of the independent variables. What this means is that certain (at least one) of the independent variables appear to influence systematically the dependent variable (as indicated by the high R^2), but we cannot tell which ones.

More formally, the problem is that a high degree of multicollinearity results in large variances for the estimators of the coefficients. Recall that a large variance implies that a given percentage (e.g., 95%) confidence interval for the corresponding parameter will be relatively wide; a large range of values of the parameter, perhaps including the value zero, will be consistent with our interval. This suggests that, even if the corresponding independent variable has an important effect on the dependent variable, the multicollinearity problem may make it quite difficult for us to estimate accurately the effect of that variable. Consequently, we may have little confidence in any policy prescriptions based on these estimates.

In order to see that imperfect multicollinearity results in large variances (and, hence, large standard deviations) for our estimators, recall from Chapter 4 that the variance of the estimator $\hat{b}_i$ is

$$\text{var}(\hat{b}_i) = \frac{\sigma_u{}^2}{\sum \hat{v}_{it}{}^2},\tag{6.5}$$

where $\hat{v}_{it}$ is the residual in the regression of the ith regressor, X_{it}, on all of the other regressors in the model: $\hat{v}_{it} = X_{it} - \hat{X}_{it}$. Now, if there is a close, or tight, linear relationship among the independent variables, $\hat{v}_{it}$ will tend to be small because the calculated value, $\hat{X}_{it}$, will be close to the actual value of the regressor, X_{it}. It follows that the denominator in (6.5) will tend to be small, with a resulting large variance of $\hat{b}_i$.

It is important to interpret correctly what all this means. Note that it does *not* imply that the estimators of the coefficients are biased; they are still unbiased, as we proved formally in the Appendix to Chapter 4. What multicollinearity does cause is an imprecision in our estimators: they have a large variance and consequently are not very reliable. The problem, as we discussed earlier, is the difficulty of determining for each independent variable its particular influence, apart from the others, on the dependent variable.

A FURTHER COMMENT

We have thus far assumed implicitly that *all* of the regressors of the model are highly interrelated. This need not be the case. Suppose a regression model contains the regressors X_{1t}, X_{2t}, and X_{3t}. Suppose also that X_{1t} and X_{2t} are highly (but imperfectly) related, but X_{3t} is relatively unrelated to X_{1t} and X_{2t}. Then, the variance formula in (6.5) suggests that the variance of the estimators corresponding to the coefficients of X_{1t} and X_{2t}, say $\hat{a}_1$ and $\hat{a}_2$, will be large; however, the variance of $\hat{a}_3$, the estimator of the coefficient of X_{3t}, *need not* be large. Intuitively, if X_{3t} is not highly related to X_{1t} and X_{2t}, $\hat{v}_{3t}^2$ could generally be large, since $\hat{X}_{3t}$ would be a relatively poor predictor of X_{3t} (i.e., X_{3t} cannot be well explained by X_{1t} and X_{2t}).

We now give a formula which may be useful in interpreting the multicollinearity problem. The expression $\sum \hat{v}_{it}^2$ appearing in the denominator of (6.5) is an error sum of squares obtained by regressing X_{it} on all of the other regressors in the regression model. Denote this error sum of squares as ESS_i. Let $\text{TSS}_i = \sum X_{it}^2$. Then $\text{TSS}_i = \text{RSS}_i + \text{ESS}_i$, where $\text{RSS}_i = \text{TSS}_i - \text{ESS}_i$. Clearly, $\text{ESS}_i \geq 0$, $\text{TSS}_i \geq 0$. It can also be shown that $\text{RSS}_i \geq 0$.* Therefore, $\text{TSS}_i \geq \text{RSS}_i$, and $\text{TSS}_i \geq \text{ESS}_i$.

Let $r_i^2 = \text{RSS}_i/\text{TSS}_i$. Then $0 \leq r_i^2 \leq 1$. Clearly the more highly related is X_{it} to the other regressors, the smaller will be ESS_i, and hence the closer to unity will be r_i^2. Conversely, the weaker the relation of X_{it} to the other regressors, the larger will be ESS_i, and consequently the closer will be r_i^2 to zero. r_i^2 is therefore similar to a multiple coefficient of determination relating X_{it} to the other regressors of the model.

Now express the denominator of the variance formula (6.5) as $\text{ESS}_i = \text{TSS}_i - \text{RSS}_i \equiv \text{TSS}_i(1 - r_i^2)$. It follows that $\text{var}(\hat{b}_i)$ can be expressed as

$$\text{var}(\hat{b}_i) = \frac{\sigma_u^2}{\text{TSS}_i(1 - r_i^2)} \equiv \frac{\sigma_u^2}{\sum X_{it}^2(1 - r_i^2)} \tag{6.6}$$

The expression in (6.6) clearly indicates the effect of partial multicollinearity on the variance of an estimator. The absence of partial multicollinearity corresponds to the case $r_i^2 = 0$. The problem worsens, leading to larger variances, as r_i^2 increases toward unity. Finally note that r_i^2 need not be equally large for all $i = 1, \ldots, k$.

---

* See (4A.5) in the Appendix to Chapter 4, and note that for the kth regressor $\text{TSS}_k = \sum X_{kt}^2$, $\text{ESS}_k = \sum \hat{v}_{kt}^2$, $\text{RSS} = \sum \hat{X}_{kt}^2$ since $(\sum \hat{X}_{kt}\hat{V}_{kt}) = 0$.

SOME SOLUTIONS

Multicollinearity is not an easy problem to resolve. Where possible, the researcher can always try to increase the precision of his estimators (that is, reduce their variance) by increasing the number of observations. For instance, however small the $\hat{v}^2$'s are in (6.5), it is clear that var($\hat{b}_i$) decreases as n increases. But obviously it is not always possible to increase the sample size, and, where the multicollinearity is sufficiently serious, it may still not help very much, unless the sample is increased a great deal.

An alternative approach is to introduce some additional information that can be used to estimate the values of the individual coefficients. For instance, suppose that we want to estimate the production function expressed in equation (6.7) for some particular commodity:

$$Q_t = AL_t^\alpha K_t^\beta e^{u_t}, \tag{6.7}$$

where Q_t is the quantity produced in period t, L_t is the hours of labor input, K_t is the input of capital, u_t is our disturbance term, and A, α, and β are the parameters we want to estimate. Recall that by using the logarithmic transformation we can put (6.7) in the estimable form

$$Q_t^* = A^* + \alpha L_t^* + \beta K_t^* + u_t, \tag{6.8}$$

where the asterisks indicate that these are the logs of the variables in equation (6.7). For purposes of illustration, suppose we have a partial multicollinearity problem in that L and K are highly correlated in our sample. In this case (among other things), the high correlation between L and K would result in large variances of the estimators of the elasticity parameters, α and β, of the production function.

Now let us assume that on the basis of information from another source, we have solid evidence that this industry is characterized by constant returns to scale. From our discussion of production functions in the last chapter, this implies that $(\alpha + \beta) = 1$. With this information, we can substitute $\beta = (1 - \alpha)$ into (6.7) to obtain

$$Q_t = AL_t^\alpha K_t^{(1-\alpha)} e^{u_t}. \tag{6.9}$$

Taking logs, we now get

$$Q_t^* = A^* + \alpha L_t^* + (1 - \alpha)K_t^* + u_t, \tag{6.10}$$

where the asterisks again denote the logs of the original variables. Rearranging terms in (6.10), we obtain

$$Q_t^* - K_t^* = A^* + \alpha(L_t^* - K_t^*) + u_t, \tag{6.11}$$

or

$$Y_t^* = A^* + \alpha Z_t^* + u_t,$$

where $Y_t^* = (Q_t^* - K_t^*)$ and $Z_t^* = (L_t^* - K_t^*)$.

Our *a priori* information enables us to reduce our model to one in which there is only one independent variable, Z_t^*. The reader should note that, even if L_t^* and K_t^* are very strongly related, there will still generally be no difficulty resulting from multicollinearity in estimating (6.11). For instance, suppose that $L_t^* = 4K_t^*$; we would have no estimation problems because our model in (6.11) would reduce to*

$$Y_t^* = A^* + \alpha(3K_t^*) + u_t. \qquad (6.12)$$

In brief, the additional information that the industry is characterized by constant returns to scale would enable us to obtain estimators with smaller variances for the parameters A^* and α. Our estimator of β will then simply be

$$\hat{\beta} = 1 - \hat{\alpha}. \qquad (6.13)$$

CONSEQUENCES FOR PREDICTION

In many instances, no supplementary information may be available, and the researcher will simply be stuck with a set of rather unreliable parameter estimates. It may provide some comfort to know that, even in this case, the estimated equation may be reasonably satisfactory for purposes of forecasting. To take an extreme example, consider the following relationship which, because of the way the variables are defined, exhibits *perfect* multicollinearity:

$$Y_t = b_0 + b_1 X_{1t} + b_2 X_{2t} + u_t, \qquad (6.14)$$

where $X_{1t} = 3X_{2t}$. As noted earlier, because X_1 bears a perfect linear relationship to X_2, we cannot estimate b_1 and b_2. However, for purposes of prediction, we are not interested in the values of b_1 and b_2 per se, but rather in the mean value of Y_t corresponding to X_1 and X_2, namely,

$$\begin{aligned} Y_t^m &= b_0 + b_1 X_{1t} + b_2 X_{2t} \\ &= b_0 + (3b_1 + b_2)X_{2t}. \end{aligned} \qquad (6.15)$$

From our discussion above, we know that we *can* estimate the mean value of Y_t by the estimator

$$\hat{Y}_t = \hat{b}_0 + \hat{b}^* X_{2t}, \qquad (6.16)$$

---

* This example demonstrates that we would have difficulty only if $L_t^* - K_t^*$ is equal to a constant. This would occur when L_t is exactly proportional to K_t; that is, when $L_t = dK_t$, where d is a constant. For this special case, $Z_t^* = (L_t^* - K_t^*)$ in equation (6.11) would be a constant, and we would be unable to obtain an estimator for α. In this respect, recall from our discussion of the bivariate-regression model in Chapter 2 that the independent variable must take on at least two distinct values in order for us to be able to estimate the regression coefficients.

where $\hat{b}^*$ is our estimator of the sum $(3b_1 + b_2)$. Although we cannot estimate the effects of X_1 and X_2 on Y, we can make predictions concerning the value of Y corresponding to any value of X_{2t}, so long as the relationship $X_{1t} = 3X_{2t}$ continues to hold.* Although its proof is beyond the scope of this book, a similar conclusion extends to the case of less-than-perfect multicollinearity. Specifically, even though our estimators of the separate effects of the independent variables may have large variances, our estimator, $\hat{Y}_t$, of their combined effect on Y_t, which would be given by the mean of Y_t, Y_t^m, may have a small variance. Since our predictions involve estimating the mean of Y_t and since we may be able to estimate that mean quite accurately, multicollinearity may not prove too troublesome for purposes of forecasting.

6.2 THE PROBLEM OF AUTOCORRELATION

One of the basic assumptions in the regression model is that the value of the disturbance term in one period is independent of its value in any other period, so that

$$\text{cov}(u_t, u_s) = 0 \qquad \text{for } t \neq s.$$

This implies that, for given values of the regressors, Y_t will differ from its mean value, Y_t^m, by an amount that is independent of the size of the discrepancy in any other period. Corresponding to a regression model of the form

$$Y_t = b_0 + b_1 X_t + u_t,$$

we would expect to have a scatter diagram like that in Figure 6.1, where the observed points are "randomly scattered" about the regression line.

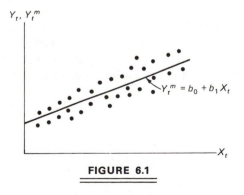

FIGURE 6.1

---

* It should be evident that the quality or precision of our prediction depends on two considerations: (1) the precision of our estimator of the mean value of Y_t (that is, the variance of $\hat{Y}_t$ as an estimator of Y_t^m); and (2) the size of the variance of the disturbance term u_t. Unfortunately, the formulas describing the precision of our forecast in the multiple-regression framework require statistical concepts beyond those used here.

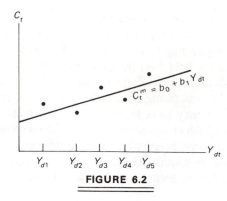

FIGURE 6.2

Suppose, however, that $\text{cov}(u_t, u_s) \neq 0$, so that the successive values of the disturbance term are not independent of one another. For example, consider an individual whose consumption behavior can be described by

$$C_t = b_0 + b_1 Y_{dt} + u_t, \tag{6.17}$$

but where the value of u_t is not independent of its earlier values. If, for instance, our individual spends "too much" in period 1 (as a result, perhaps, of an unexpected visit by friends) so that $u_1 > 0$, he will attempt to compensate in period 2 by spending less than usual, so that we would expect $u_2 < 0$. Note that this would imply that, more generally, u_t has a negative correlation with u_{t+1}. If the level of income were to increase in successive periods, such a negative association between successive values of the disturbance term would be expected to generate a scatter diagram somewhat like that depicted in Figure 6.2. If we were to plot the values of the disturbance term over time, we would then expect to observe a pattern such as that in Figure 6.3.

Alternatively, it could be the case that the values of the disturbance term exhibit a positive correlation over time. For example, as a result of inertia or sluggish adjustment in behavior, we might find that a positive value of u is typically followed by another positive value of u, and conversely, so that

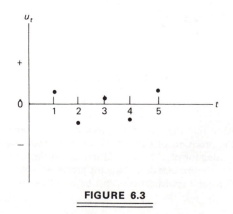

FIGURE 6.3

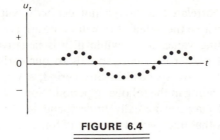

FIGURE 6.4

$\operatorname{cov}(u_t, u_{t+1}) > 0$. Assuming that the values of the disturbance terms are in part determined by external forces (formally specified below) whose effects alternate randomly from positive to negative, we might expect a pattern of values over time for u in which there are various "runs" of positive and negative values. For example, if the external forces produce a positive value of u, it would tend to be followed by further positive values; if then a negative value is produced, it would tend to be followed by additional negative values, and so on. One such pattern is outlined in Figure 6.4.

This problem of an interdependence among successive values of the disturbance term is known as *autocorrelation*. We shall show that, under certain assumptions, it is still true that for any given observation $E(u_t) = 0$; further, under our assumptions, the disturbance term will still be uncorrelated with the independent variables so that our estimators of the coefficients will remain unbiased. As we shall see, the problem that autocorrelation introduces concerns the variance of our estimators. Specifically, the formulas we have derived for the variances do not hold if there is autocorrelation. If we continue to use these formulas, we shall generate erroneous t ratios, which will render invalid our tests of hypotheses about the values of the parameters of our model. As a result, we might, for instance, accept as statistically significant an estimated value for a parameter that in fact is not significantly different from zero.

AN AUTOREGRESSIVE MODEL

To formalize our treatment, assume that the autoregressive process (the manner in which one disturbance term relates to another) takes the form

$$u_t = \gamma u_{t-1} + \varepsilon_t, \qquad t = \ldots, -2, -1, 0, 1, 2, \ldots, \qquad (6.18)$$

where ε_t is a normally distributed random variable that has a mean of zero, $E(\varepsilon_t) = 0$, is independent of its value in any other time period so that $\operatorname{cov}(\varepsilon_t, \varepsilon_s) = 0$, and has a constant variance, $E(\varepsilon_t)^2 = \sigma_\varepsilon^2$. We also assume, for reasons given below, that γ is less than unity in absolute value: $|\gamma| < 1$. In brief, we are assuming that the value of the disturbance term in *any* period is related to its immediately preceding value by a simple linear regression model. Note that (6.18) is assumed to hold for all time periods, both past and future. In this model, the successive values of the disturbance terms, the u's, are correlated, although not perfectly, with one another. In particular, if γ is positive the value of u_t will be positively correlated with its immediately preceding value, u_{t-1}, while if γ is negative this correlation will be negative. The latter case corresponds to our earlier example of the individual who, if he "overspends" in one period, say t, attempts to compensate by underspending in the following period. Note from (6.18), however, that our individual may not actually underspend in the following period, $(t + 1)$, because another unexpected event may force him again to overspend (e.g., $\varepsilon_{t+1} > 0$).

We shall show first that, under the autoregressive scheme represented by equation (6.18), $E(u_t) = 0$. Noting, from (6.18), that

$$u_{t-1} = \gamma u_{t-2} + \varepsilon_{t-1}, \tag{6.19}$$

and substituting (6.19) for u_{t-1} in (6.18), we obtain

$$u_t = \gamma(\gamma u_{t-2} + \varepsilon_{t-1}) + \varepsilon_t = \varepsilon_t + \gamma \varepsilon_{t-1} + \gamma^2 u_{t-2}. \tag{6.20}$$

Recalling that (6.18) holds for all periods, if we next substitute for u_{t-2}, then u_{t-3}, and so on, we obtain the expression

$$u_t = \varepsilon_t + \gamma \varepsilon_{t-1} + \gamma^2 \varepsilon_{t-2} + \gamma^3 \varepsilon_{t-3} + \cdots, \tag{6.21}$$

which does not include a lagged value of u because its coefficient would be γ raised to an infinite power (which would equal zero). Taking the expected value of u_t in (6.21), we have

$$\begin{aligned} E(u_t) &= E(\varepsilon_t + \gamma \varepsilon_{t-1} + \gamma^2 \varepsilon_{t-2} + \gamma^3 \varepsilon_{t-3} + \cdots) \\ &= E(\varepsilon_t) + \gamma E(\varepsilon_{t-1}) + \gamma^2 E(\varepsilon_{t-2}) + \gamma^3 E(\varepsilon_{t-3}) + \cdots = 0, \end{aligned} \tag{6.22}$$

since $E(\varepsilon_s) = 0$ for $s = t, t - 1, t - 2, \ldots$. The expected value of the disturbance term is still zero. Similarly, we can see that if we assume, as is usually done, that ε_t is independent of the value of the regressor, say X_t, in *all* time periods (ε_t is independent of X_s for all t and s), that u_t will be independent of, and hence uncorrelated with, X_t. That is, using (6.21), you should be able to show that $\text{cov}(u_t, X_t) = E(u_t X_t) = 0$.

For future reference, we note that since u_t is a linear combination of ε_t, $\varepsilon_{t-1}, \ldots$, and since all of the ε's are independent of one another, the variance of u_t is*

$$\begin{aligned} \sigma_{u_t}^2 &= \sigma_\varepsilon^2 + \gamma^2 \sigma_\varepsilon^2 + (\gamma^2)^2 \sigma_\varepsilon^2 + (\gamma^3)^2 \sigma_\varepsilon^2 + \cdots \\ &= \sigma_\varepsilon^2 [1 + \gamma^2 + (\gamma^2)^2 + (\gamma^2)^3 + \cdots] \\ &= \frac{\sigma_\varepsilon^2}{1 - \gamma^2} = \sigma_u^2, \end{aligned} \tag{6.23}$$

---

* We make use here of a basic theorem for the summation of a geometric series, which states that if

$$s = a(1 + \alpha + \alpha^2 + \alpha^3 + \cdots) \qquad \text{where } |\alpha| < 1,$$

then

$$s = \frac{a}{1 - \alpha}.$$

If $\alpha \geq 1$, then the series does not converge.

since all of the ε's have the same variance and by assumption $|\gamma| < 1$. From (6.23) we see that the variance of u_t does *not* involve t and, like the ε's, all of the u_t's have the same variance: $\sigma_{u_t}^2 = \sigma_{u_s}^2 = \sigma_u^2$. We can also see from (6.23) the reason for our assumption that $|\gamma| < 1$. Without this assumption, the series in (6.23) would not converge; the variance of u_t would be infinite.

Let us next examine the covariance of the disturbance terms. Substituting (6.18) for u_t and using (6.23), we have

$$
\begin{aligned}
E(u_t u_{t-1}) &= E[(\gamma u_{t-1} + \varepsilon_t) u_{t-1}] \\
&= \gamma E(u_{t-1}^2) + E(\varepsilon_t u_{t-1}) \qquad (6.24) \\
&= \gamma E(u_{t-1}^2) + 0 = \gamma \sigma_u^2,
\end{aligned}
$$

since, by (6.21), u_{t-1} depends only on ε_{t-1} and its further lagged values. This means that u_{t-1} and ε_t are independent, so that

$$
E(\varepsilon_t u_{t-1}) = \text{cov}(\varepsilon_t, u_{t-1}) = 0.
$$

We thus see from (6.24) that the autoregressive form in equation (6.18) does violate our assumption of a zero covariance among the disturbance terms so long as γ is nonzero.

CONSEQUENCES FOR THE VARIANCES OF THE ESTIMATORS

We shall now show that this leads to different expressions for the variances of our estimators. Suppose that we have a simple two-variable model of the form described in Chapter 2:

$$
Y_t = b_0 + b_1 X_t + u_t. \qquad (6.25)
$$

Recall that, subject to the assumptions of the model (including a zero covariance among the disturbance terms), we found that the conditional variance of the estimator, $\hat{b}_1$, is

$$
\text{var}(\hat{b}_1) = \frac{\sigma_u^2}{\sum (X_t - \bar{X})^2}. \qquad (6.26)
$$

To derive this result, we used equation (2.71), which indicates that $\hat{b}_1$ may be expressed as

$$
\hat{b}_1 = b_1 + \frac{\sum (X_t - \bar{X}) u_t}{\sum (X_t - \bar{X})^2}. \qquad (6.27)
$$

We then let $A = \sum (X_t - \bar{X})^2$, and $w_t = (X_t - \bar{X})$, and rewrite (6.27), in expanded form, as

$$
\hat{b}_1 = b_1 + \frac{w_1}{A} u_1 + \cdots + \frac{w_n}{A} u_n. \qquad (6.28)
$$

Given the values of the X's (and therefore of the w's and of A), $\hat{b}_1$ is simply a linear combination of the disturbance terms. We then derived (6.26) from

(6.28) by using the formula for the variance of a linear sum of *uncorrelated* random variables. However, if we have autocorrelation we cannot use this formula, because the u_t and consequently the terms in (6.28) are not uncorrelated. This means that (6.26) is no longer the correct expression for the variance of $\hat{b}_1$. As a result, the tests of hypotheses using our standard formulas are no longer valid.*

THE MEAN OF THE ESTIMATORS

It is easy to see from (6.28) that autocorrelation does not lead to a bias in $\hat{b}_1$. The disturbance term, u_t, under our assumptions above, is still independent of, and therefore uncorrelated with, all the values of X_t (and hence of w_t) and still has a mean of zero. For any given values of X_t, taking the expected value of (6.28) yields

$$E(\hat{b}_1) = b_1 + \frac{w_1}{A} E(u_1) + \cdots + \frac{w_n}{A} E(u_n) = b_1. \tag{6.29}$$

Similarly, using the formula $\hat{b}_0 = \bar{Y} - \hat{b}_1\bar{X}$, you should be able to show that

$$E(\hat{b}_0) = b_0 + b_1\bar{X} + E(\bar{u}) - \bar{X}E(\hat{b}_1)$$
$$= b_0. \tag{6.30}$$

The general character of the problem of autocorrelation should now be clear. Where it is present, we have a systematic variation in the values of the disturbance term for successive observations. This pattern of variation does not lead to biased parameter estimators; however, our variance formulas no longer hold and, consequently, without further results we would be unable to test hypotheses and establish confidence intervals. Our procedure obviously leaves something to be desired. Furthermore, our intuition might suggest that, since our standard estimation procedure does not explicitly account for autocorrelation, it may not yield the most reliable estimators of the parameters. That is, if there is a pattern of variation among the disturbance terms, we should be able to do a better job of estimation and prediction if we incorporate this additional information into our calculations. We shall investigate next just how this can be done.

A GENERALIZED ESTIMATION TECHNIQUE

Suppose that our model consists of

$$Y_t = b_0 + b_1X_t + u_t \tag{6.31}$$

and

$$u_t = \gamma u_{t-1} + \varepsilon_t, \tag{6.32}$$

---

* Using (6.28), you should be able to show that, if we have autocorrelation, the variance of $\hat{b}_1$, formally $E(\hat{b}_1 - b_1)^2$, involves the expected value of the cross-product terms of (6.28); in the absence of autocorrelation, all the cross-product terms are zero and thus drop out, leaving us with the expression in (6.26) for the variance of $\hat{b}_1$.

where $|\gamma| < 1$, and where ε_t satisfies all the assumptions we made above. Our problem is how to use the information provided in (6.32) to improve upon our estimators of the parameters in equation (6.31).

Assume initially that the value of γ is known. If we take a lagged form of (6.31) and multiply through by γ, we obtain

$$\gamma Y_{t-1} = \gamma b_0 + \gamma b_1 X_{t-1} + \gamma u_{t-1}. \tag{6.33}$$

Subtracting (6.33) from (6.31), we have

$$Y_t - \gamma Y_{t-1} = (b_0 - \gamma b_0) + (b_1 X_t - \gamma b_1 X_{t-1}) + (u_t - \gamma u_{t-1}). \tag{6.34}$$

From (6.32), we see, by rearranging terms, that

$$\varepsilon_t = (u_t - \gamma u_{t-1}),$$

which, when substituted for the last term in (6.34), gives us

$$Y_t - \gamma Y_{t-1} = (b_0 - \gamma b_0) + (b_1 X_t - \gamma b_1 X_{t-1}) + \varepsilon_t. \tag{6.35}$$

We can rewrite (6.35) as

$$Y_t' = B + b_1 X_t' + \varepsilon_t, \tag{6.36}$$

where

$$Y_t' = Y_t - \gamma Y_{t-1},$$

$$B = b_0 - \gamma b_0,$$

$$X_t' = X_t - \gamma X_{t-1}.$$

Note that in translating (6.31) into (6.36), one observation is lost because of the lagging and subtracting in (6.34).

Equation (6.36) is in the standard form for the regression model; in particular, ε_t (unlike u_t) satisfies all our assumptions concerning the properties of the disturbance term. We can, therefore, simply follow the estimation procedure we set out earlier: we impose the conditions $\sum_{t=2}^{n} \hat{\varepsilon}_t = 0$ and $\sum_{t=2}^{n} (X_t' \hat{\varepsilon}_t) = 0$ and thereby derive two normal equations the solution of which gives us our estimators, $\hat{B}$ and $\hat{b}_1$, for our two parameters in (6.36). From this, we can then estimate b_0 by

$$\hat{b}_0 = \frac{\hat{B}}{1 - \gamma}. \tag{6.37}$$

It can also be shown that

$$\text{var}(\hat{b}_0) = \left(\frac{1}{1 - \gamma}\right)^2 \text{var}(\hat{B}), \tag{6.38}$$

since $\hat{b}_0$ is perfectly and linearly related to $\hat{B}$. Since ε_t satisfies all of our standard assumptions, the variances of $\hat{B}$ and $\hat{b}_1$ would be given by our standard formulas,

$$\text{var}(\hat{B}) = \frac{\sigma_\varepsilon^2 \sum\limits_{t=2}^{n} (X_t')^2}{n' \sum\limits_{t=2}^{n} (X_t' - \bar{X}')^2},$$

$$\text{var}(\hat{b}_1) = \frac{\sigma_\varepsilon^2}{\sum\limits_{t=2}^{n} (X_t' - \bar{X}')^2}$$

(6.39)

where $n' = n - 1$, since one observation was lost in lagging and subtracting to obtain X_t'.

We can now, at least in principle, test hypotheses and construct valid confidence intervals if we estimate our basic parameters in terms of (6.36). We also point out that the estimators obtained from (6.36) are "efficient"; intuitively* this means that if the sample size is large, the variances of our estimators from (6.36) would be less than or equal to the variances of any other unbiased estimators of B and b_1. The reason we cannot say that our estimators will have the smallest variances regardless of the sample size is that our technique involves the loss of one observation. Essentially, the importance of this one observation becomes negligible as the sample size increases.**

We have found a technique with desirable properties for incorporating available information about the relationship among the disturbance terms themselves into our estimation procedure. In particular, we transform the regression model with autocorrelated disturbance terms into one that satisfies all the assumptions of our basic regression model (including zero covariance between the disturbance terms) and then simply apply our standard techniques. The difficulty with implementing this procedure is that γ is, in general, unknown; we must first estimate the value of γ.†

---

* The following is not a formal definition of an efficient estimator. Such a definition is beyond the scope of this book and is unnecessary for understanding the results that are to come.

** Efficiency is usually defined in terms of what is called the mean square error, M.S.E. That is, let $\hat{\alpha}$ be an estimator of α. Then the M.S.E. of $\hat{\alpha}$ is equal to the sum of its variance, $\sigma_{\hat{\alpha}}^2$, and the square of its *bias*, $[E(\hat{\alpha}) - \alpha]^2$. In our case above, our estimators were unbiased so that the M.S.E. was equal to the variance. In any event, omitting a few subtleties, if $\hat{\alpha}$ is an efficient estimator of α, we would "expect" (if our sample is large) that the M.S.E. of $\hat{\alpha}$ would be less than or equal to the M.S.E. of any other consistent estimator of α.

† One often sees in the literature regression equations in which all of the variables involved are in first-difference form; that is, for the two-variable case, $(Y_t - Y_{t-1})$ is regressed on $(X_t - X_{t-1})$. From (6.36) we can see that such an equation is a *special case* of an autoregressive model in which $\gamma = 1$. Note from (6.23) that for such a model the variance of u_t would be infinite. Furthermore, this procedure is quite restrictive, since the results are conditional on $\gamma = 1$.

We can do this by looking at the residuals from our original equation (6.31). Recalling that $E(u_t) = 0$ and $\text{cov}(u_t, X_t) = E(u_t X_t) = 0$, we can derive unbiased estimators of the parameters in (6.31) by imposing the conditions $\sum_{t=1}^{n} \hat{u}_t = 0$ and $\sum_{t=1}^{n} (\hat{u}_t X_t) = 0$. This gives us the usual normal equations

$$\sum Y_t = n\hat{b}_0 + \hat{b}_1 \sum X_t,$$
$$\sum (X_t Y_t) = \hat{b}_0 \sum X_t + \hat{b}_1 \sum X_t^2, \qquad (6.40)$$

which we can solve for the unbiased estimators, $\hat{b}_0$ and $\hat{b}_1$. We can then use $\hat{b}_0$ and $\hat{b}_1$ to obtain an estimator, $\hat{u}_t$, for the value of the disturbance term:

$$\hat{u}_t = Y_t - \hat{Y}_t = Y_t - (\hat{b}_0 - \hat{b}_1 X_t). \qquad (6.41)$$

To estimate γ, we simply substitute the values for $\hat{u}$ into a relationship "suggested" by (6.32), namely,

$$\hat{u}_t = \gamma \hat{u}_{t-1} + \varepsilon_t. \qquad (6.42)$$

Consider (6.42) as a regression model. Since ε_t is independent of u_{t-1}, let us take ε_t to be uncorrelated with $\hat{u}_{t-1}$.* With this assumption, we may estimate γ in (6.42) by our standard technique. Specifically (as somewhat of a review), rewrite (6.42) as

$$\hat{u}_t = \hat{\gamma} \hat{u}_{t-1} + \hat{\varepsilon}_t, \qquad (6.43)$$

where $\hat{\varepsilon}_t = (\hat{u}_t - \hat{\gamma} \hat{u}_{t-1})$ is the estimator of the disturbance term, and $\hat{\gamma}$ is our estimator of γ. Our assumption that $\text{cov}(\varepsilon_t, \hat{u}_{t-1}) = 0$ suggests that we impose the condition (recalling that one observation would be lost) $\sum_{t=2}^{n} (\hat{\varepsilon}_t \hat{u}_{t-1}) = 0$. To do this, we multiply the terms in (6.43) by $\hat{u}_{t-1}$, sum over the sample, and then impose our condition to get

$$\sum_{t=2}^{n} (\hat{u}_t \hat{u}_{t-1}) = \hat{\gamma} \sum_{t=2}^{n} (\hat{u}_{t-1})^2 + \sum_{t=2}^{n} (\hat{\varepsilon}_t \hat{u}_{t-1}) = \hat{\gamma} \sum_{t=2}^{n} (\hat{u}_{t-1})^2. \quad (6.44)$$

From (6.44) our estimator of γ is

$$\hat{\gamma} = \frac{\sum_{t=2}^{n} (\hat{u}_t \hat{u}_{t-1})}{\sum_{t=2}^{n} (\hat{u}_{t-1})^2}. \qquad (6.45)$$

---

* Somewhat more formally, the dependence between ε_t and $\hat{u}_{t-1}$ diminishes to zero as the sample size increases without limit. That is, if the sample size is small, ε_t and $\hat{u}_{t-1}$ will be correlated because $\hat{u}_{t-1}$ depends on $\hat{b}_0$ and $\hat{b}_1$ which, in turn, depend on all of the ε's, including ε_t. However, as the size of the sample increases, since $\hat{b}_0$ and $\hat{b}_1$ are consistent, they converge in probability terms to b_0 and b_1. Therefore, in the limit $\hat{u}_{t-1}$ will diverge from u_{t-1} with a probability of zero. Equation (6.42) may be assumed to hold, with probability equal to one, only if the sample is of infinite size. In brief, we should look upon (6.42) as an approximate (or large-sample) equation.

We can now employ the procedure we described earlier, using $\hat{\gamma}$ instead of γ, to obtain estimators of the coefficients in our regression model. For the two-variable case, we would now have

$$b_1 = \frac{\displaystyle\sum_{t=2}^{n} (X_t^* - \bar{X}^*)Y_t^*}{\displaystyle\sum_{t=2}^{n} (X_t^* - \bar{X}^*)^2} \tag{6.46}$$

and

$$b_0 = \frac{\hat{B}}{1 - \hat{\gamma}}, \tag{6.47}$$

where

$$X_t^* = X_t - \hat{\gamma}X_{t-1},$$

$$Y_t^* = Y_t - \hat{\gamma}Y_{t-1},$$

and

$$\hat{B} = \bar{Y}^* - b_1\bar{X}^*.$$

Similarly, subject to the discussion below, we would take as our variance formulas

$$\text{var}(b_0) = \frac{1}{(1 - \hat{\gamma})^2} \text{var}(\hat{B}),$$

$$\text{var}(b_1) = \frac{\sigma_\varepsilon^2}{\displaystyle\sum_{t=2}^{n} (X_t^* - \bar{X}^*)^2}, \tag{6.48}$$

where

$$\text{var}(\hat{B}) = \frac{\sigma_\varepsilon^2 \displaystyle\sum_{t=2}^{n} (X_t^*)^2}{n' \displaystyle\sum_{t=2}^{n} (X_t^* - \bar{X}^*)^2}, \tag{6.49}$$

where again $n' = n - 1$. In brief, once we transform our equation by using $\hat{\gamma}$, we would treat $\hat{\gamma}$ as if it were γ and would use all of our standard formulas. This includes the estimation of σ_ε^2 in the variance formulas above. Specifically, it should be clear from (6.36) that our estimator of σ_ε^2 would be

$$\hat{\sigma}_\varepsilon^2 = \sum_{t=2}^{N} \frac{(Y_t^* - \hat{B} - b_1 X_t^*)^2}{(n' - 2)} \tag{6.49}$$

Consider now the issues of hypothesis testing and confidence intervals. From (6.45) we see that $\hat{\gamma}$ depends upon estimated disturbance terms. Moreover, from (6.46) we see that b_1 depends upon $\hat{\gamma}$ in a nonlinear way. It follows that b_1 depends, among other things, upon estimated disturbance terms in a nonlinear way. Furthermore, since the estimated disturbance terms depend in part upon the actual values of the disturbance terms [see (6.41) and (6.25)], it follows that b_1 depends upon the actual disturbance terms in a nonlinear way. Because of this, $\hat{b}_1$ is *not* normally distributed, and the ratio $(\hat{b}_1 - b_1)/\hat{\sigma}_{b_1}$ is *not* a "*t*" variable with $(n - 2)$ degrees of freedom, where $\hat{\sigma}_{b_1}$ is the estimated standard deviation of $\hat{b}_1$. Similar results apply to $\hat{B}$ and $\hat{b}_0$, since they too depend upon $\hat{y}$ in a nonlinear way.

Fortunately, hypotheses can be tested in an "approximate" way, or "approximate" confidence intervals established, by assuming that the ratios $(\hat{b}_0 - b_0)/\hat{\sigma}_{b_0}$, $(\hat{b}_1 - b_1)/\hat{\sigma}_{b_1}$, and $(\hat{B} - B)/\hat{\sigma}_B$ are *standard normal variables*. If the sample size were infinite, these ratios would indeed be standard normal variables. In the typical case of a finite sample, the normality assumption must be viewed as an approximation. Therefore tests of hypotheses, or confidence intervals based on this normality assumption, must be viewed as approximate. In a similar vein, we note that the variance formulas above, for the case in which $\hat{y}$ is used, are also approximate in that they only hold strictly in the case of an infinite sample.

It follows from the above discussion that an approximate 95 percent confidence interval for b_1 would be $(\hat{b}_1 \pm 1.96\,\sigma_{b_1})$. If one were interested in testing the hypothesis $H_0 : b_1 = 0$ against $H_1 : b_1 \neq 0$ at a 5 percent level of significance, the null hypothesis H_0 would be accepted if $|\hat{b}_1/\hat{\sigma}_{b_1}| < 1.96$, and rejected otherwise. Thus, we would again be interested in what we will continue to call a t ratio, $\hat{b}_1/\hat{\sigma}_{b_1}$; the only difference is that the exact critical value relates to the normal distribution, rather than the t distribution. For this reason, researchers often calculate and report the ratios of their regression results for the convenience of their readers.

In passing we point out that the estimators based on $\hat{y}$ are no longer unbiased, but they do have the desirable property of consistency.* Furthermore, these estimators are also efficient so that, at least in large samples, no better consistent estimators of the parameters are available.

AN EXTENSION TO THE MULTIPLE-REGRESSION MODEL

The extension of the above technique to the multiple-regression case is straightforward. For instance, suppose we maintain all of our above assumptions except that we now have k regressors. Our model would then be

$$Y_t = b_0 + b_1 X_{1t} + \cdots + b_k X_{kt} + u_t,$$
$$u_t = \gamma u_{t-1} + \varepsilon_t. \tag{6.50}$$

We would proceed by first estimating the regression parameters, $b_0, b_1, \ldots, b_k$, by our standard technique, and then the disturbance term by $\hat{u}_t = Y_t - \hat{Y}_t$. We would next estimate γ by (6.45), and then transform the dependent

* For a formal presentation of the issues involved in the above analysis, see Arthur S. Goldberger, *Econometric Theory* (New York: Wiley, 1964), chap. 6.

variable to $Y_t^* = Y_t - \hat{\gamma}Y_{t-1}$, and the independent variables correspondingly to $X_{it}^* = X_{it} - \hat{\gamma}X_{i(t-1)}$. We would now consider the regression model

$$Y_t^* = B + b_1 X_{1t}^* + \cdots + b_k X_{kt}^* + \varepsilon_t, \qquad (6.51)$$

and would estimate $B, b_1, \ldots, b_k$, as well as the variances of our estimators, by our standard techniques. Our results for b_0 would be derived from those for B exactly as above. The parameter estimators would again be biased, but consistent and efficient. Finally, we would again test hypotheses or construct confidence intervals by assuming that the ratios $(\hat{b}_i - b_i)/\hat{\sigma}_{b_i}$ are standard normal variables. As in the case above, such tests of hypotheses, confidence intervals, or even our variance formulas for the parameter estimators would be strictly valid only in the infinite-sample case, so that we must interpret our results as "approximate" for samples of finite size.

In passing, we point out that the technique we have just discussed is not the only technique for correcting for autocorrelation. Two other widely used techniques are the so-called Cochrane-Orcutt, and the Hildreth-Lu methods.* However, for the model we have considered, these techniques are equivalent to ours in that they produce estimators whose large-sample properties are *identical* to those of our estimators (i.e., the estimators are consistent and efficient).

THE DURBIN-WATSON TEST FOR AUTOCORRELATION

Let us assume that, if the disturbance terms of the regression model are autocorrelated, the relationship takes the form given by our above model (6.32). At this point we have a method for dealing with the problem of autocorrelation, but we have not yet established a means for testing whether or not we have autocorrelated disturbance terms in the first place. Alternatively, our estimation procedure above is based on the *assumption* that, in (6.32), $\gamma \neq 0$; clearly it would be desirable to be able to test this hypothesis.

A straightforward procedure would be to take $\gamma = 0$ as our null hypothesis and then see if we can reject this hypothesis in favor of $\gamma \neq 0$ at a specified level of significance. Similar to our approach in Chapter 3, we would establish a confidence interval about our estimator for γ. If our interval around $\hat{\gamma}$ includes zero, we would accept the null hypothesis that $\gamma = 0$; if it does not (because $\hat{\gamma}$ is either sufficiently negative or positive), we would reject the hypothesis $\gamma = 0$. In this latter case we would be accepting the hypothesis of autocorrelated disturbance terms. We would then use the modified estimation procedure we have developed in this section.

---

* For a discussion of these and other methods, see S. Goldfeld and R. Quandt, *Non-Linear Methods in Econometrics* (Amsterdam: North Holland, 1972), pp. 183–186.

Fortunately, a test of this general kind concerning autocorrelation has been developed by J. Durbin and G. Watson.* The test uses what is usually referred to as the Durbin-Watson d statistic, which is based on the sum of the squared differences in *successive* values of the estimated disturbance terms:

$$d = \frac{\sum\limits_{t=2}^{n} (\hat{u}_t - \hat{u}_{t-1})^2}{\sum\limits_{t=1}^{n} \hat{u}_t^2}. \qquad (6.52)$$

Somewhat intuitively, we can see that, if we have positive autocorrelation, the successive values of the disturbance terms will tend to be abnormally close to one another; a positive value of the disturbance term in time t would most likely be followed by another positive value in $(t + 1)$. This suggests that the terms in the numerator of (6.52) will be relatively small; we would therefore expect positive autocorrelation to result in small values for d. Conversely, negative autocorrelation tends to generate large differences between successive values of u_t. The signal for this type of autocorrelation is an unusually large value of d.

Suppose that our assumption from the original regression model that $E(u_s u_t) = 0$ for $s \neq t$ is correct, so that we have no autocorrelation. In this case, we would also expect the covariance between the estimated residuals $\hat{u}_t$ and $\hat{u}_{t-1}$ to be approximately zero. When this is true, we can see by expanding the numerator of the expression for the d statistic in (6.52) that if n is large, d should have a value "close" to 2:**

$$d = \frac{\sum\limits_{t=2}^{n} (\hat{u}_t - \hat{u}_{t-1})^2}{\sum\limits_{t=1}^{n} \hat{u}_t^2} \doteq \frac{2 \sum\limits_{t=2}^{n} \hat{u}_t^2 - 2 \sum\limits_{t=2}^{n} (\hat{u}_t \hat{u}_{t-1})}{\sum\limits_{t=1}^{n} \hat{u}_t^2}$$

$$= \frac{\left[2 \sum\limits_{t=2}^{n} \hat{u}_t^2/(n-1) \right] - \left[2 \sum\limits_{t=2}^{n} \hat{u}_t \hat{u}_{t-1}/(n-1) \right]}{\left[\sum\limits_{t=1}^{n} \hat{u}_t^2/(n-1) \right]} \qquad (6.53)$$

$$\doteq 2,$$

* J. Durbin and G. S. Watson, "Testing for Serial Correlation in Least-Squares Regression," parts I and II, *Biometrika* 37 (1950), pp. 409–428 and 38 (1951), pp. 159–178. See also the discussion of the test in Arthur S. Goldberger, *Econometric Theory* (New York: Wiley, 1964), pp. 243–244; and in J. Johnston, *Econometric Methods*, 2nd ed. (New York: McGraw-Hill, 1972), pp. 249–254.

** If the sample size, n, were infinite, d would take on the value of 2 with a probability equal to unity.

since $\sum_{t=2}^{n} (\hat{u}_t \hat{u}_{t-1})/(n-1) \doteq 0$, $\sum_{t=2}^{n} \hat{u}_t^2 \doteq \sum_{t=1}^{n} \hat{u}_t^2$, and $\sum_{t=2}^{n} \hat{u}_t^2 \doteq \sum_{t=2}^{n} \hat{u}_{t-1}^2$.

Actually, as somewhat of a generalization, it follows from (6.53) that if n is large, and if we assume our above autoregressive model, $u_t = \gamma u_{t-1} + \varepsilon_t$:

$$
\begin{aligned}
d &\doteq \frac{2 \operatorname{var}(u_t) - 2 \operatorname{cov}(u_t, u_{t-1})}{\operatorname{var}(u_t)} \\
&= \frac{2\sigma_u^2 - 2\gamma\sigma_u^2}{\sigma_u^2} = 2(1 - \gamma),
\end{aligned}
\tag{6.54}
$$

since $\hat{u}_t$ is a consistent estimator of u_t, and, from (6.24), $\operatorname{cov}(u_t, u_{t-1}) = \gamma\sigma_u^2$. In brief, we see that

$$
\begin{aligned}
\gamma &= 0 &&\text{suggests} && d \doteq 2, \\
\gamma &= 1 &&\text{suggests} && d \doteq 0, \\
\gamma &= -1 &&\text{suggests} && d \doteq 4.
\end{aligned}
\tag{6.55}
$$

What all this suggests is that, if we wish to test the null hypothesis of no autocorrelation, $H_0 : \gamma = 0$, against the alternative that we do have auto-correlation, $H_1 : \gamma \neq 0$, we would accept H_0 if d has a value that is sufficiently close to 2, and would accept H_1 otherwise. Alternatively, values of d that are close to zero or to 4 would lead us to accept $H_1 : \gamma \neq 0$.

Unfortunately, because of certain statistical properties of the d statistic, the problem is a bit more complex than this. In particular, the regions for d corresponding to the acceptance and rejection of the null hypothesis of zero autocorrelation do not fully exhaust all the possible values of d, so that there exists a range of values *within which we can neither accept nor reject* H_0. Specifically, for the two-tailed Durbin-Watson test, with $H_0 : \gamma = 0$ against $H_1 : \gamma \neq 0$, we have a set of five regions for the value of d as depicted in Figure 6.5. If d is less than d_l or greater than $(4 - d_l)$, we reject the null hypothesis in favor of the alternative, which implies autocorrelation. In contrast, if d has a value in the neighborhood of 2, or more precisely between d_u and $(4 - d_u)$, we accept the null hypothesis of no autocorrelation. If, however, the value of d lies between d_l and d_u or between $(4 - d_u)$ and $(4 - d_l)$, the Durbin-Watson test is inconclusive; for these values of d, we

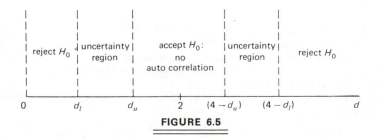

FIGURE 6.5

cannot, at a specified level of significance, conclude either that we do or do not have autocorrelation among the disturbance terms. That is, unlike our previous tests, the Durbin-Watson test, because of certain statistical difficulties, involves regions of uncertainty.

The procedure for the one-tailed test follows directly from the above. For instance, suppose we are interested in the hypothesis $H_0:\gamma = 0$ against $H_1:\gamma > 0$. We would then accept H_0 if d were sufficiently "far" from zero. More formally, in terms of Figure 6.5, we would accept H_0 if $d > d_u$, reject H_0 if $d < d_l$, and have an inconclusive test if $d_l < d < d_u$. Similarly, if the alternative were $\gamma < 0$, we would accept H_0 if $d < 4 - d_u$, reject H_0 if $d > 4 - d_l$, and have an inconclusive test if $4 - d_u < d < 4 - d_l$.

A table of values of d_u and d_l is reproduced as Statistical Table 4 at the end of the book. To find the particular value of d_u and d_l for the problem at hand, we need to know the significance level of the test, if it is a one- or two-tailed test, the sample size n, and the number of independent variables, k', in the regression equation.* Turning to Statistical Table 4, we find, for example, that at a 5 percent level of significance ($\alpha = 0.05$) for a two-tailed test, if we have 50 observations, $n = 50$, and an equation with three independent variables, $k' = 3$, then $d_l = 1.34$ and $d_u = 1.59$. In obtaining these figures, note that the values of d_u and d_l given in the table correspond to the $2\frac{1}{2}$ percent level (that is, $2\frac{1}{2}$ percent on each tail). In this case, the five regions in Figure 6.5 would be

a. $(0, d_l) = (0, 1.34)$,
b. $(d_l, d_u) = (1.34, 1.59)$,
c. $(d_u, 4 - d_u) = (1.59, 2.41)$,
d. $(4 - d_u, 4 - d_l) = (2.41, 2.66)$,
e. $(4 - d_l, 4) = (2.66, 4.00)$.

We would then use equation (6.52) to compute the actual value of d from the observed values of our variables and determine in which of the five regions it lies to see whether or not we must worry about autocorrelation among the disturbance terms.

AN APPLICATION

To review our treatment of autocorrelation, it may prove helpful to conclude with an actual numerical illustration. Suppose that we want to estimate a simple consumption function of the form

$$C_t = b_0 + b_1 Y_{dt} + u_t, \tag{6.56}$$

where (as earlier) C_t is consumption expenditure and Y_{dt} is disposable income. We have available the set of annual observations on aggregate consumption

---

* k' does not include the constant term. For instance, k' could be defined as the number of slope parameters.

spending and disposable income for the United States for the years 1951–1969, which appear in Table 6.1. If we regress C on Y_d using the data in Table 6.1, we get

$$\hat{C}_t = 3.29 + 0.906Y_{dt}, \qquad n = 19, \qquad (6.57)$$
$$(1.5) \quad (162.0) \qquad R^2 = 0.999,$$

where the values of the t ratios appear below the estimates of the coefficients. The equation obviously explains most of the variation in consumption (as indicated by an R^2 of virtually unity); moreover, the variance of $\hat{b}_1$ is extremely small, as evidenced by the enormous value of the corresponding t ratio.

Let us now examine the estimated values of the disturbance terms to see if we find any evidence of autocorrelation. Most computer programs for regression analysis calculate the value of the Durbin-Watson d statistic so that this question can be answered at a glance. However, to provide more familiarity with this technique, Table 6.2 shows the actual sequence of calculations. To compute the estimated disturbance terms, we first use our estimated equation (6.57) to calculate the predicted value for consumption for each year and then subtract this from actual consumption to obtain the estimates of the disturbance terms that appear in the fourth column. If you simply look down this column, you will notice that there are successions of

TABLE 6.1[a]

Year	Consumption Expenditure	Disposable Income
1951	206.3	226.6
1952	216.7	238.3
1953	230.0	252.6
1954	236.5	257.4
1955	254.4	275.3
1956	266.7	293.2
1957	281.4	308.5
1958	290.1	318.8
1959	311.2	337.3
1960	325.2	350.0
1961	335.2	364.4
1962	355.1	385.5
1963	375.0	404.6
1964	401.2	438.1
1965	432.8	473.2
1966	466.3	511.9
1967	492.1	546.3
1968	536.2	591.0
1969	579.6	634.2

[a] Data are in billions of current U.S. dollars.

SOURCE: *Economic Report of the President* (Washington, D.C.: U.S. Government Printing Office, Jan. 1972), p. 212.

TABLE 6.2

CALCULATION OF DURBIN-WATSON d STATISTIC[a]

Year	Actual Consumption (C_t)	Predicted Consumption $(\hat{C}_t)$	$\hat{u}_t = C_t - \hat{C}_t$	$\hat{u}_t^2$	$\hat{u}_{t-1}$	$\hat{u}_t - \hat{u}_{t-1}$	$(\hat{u}_t - \hat{u}_{t-1})^2$
1951	206.3	208.6	-2.3	5.2			
1952	216.7	219.2	-2.5	6.2	-2.3	-0.2	0.0
1953	230.0	232.1	-2.1	4.6	-2.5	0.4	0.1
1954	236.5	236.5	0	0	-2.1	2.1	4.6
1955	254.4	252.7	1.7	2.9	0	1.7	2.8
1956	266.7	268.9	-2.2	5.0	1.7	-3.9	15.3
1957	281.4	282.8	-1.4	1.9	-2.2	0.8	0.7
1958	290.1	292.1	-2.0	4.1	-1.4	-0.6	0.4
1959	311.2	308.9	2.3	5.4	-2.0	4.3	18.8
1960	325.2	320.4	4.8	23.1	2.3	2.5	6.2
1961	335.2	333.4	1.8	3.1	4.8	-3.0	9.3
1962	355.1	352.4	2.7	7.4	1.8	1.0	0.9
1963	375.0	369.9	5.1	26.5	2.7	2.4	5.8
1964	401.2	400.2	1.0	1.0	5.1	-4.2	17.2
1965	432.8	432.0	0.8	0.6	1.0	-0.2	0.0
1966	466.3	467.1	-0.8	0.6	0.8	-1.6	2.4
1967	492.1	498.2	-6.1	36.7	-0.8	-5.4	28.8
1968	536.2	538.7	-2.5	6.4	-6.1	3.6	13.0
1969	579.6	577.9	1.7	3.0	-2.5	4.3	18.2

$$\sum \hat{u}_t^2 = 143.7 \qquad \sum (\hat{u}_t - \hat{u}_{t-1})^2 = 144.5$$

$$d = \frac{\sum (\hat{u}_t - \hat{u}_{t-1})^2}{\sum \hat{u}_t^2} = \frac{144.5}{143.7} = 1.01$$

[a] Figures may not sum precisely due to rounding.

estimated disturbance terms with negative values followed by series of positively valued terms. This should make us immediately suspicious, for it suggests the presence of positive autocorrelation among the disturbance terms and leads us to expect a relatively low value for the d statistic. The value for the d statistic is indeed well below 2; it is 1.01. If we refer back to Statistical Table 4 for the Durbin-Watson d statistic, we find that, for a two-tailed test,* if $n = 19$, $k' = 1$, and $\alpha = 0.05$, the value for d_l, the lower bound, is 1.06. Our d statistic falls below this lower bound, and we reject the null hypothesis of no autocorrelation in favor of the alternative hypothesis of autocorrelated disturbance terms, $\gamma \neq 0$.

To employ the procedure described earlier to correct for the autocorrelation, we must first estimate the relationship among the disturbance terms. We assume that this relationship is of the form

$$u_t = \gamma u_{t-1} + \varepsilon_t,$$

where ε_t satisfies all the assumptions we made above. Taking our estimated values for the disturbance terms in Table 6.2, we use the expression in (6.45) to estimate the value of γ:

$$\hat{\gamma} = \frac{\sum\limits_{t=2}^{n} \hat{u}_t \hat{u}_{t-1}}{\sum\limits_{t=2}^{n} \hat{u}_{t-1}^2} = 0.48. \tag{6.58}$$

With an estimated value for γ of 0.48, we then calculate:

$$C_t^* = C_t - \hat{\gamma}C_{t-1} = C_t - 0.48C_{t-1},$$

$$Y_{dt}^* = Y_{dt} - \hat{\gamma}Y_{d(t-1)} = Y_{dt} - 0.48Y_{d(t-1)}.$$

Regressing C^* on Y_d^*, we find that

$$\hat{C}_t^* = 2.12 + 0.905Y_{dt}^*, \qquad n = 18, \tag{6.59}$$
$$\quad (1.0) \quad\ (98.9) \qquad\qquad R^2 = 0.998.$$

Finally, our estimates of the constant term and the associated variance are

$$\hat{b}_0 = \frac{\hat{B}}{1 - \hat{\gamma}} = \frac{2.12}{(1 - 0.48)} = 4.08$$

$$\widehat{\text{var}}(\hat{b}_0) = \frac{1}{(1 - \hat{\gamma})^2}\widehat{\text{var}}(\hat{B}) = \frac{1}{(1 - 0.48)^2}(4.2) = 15.5.$$

---

* Hypotheses should be formulated *prior* to examining the results; it is for this reason that we are using a two-tailed test. The implication is that, before we actually examined the residuals, we presumably had no reason to expect that, if we had autocorrelation, it would be positive.

Our estimated equation, corrected for autocorrelation, thus is*

$$\hat{C}_t = 4.08 + 0.905 Y_{dt}.$$

$$(1.0) \quad (98.9)$$

Note that, although in this case the estimated value for the MPC, b_1, is virtually the same as in the ordinary regression equation (6.57), the corresponding t ratio is considerably lower (although still extremely large) when we correct for autocorrelation. In other cases, this might have made the difference between rejecting or accepting the null hypothesis of a value of zero for the parameter.

AUTOCORRELATION AND LAGGED DEPENDENT VARIABLES

The Durbin-Watson test is not valid if the regression model contains a lagged value of the dependent variable as one of its regressors. To see the issues involved, consider the model

$$Y_t = b_0 + b_1 X_{1t} + \cdots + b_k X_{kt} + a Y_{t-1} + u_t \qquad (6.60)$$

$$u_t = \gamma u_{t-1} + \varepsilon_t, \qquad t = \ldots, -2, -1, 0, 1, 2, \ldots \qquad (6.61)$$

where ε_t has zero mean, $E(\varepsilon_t) = 0$, constant variance, $E(\varepsilon_t^2) = \sigma_\varepsilon^2$, and $E(\varepsilon_t \varepsilon_s) = 0$ if $t \neq s$. Also assume that $|\gamma| < 1$, and $|a| < 1$. This model is identical to the model in (6.50) except that (6.60) contains Y_{t-1} as a regressor, and (6.50) does not. We have assumed that $|a| < 1$ for the same reason that we assumed that $|\gamma| < 1$.**

At this juncture, note that since Y_t depends on u_t in (6.60), Y_t and u_t are correlated. Similarly, since Y_{t-1} through the lagged version of (6.60), depends on u_{t-1}, it can be shown that these two variables are also correlated. Finally, at least on an intuitive level, it follows that if $\gamma \neq 0$, Y_{t-1} is correlated with u_t because, through (6.61), u_t depends on u_{t-1}, and Y_{t-1} is correlated with u_{t-1}.

If we estimate (6.60) by our usual instrumental-variable procedure, one of our normal equations, namely $\sum_{t=1}^{N} (Y_{t-1} \hat{u}_t) = 0$, will correspond to the assumption that $\text{cov}(Y_{t-1}, u_t) = 0$. However, we have noted that if $\gamma \neq 0$, $\text{cov}(Y_{t-1}, u_t) \neq 0$. Therefore, if $\sum (Y_{t-1} \hat{u}_t) = 0$ is used as one of our normal equations, our estimators will be biased. It can be shown that they will also be inconsistent. The major problem in all this is that the biases and inconsistencies involved are such that the Durbin-Watson d statistic will tend toward 2 even if $\gamma \neq 0$. Recall that the d statistic will also tend toward 2 if $\gamma = 0$. Also recall that values of d near 2 lead to an acceptance of the hypothesis of no autocorrelation, $\gamma = 0$. The implication of all this is that if the Durbin-Watson test is used in cases involving a lagged dependent variable, the re-

---

* The t ratio for the constant term is calculated by dividing the standard deviation of $\hat{b}_0$ (the square root of its variance) into $\hat{b}_0$.

** This assumption is needed for the model to be "stable." See the appendix to this chapter for a discussion of the role of this assumption.

searcher will typically be led to accept the hypothesis of no autocorrelation whether or not it exists! Clearly, the Durbin-Watson test should not be used in such cases.

Fortunately, another test for autocorrelation is available for the case in which a lagged dependent variable is present. This test involves the use of the Durbin h statistic.* Suppose (6.60) is estimated by the usual instrumental-variable method, and γ is correspondingly estimated by (6.45). Let $\hat{\gamma}$ and $\hat{a}$ be the estimators of γ and a so obtained, and let var$(\hat{a})$ be the estimator of the variance of $\hat{a}$ so obtained. Then, the h statistic is

$$h = \hat{\gamma}\left(\frac{n}{1 - n\,\widehat{\mathrm{var}}(\hat{a})}\right)^{1/2} \tag{6.62}$$

where n is the sample size. It can be shown that if there is no autocorrelation (i.e., $\gamma = 0$), h would be $N(0, 1)$ if the sample size were infinite. If there is autocorrelation, h will tend to be "large." More specifically, if $\gamma > 0$, h will tend to be large in a positive direction, and if $\gamma < 0$, h will tend to be large in a negative direction.

The above observations suggest the following test for autocorrelation when a lagged dependent variable is present. This test is a large sample test in that strictly speaking the results are correct, or exact, only if the sample is of infinite size.

Consider the model in (6.60), and the null hypothesis $H_0 : \gamma = 0$. Suppose the alternative hypothesis is $H_1 : \gamma \neq 0$. Then, we can test H_0 against H_1 at the 0.05 level of significance in the following way:

1. Estimate (6.60) in the usual fashion using the instrumental-variable technique from Chapter 4 and note the value of $\widehat{\mathrm{var}}(\hat{\gamma})$ so obtained.
2. From the residuals, calculate $\hat{\gamma}$ as in (6.45). Alternatively, if the program provides a value for the Durbin-Watson d statistic, we can use the approximation $\hat{\gamma} = 1 - d/2$. This approximation is based on (6.54).
3. Compute the value for the Durbin h statistic.
4. Reject H_0 if $|h| > 1.96$, and accept H_0 otherwise.

Two variations on this test should be obvious. Specifically, if H_1 were $\gamma > 0$, and we maintain 0.05 as our level of significance, we would reject H_0 if $h > 1.645$; if H_1 were $\gamma < 0$, we would reject H_0 if $h < -1.645$. Tests at other levels of significance (e.g., 0.01) are straightforward and are left for the reader to develop.

The test based on the h statistic has its limitations. For example, in light of (6.62) it should be clear that the test breaks down if

$$n\,\widehat{\mathrm{var}}(\hat{a}) \geq 1 \tag{6.63}$$

since h will involve the square root of a negative number. In such cases h will not be defined. This, incidentally, is not just a point of theoretical curiosity;

---

* J. Durbin, "Testing for Serial Correlation in Least Squares Regression When Some of the Regressors are Lagged Dependent Variables," *Econometrica* 38 (1970), pp. 410–421.

it often happens in practice. In such cases, there is an alternative test that can be used. This test is also a large sample test. In practice, therefore, its results are also approximate.

Again, let the null hypothesis be $H_0 : \gamma = 0$ and the alternative be $H_1 : \gamma \neq 0$. Then, taking the level of significance to be 0.05, the proposed test is:

1. Estimate the basic equation, say (6.60), by our standard instrumental-variable technique.
2. Next, obtain the estimated disturbance terms, $\hat{u}_t$.
3. Using the results from step 2, estimate the following regression equation:

$$\hat{u}_t = a_0 + a_1\hat{u}_{t-1} + a_2 Y_{t-1} + c_1 X_{1t} + \cdots + c_k X_{kt} + \varepsilon_t \qquad (6.64)$$

   in the usual way. Note that (6.64) contains, as regressors, the lagged esti-mated disturbance term and all of the regressors in the original model (6.60).
4. Obtain the t-ratio corresponding to a_1, namely $\hat{a}_1/\hat{\sigma}_{\hat{a}1}$. It can be shown that $\hat{a}_1/\hat{\sigma}_{\hat{a}1}$ would be $N(0, 1)$ if $\gamma = 0$ and N were infinite. Based on this, the test involves rejecting H_0 if $|\hat{a}_1/\hat{\sigma}_{\hat{a}1}| > 1.96$ and accepting H_0 otherwise. If the alternative hypothesis were $H_1 : \gamma > 0$, we would reject H_0 if $\hat{a}_1/\hat{\sigma}_{\hat{a}1} > 1.645$. The case in which the alternative is $H_1 : \gamma < 0$ is left to the reader.

6.3 HETEROSCEDASTICITY

In this section we turn to another problem arising from the violation of one of the assumptions concerning the disturbance terms. Recall that in our basic regression model we postulated that

$$\text{var}(u_t) = E(u_t^2) = \sigma_u^2.$$

That is, we assumed that the disturbance terms all have the same variance, σ_u^2. This condition of a constant variance is known as *homoscedasticity*. It may be the case, however, that all of the disturbance terms do not have the same variance. This condition of nonconstant variance is known in the liter-ature as *heteroscedasticity*. As an example, in studying the levels of consump-tion expenditure of families with different disposable incomes, we might find that the variance in consumption rises with the level of income. For instance, families with larger incomes may simply have more flexibility concerning consumption. Such a condition is illustrated in Figure 6.6, where we see that the variation of the hypothetical set of points seems to increase at higher levels of income. In a case such as this, we would probably assume that the disturbance term in the consumption function is heteroscedastic.

A FORMAL MODEL

More formally, suppose that we have a consumption function of the form

$$C_t = b_0 + b_1 Y_{dt} + b_2 A_t + u_t, \qquad (6.65)$$

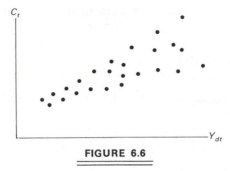

FIGURE 6.6

where

C_t = consumption expenditure of the tth household,
Y_{dt} = disposable income of the tth household,
A_t = liquid assets of the tth household, and
u_t = disturbance term,

where we now assume that, for any given set of values of the regressors, u_t is a normally distributed variable, which is not autocorrelated, and whose *variance* is proportional to the income of the tth household: $\text{var}(u_t) = Y_{dt}\sigma_u^2$. Thus, the higher the level of income, the larger the variance in consumption we would expect to observe.

In our previous models, we assumed that the disturbance term was independent of all of the regressors. We can no longer make this assumption, because we have now specified that the variance of the disturbance term *depends* on the value of one of the regressors, Y_{dt}. The disturbance term cannot, therefore, be independent of that variable. *Unless we make a further assumption*, we will not be able to implement our standard estimation procedure, because the value of the covariance between the disturbance term and the regressor, Y_{dt}, will not be zero. As we will show, the further assumption that enables us both to account for the heteroscedasticity *and* to assume that the covariance between the disturbance term and each regressor is zero is that, *whatever* the values of the regressors, Y_d and A, for any observation, the mean of the disturbance term is zero. More formally, for any given values of Y_{ds} and A_s, $E(u_t) = 0$, for all t and s. In relation to equation (6.65), the implication of this is that the mean of C_t, C_t^m, is still $C_t^m = b_0 + b_1 Y_{dt} + b_2 A_t$.

Another implication of this assumption is that the disturbance term is *not correlated* with either of the regressors: $\text{cov}(u_t, Y_{dt}) = \text{cov}(u_t, A_t) = 0$. For instance, if u_t were correlated with Y_{dt}, its value would be *expected* to increase or decrease as Y_{dt} increased. However, our assumption that the mean of u_t is zero for any value of Y_{dt} implies that this is not so; as Y_{dt} increases, the expected value of u_t remains constant, namely, zero. It follows that u_t and Y_{dt} are not correlated.

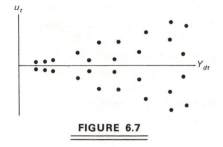

FIGURE 6.7

This conclusion may seem confusing in light of our assumption that the variance of u_t increases with Y_{dt}. However, a glance at Figure 6.7 should dispel the confusion. From the hypothetical set of points, it is apparent that the *variance* of u_t increases with Y_{dt}. But it is also clear that u_t would not be correlated with Y_{dt} because, for any value of Y_{dt}, the mean value of u_t is zero.

Note above that u_t and Y_{dt} (and u_t and A_t) are not correlated, because the mean of u_t is zero *for any given value of Y_{dt}* (and also of A_t). If we had only assumed that the mean of u_t is zero without stating the condition "*for any given value of Y_{dt}*," we could not have reached this result. As an example, suppose that X_1 is a variable whose mean is zero, $E(X_1) = 0$. Let $X_2 = 2X_1$. Then the mean of X_2 would be zero, $E(X_2) = 2E(X_1) = 0$. However, the mean of X_2 would not be zero *for any given value of X_1*. For example, if $X_1 = 3$, the mean of X_2 would be 6. In this case, X_1 and X_2 would be perfectly correlated.

Before turning to problems of estimation, we should make one last point which may not be obvious to all readers. In Figure 6.8 (a refined version of 6.7), we see that the points corresponding to (vertically about) any value of Y_d seem to have a mean value of zero. This reflects the assumption that the

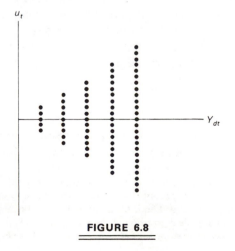

FIGURE 6.8

mean of u is zero for any given value of Y_d. Now note that the mean value of *all* the points in the figure also looks to be zero. This corresponds to the condition that the mean (sometimes called the "overall mean") of u is zero. It should now be clear that the assumption that the mean of u corresponding to any given value of Y_d is zero implies that the overall mean of u is also zero. The converse, however, is not true. For instance, the mean of u could be negative for some values of Y_d and positive for others, but u could still have an overall mean of zero.

CONSEQUENCES FOR OUR ESTIMATORS

What happens when we use our ordinary estimation procedure on an equation with heteroscedastic disturbance terms? Somewhat intuitively, since the mean of the disturbance term is still zero and since u_t is still uncorrelated with each of the independent variables [so that $E(u_t Y_{dt}) = 0$ and $E(u_t A_t) = 0$ in equation (6.65)], our parameter estimators will still be consistent and unbiased.* Essentially, the point is that our conditions $E(u_t) = 0$, $E(u_t Y_{dt}) = 0$, and $E(u_t A_t) = 0$ still suggest that we set $\sum \hat{u}_t = 0$, $\sum (\hat{u}_t Y_{dt}) = 0$, and $\sum (\hat{u}_t A_t) = 0$; there is nothing basically wrong with our normal equations. However, like the case of autocorrelation, there will be different expressions for the *variances* of our parameter estimators; once again, if we continue to use our usual formulas to estimate these variances, our resulting tests of hypotheses and confidence intervals will be suspect.

This should be clear, since our basic regression model assumes a constant variance and our estimation procedure produces an estimator of this constant. However, with heteroscedasticity the variance of the disturbance terms is not the same; it is itself a variable. This means that our standard estimator will in fact represent some kind of average of the differing variances of the disturbance terms; as such, this estimator really has little meaning and does not, for example, allow us to construct valid confidence intervals (or t ratios) for the parameters of the equation. Like the case of autocorrelation, we can obtain more reliable estimators of our coefficients (that is, estimators with smaller variances) and can generate estimators of their variances by incorporating into our estimation procedure information concerning the true properties of the disturbance term.

AN ESTIMATION PROCEDURE

To examine this problem further, let us return to our consumption relationship in equation (6.65), where we specified $\text{var}(u_t) = Y_{dt}\sigma_u^2$. We shall now

---

* The interested reader can prove that our standard estimators are still unbiased by working back through the argument in the appendix to Chapter 4. In doing so, you should note that the only assumption needed in the derivation is the assumption that the mean of the disturbance terms is zero *for any values of the regressors*. In the standard model, this condition followed from the independence assumption; in our heteroscedastic model, we explicitly made this assumption.

show that, if we simply divide through (6.65) by $\sqrt{Y_{dt}}$, we obtain an equation with a homoscedastic disturbance term. Performing this division gives us

$$\frac{C_t}{\sqrt{Y_{dt}}} = b_0\left(\frac{1}{\sqrt{Y_{dt}}}\right) + b_1\sqrt{Y_{dt}} + b_2\left(\frac{A_t}{\sqrt{Y_{dt}}}\right) + u_t^*, \qquad (6.66)$$

where

$$u_t^* = \frac{u_t}{\sqrt{Y_{dt}}}.$$

Since the mean value of u_t is zero for any given level of Y_{dt}, we have*

$$E(u_t^*) = E\left(\frac{u_t}{\sqrt{Y_{dt}}}\right) = \left(\frac{1}{\sqrt{Y_{dt}}}\right)E(u_t) = 0. \qquad (6.67)$$

Turning now to the variance of u_t^*, we have, under the same assumptions, that

$$\text{var}(u_t^*) = E(u_t^*)^2 = E\left(\frac{u_t^2}{Y_{dt}}\right) = \frac{1}{Y_{dt}}E(u_t^2)$$

$$= \frac{1}{Y_{dt}}(Y_{dt})\sigma_u^2 = \sigma_u^2. \qquad (6.68)$$

We see that our transformed model (6.66) is one in which the disturbance terms, the u_t^*, have a mean of zero and a constant variance.

Continuing our analysis, it is not difficult to see that u_t^* is uncorrelated with the independent variables of (6.66). For instance, for any given set of values of the regressors of (6.66), or, equivalently, for any given values of the regressors, $E(u_t^*) = (1/\sqrt{Y_{dt}})E(u_t) = 0$. It follows from our results above that u_t^* is uncorrelated with the regressors of (6.66), and so

(1) $$E\left[u_t^*\left(\frac{1}{\sqrt{Y_{dt}}}\right)\right] = 0,$$

(2) $$E(u_t^*\sqrt{Y_{dt}}) = 0,$$

(3) $$E\left[u_t^*\left(\frac{A_t}{\sqrt{Y_{dt}}}\right)\right] = 0.$$

In brief, if for each observation, we simply divide C_t, Y_{dt}, and A_t by $\sqrt{Y_{dt}}$, the corresponding regression model for this new set of "corrected" observed values would be (6.66), and this model would satisfy all of our basic assumptions. We could then simply use our standard estimation procedure to obtain, in this case, unbiased estimators of both the regression parameters and

---

* The meaning of (6.67) should be clear. If Y_{dt} is given as 900, $E(u_t^*) = E(u_t)/30 = 0$, since the mean of u_t is zero for any value of Y_{dt}.

the variances of the estimators.* Specifically, using assumptions (1)–(3), our normal equations would be**

$$\sum \left(\frac{C_t}{Y_{dt}}\right) = \hat{b}_0 \sum \left(\frac{1}{Y_{dt}}\right) + \hat{b}_1 n + \hat{b}_2 \sum \left(\frac{A_t}{Y_{dt}}\right),$$

$$\sum C_t = n\hat{b}_0 + \hat{b}_1 \sum Y_{dt} + \hat{b}_2 \sum A_t, \qquad (6.69)$$

$$\sum \left(\frac{C_t A_t}{Y_{dt}}\right) = \hat{b}_0 \sum \left(\frac{A_t}{Y_{dt}}\right) + \hat{b}_1 \sum A_t + \hat{b}_2 \sum \left(\frac{A_t^2}{Y_{dt}}\right).$$

The example we have just considered also provides some further insight into the problem of heteroscedasticity. Our normal estimation procedure weights each observation equally in generating parameter estimators. Our illustration suggests, however, that with heteroscedasticity we should use different weights for the observations; more specifically, for the example considered, we should weight each observation by $(1/\sqrt{Y_{dt}})$. This says that observations corresponding to a larger variance should be given less weight than those corresponding to smaller variances. Intuitively, this makes some sense. An observation corresponding to a small variance will be more likely to be "close" to the true regression line†; in our estimation procedure, we should in some sense want to pay more attention to those points that we have reason to believe lie nearer the true regression line than those that, on average, will be farther away. The observations that correspond to a smaller variance are simply more valuable in estimating the position of the regression line than those whose expected deviation from the line is greater.

---

* Unlike our previous models, equation (6.66), which corresponds to the normal equations in (6.69), does not have a constant term. As a result, there is a subtle change in the formulas for the variances of our estimators. Specifically, the $\hat{v}_{it}$ terms in these formulas would now be defined as the residuals from the regression, *which does not have a constant term*, of the ith regressor on the other regressors. For example, the variance of $\hat{b}_2$ in (6.69) would be $\sigma_u^2 / \sum \hat{v}_{2t}^2$, where $\hat{v}_{2t}$ is the residual from the regression

$$\frac{A_t}{\sqrt{Y_{dt}}} = \gamma_1 \left(\frac{1}{\sqrt{Y_{dt}}}\right) + \gamma_2(\sqrt{Y_{dt}}) + v_{2t}.$$

** We should point out that the above normal equations were derived by imposing the assumptions (1)–(3). In this case, the assumption $E(u_t^*) = 0$ was not used. That is, although we have only three parameters to estimate, b_0, b_1, b_2, we have *four assumptions* concerning the disturbance term. This "apparent" problem of having too many assumptions usually arises in the course of solving the heteroscedasticity problem. The solution is, in general, to do exactly what we did above: use only the assumptions that correspond to the covariances of the regressors in the transformed model. This implies that we should disregard the assumption that the mean of the disturbance term in the transformed equation is zero. Although the proof is beyond the scope of this book, it can be shown that, if this procedure is followed, the resulting estimators of b_0, b_1, and b_2 will have smaller variances than if we impose the zero-mean condition and two (any two) of the above three assumptions.

† By the true regression line, we refer to the *mean* equation relating the dependent variable to the independent variables.

HETEROSCEDASTICITY: FURTHER APPROACHES

How do you know *when* you have heteroscedasticity and how, more generally, do you alter your estimation procedure to cope with it? These are not easy questions to answer (and they are often, unfortunately, ignored). A sensible approach is *first* to examine the relationship under study and see if there is any reason to believe that the disturbance terms will not be homoscedastic. Heteroscedasticity is often suggested by the very formulation of the model itself. For example, suppose that we consider the hypothesis that the level of profits, measured in dollar terms (call it π), depends on the size of the business enterprise, as indicated say by the value of its assets (A). We might postulate the relationship

$$\pi_t = b_0 + b_1 A_t + u_t, \tag{6.70}$$

where we have observations on π and A for n business firms. In this instance, it would be hard to believe that the disturbance terms have the same variance; surely, the variance in *dollar profits* will be greater among firms like General Motors and Standard Oil than among the local candy store and the community hardware shop, solely because of the great difference in the absolute size of their profits. The point here is simply that we would have strong reason to expect a positive relationship between the value of A_t and the variance of u_t. There may, incidentally, be other independent variables in equation (6.70), but the problem of heteroscedasticity normally focuses on the relationship between one of independent variables and the variance of the disturbance term. At any rate, in a case such as this, the likelihood of heteroscedasticity is very great.

There are basically two approaches we could take to solve the heteroscedasticity problem associated with a model such as the one above. First, we could try to reformulate the relationship in such a way as to remove the presumption of heteroscedasticity. That is, we could look upon heteroscedasticity as being the result of a poorly formulated model; we would effectively solve the problem by specifying a better model. In terms of our preceding example, it may make more sense to examine the relationship between the *rate* of profit [that is, $\pi^* = (\pi/A)$] and firm size than between π and A. We might then estimate the equation

$$\pi_t^* = b_0 + b_1 A_t + u_t, \tag{6.71}$$

and, with no particular reason to expect profit *rates* to vary more substantially among larger or smaller firms, we could with somewhat greater confidence assume a constant variance among the disturbance terms.

Second, we can try to determine the pattern of the heteroscedasticity and incorporate this information into our estimation procedure. For instance, in the consumption function (6.65) we examined earlier, we assumed that we knew this pattern: the variance of u_t was proportional to the level of income. We solved the problem by dividing the terms in the regression model by the square root of income. However, in many cases we may not have any reason to assume a particular pattern. For example, in the profit-asset model (6.70), is the variance of the disturbance term proportional to the level of assets, A_t, to A_t^2, or to some other function of A_t? We may not know the answer to these questions on an *a priori* basis.

The determination of the pattern of heteroscedasticity is a difficult problem. Some of the proposed solutions are beyond the scope of this book.* Fortunately, however, there is a straightforward and intuitively appealing technique by which, under certain assumptions, we can both test for the presence of heteroscedasticity and estimate its pattern. Moreover, this technique draws on material we have developed in earlier chapters, which should make it relatively easy to understand and may also provide a useful review.

Suppose that we want to estimate the relationship

$$Y_t = b_0 + b_1 X_{1t} + b_2 X_{2t} + u_t, \tag{6.72}$$

and we suspect that the variance of u_t may be systematically related to the value of, say, X_{2t}; that is, we think that

$$\sigma_{u_t}^2 = f(X_{2t}). \tag{6.73}$$

If we knew the specific form of the function $f(X_{2t})$, we could (as earlier) solve the problem of heteroscedasticity by simply dividing our equation (6.72) by $\sqrt{f(X_{2t})}$, because the variance of the resulting disturbance term, $u_t^* = (u_t/\sqrt{f(X_{2t})})$, would be a *constant*, namely unity.** The new equation would thus satisfy the assumption of homoscedasticity, and we could proceed as usual.

The problem we face is that the function $f(X_{2t})$ is not known. Our procedure will be first to approximate and estimate $f(X_{2t})$, and then, as suggested above, to divide (6.72) by the square root of our estimate of $f(X_{2t})$. We shall then be able to use the modified regression equation to derive a set of normal equations that we can solve for the estimators of our parameters.

First note that our assumption of heteroscedasticity in (6.73) implies, for a given value of X_{2t}, that

$$E(u_t^2) = f(X_{2t}). \tag{6.74}$$

Now let

$$\varepsilon_t = u_t^2 - f(X_{2t}) \tag{6.75}$$

---

* For a more advanced treatment, see J. Johnston, *Econometric Methods*, 2nd ed. (New York: McGraw-Hill, 1972), pp. 214–221.

** Note that, for a given value of X_{2t}:

$$E(u_t^{*2}) = E\left[\frac{u_t^2}{f(X_{2t})}\right] = \frac{1}{f(X_{2t})} E(u_t^2) = \frac{f(X_{2t})}{f(X_{2t})} = 1.$$

and notice that for a given value of X_{2t},

$$E(\varepsilon_t) = E(u_t^2) - f(X_{2t})$$
$$= f(X_{2t}) - f(X_{2t}) = 0.$$

The mean of ε_t is zero.

Let us now solve (6.75) for u_t^2 to obtain

$$u_t^2 = f(X_{2t}) + \varepsilon_t. \tag{6.76}$$

The interpretation of (6.76) is straightforward. The variable u_t^2 is expressed as the sum of its mean, $f(X_{2t})$, and a variable, ε_t, that reflects its deviation from its mean. Note that (6.76) looks very much like a regression model.

For the moment, assume that we have observations on u_t. Furthermore, let us assume that our prior knowledge of the relationship suggests that, if u_t is heteroscedastic as in (6.74), the function $f(X_{2t})$ may be "adequately" approximated by a polynomial of degree k.* Under these assumptions, we can transform (6.76) into a regression model that is of the standard form:

$$u_t^2 = a_0 + a_1 X_{2t} + \cdots + a_k X_{2t}^k + \varepsilon_t. \tag{6.77}$$

We have already seen that, for any given value of X_{2t}, $E(\varepsilon_t) = 0$. We have also seen above that this zero-mean condition implies that ε_t is *uncorrelated* with X_{2t}. Since a given value of X_{2t} implies a given value of all of the powers of X_{2t} appearing in (6.77), it follows that ε_t is also uncorrelated with each of these powers of X_{2t}.** This means that we can treat (6.77) as a regression model with a disturbance term, ε_t, which satisfies the conditions that generate the normal equations.

Suppose that we estimate (6.77) with our standard technique by setting

$$\sum \hat{\varepsilon}_t = 0, \ \sum (\hat{\varepsilon}_t X_{2t}) = 0, \ \ldots, \ \sum (\hat{\varepsilon}_t X_{2t}^k) = 0.$$

Then it can be shown that, with some further assumptions, the resulting estimators $\hat{a}_0, \ldots, \hat{a}_k$ are consistent. A consistent estimator of $f(X_{2t})$ would thus be

$$\widehat{f(X_{2t})} = \hat{a}_0 + \hat{a}_1 X_{2t} + \cdots + \hat{a}_k X_{2t}^k. \tag{6.78}$$

The remainder of the procedure should now be evident. Specifically, we would divide our original model (6.72) across by $\hat{f}_t = [\widehat{f(X_{2t})}]^{1/2}$ and then obtain our estimators of b_0, b_1, and b_2 from the normal equations:

$$\sum \left(\frac{Y_t}{\hat{f}_t}\right) = \hat{b}_0 \sum \left(\frac{1}{\hat{f}_t}\right) + \hat{b}_1 \sum \left(\frac{X_{1t}}{\hat{f}_t}\right) + \hat{b}_2 \sum \left(\frac{X_{2t}}{\hat{f}_t}\right),$$

---

* Typically, k would be taken as $k \leq 3$. On a formal level, the results in this section hold only if the polynomial "approximation" is *perfect*. Since in practice this is not likely to be true, we must take all of these results as *approximate*.

** For example, if the mean of ε_t is zero given that $X_{2t} = 3$, it is also zero given that $X_{2t}^2 = 9$.

$$\sum \left(\frac{Y_t X_{1t}}{\hat{f}_t} \right) = \hat{b}_0 \sum \left(\frac{X_{1t}}{\hat{f}_t} \right) + \hat{b}_1 \sum \left(\frac{X_{1t}^2}{\hat{f}_t} \right) + \hat{b}_2 \sum \left(\frac{X_{1t} X_{2t}}{\hat{f}_t} \right),$$

$$\sum \left(\frac{Y_t X_{2t}}{\hat{f}_t} \right) = \hat{b}_0 \sum \left(\frac{X_{2t}}{\hat{f}_t} \right) + \hat{b}_1 \sum \left(\frac{X_{1t} X_{2t}}{\hat{f}_t} \right) + \hat{b}_2 \sum \left(\frac{X_{2t}^2}{\hat{f}_t} \right).$$

Because $\hat{f}_t$ is a consistent estimator of f_t, it can be shown that, under our assumptions, the resulting estimators $\hat{b}_0$, $\hat{b}_1$, and $\hat{b}_2$ are *consistent* and *efficient*. In addition, if the sample were of infinite size, our usual variance formulas would hold. Let $\hat{\sigma}_{\hat{b}_i}^2$, $i = 0, 1, 2$, denote the estimator of the variance of $\hat{b}_i$ which is given by our usual formula. Then, hypotheses can be tested and confidence intervals established by assuming that $(\hat{b}_i - b_i)/\hat{\sigma}_{\hat{b}_i}$ is a standard normal variable. Again, such a result would be strictly correct only in the case of an infinite sample, so that in practice we must view our results as approximate. In a manner similar to that for the autocorrelation model, the reason for the complication is that the estimator $\hat{b}_i$ is nonlinear in disturbance terms through its dependence upon $\hat{f}_t$.

The obvious difficulty in the above procedure is that, in practice, we would not have observations on u_t^2. Before implementing this procedure, we would first have to estimate the values of u_t^2. This we can easily do, however, because we can obtain consistent estimators of the parameters, and, therefore, of the disturbance terms of our original heteroscedastic model (6.72) by our standard technique. We simply estimate the parameters in (6.72) in the usual way and then take as our estimator of the disturbance terms, $\hat{u}_t = Y - \hat{b}_0 - \hat{b}_1 X_{1t} - \hat{b}_2 X_{2t}$. It can be shown that, if the above procedure is carried out with u_t^2 replaced by $\hat{u}_t^2$, all of the above results still hold.

A TEST FOR HETEROSCEDASTICITY

We now have a technique for correcting our estimation procedure in the presence of heteroscedastic disturbance terms. To conclude this section, let us return to the issue of determining whether or not the regression model is in fact heteroscedastic. We discussed earlier (in our hypothetical regression of firms' profits on their assets) how we can simply examine the regression equation to see if the formulation of the model itself suggests the likelihood of heteroscedasticity. It would be desirable, however, to have a more formal procedure for deciding if we have heteroscedastic disturbance terms. We shall suggest such a test here. The hypothesis we shall test is that the disturbance terms in our original model (6.72) are heteroscedastic as specified in (6.73). We should understand that the formal specification of (6.73) is that "if the disturbance terms u_t are heteroscedastic, the manner in which they are heteroscedastic is given by (6.73)."

We shall now use our polynomial approximation of $f(X_{2t})$ to develop our test. Specifically, a test of the specification in (6.73) can be carried out by testing the joint hypotheses in (6.77) that $H_0 : a_1 = a_2 = \cdots = a_k = 0$. If H_0 is accepted, we would conclude that the variance of u_t does not depend on

X_{2t}; we would then take u_t to be homoscedastic. If H_0 is rejected, however, we would conclude that u_t is heteroscedastic and so would then proceed to go through the above estimation technique for its correction.*

We can construct a large sample test of the hypothesis H_0 above in terms of a variation on the procedure suggested in Appendix B to Chapter 5. Specifically, again, let $\hat{u}_t$ be the tth estimated disturbance term of the model (6.72) which is obtained by applying our standard procedure to that model. Let ESS_u be the error sum of squares obtained by regressing $\hat{u}_t^2$ on the $(k + 1)$ variables of (6.77), namely, the constant term, $X_{2t}, \ldots, X_{2t}^k$, and let $\hat{\sigma}_\varepsilon^2$ be the corresponding estimate of the variance of the disturbance term obtained in our usual fashion, namely, as $\text{ESS}_u/(N - k - 1)$, where N is the sample size. Finally, let ESS_R be the error sum of squares obtained by regressing $\hat{u}_t^2$ on only the constant term. In this case, $\text{ESS}_R = \sum_{t=1}^N (\hat{u}_t^2 - A)^2$, where $A = \sum_{t=1}^N \hat{u}_t^2/N$. Then, it can be shown that, if $N = \infty$, $(\text{ESS}_R - \text{ESS}_u)/\hat{\sigma}_\varepsilon^2$ is a chi-square variable with k degrees of freedom. In a manner that is similar to the discussion in Appendix B to Chapter 5, it can be demonstrated that, if H_0 is false so that the disturbance term is heteroscedastic in the nature of (6.77), ESS_R will tend to be large relative to ESS_u. Therefore, "large" values of our chi-square statistic $(\text{ESS}_R - \text{ESS}_u)/\hat{\sigma}_\varepsilon^2$ would lead one to reject H_0. Denote a chi-square variable with k degrees of freedom as χ_k^2. Then, assuming a 5 percent level of significance of the test, "large" values of our statistic would be defined to be all values that exceed $\chi_{k,0.95}^2$ where $\text{Prob}(\chi_k^2 \leq \chi_{k,0.95}^2) = 0.95$. The value of $\chi_{k,0.95}^2$ can be obtained from any tabulated table for the chi-square variable.

In practice, of course, the sample size would not be infinite and so the results of our test would only be approximate. As a point of interest, we note that, if $N = \infty$, this chi-square test can be shown to be *equivalent* to the F test that one would construct by following the procedure outlined in Appendix B to Chapter 5 with respect to equation (6.77) after u_t^2 is replaced by $\hat{u}_t^2$.

Finally, we point out that although we have developed our test for heteroscedasticity in terms of a single independent variable, it is a straightforward matter to generalize the test to the case where several independent variables are the source of the heteroscedasticity. Suppose, for example, that in (6.72) the variance of the disturbance term depends on both X_{1t} and X_{2t}, say as

$$\sigma_{u_t}^2 = g(X_{1t}, X_{2t}). \tag{6.79}$$

Assuming again that the function is not known, our procedure would essentially be the same as that described above except that (6.77) would be replaced by a polynomial in both X_{1t} and X_{2t}.

For purposes of illustration, suppose $k = 2$. Then (6.77) could be replaced by

$$u_t^2 = a_0 + a_1 X_{2t} + a_2 X_{2t}^2 + b_1 X_{1t} + b_2 X_{1t}^2 + c_1 X_{1t} X_{2t} + \varepsilon_t. \tag{6.80}$$

---

* Formally, before proceeding to "correct" for it, we should obtain a new sample. In many cases, however, this is not feasible and so we would continue to work with our original sample.

The test for homoscedasticity would then relate to the null hypothesis $H_0: a_1 = a_2 = b_1 = b_2 = c_1 = 0$. Specifically, let ESS_u be the error sum of squares obtained from the regression of $\hat{u}_t^2$ on the constant term, X_{2t}, X_{2t}^2, X_{1t}, X_{1t}^2, and $X_{1t}X_{2t}$. Since this regression has six coefficients, we would take our estimate of σ_e^2 as $\hat{\sigma}_e^2 = ESS_u/(n - 6)$. Let ESS_R again be the error sum of squares obtained from the regression of $\hat{u}_t^2$ on only the constant term. In this case, it can be shown that if the sample size were infinite, $(ESS_R - ESS_u)/\hat{\sigma}_e^2$ would be a chi-square variable with 5 degrees of freedom. Note that the model determining ESS_u, in this case, has five nonconstant regressors.* If we again take 0.05 as our level of significance, we would reject H_0, in this case, if $(ESS_R - ESS_u)/\hat{\sigma}_e^2 > \chi_{5;0.95}^2$. Again, the results of this test are only approximate since, in practice, the sample size is typically finite.

Some final observations are in order. If the degree of the polynomial approximating the pattern of heteroscedasticity is taken to be small, for example, $k \leq 2$, interaction terms would typically be considered. For instance, $X_{1t}X_{2t}$ appears in (6.80). However, if k is taken to be large, say $k \geq 3$, we would not typically consider all possible interaction terms. The reason for this is that if k is large and all possible interaction terms are included in the model, the number of regressors would be "very large." This could lead to problems of multicollinearity.

If the sample is infinite but k, the degree of the polynomial, is finite (no matter how large) then all possible interactions should, in principle, be considered in order to make the test as "good as possible." "As good as possible" is taken to mean that, for a given Type 1 error, the Type 2 error is minimized. However, in practice the sample size, n, is finite. For this case, there are no results which indicate just how many (if any) of the interaction terms should be considered in order to make the test "as good as possible." The only guidance we offer on this issue is as follows. Let p be the total number of regressors in the model determining the error sum of squares which we have denoted as ESS_u. Then we suggest that the number of terms in the polynomial be chosen in such a way that $(n - p) \geq 25$. This suggestion is based only on our intuition.

ANOTHER TEST FOR HETEROSCEDASTICITY: THE GOLDFELD-QUANDT TEST

We turn now to a second test for heteroscedasticity that, if certain conditions are satisfied, is quite simple and appealing. In particular, suppose we believe that one of the independent variables is the likely source of heteroscedasticity. Further, suppose that the relationship between this variable and the variance of the disturbance term is monotonic. By this we will mean that the variance of the disturbance term either consistently increases with the value of the independent variable, or consistently decreases with the value of the independent variable. As an example, in our earlier discussion concerning equation (6.70), we suggested the possibility that the variance of dollar profits

---

*In general the degrees of freedom of the chi-square variable corresponding to $(ESS_R - ESS_u)/\hat{\sigma}_e^2$ is equal to the number of nonconstant regressors determining ESS_u.

may increase with the assets of the firm; this would be a case of a monotonically increasing relationship between the variance of the disturbance term and an independent variable.

If the variance of the disturbance term is monotonically related to one of the regressors, and the disturbance terms are normally distributed, we can employ the Goldfeld-Quandt test for the presence of heteroscedasticity.* This test has some appealing properties. In contrast to our large-sample test in the preceding section, the Goldfeld-Quandt test is an exact small-sample test; we do not have to regard it as an approximation for less than infinite samples.

Consider the following linear regression model

$$Y_t = b_0 + b_1 X_{1t} + \cdots + b_h X_{ht} + \cdots + b_k X_{kt} + u_t, \qquad (6.81)$$

where X_h is the independent variable that we suspect is the source of the heteroscedasticity. Assume that the disturbance terms are normally distributed and that, if heteroscedasticity is present, it is because the variance of the disturbance term is monotonically related to X_h. Given these assumptions, the procedure for the Goldfeld-Quandt test is as follows:

1. Order all the observations by the values of X_h. If the suspected relationship between X_h and the variance of the disturbance term is monotonic and positive, then the first of the reordered observations should correspond to the smallest value of X_h, the second to the next smallest value of X_h, and so on. In contrast, if the suspected relationship between X_h and the variance of the disturbance term is monotonic and negative, then the first of the reordered observations should correspond to the largest value of X_h, the next to the second largest, and so on. If the observations are reordered in this fashion and if heteroscedasticity is present, the variance of the ith and jth disturbance terms will be such that $\text{var}(u_i) \leq \text{var}(u_j)$ if $i \leq j$.

   As an illustration of the reordering, consider the model

$$Y_t = a_0 + a_1 X_{1t} + a_2 X_{2t} + u_t, \qquad t = 1, 2, \ldots, 6 \qquad (6.82)$$

and suppose we assume that $\text{var}(u_t)$ *increases* with the value of X_{1t}. Then, if the original sample is

	Y	X_1	X_2
$t = 1$	10	2	15
$t = 2$	12	1	27
$t = 3$	−1	10	0
$t = 4$	5	9	5
$t = 5$	3	27	1
$t = 6$	0	5	10

(6.83)

* S. M. Goldfeld and R. E. Quandt, "Some Tests for Homoscedasticity," *Journal of the American Statistical Association*, Vol. 60 (1965), pp. 539–547.

the reordered sample is

Y	X_1	X_2
12	1	27
10	2	15
0	5	10
5	9	5
−1	10	0
3	27	1

(6.84)

If var(u_t) was assumed to *decrease* with the value of X_{1t}, the reordered sample would be

Y	X_1	X_2
3	27	1
−1	10	0
5	9	5
0	5	10
10	2	15
12	1	27

(6.85)

2. Omit d observations from the middle of the reordered sample. Although this number d is somewhat arbitrary, a reasonable rule of thumb is to take d as roughly $n/3$, where n is the size of the original sample. In addition d should be chosen in such a way that $(n - d)$ is an even integer. For example, if $n = 61$, d could be taken to be 21 so that $n - d = 40$ is even. If this is done, the original sample will be broken up into two subsamples, each containing $(n - d)/2$ observations.

To illustrate, if (6.83) were the original sample, and (6.84) the reordered sample, $d = 6/3 = 2$ and so the middle two observations in (6.84) would be dropped. The first subsample would then be the first $(n - d)/2 = (6 - 2)/2 = 2$ observations.

Y	X_1	X_2
12	1	27
10	2	15

(6.86)

and the second subsample would be

Y	X_1	X_2
−1	10	0
3	27	1

(6.87)

3. Estimate *separate* regression equations for the two resulting subsamples.
4. Calculate the error sum of squares for each of the regression equations. Let ESS_1 be the ESS for the first subsample and ESS_2 be the ESS for the second subsample. Note that if heteroscedasticity is present, the first subsample will have disturbance terms whose variances are less than those of the second subsample.
5. To simplify notation, let p be the number of regression coefficients. For example, $p = K + 1$ in (6.81). Then, it can be shown that (ESS_2/ESS_1) is distributed *exactly* as an F variable with $(n − d − 2p)/2$ degrees of freedom in both the numerator and denominator. Given this, we would then reject the null hypothesis, H_0, of homoscedastic disturbance terms at the chosen level of significance if ESS_2/ESS_1 is greater than the critical value of the F distribution as found in the F table.

As an illustration, let $e = (n − d − 2p)/2$ and denote an F variable with e degrees of freedom in both the numerator and denominator as $F_{e,e}$. Let $F_{e,e}^{0.95}$ be the value from the F table which is such that $\text{Prob}(F_{e,e} \leq F_{e,e}^{0.95}) = 0.95$. Then if we again take the level of significance to be 0.05, we would reject H_0 if $ESS_2/ESS_1 > F_{e,e}^{0.95}$.

The Goldfeld-Quandt test is thus quite a simple and straightforward test to employ. Moreover, the general rationale for the test is readily apparent. Somewhat intuitively, if the variance of the disturbance term is indeed monotonically related to the suspect independent variable, then we should expect the squares of the estimated disturbance terms to be larger in the second subsample than in the first. Therefore, large values of ESS_2/ESS_1 lead to a rejection of H_0. If the estimated disturbance terms are roughly of the same size in both subsamples, then the value of ESS_2/ESS_1 will typically be around unity; hence, we will be led to accept the null hypothesis of homoscedastic disturbance terms, because the critical value of the F distribution is larger than unity for significance levels of 0.05 or 0.01 and for equal degrees of freedom in the numerator and the denominator.

Two final points should be noted. First, the Goldfeld-Quandt test is valid even if no observations from the middle of the reordered sample are omitted. However, experiments have shown that the elimination of some observations improves the test because the size of the Type 2 error decreases—up to a point. The issue is that the omitted observations make the first and second portions of the reordered sample "more different." Thus, it becomes easier to detect differences in the variances of the disturbance terms in the two subsamples.

The second point is that our discussion above has implicitly assumed that $(n - d)/2 > p$. If $(n - d)/2 < p$, the test cannot be carried out because there will not be enough observations in each portion of the sample to estimate the coefficients of the regression model and hence to determine ESS_1 and ESS_2. If $(n - d)/2 = p$, the number of observations in each portion of the sample is equal to the number of parameters being estimated. In this case it can be shown that, unless there is perfect multicollinearity, both ESS_1 and ESS_2 will be zero, and so again the test cannot be implemented. We suggest that if d is taken to be approximately $n/3$, and it turns out that $(n - d)/2 \leq p$, then no observations be dropped from the middle of the reordered sample (i.e., d be taken to be zero). If this is done, and n is even, there will be $n/2$ observations in each of the two reordered samples. If $n/2 > p$, the test should be carried out as described above. In this case H_0 would be rejected, if the level of significance is 0.05 and $ESS_2/ESS_1 > F_{(n-2p)/2;(n-2p)/2}^{0.95}$. If n is odd, we suggest putting $n_1 = (n + 1)/2$ observations in the first subsample, and $n_2 = n - n_1$ in the second. The test would then be carried out as above except now H_0 would be rejected if $ESS_2/ESS_1 > F_{(n_1-p)/2;(n_2-p)/2}^{0.95}$. Finally, if $n/2 \leq p$, the Goldfeld-Quandt test should not be considered.

SOME COMMENTS ON THE TWO TESTS FOR HETEROSCEDASTICITY

We have suggested two tests for heteroscedasticity. There are still others. The reason for this is that no single test is ideal in all possible circumstances. One set of circumstances suggests the use of one test, while another suggests the use of another test. The researcher should be able to use one of the two tests we have suggested in most cases considered in practice.

To see the issues involved recall that, given the underlying assumptions, the Goldfeld-Quandt test is appealing because it is a small sample test; that is, it is not based upon an approximation to a case involving an infinite sample. Therefore, the results are exact; they are not approximations. For example, a Goldfeld-Quandt test constructed with a 0.05 level of significance really has a Type 1 error of 0.05. In addition, experiments have shown that, again given the underlying assumptions, Type 2 errors for a Goldfeld-Quandt test are reasonably small. Therefore, if the underlying assumptions are satisfied, the Goldfeld-Quandt test is a good test to use.

However, the underlying assumptions may not hold. For instance, the disturbance terms may not be normally distributed. If they are not, the results of the Goldfeld-Quandt test must be viewed as approximations. Clearly, on an intuitive level, the closeness of the approximations would depend upon just how different from normality the disturbance terms are. In practice, economists seem willing to assume that the disturbance terms are normal so that this assumption is typically not of much concern. We are not endorsing this "view," just reporting it!

More serious for the procedure itself is the assumption that if heteroscedasticity is present, it is because the variance of the disturbance term relates to *one* of the regressors in a *monotonic way*. This is the assumption that enables the researcher to reorder the sample in such a way that the variance of the disturbance term never decreases. This is the cornerstone of the test. Clearly, if the variance of the disturbance term relates to more than one regressor, or if only to one regressor in something other than a monotonic fashion, the researcher would not generally be able to reorder the sample as described and hence would not be able to carry out the test.

In such cases, the researcher could use the test we described in the preceding section. That test is not limited to cases in which only one regressor is involved in the heteroscedasticity. Furthermore, it does not require the regressors involved in the heteroscedasticity to be so involved in a monotonic fashion. Indeed, very complex patterns of heteroscedasticity could be considered by simply taking the degree of the approximating polynomial [e.g., k in (6.73)] to be large. We also note that this test is not based upon the assumption that the disturbance terms are normally distributed.

However, this test also has its limitations. Specifically, it is a large sample test; since in practice, the researcher will have a finite sample, this means that the researcher cannot be sure of the properties of the test he is using—for example, the size of the Type 1 error! Also, in this test, the size of the Type 2 error could be large if the sample size is small.

HETEROSCEDASTICITY: A CONSEQUENCE OF AGGREGATION

We shall conclude our treatment of heteroscedasticity with an actual case that arose in the context of estimating the demand for wheat in the United States.* The source of the heteroscedasticity was, in this instance, somewhat different from those we have examined thus far. In particular, the study proceeded by setting forth a standard sort of demand function:

$$Q_t = b_0 + b_1 P_t^w + b_2 P_t^g + b_3 Y_t + b_4 D_t + b_5 S_{1t} + b_6 S_{2t} + b_7 S_{4t} + u_t. \quad (6.88)$$

In this equation, the demand for wheat in period $t (Q_t)$ depends on the current price of wheat (P_t^w), the price of other grains (P_t^g), the level of per capita income (Y_t), and four dummy variables. The dummy variable D_t accounts for the cost of certain marketing certificates that domestic food processors had to buy during only part of the period under consideration; D_t takes on a value of unity for those periods during which the market certificates were in effect and a value of zero for the remaining periods. The remaining dummy variables, S_1, S_2, and S_4, are seasonal dummies for, respectively, the first, second, and fourth calendar quarters.

The source of the problem, in this case, was the nature of the data. The

---

* This study involved one of the authors. See David F. Bradford and Harry H. Kelejian, *A Quarterly Demand Model for Wheat* (unpublished manuscript, 1976).

U.S. Department of Agriculture provides periodic figures on quantities and prices of wheat and other grains. Data on these variables are available on a quarterly basis since the third quarter of 1964; prior to that time, however, figures relating to the demand variable for wheat are available *only* in semiannual form.

For example, the available observation on the demand variable prior to the third quarter of 1964 relates to the *first half* (first two quarters) of 1964; the available observation prior to this relates to the *second half* (last two quarters) of 1963, and so on. There is thus an obvious problem if we want to use data before and after the third quarter of 1964 to estimate a single demand function. How can we use both semiannual and quarterly data to estimate a single regression equation?

Using a more general formulation, suppose the regression model explaining the quarterly values of a dependent variable, Y_t, is

$$Y_t = a_0 + a_1 X_{1t} + \cdots + a_n X_{nt} + u_t, \qquad (6.89)$$

where the time subscript t refers to calendar quarters, and where the disturbance term u_t satisfies all of our standard assumptions. Specifically, assume that u_t is independent of all lagged, current, and future values of the regressors, is not autocorrelated, has a mean of zero, $E(u_t) = 0$, and a constant variance, $E(u_t^2) = \sigma_u^2$.

Assume that quarterly observations on the dependent variable are only available for periods $t = T, T + 1, T + 2, \ldots, T + N$. For periods prior to T, we have only the nonoverlapping semiannual observations, $(Y_{T-1} + Y_{T-2})$, $(Y_{T-3} + Y_{T-4}), \ldots, (Y_{T-\mathscr{S}} + Y_{T-\mathscr{S}-1})$, where $\mathscr{S}$ is an odd integer that indicates the number of available semiannual observations. This will be discussed below. In the example above, $(Y_{T-1} + Y_{T-2})$ relates to the first half of 1964, $(Y_{T-3} + Y_{T-4})$ relates to the second half of 1963, and so on. Returning to our model (6.89), we assume that quarterly observations are available for each of the regressors for all periods of interest (e.g., in the example above, before and after the third quarter of 1964).

If (6.89) is the regression model explaining the quarterly variable Y_t, it follows that the regression model for the semiannual variable $(Y_{T-j} + Y_{T-j-1})$ is

$$(Y_{T-j} + Y_{T-j-1}) = 2a_0 + a_1(X_{1,T-j} + X_{1,T-j-1}) + \cdots$$
$$+ a_n(X_{n,T-j} + X_{n,T-j-1}) + (u_{T-j} + u_{T-j-1}), \quad (6.90)$$
$$j = 1, 3, 5, \ldots, \mathscr{S},$$

where $\mathscr{S}$ is an odd integer whose value determines (in a manner discussed below) the number of available semiannual observations. The model in (6.90) is obtained by simply summing the right-hand side of (6.89) for the quarters that correspond to the dependent variable, namely, $T - j$ and $T - j - 1$.

Under our assumptions, the disturbance term $(u_{T-j} + u_{T-j-1})$ in the semiannual model (6.90) has a mean of zero, is not autocorrelated since the quarterly components are nonoverlapping, and is independent of all lagged, current, and future values of the regressors; it also has a *constant variance*, namely,

$$E(u_{T-j} + u_{T-j-1})^2 = 2\sigma_u^2. \tag{6.91}$$

Therefore, the model in (6.90), which relates to our semiannual observations, satisfies all of our standard assumptions. The quarterly model in (6.89), however, also satisfies all of our standard assumptions, *and contains the same unknown parameters*. We shall now demonstrate that these two models can be combined into one model that also satisfies all of our standard assumptions, and permits *both* the quarterly and semiannual data to be used in the estimation of its parameters.

First, note that our available observations on the dependent variable can be ordered according to calendar time, from earliest to latest, as

$$(Y_{T-\mathscr{S}} + Y_{T-\mathscr{S}-1}), (Y_{T-\mathscr{S}+2} + Y_{T-\mathscr{S}+1}), \ldots, (Y_{T-5} + Y_{T-6}),$$
$$(Y_{T-3} + Y_{T-4}), (Y_{T-1} + Y_{T-2}), Y_T, Y_{T+1}, \ldots, Y_{T-N}. \tag{6.92}$$

Note that, if $\mathscr{S} = 5$, we would have three semiannual observations, namely, $(Y_{T-5} + Y_{T-6})$, $(Y_{T-3} + Y_{T-4})$, and $(Y_{T-1} + Y_{T-2})$. Note also that $(5 + 1)/2 = 3$. As another example, it should be clear that, if $\mathscr{S} = 3$, we would have two semiannual observations. Note again that $(3 + 1)/2 = 2$. These illustrations should make it clear that, in general, for any odd integer $\mathscr{S}$, the number of semiannual observations is $(\mathscr{S} + 1)/2$. Therefore, the total number of observations listed in (6.92) is $\{[(\mathscr{S} + 1)/2] + [N + 1]\}$.

Let us now denote the $\{[(\mathscr{S} + 1/2)] + [(N + 1)]\}$ observations in (6.92) by y_t, $t = 1, 2, \ldots, \{[(\mathscr{S} + 1)/2] + [N + 1]\}$. That is, y_1 indicates the earliest observation in (6.92), namely, $(Y_{T-\mathscr{S}} + Y_{T-\mathscr{S}-1})$, y_2 indicates the next, and so on. In a similar manner, we see that there are $[(\mathscr{S} + 1)/2]$ semiannual observations for each of the regressors in (6.90)*; in addition, we have assumed that quarterly observations on each regressor are available for each of the periods for which we have quarterly data on the dependent variable—that is, for periods $T, T + 1, \ldots, T + N$. Let x_{jt}, $t = 1, \ldots, \{[(\mathscr{S} + 1)/2] + [N + 1]\}$, denote the $\{[(\mathscr{S} + 1)/2] + [N + 1]\}$ semiannual *and* quarterly observations on the regressor X_{jt}, which are arranged according to calendar times in a manner exactly analogous to (6.92). Then our results in (6.89) and (6.90) imply that y_t is related to $x_{1t}, x_{2t}, \ldots, x_{nt}$ as

$$y_t = a_0 x_{0t} + a_1 x_{1t} + \cdots + a_n x_{nt} + v_t,$$
$$t = 1, 2, \ldots, \left(\frac{\mathscr{S} + 1}{2}\right) + (N + 1), \tag{6.93}$$

---

* Because we have assumed that quarterly observations on the regressors are available, observations on the semiannual forms of these variables can easily be constructed.

where $x_{0t} = 2$ if t corresponds to a semiannual observation, $t \le [(\mathscr{S} + 1)/2]$, and $x_{0t} = 1$ otherwise; and where v_t is a disturbance term which satisfies all of our standard assumptions except that it is heteroscedastic. Specifically, $E(v_t^2) = 2\sigma_u^2$, if $t \le [(\mathscr{S} + 1)/2]$, and $E(v_t^2) = \sigma_u^2$, otherwise.

The model in (6.93) can be converted into one that satisfies *all* of our standard assumptions. Specifically, let $d_t = \sqrt{2}$, if $t \le [(\mathscr{S} + 1)/2]$, and $d_t = 1$, otherwise. Then, following the procedure outlined in previous sections, we can eliminate the problem of heteroscedasticity by dividing (6.93) across by d_t. The resulting model is then

$$\left(\frac{y_t}{d_t}\right) = a_0\left(\frac{x_{0t}}{d_t}\right) + a_1\left(\frac{x_{1t}}{d_t}\right) + \cdots + a_n\left(\frac{x_{nt}}{d_t}\right) + w_t, \qquad (6.94)$$

$$t = 1, 2, \ldots, \left(\frac{\mathscr{S} + 1}{2}\right) + (N + 1),$$

where $w_t = v_t/d_t$. Clearly, $E(w_t^2) = \sigma_u^2$ for all $t = 1, 2, \ldots, [(\mathscr{S} + 1)/2] + (N + 1)$.

The model in (6.94) satisfies all of our standard assumptions and relates to all of our available semiannual and quarterly observations on the dependent variable. This model can be estimated by our standard procedure. Specifically, the normal equations would be determined by the conditions

$$\sum \hat{w}_t\left(\frac{x_{0t}}{d_t}\right) = 0, \ldots, \sum \hat{w}_t\left(\frac{x_{nt}}{d_t}\right) = 0, \qquad (6.95)$$

where each summation is from $t = 1, \ldots, \{[(\mathscr{S} + 1)/2] + [N + 1]\}$, and where $\hat{w}_t = (y_t/d_t) - \hat{a}_0(x_{0t}/d_t) - \cdots - \hat{a}_n(x_{nt}/d_t)$, where $\hat{a}_0, \ldots, \hat{a}_n$ are the estimators of $a_0, \ldots, a_n$.

We note that, once the estimators $\hat{a}_0, \ldots, \hat{a}_n$ are obtained, the value of y_t would be explained by the model as

$$\left(\frac{\hat{y}_t}{d_t}\right) = \hat{a}_0\left(\frac{x_{0t}}{d_t}\right) + \cdots + \hat{a}_n\left(\frac{x_{nt}}{d_t}\right), \qquad (6.96)$$

or, canceling d_t, as

$$\hat{y}_t = \hat{a}_0 x_{0t} + \cdots + \hat{a}_n x_{nt}. \qquad (6.97)$$

This means that the latest quarterly values would be explained as

$$\hat{Y}_t = \hat{a}_0 + \hat{a}_1 X_{1t} + \cdots + \hat{a}_n X_{nt}, \qquad t = T, T + 1, \ldots, T + N; \quad (6.98)$$

the semiannual values would be explained as

$$(\hat{Y}_{T-j} + \hat{Y}_{T-j-1}) = 2\hat{a}_0 + \hat{a}_1(X_{1,T-j} + X_{1,T-j-1})$$

$$+ \cdots + \hat{a}_n(X_{n,T-j} + X_{n,T-j-1}), \qquad j = 1, 3, 5, \ldots, \mathscr{S}.$$

6.4 PROBLEMS IN THE SELECTION OF VARIABLES

To this point we have assumed that the variables of the regression model are somehow given to us and that our only problem is to estimate the model, test hypotheses, correct for autocorrelation, and so on. However, in practice we must select the variables to include in the model. The experimenter typically draws upon a theory relating to the determination of the *dependent* variable and then attempts to specify the *independent* variables that best describe the theory. In doing this, it is possible to make two sorts of errors. First, he may fail to include an important independent variable in his model. That is, he may simply overlook an important factor determining the dependent variable. Second, he may assume that a particular factor is important in determining the dependent variable when in fact it is not. If so, he would be led to include an unnecessary variable in the model. In this section we consider the consequences of each of these types of errors.

AN OMITTED VARIABLE

Consider first the case where we omit a regressor from the hypothesized relationship. For example, suppose that the true (but unknown to us) relationship is

$$Y_t = b_0 + b_1 X_{1t} + b_2 X_{2t} + u_t, \qquad (6.99)$$

where u_t is a disturbance term that satisfies all of our standard assumptions. We overlook X_2, however, and instead consider the equation

$$Y_t = b_0 + b_1 X_{1t} + r_t, \qquad (6.100)$$

where we take r_t as our disturbance term. We shall now show that, if we were to estimate (6.100) by our standard technique, the resulting estimators of b_0 and b_1 would, in general, be *biased* and *inconsistent*. The reason is that the failure to include X_2 in the model would generally lead to violations of our key assumptions concerning the disturbance term, in this case, r_t.

More specifically, in comparing (6.99) to (6.100) we see that the disturbance term in the model being considered depends, in part, on X_{2t}:

$$r_t = b_2 X_{2t} + u_t. \qquad (6.101)$$

Taking expected values, we see that

$$E(r_t) = E(b_2 X_{2t}) + E(u_t) = b_2 \mu_2 + 0 = b_2 \mu_2, \qquad (6.102)$$

where μ_2 is the mean of the X_{2t}. Clearly, the expected value of the disturbance term, r_t, will in general not be zero, except when $b_2 = 0$, which would imply that Y_t does not depend on X_{2t}.* Thus, we see that, if Y is a function of X_2

---

* The one other case where $E(r_t) = 0$ is the accidental and unusual instance in which $\mu_2 = 0$.

but we do not include X_2 in the regression equation, the disturbance term in the equation we do consider will typically have a mean that is nonzero. In addition it should be evident that r_t will be correlated with X_{1t} if X_{2t} is correlated with X_{1t}; as a result, $\text{cov}(r_t, X_{1t})$ will generally not be zero. It follows, at least intuitively, that under such conditions our estimators of b_0 and b_1 would be biased and inconsistent. For instance, if $E(r_t) \neq 0$, but our first normal equation is obtained by setting $\sum \hat{r}_t = 0$, our procedure is simply not internally consistent.

It may be helpful to consider at a more intuitive level the character of this bias. Suppose that we want to estimate a consumption function and the true relationship is

$$C_t = b_0 + b_1 Y_{dt} + b_2 A_t + u_t, \qquad (6.103)$$

where

C_t = consumption expenditure in period t,
Y_{dt} = disposable income in period t,
A_t = stock of liquid assets in period t, and
u_t = the disturbance term.

We would expect A_t to have a positive effect on C_t so that $b_2 > 0$; suppose also that A_t and Y_t have a positive correlation: as disposable income rises, so typically does the value of liquid assets (and conversely). Assume, however, that the equation we actually estimate omits A_t:

$$C_t = b_0 + b_1 Y_{dt} + r_t. \qquad (6.104)$$

In this case (as above), the expected value of the disturbance term in the equation we choose to estimate will not in general be zero:

$$E(r_t) = E(b_2 A_t) + E(u_t) = b_2 \mu_A + 0 = b_2 \mu_A \neq 0, \qquad (6.105)$$

where μ_A is the mean of A_t. Similarly, r_t would be expected to be correlated with Y_{dt}. We shall therefore obtain biased estimators of b_0 and b_1 (where the latter is the MPC). Moreover, because of the positive effect of A_t on C_t ($b_2 > 0$) and the positive correlation of A_t and Y_{dt}, we shall typically get an overestimate of the MPC; that is, $E(\hat{b}_1) > b_1$. Intuitively, the reason for this is that Y_{dt} in equation (6.104) serves as a proxy variable for both itself and for A_t; it, in a sense, gets credit for the positive effects on C_t of both Y_{dt} and A_t. The point is that, as Y_{dt} rises, so typically does A_t, but with the absence of A_t from the estimated equation the positive effect of A_t on C_t is attributed to Y_{dt}; as a result, the measured influence of Y_{dt} on C_t is exaggerated. If, instead, A_t were negatively correlated with C_t but were still positively related to Y_{dt}, then our estimator of b_1 (in the absence of A_t) would typically be biased downward; the negative effect of A_t on C_t would be reflected to some extent in $\hat{b}_1$. Finally, we note that the direction of the biases in these cases would in general be reversed if Y_{dt} and A_t were negatively related. The important point of all this is not so much to determine the direction of bias, but rather to realize that our estimators will be biased and inconsistent if an important variable has been omitted from our equation. In fact, for most regression models in which there are many independent variables, the direction of bias cannot usually be determined.

TOO MANY VARIABLES

Let us consider next the case of too many regressors. Suppose, for example, that the true relationship is

$$Y_t = b_0 + b_1 X_{1t} + b_2 X_{2t} + u_t, \tag{6.106}$$

where we assume that the disturbance term is independent of all values of the regressors and satisfies all of our other standard assumptions. This equation says that we do not have to include X_{3t} in our model, because Y_t does not depend on it; that is,

$$b_3 = 0.$$

Note, however, that this does not prevent us from writing our model as

$$Y_t = b_0 + b_1 X_{1t} + b_2 X_{2t} + b_3 X_{3t} + u_t, \tag{6.107}$$

where $b_3 = 0$. You may recall from our discussion in Appendix B to Chapter 5 that, because zero is a constant, there is nothing basically wrong in having a regression coefficient whose value is zero.

Suppose that we do not know that b_3 is in fact zero. As a result, we consider (6.107) as our model and proceed to generate estimators of b_0, b_1, b_2, and b_3 in the usual manner. The question we must consider is whether our standard estimation technique will still give us unbiased estimators of the regression coefficients and of the variances of our estimators. The answer, fortunately, is yes, if none of our basic assumptions concerning the disturbance term in (6.107) are violated. For example, suppose that u_t is independent of X_{3t}. Then, in (6.107) we would have a regression model whose disturbance term has a mean of zero, is independent and therefore uncorrelated with all of the regressors, and satisfies all of our other assumptions. It follows that the estimators of b_0, b_1, b_2, and b_3 are unbiased.* Somewhat intuitively, if we did not know that the effect of X_{3t} on Y_t were zero, the data would tell us so in the sense that our estimator of b_3 would be unbiased: $E(\hat{b}_3) = b_3 = 0$. Alternatively, if we were to test the null hypothesis $b_3 = 0$ at the 5 percent level of significance, we would have a 95 percent chance of accepting it.

---

* This is the usual case considered in the literature. It can be shown that if X_{3t} is only *uncorrelated* with the disturbance term, our estimators, under some further assumptions, will still be *consistent*. Finally, it should be obvious, that if X_{3t} were correlated with the disturbance term, our estimators would be both biased and inconsistent.

SOME FURTHER COMMENTS

The results above might seem to imply that there is nothing to be lost by including a whole set of regressors of highly dubious importance in the equation to be estimated. This, however, is not the case. Note first that, even if these regressors are independent of the disturbance term so that none of our assumptions would be violated, it is still possible for us to reject a null hypothesis concerning whether or not a particular parameter is zero. In other words, we could make a Type 1 error.

Second, and probably more important, the variance of the parameter estimators, given the sample size, increases in general with the number of regressors. That is, if we knew that $b_3 = 0$ and so obtained our estimator of say, b_2, from (6.106), that estimator would, in general, have a smaller variance than the estimator of b_2 obtained from (6.107). In a sense, by using (6.107) we are asking more of our available data, since we must estimate four, instead of three, parameters. Alternatively, model (6.106), unlike (6.107), incorporates the information that $b_3 = 0$, and the variance of the estimators reflects this additional information. There is, then, a cost associated with increasing the number of independent variables: larger variances resulting in less precise estimators of the coefficients. In consequence, confidence intervals become wider, and we may reject as statistically insignificant a variable that in fact does have a systematic effect on the dependent variable.

This puts us in a dilemma. If we leave something out, we get biased results; however, if we put too much in, the variance of our estimators increases. What this indicates is the need for some care and judgment in the selection of the set of independent variables. For example, even though you may be interested in the relationship between only two variables (as in the illustration in Chapter 4 where the researcher was attempting to determine the effect of the sales-tax rate on retail sales in central cities), it is essential to include in the model the other variables that determine the value of the dependent variable. The failure to include the other regressors will result, in general, in a biased estimator of the coefficient with which you are concerned. Returning to the illustration, the estimated effect of a higher tax rate on the volume of central-city sales will tend to be biased unless the other variables that determine retail sales in the city are included in the equation. On the other hand, there is no reason to include as a regressor every variable for which you can find data; you should select those variables that you believe on *a priori* grounds influence the dependent variable.

One approach economists frequently use is to "try" a variable that they think may be of importance and then drop it from the equation should it turn out not to be significantly different from zero. Suppose, for instance, that we estimate the equation

$$Y_t = b_0 + b_1 X_{1t} + b_2 X_{2t} + u_t, \qquad (6.108)$$

where we have only some rather tenuous reasons to believe that X_2 influences Y. And we find that indeed we cannot reject the null hypothesis that $b_2 = 0$.

An intuitively appealing procedure to reduce the variance of our estimator of b_1 would be to remove X_2 from the equation and estimate the revised equation

$$Y_t = b_0 + b_1 X_{1t} + u_t. \tag{6.109}$$

While this widely employed technique has a certain pragmatic value in terms of eliminating variables of no apparent importance, one should be aware that the way in which it is normally used entails complications. As one example, if the original set of data is "reused" to estimate (6.109), an element of circularity is introduced and the resulting estimators can be shown to be *biased*. This element of circularity enters because the model (6.109) would have been *formulated* on the basis of a test performed on the data that are being used to estimate the model. Clearly, the scientific method requires researchers to formulate their models before analyzing the data that will be used to estimate them.

There are other problems associated with this sequential method, some of which arise even if a new set of data is used to estimate (6.109). A full discussion of these problems is beyond the scope of this book. However, the reader should be aware that certain problems may arise whenever a test result is used to select the model that is used to estimate a parameter. This is precisely what we are doing above where the parameter b_1 is estimated in terms of (6.108) if X_2 is statistically signifcant and from (6.109) if X_2 is not significant. In such instances, the standard properties of the estimators may no longer hold; for example, the estimators may be biased, their variances may no longer be given by the standard formulas, and they may no longer be normally distributed. Despite the fact that such sequential methods are widely used in economics, the associated problems are typically (and unfortunately) ignored!

APPENDIX.
A Note on Stability

In equation (6.60), we assumed that $|a| < 1$. The reason for this is that the suggested tests for autocorrelation in the text will not be valid unless $|a| < 1$. In this appendix we will explain the importance of this assumption.

In reference to (6.60) let

$$Z_t = b_0 + b_1 X_{1t} + \cdots + b_k X_{kt} + u_t, \qquad t = \ldots, -2, -1, 0, 1, 2, \ldots. \quad (6A.1)$$

Clearly Z_t is the net sum, at t, of all the components of Y_t except for aY_{t-1}.

Given this observation Y_t can be expressed as

$$Y_t = aY_{t-1} + Z_t, \qquad t = \ldots, -2, -1, 0, 1, 2, \ldots. \quad (6A.2)$$

The relationship in (6A.2) implies that

$$Y_{t-1} = aY_{t-2} + Z_{t-1}. \quad (6A.3)$$

Substituting (6A.3) into (6A.2) we obtain

$$Y_t = a^2 Y_{t-2} + aZ_{t-1} + Z_t. \quad (6A.4)$$

The relationship in (6A.2) also implies that

$$Y_{t-2} = aY_{t-3} + Z_{t-2}. \quad (6A.5)$$

Substituting (6A.5) into (6A.4) yields

$$Y_t = a^3 Y_{t-3} + a^2 Z_{t-2} + aZ_{t-1} + Z_t. \quad (6A.6)$$

Note that in (6A.2), (6A.4), and (6A.6), Y_t is expressed in terms of a lagged value of Y_t which is multiplied by the parameter a which is raised to a power. The power to which a is raised is the same as the lag in Y_t. Thus, in (6A.6), for instance, Y_t is lagged three periods, and a is raised to the power 3. Y_t is related to Z_t, Z_{t-1}, and Z_{t-2} in a similar fashion.

Consider the value of Y_t which is lagged t periods, namely $Y_{t-t} = Y_0$. If we continue the substitutions which lead to (6A.6), we can express Y_t in terms of Y_0 as

$$Y_t = a^t Y_0 + a^{t-1} Z_1 + a^{t-2} Z_2 + \cdots + aZ_{t-1} + Z_t. \quad (6A.7)$$

As an illustration, (6A.7) means that

$$Y_1 = aY_0 + Z_1$$
$$Y_2 = a^2 Y_0 + aZ_1 + Z_2 \qquad (6A.8)$$
$$Y_3 = a^3 Y_0 + a^2 Z_1 + aZ_2 + Z_3, \text{ etc.}$$

Consider now the case in which $|a| < 1$. In this case we see that the dependence of Y_t on its value t periods ago, namely Y_0, involves a^t which decreases in absolute value as t increases. Among other things, this means that the dependence of Y_2 on Y_0 will be greater in absolute value than the dependence of Y_3 on Y_0. Similarly, the dependence of Y_3 on Y_0 will be greater in absolute value than that of Y_4 on Y_0, and so forth.

If certain technical conditions concerning the components of Z_t are satisfied,* and the substitution process leading to (6A.7) repeated indefinitely, we would obtain, if $|a| < 1$,**

$$Y_t = Z_t + aZ_{t-1} + a^2Z_{t-2} + a^3Z_{t-3} + \cdots . \qquad (6A.9)$$

We have not included a lagged value of Y_t in the right-hand side of (6A.9) because its coefficient would be zero if $|a| < 1$.

Consider now the case in which $|a| \geq 1$. In this case, the above argument leading to (6A.9) will not hold since a^t will not decrease in absolute value as t increases. Also, note in light of (6A.7) and (6A.8), that the dependence of Y_3 on Y_0 will be *at least as large* in absolute value as the dependence of Y_2 on Y_0. Similarly, the dependence of Y_4 on Y_0 will be at least as large in absolute value as that of Y_3 on Y_0, and so on. Indeed, if $|a| > 1$, the dependence of Y_t on Y_0 in absolute value will *increase* as t increases. This should be clear from (6A.7) and (6A.8).

In general let Y_t be the value of the dependent variable of a given model at time t. Let Y_0 be the value of that variable at time zero. Then, if the model implies that the dependence of Y_t on Y_0 eventually diminishes to zero as $t \to \infty$, that model is said to be *stable*. If this dependence does not diminish to zero as $t \to \infty$, the model is *not* stable, or is said to be *unstable*. Somewhat intuitively, if the model is unstable, the value of the dependent variable at one point in time will forever influence its future values. If the model is stable, it will not forever influence future values.

Our discussion above suggests that the model in (6.60) is stable if $|a| < 1$.† It is not stable if $|a| > 1$. Note that the condition for stability in (6.60) does not relate to the coefficients $b_0, b_1, \ldots, b_k$.

---

* On an intuitive level, these conditions imply that the probability is zero that the lagged values of Z_t will be infinite.

** In this substitution process one would use the relationships $Y_0 = aY_{-1} + Z_0$, $Y_{-1} = aY_{-2} + Z_{-1}$, and so on.

† We are again assuming those technical conditions concerning the lagged value of Z_t.

QUESTIONS

1. Consider the model
$$Y_t = a + bX_t + u_t,$$
with observations

X	1	2	3	4	5	6	7	8	9	10	11	12	13	14	15
Y	2	2	2	1	3	5	6	6	10	10	10	12	15	10	11

Using a Type 1 error of $\alpha = 0.05$, test for autocorrelation. Assume the standard conditions.

2. Consider the linear production model
$$Q_t = a + bL_t + cK_t + u_t,$$
in which total output for the economy at time t, Q_t, is related to total labor and capital inputs L_t and K_t.
   a. Can it plausibly be argued that u_t in the model above is heteroscedastic? Discuss.
   b. Suppose that capital is ignored and hence the model $Q_t = a + bL_t + u_t$ is estimated. Explain why the estimator of b will probably be upwardly biased.

3. Suppose the consumption function for each individual, i, at time t is
$$C_{it} = a + b_1 Y_{it} + b_2 Y_{it}^2 + u_{it}, \qquad i = 1, \ldots, N. \tag{1}$$

Let C_t and Y_t be average consumption expenditure and average income at time t. That is,
$$C_t = \sum_{i=1}^{N} \frac{C_{it}}{N}, \qquad Y_t = \sum_{i=1}^{N} \frac{Y_{it}}{N}. \tag{2}$$

Then, in light of the individual consumption equations, (1), we might consider the *macro time-series* regression model:
$$C_t = a + b_1 Y_t + b_2 Y_t^2 + u_t, \qquad t = 1, \ldots, T. \tag{3}$$

   a. Demonstrate that our macro time-series model would have a specification error. This error may be termed an *aggregation bias* since it arises due to the "adding" up of the micro relationships.
   b. Suppose that $b_2 = 0$ and so there is no *aggregation bias*. Suppose we have observations on $N = 3$ individuals for $T = 2$ years. Write out, in notational form, the observation matrix corresponding to equation (1).
   c. Why will we generally have an *aggregation bias* if our postulated *cross-sectional* regression model contains a nonlinearity such as Y_{it}^2 above?

4. Consider the following demand for money equation:

$$M_{dt} = b_0 + b_1 i_t + b_2 i_{(t-1)} + b_3(\Delta i_t) + u_t,$$

where M_{dt} is the demand for money, i_t is the rate of interest, and $\Delta i_t = i_t - i_{t-1}$. We assume that i_{t-1} reflects the effects of habits, or inertia, and that Δi_t reflects an "expectations effect" stemming from recent changes in interest rates.

a. Show that, without further information, it is impossible to estimate b_1, b_2, and b_3.

b. Put the equation in a form that could be estimated and used to predict values of M_{dt}.

5. Assume the following production function;

$$Q_t = A L_{1t}{}^{\alpha_1} L_{2t}{}^{\alpha_2} K_t{}^{\alpha_3} e^{u_t},$$

where L_1 = the number of production workers, L_2 = the number of non-production workers, K = the stock of capital, u is the disturbance term, and the subscript t refers to time periods. Suppose that the firm always employs 10,000 workers; then $L_{1t} + L_{2t} = 10,000$. Can we estimate α_1, α_2, and α_3? Explain.

6. Consider the model

$$Y_t = a + bX_t + u_t,$$

$$u_t = \rho u_{t-1} + \varepsilon_t.$$

Suppose that we calculate $\hat{b}$ by the usual formula:

$$\hat{b} = \frac{\sum (X_t - \bar{X})(Y_t - \bar{Y})}{\sum (X - \bar{X})^2}.$$

Show that, because of the autocorrelation, our usual formula for the variance of $\hat{b}$, namely,

$$\sigma_b{}^2 = \frac{\sigma_u{}^2}{\sum (X_t - \bar{X})^2}$$

no longer holds.

7. Take the consumption function to be of the form

$$C_t = b_0 + b_1 Y_t + b_2 A_t + u_t,$$

where, for any values of Y_t and A_t we assume that $E(u_t) = 0$, and var$(u_t) = Y_t^2 \sigma_u^2$. Transform the above equation into one in which the disturbance term is homoscedastic and then derive the normal equations.

8. Consider the model

$$I_t = a_0 + a_1 \Delta Y_t + a_2 r_t + \varepsilon_t,$$

$$\varepsilon_t = \rho_1 \varepsilon_{t-1} + \rho_2 \varepsilon_{t-2} + u_t,$$

where I = investment, ΔY = the change in income, and r_t = the interest rate. Assume that u_t is independent of all the regressors, is not autocorrelated, has a mean of zero, and a constant variance. Outline a procedure for obtaining estimates of a_0, a_1, and a_2 that accounts for the autocorrelation when ρ_1 and ρ_2 are not known.

CHAPTER 7
Systems of Equations

To this point we have studied the estimation of a single equation in isolation from the larger economic model of which it may be a part. For example, the demand equation for a particular commodity is typically one in a system of equations that determines the equilibrium price and quantity in the market for that commodity; the economic model for a market will generally include a demand equation, a supply equation, and a third equation describing the equilibrating process in the market (e.g., that quantity demanded is brought into equality with quantity supplied). In this chapter we shall consider explicitly the problems that may arise when the equation we seek to estimate is interrelated with other equations in our more complete model. In particular, we shall find that, under certain circumstances, our regular estimation procedure no longer gives us unbiased (or even consistent) estimators of the coefficients; for such cases we shall have to modify our estimation technique.

7.1 SIMULTANEOUS-EQUATION BIAS

Recall that, in the initial presentation of the regression model in Chapter 2, we made two crucial assumptions concerning properties of the regression equation

$$Y_t = b_0 + b_1 X_t + u_t.$$

We assumed that the mean of the disturbance term is zero, $E(u_t) = 0$, and that the disturbance term is independent of the regressor so that the covariance between the disturbance term and the independent variable is zero, $E(X_t u_t) = 0$. As suggested by these assumptions, we then, in our estimation procedure, set

$$\sum \hat{u}_t = 0 \quad \text{and} \quad \sum (X_t \hat{u}_t) = 0.$$

This gave us our two normal equations, which we solved for our parameter estimators, $\hat{b}_0$ and $\hat{b}_1$; we were then able to show that these estimators of the coefficients were unbiased.

We also saw that the absence of bias in these estimators depends on the validity of our assumptions. In review, suppose that the covariance between X_t and u_t were not zero: $\text{cov}(X_t, u_t) = E(X_t u_t) \neq 0$. Assume, for example, that the covariance is positive. This implies that larger-than-mean values of

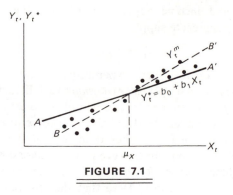

FIGURE 7.1

u_t (that is, positive values since the mean of u_t is zero) will be associated with larger-than-mean values of X_t, and vice versa. This, in turn, implies that the mean value of Y_t will be greater than $Y_t^* = (b_0 + b_1X_t)$ when X_t is larger than its mean value, μ_X, and less than Y_t^* when X_t is less than μ_X. In terms of the hypothetical scatter diagram in Figure 7.1, suppose the relationship involving Y_t^* is represented by the line AA'. Then, our expectations would be that, since positive values of u_t would typically occur when X_t is large, while negative values of u_t would usually accompany smaller values of X_t, the observed scatter of points should lie about some curve such as BB'. If we were to assume incorrectly that $E(X_tu_t) = 0$ and, accordingly, impose the condition $\sum (X_t\hat{u}_t) = 0$, we would end up estimating the parameters of the relationship BB'. That is, we would end up estimating the relationship between Y_t and X_t that is expected to be in the "middle" of all of the points in the scatter diagram. This would result in biased estimators of the coefficients b_0 and b_1; in this case we would tend to underestimate the value of b_0 (the vertical intercept of AA') and overestimate b_1 (the slope of AA'). We stress that this bias does not diminish in importance as the sample size becomes large. Our estimators are not only biased; they are also inconsistent!

Let us now reconsider our simple consumption function where*

$$C_t = b_0 + b_1Y_t + u_t. \tag{7.1}$$

In (7.1), we assume that the disturbance term u_t is normally distributed, has a mean of zero, $E(u_t) = 0$, a constant variance, $E(u_t^2) = \sigma_u^2$, and is not autocorrelated. We do not assume that u_t is independent of, or uncorrelated with, Y_t, for reasons we now discuss.

We know from macroeconomic theory that there is (at least) one additional equation in this model. This is an equilibrium statement that says that the

---

* In the simple model we develop in this section, we shall not distinguish between total income and disposable income. Following the convention in most textbooks, we shall denote income by Y and simply regard consumption as a function of income.

level of output and income adjusts so as to make aggregate demand $(C_t + I_t)$ equal to aggregate supply (Y_t):

$$Y_t = C_t + I_t, \tag{7.2}$$

where I_t is the level of investment expenditure by individuals and business firms.* Let us assume that I_t is an *exogenous* variable; this means that its value at any time t is determined by factors outside our model. For instance, investment expenditure might be determined by force of habit (one period's investment is always 2 percent higher than that of the preceding period), or by sociological conditions. In any event, we shall assume for purposes of this model that these "outside forces," whatever they may be, are unrelated to our disturbance term, u_t, in (7.1) so that the covariance between I_t and u_t is zero:

$$E(I_t u_t) = \text{cov}(I_t, u_t) = 0.$$

We shall now demonstrate that, because of the relationship between Y_t and C_t in equation (7.2), the covariance between income, Y_t, and the disturbance term, u_t, in (7.1) is *not* zero. This is easily seen if we substitute the expression for C_t in (7.1) into (7.2) to obtain

$$Y_t = b_0 + b_1 Y_t + u_t + I_t. \tag{7.3}$$

Solving (7.3) for Y_t gives us

$$Y_t = \frac{b_0}{1 - b_1} + \frac{I_t}{1 - b_1} + \frac{u_t}{1 - b_1}. \tag{7.4}$$

If we next multiply (7.4) by u_t and take expected values, we get**

$$\text{cov}(Y_t, u_t) = E(Y_t u_t) = E\left(\frac{b_0 u_t}{1 - b_1} + \frac{I_t u_t}{1 - b_1} + \frac{u_t^2}{1 - b_1}\right)$$

$$= \frac{b_0}{1 - b_1} E(u_t) + \frac{1}{1 - b_1} E(I_t u_t) + \frac{1}{1 - b} E(u_t^2). \tag{7.5}$$

Since the mean value of u_t is zero and we assume a zero covariance between u_t and I_t, the first two terms in the last form of (7.5) are zero, but the last term is nonzero. Specifically, we have

$$E(Y_t u_t) = \frac{1}{1 - b_1} E(u_t^2) = \frac{\sigma_u^2}{1 - b_1} \neq 0. \tag{7.6}$$

---

* Equation (7.2) is obviously a highly simplified equilibrium statement in which we are neglecting government and net foreign demand; we could easily incorporate these latter components of demand into the model, but this is unnecessary for the problem we are considering here.

** Again recall that since the mean of u_t is zero, the covariance between u_t and Y_t is $E(u_t Y_t)$, since

$$E[(u_t - 0)(Y_t - \mu_Y)] = E(u_t Y_t) - E(u_t \mu_Y)$$

$$= E(u_t Y_t) - \mu_Y E(u_t) = E(u_t Y_t),$$

where μ_Y is the mean of Y_t.

We see that, because of the additional equation (7.2), we can no longer assume that the covariance between the independent variable, Y_t, and the disturbance term, u_t, in (7.1) is zero. Equation (7.6) indicates that one of the basic assumptions of our regression model is invalid; the application of our standard estimation procedure will, for reasons given a bit earlier, generate biased and inconsistent estimators of b_0 and b_1.

It may prove helpful to supplement our formal treatment with a more intuitive discussion of the source of this bias. In equation (7.1) we have postulated that consumption expenditure in time t, C_t, depends on income in the same period, Y_t. However, we see from (7.2) that Y_t also depends on C_t. We have "causation" running in both directions: the two variables are interdependent. When we estimate (7.1) by our standard technique, we determine the pattern of the statistical association between C_t and Y_t. If causation were unambiguously in the direction of Y_t to C_t, then we could interpret our estimates as indicating the effect of Y_t on C_t. However, in the case of interdependency [as revealed by (7.2)], this measured statistical association between C_t and Y_t reflects the *mix* of effects of the variables on each other. Our estimates can no longer be interpreted as an unambiguous measurement of the effect of one variable, here Y_t, on the other, C_t. What we shall need is a revised estimation technique that will allow us to unravel the two effects; we need a means to unscramble the effect of Y_t on C_t from that of C_t on Y_t.

This is the problem of *simultaneous-equation bias*. It generally arises whenever the value of one of the independent variables is itself a function of the dependent variable. Consider the multiple-regression model

$$Y_t = b_0 + b_1 X_{1t} + b_2 X_{2t} + u_t, \qquad (7.7)$$

where X_{1t} is a regressor that satisfies our usual conditions in that it is independent of the disturbance term. If it is true that X_{2t} depends on Y_t, then we have a second equation to worry about—perhaps of the form

$$X_{2t} = c_0 + c_1 Y_t + r_t, \qquad (7.8)$$

where r_t is a disturbance term that is also assumed to be independent of X_{1t}. We leave it as an exercise to show (as before) that, in general,

$$E(X_{2t} u_t) \neq 0.$$

This set of equations implies a violation of one of the key assumptions of the regression model, and any attempt to employ our usual procedures to estimate (7.7) will yield biased and inconsistent estimators of *all* the parameters in the equation.

Henceforth we shall only refer to the *consistency* property, or lack of it, of our estimators. The reason for this is that econometricians generally "solve the systems problem" by constructing *consistent* estimators, because unbiased estimators are generally not available for parameters in equations that are part of a larger system of equations.

7.2 TWO-STAGE LEAST SQUARES: A SIMPLE CASE

Econometricians have in recent years developed a number of different techniques to deal with the estimation problems relating to systems of simultaneous equations.* We shall develop one of them here: two-stage least squares (TSLS). This particular technique has a number of attractive characteristics. First, it is intuitively appealing: it is relatively easy to understand and is based largely on procedures we have already developed in this book. Second, under the usual conditions, if the equation under consideration *can* be estimated, TSLS (unlike some other techniques) always works; it will generate consistent estimators of estimable parameters.** Third, TSLS is what we might call a "limited-information" procedure. By this we mean that one may estimate a given equation that is contained in a simultaneous-equation framework by the TSLS technique with only "vague" knowledge of the other equations. Many other techniques require much more detailed information for their implementation. And fourth, TSLS makes relatively modest computational demands.

AN ILLUSTRATION: CONSISTENT ESTIMATORS

We shall first provide an intuitive introduction to TSLS. Recall that formally our problem is that the presence of "two-way causation" results in a non-zero covariance between the disturbance term and one (or more) of the independent variables. If we want to use our standard estimation procedure ($OLSQ$),† we must somehow get rid of this nonzero covariance so that our equation will satisfy the assumptions of our regression model. This is precisely what TSLS does. It is a two-step estimation procedure. In the first step, we "purge," or eliminate from, the independent variable(s) that part which is correlated with the disturbance term; this involves generating a revised set of values for the suspect independent variables. These "revised" values are no longer correlated with the disturbance term so that the second step is simply to estimate the parameters with our standard technique.

---

* For more advanced treatments of the estimation of systems of equations, see J. Johnston, *Econometric Methods*, 2nd ed. (New York: McGraw-Hill, 1972), chaps. 12 and 13, and Arthur S. Goldberger, *Econometric Theory* (New York: Wiley, 1964), chap. 7.

** As we shall see shortly, some equations, or certain parameters therein, simply cannot be estimated. Actually, in a different context, the one of multicollinearity, we have already encountered equations in which there were parameters that we were unable to estimate.

† Recall from Chapter 2 that our instrumental-variable estimation technique has a "least-squares" property in that the procedure is equivalent to minimizing the sum of the squared deviations of the observed points from the estimated regression line. For this reason, we may refer to our standard results as the ordinary least-squares (OLSQ) results and may abbreviate reference to our standard procedure as OLSQ inasmuch as the results are identical. This notation is a convenient way to distinguish our standard procedure, OLSQ, from TSLS.

To see how this works, let us return to our simple two-equation model of national income, where we had

$$C_t = b_0 + b_1 Y_t + u_t, \tag{7.1}$$

$$Y_t = C_t + I_t. \tag{7.2}$$

As earlier, substituting the expression for C_t in (7.1) into (7.2) and solving for Y_t gives us

$$Y_t = \frac{b_0}{1 - b_1} + \frac{I_t}{1 - b_1} + \frac{u_t}{1 - b_1}. \tag{7.4}$$

We can simplify our notation by writing (7.4) as

$$Y_t = a_0 + a_1 I_t + q_t, \tag{7.9}$$

where

$$a_0 = \frac{b_0}{1 - b_1},$$

$$a_1 = \frac{1}{1 - b_1},$$

$$q_t = \frac{u_t}{1 - b_1}.$$

We now have Y_t solely as a function of I_t and the disturbance term q_t; notice that q_t (like u_t) has a mean of zero. Suppose, for the moment, that we know the values of a_0 and a_1. Under this assumption, we would be able to derive values for the mean of Y_t, Y_t^m, associated with any given value for I_t:

$$Y_t^m = a_0 + a_1 I_t. \tag{7.10}$$

We can also see from (7.9) that

$$Y_t = Y_t^m + q_t. \tag{7.11}$$

Returning to our original consumption equation, (7.1), we substitute the expression in (7.11) for Y_t to get

$$C_t = b_0 + b_1(Y_t^m + q_t) + u_t$$
$$= b_0 + b_1 Y_t^m + (b_1 q_t + u_t). \tag{7.12}$$

Noting that $q_t = u_t/(1 - b_1)$, we can write (7.12) as

$$C_t = b_0 + b_1 Y_t^m + \frac{u_t}{1 - b_1} \tag{7.13}$$
$$= b_0 + b_1 Y_t^m + q_t.$$

We shall now show that equation (7.13), unlike (7.1), satisfies the basic assumptions of our regression model. First, we can see that the disturbance term has a zero mean:

$$E(q_t) = E\left(\frac{u_t}{1 - b_1}\right) = \frac{1}{1 - b_1} E(u_t) = 0.$$

And second, we find that the independent variable is no longer correlated with the disturbance term. If we multiply (7.10) by q_t and take the expected value, we get

$$
\begin{aligned}
E(Y_t^m q_t) &= E(a_0 q_t + a_1 I_t q_t) \\
&= \left(\frac{a_0}{1 - b_1}\right) E(u_t) + \left(\frac{a_1}{1 - b_1}\right) E(I_t u_t) = 0,
\end{aligned}
\tag{7.14}
$$

since the expected value of u_t is zero and since, by assumption, I_t is independent of u_t.* We could, therefore, use our regular estimation procedure to obtain consistent estimators of b_0 and b_1. We would impose the conditions $\sum \hat{q}_t = 0$ and $\sum (Y_t^m \hat{q}_t) = 0$ to generate the normal equations

$$\sum C_t = n\hat{b}_0 + \hat{b}_1 \sum Y_t^m,$$

$$\sum (C_t Y_t^m) = \hat{b}_0 \sum Y_t^m + \hat{b}_1 \sum (Y_t^m)^2,$$

which we could solve for $\hat{b}_0$ and $\hat{b}_1$. Notice further that these equations are exactly what we would have obtained if we had simply replaced Y_t by Y_t^m in our original equation (7.1) and then proceeded to derive the normal equations in the usual manner.

In review, to deal with the systems problem we first determined the mean value of income, Y_t^m, associated with each value of investment, I_t. The second step was simply to substitute this new variable for Y_t in the original equation and then estimate the parameters in the usual way. Of course, when we substituted Y_t^m for Y_t in our basic equation (7.1), we noticed that the disturbance term, q_t, in our resulting equation (7.13) was not the same as our original disturbance term, u_t. *For our purposes*, this is really an unimportant change, in effect one in notation only, because q_t was shown to have the same basic properties as u_t.

The TSLS procedure consists in effect of purging the independent variable, Y_t, of that component, q_t, that is correlated with the original disturbance term, u_t. Recall that $Y_t = Y_t^m + q_t$, and, as we have shown, Y_t^m is uncorrelated with q_t (and therefore with u_t). When we use Y_t^m in place of Y_t, we have effectively subtracted q_t from Y_t: $Y_t^m = Y_t - q_t$. In a sense, we have removed that part of Y_t that embodies the effect of the disturbance component of the dependent variable (C_t) on the regressor (Y_t); in this way, we are able, with TSLS, to unravel the effects that were previously intertwined.

While in principle this procedure appears unimpeachable, the difficulty

---

* It is also clear that the disturbance term, q_t, will not be autocorrelated (since u_t is not autocorrelated), and will have a constant variance, namely, $[\sigma_u^2/(1 - b_1)^2]$. In addition, q_t will be normally distributed since u_t is so distributed.

is that in practice we cannot implement it directly because we shall not know the values of Y_t^m. Recall that in equation (7.10),

$$Y_t^m = a_0 + a_1 I_t, \tag{7.10}$$

we assumed that the values of a_0 and a_1 were known. This will not in general be true, but we can estimate their values. If we look back at an equation we derived from the original model, namely (7.9), we can verify that it satisfies all the assumptions of the basic regression model:

$$Y_t = a_0 + a_1 I_t + q_t. \tag{7.9}$$

We can obtain estimators of a_0 and a_1, say $\hat{a}_0$ and $\hat{a}_1$, from the normal equations we generate by setting $\sum \hat{q}_t = 0$ and $\sum (\hat{q}_t I_t) = 0$. We can then use $\hat{a}_0$ and $\hat{a}_1$ to obtain an estimator of Y_t^m:

$$\hat{Y}_t^m = \hat{a}_0 + \hat{a}_1 I_t. \tag{7.15}$$

Recalling our notation from previous chapters, we see that $\hat{Y}_t^m$ is nothing more than the calculated value of Y_t corresponding to the regression (7.9): $\hat{Y}_t^m \equiv \hat{Y}_t$.

The second stage is to employ $\hat{Y}_t$ (instead of Y_t^m) to estimate the consumption equation; that is, we would take as our regression model

$$C_t = b_0 + b_1 \hat{Y}_t + u_t^*, \tag{7.16}$$

where $u_t^* = u_t + b_1 \hat{q}_t$, since $Y_t = \hat{Y}_t + \hat{q}_t$. Following the usual procedure we would then simply impose the conditions $\sum \hat{u}_t^* = 0$ and $\sum (\hat{u}_t^* \hat{Y}_t) = 0$ to obtain the normal equations

$$\sum C_t = n\hat{b}_0 + \hat{b}_1 \sum \hat{Y}_t,$$

$$\sum (C_t \hat{Y}_t) = \hat{b}_0 \sum \hat{Y}_t + \hat{b}_1 \sum \hat{Y}_t^2,$$

which we would solve for $\hat{b}_0$ and $\hat{b}_1$.* It can be shown that, under general conditions, $\hat{b}_0$ and $\hat{b}_1$ thus obtained are consistent.

---

*As a technical point, note that a_0 and a_1 in (7.9) would be estimated by imposing the conditions

$$\sum \hat{q}_t = 0 \quad \text{and} \quad \sum (\hat{q}_t I_t) = 0.$$

Since $\hat{Y}_t = \hat{a}_0 + \hat{a}_1 I_t$, it follows that $\sum (\hat{q}_t \hat{Y}_t) = 0$. Now because $u_t^* = u_t + b_1 \hat{q}_t$ in (7.16), we have that

$$\sum u_t^* = \sum u_t \quad \text{and} \quad \sum (u_t^* \hat{Y}_t) = \sum (u_t \hat{Y}_t).$$

These conditions suggest that, to estimate (7.16), we set

$$\sum \hat{u}_t^* = \sum \hat{u}_t = 0 \quad \text{(since } E(u_t) = 0\text{)},$$

$$\sum (\hat{u}_t^* \hat{Y}_t) = \sum (\hat{u}_t \hat{Y}_t) = 0 \quad \text{(since } E(u_t Y_t^m) = 0\text{)}.$$

In other words, the $\hat{q}_t$ component of u_t^* *does not play any role* in the estimation of (7.16). We will see the consequences of this for the variance formulas below.

In summary, for our illustrative case, the TSLS estimation procedure consists of, first, regressing the suspect independent variable, Y_t, on the exogenous variable, I_t, and using this estimated equation to generate a new independent variable, $\hat{Y}_t$. The second step is to replace Y_t by $\hat{Y}_t$ in our original equation, and then estimate our equation in the usual way. Under this procedure, we note that the disturbance term in the second stage, u_t^*, is a slight modification of the original one, u_t.

SOME FURTHER RESULTS

Before generalizing our technique we should note that, once we have consistent estimators of b_0 and b_1, we can easily obtain a consistent estimator of the original disturbance term u_t in (7.1) by the obvious formula

$$\hat{u}_t = C_t - (\hat{b}_0 + \hat{b}_1 Y_t).$$

With this, we obtain a consistent estimator of the variance of u_t by our usual expression:

$$\hat{\sigma}_u^2 = \frac{\sum \hat{u}_t^2}{n - 2}. \tag{7.17}$$

Another attraction of the TSLS technique is that, once Y_t is replaced by $\hat{Y}_t$, our old formulas for the variances of $\hat{b}_0$ and $\hat{b}_1$ still hold except for a change in interpretation. Referring to (7.16) and recalling that the sample average of $\hat{Y}_t$ is $\bar{\hat{Y}} = \bar{Y}$, the usual formulas,

$$\sigma_{b_0}^2 = \sigma_u^2 \left[\frac{\sum \hat{Y}_t^2}{n \sum (\hat{Y}_t - \bar{Y})^2} \right], \tag{7.18}$$

$$\sigma_{b_1}^2 = \sigma_u^2 \left[\frac{1}{\sum (\hat{Y}_t - \bar{Y})^2} \right], \tag{7.19}$$

can be shown to hold if the sample is infinitely large. Since we never have samples that are of infinite size, we must again interpret these formulas as approximations.

The alert reader will have noticed a subtle difference in these variance formulas. Specifically, since our estimation procedure at the second stage involves equation (7.16) where the disturbance term is u_t^* (not u_t), it would appear that our expressions for the variances of $\hat{b}_0$ and $\hat{b}_1$ in (7.18) and (7.19) should include the variance of u_t^*, say σ_u^{2*}, instead of σ_u^2. However, this is not the case. The reason for this is that the $\hat{q}_t$ component of u_t^*,

$$u_t^* = u_t + b_1 \hat{q}_t,$$

cancels out in the expressions for $\hat{b}_0$ and $\hat{b}_1$. It follows that the values of both of these estimators can be shown to depend, not on u_t^*, but on u_t. Consequently, the variances of $\hat{b}_0$ and $\hat{b}_1$ depend on the variance of u_t, and not on that of u_t^*.

To see this, note that our estimator, $\hat{b}_1$, would be

$$\hat{b}_1 = \frac{\sum (\hat{Y}_t - \bar{Y}) C_t}{\sum (\hat{Y}_t - \bar{Y})^2}. \tag{7.20}$$

Substituting (7.16) for C_t into (7.20) and simplifying, we obtain

$$\hat{b}_1 = b_1 + \frac{\sum (\hat{Y}_t - \bar{Y})u_t^*}{\sum (\hat{Y}_t - \bar{Y})^2}.$$ (7.21)

Since $\sum \hat{q}_t = 0$ and $\sum (\hat{q}_t \hat{Y}_t) = 0$, we have that

$$\sum (\hat{Y}_t u_t^*) = \sum (\hat{Y}_t u_t) + b_1 \sum (\hat{Y}_t \hat{q}_t) = \sum (\hat{Y}_t u_t),$$

$$\sum (\bar{Y}u_t^*) = \bar{Y} \sum u_t + \bar{Y}b_1 \sum \hat{q}_t = \bar{Y} \sum u_t.$$

We can now express $\hat{b}_1$ as

$$\hat{b}_1 = b_1 + \frac{\sum (\hat{Y}_t - \bar{Y})u_t}{\sum (\hat{Y}_t - \bar{Y})^2}.$$ (7.22)

It follows, at least intuitively, that the large-sample variance of $\hat{b}_1$ will involve the variance of u_t, not u_t^*. We leave it for the reader to show that $\hat{b}_0$ can also, for the same reasons, be expressed in terms of u_t.

Although σ_u^2 is usually unknown, we can obtain consistent estimators of the variances of $\hat{b}_0$ and $\hat{b}_1$ by simply replacing σ_u^2 by its consistent estimator:

$$\hat{\sigma}_{\hat{b}_0}^2 = \hat{\sigma}_u^2 \left[\frac{\sum \hat{Y}_t}{n \sum (\hat{Y}_t - \bar{Y})^2} \right]$$ (7.23)

and

$$\hat{\sigma}_{\hat{b}_1}^2 = \hat{\sigma}_u^2 \left[\frac{1}{\sum (\hat{Y}_t - \bar{Y})^2} \right].$$ (7.24)

Finally, hypotheses can be tested, or confidence intervals established, by assuming that the ratio $(\hat{b}_i - b_i)/\hat{\sigma}_{\hat{b}_i}$, $(i = 0, 1)$, is a standard normal variable. Again, in practice the sample size would be finite and so such results must be viewed as approximate. The reason for the complication in this case is the nonlinearity of $\hat{b}_0$ and $\hat{b}_1$ with respect to disturbance terms through their dependence upon $\hat{Y}_t$ [e.g., see (7.22)].

7.3 SYSTEMS OF EQUATIONS: A MORE GENERAL DISCUSSION *

MODEL SPECIFICATION

We shall now generalize our discussion of simultaneous-equation models. Consider the multiple-regression system of equations

$$Y_{1t} = b_0 + b_1 Y_{2t} + b_2 Y_{3t} + a_1 X_{1t} + \cdots + a_k X_{kt} + u_t,$$ (7.25)

$$Y_{2t} = c_0 + c_1 Y_{3t} + c_2 Y_{1t} + d_1 Z_{1t} + \cdots + d_r Z_{rt} + \varepsilon_t,$$ (7.26)

$$Y_{3t} = g_0 + g_1 Y_{2t} + g_2 Y_{1t} + h_1 W_{1t} + \cdots + h_s W_{st} + e_t,$$ (7.27)

---

* For ease of exposition we present the following discussion in terms of a three-equation model. However, the results apply as well to models of all sizes.

where u_t, ε_t, and e_t are disturbance terms. We assume that each of these disturbance terms has a zero mean,

$$E(u_t) = 0, \qquad E(\varepsilon_t) = 0, \qquad E(e_t) = 0,$$

a constant variance,

$$E(u_t^2) = \sigma_u^2, \qquad E(\varepsilon_t^2) = \sigma_\varepsilon^2, \qquad E(e_t^2) = \sigma_e^2,$$

that they are not autocorrelated, and that they are normally distributed. In addition, we shall assume that these disturbance terms are uncorrelated with all of the X_t's, Z_t's, and W_t's appearing in the system (7.25)–(7.27). Although our notation may suggest otherwise, we allow for the possibility that one or more of these variables may appear in more than one equation. In other words, the X_t's, Z_t's, and W_t's may have elements in common.

It should be clear that we cannot assume that the disturbance terms are also uncorrelated with Y_{1t}, Y_{2t}, and Y_{3t}. Indeed, in general, each Y_t will be correlated with *all* three disturbance terms. For instance, equation (7.25) immediately tells us that Y_{1t} depends on u_t, so that these two variables will typically be correlated. Moreover, equation (7.26) indicates that Y_{2t} depends on Y_{1t} and hence on u_t. We see that Y_{2t} will, in general, also be correlated with u_t. Similarly, (7.27) implies that Y_{3t} will generally be correlated with u_t. This argument can obviously be extended to demonstrate nonzero covariance of Y_{1t}, Y_{2t}, and Y_{3t} with the other two disturbance terms ε_t and e_t. In brief, if two variables are involved in a feedback relationship, each variable will generally be correlated with the disturbance term in the equation for the other.

In this three-equation model, Y_{1t}, Y_{2t}, and Y_{3t} are *endogenous* variables; their values are determined at time t by the model specified in equations (7.25)–(7.27). These are the variables whose values our model explains. The other variables (the X_t's, Z_t's, and W_t's) in this system are called *predetermined* variables. They are uncorrelated with the disturbance terms, and their values at time t are *not* determined by the model at time t. We shall examine shortly exactly how they are determined. In the meantime, it should be clear that the values of the predetermined variables, along with the values of the disturbance terms, determine at time t the values of the endogenous variables of our model. For instance, in general, a set of linear equations such as (7.25), (7.26), and (7.27) can be solved for the endogenous variables Y_{1t}, Y_{2t}, and Y_{3t} in terms of the predetermined variables and the disturbance terms. That is, we could solve equations (7.25)–(7.27) so as to express each Y_t in the form

$$Y_{1t} = l_0 + \sum_{i=1}^{k} l_i X_{it} + \sum_{i=k+1}^{k+r} l_i Z_{it} + \sum_{i=k+r+1}^{k+r+s} l_i W_{it}$$

$$+ \alpha_1 u_t + \alpha_2 \varepsilon_t + \alpha_3 e_t, \qquad (7.28)$$

$$Y_{2t} = m_0 + \sum_{i=1}^{k} m_i X_{it} + \sum_{i=k+1}^{k+r} m_i Z_{it} + \sum_{i=k+r+1}^{k+r+s} m_i W_{it}$$

$$+ \gamma_1 u_t + \gamma_2 \varepsilon_t + \gamma_3 e_t, \qquad (7.29)$$

$$Y_{3t} = d_0 + \sum_{i=1}^{k} d_i X_{it} + \sum_{i=k+1}^{k+r} d_i Z_{it} + \sum_{i=k+r+1}^{k+r+s} d_i W_{it}$$

$$+ \beta_1 u_t + \beta_2 \varepsilon_t + \beta_3 e_t. \qquad (7.30)$$

Here we can see that the values of the predetermined variables and of the disturbance terms completely determine the values of the endogenous variables. This suggests that the predetermined variables and the disturbance terms have something in common; specifically, *neither* is determined by the model at time t, and *both* are necessary in determining the values of the endogenous variables. That is, of course, true. However, there is a major difference: we assume that, unlike the disturbance terms, we *know*, or we observe, the values of the predetermined variables in every time period t. In other words, if we had observations on the values of a particular disturbance term, we could consider that disturbance term to be a predetermined variable. Alternatively, we might view a disturbance term as an unobservable predetermined variable that has a mean of zero and is uncorrelated with all of the observed predetermined variables.

As a summary, we present in Figure 7.2 a schematic representation of the causal structure of the set of relationships in (7.25)–(7.27). Note (as indicated by the arrows) that the predetermined variables and the disturbance terms influence directly the values of the endogenous variables, but are *not* in turn influenced by them. In contrast, there is a *feedback* relationship (or interdependency) among the endogenous variables; Y_{1t}, for example, is dependent on Y_{2t} and Y_{3t}, but also affects the values of Y_{2t} and Y_{3t}.

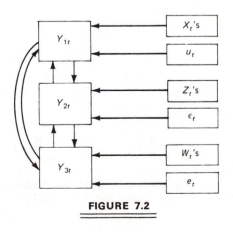

FIGURE 7.2

THE NATURE OF THE PREDETERMINED VARIABLES

The predetermined variables themselves come in two forms. First, there are *exogenous* variables. As we indicated in our discussion of the simple consumption model, (7.1) and (7.2), these are the variables whose values are determined by forces external to our model. Somewhat more formally, the values of the exogenous variables are assumed tc depend on variables that are not related in any way to the endogenous variables, or to the disturbance terms, of our model. In a sense these variables are "beyond" the scope of our analysis.* We simply take their values as given without attempting to explain them. An example of a variable that *might* be taken to be exogenous in a consumption equation would be family size. This is a variable we could consider to be "fed in" by the social system to the economic model; it is important in determining economic variables, such as consumption, but (at least in the short run) may not in turn be influenced by the economic variables in our particular model. Another example of an exogenous variable would be the amount of rainfall per year in an equation explaining the production of wheat. In the first case (family size), one might consider *extending* the scope of the analysis to explain the exogenous variable; for instance, the size of the family might be explained in terms of employment opportunities, and so forth. If so, this variable would no longer be exogenous. In the second case, we would probably regard the amount of rainfall as beyond any plausible extension of the analysis.

The second type of predetermined variable is the *lagged endogenous* variable. For example, in the consumption model

$$C_t = b_0 + b_1 Y_t + b_2 Y_{t-1} + u_t, \tag{7.31}$$

$$Y_t = C_t + I_t, \tag{7.32}$$

we can see that, under our usual assumptions, Y_t is correlated with u_t because, solving the equations for Y_t, we find (as noted earlier) that Y_t depends on u_t:

$$Y_t = \left(\frac{b_0}{1 - b_1}\right) + \left(\frac{b_2}{1 - b_1}\right) Y_{t-1} + \left(\frac{1}{1 - b_1}\right) I_t + \left(\frac{1}{1 - b_1}\right) u_t. \tag{7.33}$$

However, this is not true of Y_{t-1}; the value of Y_{t-1} was determined in the previous period, and its value cannot depend on C_t, u_t, or the value of any other variable in time t. For instance, replacing t by $(t - 1)$ in (7.33), we find that Y_{t-1} depends on u_{t-1}, not u_t:

$$Y_{t-1} = \left(\frac{b_0}{1 - b_1}\right) + \left(\frac{b_2}{1 - b_1}\right) Y_{t-2} + \left(\frac{1}{1 - b_1}\right) I_{t-1} + \left(\frac{1}{1 - b_1}\right) u_{t-1}.$$

---

* Defining "the scope of analysis" is not a simple task! The problem is that a more complete analysis requires a "wider scope," but this typically increases the complexity of the model.

This implies that, if the value of the disturbance term u_t is independently determined in each and every period (so that u_t is not autocorrelated), then u_t and Y_{t-1} should be uncorrelated. In brief, because the value of Y_{t-1} is not determined by the model *during time t* and because it is uncorrelated with the disturbance term at time t, we can classify Y_{t-1} as a predetermined variable. Under certain conditions, we can simply treat all lagged endogenous variables as predetermined variables.* Our basic assumption of zero covariance between the predetermined variables and the disturbance terms holds *both* for the exogenous and the lagged endogenous variables in our system.

STRUCTURAL AND REDUCED-FORM EQUATIONS

Before considering the problem of generalizing our estimation technique, we need to make one final distinction. The basic equations such as (7.25), (7.26), (7.27) that explain the behavior and interrelations of our endogenous variables are called *structural* equations. These are the equations *suggested by economic theory*. In terms of our earlier simple model of income determination, we postulated a system of two structural equations:

$$C_t = b_0 + b_1 Y_t + u_t, \tag{7.1}$$

$$Y_t = C_t + I_t. \tag{7.2}$$

These equations embody our theoretical propositions that consumption expenditure depends on income (7.1), and that aggregate output moves to an equilibrium level at which it is equal to aggregate demand (7.2). The structural equations, we repeat, are a formal statement of our basic economic model.

If the structural equations are solved for the endogenous variables in terms of the predetermined variables and the disturbance terms, such as in (7.28)–(7.30), the resulting equations are called the *reduced-form equations*. These are the equations that describe how each endogenous variable is causally determined by the predetermined variables and the disturbance terms.

As an example, if we solve the structural equations (7.1) and (7.2) for the two endogenous variables, we obtain

$$C_t = \frac{b_0}{1 - b_1} + \frac{b_1 I_t}{1 - b_1} + \frac{u_t}{1 - b_1}, \tag{7.34}$$

$$Y_t = \frac{b_0}{1 - b_1} + \frac{I_t}{1 - b_1} + \frac{u}{1 - b_1}. \tag{7.35}$$

---

* The exception to this is the case where the disturbance terms are autocorrelated; in this instance, a lagged endogenous variable may be correlated with the disturbance terms at time t in the model. For the interested reader, we discuss in the Appendix to this chapter how to estimate a model embodying both the systems problem and autocorrelated disturbance terms. You may find this helpful in seeing how econometricians deal with more than one estimation problem in the same model.

We can rewrite (7.34) and (7.35) as

$$C_t = a_0 + a_1 I_t + q_t, \tag{7.34A}$$

$$Y_t = d_0 + d_1 I_t + q_t, \tag{7.35A}$$

where $a_0 = d_0 = b_0/(1 - b_1)$, $a_1 = b_1(1 - b_1)$, $d_1 = 1/(1 - b_1)$, and $q_t = u_t/(1 - b_1)$. Equations (7.34A) and (7.35A), or (7.34) and (7.35), would be the reduced-form equations for C_t and Y_t, respectively. Note that these reduced-form equations imply that both C_t and Y_t are completely determined by I_t and u_t.

As another example, consider the wage-price model

$$\dot{W}_t = a_1 + b_1 \dot{P}_t + c_1 R_{t-1} + \varepsilon_{1t}, \tag{7.36}$$

$$\dot{P}_t = a_2 + b_2 \dot{W}_t + b_3 \dot{T}_{t-1} + \varepsilon_{2t}, \tag{7.37}$$

where $\dot{W}_t$ and $\dot{P}_t$ are, respectively, the percentage change in money wages and consumer prices, R_{t-1} is last period's unemployment rate, $\dot{T}_{(t-1)}$ is the percentage change in last period's prices of raw materials, and ε_{1t} and ε_{2t} are the disturbance terms. Equation (7.36) and (7.37) are the structural equations of the model. They represent the assumptions that wage changes depend on price changes and labor market conditions (as represented by the rate of unemployment in the preceding period), while price changes, in turn, depend on changes in wages and changes in other costs that we represent by changes in the price of raw materials during the preceding period. The endogenous variables are $\dot{W}_t$ and $\dot{P}_t$, while the predetermined variables are $R_{(t-1)}$ and $\dot{T}_{(t-1)}$. In this case both predetermined variables are lagged *exogenous* variables.* There are no lagged endogenous variables. Finally, if we solve (7.36) and (7.37) for $\dot{W}_t$ and $\dot{P}_t$, we obtain the reduced-form equations

$$\dot{W}_t = d_0 + d_1 \dot{T}_{t-1} + d_2 R_{t-1} + d_3 \varepsilon_{1t} + d_4 \varepsilon_{2t}, \tag{7.38}$$

$$\dot{P}_t = e_0 + e_1 \dot{T}_{t-1} + e_2 R_{t-1} + e_3 \varepsilon_{1t} + e_4 \varepsilon_{2t}, \tag{7.39}$$

where

$$d_0 = \frac{a_1 + b_1 a_2}{1 - b_1 b_2}, \quad d_1 = \frac{b_1 b_3}{1 - b_1 b_2}, \quad d_2 = \frac{c_1}{1 - b_1 b_2},$$

$$d_3 = \frac{1}{1 - b_1 b_2}, \quad d_4 = \frac{b_1}{1 - b_1 b_2},$$

* One may object to the narrow "scope of analysis" in (7.36) and (7.37). That is, a full explanation of the wage-price spiral should include equations explaining the rate of un-employment (i.e., the rate of unemployment should not be considered exogenous to a model of the wage-price spiral). However, as mentioned above, the cost of such a more complete explanation would be increased complexity. Again, just where to draw the line concerning the scope of analysis depends on the judgment of the researcher.

and

$$e_0 = \frac{a_2 + b_2 a_1}{1 - b_1 b_2}, \qquad e_1 = \frac{b_3}{1 - b_1 b_2}, \qquad e_2 = \frac{b_2 c_1}{1 - b_1 b_2},$$

$$e_3 = \frac{b_2}{1 - b_1 b_2}, \qquad e_4 = \frac{1}{1 - b_1 b_2}.$$

Notice that the reduced-form equations are *linear* in the predetermined variables and in the disturbance terms.

7.4 TWO-STAGE LEAST SQUARES: A GENERALIZATION

AN OVERVIEW

Let us now return to our estimation problem. Consider once again the set of equations (7.25) through (7.27), and suppose that we want to estimate the

$$Y_{1t} = b_0 + b_1 Y_{2t} + b_2 Y_{3t} + a_1 X_{1t} + \cdots + a_k X_{kt} + u_t, \qquad (7.25)$$

$$Y_{2t} = c_0 + c_1 Y_{3t} + c_2 Y_{1t} + d_1 Z_{1t} + \cdots + d_r Z_{rt} + \varepsilon_t, \qquad (7.26)$$

$$Y_{3t} = g_0 + g_1 Y_{2t} + g_2 Y_{1t} + h_1 W_{1t} + \cdots + h_s W_{st} + e_t. \qquad (7.27)$$

coefficients of equation (7.25) in this model. The procedure under TSLS is, first, to regress the endogenous variables appearing in our equation, Y_{2t} and Y_{3t} (that is, the regressors that are correlated with the disturbance term), on *all* the predetermined variables in the three-equation model. Specifically, we would estimate, by our usual procedure, the equation

$$Y_{2t} = m_0 + m_1 X_{1t} + \cdots + m_k X_{kt} + m_{(k+1)} Z_{1t} + \cdots + m_{(k+r)} Z_{rt}$$

$$+ m_{(k+r+1)} W_{1t} + \cdots + m_{(k+r+s)} W_{st} + \theta_{1t}, \qquad (7.40)$$

where θ_{1t} is the disturbance term.* Likewise, we would regress Y_{3t} on precisely the *same* set of independent variables. We would then use the estimated equations to determine the calculated values: $\hat{Y}_{2t}$ and $\hat{Y}_{3t}$. The second step is to substitute $\hat{Y}_{2t}$ and $\hat{Y}_{3t}$ for Y_{2t} and Y_{3t}, respectively, in equation (7.25), more or less put a "star" on the disturbance term, and then proceed as usual to generate the second-stage normal equations and solve them for our estimators: $\hat{b}_0, \hat{b}_1, \hat{b}_2,$ and $\hat{a}_1, \hat{a}_2, \ldots, \hat{a}_k$. Again $\hat{Y}_{2t}$ and $\hat{Y}_{3t}$ turn out to be estimators of that component, respectively, of Y_{2t} and Y_{3t}, which is uncorrelated with the disturbance term of our equation, u_t.

* As we will show formally, the disturbance term, θ_{1t}, is a weighted sum of the three disturbance terms ($\gamma_1 u_t + \gamma_2 \varepsilon_t + \gamma_3 e_t$) like in equation (7.29).

A FORMALIZATION

To see this more clearly, note that, since our three-equation model is linear, the solution (or reduced-form equation) for, say, Y_{2t} will be linear in the X_t's, Z_t's, W_t's, *and* in u_t, ε_t, and e_t. To economize on notation, denote the sum of all the terms in the reduced-form equation (see 7.29) with the exception of the disturbance terms as Y_{2t}^m; that is, Y_{2t}^m is a linear combination of the X's, Z's, and W's*:

$$Y_{2t}^m = m_0 + m_1 X_{1t} + \cdots + m_k X_{kt} + m_{(k+1)} Z_{1t} + \cdots$$
$$+ m_{(k+r)} Z_{rt} + m_{(k+r+1)} W_{1t} + \cdots + m_{(k+r+s)} W_{st}. \qquad (7.41)$$

We can now express the reduced-form equation for Y_{2t} more simply as

$$Y_{2t} = Y_{2t}^m + \gamma_1 u_t + \gamma_2 \varepsilon_t + \gamma_3 e_t, \qquad (7.42)$$

where γ_1, γ_2, and γ_3 are constants.

Note next that

$$E(\gamma_1 u_t + \gamma_2 \varepsilon_t + \gamma_3 e_t) = \gamma_1 E(u_t) + \gamma_2 E(\varepsilon_t) + \gamma_3 E(e_t) = 0,$$

since all the disturbance terms have mean values of zero. Let us combine these three terms into a single composite disturbance term:

$$\theta_{1t} = \gamma_1 u_t + \gamma_2 \varepsilon_t + \gamma_3 e_t. \qquad (7.43)$$

We can then write (7.42) in the form

$$Y_{2t} = Y_{2t}^m + \theta_{1t}, \qquad (7.44)$$

where $E(\theta_{1t}) = 0$. Similarly, we could show that

$$Y_{3t} = Y_{3t}^m + \theta_{2t}, \qquad (7.45)$$

where $E(\theta_{2t}) = 0$, and Y_{3t}^m is a linear combination of the X_t's, Z_t's, and W_t's [see (7.30)]. Finally, exactly as in the simple case of one regressor, we could use (7.44) and (7.45) to rewrite the first of our structural equations, (7.25), as

$$Y_{1t} = b_0 + b_1 Y_{2t}^m + b_2 Y_{3t}^m + a_1 X_{1t} + \cdots + a_k X_{kt} + q_{1t} \qquad (7.46)$$

where

$$q_{1t} = u_t + b_1 \theta_{1t} + b_2 \theta_{2t},$$

and so $E(q_{1t}) = 0$.

The analogy with the simple case should now be clear; if we had observations on Y_{2t}^m and Y_{3t}^m, we could simply estimate (7.46) in the usual manner. The reason for this is that, since Y_{2t}^m and Y_{3t}^m depend only on the X_t's, Z_t's,

---

* For example, with respect to the model (7.36) and (7.37),

$$\dot{W}_t^m = d_0 + d_1 \dot{T}_{(t-1)} + d_2 R_{(t-1)},$$

where the d_i are defined in (7.38).

and W_t's, and since these predetermined variables are uncorrelated with the disturbance terms, it follows that $Y_{2t}{}^m$ and $Y_{3t}{}^m$ must also be uncorrelated with the disturbance terms. As in the simple case, we do not know $Y_{2t}{}^m$ and $Y_{3t}{}^m$ and must first estimate them (by $\hat{Y}_{2t}$ and $\hat{Y}_{3t}$) before "proceeding as usual."

We point out that, as in the earlier two-variable case, the estimators generated by the TSLS procedure are generally biased, but *consistent*. We also note that, with consistent estimators of the regression parameters, we may construct a consistent estimator of the disturbance term, say in (7.25), from the expression

$$\hat{u}_t = Y_{1t} - (\hat{b}_0 + \hat{b}_1 Y_{2t} + \hat{b}_2 Y_{3t} + \hat{a}_1 X_{1t} + \cdots + \hat{a}_k X_{kt}). \quad (7.47)$$

We may then obtain a consistent estimator of the variance of that disturbance term by*

$$\hat{\sigma}_u{}^2 = \sum_{t=1}^{n} \frac{\hat{u}_t{}^2}{n - k - 3}. \quad (7.48)$$

We also state without proof that, once the endogenous regressors are replaced by their calculated counterparts, all of our variance formulas for the parameter estimators go through, again as large-sample results, exactly as in the case of one regressor. For instance, again referring to equation (7.25), the large-sample variance of the TSLS estimator $\hat{b}_1$ would be

$$\sigma_{\hat{b}_1}{}^2 = \sigma_u{}^2 \left(\frac{1}{\sum \hat{v}_{1t}{}^2} \right), \quad (7.49)$$

where $\hat{v}_{1t}$ is the residual in the regression of $\hat{Y}_{2t}$ on $\hat{Y}_{3t}, X_{1t}, \ldots, X_{kt}$. Note again that $\hat{Y}_{2t}$ and $\hat{Y}_{3t}$ are the regressors in the second stage whose coefficients are b_1 and b_2. Similarly, we see again that the variance formula in (7.49) involves the variance of u_t, not the disturbance term which would correspond to the second-stage regression: $u_t{}^* = u_t + b_1 \hat{v}_{1t} + b_2 \hat{v}_{2t}$. Finally, since $\sigma_u{}^2$ would generally be unknown, a consistent estimator of the variance of $\hat{b}_1$ would be

$$\hat{\sigma}_{\hat{b}_1}{}^2 = \hat{\sigma}_u{}^2 \left(\frac{1}{\sum \hat{v}_{1t}{}^2} \right). \quad (7.50)$$

Similar formulas hold for the other parameter estimators.

Using these formulas, we may test hypotheses and establish confidence intervals by again using the normal distribution as an approximation. In practice, such results must be viewed as approximate, since the sample size would be finite.

TSLS WITH MISSING VARIABLES

One further practical matter requires clarification. In (7.25), our first-stage procedure under TSLS was to regress each of the endogenous regressors

---

* We divide by $(n - k - 3)$ in (7.48) because there are $(k + 3)$ parameters in the corresponding regression model (7.46).

on *all* the predetermined variables in the model. Now it may be the case that data are not available for all these variables. Suppose we did not have observed values for Z_{1t} and W_{1t} from equations (7.26) and (7.27), respectively. This will not in general prevent us from using TSLS to estimate (7.25). Our first-stage procedure in this case simply becomes the regressing of Y_{2t} and Y_{3t} on all the *available* predetermined variables (i.e., those other than Z_{1t} and W_{1t}, in our example). We would then use these first-stage equations to obtain $\hat{Y}_{2t}$ and $\hat{Y}_{3t}$; if we then replace Y_{2t} and Y_{3t} by $\hat{Y}_{2t}$ and $\hat{Y}_{3t}$, respectively, we could proceed as before with our second-stage estimation and all the formulas and results we have described earlier will still hold. We may thus be able to employ the TSLS technique with less than complete data!

We shall present a somewhat more formal discussion of just why this is so. Consider first the argument as it relates to Y_{2t}. Since data on Z_{1t} and W_{1t} are not available, our first-stage regression would be similar to (7.40), differing only by the absence of Z_{1t} and W_{1t}:

$$Y_{2t} = \pi_0 + \pi_1 X_{1t} + \cdots + \pi_k X_{kt} + \pi_{(k+1)} Z_{2t} + \cdots + \pi_{(k+r-1)} Z_{rt}$$
$$+ \pi_{(k+r)} W_{2t} + \cdots + \pi_{(k+r+s-2)} W_{st} + \theta_{3t}. \qquad (7.51)$$

We generate $\hat{Y}_{2t}$ from estimators of the parameters of this model obtained by setting

$$\sum \hat{\theta}_{3t} = 0, \qquad \sum (\hat{\theta}_{3t} X_{jt}) = 0, \qquad \sum (\hat{\theta}_{3t} Z_{it}) = 0, \qquad \sum (\hat{\theta}_{3t} W_{mt}) = 0,$$
$$(7.52)$$

for $j = 1, \ldots, k$; $i = 2, \ldots, r$, and $m = 2, \ldots, s$. More explicitly, we have

$$\hat{Y}_{2t} = \hat{\pi}_0 + \hat{\pi}_1 X_{1t} + \cdots + \hat{\pi}_k X_{kt} + \hat{\pi}_{(k+1)} Z_{2t} + \cdots + \hat{\pi}_{(k+r-1)} Z_{rt}$$
$$+ \hat{\pi}_{(k+r)} W_{2t} + \cdots + \hat{\pi}_{(k+r+s-2)} W_{rt}. \qquad (7.53)$$

As usual, we may express Y_{2t} as

$$Y_{2t} = \hat{Y}_{2t} + \hat{\theta}_{3t}, \qquad (7.54)$$

where $\hat{\theta}_{3t}$ is defined as $(Y_{2t} - \hat{Y}_{2t})$. Again, because $\hat{Y}_{2t}$ depends only on $X_{1t}, \ldots, X_{kt}, Z_{2t}, \ldots, Z_{rt}$, and $W_{2t}, \ldots, W_{st}$, it follows from (7.52) that

$$\sum (\hat{Y}_{2t} \hat{\theta}_{3t}) = 0. \qquad (7.55)$$

We can obtain an analogous expression for Y_{3t} by regressing Y_{3t} on the *same set* of predetermined variables to obtain $\hat{Y}_{3t}$. Noting that

$$Y_{3t} = \hat{Y}_{3t} + \hat{\theta}_{4t}, \qquad (7.56)$$

where $\hat{\theta}_{4t} = Y_{3t} - \hat{Y}_{3t}$, we would have

$$\sum (\hat{Y}_{3t} \hat{\theta}_{4t}) = 0. \qquad (7.57)$$

Finally, since $\hat{Y}_{2t}$ and $\hat{Y}_{3t}$ are both linear combinations of $X_{1t}, \ldots, X_{kt}$, $Z_{2t}, \ldots, Z_{rt}$, and $W_{2t}, \ldots, W_{st}$, we have, from (7.52) and the corresponding conditions for $\hat{\theta}_{4t}$,

$$\sum (\hat{Y}_{2t}\hat{\theta}_{4t}) = 0 = \sum (\hat{Y}_{3t}\hat{\theta}_{3t}). \tag{7.58}$$

Let us now return to equation (7.25). Substituting (7.54) and (7.56) for Y_{2t} and Y_{3t}, respectively, we obtain

$$Y_{1t} = b_0 + b_1\hat{Y}_{2t} + b_2\hat{Y}_{3t} + a_1X_{1t} + \cdots + a_kX_{kt} + u_t', \tag{7.59}$$

where

$$u_t' = b_1\hat{\theta}_{3t} + b_2\hat{\theta}_{4t} + u_t.$$

It follows from (7.52) and the corresponding conditions for $\hat{\theta}_{4t}$ that

$$\sum u_t' = \sum u_t, \qquad \sum (u_t'\hat{Y}_{2t}) = \sum (u_t\hat{Y}_{2t}),$$

$$\sum (u_t'\hat{Y}_{3t}) = \sum (u_t\hat{Y}_{3t}), \qquad \sum (X_{jt}u_t') = \sum (X_{jt}u_t), \tag{7.60}$$

for $j = 1, \ldots, k$. That is, the conditions in (7.60) suggest that, for purposes of estimation, we may treat u_t' in exactly the same manner as we would u_t.

For instance, as in the two-variable case, the conditions in (7.60) suggest that, for purposes of estimating (7.59), we set

$$\sum \hat{u}_t' = \sum \hat{u}_t = 0 \qquad \text{(since } E(u_t) = 0\text{).}$$

$$\left.\begin{aligned}\sum (\hat{u}_t'\hat{Y}_{2t}) = \sum (\hat{u}_t\hat{Y}_{2t}) = 0 \\ \sum (\hat{u}_t'\hat{Y}_{3t}) = \sum (\hat{u}_t\hat{Y}_{3t}) = 0\end{aligned}\right\} \begin{aligned}&\text{since } u_t \text{ is uncorrelated with all the} \\ &\text{predetermined variables upon which} \\ &\hat{Y}_{2t} \text{ and } \hat{Y}_{3t} \text{ depend.}\end{aligned} \tag{7.61}$$

$$\sum (\hat{u}_t'X_{jt}) = \sum (\hat{u}_tX_{jt}) = 0 \qquad \text{(since } E(u_tX_{jt}) = 0, \text{ for } j = 1, 2, \ldots, k\text{).}$$

It can be shown that if the parameters of (7.59) are estimated by imposing the conditions in (7.61), our usual procedure, the resulting estimators will be consistent.

In brief, if we compare (7.59) to (7.25), we see that, again, all we have to do is replace Y_{2t} and Y_{3t} by $\hat{Y}_{2t}$ and $\hat{Y}_{3t}$, change the notation of the disturbance term, and proceed as usual.

This, incidentally, is a very attractive characteristic of the TSLS procedure. To estimate the equation of interest, it is not necessary to estimate the whole system of equations; it may not even be necessary to specify fully and have complete data for the other equations in the model. All that is needed is an "adequate set" of predetermined variables from the system of equations on which to regress the endogenous independent variables (those correlated with the disturbance term). We shall discuss below just what we mean by an "adequate set" of predetermined variables. At this stage we point out that the adequate set of predetermined variables must always include *all of the predetermined variables appearing in the equation being estimated.* For instance, in the above estimation of (7.25), we assumed that Z_{1t} and W_{1t} were not available for the determination of $\hat{Y}_{2t}$ and $\hat{Y}_{3t}$. Their omission is acceptable, because neither Z_{1t} nor W_{1t} appears in the structural equation (7.25). If, however, X_{1t} were not used in constructing $\hat{Y}_{2t}$ and $\hat{Y}_{3t}$, the above procedure would not lead to consistent estimators. To see this, note that if X_{1t} were not so used, we could not deduce from (7.52) that $\sum (\hat{\theta}_{3t} X_{1t}) = 0$, because Y_{2t} would not have been regressed on X_{1t}; in fact, this sum will generally be nonzero. In this instance, the corresponding equation for X_{1t} in (7.60) will not typically hold:

$$\sum (u_t' X_{1t}) \neq \sum (u_t X_{1t}).$$

We would clearly *not* be justified in setting the corresponding sum in (7.61) equal to zero.

Finally, we note that, although we do not have to use all of the predetermined variables in the system in the first stage of our TSLS procedure, there is a benefit in doing so. It can be shown that, in general, the more predetermined variables of the model one uses in the first stage of the TSLS procedure, the smaller will be the large-sample variances of the estimators of the coefficients that we generate in the second stage. Although its proof is beyond the scope of this book, this result should not be surprising. If more "information" in the form of additional predetermined variables is used in the first stage, the second-stage estimators should be correspondingly improved. We turn now to the problem of just what constitutes an adequate set of predetermined variables by considering what has become known as the "identification problem."

7.5 THE IDENTIFICATION PROBLEM*

You may remember that, in the introduction to TSLS, we mentioned that one of its virtues was that, if the equation *can* be estimated, TSLS always works in the sense that it will provide consistent estimators of the coefficients. However, there may arise situations with systems of equations where it is impossible to estimate the values of some (or perhaps all) of the parameters.

EXAMPLE 1

Consider the following simple model of the market for a particular commodity:

$$Q_t^d = a_0 + a_1 P_t + u_t, \tag{7.62}$$

$$Q_t^s = b_0 + b_1 P_t + \varepsilon_t, \tag{7.63}$$

$$Q_t^d = Q_t^s = Q_t. \tag{7.64}$$

The model consists of three equations: a demand function (7.62), a supply

---

* The classic work on this subject is Franklin M. Fisher, *The Identification Problem in Econometrics* (New York: McGraw-Hill, 1966). The following discussion draws, in part, upon this work.

function (7.63), and a market-equilibrium statement (7.64), where Q_t^d and Q_t^s are, respectively, the quantity demanded and the quantity supplied at time t, P_t is the price of the commodity at t, and u_t and ε_t are the respective disturbance terms, which have zero means, constant variances, are not auto-correlated, and are normally distributed. Equation (7.64) allows us to set Q_t^d and Q_t^s equal to Q_t, the quantity actually traded during period t. The implication is that price adjusts so as to make the quantity demanded equal to the quantity supplied during each time period.

Suppose that we are interested in estimating the parameters in the demand equation. We note first that P_t is correlated with u_t so that our standard estimation procedure will give us inconsistent estimators of the coefficients. To see this, set the expressions on the right-hand side of equations (7.62) and (7.63) equal to one another to get

$$a_0 + a_1 P_t + u_t = b_0 + b_1 P_t + \varepsilon_t. \tag{7.65}$$

Solving (7.65) for P_t gives us our reduced-form equation for P_t:

$$P_t = \frac{(b_0 - a_0)}{(a_1 - b_1)} + \frac{\varepsilon_t}{(a_1 - b_1)} - \frac{u_t}{(a_1 - b_1)}. \tag{7.66}$$

Multiplying (7.66) by u_t and taking the expected value yields

$$\begin{aligned} E(P_t u_t) &= E\left[\frac{(b_0 - a_0)u_t}{(a_1 - b_1)} + \frac{\varepsilon_t u_t}{(a_1 - b_1)} - \frac{u_t^2}{(a_1 - b_1)} \right] \\ &= \frac{(b_0 - a_0)}{(a_1 - b_1)} E(u_t) + \frac{E(\varepsilon_t u_t)}{(a_1 - b_1)} - \frac{E(u_t^2)}{(a_1 - b_1)} \\ &= 0 + \frac{\operatorname{cov}(\varepsilon_t, u_t)}{(a_1 - b_1)} - \frac{\sigma_u^2}{(a_1 - b_1)}. \end{aligned} \tag{7.67}$$

Since there is no reason to expect $\operatorname{cov}(\varepsilon_t, u_t)$ and σ_u^2 to be equal, we can assume, in general, that

$$E(P_t u_t) = \operatorname{cov}(P_t, u_t) \neq 0. \tag{7.68}$$

Since (7.68) is, in general, nonzero, the regressor, P_t, is correlated with u_t, and so we have a systems problem. To resolve the problem, suppose that we attempt to estimate (7.62) by two-stage least squares (TSLS). The first stage, you will recall, consists of regressing the endogenous independent variable (here P_t) on all the predetermined variables in the model. A glance at the three-equation model suggests, however, that there are no predetermined variables in the system!* Our reduced-form equation for P_t, namely

---

* Actually, as we discuss below, the constant term may be considered as a predetermined variable. If so, the reduced-form equation for P_t, (7.66), would contain one predetermined variable. However, as we shall see, we would still be unable to estimate our demand equation (7.62).

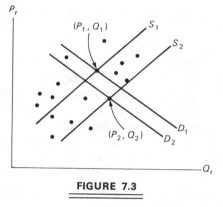

FIGURE 7.3

(7.66), has no predetermined variables on the right side. We cannot employ the TSLS estimation technique.

The demand function in this instance (and the supply equation as well) is *unidentified*, which is to say that we cannot estimate its parameters. Note that the identification problem is not a data problem; no matter how many observations on price and quantity we might obtain, we still would not be able to estimate the coefficients of either the demand or the supply equations. The identification problem is one of *specification*: it is the structure of the model and the nature of the available information that prevents its estimation.

It is instructive to see an intuitive argument supporting this conclusion. In Figure 7.3 we have a scatter diagram depicting observations on price and quantity purchased at different points in time. These points represent the information at hand with which we must estimate the demand and supply curves. The problem we face is that each point in the diagram is determined by *both* the demand and supply curves. That is, the demand *and* supply schedules shift from period to period (because ε_t and u_t change) with resulting variations over time in price and quantity in the market. This is illustrated in Figure 7.3 by the two sets of demand and supply curves at time 1 and time 2, which determine P_1 and Q_1, and P_2 and Q_2. What we observe is a scatter of points such as that in Figure 7.3. However, there are no points, *that we know of*, that resulted from a change in demand only. If there were, we could use these points to estimate the coefficients of the supply curve. For example, in Figure 7.4, if we knew that points A, B, and C were generated by three different demand curves moving along the *same* supply curve, it should seem clear intuitively that we could use these three points to estimate the slope and intercept parameters of the supply curve. But in Figure 7.3, since we have no way of separating those points that resulted from a change in demand only, we are unable to estimate the supply curve. Since the same argument applies to the demand curve, we see that there is simply no way from the scatter of points in Figure 7.3 that we can "identify" either the demand or supply curve.

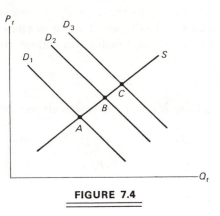

FIGURE 7.4

EXAMPLE 2

Consider next a variation on our supply-demand model:

$$Q_t^d = a_0 + a_1 P_t + a_2 P_{t-1} + u_t, \tag{7.69}$$

$$Q_t^s = b_0 + b_1 P_t + b_2 P_{t-1} + \varepsilon_t, \tag{7.70}$$

$$Q_t^d = Q_t^s = Q_t. \tag{7.71}$$

The three-equation model, (7.69)–(7.71), is identical to our earlier model with the sole exception that a lagged price variable, P_{t-1}, appears in both the demand and supply equations.* Because the disturbance terms are assumed not to be autocorrelated, P_{t-1} would not be correlated with either u_t or ε_t and may, therefore, be taken to be a predetermined variable. The current price variable, P_t, however, is again correlated with u_t and with ε_t so that we must use a modified technique to estimate the demand and supply equations.

Suppose that we attempt to use TSLS to estimate the parameters in the demand equation. We would first regress P_t on all the predetermined variables in the model, in this case P_{t-1}, and then construct the calculated value of P_t, say,

$$\hat{P}_t = \hat{c}_0 + \hat{c}_1 P_{t-1}. \tag{7.72}$$

We would then substitute $\hat{P}_t$ for P_t in (7.69) and, in the second-stage, attempt to estimate the equation,

$$Q_t^d = a_0 + a_1 \hat{P}_t + a_2 P_{t-1} + u_t^*, \tag{7.73}$$

where, of course, $Q_t^d = Q_t$. However, in light of (7.72), once again our estimation procedure breaks down, because the values of $\hat{P}_t$ would be

* The presence of P_{t-1} might indicate that buyers and sellers behave somewhat on the basis of past habits or information, or, alternatively, that expected future prices influence decisions where both P_t and P_{t-1} affect expectations.

perfectly and linearly related to those of P_{t-1}. This is the case of perfect multicollinearity, which will not permit us to generate separate estimators of a_0, a_1, and a_2. Our supply and demand equations are still unidentified.

EXAMPLE 3

Let us explore yet a third form of our supply-demand model:

$$Q_t^d = a_0 + a_1 P_t + a_2 Y_t + u_t, \tag{7.74}$$

$$Q_t^s = b_0 + b_1 P_t + \varepsilon_t, \tag{7.75}$$

$$Q_t^d = Q_t^s = Q_t. \tag{7.76}$$

This model is similar to our original one except that an additional variable, the level of income (Y_t), appears in the demand equation. For purposes of this example, assume that Y_t is independent of both u_t and ε_t. Let us see if, in this instance, we can estimate either the demand or supply functions. Consider first the demand equation, (7.74). Aside from the constant term, there is one predetermined variable in the system: Y_t. So we first regress P_t on Y_t to obtain $\hat{P}_t$ as, say, $\hat{P}_t = \hat{h}_0 + \hat{h}_1 Y_t$. Substituting $\hat{P}_t$ for P_t in the demand equation (7.74), we see that, as in the previous case, we cannot obtain estimators for a_0, a_1, and a_2 because we would again have perfect multicollinearity. However, we now *can* estimate the coefficients in the supply equation, (7.75). That is, if P_t is replaced by $\hat{P}_t$ in (7.75), we can proceed with our TSLS procedure, because we are not confronted with a multicollinearity problem. We find that we *can* obtain consistent estimators of b_0 and b_1 by regressing Q_t on $\hat{P}_t$. In this case, we can estimate the coefficients of the supply equation, but not the demand equation.

An intuitive justification, or clarification, for this result can be given geometrically. We would again have a scatter diagram between P_t and Q_t similar to that in Figure 7.3. However, we now have *additional information* relating to the separation of those points that resulted from a change in demand only. In particular, we see from the specification of our equations that the demand and supply curves shift when the disturbance terms, ε_t and u_t, change. However, in addition to this effect of the disturbance terms, the demand curve, and *not* the supply curve, will shift if Y_t changes. In terms of our scatter diagram, this implies that, *if* the disturbance terms could be held constant at zero, we would observe a set of points corresponding to the different values of Y_t that would trace out the supply curve. Such a situation is depicted in Figure 7.5. In this case, we could estimate the supply curve, *if* we could somehow account for the fact that the disturbance terms will not usually be zero but, instead, will take on different values from period to period. Somewhat intuitively, this variation of the disturbance terms is accounted for by our assumption that the disturbance terms are independent of, and therefore uncorrelated with, the level of income, Y_t. This condition,

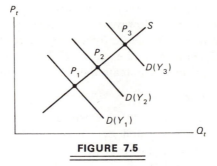

FIGURE 7.5

and the assumption that the disturbance terms have a zero mean, enable us by our estimation technique more or less to "average out" the effect of the disturbance terms. Alternatively, the curves in Figure 7.5 could be looked upon as "mean" curves corresponding to each level of income; that is, for any given value of Y_t, $E(u_t) = E(\varepsilon_t) = 0$, so that the mean effect of the disturbance terms on the position of the curves in Figure 7.5 is zero. Note, however, that there is no corresponding argument that suggests that we can estimate the demand curve, because there is no variable in the supply function that (by virtue of *not appearing* in the demand function) would generate shifts in the supply curve along the demand curve. In this third case the supply equation is identified, but the demand equation is not.

A MORE GENERAL PRESENTATION

We shall now consider some examples that are a bit more general. Suppose that the first structural equation of a system of simultaneous equations is

$$Y_{1t} = b_0 + b_1 X_{1t} + b_2 Y_{2t} + b_3 Y_{3t} + \varepsilon_t, \tag{7.77}$$

where Y_{1t}, Y_{2t}, and Y_{3t} are endogenous variables, X_{1t} is a predetermined variable, and the disturbance term ε_t satisfies all of the usual assumptions. Suppose also that the complete system of which this equation is a member contains only one additional predetermined variable, say, X_{2t}. Then, to estimate (7.77) we would use our TSLS procedure, since both Y_{2t} and Y_{3t} would be expected to be correlated with ε_t. Regressing Y_{2t} and Y_{3t} on X_{1t} and X_{2t}, we would obtain $\hat{Y}_{2t}$ and $\hat{Y}_{3t}$:

$$\hat{Y}_{2t} = \hat{\gamma}_0 + \hat{\gamma}_1 X_{1t} + \hat{\gamma}_2 X_{2t}, \tag{7.78}$$

$$\hat{Y}_{3t} = \hat{\alpha}_0 + \hat{\alpha}_1 X_{1t} + \hat{\alpha}_2 X_{2t}. \tag{7.79}$$

If we then substitute (7.78) and (7.79) into (7.77), our second-stage regression model would be

$$Y_{1t} = b_0 + b_1 X_{1t} + b_2 \hat{Y}_{2t} + b_3 \hat{Y}_{3t} + \varepsilon_t^*. \tag{7.80}$$

where ε_t^* is our new disturbance term. We would then attempt to estimate (7.80) in the usual manner. However, our procedure would again break down because of *perfect multicollinearity* among the regressors. To see this, multiply equation (7.78) by $\hat{\alpha}_2$ and equation (7.79) by $\hat{\gamma}_2$, and then subtract the latter from the former to eliminate the X_{2t} term and obtain

$$\hat{Y}_{2t}\hat{\alpha}_2 - \hat{Y}_{3t}\hat{\gamma}_2 = (\hat{\alpha}_2\hat{\gamma}_0 - \hat{\alpha}_0\hat{\gamma}_2) + (\hat{\gamma}_1\hat{\alpha}_2 - \hat{\alpha}_1\hat{\gamma}_2)X_{1t}. \qquad (7.81)$$

Equation (7.81) indicates that there exists a perfect linear relationship between the values of $\hat{Y}_{2t}$, $\hat{Y}_{3t}$, and X_{1t}. It follows that one of our normal equations will not be linearly independent of the others and so the parameters of (7.80) cannot be estimated.

We can understand this result by considering the normal equations corresponding to (7.80). We obtain the first two normal equations by setting $\sum \hat{\varepsilon}_t^* = 0$ and $\sum (\hat{\varepsilon}_t^* X_{1t}) = 0$. The third normal equation, which we generate by setting $\sum (\hat{\varepsilon}_t^* \hat{Y}_{2t}) = 0$, is independent of the first two because $\hat{Y}_{2t}$ depends on X_{2t} [see (7.78)]; if it did not, our third normal equation would be equal to $\hat{\gamma}_0$ times the first, plus $\hat{\gamma}_1$ times the second. In a sense, X_{2t} "separates" the third normal equation from the first two. However, trouble develops when we turn to the fourth normal equation, which we obtained by setting $\sum (\hat{Y}_{3t}\hat{\varepsilon}_t^*) = 0$. We have in effect already used X_{2t} to separate the third normal equation from the first two. Can we use it again to separate the fourth from the first three? As we have seen, the answer is no, because the values of $\hat{Y}_{3t}$ are perfectly and linearly related to those of X_{1t} and $\hat{Y}_{2t}$.* Somewhat intuitively, each linearly independent normal equation requires new information—a new variable! Since there are none left, the parameters of (7.80) or (7.77) are not identified for lack of an independent fourth normal equation.**

Suppose that the system of equations containing (7.77) includes two additional predetermined variables, say X_{2t} and X_{3t}. Then in the first-stage, (7.78) and (7.79) would include an additional independent variable: X_{3t}. If, as before, we now eliminate X_{2t} from these first-stage equations, we would end up with a linear equation relating $\hat{Y}_{2t}$, $\hat{Y}_{3t}$, X_{1t}, and X_{3t}. Because of this X_{3t} term, $\hat{Y}_{3t}$ *would not* be a perfect combination of X_{1t} and $\hat{Y}_{2t}$. In this

---

* You should be able to show that, in light of (7.81), the fourth normal equation will be equal to $(\hat{\alpha}_0\hat{\gamma}_2 - \hat{\alpha}_2\hat{\gamma}_0)/\hat{\gamma}_2$ times the first, plus $(\hat{\alpha}_1\hat{\gamma}_2 - \hat{\gamma}_1\hat{\alpha}_2)/\hat{\gamma}_2$ times the second, plus $\hat{\alpha}_2/\hat{\gamma}_2$ times the third.

** An even simpler illustration of this case is the model

$$Y_{1t} = b_0 + b_1 Y_{2t} + b_3 Y_{3t} + u_t,$$

where Y_{2t} and Y_{3t} are endogenous variables and there exists only one predetermined variable (say, Z_t) in the rest of the system of equations. In this instance, our first-stage regressions and calculations would generate $\hat{Y}_{2t}$ and $\hat{Y}_{3t}$. However, the values of both $\hat{Y}_{2t}$ and $\hat{Y}_{3t}$ would be exact linear combinations of those of Z_t and would be perfectly correlated with one another. Our estimation procedure would clearly fail because of perfect multicollinearity among the regressors.

case, we would not have perfect multicollinearity in the second stage of our TSLS procedure, and equation (7.77) would now be identified. Clearly this conclusion would hold if more than two additional predetermined variables appeared in the system of which equation (7.77) is a member. That is, our equation in question seems to be identified if the number of additional predetermined variables in the system [those not appearing in equation (7.77)] is greater than or equal to two, the number of endogenous regressors.

One final point should be made. The first normal equation, which we obtain by setting $\sum \hat{\varepsilon}_t^* = 0$, can be thought of as corresponding to the constant term.* Alternatively, we can think of the constant term as a predetermined variable. As such, we find, as our example below indicates, that if the equation we are estimating does not have a constant term in it, but one or more of the other equations of the system do, we can count the constant term as one of the predetermined variables of the system that does not appear in our equation to be estimated.

For example, consider the two-equation model

$$Y_{1t} = b_1 Y_{2t} + b_2 X_t + \varepsilon_{1t}, \qquad (7.82)$$

$$Y_{2t} = a_1 + a_2 Y_{1t} + \varepsilon_{2t}, \qquad (7.83)$$

where X_t is a predetermined variable and ε_{1t} and ε_{2t} are disturbance terms that satisfy our basic assumptions. At first glance the reader may suspect that we shall not be able to apply our TSLS procedure to (7.82), since we have only one predetermined variable, X_t, in the system and that variable appears in the equation we want to estimate. We find, however, that because the "constant term" is excluded from (7.82), we can employ TSLS to estimate (7.82), because the excluded constant term in a sense provides us with the additional needed "predetermined" variable. For instance, from the first stage of our TSLS procedure we would obtain

$$\hat{Y}_{2t} = \hat{c}_1 + \hat{c}_2 X_t. \qquad (7.84)$$

Condition (7.84) implies that of the three normal equations obtained by setting

$$N_1 : \sum \hat{\varepsilon}_{1t}^* = 0, \qquad N_2 : \sum (\hat{\varepsilon}_{1t}^* \hat{Y}_{2t}) = 0, \qquad N_3 : \sum (\hat{\varepsilon}_{1t}^* X_t) = 0, \qquad (7.85)$$

only two will be independent. But since (7.82) does not contain a constant term, we only need two normal equations! We would simply take the

---

* For instance, equation (7.80) can be expressed as

$$Y_{1t} = b_0 X_{0t} + b_1 X_{1t} + b_2 \hat{Y}_{2t} + b_3 \hat{Y}_{3t} + \varepsilon_t^*,$$

where X_{0t} is defined to be unity in every period; $X_{0t} \equiv 1$, for all t. Thus, the condition $\sum \hat{\varepsilon}_t^* = 0$ can be thought of as $\sum (\hat{\varepsilon}_t^* X_{0t}) = 0$.

equations corresponding to N_2 and N_3 in (7.85), because these conditions correspond to the regressors in our equation (7.82).

A GENERAL STATEMENT*

With this as background, let us now state the general rule for obtaining consistent estimators with TSLS: *in order to use TSLS to generate consistent estimators of the parameters in a regression equation, the number of endogenous variables that appears as regressors in the equation to be estimated cannot exceed the number of predetermined variables that both appear in the model as a whole and are excluded from that equation.* Alternatively, in general, a particular equation in a model is identified (and can be consistently estimated) if $K_2 \geq K_1$, where K_2 equals the number of predetermined variables in the model *excluded* from the given equation and K_1 is the number of endogenous variables appearing as regressors in that equation.**

Looking back at the earlier examples, we see that, in our simple income-determination model, we were able to estimate the consumption equation because we had one endogenous variable as a regressor (Y_t) and one predetermined variable (I_t) that was part of the model but did not appear in the consumption equation. We were unable to estimate either the supply or demand equations in our first two supply-demand models; in both of these cases we had one endogenous regressor but no excluded predetermined variables. Finally, in our third example, the supply equation was identified, since the one endogenous regressor in the supply function (P_t) was matched by a predetermined variable (Y_t) appearing only in the demand equation; there was, however, no predetermined variable excluded from the demand function, so that we found ourselves unable to estimate that equation.

The rationale for this rule should be clear from the earlier examples. Where there are an insufficient number of predetermined variables excluded from the equation, our TSLS estimation procedure will break down because of perfect multicollinearity in the second stage. Let us emphasize in conclusion that this is not a particular deficiency of TSLS *per se*; other estimation techniques are also unable to provide consistent estimators of unidentified equations. It is the structure of the model itself and the character of the available information that prevent the unraveling of the interdependencies among the variables.

---

* The general statements given here hold in the context of our analysis. For example, we have not considered cases in which the researcher knows the values of certain variances, relationships between particular parameters, etc. However, it is fair to say that the analysis we have presented here is the one encountered in practice in the large majority of cases.

** We must use the phrase "in general," because these are actually necessary, but not sufficient, conditions for an equation to be identified. [See Arthur S. Goldberger, *Econometric Theory* (New York: Wiley, 1964), pp. 306–329]. A discussion of the sufficient conditions is beyond the scope of this book. However, from a practical point of view, the conditions usually considered in practice are the ones we have discussed here.

7.6 TSLS ESTIMATION: TWO ILLUSTRATIONS

To provide greater familiarity with the TSLS estimation procedure, we shall conclude this chapter by considering two examples. The first, involving the estimation of a hypothetical demand curve for a particular commodity, will permit us simply to follow through the mechanics of the technique. The second draws on an actual empirical study from the recent journal literature on local public finances.

A DEMAND AND SUPPLY MODEL

Consider first the following simple model of the market for an agricultural commodity, say artichokes:

$$Q_t^d = b_0 + b_1 P_t + b_2 Y_t + u_t, \tag{7.86}$$

$$Q_t^s = a_0 + a_1 P_{t-1} + a_2 W_t + e_t, \tag{7.87}$$

$$Q_t^d = Q_t^s = Q_t. \tag{7.88}$$

Equation (7.86), the demand function, indicates that the quantity demanded in period t depends on price (P_t) and income (Y_t). The supply equation (7.87) states that the production of artichokes depends on P_{t-1}, the price in the previous period (when planting decisions must be made), and on the weather, W_t. We shall use inches of rainfall as our measure of weather conditions. Finally, we have our standard market-clearing equation (7.88), which implies that price in time t adjusts so as to make quantity demanded equal to quantity supplied.

Let us assume that Y_t and W_t are determined by factors outside the system: they are exogenous variables. Furthermore, let us assume that the disturbance terms, u_t and e_t, have zero means, constant variances, are normally distributed, are not autocorrelated, and are independent of the predetermined variables. Suppose that we want to estimate the coefficients in the demand function for artichokes. We notice first that one of the regressors, namely, P_t, is an endogenous variable that we would expect to be correlated with the disturbance terms of the model. Since the use of OLSQ will generate inconsistent estimators of the coefficients, we shall employ TSLS to estimate (7.86). Second, we note that the demand equation is identified: it contains one endogenous regressor, but there are two predetermined variables (P_{t-1} and W_t) that appear in the system but not in the demand equation itself. Assuming that we have data for these variables, we should be able to estimate this demand function with TSLS.

We have assembled a set of hypothetical data for the variables in the model, which appear in Table 7.1. Notice that there are only ten observations, hardly enough to justify the use of an estimation technique that provides "large-sample" results. We emphasize that the purpose of this example is simply to follow through the steps in the TSLS estimation procedure with some actual numbers.

Our first operation is to regress the endogenous independent variable in the demand equation (that is, P_t) on all the predetermined variables in the system. Aside from the constant term, there are three such predetermined variables: two exogenous variables (Y_t and W_t) and one lagged endogenous variable (P_{t-1}). The estimated regression equation is

$$\hat{P}_t = -8.60 + 3.75Y_t - 0.22W_t + 0.42P_{t-1}. \qquad (7.89)$$

We now use (7.89) to compute a "corrected" set of values for P_t. That is, for each period $t = 1, \ldots, 10$, we substitute the values for Y_t, W_t, and P_{t-1} into (7.89) and calculate the corresponding value for $\hat{P}_t$. This new "purged" series of values for the price variable (along with the observed values, P_t) appears in Table 7.2.* The second stage in the TSLS procedure is to substitute $\hat{P}_t$ for P_t in our demand equation and then simply estimate the new equation in the usual way. Regressing Q_t on Y_t and $\hat{P}_t$ gives us

$$\hat{Q}_t = -39.9 - 1.3\hat{P}_t + 9.5Y_t, \qquad (7.90)$$
$$\quad\;\; (2.9) \quad\;\; (3.7) \quad\; (4.1)$$

where the numbers in parentheses are the corresponding absolute values of the t ratios. We thus have $\hat{b}_0 = -39.9$, $\hat{b}_1 = -1.3$, and $\hat{b}_2 = 9.5$.

If we had simply used ordinary least squares (OLSQ) to estimate the demand for artichokes (that is, if we had used P_t instead of $\hat{P}_t$), we would have obtained

$$\hat{Q}_t = -25.1 - 0.7P_t + 6.2Y_t. \qquad (7.91)$$
$$\quad\;\; (1.9) \quad\;\; (2.1) \quad\; (2.8)$$

TABLE 7.1

HYPOTHETICAL DATA FOR THE MARKET FOR ARTICHOKES[a]

Period (t)	Quantity (Q)	Unit Price (P)	Income (Y)	Rainfall (W)
1	11	20	8.1	42
2	16	18	8.4	58
3	11	22	8.5	35
4	14	21	8.5	46
5	13	27	8.8	41
6	17	26	9.0	56
7	14	25	8.9	48
8	15	27	9.4	50
9	12	30	9.5	39
10	18	28	9.9	52

[a] The units for these variables might be

      Q = tons of artichokes,
      P = unit price of artichokes (in cents),
      Y = average annual family income (in thousands of dollars),
      W = annual rainfall in inches.

* Note that we have only nine observations for $\hat{P}_t$; in the process of using the lagged variable, P_{t-1}, in (7.89), we "lost" one observation.

TABLE 7.2

Period	P_t	$\hat{P}_t$
1	20.0	—
2	18.0	18.5
3	22.0	23.1
4	21.0	22.4
5	27.0	24.2
6	26.0	24.2
7	25.0	25.1
8	27.0	26.1
9	30.0	29.8
10	28.0	29.7

Notice the differences between the estimated coefficients in (7.90) and (7.91). Our TSLS equation indicates that the demand for artichokes is a good deal more responsive to changes in price and in income than does the OLSQ equation. In view of the small number of observations in our sample, we clearly could not have much confidence that, in a case like this, our TSLS estimates were the more reliable. If, however, these results were based on a large sample of observed values for the variables (and, of course, on actual, rather than hypothetical, data!), there would be good reason, because of the inconsistency of the OLSQ estimators, to prefer the results based on the TSLS technique.

A MODEL OF LOCAL PUBLIC FINANCE

Having worked through the mechanics of TSLS with some hypothetical figures, we turn next to an actual empirical study employing the TSLS technique. A problem of genuine concern and interest, not only to economists, but also to local public officials, is the impact of local fiscal policies on individual decisions. Do high local property taxes, for example, discourage the entry of potential new residents and business? How much do residents (actual and potential) care about the quality of local schools? Enough to influence their location decisions? These are not easy questions to answer, but they are for obvious reasons on the minds of local officials.

Some years ago, Charles Tiebout advanced a theoretical model of local finance that deals with some of these issues.* Tiebout postulated a system composed of a large number of communities offering differing outputs of public services in which mobile consumers selected their community of residence in accordance with their preferences for these services. For example, people who have a high demand for education would presumably group together in communities with superior schools. One attraction of the Tiebout

---

*Charles Tiebout, "A Pure Theory of Local Expenditures," *Journal of Political Economy*, 64 (Oct. 1956), pp. 416–424.

model is that it provides a mechanism through which people can express and satisfy their demands for local services: their location decision (or, as it is sometimes described, by "voting with their feet.")

At an empirical level, however, the question remains as to whether or not (at least some) people behave in this manner. The obstacles to the perfect mobility envisioned in the Tiebout model are many: moving costs, job location and commuting costs, and so forth. Nevertheless, when one looks at the structure and mobility within our metropolitan areas, behavior of a Tiebout type does not seem entirely implausible: individuals working in a central city frequently have a wide choice of suburban communities in which to reside, and the quality of local public schools, for instance, may be of real importance in the choice of a community of residence.

But how can we test for the presence of such behavior? One approach is to ask ourselves what we would expect to observe if behavior of the Tiebout type is of importance. If in fact fiscal variables such as school quality and tax burdens are significant factors in individual location decisions, we might expect to find that they would exhibit some influence on property values. For example, a community with superior schools would, other things equal, be a relatively desirable place to live; in their attempt to locate in such a community, people would tend to bid up property values above their levels elsewhere. Likewise, high tax rates should, other things equal, tend to depress the value of local property. In short, in a Tiebout world, we would expect to see fiscal differentials among communities manifest themselves in terms of intercommunity differences in property values. This suggests that we might examine the relationship between fiscal variables and property values across different communities. We could postulate a relationship of the general form

$$V_t = b_0 + b_1 X_{1t} + \cdots + b_k X_{kt} + b_{(k+1)} Z_{1t} + \cdots + b_{(k+l)} Z_{lt}$$
$$+ b_{(k+l+1)} T_t + u_t, \qquad (7.92)$$

where

V_t is some measure of local property values in the tth community,

X_{1t} through X_{kt} are the nonfiscal variables that influence local property values,

Z_{1t} through Z_{lt} are levels of output of l different public services,

T_t is the local property tax rate, and

u_t is our disturbance term.

Then, using data from a sample of communities, we could estimate this equation and see if we discover any systematic relationships between our public service and tax variables and local property values.

We shall now describe just such a study.* Using a sample of 53 residential

---

* W. E. Oates, "The Effects of Property Taxes and Local Public Spending on Property Values: An Empirical Study of Tax Capitalization and the Tiebout Hypothesis," *Journal of Political Economy*, 77 (Nov–Dec. 1969), pp. 957–971.

municipalities in northeastern New Jersey (all within the greater New York metropolitan area), this study entailed the estimation of an equation similar to (7.92). The U.S. Censuses of Population and Housing provide a substantial amount of information concerning the population and housing character- istics of municipalities in the United States. Supplementing this data with budgetary information on local expenditures and tax rates from New Jersey sources, it was possible to assemble some measures of the variables in (7.92). As an index of local property values, the study used*

V_t = the median value of owner-occupied dwellings in the tth municipality.

The value of dwelling units in a given community obviously depends on a number of nonfiscal variables: the proximity of the municipality to the central city, the physical characteristics of housing units, and various in- tangible "environmental" considerations; these are the X_{it} in (7.92). To measure these influences, the study used as regressors the distance of the municipality in miles from New York City (M_t), the median number of rooms per owner-occupied house in the municipality (R_t), the percentage of houses in the municipality built since 1950 (N_t) as a measure of the age of the housing stock, and, as a proxy variable for the intangible character- istics of the community, median family income (Y_t) in the municipality. The presumption here is that higher-income families will tend to select residences in more "attractive" communities; median family income thus represents a measure of the intangible features of residence in the community. For fiscal variables, the study included the effective or true tax rate (T_t) on local property (the nominal rate corrected for varying assessment practices) and, as a measure of local services, the expenditure per pupil (E_t) in the local public schools.** The first step was simply to regress V_t on this set of in- dependent variables using ordinary least squares; this generated the estimated equation†

$$\hat{V} = -21 - 3.6 \log T + 3.2 \log E - 1.4 \log M$$
$$\quad\;\; (2.4) \quad\;\; (4.1) \qquad\quad (2.1) \qquad\quad (4.8)$$

$$+ 1.7R + 0.05N + 1.5Y + 0.3P, \qquad R^2 = 0.93. \qquad (7.93)$$
$$(4.1) \quad\;\; (3.9) \quad\;\; (8.9) \quad\; (3.6)$$

We find that all the regressors possess estimated coefficients with the expected sign and, from their t ratios, we see that, had we considered any of the null

---

* All these data were for the year 1960.

** For a more detailed description (and justification) of these variables and of the particular transformations used in the actual regression equation, see the article itself.

† The variable P is the percentage of families in the municipality with incomes less than $3000. This serves to correct a deficiency in the income variable Y_t; see pp. 962–963 of the article.

hypotheses of no relationship (e.g., $H_0 : b_i = 0$; $H_1 : b_i \neq 0$), we would have rejected it at the 5 percent level of significance. At first glance, the results would appear to support a model of individual behavior in which fiscal variables do exert a significant influence on location decisions: the higher are tax rates (other things held constant), the lower is the value of a typical dwelling unit, and, conversely, the larger is expenditure per pupil, the higher is its value. People would appear willing to pay more to live in communities with relatively low tax rates and superior schools.

A little thought about our regression model and estimation procedure raises some serious problems. While we might be willing to regard the physical and certain environmental characteristics of a municipality as exogenous variables, our two fiscal variables are clearly endogenous. The tax rate, for example, depends on the size of the public budget and on the tax base which, of course, depends in part on property values. Likewise, the level of spending on schools will be determined by tax rates (and, therefore, property values) along with income and other characteristics of the population.* In fact, one could argue quite plausibly that the observed negative relationship in (7.93) between tax rates and the value of dwelling units simply reflects the fact that with more valuable property a given amount of revenues can be raised with a lower tax rate; that is, V is determining T, not vice versa. What all this amounts to is that we must consider the consequences of two additional equations in our system of the general form

$$T_t = f(V_t, E_t, \ldots), \tag{7.94}$$

$$E_t = g(T_t, Y_t, \ldots). \tag{7.95}$$

Equation (7.94) indicates that the tax rate is a function of the level of public spending and other variables (such as V_t) that determine the size of the tax base, while (7.95) says that school spending is a function of the tax rate, income, and other variables reflecting relevant characteristics of the tth community's population. In brief, our fiscal variables [in this case $(\log T_t)$ and $(\log E_t)$] are *endogenous* variables in our model. This means that they are likely to be correlated with the disturbance terms and, as a result, our estimated coefficients in (7.93) are subject to simultaneous-equation bias. OLSQ is not the appropriate technique for estimating our regression model.

For this reason, the study goes back and reestimates the equation using TSLS. This means that we must regress the two endogenous variables, $E_t' = (\log E_t)$ and $T_t' = (\log T_t)$, on the predetermined variables in the system, generate the purged variables $\hat{E}_t' = (\widehat{\log E_t})$ and $\hat{T}_t' = (\widehat{\log T_t})$, and

---

*Tax rates influence public spending because they in effect represent the "price" of public services. For example, residents living in a community with a relatively large commercial and industrial tax base can "purchase" units of education at a relatively low "price," because a large part of spending per pupil comes from taxes paid by local business. We would expect the residents of such a community to select a larger school budget than they would in the absence of the large commercial-industrial tax base.

then estimate the original equation with $\hat{E}_t' = (\widehat{\log E_t})$ and $\hat{T}_t' = (\widehat{\log T_t})$ in place of log E_t and log T_t.* At this point the study makes use of one of the attractive properties of TSLS. Recall from our earlier discussion that TSLS does not require the complete specification of the other equations in the model; that is, we do not have to specify fully and obtain data on *all* the independent variables in (7.94) and (7.95). We do need information on some of them. More specifically, in order for our procedure to work, we know that we must have at least two predetermined variables in addition to those appearing in (7.93). The procedure in the study was to isolate a number of additional predetermined variables that would enter as regressors in equations (7.94) and (7.95); these are variables that influence tax rates and expenditures on schools, variables such as the value of commercial-industrial property per capita, the educational levels of the population, the percentage of the population enrolled in the schools, and so forth.** After regressing log E_t and log T_t on these predetermined variables and then calculating $\widehat{\log E_t}$ and $\widehat{\log T_t}$, the study estimates the second-stage regression equation to obtain

$$\hat{V} = -29 - 3.6 \log T + 4.9 \log E - 1.3 \log M + 1.6R$$
$$\quad (2.3) \qquad (3.1) \qquad\quad (2.1) \qquad\quad (4.0) \qquad\quad (3.6)$$

$$+ 0.06N + 1.5Y + 0.3P. \qquad (7.96)$$
$$\quad (3.9) \qquad (7.7) \qquad (3.1)$$

It is interesting in this case that, unlike our earlier example, the estimated coefficients in the TSLS equation are generally quite close to the OLSQ estimates. They all have the same sign, about the same value, and approximately the same t ratios; the only notable difference is that the estimated coefficient on the school-spending variable is noticeably larger in the TSLS equation than in the OLSQ equation [although even here the OLSQ estimate, 3.2, lies within a 95 percent confidence interval for the parameter constructed with the information in (7.96)]. The results suggest that, in this particular study, the inconsistency introduced by our simultaneity problem was apparently not too serious. In other cases, OLSQ and TSLS estimates may be quite different. At any rate, we find here that the results provide evidence consistent with a model in which individuals do consider local fiscal variables in their choice of a suburban municipality.

---

* The reader should note that the "purged" variables are *not* log $(\hat{T}_t)$ and log $(\hat{E}_t)$. That is, *we do not* first regress T_t and E_t on the predetermined variables in order to obtain $\hat{T}_t$ and $\hat{E}_t$ and *then take logs*. Instead, we treat log T_t and log E_t as transformed variables, T_t' and E_t', and regress T_t' and E_t' on the predetermined variables in order to obtain $\hat{T}_t'$ and $\hat{E}_t'$. This subtle point must be noted, because, as we show in Chapter 8, the use of log $(\hat{T}_t)$ and log $(\hat{E}_t)$ would lead to inconsistent estimators!

** There were actually seven additional predetermined variables used to generate $\widehat{\log E_t}$ and $\widehat{\log T_t}$; a complete listing appears on p. 965 of the cited article.

APPENDIX.

Autocorrelated Disturbance Terms in a Simultaneous-Equation Model*

In the text both of Chapters 6 and 7, we examined a number of difficulties in estimation that arise when the assumptions of our basic regression model are not satisfied. Our procedure was to consider each of these problems in turn and to develop more or less satisfactory ways of modifying our estimation procedures to deal with them. In some instances, however, several of these estimation problems may arise side by side in the same regression model, and it is not always clear just how we should proceed. In this appendix we want to consider just such a case, a model plagued both by a systems problem and autocorrelated disturbance terms, and explore how we can estimate such a model. This, we hope, will provide some insight into the methods by which econometricians treat *at the same time* two (or more) estimation problems.

Suppose we are interested in the following equations of a system of simultaneous equations:

$$Y_{1t} = b_0 + b_1 X_{1t} + b_2 Y_{2t} + b_3 Y_{3(t-1)} + u_t, \tag{7A.1}$$

$$u_t = \rho u_{t-1} + \varepsilon_t, \qquad -1 < \rho < 1, \tag{7A.2}$$

where X_{1t} is an exogenous variable, Y_{2t} is a current endogenous variable, $Y_{3(t-1)}$ is a lagged endogenous variable, and u_t is our disturbance term. In contrast to our previous examples, we now assume that the disturbance term is autocorrelated, as described by equation (7A.2), where ε_t is a normally distributed disturbance term that is independent and therefore uncorrelated with all of the *exogenous* variables (and all of their lagged values) in the system. We also assume that ε_t is not autocorrelated $[E(\varepsilon_s \varepsilon_t) = 0$ for $s \neq t]$, has a mean of zero, $[E(\varepsilon_t) = 0]$, and a constant variance $[E(\varepsilon_t^2) = \sigma^2]$.

If ρ were zero in equation (7A.2), we would simply treat $Y_{3(t-1)}$ as a predetermined variable, and proceed as described in the text. However, since we assume here that $\rho \neq 0$, we have further difficulties. Because of the autocorrelation, we would expect $Y_{3(t-1)}$ to be correlated with u_t. To see this, note that, since Y_{3t} is an endogenous variable, $Y_{3(t-1)}$ would depend, in general, on $Y_{1(t-1)}$, which, in turn, depends on $u_{(t-1)}$. It follows that $Y_{3(t-1)}$ would depend on $u_{(t-1)}$ and so would be correlated with u_t in the light of equation (7A.2). This means that we cannot treat $Y_{3(t-1)}$ as a predetermined variable. The generalization of this should be clear: *if the disturbance terms are autocorrelated, lagged endogenous variables will generally be correlated with the disturbance terms.*

* In varying degrees, the following discussion draws upon the work of Ray C. Fair, "The Estimation of Simultaneous Equation Models with Lagged Endogenous Variables and First Order Serially Correlated Errors," *Econometrica*, 38 (May 1970), pp. 507–516; and J. Phillip Cooper, "Asymptotic Covariance Matrix of Procedures for Linear Regression in the Presence of First Order Serially Correlated Disturbances," *Econometrica*, 40 (March 1972), pp. 305–310.

Note that we may still take the *exogenous variables* to be predetermined variables, because they remain uncorrelated with the disturbance terms. We can see this by the repeated lagging and substitution of u_t in equation (7A.2), which gives us

$$u_t = \varepsilon_t + \rho\varepsilon_{t-1} + \rho^2\varepsilon_{t-2} + \cdots. \tag{7A.3}$$

Since u_t depends ultimately on the current and lagged values of ε_t, and since the current and lagged values of ε_t are, by assumption, independent of the exogenous variables, it follows that u_t must be uncorrelated with the exogenous variables. In equation (7A.1), we can thus presume X_{1t} to be uncorrelated with u_t.

We must now modify our TSLS technique to account for the autocorrelation. As one might suspect from our work in previous chapters, we shall first obtain an estimator of ρ, transform equation (7A.1) to rid it of the autocorrelated disturbance term, and then proceed with our TSLS estimation procedure.

Unfortunately, deriving an estimator of ρ is not as simple a process as in Chapter 5, where we considered autocorrelation in isolation. If equation (7A.1) suffered only from autocorrelation, the procedure, as described in Chapter 5, would be to obtain consistent estimators, $\hat{b}_0, \ldots, \hat{b}_3$, of $b_0, \ldots, b_3$ by OLSQ and use them to estimate u_t by $\hat{u}_t = Y_{1t} - (\hat{b}_0 + \hat{b}_1 X_{1t} + \hat{b}_2 Y_{2t} + \hat{b}_3 Y_{3(t-1)})$. From $\hat{u}_t$ we would compute $\hat{\rho}$ from equation (6.45). But, since (7A.1) also has a systems problem, we cannot simply apply OLSQ to (7A.1), since the resulting estimators of $b_0, \ldots, b_3$ would be inconsistent, thereby producing an inconsistent estimator of ρ. We must estimate (7A.1) by the TSLS method.

To implement this TSLS procedure, we observe that because $Y_{3(t-1)}$ is correlated with u_t, we treat it as if it were a current endogenous variable, say, $Z_t = Y_{3(t-1)}$. To simplify notation, let X_t denote all the exogenous variables (including X_{1t}) in the system at time t. Then the first stage of our TSLS procedure would be to obtain the "corrected" or "purged" values of *both* Z_t and of Y_{2t}, namely, $\hat{Z}_t$ and $\hat{Y}_{2t}$.

Now we would typically obtain $\hat{Y}_{2t}$ by regressing Y_{2t} on all of the exogenous variables in the system, X_t.* Similarly, in an attempt to synchronize time periods, we would construct $\hat{Z}_t = \hat{Y}_{3(t-1)}$ by regressing Z_t on all of the lagged values of the exogenous variables, X_{t-1}. However, in order to ensure the technical conditions of the TSLS procedure, we construct $\hat{Y}_{2t}$ and $\hat{Z}_t$ by regressing Y_{2t} and Z_t on *both* the variables denoted by X_t and by X_{t-1} (e.g., among others, on both X_{1t} and $X_{1(t-1)}$).** Once we have constructed $\hat{Y}_{2t}$ and $\hat{Z}_t$, the remainder of our technique should be obvious. That is, we would estimate the parameters of (7A.1) by first replacing Y_{2t} and $Y_{3(t-1)}$ by $\hat{Y}_{2t}$ and $\hat{Y}_{3(t-1)}$, respectively, more or less put a "star" on the disturbance term, and then derive the normal equations in the second stage by our standard technique.

If we were only interested in obtaining consistent estimators for b_0, b_1, b_2, and b_3, we could simply solve our normal equations for $\hat{b}_0, \ldots, \hat{b}_3$ and be finished with

---

* Recall that, because of the autocorrelation, we must treat lagged endogenous variables as current endogenous variables. Therefore, exogenous variables are the only predetermined variables in the system.

** The reader should be able to show that if $\hat{Y}_{2t}$ were constructed by regressing Y_{2t} only on X_t, and $\hat{Z}_t$ were constructed by regressing Z_t only on X_{t-1}, then, in general, the conditions described in (7.61) would not hold. That is, if we let $Y_{2t} = \hat{Y}_{2t} + \hat{\theta}_{1t}$, and $Z_t = \hat{Z}_t + \hat{\theta}_{2t}$, then $\sum (\hat{\theta}_{1t}\hat{Z}_t) \neq 0$ and $\sum (\hat{\theta}_{2t}\hat{Y}_{2t}) \neq 0$. (Hint: $\hat{\theta}_{1t}$ would be such that, for any current exogenous variable such as $X_{1t}, \sum (\hat{\theta}_{1t}X_{1t}) = 0$. However $\hat{Z}_t$ would depend on $X_{1(t-1)}$.)

it. However, we usually want to determine the variances and associated t ratios for our estimators so that we can establish confidence intervals and test hypotheses. Unfortunately, if we stop at this point with our estimation procedure, we cannot obtain these variances and t ratios, because the *autocorrelation* problem is still with us and invalidates all of our variance formulas. We are forced to make further modifications.

Since our use of TSLS has produced consistent estimators, $\hat{b}_0$, $\hat{b}_1$, $\hat{b}_2$, and $\hat{b}_3$, of the parameters of (7A.1), we can obtain a consistent estimator of the disturbance term u_t by

$$\hat{u}_t = Y_{1t} - (\hat{b}_0 + \hat{b}_1 X_{1t} + \hat{b}_2 Y_{2t} + \hat{b}_3 Y_{3(t-1)}). \qquad (7A.4)$$

Using our procedure from Chapter 5, we now obtain a consistent estimator of ρ:

$$\hat{\rho} = \frac{\sum_{t=2}^{n} \hat{u}_{t-1} \hat{u}_t}{\sum_{t=2}^{n} \hat{u}_{t-1}^2}. \qquad (7A.5)$$

This, you will recall, is the estimator of ρ suggested by equation (7A.2). As described in Chapter 5, we now lag equation (7A.1), multiply the lagged equation by $\hat{\rho}$, and then subtract our resulting equation from (7A.1) to obtain*

$$Y_{1t}{}^* = B + b_1 X_{1t}{}^* + b_2 Y_{2t}{}^* + b_3 Y_{3(t-1)}^* + \varepsilon_t, \qquad (7A.6)$$

where $B = (b_0 - \hat{\rho} b_0)$, and

$$Y_{1t}{}^* = Y_{1t} - \hat{\rho} Y_{1(t-1)}, \qquad X_{1t}{}^* = X_{1t} - \hat{\rho} X_{1(t-1)},$$

$$Y_{2t}{}^* = Y_{2t} - \hat{\rho} Y_{2t(t-1)}, \qquad Y_{3(t-1)}^* = Y_{3(t-1)} - \hat{\rho} Y_{3(t-2)}.$$

Having effectively eliminated the autocorrelation problem, we can now proceed in a manner similar to that described earlier with one exception. In the above, we used all of the exogenous variables, X_t, and their lags, X_{t-1}, to construct the corrected values of Y_{2t} and $Y_{3(t-1)}$. We are now concerned with the endogenous variables $Y_{2t}{}^*$ and $Y_{3(t-1)}^*$ in (7A.6).** These variables are, respectively, linear combinations of Y_{2t} and $Y_{3(t-1)}$ *and their first lags*. Therefore, in another attempt to synchronize variables, we construct $\hat{Y}_{2t}{}^*$ and $\hat{Y}_{3(t-1)}^*$ by regressing $Y_{2t}{}^*$ and, say, $Z_t^* = Y_{3(t-1)}^*$ on the corresponding linear combinations of X_t and X_{t-1}, namely, $X_t^* = (X_t - \hat{\rho} X_{t-1})$ and $X_{t-1}^* = (X_{t-1} - \hat{\rho} X_{t-2})$. As an example, one of the variables denoted by X_t^* would be $X_{1t}{}^* = (X_{1t} - \hat{\rho} X_{1(t-1)})$.

Once we have calculated $\hat{Y}_{2t}{}^*$ and $\hat{Y}_{3(t-1)}^*$, we would substitute them into (7A.6) in place of $Y_{2t}{}^*$ and $Y_{3(t-1)}^*$, more or less put a star on the disturbance term, ε_t, and then derive our second-stage normal equations. It can be shown that under general conditions, the resulting estimators are consistent and have large-sample variances given by our standard formulas, so that we can establish confidence intervals and test hypotheses in the standard way. Note that our estimator of b_0 would be

---

* Again, equation (7A.6) is strictly correct in terms of probability only if the sample is of infinite size. The reason for this, of course, is that $\hat{\rho}$ is only a consistent estimator of ρ.

** We must still consider $Y_{3(t-1)}^*$ as an endogenous variable because of some problems involved in using $\hat{\rho}$ instead of the true parameter ρ in (7A.6).

$\hat{b}_0 = \hat{B}/(1 - \hat{\rho})$. Similarly, the large-sample variance of $\hat{b}_0$ would be

$$\text{var}(\hat{b}_0) = \frac{1}{(1 - \hat{\rho})^2} \text{var}(\hat{B}).$$

We now summarize and generalize our results. If a given equation in a system of simultaneous equations has autocorrelated disturbance terms, the lagged endogenous regressors in that equation must be treated as endogenous variables. We proceed to estimate such an equation by first regressing the current endogenous regressors *and* the lagged endogenous regressors on all of the exogenous variables of the system and their lagged values, in order to construct the calculated values. We then replace the current and lagged endogenous regressors by these "purged" values, and proceed as usual to obtain consistent estimators of the coefficients in the regression equation. Using these TSLS estimators, we next generate a consistent estimator of the disturbance term which, in turn, we use to obtain an estimator of ρ, $\hat{\rho}$, in the autocorrelation scheme. Using $\hat{\rho}$, we can then transform our original equation to rid it of autocorrelation. We now employ our TSLS procedure again, remembering that here too we must treat lagged endogenous regressors as endogenous (not predetermined) variables. We regress our "transformed" values of the current endogenous and lagged endogenous regressors on the transformed current *and* lagged exogenous variables, replace these regressors by their corrected or "purged" counterparts, and proceed to implement the second stage of the TSLS procedure.

QUESTIONS

1. Consider the model

$$C_t = b_0 + b_1 C_{t-1} + b_2 Y_t + \varepsilon_{1t}, \qquad (1)$$

$$Y_t = I_t + C_t, \qquad (2)$$

$$I_t = a_0 + a_1 Y_t + a_2 Y_{t-1} + a_3 r_t + \varepsilon_{2t}, \qquad (3)$$

where C, I, Y, and r are, respectively, consumer expenditures, investment, income, and the interest rate. Assume that ε_1 and ε_2 are not autocorrelated and are independent of r_t.

   a. List the endogenous variables and the predetermined variables in the model.

   b. How would you estimate equation (1)?

   c. How would you estimate equation (3)?

2. Take as a model of wage-price behavior:

$$\dot{W}_t = a_0 + a_1 (UN)_t + a_2 \dot{P}_t + \varepsilon_{1t},$$

$$\dot{P}_t = b_0 + b_1 \dot{M}_t + b_2 (UN)_t + b_3 \dot{W}_t + \varepsilon_{2t},$$

where

$$\dot{W} = \text{the percentage change in wages,}$$
$$UN = \text{the rate of unemployment,}$$
$$\dot{P} = \text{the percentage change in prices,}$$
$$\dot{M}_t = \text{the percentage change in the money supply, and}$$
$$\varepsilon_1 \text{ and } \varepsilon_2 = \text{disturbance terms.}$$

Assume that ε_{1t} and ε_{2t} have zero means, constant variances, are not autocorrelated, and are independent of $(UN)_t$ and $\dot{M}_t$.

   a. Are the above equations identified? Explain.

   b. Outline an estimation procedure for the identified equation.

3. Consider the model

$$L_t = a_0 + a_1 W_t + a_2 S_t + u_{1t}, \qquad (1)$$

$$W_t = b_0 + b_1 L_t + b_2 P_t + u_{2t}, \qquad (2)$$

where

$$L = \text{the amount of labor employed,}$$
$$W = \text{the wage rate,}$$
$$S = \text{sales, and}$$
$$P = \text{a measure of the productivity of labor.}$$

   a. Obtain the reduced-form equations for L_t and W_t.

   b. Outline a technique for estimating equation (1).

4. Assume that the demand for shoes by an individual is described by

$$D_{it} = a_0 + a_1 P_t + a_2 D_{i(t-1)} + u_{it}, \tag{1}$$

where D_{it} is the ith individual's demand for shoes at time t, and P_t is the price he faces. Suppose that

$$u_{it} = \rho u_{i(t-1)} + \varepsilon_{it}, \qquad -1 < \rho < 1,$$

where ε_{it} has a zero mean, a constant variance, is not autocorrelated, and is independent of P_t and all of its lagged values.

a. Argue intuitively that the lagged dependent variable, $D_{i(t-1)}$ is correlated with the disturbance term.

b. Assume that equation (1) is not part of a system of equations. Demonstrate that it can nevertheless be estimated by TSLS.

5. Consider the following multiple-regression model:

$$Y_t = b_0 + b_1 X_{1t} + b_2 X_{2t} + u_{1t}, \tag{1}$$

$$X_{2t} = c_0 + c_1 Y_t + u_{2t}. \tag{2}$$

Show that, under our usual assumptions, $E(X_{2t} u_{1t}) \neq 0$.

6. Consider the wage-price model

$$\dot{W}_t = a_0 + a_1 \dot{P}_t + a_2 (UN_t) + \varepsilon_{1t}, \tag{1}$$

$$\dot{P}_t = b_0 + b_1 \dot{W}_t + \varepsilon_{2t}, \tag{2}$$

where

$\dot{W} = $ the percentage change in money wages,
$\dot{P} = $ the percentage changes in prices, and
$UN = $ the rate of unemployment.

a. Show that TSLS will not "work" if we attempt to estimate equation (1).

b. Does the TSLS procedure also break down if we attempt to estimate equation (2)? Explain.

7. Assume the following structural equation, which is part of a system of simultaneous equations:

$$Y_{1t} = b_0 + b_1 X_{1t} + b_2 Y_{2t} + b_3 Y_{3t} + u_{1t},$$

where Y_{1t}, Y_{2t}, and Y_{3t} are endogenous variables, and X_{1t} is a predetermined variable. Suppose that the complete system of which this equation is a member contains ten additional predetermined variables. However, suppose that we have observations on only one of them, say X_2.

a. Is the equation identified? Why or why not?

b. Can we estimate this equation by TSLS? Explain.

8. Consider the two-equation model

$$Y_{1t} = a_1 + b_1 X_t^2 + c_1 Y_{2t} + \varepsilon_{1t}, \tag{1}$$

$$Y_{2t} = a_2 + b_2 X_t + c_2 Y_{1t} + \varepsilon_{2t}, \tag{2}$$

where X_t is a predetermined variable and ε_1 and ε_2 satisfy our standard assumptions.

a. Are both equations identified? Why or why not?

b. Derive the reduced-form equations.

c. Outline a procedure for estimating the first equation in the above model.

9. Suppose that private investment spending is such that

$$I_{it} = a + b_1 r_{it} + b_2 S_{i(t-1)} + u_{it}, \qquad i = 1, \ldots, N,$$

$$r_{it} = r_t + b_3 I_{it} + \varepsilon_{it},$$

where

$$I_{it} = \text{investment expenditures of the } i\text{th firm at time } t,$$
$$r_{it} = \text{the rate of interest it must pay for investment funds,}$$
$$S_{i(t-1)} = \text{its sales in period } t - 1, \text{ and}$$
$$r_t = \text{the economy-wide average interest rate for investment funds.}$$

We assume that these N firms are large so that the level of their investment expenditure affects the interest rate they face. Assume the standard conditions concerning u_{it} and ε_{it}. Assume also that we have *only* cross-sectional data.

a. Discuss whether or not the equations are identified.

b. Obtain the reduced-form equation for I_{it}.

CHAPTER 8
Simultaneous Equation Models That Are Nonlinear

All of the simultaneous equation models discussed in Chapter 7 were linear in the endogenous variables. However, many (if not most) of the models economists consider in practice are not linear in the endogenous variables. For example, many economic models contain wages, say, W, and prices, say, P, as endogenous variables. These models typically also explain the demand for labor in terms of the real wage rate, W/P. Clearly, the real wage variable, W/P, must be explained by the model; it is endogenous if W and P are endogenous. It should also be clear that W/P is a nonlinear function of endogenous variables.

Other examples of nonlinearities in the endogenous variables abound. For instance, total revenue, say, R, is usually defined as the *product* (PQ), where P is price, and Q is the number of units sold. Again, if P and Q are endogenous, models that also incorporate total revenues (perhaps as a component of profits) must be regarded as nonlinear. Similar considerations relate to models that incorporate the wage bill, defined as the *product* of the wage rate, W, and the units of labor purchased per unit time, L. Likewise, note that most macro models explain some measure of the general level of prices (e.g., a GNP deflator), as well as the real (deflated) and current values of most, or all, of the economic variables considered. As an example, such models usually explain GNP in current, as well as in constant, dollars. Our discussion thus far suggests that models that contain both current and price deflated values of endogenous variables must be regarded as nonlinear in the endogenous variables, if the price deflator is endogenous.

Still further examples of nonlinearities stem from production functions that are nonlinear in the endogenous factors of production; from Phillips curves, which are formulated in terms of the reciprocal of the endogenously determined unemployment rate; and finally, from the very definition of many of the variables economists seek to explain. For instance, the unemployment rate is defined as the *ratio* of the number of unemployed workers to the labor force. If macro models seek to explain the size of the labor force, as well as the number of unemployed workers, they must be regarded as nonlinear.

In this chapter, we shall discuss the analysis of such models. In particular, we shall extend our analysis of the identification problem and the application of two-stage least squares to models that incorporate nonlinear forms of the endogenous variables, but are linear in the parameters.* In the Appendix to this chapter we extend our results concerning estimation to models that also contain nonlinearities in the parameters. We should caution the reader that nonlinearities do introduce some further complexities into the analysis. Consequently, some parts of this chapter may require extra concentration. However, the analysis draws directly and *solely* on the material from the preceding chapters; in fact, it may even prove a little surprising to see how far we can go on the basis of this material.

8.1 THE ANALYTIC FRAMEWORK

First, we must define more formally the type of nonlinear model with which the analysis is concerned. In so doing, we shall not set forth the most general form of model but, instead, the most typical. Most of the models considered in practice should fit into our framework of analysis. We start with a two-equation model and then generalize the results.

A TWO-EQUATION ILLUSTRATION

Consider the following illustrative model:

$$Y_{1t} = a_0 + a_1 Y_{2t} + a_2[Y_{1t}Y_{2t}/X_{1t}] + a_3 X_{2t} + \varepsilon_{1t}, \tag{8.1}$$

$$Y_{2t} = b_0 + b_1 Y_{1t} + b_2[(Y_{1t} - 2Y_{2t})^2 e^{X_{3t}}] + b_3 X_{4t} + \varepsilon_{2t}, \tag{8.2}$$

where X_{1t}, X_{2t}, X_{3t}, and X_{4t} are exogenous variables, ε_{1t} and ε_{2t} are disturbance terms, and Y_{1t} and Y_{2t} are the variables that the model is supposed to explain (i.e., they are endogenous). Assume that ε_{1t} and ε_{2t} are independent of the exogenous variables X_{1s}, X_{2s}, X_{3s}, and X_{4s} for all t and s, and that $E(\varepsilon_{it}) = 0$, and $E(\varepsilon_{it}^2) = \sigma_i^2$, for $i = 1, 2$. Also, assume that ε_{1t} and ε_{2t} are independent of ε_{1s} and ε_{2s} for all $t \neq s$, so that neither disturbance term is autocorrelated.

There are two central features concerning the model described in (8.1) and (8.2) that should be noted. The first is that the model is *linear* in the regression parameters $a_0, \ldots, a_3, b_0 \ldots, b_3$. The second is that the model is nonlinear in the endogenous variables because of the variables that appear in brackets

---

* The classic reference for the identification problem in both linear and nonlinear econometric models is F. Fisher, *The Identification Problem in Econometrics* (New York: McGraw-Hill, 1966). Our discussion of the identification problem will draw heavily on H. H. Kelejian, "Identification of Nonlinear Systems: An Interpretation of Fisher," Princeton University, Econometric Research Program, Research Paper No. 22 (Revised), 1970. Our discussion of the two-stage least-squares procedure will follow H. H. Kelejian, "Two Stage Least Squares and Econometric Models Linear in the Parameters but Nonlinear in the Endogenous Variables," *Journal of the American Statistical Association* June 1971, vol. 66, pp. 373–374.

corresponding to the parameters a_2 and b_2. It should be noted that the values of these bracketed variables can be determined from the values of the variables Y_{1t}, Y_{2t}, X_{1t}, X_{3t}. Alternatively, the variables in brackets can be viewed as known functions of these four variables. By a known function we mean a function whose form is known and which does not contain unknown parameters. For example, the bracketed variable corresponding to b_2 is *not* of the form $[(Y_{1t} - \gamma_1 Y_{2t})^2 e^{\gamma_2 X_{3t}}]$, where γ_1 and γ_2 are parameters whose values are *unknown*. If it were, the model would not be linear in the parameters.

Assume now that, for any given set of values of the parameters in (8.1) and (8.2) which is consistent with the theory of that model (e.g., the marginal propensity to consume cannot be negative), the model can be solved for the endogenous variables, Y_{1t} and Y_{2t}, in terms of the exogenous variables, X_{1t}, ..., X_{4t}, and the disturbance terms, ε_{1t} and ε_{2t}. For some sets of possible parameter values, we may be able to obtain an explicit solution by simple means, for example, if $a_2 = b_2 = 0$. For other sets of parameter values, we may only be able to obtain a numerical solution; for example, we may only be able to deduce the numerical values of Y_{1t} and Y_{2t} that correspond to a particular set of numerical values of the exogenous variables and the disturbance terms. In either case, however, the values of the endogenous variables, Y_{1t} and Y_{2t}, as dictated by the model, will depend on the values of the exogenous variables and the disturbance terms. We shall henceforth refer to this phenomenon by saying that the solution of the model for the endogenous variables depends on, or is a function of, the exogenous variables and the disturbance terms.

Because the solution of (8.1) and (8.2) for Y_{1t} and Y_{2t} depends in part on the disturbance terms, one cannot generally assume that these endogenous variables and the disturbance terms are independent, or even uncorrelated.* This conclusion is evident from the discussion in Chapter 7. Consider now the bracketed variable corresponding to a_2. The value of this variable depends on Y_{1t}, Y_{2t}, and X_{1t}. Since the values of Y_{1t} and Y_{2t} depend in part on the disturbance terms, it follows that the value of this bracketed variable itself depends in part on the disturbance terms. In consequence, it will, in general, be correlated with the disturbance terms. Similarly, we may conclude that the bracketed variable corresponding to b_2 will usually be correlated with the disturbance terms. To generalize further, we conclude that any function of one or more endogenous variables will, in general, be correlated with the disturbance terms.

---

* For more advanced readers we note that a set of nonlinear equations generally has more than one solution. Our discussion will proceed under the assumption that, if the model's equations define more than one solution, all but one of them are ruled out by certain (unstated) restrictions on the variables in the model, for example, prices cannot be negative, and so on. As an illustration, the set of two equations $x^2 + y^2 = 20$, $|x| = 2|y|$ has four possible solutions, namely, $(x = 4, y = 2)$, $(x = -4, y = 2)$, $(x = 4, y = -2)$, and $(x = -4, y = -2)$. If we assert, however, that both x and y must be positive, the only solution of the model is $x = 4$, $y = 2$.

SOME CLARIFYING COMMENTS

Before proceeding we should be explicit about a few points that may not be evident to all of our readers. Suppose a model has M endogenous variables, $Y_{1t}, \ldots, Y_{Mt}$, and G exogenous variables, $X_{1t}, \ldots, X_{Gt}$. Let it also have M disturbance terms, $\varepsilon_{1t}, \ldots, \varepsilon_{Mt}$. As in the case above, assume that the model can be solved for the endogenous variables in terms of the exogenous variables and the disturbance terms. Denote these solutions as

$$Y_{1t} = F_1(X_{1t}, \ldots, X_{Gt}, \varepsilon_{1t}, \ldots, \varepsilon_{Mt})$$

$$\cdot \quad \cdot \quad \cdot \quad \cdot \quad \cdot \quad \cdot$$
$$\cdot \quad \cdot \quad \cdot \quad \cdot \quad \cdot \quad \cdot$$
$$\cdot \quad \cdot \quad \cdot \quad \cdot \quad \cdot \quad \cdot$$

$$Y_{Mt} = F_M(X_{1t}, \ldots, X_{Gt}, \varepsilon_{1t}, \ldots, \varepsilon_{Mt}).$$

In general, if the model is a nonlinear one, the functions above describing the dependence of the endogenous variables on the disturbance terms and the exogenous variables *will not be linear*. Suppose the model also contains $(Y_{1t}^2 + Y_{3t}Y_{5t})$—or, more generally, $K(Y_{1t}, \ldots, Y_{Mt})$—as a variable. Then, the model solution values for these variables are, respectively, $F_{1t}^2 + F_{3t}F_{5t}$, and $K(F_{1t}, \ldots, F_{Mt})$, where we have simplified notation by denoting $F_i(X_{1t}, \ldots, X_{Gt}, \varepsilon_{1t}, \ldots, \varepsilon_{Mt})$ as F_{it}. Clearly, in a nonlinear model, functions of the endogenous variables will *not* depend on the disturbance terms and the exogenous variables in a linear manner! They will, however, typically be correlated with the disturbance terms, because their values *in part* are determined by the values of the disturbance terms.

For purposes of estimation, we may define a variable to be endogenous if it is correlated with the disturbance terms. Therefore, we shall refer to constructed variables that are functions of one or more endogenous variables as *functions of endogenous variables*, or simply as *endogenous variables*. Note that it is irrelevant whether or not a function of endogenous variables also involves exogenous variables; the constructed variable will generally be correlated with the disturbance terms solely because of its dependence on one or more endogenous variables. In passing, we note that the two-equation model in (8.1) and (8.2) determines all *four* of its endogenous variables in terms of the exogenous variables and the disturbance terms; for example, if Y_{1t} and Y_{2t} can be expressed in terms of exogenous variables and disturbance terms, so can the constructed variable $[Y_{1t}Y_{2t}/X_{1t}]$.

ANOTHER ILLUSTRATION

As a point of contrast to (8.1) and (8.2), consider the two-equation model

$$\log(Y_{1t}) = a_0 + a_1 Y_{2t}^3 + a_2 X_{1t} + \varepsilon_{1t}, \tag{8.3}$$

$$Y_{2t}^3 = b_0 + b_1[\log(Y_{1t})] + b_2 X_{2t} + \varepsilon_{2t}, \tag{8.4}$$

where Y_{1t} and Y_{2t} are endogenous variables, X_{1t} and X_{2t} are exogenous variables, and ε_{1t} and ε_{2t} are disturbance terms. Assume that the disturbance terms have all of the desirable properties described in reference to the model above.

At first glance, this model may appear to be nonlinear. However, for purposes of estimation, it is linear. To see this, define the variables Z_{1t} and Z_{2t} as

$$Z_{1t} = \log(Y_{1t}), \quad Z_{2t} = Y_{2t}^{3}. \tag{8.5}$$

Then, in terms of these variables the model in (8.3) and (8.4) can be expressed as

$$Z_{1t} = a_0 + a_1 Z_{2t} + a_2 X_{1t} + \varepsilon_{1t}, \tag{8.6}$$

$$Z_{2t} = b_0 + b_1 Z_{1t} + b_2 X_{2t} + \varepsilon_{2t}. \tag{8.7}$$

In this form the model is seen to be a two-equation model which is *linear* in the parameters and in the two endogenous variables, Z_{1t} and Z_{2t}. Therefore, its parameters can be estimated in terms of the procedures described in Chapter 7. We conclude that, for purposes of estimation, the model in (8.3) and (8.4) is linear.

The model in (8.3) and (8.4) can be reduced, for estimation purposes, to a linear model because the number of equations, namely, two, is equal to the number of endogenous variables. Now recall that the two-equation model in (8.1) and (8.2) has *four* endogenous variables. Because the number of endogenous variables in (8.1) and (8.2) *exceeds* the number of equations, it is not possible to express that model as a linear model in two endogenous variables. For example, suppose we define Z_{3t} and Z_{4t} as

$$Z_{3t} = \left[\frac{Y_{1t}Y_{2t}}{X_{1t}}\right]; \quad Z_{4t} = (Y_{1t} - 2Y_{2t})^2 e^{X_{3t}}. \tag{8.8}$$

Then, if the model in (8.1) and (8.2) is to be expressed as a two-equation model in terms of the two endogenous variables Z_{3t} and Z_{4t}, the variables Y_{1t} and Y_{2t} must also be expressed in terms of Z_{3t} and Z_{4t}. Y_{1t} and Y_{2t} can be expressed in terms of Z_{3t} and Z_{4t} (and X_{1t} and X_{3t}) by solving the equations in (8.8) for Y_{1t} and Y_{2t}. However, if this is done, Y_{1t} and Y_{2t} will turn out to be nonlinear in Z_{3t} and Z_{4t}. For purposes of illustration, express these relationships as

$$Y_{1t} = g_1(Z_{3t}, Z_{4t}, X_{1t}, X_{3t}), \tag{8.9}$$
$$Y_{2t} = g_2(Z_{3t}, Z_{4t}, X_{1t}, X_{3t}),$$

and note that the functions in (8.9) are not linear in Z_{3t} and Z_{4t}. Then, the model in (8.1) and (8.2) can be expressed in terms of Z_{3t} and Z_{4t} as

$$g_1(Z_{3t}, Z_{4t}, X_{1t}, X_{3t}) = a_0 + a_1 g_2(Z_{3t}, Z_{4t}, X_{1t}, X_{3t}) \\ + a_2 Z_{3t} + a_3 X_{2t} + \varepsilon_{1t}, \tag{8.10}$$

$$g_2(Z_{3t}, Z_{4t}, X_{1t}, X_{3t}) = b_0 + b_1 g_1(Z_{3t}, Z_{4t}, X_{1t}, X_{3t}) \\ + b_2 Z_{4t} + b_3 X_{4t} + \varepsilon_{2t}. \tag{8.11}$$

Clearly, the model in (8.10) and (8.11) is not a linear model in the endogenous variables Z_{3t} and Z_{4t}.

A GENERALIZATION

The results above suggest that, despite appearances, a model that has the same number of endogenous variables as equations can be viewed as a linear model for purposes of estimation; if the number of endogenous variables *exceeds* the number of equations, the model will not, in general, reduce to a linear model. More formally, consider a simultaneous equation model that has K equations and which uniquely determines the values of all of its endogenous variables in terms of its exogenous variables and disturbance terms.* Assume that this model is *linear* in the parameters. Suppose, moreover, that the number of variables appearing in the model that depend on one or more of the endogenous variables is K^*. Finally, assume that none of these K^* variables can be expressed as a linear combination of the others (i.e., they are not multicollinear).** Then the model is nonlinear if $K^* > K$. If $K^* = K$ the model can be expressed as a linear model for purposes of estimation. We do not consider the case in which $K^* < K$, because this corresponds to an overdetermined system (i.e., there are more equations than variables). Unless some of the equations are redundant, such models are not, in general, internally consistent.†

8.2 THE IDENTIFICATION PROBLEM

AN ILLUSTRATION

Consider the following two-equation model

$$Y_{1t} = a_0 + a_1 g(Y_{2t}) + a_2 X_t + \varepsilon_{1t}, \tag{8.12}$$

$$Y_{2t} = b_0 + b_1 Y_{1t} + \varepsilon_{2t}, \tag{8.13}$$

where $g(Y_{2t})$ is a known nonlinear function of Y_{2t}, and where X_t is an exogenous variable which is assumed to be independent of the disturbance terms, ε_{1t} and ε_{2t}, for all t and s. Assume that the disturbance terms satisfy all of the desirable properties: they have a zero mean and a constant variance, and are not autocorrelated.

---

* Again, a nonlinear model will uniquely determine the values of all of its endogenous variables if all solutions but one can be ruled out because of the various restrictions the variables must satisfy.

** This assumption is made in order to rule out redundancies. For example, without this assumption, a model containing Y_{1t}, Y_{2t}, $2Y_{1t}$, and $3Y_{2t}$ would be listed as containing four endogenous variables.

† As a simple illustration, the *two*-equation system, in *one* variable: $3 + 2X = 5$, $X + 10 = 15$, is not consistent because the first equation implies $X = 1$ while the second implies $X = 5$.

The discussion in Chapter 7 suggests that the parameters of (8.12) are not identified. The reason for this is that (8.12) contains one endogenous variable on the right-hand side of the equation, but it does not exclude any predetermined variables. Therefore, according to the argument of Chapter 7, if an attempt is made to estimate (8.12) by TSLS, the effort will fail because of perfect multicollinearity in the second stage of the procedure. However, the model in (8.12) and (8.13) is not a linear model, and so the results of Chapter 7 concerning identification do not apply. In particular, we shall see that, under some fairly general further assumptions, equation (8.12) is identified.

To see this, assume that the two-equation model in (8.12) and (8.13) uniquely determines the values of the endogenous variables, Y_{1t} and Y_{2t}, in terms of the exogenous variable, X_t, and the disturbance terms, ε_{1t} and ε_{2t}. To simplify notation, let

$$Z_t = g(Y_{2t}). \tag{8.14}$$

Then, if the model determines the value of Y_{2t} in terms of X_t, ε_{1t}, and ε_{2t}, it also determines the value of Z_t in terms of these variables. Denote this dependence as

$$Z_t = h(X_t, \varepsilon_{1t}, \varepsilon_{2t}), \tag{8.15}$$

and note that, since the model is nonlinear, the function h in (8.15) will generally be nonlinear.

If ε_{1t} and ε_{2t} were identically (always) equal to zero, Z_t would be completely determined by X_t. Therefore, if observations on Z_t and X_t were graphed, a curve would be traced whose equation could be obtained from (8.15) by setting $\varepsilon_{1t} = \varepsilon_{2t} = 0$, namely,

$$Z_t = h(X_t, 0, 0). \tag{8.16}$$

As an illustration, we have traced such a curve in Figure 8.1. The curve is purposely drawn in a nonlinear fashion, because the nonlinear model of (8.12)

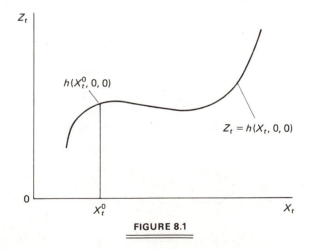

FIGURE 8.1

and (8.13) implies that, in general, the dependence of the variable $Z_t = g(Y_{2t})$ on the exogenous variable X_t will not be linear.

Consider now the more typical case in which ε_{1t} and ε_{2t} are not identically equal to zero. In this case, (8.15) implies that Z_t will not be completely determined by X_t. However, again by reference to (8.15), Z_t will not be independent of X_t because X_t is one of the elements determining Z_t. For purposes of illustration, assume that we have an infinite sample of observations on Z_t and X_t. Then, our discussion indicates that if these observations are plotted, the scatter of points will indicate a curve that reflects the partial dependence of Z_t on X_t. Such a scatter diagram is depicted in Figure 8.2.

Regarding Figure 8.2, note first that all of the points in the diagram do not lie on the indicated curve, because X_t is only one of the factors determining Z_t. Second, there are many ways in which one can trace out a curve in terms of a scatter diagram. The curve indicated in Figure 8.2 is the curve that gives the mean value of Z_t corresponding to given values of X_t. For example, corresponding to $X_t = X_t^0$, the mean value of Z_t is given by the height of the curve, $G(X_t^0)$. Third, we have purposely drawn the curve in Figure 8.2 differently from the curve in Figure 8.1. The reason for this is that, in general, the curve as defined in Figure 8.1 will be different from the "mean-relationship" curve in Figure 8.2. Although this may appear to be counterintuitive, it can easily be explained. For example, corresponding to the given value of X_t, namely, X_t^0, the mean value of Z_t is, from (8.15),

$$E(Z_t) = E[h(X_t^0, \varepsilon_{1t}, \varepsilon_{2t})]. \tag{8.17}$$

If the function h in (8.17) is nonlinear in ε_{1t} and ε_{2t}, our results in Appendix B to Chapter 1, most specifically (1B.12), imply that

$$E[h(X_t^0, \varepsilon_{1t}, \varepsilon_{2t})] \neq h(X_t^0, E(\varepsilon)_{1t}, E(\varepsilon)_{2t}) = h(X_t^0, 0, 0). \tag{8.18}$$

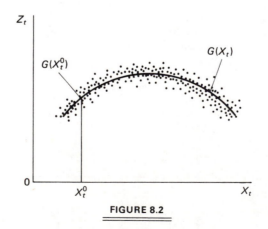

FIGURE 8.2

Therefore, the value of the curve in Figure 8.1 corresponding to $X_t = X_t^0$, namely, $h(X_t^0, 0, 0)$, is not equal to the corresponding value of the curve in Figure 8.2, which is

$$G(X_t^0) = E[h(X_t^0, \varepsilon_{1t}, \varepsilon_{2t})]. \tag{8.19}$$

As stated, the curve in Figure 8.2 gives the mean value of Z_t corresponding to any value of X_t. Define

$$V_t = Z_t - G(X_t). \tag{8.20}$$

Then, the mean value of V_t corresponding to any given value of X_t is zero. For instance, when X_t is X_t^0, the mean value of V_t is

$$E[V_t] = E[Z_t] - G(X_t^0) = G(X_t^0) - G(X_t^0) = 0. \tag{8.21}$$

We recall from Section 6.3 of Chapter 6 that, since the mean of V_t is zero *for any given value of X_t*, the overall mean of V_t is also zero, and V_t is uncorrelated with X_t.

The terms in (8.20) can be rearranged as

$$Z_t = G(X_t) + V_t. \tag{8.22}$$

The relationship in (8.22) is very similar to those from which we derived the polynomial regression models in Section 5.3. Specifically, from (8.22) we see that the tth value of Z_t is related in a nonlinear way to the tth value of an independent variable, X_t, and to a term, V_t, which can be viewed as a disturbance term in that it has a mean value of zero corresponding to any given value of the independent variable. For purposes of illustration, assume, as we did in Section 5.3, that

$$G(X_t) \doteq b_0 + b_1 X_t + b_2 X_t^2 + \cdots + b_k X_t^k. \tag{8.23}$$

Then, from (8.22), we have

$$Z_t \doteq b_0 + b_1 X_t + b_2 X_t^2 + \cdots + b_k X_t^k + V_t. \tag{8.24}$$

For simplicity of presentation we now assume that (8.23), and therefore (8.24), holds as an *equality*. We stress that this assumption is made only for purposes of exposition; it will become evident that the results below do not depend on this assumption.

Assume now that we have n observations on the variables of the model (8.12) and (8.13). Then, since Z_t is a known function of Y_{2t}, namely, $Z_t = g(Y_{2t})$, we can obtain n observations on Z_t. We could therefore view (8.24) as a regression model. In terms of this model, the calculated value of Z_t is

$$\hat{Z}_t = \hat{b}_0 + \hat{b}_1 X_t + \hat{b}_2 X_t^2 + \cdots + \hat{b}_k X_t^k, \tag{8.25}$$

where $\hat{b}_0, \ldots, \hat{b}_k$ are obtained in the usual manner.

Consider now the problem of estimation concerning (8.12). The endogenous variable on the right-hand side is $g(Y_{2t})$, which is our Z_t variable. To apply the TSLS procedure to (8.12), we could replace Z_t by its calculated value given in (8.25), namely, $\hat{Z}_t$. If we do this, the second stage will *not be characterized by perfect multicollinearity*. Since the dependence of $\hat{Z}_t$ on X_t is nonlinear in form, $\hat{Z}_t$ will not be a perfect linear function of X_t. The suggestion is that the parameters of (8.12) can be consistently estimated, and so the equation is identified!

A REFINEMENT

In the analysis above, we assumed that the mean function $G(X_t)$ in (8.22) can be expressed as a polynomial in X_t. In this section, we demonstrate that this assumption is not necessary for the identification, and therefore the consistent estimation, of equation (8.12). We also demonstrate that, if the model in (8.12) and (8.13) were *linear* in that $g(Y_{2t}) = Y_{2t}$, equation (8.12) could *not* be consistently estimated in terms of a procedure similar to that described above. More explicitly, assume $g(Y_{2t}) = Y_{2t}$. Also assume that Y_{2t} is regressed on the powers of X_t, say, X_t, X_t^2, ..., X_t^k, and the calculated value of Y_{2t} is correspondingly obtained as, say,

$$\hat{Y}_{2t} = \hat{a}_0 + \hat{a}_1 X_t + \cdots + \hat{a}_k X_t^k. \tag{8.26}$$

Then, if the TSLS procedure is applied to (8.12) with Y_{2t} replaced by $\hat{Y}_{2t}$, the resulting estimators will not be consistent!

It will be convenient first to demonstrate the latter proposition, and then the former. To begin, note that, if $g(Y_{2t}) = Y_{2t}$, the solution of the linear model (8.12) and (8.13) for Y_{2t} (i.e., the reduced form equation) may be expressed as

$$Y_{2t} = \pi_0 + \pi_1 X_t + \psi_t, \tag{8.27}$$

where, for any given value of X_t, the mean of the variable ψ_t is zero, $E(\psi_t) = 0$.* Thus, for the linear case, the mean value of Y_{2t} corresponding to a given value of X_t is linear in X_t, namely, $(\pi_0 + \pi_1 X_t)$. It follows that the regression model relating Y_{2t} to X_t, X_t^2, ..., X_t^k can be expressed as

$$Y_{2t} = \pi_0 + \pi_1 X_t + \pi_2 X_t^2 + \cdots + \pi_k X_t^k + \psi_t, \tag{8.28}$$

where $\pi_2 = \pi_3 = \cdots = \pi_k = 0$.

Let the calculated value of Y_{2t} from the regression of Y_{2t} on X_t, X_t^2, ..., X_t^k be

$$\hat{Y}_{2t} = \hat{\pi}_0 + \hat{\pi}_1 X_t + \hat{\pi}_2 X_t^2 + \cdots + \hat{\pi}_k X_t^k. \tag{8.29}$$

Then, from (8.28) and the assumptions of the model (8.12) and (8.13), we have $E(\hat{\pi}_2) = E(\hat{\pi}_3) = \cdots = E(\hat{\pi}_k) = 0$.** It can also be shown, under some further

---

* It should be clear from Section 7.4 that ψ_t is just a linear combination of the disturbance terms ε_{1t} and ε_{2t}.

** The model in (8.28) corresponds to the general linear model we considered in Chapter 4. In that chapter we showed, for the model considered, that the parameter estimators are unbiased.

and reasonable technical assumptions, that $\hat{\pi}_0$, $\hat{\pi}_1$, ..., $\hat{\pi}_k$ are consistent estimators of their respective parameters; therefore, $\hat{\pi}_2$, ..., $\hat{\pi}_k$ converge in probability to *zero*. The implications of this are as follows. If $g(Y_{2t}) = Y_{2t}$, *and* the sample size is infinite, $\hat{Y}_{2t}$ will converge to $(\pi_0 + \pi_1 X_t)$ with probability equal to one. Therefore, if the model is linear and if the sample size is infinite, the TSLS procedure, with Y_{2t} replaced by $\hat{Y}_{2t}$ in (8.29), will be characterized by perfect multicollinearity in the second stage with probability equal to one. The method will break down, and so the procedure is not consistent. Note, however, that in finite samples, $\hat{\pi}_2$, $\hat{\pi}_3$, ..., $\hat{\pi}_k$ will generally *not* be zero. Therefore, if the sample size is finite, one will be able to implement the TSLS procedure, because $\hat{Y}_{2t}$ in (8.29) will not be perfectly multicollinear with the constant term and with X_t. However, we stress that the *procedure* is not consistent, because the consistency property relates to the case of an infinite sample.

Consider now the nonlinear case in which $g(Y_{2t}) \neq Y_{2t}$. We have already shown that, in this case, $g(Y_{2t})$ may be expressed [see (8.22)] as

$$g(Y_{2t}) = G(X_t) + V_t, \tag{8.30}$$

where the mean value of V_t corresponding to any value of X_t is zero. We have also indicated that the mean function $G(X_t)$ will typically be nonlinear in X_t.

If $g(Y_{2t})$ is regressed on the first k powers of X_t, and if the sample size were infinite, the resulting estimated curve, say,

$$\widehat{g(Y_{2t})} = \hat{a}_0 + \hat{a}_1 X_t + \cdots + \hat{a}_k X_t^k, \tag{8.31}$$

would be the best approximating polynomial of degree k to the curve $G(X_t)$.* If $G(X_t)$ is nonlinear, the best approximating polynomial will generally not be a linear one. Indeed, it will typically be the case that the approximation will

---

*To the more formal readers, denote the kth-degree polynomial in X_t as $P(X_t, \alpha)$ where α denotes its parameters. Then, the least-squares procedure will pick α to minimize

$$L = \sum_{t=1}^{n} [g(Y_{2t}) - P(X_t, \alpha)]^2,$$

or, for purposes of presentation, L/n. Recalling that $V_t = g(Y_{2t}) - G(X_t)$, L/n can be expressed as

$$\frac{L}{n} = \frac{\sum [g(Y_{2t}) - G(X_t) + G(X_t) - P(X_t, \alpha)]^2}{n}$$

$$= \frac{\sum V_t^2}{n} + 2\frac{\sum D_t V_t}{n} + \frac{\sum D_t^2}{n}$$

where $D_t = G(X_t) - P(X_t, \alpha)$. Note that the value of D_t is determined by the value of X_t. In reference to (8.30) we saw that the mean value of V_t is zero, corresponding to any value of X_t. It follows that the mean value of V_t is zero corresponding to any value of D_t. Our discussion in Section 6.3 indicates that V_t is, therefore, uncorrelated with D_t; because of this, it can be shown, under reasonable further assumptions, that the probability limit of the cross-product term above is zero. Therefore, it should be clear that, in the infinite sample case, L/n will be minimized by choosing α to minimize $\sum D_t^2/n$, since this is the only component of L/n that involves α.

improve as higher powers of the polynomial are considered. It follows that, if the sample size is infinite, $\widehat{g(Y_{2t})}$ in (8.31) will not, in general, reduce to a linear function in X_t. Consequently, we would not expect the TSLS procedure to collapse in the infinite sample case.

A RULE FOR IDENTIFICATION OF NONLINEAR MODELS

By now the reader should be convinced that the rules for identification of linear models cannot be applied, without modification, to nonlinear models. We now give the corresponding rules for nonlinear models. Then, we shall give illustrations that suggest that the rules are plausible.

Consider an M equation model that is linear in parameters, but nonlinear in the endogenous variables. Each equation of this model will usually relate, or be associated with, a given economic variable. This variable typically appears on the left-hand side of the equation and its coefficient is, implicitly, unity. We shall refer to these variables as *basic endogenous variables*. For example, the basic endogenous variables of the model in (8.12) and (8.13) are Y_{1t} and Y_{2t}. Let us denote all of the other endogenous variables that appear in the model as *additional endogenous variables*. For example, the model of (8.12) and (8.13) contains only one additional endogenous variable, namely, $g(Y_{2t})$. Our discussion in Section 8.1 implies that, if a model does not contain any additional endogenous variables, the model is, for purposes of estimation, a linear one.

Assume that the disturbance terms of the models have zero means, are not autocorrelated, and are independent of all of the values of the exogenous variables appearing in the model. Assume also that the basic endogenous variables of the model can be expressed in terms of the disturbance terms, the exogenous variables, the lagged endogenous variables (if any), and the *additional endogenous variables*. For example, consider the model given by (8.12) and (8.13). Equation (8.12) is in the required form since a basic endogenous variable does not appear on the right-hand side; a similar expression for Y_{2t} can easily be obtained by simply substituting (8.12) for Y_{1t} in (8.13).

Finally, assume that the solution of the model for the basic endogenous variables in terms of the exogenous variables, the lagged endogenous variables, and the disturbance terms is unique. If this assumption did not hold, the model would be incomplete in that it would not determine, or explain, the variables it was constructed to explain.

Under these conditions and a few additional technical assumptions, it can be shown that the parameters of a given equation of the model, say, the ith, can be consistently estimated, and therefore are identified, if

$$A_{1i} \geq A_{2i}, \tag{8.32}$$

where A_{2i} is the number of *basic endogenous variables* appearing on the right-hand side of the ith equation and A_{1i} is the number of *predetermined variables and additional endogenous variables* appearing in the model but not appearing in the ith equation. In nonlinear systems such as the ones we are considering, a predetermined variable is defined to be any variable appearing in the model that is not correlated with the current values of the disturbance terms. Therefore, a predetermined variable would be any variable appearing in the model whose value does not depend on the contemporaneous values of one or more of the basic endogenous variables (e.g., its value would only depend on exogenous variables and lagged endogenous variables).

Taken by itself, the counting rule in (8.32) is a necessary condition for the identification of the ith equation of the model under consideration. This means that, if the ith equation is identified, (8.32) holds, but (8.32) in and of itself cannot guarantee that the ith equation is, in fact, identified. In nonlinear models, the "additional technical" conditions that must be satisfied in order to guarantee that a given equation of the model is identified are difficult to determine and would rarely be considered in practice. The typical procedure would be to check for (8.32) and then, if (8.32) is satisfied, assume that the further "technical conditions" that are sufficient for identification hold.

The counting rule given in (8.32) differs from the one that would be suggested by the results of Chapter 7, because the additional endogenous variables are grouped with the predetermined variables, rather than with the basic endogenous variables. Before attempting to justify the rule in (8.32), let us apply the rule to the model in (8.12) and (8.13). For equation (8.12) we have (setting $i = 1$) $A_{11} = 0$, since none of the predetermined variables are excluded from the equation, and $A_{21} = 0$, since no basic endogenous variables appear on the right-hand side. Therefore, (8.32) holds $(0 \geq 0)$ and so, assuming the further technical conditions, (8.12) is identified. For equation (8.13) we have $A_{12} = 2$, since $g(Y_{2t})$ and X_t are excluded from (8.13), and $A_{22} = 1$, since Y_{1t} appears on the right-hand side. Therefore, $A_{12} \geq A_{22}$; thus, assuming the further technical conditions, equation (8.13) is also identified.

A JUSTIFICATION OF THE RULE

Let us now see why the additional endogenous variables are grouped with the predetermined variables for purposes of identification. Considering again the simple model in (8.12) and (8.13), we see that this model is nonlinear because of the additional endogenous variable $g(Y_{2t})$. However, we have shown in (8.30) that $g(Y_{2t})$ can be expressed as the sum of two components. The first is a nonlinear function of X_t, namely, $G(X_t)$, and the second, namely, V_t, is a disturbance term that has a mean value of zero corresponding to any given value of X_t. We have also demonstrated that $G(X_t)$ can be approximated in terms of the polynomial regression of $g(Y_{2t})$ on the powers of X_t; see, for example, (8.31).

If (8.30) is subsituted into (8.12), the two-equation model (8.12) and (8.13) can be expressed as

$$Y_{1t} = a_0 + a_1 G(X_t) + a_2 X_t + w_t, \tag{8.33}$$

$$Y_{2t} = b_0 + b_1 Y_{1t} + \varepsilon_{2t}, \tag{8.13}$$

where $w_t = \varepsilon_{1t} + a_1 V_t$. Since w_t is just a linear combination of ε_{1t} and V_t, it can be regarded as a disturbance term that has a mean value of zero corresponding to any given value of X_t. Therefore, w_t is not correlated with either X_t or $G(X_t)$.

Equations (8.33) and (8.13) can be regarded as a two-equation *linear* model in the dependent variables Y_{1t} and Y_{2t}, which contains the constant term, $G(X_t)$, and X_t as predetermined variables. Note that this model contains the *same regression parameters* as the original model (8.12) and (8.13), namely, a_0, a_1, a_2, b_0, and b_1. Also note that, aside from the disturbance terms, it can be obtained from the original model by simply replacing the additional endogenous variable $g(Y_{2t})$ by its "mean function" in X_t, namely, $G(X_t)$. It should be clear that, if (8.33) and (8.13) are identified, then (8.12) and (8.13) must also be identified—they have the same parameters.

For purposes of presentation, we shall continue our discussion by assuming that observations on $G(X_t)$ can be determined once X_t is observed. This assumption is not necessary, but it does simplify the discussion. One way to rationalize this assumption is to suppose that $G(X_t)$ can be perfectly approximated by a kth degree polynomial in X_t, and that this polynomial can be consistently estimated by regressing $g(Y_{2t})$ on the powers of X_t. For example, under these conditions, the value of $G(X_t)$ would be determined from that of X_t [see (8.31)] as

$$G(X_t) = \hat{a}_0 + \hat{a}_1 X_t + \cdots + \hat{a}_k X_t^k. \tag{8.34}$$

Since we are only considering the large sample case, $n = \infty$, we can permit "very large" values of k.

If observations on $G(X_t)$ are available, the model in (8.33) and (8.13) fits directly into the framework of the linear models considered in Chapter 7. Specifically, we see that, assuming the further technical conditions, (8.33) is identified because the right-hand side of the equation contains only predetermined variables. Alternately, in the notation of Chapter 7, (8.33) is identified since $K_2 \geq K_1$, because K_1 and K_2 are both zero, where K_2 is the number of predetermined variables excluded from the equation and K_1 is the number of right-hand side endogenous variables. Note that this result concerning K_1 and K_2 is identical to the result above concerning A_{11} and A_{21}, and can be obtained from the original equations (8.12) and (8.13) by simply classifying the additional endogenous variable $g(Y_{2t})$ as a predetermined variable. Similarly, concerning (8.13) we have $K_2 \geq K_1$, since $K_2 = 2$ [$G(X_t)$ and X_t are excluded] and $K_1 = 1$ (since Y_{1t} is included). Note again that this result can be obtained by simply classifying $g(Y_{2t})$ as a predetermined variable in the original nonlinear model (8.12) and (8.13).

A GENERALIZATION OF THE JUSTIFICATION OF THE IDENTIFICATION RULE

The above result can be generalized. To show this, we first give a result that corresponds to (8.30) for a more general model.

In general, an m equation nonlinear model of the form we are considering may contain many additional endogenous, as well as predetermined, variables, Under very reasonable assumptions, each of these additional endogenous variables can be expressed as the sum of two components. One component [similar to $G(X_t)$ above] will give the mean value of the additional endogenous variable corresponding to given values of the predetermined variables; the other will be a disturbance term whose mean is zero for any given set of values of the predetermined variables. As an illustration, assume that $(Y_{1t} Y_{2t})$ is an additional endogenous variable and X_{1t}, X_{2t}, and X_{3t} are the predetermined variables of a nonlinear model. Then, $(Y_{1t} Y_{2t})$ can, under reasonable assumptions, be expressed as

$$(Y_{1t} Y_{2t}) = H(X_{1t}, X_{2t}, X_{3t}) + \psi_t, \qquad (8.35)$$

where $H(X_{1t}, X_{2t}, X_{3t})$ is a function of X_{1t}, X_{2t}, and X_{3t}, and ψ_t is a variable that has a mean of zero corresponding to any given set of values of X_{1t}, X_{2t}, and X_{3t}. For example, if $H(X_{1t}, X_{2t}, X_{3t}) = (X_{1t}^2 + X_{2t})e^{X_{3t}}$, and if $X_{1t} = 3$, $X_{2t} = 5$, and $X_{3t} = 0$, the corresponding mean value of $(Y_{1t} Y_{2t})$ would be

$$H(3, 5, 0) = (9 + 5)e^0 = 14. \qquad (8.36)$$

Alternatively, assume that we have a sample of observations on X_{1t}, X_{2t}, X_{3t}, Y_{1t}, and Y_{2t}. Assume that the observations on X_{1t}, X_{2t}, and X_{3t} are used to construct observations (as in the illustration above) on H_t where

$$H_t = (X_{1t}^2 + X_{2t})e^{X_{3t}}. \qquad (8.37)$$

Then, if the sample were infinite, a scatter diagram between $Y_{1t} Y_{2t}$ (on the vertical axis) and H_t would consist of points lying about a 45° line which passes through the origin.

Consider now a more general m equation, nonlinear model, which is linear in the parameters. Let the basic endogenous variables be $Y_{1t}, \ldots, Y_{mt}$; let the additional endogenous variables be $g_{1t} = g_1(Y_{1t}, \ldots, Y_{mt})$, $g_{2t} = g_2(Y_{1t}, \ldots, Y_{mt}), \ldots, g_{rt} = g_r(Y_{1t}, \ldots, Y_{mt})$;* and let the predetermined variables be $X_{1t}, \ldots, X_{pt}$. Our arguments above suggest that, under reasonable assumptions, g_{it} may be expressed as

$$g_{it} = H_i(X_{1t}, \ldots, X_{pt}) + \psi_{it} \qquad i = 1, \ldots, r, \qquad (8.38)$$

where the mean of ψ_{it} is zero for any given set of values of $X_{1t}, \ldots, X_{pt}$. The remainder of our argument may now be evident. The nonlinear model we are

---

*The additional endogenous variables may, in general, be functions of the predetermined variables, as well as the basic endogenous variables. We have not accounted for this for purposes of notational simplification.

considering can be reduced to a linear model by simply replacing each additional endogenous variable by its expression in (8.38), and then grouping disturbance terms at the end of the right-hand side of each equation.* The resulting linear model will contain $Y_{1t}, \ldots, Y_{mt}$ as endogenous variables, and $X_{1t}, \ldots, X_{pt}, H_{1t}, \ldots, H_{rt}$, as predetermined variables, where

$$H_{it} = H_i(X_{1t}, \ldots, X_{pt}), \qquad i = 1, \ldots, r. \tag{8.39}$$

This linear model will contain the same regression parameters as the original nonlinear model. If the rules concerning identification given in Chapter 7 are applied to each equation of this linear model, the results will clearly be identical to those that would be obtained by applying (8.32).

There is one point that relates to the "further technical assumptions" we have mentioned, that may be instructive to outline. The results we have just obtained are based on the implicit assumption that the predetermined variables $X_{1t}, \ldots, X_{pt}, H_{1t}, \ldots, H_{mt}$ are not multicollinear. If these variables are multicollinear, our result in (8.32) will not hold. For instance, consider again the linear model that results from the application of (8.38) to the nonlinear model indicated above. Suppose the right-hand side of the first equation of this model contains *three* basic endogenous variables, say, Y_{2t}, Y_{3t}, and Y_{4t}, the constant term, and the predetermined variable, X_{1t}. Suppose this equation excludes X_{2t}, X_{3t}, and H_{1t}, but $H_{1t} = X_{2t} + X_{3t}$. Would we conclude that, subject to "further technical conditions," our equation is identified? Absolutely not! For instance, suppose we were to attempt to apply the TSLS procedure to the estimation of the parameters of the first equation of the linear model. In the first stage, we would attempt to calculate $\hat{Y}_{2t}$, $\hat{Y}_{3t}$, and $\hat{Y}_{4t}$ by regressing each of the variables, Y_{2t}, Y_{3t}, and Y_{4t}, on the constant term, X_{1t}, X_{2t}, X_{3t}, and H_{1t}. However, our first stage efforts would break down because of perfect multicollinearity due to the linear relationship $H_{1t} = X_{2t} + X_{3t}$. Clearly, the equation is not identified because only *two* "nonmulticollinear" variables are omitted from the equation, whereas it contains *three* endogenous variables on the right-hand side.

There are conditions under which one can deduce whether or not the set of predetermined variables $X_{1t}, \ldots, X_{pt}, H_{1t}, \ldots, H_{mt}$ is multicollinear. In addition, the results we have presented can be modified to account for this case. However, the arguments are complex, and this case of perfect

---

*As an example, suppose the first equation is

$$Y_{1t} = a_0 + a_1 Y_{2t} + a_2 g_{1t} + a_3 g_{2t} + a_4 X_{1t} + \varepsilon_{1t};$$

then, (8.38) implies that this equation can be rewritten as

$$Y_{1t} = a_0 + a_1 Y_{2t} + a_2 H_{1t} + a_3 H_{2t} + a_4 X_{1t} + (\varepsilon_{1t} + a_2 \psi_{1t} + a_3 \psi_{2t}),$$

where $(\varepsilon_{1t} + a_2 \psi_{1t} + a_3 \psi_{2t})$ would be taken as a disturbance term.

multicollinearity is only rarely encountered in practice. We therefore conclude the discussion by referring the advanced reader to other sources,* and again remind other readers that our analysis is not quite complete.

8.3 TWO-STAGE LEAST-SQUARES ESTIMATION

In this section we outline a two-stage least-squares procedure for estimating econometric models that are linear in the parameters, but nonlinear in the endogenous variables. The suggested procedure is a direct generalization of the one outlined in Section 8.2.

AN OUTLINE OF THE PROCEDURE

Assume that the ith equation of an econometric model of the sort we are considering is identified. Then, under reasonable conditions, that equation can be consistently estimated by the following procedure:

Step 1. Obtain the calculated values of each basic endogenous variable that appears on the right-hand side of the equation by regressing that variable on the predetermined variables that appear in the model and, *perhaps*, on powers (e.g., the squares, cubes, etc.) of those variables. We shall elaborate below on the issue as to whether or not powers of the predetermined variables should be used.

Step 2. Obtain the calculated values of the additional endogenous variables in the same manner as that described in (1).

Step 3. Replace the basic and the additional endogenous variables in the ith equation with their calculated values, and then estimate the parameters of the equation by least squares.

It can be shown that, under reasonable conditions, the parameter estimators obtained by this two-stage procedure are consistent. We now outline some of the subtleties of the procedure.

Note 1. Typically, if the model contains many predetermined variables, powers of these predetermined variables would not be used in the first stage *unless their absence leads to perfect multicollinearity in the second stage.* The issue is that the desirable property of the estimation procedure, namely, consistency, is a large sample property ($n = \infty$). If the sample size is infinite, it can be shown, under reasonable conditions, that the use of higher and higher

---

* See Chapter 5 of F. Fisher, *The Identification Problem in Econometrics* (New York: McGraw-Hill, 1966), and H. H. Kelejian, "Identification of Nonlinear Systems: An Interpretation of Fisher," Princeton University, Econometric Research Program, Research Paper No. 22 (Revised), 1970. A nice overall review of the issues involved is given in Chapter 8 of S. Goldfeld and R. Quandt, *Nonlinear Methods in Econometrics* (Amsterdam: North Holland, 1972).

powers of the predetermined variables (along with all of their lower powers) in the first stage will lead to smaller and smaller variances of the estimators obtained in the second stage. The rationale is that the polynomial regressions of the first stage become better and better approximations to the corresponding mean functions as higher and higher powers are considered [see (8.31) and footnote on page 293]. However, in practice the sample size is finite. Therefore, the number of independent variables considered in the first stage (which depends in part on the number of powers considered) must be limited.* Indeed, it can be shown that, if so many powers of the variables are considered that the number of variables in the first stage is equal to the number of observations, the two-stage least-squares procedure reduces to ordinary least squares** and, therefore, generates inconsistent estimators. We therefore have a dilemma. To reduce the large sample variance, the number of variables in the first stage should be increased. On the other hand, if the sample size is finite, as the number of variables used in the first stage approaches the sample size, the two-stage least-squares estimators become more and more like the least-squares estimators—which are not consistent! The optimal ratio between the sample size and the number of variables used in the first stage is an open question. However, we suggest that, if possible, the difference between the sample size and the number of variables used in the first stage be at least 20.

Note 2. Let w be the number of predetermined variables in the model, and N the sample size. Then, in (1) it was implicitly assumed that $(N - w) \geq 20$ so that only the number of *powers* of the predetermined variables had to be restricted in the first stage. However, in some large-scale models, w may be at least as large as N, or in any event it may be the case that $(N - w) < 20$. For such models, the number of predetermined variables in linear form, entering the first stage must be restricted for reasons that are identical to those given in (1) above. There are various ways of selecting the set of predetermined variables that will enter the first stage regressions. However, in order for the resulting estimators to be consistent, this set of predetermined variables *must* include all the predetermined variables in the equation being estimated, and must include *at least* as many predetermined variables that are not contained in the equation as there are right-hand-side basic endogenous and additional endogenous variables. Although the model we are now considering is a nonlinear one, the reasons for this are exactly the same as those given in Sections 7.4 and 7.5 of Chapter 7 for the case of linear models. Our following discussion of the issue described in (3) will make this evident.

---

* For example, the regression model $Y_t = b_0 + b_1 X_{1t} + b_2 X_{2t} + b_3 X_{2t}^2 + b_4 X_{2t}^2 + \varepsilon_t$ contains (including the constant term) five independent variables.

** Two-stage least squares will reduce to ordinary least squares if the calculated values of the endogenous variables are *equal* to the corresponding actual values. Ignoring a theoretical subtlety, this is precisely what happens if the sample size is equal to the number of variables (including the constant term) used in the first stage. This result should be evident: if there are N values of a variable that are to be explained in terms of N variables and, therefore, N parameters, the explanation should be perfect.

Note 3. The same set of (first stage) independent variables must be used in obtaining *all* the calculated variables to be used in the second stage. To be explicit, suppose the ith equation is

$$Y_{it} = b_0 + b_1 Y_{1t} + b_2(Y_{2t} Y_{3t}) + b_3 Y_{2t}^2 + a_1 X_{1t} + \varepsilon_{it}. \qquad (8.40)$$

Assume, moreover, that the complete model also contains the predetermined variables X_{2t} and X_{3t}. Let $\hat{Y}_{1t}$ be obtained from the regression*

$$Y_{1t} = \alpha_0 + \alpha_1 X_{1t} + \alpha_2 X_{2t} + \alpha_3 X_{3t} + \alpha_4 X_{1t}^2 + \alpha_5 X_{2t}^2 + V_{1t}. \qquad (8.41)$$

Let $Z_{1t} = (Y_{2t} Y_{3t}))$, and $Z_{2t} = Y_{2t}^2$. Then $\hat{Z}_{1t}$ *must* be obtained by regressing Z_{1t} on the constant term, $X_{1t}, X_{2t}, X_{3t}, X_{1t}^2, X_{2t}^2$. Likewise, $\hat{Z}_{2t}$ *must* be obtained by regressing Z_{2t} on the same set of variables. If the same set of variables is not used in determining $\hat{Y}_{1t}, \hat{Z}_{1t}$, and $\hat{Z}_{2t}$, the estimators obtained in the second stage will not be consistent. We shall indicate below just why this is so.

Note 4. In describing the procedure with respect to (8.40), we indicated that $Z_{1t} = (Y_{2t} Y_{3t})$ and $Z_{2t} = Y_{2t}^2$ should be replaced in the second stage by $\hat{Z}_{1t}$ and $\hat{Z}_{2t}$. It can be shown that, if $(Y_{2t} Y_{3t})$ and Y_{2t}^2 are, instead, replaced by $(\hat{Y}_{2t} \hat{Y}_{3t})$ and $(\hat{Y}_{2t})^2$, where $\hat{Y}_{2t}$ and $\hat{Y}_{3t}$ are obtained by regressing Y_{2t} and Y_{3t} on the first stage regressors, the resulting estimators of the regression parameters obtained from the second stage regression will not be consistent. More generally, let $g_{1t} = g_1(Y_{1t}, \ldots, Y_{mt})$ be an additional endogenous variable that appears as a regressor in the equation of interest. Then, consistent estimation of the regression parameters requires that g_{1t} be replaced in the second stage by $\hat{g}_{1t}$, which is obtained by regressing g_{1t} on the predetermined variables (and perhaps their powers). If, in the second stage, g_{1t} is replaced by $g_1(\hat{Y}_{1t}, \ldots, \hat{Y}_{mt})$, where each $\hat{Y}_{jt}$ is obtained by regressing Y_{jt} on the predetermined variables (and perhaps their powers), the estimators of the regression parameters will not be consistent. Before examining the rationale for this, we return to the explanation of why the same set of first stage regressors must be used in determining the calculated values of all the endogenous variables.

JUSTIFICATIONS FOR SOME OF THE SUBTLETIES

Consider again equation (8.40). Assume that the predetermined variables of the model of which (8.40) is a part are the constant term, X_{1t} and X_{2t}. For purposes of illustration, suppose the variables used in the first stage are the constant term X_{1t}, X_{2t}, X_{1t}^2, and X_{2t}^2. Denote the calculated value of Y_{1t} obtained by regressing Y_{1t} on these variables as $\hat{Y}_{1t}$. Then $\hat{Y}_{1t}$ will be a linear combination of the regressors, say,

$$\hat{Y}_{1t} = \hat{d}_0 + \hat{d}_1 X_{1t} + \hat{d}_2 X_{2t} + \hat{d}_3 X_{1t}^2 + \hat{d}_4 X_{2t}^2, \qquad (8.42)$$

---

* Note (8.41) does not contain X_{3t}^2. We have done this *only* to illustrate that, because the first stage regression contains the squares of X_{1t} and X_{2t}, it *need not* also contain the square of X_{3t}.

where $\hat{a}_0, \ldots, \hat{a}_4$ are the estimated parameters in the first stage regression.

Let $\hat{\phi}_{1t}$ be the estimated residual from the first stage regression, namely,

$$\hat{\phi}_{1t} = Y_{1t} - \hat{Y}_{1t}. \tag{8.43}$$

Then, we know from our results of previous chapters that $\sum (\hat{\phi}_{1t} \hat{Y}_{1t}) = 0$, since the normal equations of the first stage are based on the conditions

$$\sum \hat{\phi}_{1t} = 0, \qquad \sum (\hat{\phi}_{1t} X_{1t}) = 0, \qquad \sum (\hat{\phi}_{1t} X_{2t}) = 0,$$
$$\sum (\hat{\phi}_{1t} X_{1t}^2) = 0, \qquad \sum (\hat{\phi}_{1t} X_{2t}^2) = 0. \tag{8.44}$$

Now let $Z_{1t} = (Y_{2t} Y_{3t})$, and let $\hat{Z}_{1t}$ be the calculated value of Z_{1t} obtained by regressing Z_{1t} on the *same* first stage regressors, namely, the constant term, X_{1t}, X_{2t}, X_{1t}^2, and X_{2t}^2. Let $\hat{\phi}_{2t}$ be the corresponding estimated residual

$$\hat{\phi}_{2t} = Z_{1t} - \hat{Z}_{1t}. \tag{8.45}$$

We note that the regression equation from which $\hat{Z}_{1t}$ is calculated is based on the conditions

$$\sum \hat{\phi}_{2t} = 0, \qquad \sum (\hat{\phi}_{2t} X_{1t}) = 0, \qquad \sum (\hat{\phi}_{2t} X_{2t}) = 0,$$
$$\sum (\hat{\phi}_{2t} X_{1t}^2) = 0, \qquad \sum (\hat{\phi}_{2t} X_{2t}^2) = 0. \tag{8.46}$$

We also note that the conditions in (8.46) imply $\sum (\hat{\phi}_{2t} \hat{Z}_{1t}) = 0$. Finally, let $Z_{2t} = Y_{2t}^2$, and let $\hat{Z}_{2t}$ be the calculated value of Z_{2t} obtained by regressing Z_{2t} on the *same* set of regressors. Let the estimated residual from this regression be

$$\hat{\phi}_{3t} = Z_{2t} - \hat{Z}_{2t}, \tag{8.47}$$

and note that $\hat{\phi}_{3t}$ would satisfy the conditions

$$\sum (\hat{\phi}_{3t}) = 0, \qquad \sum (\hat{\phi}_{3t} X_{1t}) = 0, \qquad \sum (\hat{\phi}_{3t} X_{2t}) = 0,$$
$$\sum (\hat{\phi}_{3t} X_{1t}^2) = 0, \qquad \sum (\hat{\phi}_{3t} X_{2t}^2) = 0. \tag{8.48}$$

Also note that the conditions in (8.48) imply that $\sum (\hat{\phi}_{3t} \hat{Z}_{2t}) = 0$. Moreover, because $\hat{Y}_{1t}, \hat{Z}_{1t}$, and $\hat{Z}_{2t}$ are linear combinations of the *same set of variables*, the conditions in (8.44), (8.46), and (8.48) imply that

$$\sum (\hat{\phi}_{it} \hat{Y}_{1t}) = 0, \qquad \sum (\hat{\phi}_{it} \hat{Z}_{1t}) = 0, \qquad \sum (\hat{\phi}_{it} \hat{Z}_{2t}) = 0, \tag{8.49}$$

for $i = 1, 2, 3$. That is, the sum of the cross products of the residuals from one first stage regression, with the calculated values of a variable from another first stage regression, is zero.

One more preliminary result is needed. In (8.42) the calculated value of Y_{1t} is related to the first stage regressors via the parameter estimators $\hat{a}_0, \ldots, \hat{a}_4$. If the sample were infinite, these estimators would converge to constants. Denote these constants, respectively, as $d_0, \ldots, d_4$. Similarly, denote the "large" sample value of $\hat{Y}_{1t}$ as Y_{1t}^m, where

$$Y_{1t}^m = d_0 + d_1 X_{1t} + d_2 X_{2t} + d_3 X_{1t}^2 + d_4 X_{2t}^2. \tag{8.50}$$

In a corresponding manner, let the large sample values of $\hat{Z}_{1t}$ and $\hat{Z}_{2t}$ be $Z_{1t}{}^m$ and $Z_{2t}{}^m$.

Let us now demonstrate that consistency of the two-stage least-squares estimators requires the same set of regressors in all the first stage regressions. Equations (8.43), (8.45), and (8.47) can be rearranged as

$$Y_{1t} = \hat{Y}_{1t} + \hat{\phi}_{1t},$$
$$Z_{1t} = \hat{Z}_{1t} + \hat{\phi}_{2t}, \qquad (8.51)$$
$$Z_{2t} = \hat{Z}_{2t} + \hat{\phi}_{3t}.$$

Substituting the equations of (8.51) into the equation being estimated, namely, (8.40), yields

$$Y_{it} = b_0 + b_1 \hat{Y}_{1t} + b_2 \hat{Z}_{1t} + b_3 \hat{Z}_{2t} + a_1 X_{1t} + \acute{W}_t, \qquad (8.52)$$

where $W_t = b_1 \hat{\phi}_{1t} + b_2 \hat{\phi}_{2t} + b_3 \hat{\phi}_{3t} + \varepsilon_{it}$. In a manner similar to our discussion in Chapter 7, we note that the only relevant component of the disturbance term W_t is ε_{it}, since

$$\sum W_t = \sum \varepsilon_{it}, \qquad \sum (\hat{Z}_{2t} W_t) = \sum (\hat{Z}_{2t} \varepsilon_{it}),$$
$$\sum (W_t \hat{Y}_{1t}) = \sum (\hat{Y}_{1t} \varepsilon_{it}), \qquad \sum (X_{1t} W_t) = \sum (X_{1t} \varepsilon_{it}), \qquad (8.53)$$
$$\sum (W_t \hat{Z}_{1t}) = \sum (\hat{Z}_{1t} \varepsilon_{it}).$$

Therefore, the suggestion is to estimate (8.52) by our typical procedure which is equivalent to least squares, and which is given by the conditions [see (8.53)]

$$\sum \hat{W}_t = 0, \qquad \text{since } E[\sum \varepsilon_{it}] = 0;$$
$$\sum (\hat{W}_t \hat{Y}_{1t}) = 0, \qquad \text{since } E[\sum (Y_{1t}{}^m \varepsilon_{it})] = 0;$$
$$\sum (\hat{W}_t \hat{Z}_{1t}) = 0, \qquad \text{since } E[\sum (Z_{1t}{}^m \varepsilon_{it})] = 0; \qquad (8.54)$$
$$\sum (\hat{W}_t \hat{Z}_{2t}) = 0, \qquad \text{since } E[\sum (Z_{2t}{}^m \varepsilon_{it})] = 0;$$
$$\sum (\hat{W}_t X_{1t}) = 0, \qquad \text{since } E[\sum (X_{1t} \varepsilon_{it})] = 0.$$

It can be shown, under reasonable conditions, that the estimators of the parameters in (8.52) obtained in this manner are consistent.

If the same set of regressors had *not been used* in calculating $\hat{Y}_{1t}$, $\hat{Z}_{1t}$, and $\hat{Z}_{2t}$, the conditions in (8.49) would not hold. Consequently, all of the conditions in (8.53) would not hold. Therefore, if (8.52) is estimated by our usual procedure (which is equivalent to the least-squares procedure), the resulting estimators would be based on normal equations that are not "consistent" with the specifications of the model. As an illustration, suppose $\hat{Z}_{2t}$ is based on regressors that are not the same as those underlying $\hat{Y}_{1t}$ and $\hat{Z}_{1t}$. Then, in general, there is no reason for the sum of cross products of $\hat{\phi}_{1t}$ and $\hat{Z}_{2t}$, or of $\hat{\phi}_{2t}$ and $\hat{Z}_{2t}$ to be zero. We would have that, in general, $\sum (\hat{\phi}_{1t} \hat{Z}_{2t}) \neq 0$ and $\sum (\hat{\phi}_{2t} \hat{Z}_{2t}) \neq 0$. Thus, in this case

$$\sum (W_t \hat{Z}_{2t}) = b_1 [\sum (\hat{\phi}_{1t} \hat{Z}_{2t})] + b_2 [\sum (\hat{\phi}_{2t} \hat{Z}_{2t})] + \sum (\varepsilon_{it} \hat{Z}_{2t}). \qquad (8.55)$$

The normal equation obtained by setting $\sum (\hat{W}_t \hat{Z}_{2t}) = 0$ is not, in this instance, "suggested" by the assumptions of the model.* For example, (8.55) suggests that we estimate our equation by setting $\sum (\hat{W}_t \hat{Z}_{2t}) = b_1[\sum (\hat{\phi}_{1t} \hat{Z}_{2t})] + b_2[\sum (\hat{\phi}_{2t} \hat{Z}_{2t})]$. If we did this, we would have a different (and much more complex) estimation procedure.

We now return to the issue in (4). Let $g_t = g(Y_{1t}, \ldots, Y_{mt})$ be an additional endogenous variable that appears in an equation that we wish to estimate. We shall now see that, if the above two-stage procedure is carried out with $g(\hat{Y}_{1t}, \ldots, \hat{Y}_{mt})$ replacing $g(Y_{1t}, \ldots, Y_{mt})$ in the second stage, the resulting parameter estimators will be inconsistent.

Consider again the estimation of (8.40) but assume that Y_{2t}^2 is replaced in the second stage by $\hat{Y}_{2t}^2$, where $\hat{Y}_{2t}$ is obtained by regressing Y_{2t} on the first stage regressors. In this case, Y_{2t} can be expressed as

$$Y_{2t} = \hat{Y}_{2t} + \hat{\phi}_{4t}, \tag{8.56}$$

where, among other things,

$$\sum (\hat{Y}_{2t} \hat{\phi}_{4t}) = 0. \tag{8.57}$$

Squaring both sides of (8.56), we have

$$
\begin{aligned}
Y_{2t}^2 &= \hat{Y}_{2t}^2 + (\hat{\phi}_{4t}^2 + 2\hat{\phi}_{4t}\hat{Y}_{2t}) \\
&= \hat{Y}_{2t}^2 + \hat{\psi}_t
\end{aligned}
\tag{8.58}
$$

where $\hat{\psi}_t$ is equal to the term in parentheses in (8.58). It should be clear that $\hat{\psi}_t$ will not atisfy conditions similar to those given in (8.44), (8.46), and (8.48). For example, in light of (8.57) and (8.58),

$$\sum \hat{\psi}_t = \sum \hat{\phi}_{4t}^2 \neq 0.$$

It should also be clear that the disturbance term of the second stage regression will not satisfy conditions such as those in (8.53). Consequently, the resulting parameter estimators will not be consistent.

8.4 THE LARGE SAMPLE VARIANCES

Fortunately, the large sample variance formulas given in Chapter 7 for two-stage least-squares estimators in a linear system *also hold* for these estimators in the nonlinear system. For example, consider again the two-stage estimation procedure applied to (8.40) when Y_{1t}, $Z_{1t} = (Y_{2t} Y_{3t})$, and

---

* To more advanced readers we note that, if the same set of regressors is not used in all the first stage regressions, the residuals from those regressions will not be orthogonal to all of the second stage regressors. This will lead to inconsistent estimators for the same reason that TSLS will lead to inconsistent estimators in linear systems if all the "included" predetermined variables are not used in the first stage.

$Z_{2t} = Y_{2t}^2$ are replaced, respectively, by $\hat{Y}_{1t}$, $\hat{Z}_{1t}$, and $\hat{Z}_{2t}$. Then, under typical assumptions, it can be shown that a consistent estimator of the large sample variance of $\hat{b}_1$ is

$$\widehat{\text{var}(\hat{b}_1)} = \frac{\hat{\sigma}_i^2}{\sum \hat{q}_t^2} \qquad (8.59)$$

where $\hat{\sigma}_i^2$ is a consistent estimator of the variance of ε_{it}, and $\hat{q}_t$ is the tth residual in the regression of $\hat{Y}_{1t}$ on the constant term, $\hat{Z}_{1t}$, $\hat{Z}_{2t}$, and X_{1t}. The obvious consistent estimator of the variance of ε_{it} is*

$$\hat{\sigma}_i^2 = \sum_{t=1}^{n} \frac{(Y_{it} - \hat{b}_0 - \hat{b}_1 Y_{1t} - \hat{b}_2 Z_{1t} - \hat{b}_3 Z_{2t} - \hat{a}_1 X_{1t})^2}{n-5}, \qquad (8.60)$$

where n is the sample size. Similarly, as in Chapter 7, hypotheses may be tested, or confidence intervals established, by using the normal distribution as an approximation. For example, in the case above, inferences concerning b_1 would be based on the *assumption* that

$$\frac{(\hat{b}_1 - b_1)}{\sqrt{\widehat{\text{var}(\hat{b}_1)}}} \qquad (8.61)$$

is a standard normal variable. Again, as in the linear case, the results would be strictly correct only if the sample size were infinite.

8.5 AN EXAMPLE

We now give an example that should serve to illustrate and extend some of the results obtained in this chapter. Because the purpose of the example is to illustrate the mechanics of our results, we shall not be overly concerned with the realism of the model or the subtleties of the economic relationships involved.

THE MODEL

Consider the following three-equation macroeconomic model of the economy:

$$C_t = a_0 + a_1 Y_t + a_2 Y_t^2 + a_3 Y_t^3 + a_4 \left(\frac{1}{C_{t-1}}\right) + a_5 W_{t-1} + u_{1t}, \qquad (8.62a)$$

$$I_t = b_0 + b_1 (Y_t Y_{t-1})^{1/2} + b_2 r_t + b_3 T_t + u_{2t}, \qquad (8.62b)$$

$$Y_t = C_t + I_t + G_t, \qquad t = 1, \ldots, n, \qquad (8.62c)$$

---

* As a point of interest, we note that, if the sample size were infinite, $n - 5 = n = \infty$.

where C_t is aggregate consumption expenditure at time t, Y_t is total income at time t, W_{t-1} is consumer wealth at time $(t-1)$, I_t is investment expenditure at time t, r_t is the rate of interest at time t, G_t is government expenditure at time t, T_t is a time-trend variable $T_1 = 1$, $T_2 = 2$, and so on, and u_{1t} and u_{2t} are the values of disturbance terms at time t. Before we formally specify our statistical assumptions, we shall briefly describe the nature of the model.

Equation (8.62a) is a consumption function that relates consumer expenditure to income, to the previous level of consumption (a kind of habit effect), and to the consumer's wealth position in the previous period. It would, of course, be expected that income has a positive effect on consumption. However, the exact nature of this positive relationship may not be obvious; in particular, it may not be the typical linear one portrayed in many elementary texts. Figure 8.3 depicts two possible relationships between consumption expenditure and income for given values of the "other" variables involved. The cubic form used in (8.62a) is flexible enough to account for both a linear form $(a_2 = a_3 = 0)$, as well as for relationships such as those described in Figure 8.3. If we wanted additional flexibility, we could add a fourth degree term to the income variable in (8.62a).

Equation (8.62b) explains the level of investment in terms of income levels, the rate of interest, and a time-trend variable. This last variable could be viewed as representing the net sum of exogenous investment forces that are assumed to increase (if $b_3 > 0$) or decrease (if $b_3 < 0$) steadily period after period. The term $(Y_t Y_{t-1})^{1/2}$ is a variation on the accelerator principle which we include for illustrative purposes.

Equation (8.62c) is an equation that explains income as the sum of expenditures. This equation is actually an equilibrium condition which states that the income (goods and services) produced (supplied) is demanded by the

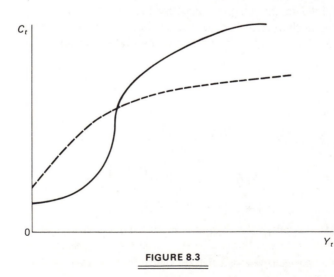

FIGURE 8.3

agents of the market, namely, by consumers, investors, and by the government.

We assume that u_{1t} and u_{2t} are not autocorrelated and have zero means, $E(u_{1t}) = E(u_{2t}) = 0$, constant variances, $E(u_{1t}^2) = \sigma_1^2$, $E(u_{2t}^2) = \sigma_2^2$, and a constant covariance $E(u_{1t}u_{2t}) = \sigma_{12}$. We also assume that government expenditure, consumer wealth, and interest rate are generated in an exogenous manner so that the disturbance terms, u_{1t} and u_{2t}, are independent of G_t, r_t, and W_{t-1}; because the trend variable T_t is deterministic, it is exogenous and, therefore, both disturbance terms are independent of it. Thus, our model in (8.62) is a three-equation model explaining C_t, I_t, and Y_t in terms of C_{t-1}, W_{t-1}, Y_{t-1}, r_t, T_t, G_t, and the disturbance terms. In a more general model, one would also attempt to explain, among other things, the rate of interest and, perhaps, government expenditure.

ANALYSIS OF THE MODEL

The basic endogenous variables of the model in (8.62) are C_t, I_t, and Y_t. The additional endogenous variables are Y_t^2, Y_t^3, and $(Y_tY_{t-1})^{1/2}$. There are, in addition to the constant term, five predetermined variables, namely, $(1/C_{t-1})$, W_{t-1}, r_t, T_t, and G_t. Of these five variables, only $(1/C_{t-1})$ is not exogenous; the model would have determined C_{t-1}, and therefore, its reciprocal, in period $t-1$.

Consider equation (8.62a). The necessary condition for the identification of this equation, namely, (8.32), is satisfied since it has only *one* right-hand-side basic endogenous variable, namely, Y_t; but it excludes *four* variables which are either additional endogenous variables, namely, $(Y_tY_{t-1})^{1/2}$, or predetermined (in this case, exogenous) variables, namely, r_t, T_t, and G_t. The necessary condition for the identification of (8.62b) is also satisfied, since this equation does not contain any right-hand-side basic endogenous variables, and it excludes five variables that are either additional endogenous variables, namely, Y_t^2 and Y_t^3, or predetermined variables, namely, $(1/C_{t-1})$, W_{t-1}, and G_t. The issue of identification concerning (8.62c) does not arise, since it does not contain parameters that must be estimated.

Consider now the problem of estimating (8.62a). To implement our TSLS procedure, we must first obtain the calculated values of Y_t, $Q_{1t} = Y_t^2$, and $Q_{2t} = Y_t^3$. To obtain these calculated values, we must specify our first stage regressors. If our sample is of, say, size $n = 50$, the regressors of the first stage might be chosen as

$$\text{the constant term, } (1/C_{t-1}),\ W_{t-1},\ r_t,\ T_t,\ G_t,\ Y_{t-1},$$
$$(1/C_{t-1})^2,\ W_{t-1}^2,\ R_t^2,\ T_t^2,\ G_t^2,\ Y_{t-1}^2. \qquad (8.63)$$

In (8.63) we have simply selected all the predetermined variables of the model and their squared values. We have not included cubic and higher-order terms or cross-product terms because one would expect these variables to be extremely highly correlated with the variables listed in (8.63). If these additional terms were added to (8.63), we *might* expect any improvement in the estimators that results because the polynomial regressions more closely approximate the mean functions to be outweighed by the loss that results as the difference between the sample size and the number of variables used in the first stage narrows (see Section 8.3). However, there is no formal basis for this belief! It may be the case that the addition of the cubic and higher-order terms and the cross-product terms would lead to improved regression parameter estimators.* In any event, the selection in (8.63) does include all the predetermined variables of (8.62a), namely, the constant term, $(1/C_{t-1})$, and W_{t-1}, and at least as many predetermined variables that are not contained in (8.62a), namely, 10, as there are right-hand-side basic endogenous and additional endogenous variables in (8.62a), namely, 3. In addition, the selection in (8.63) satisfies our *suggested condition* that the difference between the sample size (which would be 49 resulting from the loss of the first observation because of the lagged variables) and the number of variables used in the first stage (namely, 13) be at least 20.

The remainder of the procedure is now evident. We can calculate $\hat{Y}_t$, $\hat{Q}_{1t}$, and $\hat{Q}_{2t}$ in terms of the least-squares regressions of Y_t, Q_{1t}, and Q_{2t} on the variables in (8.63) for $t = 2, \ldots, n = 50$. Note, we are using the same set of first stage regressors to calculate $\hat{Y}_t$, $\hat{Q}_{1t}$, and $\hat{Q}_{2t}$. The second stage regression corresponding to the estimation of (8.62a) is then

$$C_t = a_0 + a_1 \hat{Y}_t + a_2 \hat{Q}_{1t} + a_3 \hat{Q}_{2t} + a_4(1/C_{t-1}) + a_5 W_{t-1} + k_t,$$
$$t = 2, \ldots, n = 50, \tag{8.64}$$

where k_t is the resulting disturbance term. The estimators of the parameters a_0, $a_1, a_2, a_3, a_4,$ and a_5 are then obtained in terms of the least-squares regression corresponding to (8.64). Specifically, the normal equations for this regression are given by the conditions

$$\sum_{t=2}^{50} \hat{k}_t = 0, \quad \sum_{t=2}^{50} (\hat{k}_t \hat{Y}_t) = 0, \quad \sum_{t=2}^{50} (\hat{k}_t \hat{Q}_{1t}) = 0,$$

$$\sum_{t=2}^{50} (\hat{k}_t \hat{Q}_{2t}) = 0, \quad \sum_{t=2}^{50} [\hat{k}_t(1/C_{t-1})] = 0, \quad \sum_{t=2}^{50} (\hat{k}_t W_{t-1}) = 0, \tag{8.65}$$

where $\hat{k}_t = C_t - \hat{a}_0 - \hat{a}_1 \hat{Y}_t - \hat{a}_2 \hat{Q}_{1t} - \hat{a}_3 \hat{Q}_{2t} - \hat{a}_4(1/C_{t-1}) - \hat{a}_5 W_{t-1}$, and $\hat{a}_i$, $i = 0, \ldots, 5$, denotes the estimator of a_i.

The variance of u_{1t}, σ_1^2 would then be estimated as

$$\hat{\sigma}_1^2 = \sum_{t=2}^{50} \frac{\hat{u}_{1t}^2}{(49-6)}, \tag{8.66}$$

---

* The consistency property of the TSLS estimators is a large sample property. In finite samples these estimators are biased. Therefore, just how good a TSLS estimator of a regression parameter is would depend on *both* its bias and its variance. Usually, these two attributes of an estimator are combined by adding them to obtain what is called the mean square error. Therefore, in finite samples, one could say that one TSLS estimator of a given parameter is "better" than another (which may have a different set of first stage regressors) if it has a smaller mean square error.

where $\hat{u}_{1t} = C_t - \hat{a}_0 - \hat{a}_1 Y_t - \hat{a}_2 Y_t^2 - \hat{a}_3 Y_t^3 - \hat{a}_4(1/C_{t-1}) - \hat{a}_5 W_{t-1}$.
Finally, the large sample variance of, say, $\hat{a}_2$, would be estimated as

$$\widehat{\operatorname{var}(\hat{a}_2)} = \hat{\sigma}_1^2 \left(\frac{1}{\displaystyle\sum_{t=2}^{50} \hat{Q}_{1t}^2} \right), \tag{8.67}$$

where $\hat{Q}_{1t}$ is the residual in the least-squares regression of $\hat{Q}_{1t}$ on the constant term, $\hat{Y}_t$, $\hat{Q}_{2t}$, $(1/C_{t-1}.)$, and W_{t-1}.

The mechanics concerning the estimation of (8.62b) are identical to those described for (8.62a). The only point that should be noted is that the first stage regressors underlying the estimation of (8.62b) *need not be identical* to those used for the estimation of (8.62a); it need not be the set in (8.63). Alternatively, whatever first stage regressors are chosen for the estimation of a given equation, that same set must be used in determining the calculated values of all right-hand-side basic and additional endogenous variables of *that equation*; that same set need not be used for all equations. On the other hand, there may be little motivation to change the first stage regressors, because the sample size is typically the same for all equations and similar variables are involved.

APPENDIX.

The Estimation of Models That Are Nonlinear in Both the Endogenous Variables and Parameters

In this appendix we extend our results concerning estimation to simultaneous equation models that are nonlinear in *both* the endogenous variables and the parameters. We do not consider the corresponding issue of identification, because relatively simple rules that would be considered in practice do not, as yet, exist.

The estimation procedure we present is one whose rationale can be understood on an intuitive level. However, unless one is familiar with numerical analysis and computer programming, the empirical implementation of this procedure will require the availability of a user computer program that has this procedure as an option.*

THE FRAMEWORK OF ANALYSIS

Consider a three-equation model containing the endogenous variables Y_{1t}, Y_{2t}, and Y_{3t}, and the exogenous variables, $X_{1t}, \ldots, X_{kt}$. Suppose the first equation of this model is

$$Y_{1t} = a_0 + a_1 X_{1t} e^{a_2 Y_{2t}} + a_3 X_{2t} + a_4 Y_{3t}^2 + \varepsilon_{1t}, \tag{8A.1}$$

where ε_{1t} is a disturbance term. We assume that the value of a_2 is unknown and so must be estimated along with the values of a_0, a_1, a_3, and a_4. Then, unlike all of the models we have thus far considered, (8A.1) is nonlinear in both the endogenous variables and the parameters. Note that we cannot convert (8A.1) into a model that is linear in the parameters by expressing it as

$$Y_{1t} = a_0 + a_1 Z_t + a_3 X_{2t} + a_4 Y_{3t}^2 + \varepsilon_{1t}, \tag{8A.2}$$

where Z_t is the additional endogenous variable $Z_t = X_{1t} e^{a_2 Y_{2t}}$. The reason is that the value of a_2 is not known, and so, observations on Z_t cannot be constructed from the available observations on X_{1t} and Y_{2t}.

Another example of a model that is nonlinear in both endogenous variables and parameters is the two-equation model

$$\log(Y_{1t}) = a_0 + a_1 \left(\frac{Y_{2t}}{1 + b_2 X_{2t}} \right) + a_2 \left(\frac{X_{1t}}{Y_{2t}} \right) + \varepsilon_{1t}, \tag{8A.3a}$$

$$(Y_{2t}^\alpha X_{3t}) = b_0 + b_1 Y_{1t} + b_2 Y_{1t}^2 + b_3 X_{2t} + \varepsilon_{2t}, \tag{8A.3b}$$

where Y_{1t} and Y_{2t} are the endogenous variables, X_{1t}, X_{2t}, and X_{3t} are the exogenous variables, and ε_{1t} and ε_{2t} are the disturbance terms. In this case, the "parameter nonlinearity" occurs because of the parameters α and b_2.

---

*The procedure is the nonlinear two-stage least-squares method first proposed by T. Amemiya, "The Nonlinear Two-Stage Least-Squares Estimator," *Journal of Econometrics* 2 (1974), pp. 105–110. Our discussion will be an interpretation of Amemiya's results.

We now use the models in (8A.1) and (8A.3) to illustrate two properties of the type of models we are considering in this appendix. The first is that the left-hand side of a given equation may contain unknown parameters, as in (8A.3b), but need not, as in (8A.1) and (8A.3a). Second, the disturbance term in each equation must be additive. We shall indicate below that this assumption is not very restrictive. Accepting it for the moment, we note the implication is that all terms except the disturbance term can be placed on the left-hand side of the equation, and so the disturbance term can be isolated on the right-hand side. For example, (8A.3a) can be expressed as

$$\log(Y_{1t}) - a_0 - a_1\left(\frac{Y_{2t}}{1 + b_2 X_{2t}}\right) - a_2\left(\frac{X_{1t}}{Y_{2t}}\right) = \varepsilon_{1t}. \tag{8A.4}$$

To be more general, let $Y_{1t}, \ldots, Y_{mt}$ be the endogenous variables of a model, $X_{1t}, \ldots, X_{pt}$ the exogenous variables, and $u_{1t}, \ldots, u_{mt}$ the disturbance terms. Then, we shall assume that the equation we wish to estimate, say, the ith, can be expressed in the form*

$$F_i(Y_{1t}, \ldots, Y_{mt}, X_{1t}, \ldots, X_{pt}) = u_{it}, \tag{8A.5}$$

where the left-hand side of (8A.5) is a function of one or more of the variables $Y_{1t}, \ldots, Y_{mt}, X_{1t}, \ldots, X_{pt}$, which contains unknown parameters. As an illustration, for equation (8A.3a), this function would simply be the left-hand side of (8A.4).

The assumption that the equation can be expressed in terms of an additive disturbance term, and therefore in a form such as (8A.5), is not a very restrictive assumption because of the type of models economists generally consider. For example, this assumption requires only that the particular equation of the model under consideration can be solved for the disturbance term. As an example, if the first equation of a model is of the form

$$Y_{1t} = a_0 X_{1t}^{a_1} Y_{2t}^{a_2} e^{u_{1t}}, \tag{8A.6}$$

the form corresponding to (8A.5) is

$$\log(Y_{1t}) - \log(a_0) - a_1 \log(X_{1t}) - a_2 \log(Y_{2t}) = u_{1t}. \tag{8A.7}$$

As another illustration, consider an equation of the form

$$Y_{1t} = a_0 + a_1\left(\frac{e^{a_2 Y_{2t}}}{1 + u_{1t}}\right) + a_3 X_{1t}, \tag{8A.8}$$

where the range of possible values of the disturbance term u_{1t} is such that $1 + u_{1t} > 0$. Then, the form corresponding to (8A.5) can be obtained by first noting that

$$\left(\frac{Y_{1t} - a_0 - a_3 X_{1t}}{a_1 e^{a_2 Y_{2t}}}\right) = \frac{1}{1 + u_{1t}}, \tag{8A.9}$$

so that

$$\left(\frac{a_1 e^{a_2 Y_{2t}}}{Y_{1t} - a_0 - a_3 X_{1t}}\right) - 1 = u_{1t}. \tag{8A.10}$$

---

*If every equation of the model is to be estimated, then our analysis requires that every equation be expressible in the form (8A.5).

Before turning to the issue of estimation and then to hypothesis testing, we present a preliminary result.

A PRELIMINARY RESULT

Consider the standard *single* equation regression model

$$Y_t = b_0 + b_1 X_{1t} + \cdots + b_k X_{kt} + u_t, \qquad t = 1, \ldots, N, \qquad (8A.11)$$

where the independent variables are not multicollinear, and where the disturbance term satisfies all of our standard assumptions. Specifically, we assume u_t is independent of all lagged, current, and future values of the independent variables, has a mean of zero, $E(u_t) = 0$ and a constant variance, $E(u_t^2) = \sigma_u^2$, and is not autocorrelated.

Recall that in a model such as (8A.11) the basic assumption concerning the regression coefficients $b_0, b_1, \ldots, b_k$ is that they are *constants*; that is, their values do not depend on t. Therefore, some or all these coefficients can be zero. Clearly, if all these coefficients are zero, the dependent variable $Y_t = u_t$, so that Y_t reduces to a random variable that is independent of the regressors of the model.

Let $\hat{b}_i$ be the estimator of b_i obtained by our instrumental variable technique, which is equivalent to least squares. Then, in Chapter 4 we showed that $\hat{b}_i$ is an unbiased estimator so that $E(\hat{b}_i) = b_i$. This result holds whether or not $b_i = 0$. We have also shown, in the Appendix to Chapter 4, that the variance of $\hat{b}_i$ is expressible as

$$\mathrm{var}(\hat{b}_i) = \frac{\sigma_u^2}{\sum\limits_{t=1}^{N} \hat{v}_{it}^2}, \qquad (8A.12)$$

where $\hat{v}_{it}$ is the residual in the regression of X_{it} on all the other regressors (including the constant term) in (8A.11).

The denominator of (8A.12) is the sum of N terms, and each of these terms is greater than or equal to zero. Therefore, among other things, the value of $\mathrm{var}(\hat{b}_i)$ depends on the sample size, N. It can be shown, under further technical assumptions, that if N were infinite, the denominator in (8A.12) would also be infinite, and so $\mathrm{var}(\hat{b}_i)$ would be zero.

Consider now the case in which all of the regression coefficients in (8A.11) are zero, $b_i = 0$, $i = 0, \ldots, k$. Then, for this case our results suggest that $E(\hat{b}_i) = 0$, $i = 0, \ldots, k$, and if $N = \infty$, $\mathrm{var}(\hat{b}_i) = 0$, $i = 0, \ldots, k$. Somewhat intuitively, if the regression parameters are zero and the sample size is infinite, the expected value of each regression parameter estimator would be zero, and its expected squared deviation about zero (its variance) would also be zero. We would therefore, intuitively, expect the value of each of the regression parameter estimators to be zero in such a case. The more formal statement, however, is that, if $E(\hat{b}_i) = 0$, $i = 0, \ldots, k$, and $\lim_{N \to \infty} \mathrm{var}(\hat{b}_i) = 0$, then $\lim_{N \to \infty}$, $\mathrm{Prob}(|\hat{b}_i - 0| > \delta) = \lim_{N \to \infty}$, $\mathrm{Prob}(|\hat{b}_i| > \delta) = 0$, where δ is a positive constant, however small. In words, under these conditions, the probability that $\hat{b}_i$ will differ from zero by any amount, however small, is zero (i.e., $\hat{b}_i$ converges in probability to zero).

The upshot of all this is that, if a variable that has a zero mean, a constant variance, and is not autocorrelated (such as a disturbance term) is regressed on a set of variables of which it is independent, the regression parameter estimators will converge in probability to zero, under further technical (and reasonable) assumptions. Therefore, the calculated value of such a variable, as for example, in the case above,

$$\hat{Y}_t = b_0 + b_1 X_{1t} + \cdots + b_k X_{kt},$$ (8A.13)

will also converge in probability to zero as $N \to \infty$.

THE ESTIMATION PROCEDURE

In this section, we shall first illustrate the procedure for estimating an equation that is nonlinear in both endogenous variables and parameters in terms of equation (8A.3b). We shall then generalize our results.

Assume that we have N observations on the variables of the two-equation model in (8A.3), namely, on Y_{1t}, Y_{2t}, X_{1t}, X_{2t}, and X_{3t}. Assume that X_{1t}, X_{2t}, and X_{3t} are not multicollinear. Concerning the disturbance terms, assume that they each have a mean of zero, a constant variance, and a constant covariance; that each disturbance term is independent of its values in other periods, as well as of the values of the other disturbance term in other periods; and that both disturbance terms are independent of the lagged, current, and future values of all three of the exogenous variables. The consistency property of the estimation procedure we shall describe also depends on some further technical assumptions, some of which are not very intuitive, and which would typically be assumed to hold in practice. Because their presentation and comprehension require mathematical and statistical tools that are beyond the level of this text, we shall simply assume these conditions without actually specifying them.

Equation (8A.3b) can be expressed in the form (8A.5), namely,

$$(Y_{2t}^{\alpha} X_{3t}) - b_0 - b_1 Y_{1t} - b_2 Y_{1t}^2 - b_3 X_{2t} = \varepsilon_{2t}.$$ (8A.14)

Denote the left-hand side of (8A.14) as F_t. Suppose that we select a hypothetical value for each parameter appearing on the left-hand side of (8A.14), and construct "approximate" observations on F_t, say, F_t^a, according to these values. For example, suppose we select 0.1 for α, 3.7 for b_0, -1.5 for b_1, 2.0 for b_2, and -10 for b_3. Then our "approximate" observations would be determined as

$$F_t^a = (Y_{2t}^{0.1} X_{3t}) - 3.7 + 1.5 Y_{1t} - 2 Y_{1t}^2 + 10 X_{2t}.$$ (8A.15)

Note from (8A.14) that, if the true values of the parameters were equal to our selected values, $F_t^a = F_t = \varepsilon_{2t}$ for all t; on the other hand, if one or more of our selected values is not equal to the corresponding true values, $F_t^a \neq \varepsilon_{2t}$, for all t.

Assume, for the moment, that the parameter values we select are the true values so that $F_t^a = F_t = \varepsilon_{2t}$, $t = 1, \ldots, N$. Suppose further that we run, what we shall call henceforth, a first stage regression of our constructed F_t variable on the exogenous variables of the model and their squares, namely, on X_{1t}, X_{2t}, X_{3t}, X_{1t}^2, X_{2t}^2, X_{3t}^2, and the constant term. We shall discuss the issue below concerning the selection of the first stage regressors. Returning to our analysis, let $\hat{F}_t$ denote the calculated value of F_t from this first stage regression. Then the preliminary results given in the immediately preceding section imply that, since $F_t = \varepsilon_{2t}$ is a disturbance term that satisfies all our standard assumptions, and since F_t is independent of all three exogenous variables, $\hat{F}_t$ will converge in probability to zero as $N \to \infty$. Consider the summation

$$S = \sum_{t=1}^{N} \frac{\hat{F}_t^2}{N}.$$ (8A.16)

Then it should be evident that S will also converge in probability to zero as $N \to \infty$.

Now assume that our selected parameter values are not the true values. Then, as we indicated, our constructed variable $F_t^a \neq \varepsilon_{2t}$, $t = 1, \ldots, N$. In this case, the value of F_t^a is simply a function of the variables of the equation, namely, Y_{1t}, Y_{2t}, X_{2t}, and X_{3t}. Suppose now, as in the case above, F_t^a is regressed on the first stage regressors, X_{1t}, X_{2t}, X_{3t}, X_{1t}^2, X_{2t}^2, X_{3t}^2, and the constant term. Let the resulting calculated value of F_t^b be $\hat{F}_t^a$. Then, we might expect that the average sum of squares of the calculated values, namely,

$$S^a = \sum_{t=1}^{N} \frac{(\hat{F}_t^a)^2}{N}, \tag{8A.17}$$

will not converge in probability to zero. This is precisely the case, assuming the further technical assumptions. Because S^a is a sum of squares, it can be shown, under these technical assumptions, that S^a will converge in probability to a positive number.

The main point in the above discussion is that the average of the terms $(\hat{F}_t^a)^2$ will converge to zero if the values selected for the parameters are the true ones, but will converge to a positive number otherwise. The following estimation procedure thus presents itself. Search over the possible sets of values of the regression model's parameters to find that set of values which minimizes the average of the squares of the calculated variables, $(\hat{F}_t^a)^2$. We simply take this set of values as our estimates (more formally, estimators) of the regression parameters. These estimators are consistent because, if the sample size were infinite, the average of the squares of the calculated variables, $(F_t^a)^2$, is minimized (at zero) by the true parameter values.

THE SELECTION OF THE FIRST STAGE REGRESSORS

The issues concerning the selection of the first stage regressors are very similar to those discussed in Section 8.3. For example, it will generally be the case that, if the sample size is infinite, the variances of the regression parameter estimators are inversely related to the degree of the first stage regression in the exogenous variables. Therefore, higher and higher powers (along with the lower powers) of these variables should be considered in the first stage regression. However, in practice the sample size is finite and so the number of terms used in the first stage regression must be limited. Indeed, it can be shown that, if so many terms are used in the first stage regression that their number, say, p, is equal to the sample size, N, the resulting estimators will be a type of least-squares estimators, and these estimators are not consistent.* As in Section 8.3, we have a dilemma and again suggest that p be chosen such that $(N - p) \geq 20$. The consistency property, of course, requires $(N - p)$ to be infinite. We also note, without demonstration, that the consistency property of the estimation procedure requires p to be at least as large as the number of parameters in the equation being estimated.

---

* For our more advanced readers, if $p = N$, then $\hat{F}_t^a = F_t^a$. Therefore, we would select our parameter values to minimize $\sum_{t=1}^{N}(F_t^a)^2/N$, which is equivalent to minimizing the sum of the squares of the estimated disturbance terms (i.e., a nonlinear least-squares procedure). However, least-squares procedures do not yield consistent estimators if the regression model, among other things, has endogenous variables on the right-hand side of the equation.

A REVIEW AND GENERAL OUTLINE OF THE PROCEDURE

In general, our procedure for estimating an equation that is nonlinear in both the endogenous variables and the parameters is outlined by the following steps:

1. Express the equation in the form (8A.5), and denote the left-hand side as F_t.
2. Let F_t^a be the approximate value of F_t which is determined by selecting a set of values for the parameters that appear in the equation.
3. Determine the polynomial forms of the exogenous variables that will determine the first stage regressors. Remember that the number of first stage regressors, say, p, must be at least as large as the number of parameters appearing in the equation that is being estimated. Since the sample size, N, will in practice be finite, choose p such that $(N - p)$ is at least 20.
4. Let $\hat{F}_t^a$ be the calculated value of F_t^a obtained from the regression of F_t^a on the first stage regressors.
5. Search over the possible parameter values to find the set of values that minimizes $\sum_{t=1}^{N}(\hat{F}_t^a)^2/N$. Take these values as the estimates of the corresponding parameters.

Clearly, empirical implementation of this procedure will require a knowledge of numerical analysis and computer programming, or the availability of a user computer program that contains this procedure as an option.

HYPOTHESIS TESTING, CONFIDENCE INTERVALS, AND THE LARGE SAMPLE VARIANCES: A COMMENT

Unfortunately, except for our more advanced readers, we cannot give expressions for the large sample variances of the estimators because their presentation requires mathematical tools that are beyond the level we have assumed in this book.* However, if a user computer program that contains this procedure as an option is available, it will typically (among other things) print out the estimates of the parameters and estimates of the corresponding large sample variances. It can be shown, under further technical assumptions, that if the sample size were infinite, the parameter estimators would be normally distributed. Therefore, in terms of the output of such a computer program, a hypothesis that relates to the value of a single parameter can be tested, or a confidence interval established, by again using the normal distribution as an approximation. For instance, suppose a_2 is one of the parameters and the computer output is $\hat{a} = 10$ and $\hat{\sigma}_{\hat{a}_2}^2 = 16$. Then, an approximate 95 percent confidence interval for a_2, which is based on the large sample normal distribution, would be 10 ± 4 (1.96), or 10 ± 7.84.

---

*For our more advanced readers, assume that the equation to be estimated is in the form (8A.5) and denote the left-hand-side as F_t. Assume that the equation contains the parameters a_0, ..., a_k. Let $f_{it} = (\partial F_t/\partial a_i)$, $i = 0, \ldots, k$. In general, f_{it} will involve one or more of the parameters a_0, ..., a_k. Obtain N observations on each f_{it} by replacing the parameters involved by consistent estimators. Now, let $\hat{f}_{it}$ denote the calculated value of f_{it} from the regression of f_{it} on all of the first stage regressors. Finally, let $\hat{f}_{it}$ be the tth residual from the regression of $\hat{f}_{it}$ on the k variables $\hat{f}_{jt}$, where $j \neq i$. Then, the large sample variance of $\hat{a}_i$ is consistently estimated as $\hat{\sigma}^2/\sum_{t=1}^{N}\hat{f}_{it}^2$ where $\hat{\sigma}^2$ is a consistent estimator of the variance of the equation's disturbance term.

Statistical Tables

TABLE 1

THE STANDARDIZED NORMAL DISTRIBUTION

$$Z = \frac{X - \mu}{\sigma}$$

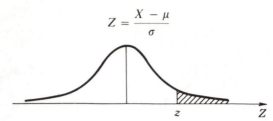

z	.00	.01	.02	.03	.04	.05	.06	.07	.08	.09
0.0	.5000	.4960	.4920	.4880	.4840	.4801	.4761	.4721	.4681	.4641
0.1	.4602	.4562	.4522	.4483	.4443	.4404	.4364	.4325	.4286	.4247
0.2	.4207	.4168	.4129	.4090	.4052	.4013	.3974	.3936	.3897	.3859
0.3	.3821	.3783	.3745	.3707	.3669	.3632	.3594	.3557	.3520	.3483
0.4	.3446	.3409	.3372	.3336	.3300	.3264	.3228	.3192	.3156	.3121
0.5	.3085	.3050	.3015	.2981	.2946	.2912	.2877	.2843	.2810	.2776
0.6	.2743	.2709	.2676	.2643	.2611	.2578	.2546	.2514	.2483	.2451
0.7	.2420	.2389	.2358	.2327	.2296	.2266	.2236	.2206	.2177	.2148
0.8	.2119	.2090	.2061	.2033	.2005	.1977	.1949	.1922	.1894	.1867
0.9	.1841	.1814	.1788	.1762	.1736	.1711	.1685	.1660	.1635	.1611
1.0	.1587	.1562	.1539	.1515	.1492	.1469	.1446	.1423	.1401	.1379
1.1	.1357	.1335	.1314	.1292	.1271	.1251	.1230	.1210	.1190	.1170
1.2	.1151	.1131	.1112	.1093	.1075	.1056	.1038	.1020	.1003	.0985
1.3	.0968	.0951	.0934	.0918	.0901	.0885	.0869	.0853	.0838	.0823
1.4	.0808	.0793	.0778	.0764	.0749	.0735	.0721	.0708	.0694	.0681
1.5	.0668	.0655	.0643	.0630	.0618	.0606	.0594	.0582	.0571	.0559
1.6	.0548	.0537	.0526	.0516	.0505	.0495	.0485	.0475	.0465	.0455
1.7	.0446	.0436	.0427	.0418	.0409	.0401	.0392	.0384	.0375	.0367
1.8	.0359	.0351	.0344	.0336	.0329	.0322	.0314	.0307	.0301	.0294
1.9	.0287	.0281	.0274	.0268	.0262	.0256	.0250	.0244	.0239	.0233
2.0	.0228	.0222	.0217	.0212	.0207	.0202	.0197	.0192	.0188	.0183
2.1	.0179	.0174	.0170	.0166	.0162	.0158	.0154	.0150	.0146	.0143
2.2	.0139	.0136	.0132	.0129	.0125	.0122	.0119	.0116	.0113	.0110
2.3	.0107	.0104	.0102	.0099	.0096	.0094	.0091	.0089	.0087	.0084
2.4	.0082	.0080	.0078	.0075	.0073	.0071	.0069	.0068	.0066	.0064
2.5	.0062	.0060	.0059	.0057	.0055	.0054	.0052	.0051	.0049	.0048
2.6	.0047	.0045	.0044	.0043	.0041	.0040	.0039	.0038	.0037	.0036
2.7	.0035	.0034	.0033	.0032	.0031	.0030	.0029	.0028	.0027	.0026
2.8	.0026	.0025	.0024	.0023	.0023	.0022	.0021	.0021	.0020	.0019
2.9	.0019	.0018	.0018	.0017	.0016	.0016	.0015	.0015	.0014	.0014
3.0	.0013	.0013	.0013	.0012	.0012	.0011	.0011	.0011	.0010	.0010

The table plots the cumulative probability $Z \geq z$.

SOURCE: Reprinted from Edward J. Kane, *Economic Statistics and Econometrics: An Introduction to Quantitative Economics*, New York: Harper & Row, Publishers, 1968.

TABLE 2

STUDENT'S *t* DISTRIBUTION

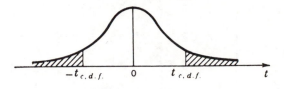

Degrees of Freedom	Probability of a Value Greater in Absolute Value than the Table Entry					
	0.01	0.02	0.05	0.1	0.2	0.3
1	63.657	31.821	12.706	6.314	3.078	1.963
2	9.925	6.965	4.303	2.920	1.886	1.386
3	5.841	4.541	3.182	2.353	1.638	1.250
4	4.604	3.747	2.776	2.132	1.533	1.190
5	4.032	3.365	2.571	2.015	1.476	1.156
6	3.707	3.143	2.447	1.943	1.440	1.134
7	3.499	2.998	2.365	1.895	1.415	1.119
8	3.355	2.896	2.306	1.860	1.397	1.108
9	3.250	2.821	2.262	1.833	1.383	1.100
10	3.169	2.764	2.228	1.812	1.372	1.093
11	3.106	2.718	2.201	1.796	1.363	1.088
12	3.055	2.681	2.179	1.782	1.356	1.083
13	3.012	2.650	2.160	1.771	1.350	1.079
14	2.977	2.624	2.145	1.761	1.345	1.076
15	2.947	2.602	2.131	1.753	1.341	1.074
16	2.921	2.583	2.120	1.746	1.337	1.071
17	2.898	2.567	2.110	1.740	1.333	1.069
18	2.878	2.552	2.101	1.734	1.330	1.067
19	2.861	2.539	2.093	1.729	1.328	1.066
20	2.845	2.528	2.086	1.725	1.325	1.064
21	2.831	2.518	2.080	1.721	1.323	1.063
22	2.819	2.508	2.074	1.717	1.321	1.061
23	2.807	2.500	2.069	1.714	1.319	1.060
24	2.797	2.492	2.064	1.711	1.318	1.059
25	2.787	2.485	2.060	1.708	1.316	1.058
26	2.779	2.479	2.056	1.706	1.315	1.058
27	2.771	2.473	2.052	1.703	1.314	1.057
28	2.763	2.467	2.048	1.701	1.313	1.056
29	2.756	2.462	2.045	1.699	1.311	1.055
30	2.750	2.457	2.042	1.697	1.310	1.055
∞	2.576	2.326	1.960	1.645	1.282	1.036

SOURCE: Reprinted from Table IV in Sir Ronald A. Fisher, *Statistical Methods for Research Workers*, 13th edition. Oliver & Boyd Ltd., Edinburgh, 1963, with the permission of the publisher and the late Sir Ronald Fisher's Literary Executor.

TABLE 3

CRITICAL VALUES FOR THE F DISTRIBUTION

5% (Roman Type) and 1% (Bold Face Type) Points for the Distribution of F.

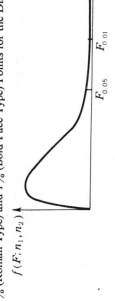

$f(F; n_1, n_2)$

$F_{0.05}$ $F_{0.01}$ F

n_1 degrees of freedom (for greater mean square)

n_2	1	2	3	4	5	6	7	8	9	10	11	12	14	16	20	24	30	40	50	75	100	200	500	∞	n_2
1	161 **4,052**	200 **4,999**	216 **5,403**	225 **5,625**	230 **5,764**	234 **5,859**	237 **5,928**	239 **5,981**	241 **6,022**	242 **6,056**	243 **6,082**	244 **6,106**	245 **6,142**	246 **6,169**	248 **6,208**	249 **6,234**	250 **6,258**	251 **6,286**	252 **6,302**	253 **6,323**	253 **6,334**	254 **6,352**	254 **6,361**	254 **6,366**	1
2	18.51 **98.49**	19.00 **99.00**	19.16 **99.17**	19.25 **99.25**	19.30 **99.30**	19.33 **99.33**	19.36 **99.34**	19.37 **99.36**	19.38 **99.38**	19.39 **99.40**	19.40 **99.41**	19.41 **99.42**	19.42 **99.43**	19.43 **99.44**	19.44 **99.45**	19.45 **99.46**	19.46 **99.47**	19.47 **99.48**	19.47 **99.48**	19.48 **99.49**	19.49 **99.49**	19.49 **99.49**	19.50 **99.50**	19.50 **99.50**	2
3	10.13 **34.12**	9.55 **30.82**	9.28 **29.46**	9.12 **28.71**	9.01 **28.24**	8.94 **27.91**	8.88 **27.67**	8.84 **27.49**	8.81 **27.34**	8.78 **27.23**	8.76 **27.13**	8.74 **27.05**	8.71 **26.92**	8.69 **26.83**	8.66 **26.69**	8.64 **26.60**	8.62 **26.50**	8.60 **26.41**	8.58 **26.35**	8.57 **26.27**	8.56 **26.23**	8.54 **26.18**	8.54 **26.14**	8.53 **26.12**	3
4	7.71 **21.20**	6.94 **18.00**	6.59 **16.69**	6.39 **15.98**	6.26 **15.52**	6.16 **15.21**	6.09 **14.98**	6.04 **14.80**	6.00 **14.66**	5.96 **14.54**	5.93 **14.45**	5.91 **14.37**	5.87 **14.24**	5.84 **14.15**	5.80 **14.02**	5.77 **13.93**	5.74 **13.83**	5.71 **13.74**	5.70 **13.69**	5.68 **13.61**	5.66 **13.57**	5.65 **13.52**	5.64 **13.48**	5.63 **13.46**	4
5	6.61 **16.26**	5.79 **13.27**	5.41 **12.06**	5.19 **11.39**	5.05 **10.97**	4.95 **10.67**	4.88 **10.45**	4.82 **10.27**	4.78 **10.15**	4.74 **10.05**	4.70 **9.96**	4.68 **9.89**	4.64 **9.77**	4.60 **9.68**	4.56 **9.55**	4.53 **9.47**	4.50 **9.38**	4.46 **9.29**	4.44 **9.24**	4.42 **9.17**	4.40 **9.13**	4.38 **9.07**	4.37 **9.04**	4.36 **9.02**	5
6	5.99 **13.74**	5.14 **10.92**	4.76 **9.78**	4.53 **9.15**	4.39 **8.75**	4.28 **8.47**	4.21 **8.26**	4.15 **8.10**	4.10 **7.98**	4.06 **7.87**	4.03 **7.79**	4.00 **7.72**	3.96 **7.60**	3.92 **7.52**	3.87 **7.39**	3.84 **7.31**	3.81 **7.23**	3.77 **7.14**	3.75 **7.09**	3.72 **7.02**	3.71 **6.99**	3.69 **6.94**	3.68 **6.90**	3.67 **6.88**	6
7	5.59 **12.25**	4.74 **9.55**	4.35 **8.45**	4.12 **7.85**	3.97 **7.46**	3.87 **7.19**	3.79 **7.00**	3.73 **6.84**	3.68 **6.71**	3.63 **6.62**	3.60 **6.54**	3.57 **6.47**	3.52 **6.35**	3.49 **6.27**	3.44 **6.15**	3.41 **6.07**	3.38 **5.98**	3.34 **5.90**	3.32 **5.85**	3.29 **5.78**	3.28 **5.75**	3.25 **5.70**	3.24 **5.67**	3.23 **5.65**	7
8	5.32 **11.26**	4.46 **8.65**	4.07 **7.59**	3.84 **7.01**	3.69 **6.63**	3.58 **6.37**	3.50 **6.19**	3.44 **6.03**	3.39 **5.91**	3.34 **5.82**	3.31 **5.74**	3.28 **5.67**	3.23 **5.56**	3.20 **5.48**	3.15 **5.36**	3.12 **5.28**	3.08 **5.20**	3.05 **5.11**	3.03 **5.06**	3.00 **5.00**	2.98 **4.96**	2.96 **4.91**	2.94 **4.88**	2.93 **4.86**	8
9	5.12 **10.56**	4.26 **8.02**	3.86 **6.99**	3.63 **6.42**	3.48 **6.06**	3.37 **5.80**	3.29 **5.62**	3.23 **5.47**	3.18 **5.35**	3.13 **5.26**	3.10 **5.18**	3.07 **5.11**	3.02 **5.00**	2.98 **4.92**	2.93 **4.80**	2.90 **4.73**	2.86 **4.64**	2.82 **4.56**	2.80 **4.51**	2.77 **4.45**	2.76 **4.41**	2.73 **4.36**	2.72 **4.33**	2.71 **4.31**	9
10	4.96 **10.04**	4.10 **7.56**	3.71 **6.55**	3.48 **5.99**	3.33 **5.64**	3.22 **5.39**	3.14 **5.21**	3.07 **5.06**	3.02 **4.95**	2.97 **4.85**	2.94 **4.78**	2.91 **4.71**	2.86 **4.60**	2.82 **4.52**	2.77 **4.41**	2.74 **4.33**	2.70 **4.25**	2.67 **4.17**	2.64 **4.12**	2.61 **4.05**	2.59 **4.01**	2.56 **3.96**	2.55 **3.93**	2.54 **3.91**	10
11	4.84 **9.65**	3.98 **7.20**	3.59 **6.22**	3.36 **5.67**	3.20 **5.32**	3.09 **5.07**	3.01 **4.88**	2.95 **4.74**	2.90 **4.63**	2.86 **4.54**	2.82 **4.46**	2.79 **4.40**	2.74 **4.29**	2.70 **4.21**	2.65 **4.10**	2.61 **4.02**	2.57 **3.94**	2.53 **3.86**	2.50 **3.80**	2.47 **3.74**	2.45 **3.70**	2.42 **3.66**	2.41 **3.62**	2.40 **3.60**	11
12	4.75 **9.33**	3.88 **6.93**	3.49 **5.95**	3.26 **5.41**	3.11 **5.06**	3.00 **4.82**	2.92 **4.65**	2.85 **4.50**	2.80 **4.39**	2.76 **4.30**	2.72 **4.22**	2.69 **4.16**	2.64 **4.05**	2.60 **3.98**	2.54 **3.86**	2.50 **3.78**	2.46 **3.70**	2.42 **3.61**	2.40 **3.56**	2.36 **3.49**	2.35 **3.46**	2.32 **3.41**	2.31 **3.38**	2.30 **3.36**	12
13	4.67 **9.07**	3.80 **6.70**	3.41 **5.74**	3.18 **5.20**	3.02 **4.86**	2.92 **4.62**	2.84 **4.44**	2.77 **4.30**	2.72 **4.19**	2.67 **4.10**	2.63 **4.02**	2.60 **3.96**	2.55 **3.85**	2.51 **3.78**	2.46 **3.67**	2.42 **3.59**	2.38 **3.51**	2.34 **3.42**	2.32 **3.37**	2.28 **3.30**	2.26 **3.27**	2.24 **3.21**	2.22 **3.18**	2.21 **3.16**	13

TABLE 3 (Continued)

n_1 degrees of freedom (for greater mean square)

n_2	1	2	3	4	5	6	7	8	9	10	11	12	14	16	20	24	30	40	50	75	100	200	500	∞	n_2
14	4.60 **8.86**	3.74 **6.51**	3.34 **5.56**	3.11 **5.03**	2.96 **4.69**	2.85 **4.46**	2.77 **4.28**	2.70 **4.14**	2.65 **4.03**	2.60 **3.94**	2.56 **3.86**	2.53 **3.80**	2.48 **3.70**	2.44 **3.62**	2.39 **3.51**	2.35 **3.43**	2.31 **3.34**	2.27 **3.26**	2.24 **3.21**	2.21 **3.14**	2.19 **3.11**	2.16 **3.06**	2.14 **3.02**	2.13 **3.00**	14
15	4.54 **8.68**	3.68 **6.36**	3.29 **5.42**	3.06 **4.89**	2.90 **4.56**	2.79 **4.32**	2.70 **4.14**	2.64 **4.00**	2.59 **3.89**	2.55 **3.80**	2.51 **3.73**	2.48 **3.67**	2.43 **3.56**	2.39 **3.48**	2.33 **3.36**	2.29 **3.29**	2.25 **3.20**	2.21 **3.12**	2.18 **3.07**	2.15 **3.00**	2.12 **2.97**	2.10 **2.92**	2.08 **2.89**	2.07 **2.87**	15
16	4.49 **8.53**	3.63 **6.23**	3.24 **5.29**	3.01 **4.77**	2.85 **4.44**	2.74 **4.20**	2.66 **4.03**	2.59 **3.89**	2.54 **3.78**	2.49 **3.69**	2.45 **3.61**	2.42 **3.55**	2.37 **3.45**	2.33 **3.37**	2.28 **3.25**	2.24 **3.18**	2.20 **3.10**	2.16 **3.01**	2.13 **2.96**	2.09 **2.89**	2.07 **2.86**	2.04 **2.80**	2.02 **2.77**	2.01 **2.75**	16
17	4.45 **8.40**	3.59 **6.11**	3.20 **5.18**	2.96 **4.67**	2.81 **4.34**	2.70 **4.10**	2.62 **3.93**	2.55 **3.79**	2.50 **3.68**	2.45 **3.59**	2.41 **3.52**	2.38 **3.45**	2.33 **3.35**	2.29 **3.27**	2.23 **3.16**	2.19 **3.08**	2.15 **3.00**	2.11 **2.92**	2.08 **2.86**	2.04 **2.79**	2.02 **2.76**	1.99 **2.70**	1.97 **2.67**	1.96 **2.65**	17
18	4.41 **8.28**	3.55 **6.01**	3.16 **5.09**	2.93 **4.58**	2.77 **4.25**	2.66 **4.01**	2.58 **3.85**	2.51 **3.71**	2.46 **3.60**	2.41 **3.51**	2.37 **3.44**	2.34 **3.37**	2.29 **3.27**	2.25 **3.19**	2.19 **3.07**	2.15 **3.00**	2.11 **2.91**	2.07 **2.83**	2.04 **2.78**	2.00 **2.71**	1.98 **2.68**	1.95 **2.62**	1.93 **2.59**	1.92 **2.57**	18
19	4.38 **8.18**	3.52 **5.93**	3.13 **5.01**	2.90 **4.50**	2.74 **4.17**	2.63 **3.94**	2.55 **3.77**	2.48 **3.63**	2.43 **3.52**	2.38 **3.43**	2.34 **3.36**	2.31 **3.30**	2.26 **3.19**	2.21 **3.12**	2.15 **3.00**	2.11 **2.92**	2.07 **2.84**	2.02 **2.76**	2.00 **2.70**	1.96 **2.63**	1.94 **2.60**	1.91 **2.54**	1.90 **2.51**	1.88 **2.49**	19
20	4.35 **8.10**	3.49 **5.85**	3.10 **4.94**	2.87 **4.43**	2.71 **4.10**	2.60 **3.87**	2.52 **3.71**	2.45 **3.56**	2.40 **3.45**	2.35 **3.37**	2.31 **3.30**	2.28 **3.23**	2.23 **3.13**	2.18 **3.05**	2.12 **2.94**	2.08 **2.86**	2.04 **2.77**	1.99 **2.69**	1.96 **2.63**	1.92 **2.56**	1.90 **2.53**	1.87 **2.47**	1.85 **2.44**	1.84 **2.42**	20
21	4.32 **8.02**	3.47 **5.78**	3.07 **4.87**	2.84 **4.37**	2.68 **4.04**	2.57 **3.81**	2.49 **3.65**	2.42 **3.51**	2.37 **3.40**	2.32 **3.31**	2.28 **3.24**	2.25 **3.17**	2.20 **3.07**	2.15 **2.99**	2.09 **2.88**	2.05 **2.80**	2.00 **2.72**	1.96 **2.63**	1.93 **2.58**	1.89 **2.51**	1.87 **2.47**	1.84 **2.42**	1.82 **2.38**	1.81 **2.36**	21
22	4.30 **7.94**	3.44 **5.72**	3.05 **4.82**	2.82 **4.31**	2.66 **3.99**	2.55 **3.76**	2.47 **3.59**	2.40 **3.45**	2.35 **3.35**	2.30 **3.26**	2.26 **3.18**	2.23 **3.12**	2.18 **3.02**	2.13 **2.94**	2.07 **2.83**	2.03 **2.75**	1.98 **2.67**	1.93 **2.58**	1.91 **2.53**	1.87 **2.46**	1.84 **2.42**	1.81 **2.37**	1.80 **2.33**	1.78 **2.31**	22
23	4.28 **7.88**	3.42 **5.66**	3.03 **4.76**	2.80 **4.26**	2.64 **3.94**	2.53 **3.71**	2.45 **3.54**	2.38 **3.41**	2.32 **3.30**	2.28 **3.21**	2.24 **3.14**	2.20 **3.07**	2.14 **2.97**	2.10 **2.89**	2.04 **2.78**	2.00 **2.70**	1.96 **2.62**	1.91 **2.53**	1.88 **2.48**	1.84 **2.41**	1.82 **2.37**	1.79 **2.32**	1.77 **2.28**	1.76 **2.26**	23
24	4.26 **7.82**	3.40 **5.61**	3.01 **4.72**	2.78 **4.22**	2.62 **3.90**	2.51 **3.67**	2.43 **3.50**	2.36 **3.36**	2.30 **3.25**	2.26 **3.17**	2.22 **3.09**	2.18 **3.03**	2.13 **2.93**	2.09 **2.85**	2.02 **2.74**	1.98 **2.66**	1.94 **2.58**	1.89 **2.49**	1.86 **2.44**	1.82 **2.36**	1.80 **2.33**	1.76 **2.27**	1.74 **2.23**	1.73 **2.21**	24
25	4.24 **7.77**	3.38 **5.57**	2.99 **4.68**	2.76 **4.18**	2.60 **3.86**	2.49 **3.63**	2.41 **3.46**	2.34 **3.32**	2.28 **3.21**	2.24 **3.13**	2.20 **3.05**	2.16 **2.99**	2.11 **2.89**	2.06 **2.81**	2.00 **2.70**	1.96 **2.62**	1.92 **2.54**	1.87 **2.45**	1.84 **2.40**	1.80 **2.32**	1.77 **2.29**	1.74 **2.23**	1.72 **2.19**	1.71 **2.17**	25
26	4.22 **7.72**	3.37 **5.53**	2.98 **4.64**	2.74 **4.14**	2.59 **3.82**	2.47 **3.59**	2.39 **3.42**	2.32 **3.29**	2.27 **3.17**	2.22 **3.09**	2.18 **3.02**	2.15 **2.96**	2.10 **2.86**	2.05 **2.77**	1.99 **2.66**	1.95 **2.58**	1.90 **2.50**	1.85 **2.41**	1.82 **2.36**	1.78 **2.28**	1.76 **2.25**	1.72 **2.19**	1.70 **2.15**	1.69 **2.13**	26

TABLE 3 (Continued)

n_1 degrees of freedom (for greater mean square)

n_2	1	2	3	4	5	6	7	8	9	10	11	12	14	16	20	24	30	40	50	75	100	200	500	∞
27	4.21 / 7.68	3.35 / 5.49	2.96 / 4.60	2.73 / 4.11	2.57 / 3.79	2.46 / 3.56	2.37 / 3.39	2.30 / 3.26	2.25 / 3.14	2.20 / 3.06	2.16 / 2.98	2.13 / 2.93	2.08 / 2.83	2.03 / 2.74	1.97 / 2.63	1.93 / 2.55	1.88 / 2.47	1.84 / 2.38	1.80 / 2.33	1.76 / 2.25	1.74 / 2.21	1.71 / 2.16	1.68 / 2.12	1.67 / 2.10
28	4.20 / 7.64	3.34 / 5.45	2.95 / 4.57	2.71 / 4.07	2.56 / 3.76	2.44 / 3.53	2.36 / 3.36	2.29 / 3.23	2.24 / 3.11	2.19 / 3.03	2.15 / 2.95	2.12 / 2.90	2.06 / 2.80	2.02 / 2.71	1.96 / 2.60	1.91 / 2.52	1.87 / 2.44	1.81 / 2.35	1.78 / 2.30	1.75 / 2.22	1.72 / 2.18	1.69 / 2.13	1.67 / 2.09	1.65 / 2.06
29	4.18 / 7.60	3.33 / 5.42	2.93 / 4.54	2.70 / 4.04	2.54 / 3.73	2.43 / 3.50	2.35 / 3.33	2.28 / 3.20	2.22 / 3.08	2.18 / 3.00	2.14 / 2.92	2.10 / 2.87	2.05 / 2.77	2.00 / 2.68	1.94 / 2.57	1.90 / 2.49	1.85 / 2.41	1.80 / 2.32	1.77 / 2.27	1.73 / 2.19	1.71 / 2.15	1.68 / 2.10	1.65 / 2.06	1.64 / 2.03
30	4.17 / 7.56	3.32 / 5.39	2.92 / 4.51	2.69 / 4.02	2.53 / 3.70	2.42 / 3.47	2.34 / 3.30	2.27 / 3.17	2.21 / 3.06	2.16 / 2.98	2.12 / 2.90	2.09 / 2.84	2.04 / 2.74	1.99 / 2.66	1.93 / 2.55	1.89 / 2.47	1.84 / 2.38	1.79 / 2.29	1.76 / 2.24	1.72 / 2.16	1.69 / 2.13	1.66 / 2.07	1.64 / 2.03	1.62 / 2.01
32	4.15 / 7.50	3.30 / 5.34	2.90 / 4.46	2.67 / 3.97	2.51 / 3.66	2.40 / 3.42	2.32 / 3.25	2.25 / 3.12	2.19 / 3.01	2.14 / 2.94	2.10 / 2.86	2.07 / 2.80	2.02 / 2.70	1.97 / 2.62	1.91 / 2.51	1.86 / 2.42	1.82 / 2.34	1.76 / 2.25	1.74 / 2.20	1.69 / 2.12	1.67 / 2.08	1.64 / 2.02	1.61 / 1.98	1.59 / 1.96
34	4.13 / 7.44	3.28 / 5.29	2.88 / 4.42	2.65 / 3.93	2.49 / 3.61	2.38 / 3.38	2.30 / 3.21	2.23 / 3.08	2.17 / 2.97	2.12 / 2.89	2.08 / 2.82	2.05 / 2.76	2.00 / 2.66	1.95 / 2.58	1.89 / 2.47	1.84 / 2.38	1.80 / 2.30	1.74 / 2.21	1.71 / 2.15	1.67 / 2.08	1.64 / 2.04	1.61 / 1.98	1.59 / 1.94	1.57 / 1.91
36	4.11 / 7.39	3.26 / 5.25	2.86 / 4.38	2.63 / 3.89	2.48 / 3.58	2.36 / 3.35	2.28 / 3.18	2.21 / 3.04	2.15 / 2.94	2.10 / 2.86	2.06 / 2.78	2.03 / 2.72	1.98 / 2.62	1.93 / 2.54	1.87 / 2.43	1.82 / 2.35	1.78 / 2.26	1.72 / 2.17	1.69 / 2.12	1.65 / 2.04	1.62 / 2.00	1.59 / 1.94	1.56 / 1.90	1.55 / 1.87
38	4.10 / 7.35	3.25 / 5.21	2.85 / 4.34	2.62 / 3.86	2.46 / 3.54	2.35 / 3.32	2.26 / 3.15	2.19 / 3.02	2.14 / 2.91	2.09 / 2.82	2.05 / 2.75	2.02 / 2.69	1.96 / 2.59	1.92 / 2.51	1.85 / 2.40	1.80 / 2.32	1.76 / 2.22	1.71 / 2.14	1.67 / 2.08	1.63 / 2.00	1.60 / 1.97	1.57 / 1.90	1.54 / 1.86	1.53 / 1.84
40	4.08 / 7.31	3.23 / 5.18	2.84 / 4.31	2.61 / 3.83	2.45 / 3.51	2.34 / 3.29	2.25 / 3.12	2.18 / 2.99	2.12 / 2.88	2.07 / 2.80	2.04 / 2.73	2.00 / 2.66	1.95 / 2.56	1.90 / 2.49	1.84 / 2.37	1.79 / 2.29	1.74 / 2.20	1.69 / 2.11	1.66 / 2.05	1.61 / 1.97	1.59 / 1.94	1.55 / 1.88	1.53 / 1.84	1.51 / 1.81
42	4.07 / 7.27	3.22 / 5.15	2.83 / 4.29	2.59 / 3.80	2.44 / 3.49	2.32 / 3.26	2.24 / 3.10	2.17 / 2.96	2.11 / 2.86	2.06 / 2.77	2.02 / 2.70	1.99 / 2.64	1.94 / 2.54	1.89 / 2.46	1.82 / 2.35	1.78 / 2.26	1.73 / 2.17	1.68 / 2.08	1.64 / 2.02	1.60 / 1.94	1.57 / 1.91	1.54 / 1.85	1.51 / 1.80	1.49 / 1.78
44	4.06 / 7.24	3.21 / 5.12	2.82 / 4.26	2.58 / 3.78	2.43 / 3.46	2.31 / 3.24	2.23 / 3.07	2.16 / 2.94	2.10 / 2.84	2.05 / 2.75	2.01 / 2.68	1.98 / 2.62	1.92 / 2.52	1.88 / 2.44	1.81 / 2.32	1.76 / 2.24	1.72 / 2.15	1.66 / 2.06	1.63 / 2.00	1.58 / 1.92	1.56 / 1.88	1.52 / 1.82	1.50 / 1.78	1.48 / 1.75
46	4.05 / 7.21	3.20 / 5.10	2.81 / 4.24	2.57 / 3.76	2.42 / 3.44	2.30 / 3.22	2.22 / 3.05	2.14 / 2.92	2.09 / 2.82	2.04 / 2.73	2.00 / 2.66	1.97 / 2.60	1.91 / 2.50	1.87 / 2.42	1.80 / 2.30	1.75 / 2.22	1.71 / 2.13	1.65 / 2.04	1.62 / 1.98	1.57 / 1.90	1.54 / 1.86	1.51 / 1.80	1.48 / 1.76	1.46 / 1.72
48	4.04 / 7.19	3.19 / 5.08	2.80 / 4.22	2.56 / 3.74	2.41 / 3.42	2.30 / 3.20	2.21 / 3.04	2.14 / 2.90	2.08 / 2.80	2.03 / 2.71	1.99 / 2.64	1.96 / 2.58	1.90 / 2.48	1.86 / 2.40	1.79 / 2.28	1.74 / 2.20	1.70 / 2.11	1.64 / 2.02	1.61 / 1.96	1.56 / 1.88	1.53 / 1.84	1.50 / 1.78	1.47 / 1.73	1.45 / 1.70

TABLE 3 (Continued)

n_1 degrees of freedom (for greater mean square)

n_2	1	2	3	4	5	6	7	8	9	10	11	12	14	16	20	24	30	40	50	75	100	200	500	∞
50	4.03 **7.17**	3.18 **5.06**	2.79 **4.20**	2.56 **3.72**	2.40 **3.41**	2.29 **3.18**	2.20 **3.02**	2.13 **2.88**	2.07 **2.78**	2.02 **2.70**	1.98 **2.62**	1.95 **2.56**	1.90 **2.46**	1.85 **2.39**	1.78 **2.26**	1.74 **2.18**	1.69 **2.10**	1.63 **2.00**	1.60 **1.94**	1.55 **1.86**	1.52 **1.82**	1.48 **1.76**	1.46 **1.71**	1.44 **1.68**
55	4.02 **7.12**	3.17 **5.01**	2.78 **4.16**	2.54 **3.68**	2.38 **3.37**	2.27 **3.15**	2.18 **2.98**	2.11 **2.85**	2.05 **2.75**	2.00 **2.66**	1.97 **2.59**	1.93 **2.53**	1.88 **2.43**	1.83 **2.35**	1.76 **2.23**	1.72 **2.15**	1.67 **2.06**	1.61 **1.96**	1.58 **1.90**	1.52 **1.82**	1.50 **1.78**	1.46 **1.71**	1.43 **1.66**	1.41 **1.64**
60	4.00 **7.08**	3.15 **4.98**	2.76 **4.13**	2.52 **3.65**	2.37 **3.34**	2.25 **3.12**	2.17 **2.95**	2.10 **2.82**	2.04 **2.72**	1.99 **2.63**	1.95 **2.56**	1.92 **2.50**	1.86 **2.40**	1.81 **2.32**	1.75 **2.20**	1.70 **2.12**	1.65 **2.03**	1.59 **1.93**	1.56 **1.87**	1.50 **1.79**	1.48 **1.74**	1.44 **1.68**	1.41 **1.63**	1.39 **1.60**
65	3.99 **7.04**	3.14 **4.95**	2.75 **4.10**	2.51 **3.62**	2.36 **3.31**	2.24 **3.09**	2.15 **2.93**	2.08 **2.79**	2.02 **2.70**	1.98 **2.61**	1.94 **2.54**	1.90 **2.47**	1.85 **2.37**	1.80 **2.30**	1.73 **2.18**	1.68 **2.09**	1.63 **2.00**	1.57 **1.90**	1.54 **1.84**	1.49 **1.76**	1.46 **1.71**	1.42 **1.64**	1.39 **1.60**	1.37 **1.56**
70	3.98 **7.01**	3.13 **4.92**	2.74 **4.08**	2.50 **3.60**	2.35 **3.29**	2.23 **3.07**	2.14 **2.91**	2.07 **2.77**	2.01 **2.67**	1.97 **2.59**	1.93 **2.51**	1.89 **2.45**	1.84 **2.35**	1.79 **2.28**	1.72 **2.15**	1.67 **2.07**	1.62 **1.98**	1.56 **1.88**	1.53 **1.82**	1.47 **1.74**	1.45 **1.69**	1.40 **1.62**	1.37 **1.56**	1.35 **1.53**
80	3.96 **6.96**	3.11 **4.88**	2.72 **4.04**	2.48 **3.56**	2.33 **3.25**	2.21 **3.04**	2.12 **2.87**	2.05 **2.74**	1.99 **2.64**	1.95 **2.55**	1.91 **2.48**	1.88 **2.41**	1.82 **2.32**	1.77 **2.24**	1.70 **2.11**	1.65 **2.03**	1.60 **1.94**	1.54 **1.84**	1.51 **1.78**	1.45 **1.70**	1.42 **1.65**	1.38 **1.57**	1.35 **1.52**	1.32 **1.49**
100	3.94 **6.90**	3.09 **4.82**	2.70 **3.98**	2.46 **3.51**	2.30 **3.20**	2.19 **2.99**	2.10 **2.82**	2.03 **2.69**	1.97 **2.59**	1.92 **2.51**	1.88 **2.43**	1.85 **2.36**	1.79 **2.26**	1.75 **2.19**	1.68 **2.06**	1.63 **1.98**	1.57 **1.89**	1.51 **1.79**	1.48 **1.73**	1.42 **1.64**	1.39 **1.59**	1.34 **1.51**	1.30 **1.46**	1.28 **1.43**
125	3.92 **6.84**	3.07 **4.78**	2.68 **3.94**	2.44 **3.47**	2.29 **3.17**	2.17 **2.95**	2.08 **2.79**	2.01 **2.65**	1.95 **2.56**	1.90 **2.47**	1.86 **2.40**	1.83 **2.33**	1.77 **2.23**	1.72 **2.15**	1.65 **2.03**	1.60 **1.94**	1.55 **1.85**	1.49 **1.75**	1.45 **1.68**	1.39 **1.59**	1.36 **1.54**	1.31 **1.46**	1.27 **1.40**	1.25 **1.37**
150	3.91 **6.81**	3.06 **4.75**	2.67 **3.91**	2.43 **3.44**	2.27 **3.14**	2.16 **2.92**	2.07 **2.76**	2.00 **2.62**	1.94 **2.53**	1.89 **2.44**	1.85 **2.37**	1.82 **2.30**	1.76 **2.20**	1.71 **2.12**	1.64 **2.00**	1.59 **1.91**	1.54 **1.83**	1.47 **1.72**	1.44 **1.66**	1.37 **1.56**	1.34 **1.51**	1.29 **1.43**	1.25 **1.37**	1.22 **1.33**
200	3.89 **6.76**	3.04 **4.71**	2.65 **3.88**	2.41 **3.41**	2.26 **3.11**	2.14 **2.90**	2.05 **2.73**	1.98 **2.60**	1.92 **2.50**	1.87 **2.41**	1.83 **2.34**	1.80 **2.28**	1.74 **2.17**	1.69 **2.09**	1.62 **1.97**	1.57 **1.88**	1.52 **1.79**	1.45 **1.69**	1.42 **1.62**	1.35 **1.53**	1.32 **1.48**	1.26 **1.39**	1.22 **1.33**	1.19 **1.28**
400	3.86 **6.70**	3.02 **4.66**	2.62 **3.83**	2.39 **3.36**	2.23 **3.06**	2.12 **2.85**	2.03 **2.69**	1.96 **2.55**	1.90 **2.46**	1.85 **2.37**	1.81 **2.29**	1.78 **2.23**	1.72 **2.12**	1.67 **2.04**	1.60 **1.92**	1.54 **1.84**	1.49 **1.74**	1.42 **1.64**	1.38 **1.57**	1.32 **1.47**	1.28 **1.42**	1.22 **1.32**	1.16 **1.24**	1.13 **1.19**
1000	3.85 **6.66**	3.00 **4.62**	2.61 **3.80**	2.38 **3.34**	2.22 **3.04**	2.10 **2.82**	2.02 **2.66**	1.95 **2.53**	1.89 **2.43**	1.84 **2.34**	1.80 **2.26**	1.76 **2.20**	1.70 **2.09**	1.65 **2.01**	1.58 **1.89**	1.53 **1.81**	1.47 **1.71**	1.41 **1.61**	1.36 **1.54**	1.30 **1.44**	1.26 **1.38**	1.19 **1.28**	1.13 **1.19**	1.08 **1.11**
∞	3.84 **6.64**	2.99 **4.60**	2.60 **3.78**	2.37 **3.32**	2.21 **3.02**	2.09 **2.80**	2.01 **2.64**	1.94 **2.51**	1.88 **2.41**	1.83 **2.32**	1.79 **2.24**	1.75 **2.18**	1.69 **2.07**	1.64 **1.99**	1.57 **1.87**	1.52 **1.79**	1.46 **1.69**	1.40 **1.59**	1.35 **1.52**	1.28 **1.41**	1.24 **1.36**	1.17 **1.25**	1.11 **1.15**	1.00 **1.00**

SOURCE: George W. Snedecor, *Statistical Methods*, 5th edition, Ames, Iowa: The Iowa State University Press, 1956, pp. 246–249. Copyright © 1956 by the Iowa State University Press; reprinted by permission. The function $F = e$ with exponent $2z$, is computed in part from Fisher's table VII(7). Additional entries are by interpolation, mostly graphical.

TABLE 4

5 PERCENT SIGNIFICANCE POINTS OF d_l AND d_u IN TWO-TAILED TESTS

n	$k' = 1$		$k' = 2$		$k' = 3$		$k' = 4$		$k' = 5$	
	d_l	d_u	d_l	d_u	d_l	d_u	d_l	d_u	d_l	d_u
15	0.95	1.23	0.83	1.40	0.71	1.61	0.59	1.84	0.48	2.09
16	0.98	1.24	0.86	1.40	0.75	1.59	0.64	1.80	0.53	2.03
17	1.01	1.25	0.90	1.40	0.79	1.58	0.68	1.77	0.57	1.98
18	1.03	1.26	0.93	1.40	0.82	1.56	0.72	1.74	0.62	1.93
19	1.06	1.28	0.96	1.41	0.86	1.55	0.76	1.72	0.66	1.90
20	1.08	1.28	0.99	1.41	0.89	1.55	0.79	1.70	0.70	1.87
21	1.10	1.30	1.01	1.41	0.92	1.54	0.83	1.69	0.73	1.84
22	1.12	1.31	1.04	1.42	0.95	1.54	0.86	1.68	0.77	1.82
23	1.14	1.32	1.06	1.42	0.97	1.54	0.89	1.67	0.80	1.80
24	1.16	1.33	1.08	1.43	1.00	1.54	0.91	1.66	0.83	1.79
25	1.18	1.34	1.10	1.43	1.02	1.54	0.94	1.65	0.86	1.77
26	1.19	1.35	1.12	1.44	1.04	1.54	0.96	1.65	0.88	1.76
27	1.21	1.36	1.13	1.44	1.06	1.54	0.99	1.64	0.91	1.75
28	1.22	1.37	1.15	1.45	1.08	1.54	1.01	1.64	0.93	1.74
29	1.24	1.38	1.17	1.45	1.10	1.54	1.03	1.63	0.96	1.73
30	1.25	1.38	1.18	1.46	1.12	1.54	1.05	1.63	0.98	1.73
31	1.26	1.39	1.20	1.47	1.13	1.55	1.07	1.63	1.00	1.72
32	1.27	1.40	1.21	1.47	1.15	1.55	1.08	1.63	1.02	1.71
33	1.28	1.41	1.22	1.48	1.16	1.55	1.10	1.63	1.04	1.71
34	1.29	1.41	1.24	1.48	1.17	1.55	1.12	1.63	1.06	1.70
35	1.30	1.42	1.25	1.48	1.19	1.55	1.13	1.63	1.07	1.70
36	1.31	1.43	1.26	1.49	1.20	1.56	1.15	1.63	1.09	1.70
37	1.32	1.43	1.27	1.49	1.21	1.56	1.16	1.62	1.10	1.70
38	1.33	1.44	1.28	1.50	1.23	1.56	1.17	1.62	1.12	1.70
39	1.34	1.44	1.29	1.50	1.24	1.56	1.19	1.63	1.13	1.69
40	1.35	1.45	1.30	1.51	1.25	1.57	1.20	1.63	1.15	1.69
45	1.39	1.48	1.34	1.53	1.30	1.58	1.25	1.63	1.21	1.69
50	1.42	1.50	1.38	1.54	1.34	1.59	1.30	1.64	1.26	1.69
55	1.45	1.52	1.41	1.56	1.37	1.60	1.33	1.64	1.30	1.69
60	1.47	1.54	1.44	1.57	1.40	1.61	1.37	1.65	1.33	1.69
65	1.49	1.55	1.46	1.59	1.43	1.62	1.40	1.66	1.36	1.69
70	1.51	1.57	1.48	1.60	1.45	1.63	1.42	1.66	1.39	1.70
75	1.53	1.58	1.50	1.61	1.47	1.64	1.45	1.67	1.42	1.70
80	1.54	1.59	1.52	1.62	1.49	1.65	1.47	1.67	1.44	1.70
85	1.56	1.60	1.53	1.63	1.51	1.65	1.49	1.68	1.46	1.71
90	1.57	1.61	1.55	1.64	1.53	1.66	1.50	1.69	1.48	1.71
95	1.58	1.62	1.56	1.65	1.54	1.67	1.52	1.69	1.50	1.71
100	1.59	1.63	1.57	1.65	1.55	1.67	1.53	1.70	1.51	1.72

SOURCE: J. Durbin and G. S. Watson, "Testing for Serial Correlation in Least Squares Regression," *Biometrika*, vol. 38 (1951), pp. 159–177. Reprinted with permission of the authors and the Trustees of Biometrika.

Answers to Questions

CHAPTER 1

1. $\bar{X} = 3$, $\sum_{t=1}^{n} (X_t - \bar{X}) = -3 + 2 + 3 - 2 = 0$.

2. $\sum_{t=1}^{n} (aX_t + bY_t + cZ_t) = (aX_1 + bY_1 + cZ_1) + \cdots + (aX_n + bY_n + cZ_n)$

$$= (aX_1 + \cdots + aX_n) + (bY_1 + \cdots + bY_n)$$

$$+ (cZ_1 + \cdots + cZ_n)$$

$$= \sum_{t=1}^{n} aX_t + \sum_{t=1}^{n} bY_t + \sum_{t=1}^{n} cZ_t$$

$$= a \sum_{t=1}^{n} X_t + b \sum_{t=1}^{n} Y_t + c \sum_{t=1}^{n} Z_t.$$

3. $\sum_{t=1}^{n} (X_t - \bar{X})(Y_t - \bar{Y}) = \sum_{t=1}^{n} [X_t(Y_t - \bar{Y}) - \bar{X}(Y_t - \bar{Y})]$

$$= \sum_{t=1}^{n} X_t(Y_t - \bar{Y}) - \sum_{t=1}^{n} \bar{X}(Y_t - \bar{Y}).$$

But since $\bar{X}$ is a constant, we can write the last term as $\bar{X}\sum_{t=1}^{n} (Y_t - \bar{Y}) = 0$.

CHAPTER 2

1. $\hat{a} = \bar{Y} - b\bar{X} = \sum_{t=1}^{n} \frac{Y_t}{n} - \bar{X} \sum_{t=1}^{n} \frac{(X_t - \bar{X})Y_t}{\sum_{t=1}^{n} (X_t - \bar{X})^2}$.

Let $A = \sum_{t=1}^{n} (X_t - \bar{X})^2$; then

$$\hat{a} = \sum_{t=1}^{n} \frac{Y_t}{n} - \frac{\bar{X}}{A} \sum_{t=1}^{n} (X_t - \bar{X})Y_t = \sum_{t=1}^{n} \left[\frac{1}{n} - \frac{\bar{X}}{A}(X_t - \bar{X}) \right] Y_t.$$

Since $W_t = (X_t - \bar{X})/A$, the answer follows.

2. a. The normal equations are

$$\sum Y_t = n\hat{a}_0 + b \sum X_t,$$

$$\sum X_t Y_t = \hat{a}_0 \sum X_t + b \sum X_t^2.$$

The computations with the observed values of of X_t and Y_t give us

$$\sum_{t=1}^{5} Y_t = 30, \quad \sum_{t=1}^{5} X_t = 12, \quad \sum_{t=1}^{5} X_t^2 = 34, \quad \sum_{t=1}^{5} X_t Y_t = 74, \quad N = 5$$

b. The normal equations yield

$$30 = 5\hat{a} + 12\hat{b},$$

$$74 = 12\hat{a} + 34\hat{b}.$$

Solving this set of equations gives us

$$\hat{a} = 5.076, \qquad \hat{b} = 0.385.$$

$$\hat{\sigma}_u^2 = \frac{\sum (Y_t - \hat{Y}_t)^2}{n - 2} = 3.077.$$

3. The argument is faulty because it neglects the existence of the disturbance term, u_t, which takes on positive and negative values, but whose *expected* value, $E(u_t)$, is zero. The relationship $C_t = a + bY_t$ is not an exact one, but is rather a mean relationship.

4. We first derive μ_Y:

$$E(Y) = E(5 - 3X) = 5 - 3E(X) = 5 - 3\mu_X = \mu_Y.$$

The covariance, therefore, is

$$\sigma_{X,Y} = E(Y - \mu_Y)(X - \mu_X) = E(5 - 3X - 5 + 3\mu_X)(X - \mu_X)$$

$$= E[-3(X - \mu_X)^2] = -3\sigma_X^2.$$

The variance of Y is $E(Y - \mu_Y)^2 = 9\sigma_X^2$; thus, $\sigma_Y = 3\sigma_X$. Therefore, the correlation coefficient is

$$\rho_{X,Y} = \frac{-3\sigma_X^2}{3\sigma_X \sigma_X} = -1.$$

5. We make use of a fundamental relationship for the variance of the sum of random variables. This relationship says that if $Y = a_0 + a_1 X_1 + a_2 X_2 + \cdots + a_n X_n$, and $X_1, \ldots, X_n$ are independent, then

$$\text{var}(Y) = a_1^2 \sigma_{X_1}^2 + a_2^2 \sigma_{X_2}^2 + \cdots + a_n^2 \sigma_{X_n}^2.$$

Applying this relationship to our problem, we get

$$\text{var}(Y) = 4 + 27 + 500 = 531.$$

6. a. The argument can be formulated as follows:

$$Y_i = a + b(T_{ci} - T_{si}) + u_i,$$

where

Y_i = the average family income in the ith city,
T_{ci} = the tax rate in the ith city,
T_{si} = the tax rate in the suburb of the ith city, and
u_i = a disturbance term.

b. A different formulation of the same proposition is

$$Y_i = a + b\frac{T_{ci}}{T_{si}} + u_i.$$

In both cases $b < 0$. That is, if T_c is high relative to T_s, we would expect the middle- and upper-income families to be living in the suburbs; thus, the average family income of those remaining in the city, Y_i, would be low.

7. Substituting (2) into (1), we obtain

$$Y_t = (a_1 + a_2) + (b_1 + b_2)X_t + \varepsilon_t.$$

Thus, the effect of X_t on the mean of Y_t would be $(b_1 + b_2)$. This problem demonstrates that we can look upon our standard bivariate regression model as being derived from another model in which the disturbance term is linearly related to the regressor as in (2).

8. Yes. To see this, substitute the disturbance relationship in equation (1) of Question 7 to obtain

$$Y_t = (a_1 + a_2) + b_1X_t + (b_2X_t^2 + \varepsilon_t).$$

Thus the model relating Y_t to X_t would have $w_t = b_2X_t^2 + \varepsilon_t$ as a disturbance term. It should be clear that w_t will not have a mean of zero; further, since X_t and X_t^2 are obviously related, w_t would be correlated with the regressor X_t. If the values of X_t are related at different points in time, so will the values of w_t. Therefore, $\text{cov}(w_t, w_s) \neq 0$. Finally, since the values of w_t would depend in part on the values of X_t, the variance of w_t would not be the same in each and every period.

9. Let A_t be the age of a child at time t and H_t be his height measured in inches. Then we might postulate

$$H_t = a + bA_t + u_t,$$

where we would expect $b > 0$. A shortcoming of this relationship is that it can obviously hold only for a limited number of years. That is, although a child will advance in age, year after year, his height will obviously reach a limit!

10. a. The regression model would be

$$Y_t = a + bX_t^m + (u_t - b\varepsilon_t).$$

b. Yes, the disturbance term would be correlated with the regressor X_t^m. To see this, note that

$$E[X_t^m(u_t - b\varepsilon_t)] = E(X_t^m u_t) - bE(X_t^m\varepsilon_t)$$

$$= 0 - b\sigma_\varepsilon^2 \neq 0,$$

since $(X_t^m\varepsilon_t) = X_t\varepsilon_t + \varepsilon_t^2$, and X_t and ε_t are independent.

CHAPTER 3

1. Let S be the population mean I.Q. We then test $H_0: S = 100$ against $H_1: S > 100$. Since we are concerned only with $S \geq 100$, we can use a one-tailed t test with $(100 - 1 = 99)$ degrees of freedom. We find that the lower bound of S is $\hat{S} - (t_{n-1;\,0.95})\hat{\sigma}_S = 110 - 1.65(2)$. Since the lower bound lies above 100, we reject $H_0: S = 100$ and accept $H_1: S > 100$.

2. Let $\bar{X}_{20}$ and $\bar{X}_{30}$ be sample averages based on samples of size 20 and 30, respectively. Then, if both samples were drawn from the same population, $E(\bar{X}_{20}) = E(\bar{X}_{30}) = \mu$, where μ is the population mean. Thus, both estimators are unbiased. However, $\bar{X}_{30}$ would be preferred because its variance would be smaller. Therefore its use would lead to narrower confidence intervals and more reliable tests of hypotheses.

3. From the results we know that $\hat{\alpha} = 0.125$. We may test the hypothesis $H_0: \alpha = 0$ against $H_1: \alpha \neq 0$ in terms of our equation by testing $H_0: (1 - \alpha) = 1$ against $H_1: (1 - \alpha) \neq 1$. The absolute value of the t ratio is

$$\left| \frac{0.875 - 1.00}{0.15} \right| = \frac{0.125}{0.15} \doteq 0.83,$$

which is substantially less than 2. We therefore accept the null hypothesis and conclude that the change in hours is not proportional to the deviation from 40.

4. Let h be the mean height. We then test $H_0: h = 70$ against $H_1: h < 70$. Since we are concerned only with $h \leq 70$, we can use a one-tailed normal test. We find that the upper bound for the value h is $(\hat{h} + 1.65\sigma_h) = 68 + 1.65(2) = 71.3$. Since $70 < 71.3$, we accept $H_0: h = 70$.

5. The normality assumption facilitates the construction of confidence intervals and the testing of hypotheses. This is demonstrated in the text. The normality assumption, however, *is not necessary* for the construction of confidence intervals or for the testing of hypotheses, but without the normality assumption, both of these tasks would be more difficult.

6. The null hypothesis would be that the mean height of people in the West is 67 in. The alternative would be that their mean height exceeds 67 in. A Type 1 error is committed if we are led to believe that they are taller when in fact they are not. The consequence would be that unnecessary retooling would take place. In addition, coats of the wrong size would be produced. A Type 2 error is committed if we are led to believe that they are not taller when in fact they are. The consequences would be that coats of the wrong size would be produced. This suggests that a Type 1 error may, in this instance, be more costly than a Type 2 error.

7. The linear regression model is not so restrictive as it first appears, because by a judicious use of various transformations it is possible to transform a wide variety of nonlinear relationships into linear forms. Letting $Z_t = 1/(1 - X_t)$, the observation matrix is

Y_t	X_t	Z_t
1	0	1
10	0.1	1.11
12	0.5	2

8. a. We test the hypothesis (at a 5 percent level of significance) by simply observing whether the absolute value of the t ratio exceeds 2 by a "significant" amount. Since it does, we reject the null hypothesis.

   b. The standard deviations are

$$\hat{\sigma}_{\hat{a}} = \frac{15}{3.1} \doteq 4.84, \qquad \hat{\sigma}_{\hat{b}} = \frac{0.81}{18.7} \doteq 0.043,$$

c. The 95 percent confidence interval is

$$0.81 \pm (t_{n-2;\,0.975})\, 0.043 = 0.81 \pm 0.091.$$

9. The hypothesis that the demand for welfare, D_t, is related to the benefit rate, B_t, may be expressed as

$$D_t = a_1 + a_2 B_t + u_{1t},$$

where we would expect $a_2 > 0$. The hypothesis that the benefit rate is related to the demand for welfare, through political pressure, may be expressed as

$$B_t = b_1 + b_2 D_{t-1} + u_{2t},$$

if we assume a lag due to the political process.

10. Let N_t be the number of firms that locate in the given state. Then, the firm location model might be expressed as

$$N_t = a_1 + b_1 \left(\frac{T_{1t}}{T_{2t}}\right) + u_{1t},$$

where T_{1t} is the tax in the given state, and T_{2t} is the average tax rate of neighboring states. We would expect $b_1 < 0$. Similarly, let P_t be some measure of pollution. Then, the pollution relationship may be expressed as

$$P_t = a_2 + b_2 N_t + u_{2t},$$

where we would expect $b_2 > 0$.

11. Solving for X_t, we have

$$X_t = \frac{5 - Z_t}{3}.$$

Substituting into the regression model, we have

$$Y_t = a + b \left(\frac{5}{3} - \frac{Z_t}{3}\right) + u_t$$

$$= (a + \tfrac{5}{3}b) - \frac{b}{3} Z_t + u_t.$$

Thus the intercept is $(a + \tfrac{5}{3}b)$ and the slope is $-b/3$.

CHAPTER 4

1. The assumptions of the model are as follows:

a. 1. The expected value of the disturbance term is zero $E(u_t) = 0$.
   2. The variance of the disturbance term is a constant $E(u_t - 0)^2 = E(u_t^2) = \sigma_u^2$.
   3. The value of the disturbance term for one observation is independent of its value for any other observation. Therefore, the covariance between disturbance terms, for any two observations, u_s and u_t, is zero:

$$\text{cov}(u_t, u_s) = 0.$$

4. The disturbance term is independent of each of the independent variables, and all of their lagged values, so that $\text{cov}(u_t, X_{it}) = 0$.
   5. None of the independent variables is a linear combination of the others.
   b. The normal equations are

   1. $\sum Y_t = n\hat{a}_0 + \hat{a}_1 \sum X_{1t} + \hat{a}_2 \sum X_{2t}$,
   2. $\sum X_{1t}Y_t = \hat{a}_0 \sum X_{1t} + \hat{a}_1 \sum X_{1t}^2 + \hat{a}_2 \sum X_{1t}X_{2t}$,
   3. $\sum X_{2t}Y_t = \hat{a}_0 \sum X_{2t} + \hat{a}_1 \sum X_{2t}X_{1t} + \hat{a}_2 \sum X_{2t}^2$.

   The first normal equation is derived by requiring that $\sum \hat{u}_t = 0$, corresponding to the assumption that $E(u_t) = 0$. The second normal equation is derived by requiring that $\sum (X_{1t}\hat{u}_t) = 0$, corresponding to the assumption that $E(X_{1t}u_t) = \text{cov}(X_{1t}, u_t) = 0$. The third normal equation is derived by requiring that $\sum (X_{2t}\hat{u}_t) = 0$, corresponding to the assumption that $E(X_{2t}u_t) = \text{cov}(X_{2t}, u_t) = 0$.
   c. $10 = 100\hat{a}_0$
   $30 = 35\hat{a}_1$
   $20 = 3\hat{a}_2$
   $\hat{a}_0 = \frac{1}{10}$
   $\hat{a}_1 = \frac{6}{7}$
   $\hat{a}_2 = \frac{20}{3}$

2. The parameters that cannot be estimated are a_1, a_2, and a_3. This is so because the third regressor, $(X_{1t} - X_{2t})$, is a linear combination of X_{1t} and X_{2t} so that we have perfect multicollinearity. This means that the corresponding normal equation is a linear combination of the normal equations corresponding to X_{1t} and X_{2t}; thus we cannot in general solve for the parameter estimators. Note that X_1X_2 is a nonlinear combination and hence presents no problems. Rewriting the equation as

$$Y_t = a_0 + (a_1 + a_3)X_{1t} + (a_2 - a_3)X_{2t} + a_4X_{1t}X_{2t} + \varepsilon_t,$$

we see that we can solve for $\hat{a}_0$, $(a_1 \widehat{+} a_3)$, $(a_2 \widehat{-} a_3)$, and $\hat{a}_4$.

3. The normal equations are

$$\sum Y_t = n\hat{b}_0 + \hat{b}_1 \sum X_{1t} + \hat{b}_2 \sum X_{2t},$$

$$\sum X_1Y_t = \hat{b}_0 \sum X_{1t} + \hat{b}_1 \sum X_{1t}^2 + \hat{b}_2 \sum X_{1t}X_{2t},$$

$$\sum X_2Y_t = \hat{b}_0 \sum X_{2t} + \hat{b}_1 \sum X_{2t}X_{1t} + \hat{b}_2 \sum X_{2t}^2.$$

The computations with the observed values of X_t and Y_t give us $n = 5$, $\sum X_1 = 8$, $\sum X_2 = 9$, $\sum Y_t = 30$, $\sum X_{1t}X_{2t} = 12$, $\sum X_{1t}^2 = 16$, $\sum X_{2t}^2 = 19$, $\sum X_{1t}Y_t = 50$, $\sum X_{2t}Y_t = 51$. Inserting these computed values into the normal equations yields

$$30 = 5\hat{b}_0 + 8\hat{b}_1 + 9\hat{b}_2,$$

$$50 = 8\hat{b}_0 + 16\hat{b}_1 + 12\hat{b}_2,$$

$$51 = 9\hat{b}_0 + 12\hat{b}_1 + 19\hat{b}_2.$$

4. The regression model could be expressed as

$$Y_i = a + b_1(T_{ci} - T_{si}) + b_2(C_{ci} - C_{si}) + b_3(H_{ci} - H_{si}) + b_4D_{ci} + u_i,$$

where

Y_i = the average income in the ith city,
T_{ci} = the tax rate in the ith city,
T_{si} = the tax rate in the corresponding ith suburb,
C_{ci} = the crime rate in the ith city,
C_{si} = the crime rate in the corresponding ith suburb,
H_{ci} = housing costs in the ith city,
H_{si} = housing costs in the corresponding ith suburb,
D_{ci} = density in the ith city (people per square mile), and
u_i = disturbance term.

The relative importance of cross-sectional and times-series data will depend on the nature of the problem. In the above regression model cross-sectional data will probably be more useful because tax rates, crime rates, costs of housing, and density tend to vary more across cities than over time within a given city. In this model we would expect all the parameters to be negative.

5. a. The perfect linear relationship

$$\bar{P}_t = \frac{\sum_{i=1}^{k} P_{it}}{k}$$

implies that the $(k + 1)$th normal equation is a linear combination of the first k normal equations. While we have $(k + 3)$ parameters to estimate, we would have only $(k + 2)$ independent normal equations. Thus, we cannot in general solve uniquely for all the parameter estimators.

b. Substituting the relationship $P_t = \sum_{i=1}^{k} (P_{it})/k$ into the demand equation and collecting terms, we get

$$D_{it} = a_0 + P_{1t}\left(a_1 + \frac{b}{k}\right) + P_{2t}\left(a_2 + \frac{b}{k}\right) + \cdots$$

$$+ P_{kt}\left(a_k + \frac{b}{k}\right) + cY_t + u_{1t}.$$

Thus we would be able to estimate a_0, $(a_i + b/k)$, and c, where $i = 1, \ldots, k$.

6. a. The equation does not have perfect multicollinearity since X_t and X_t^2 are not perfectly correlated. The normal equations are

$$\sum Y_t = nb_0 + b_1 \sum X_t + b_2 \sum X_t^2,$$

$$\sum Y_t X_t = b_0 \sum X_t + b_1 \sum X_t^2 + b_2 \sum X_t^3,$$

$$\sum Y_t X_t^2 = b_0 \sum X_t^2 + b_1 \sum X_t^3 + b_2 \sum X_t^4.$$

We note that these three equations are linearly independent and thus we can solve for b_0, b_1, and b_2.

b. $4 = 4b_0 + 8b_1 + 30b_2,$
$23 = 8b_0 + 30b_1 + 134b_2,$
$107 = 30b_0 + 134b_1 + 642b_2.$

CHAPTER 5

1. Using the logarithmic transformation, we get

$$Q_t' = B + aL_t' + bK_t' + u_t,$$

where

$$Q_t' = \log Q_t,$$
$$B = \log(1/A),$$
$$L_t' = \log L_t, \text{ and}$$
$$K_t' = \log K_t.$$

We estimate B, a, b, and take $\hat{A} = e^{-\hat{B}}$. We note that $\hat{A}$ would be biased but consistent.

2. The regression model is

$$I_t = a_0 + b_1 r_t + b_2 D_t + u_t,$$

where

$D_t = 0$ if the president is a Democrat at time t,
$D_t = 1$ otherwise (Republican president),
$r_t = $ the rate of interest, and
$u_t = $ disturbance term.

3. The model is

$$C_t = a_0 + a_1 Z_{1t} + a_2 Z_{2t} + a_3 Z_{3t} + u_t,$$

$$Z_{1t} = F_t Y_t,$$

$$Z_{2t} = Y_t^{1/2},$$

$$Z_{3t} = \frac{1}{A_t}.$$

4. To take account of a possible shift in the function, we introduce a dummy variable. The regression model is then

$$C_i = a + bY_i + cD_i + u_i,$$

where

$D_i = 0$ if the ith consumer lives in an urban area,
$D = 1$ otherwise.

Thus if the ith consumer is a rural resident, the regression is $C_t = (a + c) + bY_i + u_i$; if the ith consumer resides in an urban location, the function is $C_i = a + bY_i + u_i$.

5. a. The regression model is

$$I_t = b_0 + b_1 r_t + b_2 \Pi_t + b_3 \Delta S_t + u_t,$$

where

$I_t = $ investment expenditures,
$\Pi_t = $ the profit rate,
$\Delta S_t = $ the change in sales,
$r_t = $ the rate of interest, and
$u_t = $ the disturbance term.

b. The problem in estimating the above regression is caused by perfect multi-collinearity. Specifically, if the rate of profit is 15 percent in each and every time period, we shall be unable to estimate b_0 and b_2.

6. a. The unrestricted form of the model is

$$I_t = a_0 + a_1 r_t + b_0 S_t + b_1 S_{t-1} + \cdots + b_7 S_{t-7} + u_t.$$

b. The Almon form of the model, using $b_i = \alpha_0 + \alpha_1 i + \alpha_2 i^2$, is

$$I_t = a_0 + a_1 r_t + \alpha_0 Z_{1t} + \alpha_1 Z_{2t} + \alpha_2 Z_{3t} + u_t,$$

where $Z_{1t} = \sum_{i=0}^{7} S_{t-i}$, $Z_{2t} = \sum_{i=1}^{7} i S_{t-i}$, and $Z_{3t} = \sum_{i=1}^{7} i^2 S_{t-i}$.

c. The normal equations are

$$\sum_{t=0}^{n} I_t = n\hat{a}_0 + \hat{a}_1 \sum_{t=0}^{n} r_t + \hat{\alpha}_0 \sum_{t=0}^{n} Z_{1t}$$

$$+ \hat{\alpha}_1 \sum_{t=0}^{n} Z_{2t} + \hat{\alpha}_2 \sum_{t=0}^{n} Z_{3t},$$

$$\sum_{t=0}^{n} r_t I_t = \hat{a}_0 \sum_{t=0}^{n} r_t + \hat{a}_1 \sum_{t=0}^{n} r_t^2 + \hat{\alpha}_0 \sum_{t=0}^{n} r_t Z_{1t}$$

$$+ \hat{\alpha}_1 \sum_{t=0}^{n} r_t Z_{2t} + \hat{\alpha}_2 \sum_{t=0}^{n} r_t Z_{3t},$$

$$\sum_{t=0}^{n} Z_{1t} I_t = \hat{a}_0 \sum_{t=0}^{n} Z_{1t} + \hat{a}_1 \sum_{t=0}^{n} Z_{1t} r_t + \hat{\alpha}_0 \sum_{t=0}^{n} Z_{1t}^2$$

$$+ \hat{\alpha}_1 \sum_{t=0}^{n} Z_{1t} Z_{2t} + \hat{\alpha}_2 \sum_{t=0}^{n} Z_{1t} Z_{3t},$$

$$\sum_{t=0}^{n} Z_{2t} I_t = \hat{a}_0 \sum_{t=0}^{n} Z_{2t} + \hat{a}_1 \sum_{t=0}^{n} Z_{2t} r_t + \hat{\alpha}_0 \sum_{t=0}^{n} Z_{2t} Z_{1t}$$

$$+ \hat{\alpha}_1 \sum_{t=0}^{n} Z_{2t}{}^2 + \hat{\alpha}_2 \sum_{t=0}^{n} Z_{2t} Z_{3t},$$

$$\sum_{t=0}^{n} Z_{3t} I_t = \hat{a}_0 \sum_{t=0}^{n} Z_{3t} + \hat{a}_1 \sum_{t=0}^{n} Z_{3t} r_t + \hat{\alpha}_0 \sum_{t=0}^{n} Z_{3t} Z_{1t}$$

$$+ \hat{\alpha}_1 \sum_{t=0}^{n} Z_{3t} Z_{2t} + \hat{\alpha}_2 \sum_{t=0}^{n} Z_{3t}^2.$$

7. a. The estimate of b_2 would be

$$b_2 = \hat{\alpha}_0 + 2\hat{\alpha}_1 + 4\hat{\alpha}_2 + 8\hat{\alpha}_3 + 16\hat{\alpha}_4$$

$$= 1 + 6 + 20 + 32 - 160 = -101.$$

b. Replacing b's in the original model, we get

$$Y_t = a + \alpha_0 Z_{1t} + \alpha_1 Z_{2t} + \alpha_2 Z_{3t} + \alpha_3 Z_{4t} + \alpha_4 Z_{5t} + u_t,$$

where

$$Z_{1t} = \sum_{i=0}^{6} X_{t-i}, \qquad Z_{2t} = \sum_{i=0}^{6} i X_{t-i},$$

$$Z_{3t} = \sum_{i=1}^{6} i^2 X_{t-i}, \qquad Z_{4t} = \sum_{i=1}^{6} i^3 X_{t-i},$$

and

$$Z_{5t} = \sum i^4 X_{t-1}.$$

Since

$$\sum_{i=0}^{6} b_i = 7\alpha_0 + \sum_{i=0}^{6} i\alpha_1 + \sum_{i=0}^{6} i^2 \alpha_2 + \sum_{i=0}^{6} i^3 \alpha_3 + \sum_{i=0}^{6} i^4 \alpha_4 = 1,$$

we can solve for α_0 as follows:

$$\alpha_0 = \frac{(1 - 21\alpha_1 - 91\alpha_2 - 441\alpha_3 - 2275\alpha_4)}{7}.$$

Substituting for α_0 in the above regression, we get

$$Y_t = a + \alpha_1 Q_{1t} + \alpha_2 Q_{2t} + \alpha_3 Q_{3t} + \alpha_4 Q_{4t} + u_t,$$

where

$$Y_t^* = \left(Y_t - \frac{Z_{1t}}{7} \right),$$

$$Q_{1t} = Z_{2t} - \frac{21 Z_{1t}}{7},$$

$$Q_{2t} = Z_{3t} - \frac{91 Z_{1t}}{7},$$

$$Q_{3t} = Z_{4t} - \frac{441 Z_{1t}}{7},$$

$$Q_{4t} = Z_{5t} - \frac{2275 Z_{1t}}{7}.$$

8. Most functions that economists consider can be approximated by a polynomial. The degree of the polynomial will be determined by scope of experience, or alternatively, by the range of the variables involved. For events outside the scope of experience, a polynomial of a different degree might be appropriate. Therefore, it might be inappropriate to use our estimated equation for such prediction purposes. This is demonstrated in the following graph:

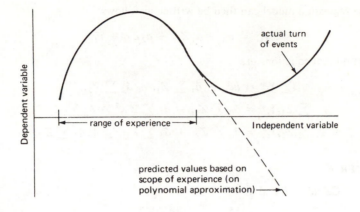

9. Lagging the equation, multiplying through by λ, then subtracting from the original equation, we have

$$Y_t = (a_0 - \lambda a_0) + a_1 X_t - a_1 \lambda X_{t-1} + \lambda Y_{t-1} + b_0 Z_t + u_t - \lambda u_{t-1}.$$

10. If $b_5 = 3$, we have $\alpha_0 + 5\alpha_1 + 25\alpha_2 = 3$. Therefore, we may solve for $\alpha_0 = 3 - 5\alpha_1 - 25\alpha_2$. The unrestricted form for the Almon model is

$$Y_t = b + \alpha_0 Z_{0t} + \alpha_1 Z_{1t} + \alpha_2 Z_{2t} + u_t,$$

where

$$Z_{0t} = \sum_{i=0}^{10} X_{t-i}, \qquad Z_{1t} = \sum_{i=1}^{10} i X_{t-i}, \qquad Z_{2t} = \sum_{i=1}^{10} i^2 X_{t-i}.$$

Substituting out α_0, we obtain the restricted form

$$Y_t^* = b + \alpha_1 Q_{1t} + \alpha_2 Q_{2t} + u_t,$$

where

$$Y_t^* = Y_t - 3 Z_{0t}, \qquad Q_{1t} = (Z_{1t} - 5 Z_{0t}),$$

and

$$Q_{2t} = (Z_{2t} - 25 Z_{0t}).$$

11. Let

$$D_t = \begin{cases} 1 & \text{if } r_t > 0.05, \\ 0 & \text{otherwise.} \end{cases}$$

Then our regression model is

$$C_t = a + b_1 Y_t + b_2 (D_t r_t) + u_t.$$

12. Let

$$\log Y_t = Y_t^*,$$

$$e^{X_{1t}} = Z_{1t},$$

$$\frac{1}{1 + X_{1t} X_{2t}} = Z_{2t}.$$

The regression model can then be written as follows:

$$Y_t^* = a_0 + a_1 Z_{1t} + a_2 Z_{2t} + u_t.$$

The normal equations are

$$\sum Y_t^* = n\hat{a}_0 + \hat{a}_1 \sum Z_{1t} + \hat{a}_2 \sum Z_{2t},$$

$$\sum Z_{1t} Y_t^* = \hat{a}_0 \sum Z_{1t} + \hat{a}_1 \sum Z_{1t}^2 + \hat{a}_2 \sum Z_{1t} Z_{2t},$$

$$\sum Z_{2t} Y_t^* = \hat{a}_0 \sum Z_{2t} + \hat{a}_1 \sum Z_{1t} Z_{2t} + \hat{a}_2 \sum Z_{2t}^2.$$

CHAPTER 6

1. *Step* 1. Calculate $\hat{b}$ and $\hat{a}$:

$$\hat{b} = \frac{\sum\limits_{t=1}^{15} (X_t - \bar{X})Y_t}{\sum\limits_{t=1}^{15} (X_t - \bar{X})^2} = \frac{255}{280} \doteq 0.91.$$

$$\hat{a} = \bar{Y} - \hat{b}\bar{X} = -0.28.$$

Thus $\hat{Y}_t = -0.28 + 0.91 X_t$, and $\hat{u}_t = Y_t - (-0.28 + 0.91 X_t)$.
Step 2. Calculate $\hat{u}_t^2$ and $(\hat{u}_t - \hat{u}_{t-1})^2$:

Y_t	$\hat{u}_t^2$	$(\hat{u}_t - \hat{u}_{t-1})^2$
0.63	1.876	—
1.54	0.211	0.828
2.45	0.203	0.828
3.36	5.570	3.648
4.27	1.612	1.188
5.18	0.032	1.188
6.09	0.008	0.008
7.00	1.000	0.828
7.91	4.368	9.548
8.82	1.392	0.828
9.73	0.073	0.828
10.64	1.850	1.188
11.55	11.903	4.369
12.46	6.052	34.928
13.37	5.617	0.008
	41.767	60.213

$$\sum \hat{u}_t^2 = 41.767,$$

$$\sum (\hat{u}_t - \hat{u}_{t-1})^2 = 60.213.$$

Therefore $d = 60.213/41.767 \doteq 1.44$, which is greater than the upper bound, 1.23, from Statistical Table 4. We therefore reject the hypothesis of autocorrelation.

2. a. It makes sense to argue that it is heteroscedastic, because it is hard to believe that while output grows over time, the variance of one of its components, the disturbance term, does not.

b. Omitting K_t from the regression leads to biased estimators of a and b because the disturbance term in the resulting equation would be $u_t^* = cK_t + u_t$. This disturbance term would, in general, not have a mean of zero, and it would be correlated with the regressor L_t. We would expect a positive bias in b because L_t would tend to get credit for both its effect, and that of capital's, on output.

3. a. Aggregating equation (1) and dividing by N, we get

$$\sum_{i=1}^{N} \frac{C_{it}}{N} = a + b_1 \sum_{i=1}^{N} \frac{Y_{it}}{N} + b_2 \sum_{i=1}^{N} \frac{Y_{it}^2}{N} + \frac{\sum u_{it}}{N}.$$

Using our definitions, we get

$$C_t = a + b_1 Y_t + b_2 \sum_{i=1}^{N} \frac{Y_{it}^2}{N} + u_t.$$

Now,

$$\sum_{i=1}^{N} Y_{it}^2 = \sum_{i=1}^{N} (Y_{it} - Y_t + Y_t)^2$$

$$= \sum_{i=1}^{N} (Y_{it} - Y_t)^2 + \sum_{i=1}^{N} Y_t^2 + 2 \sum_{i=1}^{N} Y_t(Y_{it} - Y_t).$$

The last term $2 \sum_{i=1}^{N} Y_t(Y_{it} - Y_t) = Y_t \sum_{i=1}^{N} (Y_{it} - Y_t) = 0$, since Y_t is the average value of Y_{it}. Note also that $\sum_{i=1}^{N} Y_t^2 = NY_t^2$. Thus our macro model should be, after dividing by N,

$$C_t = a + b_1 Y_t + b_2 Y_t^2 + b_2 s_t^2 + u_t,$$

where

$$s_t^2 = \sum_{i=1}^{T} \frac{(Y_{it} - Y_t)^2}{N}.$$

This s_t^2 term is a measure of the variation of income across the population. Therefore, the macro model as it appears in equation (3) is misspecified.

b. The observation matrix would be written in the two basic ways:

t	C_{it}	Y_{it}	t	C_{it}	Y_{it}
1	C_{11}	Y_{11}	1	C_{11}	Y_{11}
1	C_{21}	Y_{21}	2	C_{12}	Y_{12}
1	C_{31}	Y_{31}	1	C_{21}	Y_{21}
2	C_{12}	Y_{12}	2	C_{22}	Y_{22}
2	C_{22}	Y_{22}	1	C_{31}	Y_{31}
2	C_{32}	Y_{32}	2	C_{32}	Y_{32}

c. We shall generally have an aggregation bias, because the average of a non-linear form of a variable will not be equal to the nonlinear form of the average of the variable. For example, in the above, we saw that $\sum Y_{it}^2/N \neq Y_t^2$, where Y_t is the average of the Y_{it}. More generally, we would have $\sum_{i=1}^{N} f(X_{it})/N \neq f(X_t)$, where X_t is the average value of X_{it} across the population.

4. a. The normal equations are

(1) $\sum M_{dt} = nb_0 + b_1 \sum i_t + b_2 \sum i_{(t-1)} + b_3 \sum \Delta i_t,$

(2) $\sum i_t M_{dt} = b_0 \sum i_t + b_1 \sum i_t^2 + b_2 \sum i_t i_{(t-1)} + b_3 \sum i_t \Delta i_t,$

(3) $\sum i_{(t-1)} M_{dt} = b_0 \sum i_{t-1} + b_1 \sum i_t i_{(t-1)} + b_2 \sum i_{(t-1)}^2$
$$+ b_3 \sum i_{t-1} \Delta i_t,$$

(4) $\sum \Delta i_t M_{dt} = b_0 \sum \Delta i_t + b_1 \sum \Delta i_t i_t + b_2 \sum \Delta i_t i_{t-1} + b_3 \sum \Delta i_t^2.$

Remembering that $\Delta i_t = i_t - i_{t-1}$, we rewrite equation (4) as follows:

(5) $\sum (i_t - i_{t-1}) M_{dt} = b_0 \sum i_t - b_0 \sum i_{t-1} + b_1 \sum i_t^2 - b_1 \sum i_t i_{t-1}$
$$+ b_2 \sum i_t i_{t-1} - b_2 \sum i_{t-1}^2 + b_3 \sum i_t^2$$
$$+ b_3 \sum i_{t-1}^2 - 2b_3 \sum i_t i_{t-1}.$$

By a simple inspection it is clear that equation (5) = equation (2) − equation (3). This means that the fourth normal equation is not independent. While we have four parameter estimators to solve for, namely, b_0, b_1, b_2, and b_3, we have only three independent equations. Thus, it is impossible to estimate all the parameters.

b. Substituting for Δi_t in the demand equation and rearranging terms, we get $M_{dt} = b_0 + b_1^* i_t + b_2^* i_{t-1} + u_t$, where $b_1^* = (b_1 + b_3)$ and $b_2^* = (b_2 - b_3)$.

5. Taking the logarithmic transformation of the production function, we get

$$\log Q_t = \log A + \alpha_1 \log L_{1t} + \alpha_2 \log(10{,}000 - L_{1t}) + \alpha_3 \log K_t.$$

We can then proceed to estimate this equation by the usual procedure, since $\log L_1$ and $\log(10{,}000 - L_1)$ are not perfectly collinear.

6. From the text we know that

$$b = b + \frac{W_1 u_1}{A} + \cdots + \frac{W_n u_n}{A}, \tag{1}$$

where $W_t = X_t - \bar{X}$ and $A = \sum (X_t - \bar{X})^2$. From (1) we have

$$(b - b)^2 = \frac{W_1^2 u_1^2}{A^2} + \cdots + \frac{W_n^2 u_n^2}{A^2} + \frac{W_1 W_2 u_1 u_2}{A^2}$$
$$+ \cdots + W_i W_j u_i u_j + \cdots.$$

Thus,

$$\sigma_b^2 = E(b - b)^2 = \frac{\sigma_u^2}{\sum (X - \bar{X})^2} + E(\text{all cross-product terms}).$$

Because of autocorrelation, the expected value of the cross-product terms is no longer zero, and hence our variance formula no longer holds.

7. To rid the equation of heteroscedasticity, we divide across by Y_t:

$$\frac{C_t}{Y_t} = b_0 \frac{1}{Y_t} + b_1 + b_2 \frac{A_t}{Y_t} + u_t^*,$$

where $u_t^* = u_t/Y_t$. The normal equations are

$$\sum \frac{C_t}{Y_t^2} = b_0 \sum \frac{1}{Y_t^2} + b_1 \sum \frac{1}{Y_t} + b_2 \sum \frac{A_t}{Y_t^2},$$

$$\sum \frac{C_t}{Y_t} = b_0 \sum \frac{1}{Y_t} + nb_1 + b_2 \sum \frac{A_t}{Y_t},$$

$$\sum \frac{C_t A_t}{Y_t^2} = b_0 \sum \frac{A_t}{Y_t^2} + b_1 \sum \frac{A_t}{Y_t} + b_2 \sum \frac{A_t^2}{Y_t^2}.$$

Note that this equation has a constant term and so we use the condition $\sum \hat{u}_t^* = 0$.

8. *Step* 1. Estimate a_0, a_1, and a_2 by the usual method.

Step 2. Use the estimated coefficients to obtain a set of estimated values for the disturbance term, where

$$\hat{\varepsilon}_t = Y_t - \hat{Y}_t = Y_t - \hat{a}_0 - \hat{a}_1 \Delta Y_t - \hat{a}_2 r_t.$$

Step 3. Plug the values for $\hat{\varepsilon}_t$ into the relationship

$$\hat{\varepsilon}_t = \rho_1 \hat{\varepsilon}_{t-1} + \rho_2 \hat{\varepsilon}_{t-2} + u_t.$$

Estimate ρ_1 and ρ_2 by setting $\sum (\hat{u}_t \hat{\varepsilon}_{t-1}) = 0$ and $\sum (\hat{u}_t \hat{\varepsilon}_{t-2}) = 0$.

Step 4. Transform the original model into

$$I_t^* = a_0^* + a_1 \Delta Y_t^* + a_2 r_t^* + u_t,$$

where

$$I_t^* = I_t - \hat{\rho}_1 I_{t-1} - \hat{\rho}_2 I_{t-2},$$
$$a_0^* = a_0 - \hat{\rho}_1 a_0 - \hat{\rho}_2 a_0,$$
$$\Delta Y_t^* = \Delta Y_t - \hat{\rho}_1 \Delta Y_{t-1} - \hat{\rho}_2 \Delta Y_{t-2}, \text{ and}$$
$$r_t^* = r_t - \hat{\rho}_1 r_{t-1} - \hat{\rho}_2 r_{t-2}.$$

Step 5. Estimate a_0^*, a_1, and a_2 by the usual method. Then take

$$\hat{a}_0 = \hat{a}_0^*/(1 - \hat{\rho}_1 - \hat{\rho}_2).$$

CHAPTER 7

1. a. The endogenous variables are C_t, Y_t, and I_t. The predetermined variables are C_{t-1}, Y_{t-1}, and r_t.

b. The problem in equation (1) is that Y_t is correlated with ε_{1t}. So, the procedure is to replace Y_t by $\hat{Y}_t$. We obtain $\hat{Y}_t$ by regressing Y_t on all the predetermined variables, which are C_{t-1}, Y_{t-1}, and r_t. Thus, $\hat{Y}_t$ would be

$$\hat{Y}_t = \hat{\gamma}_0 + \hat{\gamma}_1 C_{t-1} + \hat{\gamma}_2 Y_{t-1} + \hat{\gamma}_3 r_t.$$

Equation (1) is then estimated by the usual method after Y_t is replaced by $\hat{Y}_t$. That is, the normal equations are obtained by setting to zero the following sums: $\sum \hat{\varepsilon}_1^* = 0$, $\sum (\hat{\varepsilon}_1^* C_{t-1}) = 0$, and $\sum (\hat{\varepsilon}_1^* \hat{Y}_t) = 0$.

c. To estimate equation (3) we use the same procedure as in estimating (1). The normal equations would be obtained by setting to zero the following sums: $\sum \hat{\varepsilon}_2{}^* = 0, \sum (\hat{\varepsilon}_2{}^* Y_{t-1}) = 0, \sum (\hat{\varepsilon}_2{}^* r_t) = 0$, and $\sum (\hat{\varepsilon}_2{}^* \hat{Y}_t) = 0$.

2. a. The first equation is identified since the number of predetermined variables in the model, which do not appear in the first equation, $\dot{M}_t$, is greater than or equal to the number of endogenous regressors ($\dot{P}_t$) appearing in the first equation. This is not true for the second equation, and hence it is not identified.

   b. The estimation procedure for the first equation is as follows:

   Step 1. Obtain $\hat{P}_t$ by regressing $\dot{P}_t$ on all the predetermined variables, namely, $\dot{M}_t$ and UN_t. Thus, $\hat{P}_t$ would be

   $$\hat{P}_t = \hat{\gamma}_0 + \hat{\gamma}_1 \dot{M}_t + \gamma_2 UN_t.$$

   Step 2. Replace $\dot{P}_t$ with $\hat{P}_t$ in the first equation and proceed as usual to generate the second-stage normal equations by setting to zero the following sums: $\sum \hat{\varepsilon}_{1t}^* = 0, \sum (\hat{\varepsilon}_{1t}^* UN_t) = 0, \sum (\hat{\varepsilon}_{1t}^* \hat{P}_t) = 0$.

3. a. To obtain the reduced-form equations, we solve equations (1) and (2) for L_t and W_t. The reduced forms are

   $$L_t = a_0{}^* + a_1{}^* P_t + a_2{}^* S_t + v_t,$$

   $$W_t = b_0{}^* + b_1{}^* S_t + b_2{}^* P_t + \varepsilon_t,$$

   where

   $$a_0{}^* = \frac{a_0 + a_1 b_0}{1 - a_1 b_1}, \qquad a_1{}^* = \frac{a_1 b_2}{1 - a_1 b_1}, \qquad a_2{}^* = \frac{a_2}{1 - a_1 b_1},$$

   $$v_t = \frac{a_1 u_{2t} + u_{1t}}{1 - a_1 b_1}, \qquad b_0{}^* = \frac{b_0 + b_1 a_0}{1 - a_1 b_1}, \qquad b_1{}^* = \frac{b_1 a_2}{1 - a_1 b_1},$$

   $$b_2{}^* = \frac{b_2}{1 - a_1 b_1}, \qquad \varepsilon_t = \frac{u_2 + b_1 u_{1t}}{1 - a_1 b_1}.$$

   b. The problem in equation (1) is that W_t is correlated with u_{1t}. So the procedure is to replace W_t by $\hat{W}_t$. We obtain $\hat{W}_t$ by regressing W_t on the predetermined variables, which are S_t and P_t. So $\hat{W}_t$ would be of the form

   $$\hat{W}_t = \hat{\gamma}_0 + \hat{\gamma}_1 S_t + \hat{\gamma}_2 P_t.$$

   Equation (1) is then estimated by the usual method after W_t is replaced by $\hat{W}_t$. That is, the normal equations are obtained by setting to zero the following sums: $\sum \hat{u}_{1t}{}^* = 0, \sum (\hat{u}_{1t}{}^* \hat{W}_t) = 0, \sum (\hat{u}_{1t}{}^* S_t) = 0$.

4. a. An intuitive way to see that $D_{i(t-1)}$ is correlated with u_{it} is the following: From equation (1) we see that $D_{i(t-1)}$ depends on $u_{i(t-1)}$. However, since $u_{it} = \rho u_{i(t-1)} + \varepsilon_{it}$, u_{it} also depends on $u_{i(t-1)}$. Thus, $D_{i(t-1)}$ and u_{it} are correlated because they have an element in common.

   b. If our basic equation is repeatedly solved, it turns out that D_{it} depends on P_t and all of its lagged values. More explicitly, we have

   $$D_{it} = a_0 + a_0 a_2 + a_0 a_2{}^2 + \cdots + a_1 P_t + a_1 a_2 P_{t-1} + a_1 a_2{}^2 P_{t-2}$$

   $$+ \cdots + u_{it} + a_2 u_{i(t-1)} + a_2{}^2 u_{i(t-2)} + \cdots.$$

In addition, we see that D_{it} will also depend on u_{it} and all of its lagged values. Thus, the *mean* part of D_{it} will depend only on P_t and its lagged values. If we consider the equation above, which relates D_{it} to the values of P_t and u_{it} as a reduced-form equation, we can implement the TSLS technique described in the text for a model in which all of the predetermined variables are either not known or we do not have observation on them. In other words, we can implement the TSLS procedure by regressing D_{it} on P_t and $\hat{D}_{i(t-1)}$, where $\hat{D}_{i(t-1)}$ is calculated by regressing $D_{i(t-1)}$ on P_t and *some* of its lagged values, say, for example, three of them.

5. Substituting (1) into (2), we get

$$X_{2t} = b_0{}^* + b_1{}^* X_{1t} + v_t{}^*, \tag{1'}$$

where

$$b_0{}^* = \frac{c_0 + c_1 b_0}{1 - c_1 b_2}, \qquad b_1{}^* = \frac{c_1 b_1}{1 - c_1 b_2}, \qquad v_t{}^* = \frac{c_1 u_{1t} + u_{2t}}{1 - c_1 b_2}.$$

Multiplying (1') by u_{1t} and taking expected values yields

$$E(X_{2t} u_{1t}) = b_0{}^* E(u_{1t}) + b_1{}^* E(u_{1t} X_{1t}) + \frac{c_1 E(u_{1t}{}^2)}{1 - c_1 b_2} + \frac{E(u_{1t} u_{2t})}{1 - c_1 b_2}.$$

Remembering that $E(u_{1t}) = 0$, $E(u_1 X_{1t}) = 0$, and $E(u_{1t} u_{2t}) = \text{cov}(u_1, u_2)$, we have

$$E(X_{2t} u_{1t}) = \frac{c_1 \sigma_1{}^2}{1 - c_1 b_1} + \frac{\text{cov}(u_1, u_2)}{1 - c_1 b_2} \neq 0$$

unless

$$\frac{c_1 \sigma_1{}^2}{1 - c_1 b_2} = -\frac{\text{cov}(u_1, u_2)}{1 - c_1 b_2}.$$

6. a. To show that in estimating the first equation the TSLS procedure breaks down, we proceed as follows: We first regress P_t on all of the predetermined variables in the model. This yields

$$\hat{P}_t = \hat{c}_0 + \hat{c}_1 (UN_t).$$

We next substitute $\hat{P}_t$ for P_t in the first equation. We get

$$\hat{W}_t = a_0 + a_1 \hat{P}_t + a_2 (UN_t) + \varepsilon_{1t}{}^*.$$

We note that since $\hat{P}_t$ and UN_t are perfectly correlated, it will be impossible to estimate a_1 and a_2; thus the TSLS procedure breaks down if we attempt to estimate the first equation.

b. The TSLS procedure does not break down in estimating the second equation because we are not confronted with the problem of perfect multicollinearity. We first obtain $\hat{W}_t$ by regressing it on UN_t, and then we replace W_t in the second equation by $\hat{W}_t$ and proceed as usual to derive the normal equations by setting the following sums equal to zero: $\sum \hat{\varepsilon}_{2t}{}^* = 0$, $\sum (\hat{\varepsilon}_{2t}{}^* \hat{W}_t) = 0$. The normal equations are

$$\sum \hat{P}_t = n b_0 + b_1 \sum \hat{W}_t,$$

$$\sum (\hat{P} \hat{W}_t) = b_0 \sum \hat{W}_t + b_1 \sum \hat{W}_t{}^2.$$

These equations are linearly independent, and thus we can solve them for b_0 and b_1.

7. a. The equation is identified, since the number of predetermined variables in the system that do not appear in the equation is greater than the number of endogenous regressors.

   b. We cannot estimate the equation by the TSLS procedure, because we need to have observations on at least two predetermined variables that do not appear in the equation; we have observations on only one such variable (X_{2t}). It can be shown that under this data limitation, there would be no way of estimating the regression equation in this problem.

8. a. Both equations are identified, since for each the number of excluded predetermined variables is equal to the number of endogenous regressors. Note that X_t and X_t^2 are not perfectly collinear, and therefore we can count X_t^2 as a predetermined variable that is not included in the second equation.

   b. To get the reduced form we substitute for Y_{2t} in the first equation and for Y_{1t} in the second. After rearrangement of terms, we obtain

$$Y_{1t} = a_1{}^* + b_1{}^* X_t^2 + c_1{}^* X_t + v_{1t}{}^*,$$
$$Y_{2t} = a_2{}^* + b_2{}^* X_t^2 + c_2{}^* X_t + v_{2t}{}^*,$$

where

$$a_1{}^* = \frac{a_1 + c_1 a_2}{1 - c_1 c_2},$$

$$b_1{}^* = \frac{b_1}{1 - c_1 c_2},$$

$$c_1{}^* = \frac{c_1 b_2}{1 - c_1 c_2},$$

$$v_{1t}{}^* = \frac{c_1 \varepsilon_{2t} + \varepsilon_{1t}}{1 - c_1 c_2},$$

$$a_2{}^* = \frac{a_2 + c_2 a_1}{1 - c_1 c_2},$$

$$b_2{}^* = \frac{c_2 b_1}{1 - c_1 c_2},$$

$$c_2{}^* = \frac{b_2}{1 - c_1 c_2},$$

$$v_2{}^* = \frac{c_2 \varepsilon_{1t} + \varepsilon_{2t}}{1 - c_1 c_2}.$$

   c. We use the TSLS procedure in estimating the first equation. Thus we regress Y_{2t} on all the predetermined variables to obtain, say,

$$\hat{Y}_{2t} = \hat{a}_2{}^* + \hat{b}_2{}^* X_t^2 + \hat{c}_2{}^* X_t.$$

Next we substitute $\hat{Y}_{2t}$ for Y_{2t} in first equation and proceed to estimate that equation by the usual procedure. That is, we derive the normal equation by setting the following sums equal to zero: $\sum \hat{\varepsilon}_{1t}{}^* = 0$, $\sum (\hat{\varepsilon}_t{}^* X_t^2) = 0$, $\sum (\hat{\varepsilon}_{1t}{}^* \hat{Y}_{2t}) = 0$.

9. a. The first equation is not identified because r_t would be a constant in a cross-sectional analysis; since we already have a constant in the first equation, it cannot serve as an excluded predetermined variable for r_{it}. The second equation is identified because of the exclusion of the sales variable. Suppose now that we have time-series data, say for T periods, on the variables of our model. Assume also that these N firms represent a small portion of the economy so that r_t may be taken to be exogenous. Then the first equation would be identified because r_t could be considered as an excluded predetermined variable. In this case, the investment equation would be estimated as follows. First, using the T time-series observations, regress *each* r_{it} on r_t and on the corresponding sales variable to obtain

$$\hat{r}_{it} = \hat{\gamma}_{0i} + \hat{\gamma}_{1i}S_{i(t-1)} + \hat{\gamma}_{2i}r_t, \qquad i = 1, \ldots, N.$$

Now replace each r_{it} by $\hat{r}_{it}$ and proceed to estimate the first equation by the usual procedure. In doing this note that we should have NT observations in this second stage.

b. We obtain the reduced form for I_{it} by substituting for r_{it} in the first equation. After rearranging of terms, we get

$$I_{it} = a^* + b_1^* r_t + b_2^* S_{it-1} + v_{it}^*,$$

where

$$a^* = \frac{a}{1 - b_1 b_3}, \qquad b_1^* = \frac{b_1}{1 - b_1 b_3},$$

$$b_2^* = \frac{b_2}{1 - b_1 b_3}, \qquad v_{it}^* = \frac{b_1 \varepsilon_{it} + u_{it}}{1 - b_1 b_3}.$$

INDEX